Interpersonal Skills in Organizations

Fifth Edition

SUZANNE C. DE JANASZ, Ph.D.
IMD

KAREN O. DOWD, Ph.D.
Simon Business School, University of Rochester, New York

BETH Z. SCHNEIDER, DBA

INTERPERSONAL SKILLS IN ORGANIZATIONS, FIFTH EDITION

Published by McGraw-Hill Education, 2 Penn Plaza, New York, NY 10121. Copyright © 2015 by McGraw-Hill Education. All rights reserved. Printed in the United States of America. Previous editions © 2012, 2009, and 2006. No part of this publication may be reproduced or distributed in any form or by any means, or stored in a database or retrieval system, without the prior written consent of McGraw-Hill Education, including, but not limited to, in any network or other electronic storage or transmission, or broadcast for distance learning.

Some ancillaries, including electronic and print components, may not be available to customers outside the United States.

This book is printed on acid-free paper.

2 3 4 5 6 7 8 9 0 ROV/ROV 1 0 9 8 7 6 5 4

ISBN 978-0-07-811280-5
MHID 0-07-811280-X

Senior Vice President, Products & Markets: *Kurt L. Strand*
Managing Director: *Paul Ducham*
Vice President, Content Production & Technology Services: *Kimberly Meriwether David*
Brand Manager: *Michael Ablassmeir*
Development Editor: *Laura Hurst Spell*
Marketing Manager: *Elizabeth Trepkowski*
Director, Content Production: *Terri Schiesl*
Content Project Manager: *Mary Jane Lampe*
Buyer: *Nichole Birkenholz*
Cover Designer: *Studio Montage, St. Louis, MO*
Cover Image: *Photodisc Collection/Getty Images*
Compositor: *MPS Limited*
Typeface: *10/12 Times Roman*
Printer: *R. R. Donnelley*

Dedication

From Suzanne:

To my father, Stan Cooper, who was a model of strength, courage, and perseverance; you are forever in my heart. To my children, Alex and Gabby, who, as young adults and university students, continue to make me proud in so many ways. To my friends, colleagues, and loved ones, who have been a source of inspiration, renewal, and support.

From Karen:

To my siblings Valerie, James, Joan, Mark, and Laura for their resilience, patience, and love. To my husband Tom without whom this book could not have been written. To my current and former students and colleagues from whom I learn about interpersonal skills each day.

From Beth:

To my father, Ferdinando Zuech, "Hey dad, I did it!" To my husband Jeff, who remains my rock.

About the Authors

Suzanne C. de Janasz, Ph.D., is Professor of Leadership and Organization Development at IMD in Lausanne, Switzerland. As a Fulbright Fellow, she taught at Warsaw University in Warsaw, Poland, and has had visiting stints there and at ALBA Graduate Business School in Vouliagmeni, Greece. An award-winning instructor, Suzanne currently designs and delivers programs for mid-level and senior executives in global companies, specializing in leadership, negotiations, mentoring and careers, organizational behavior and change, creativity/innovation, work–life balance, entrepreneurship, and interpersonal/managerial skills.

Suzanne's research on mentoring, careers, authenticity, work–family conflict, and leadership appears in such journals as *Academy of Management Executive, Harvard Business Review, Journal of Organizational Behavior, Journal of Vocational Behavior, British Journal of Management, Career Development International,* and *Journal of Management Education* and features frequently in domestic and international newspapers, online publications (she's a featured blogger for Huffington Post), and radio programs. Her text *Negotiation and Dispute Resolution* (co-authored with Beverly DeMarr) was published in 2013. In addition to her Fulbright Fellowship, Suzanne received the New Educator Award from the Organizational Behavior Teaching Society (OBTS) and the Jepson Fellowship from her previous university. Suzanne recently served as the Careers Division Chair in the Academy of Management, and she has held leadership roles in the Southern Management Association and the OBTS. She regularly consults with a variety of global organizations, and also serves on the boards of several nonprofit organizations.

After earning an undergraduate music degree from the University of Miami, Suzanne earned her MBA and Ph.D. degrees from the Marshall School of Business at the University of Southern California (USC). Between the two degrees, she worked for five years as an organizational consultant in the aerospace industry. Prior to joining the faculty of IMD, Suzanne taught at James Madison University and the University of Mary Washington's College of Graduate and Professional Studies, both in Virginia.

Karen O. Dowd, Ph.D., is Assistant Dean, Career Management and Corporate Engagement, Simon Business School, University of Rochester, New York. Dowd is an experienced teacher, writer, administrator, speaker, and consultant. Prior to the University of Rochester, she was at The University of Denver, the University of Notre Dame, The Empower Group in New York City, and the University of Virginia. Dowd also taught at James Madison University, where she teamed with her co-authors and the Management Department to develop a required course in Interpersonal Skills that is offered to all undergraduate business students. Karen is the co-author, with Sherrie Gong Taguchi, of *The Ultimate Guide to Getting the Career You Want* (New York: McGraw-Hill, 2003). Karen earned her doctorate from the University of Virginia, her master's degree from Indiana University South Bend, and her bachelor's degree from Saint Mary's College, Notre Dame, Indiana. She is a member of the National Association of Colleges and Employers and has served on the board of the MBA Career Services Council. She is currently head of the CSC's Asian Expansion Initiative. Karen has conducted numerous management training programs on many of the topics addressed in this book and on career management for managers. Her research interests include faculty careers, career development, candidate selection, and career branding.

Beth Zuech Schneider is a Clinical Instructor of Management at Winston Salem State University. Schneider is an experienced instructor and course administrator, having taught for several years at James Madison University and George Mason University prior to coming to WSSU. Beth is also an experienced small business owner, having owned and managed businesses in the retail, restaurant, and mail-order catalog industries. She is now serving as a small business consultant through her own business, CORE Consulting in Greensboro, NC. Beth earned her DBA from Durham University in England, her MBA from the University of Central Florida, and her BA from St. Bonaventure University. Her research interests include social entrepreneurship, international business strategy, cross-cultural management, and women's workplace issues.

Contents in Brief

Contents

**Unit 2 Interpersonal Effectiveness:
Understanding and Working with Others**

Chapter 8 Persuading Individuals and Audiences   173

Unit 3 Understanding and Working in Teams

Chapter 9 Negotiation   198

Chapter 10 Building Teams and Work Groups   236

Preface

Birth of an Idea

While we were all teaching at James Madison University, a group of executives, who served as the College of Business dean's board of advisors at the university, identified a critical ingredient missing in most business school graduates. The executives found that while students were technically competent—they could read a balance sheet, do a market analysis, and develop cash flow projections—many graduates lacked interpersonal skills or the ability to work effectively with others. The executives created a wish list of "soft skills," faculty were hired, and the Interpersonal Skills course was born. Since that time, thousands of students have taken part in this required undergraduate course.

In the beginning, the cadre of faculty dedicated to this course selected two books and additional readings to support the course objectives. In response to student and recruiter feedback, we improved continuously both the content and delivery of the course. One such improvement stemmed from students' concerns that the books were inadequate for a variety of reasons. We agreed and continued to search for a book that met our needs. Frustrated with our inability to find the interpersonal skills text for our particular audience, we decided to write it.

"I Want to Buy This Book for My Boss"

As our colleagues and students have heard about this book, a common response is not simply "Where can I buy this book," but "My boss could use this—can you send him (or her) a copy?" The truth is this book is very relevant to a variety of readers. While it was written primarily with an undergraduate student audience in mind, each of the authors is experienced working with graduate students, adult learners, and working managers. In addition to our current teaching and research responsibilities, one or more of us has been a management consultant, a corporate trainer, an internal organization development consultant, a director of a career services center at a top-tier graduate business school, or a small business owner. Because of the depth of experience we offer, we are convinced that the material, with slight modification, is very appropriate for graduate students, adult learners, and managers as well as for undergraduate students. In short, this book is appropriate for anyone who wants to improve his or her ability to interact with others in the workplace.

A Unique Focus on Developing Managerial and Interpersonal Skills

In this textbook we have included certain design elements in order to:

- Offer a variety of activities and experiential elements to meet many types of instructional needs.
- Provide coverage of areas such as diversity, project management, facilitation, and personal goal setting, which are sometimes missing or limited in other textbooks.
- Maintain an academic standard appropriate for an undergraduate audience; yet with minor adjustments the material can be utilized at a graduate or professional training level.
- Use direct and action-oriented language in order to blend academic research with practical application for each skill set.

Emphasis on Both Personal and Professional

Some texts focus solely on managerial skills but provide little if any assistance in helping the reader understand how understanding him- or herself (intrapersonal effectiveness) relates to interpersonal and managerial effectiveness. The premise and sequencing of our book is that for students to be successful as managers in business, they must first have a solid understanding of self and how the self interacts with others to facilitate organizational success. The chapters and units are designed to be interchangeable so they can be easily rearranged and presented to fit many types of courses. Accordingly, we incorporate information on personal qualities needed for success in business and provide personal examples throughout the book focusing on family and other relationships alongside professional examples focusing on the workplace.

Balance between Theory and Practice

Our book offers a balance between theory and application. The skill sets addressed in this book are timeless. We don't focus on fads but on tried-and-true principles that are proven to help individuals succeed in organizations. In our experience, students and managers benefit by having some conceptual background on the topic of interpersonal skills but relate best to practical information that can be applied immediately to school, job, or team settings. Providing tips and techniques as well as conceptual grounding based on academic research motivates the reader to learn a particular skill. Some popular interpersonal skills texts provide substantial theoretical and conceptual grounding of each skill area covered and are written primarily for a graduate audience rather than for undergraduates or working managers. In each chapter, we strike a balance by providing both sufficient conceptual material and applied material appropriate for use in real-life personal, academic, and professional situations, using conversational, user-friendly language.

Coverage of New Topics or More Thorough Coverage of Existing Topics

We have included a number of topics that are covered minimally, if at all, by other textbooks. Reviewers who have read our manuscript report that our treatment of topics such as self-disclosure and trust, stress and time management, conveying verbal messages, listening, diversity, ethical decision making, and negotiation are more thorough than what exists now. Other topics such as project management, facilitation, and problem solving are new and not addressed substantively in other books. Although some of these topics may deal with more advanced interpersonal skills, these chapters can be important for individuals who gain greater experience in their professional lives as well as impactful for graduate level students.

Focus on Experiential Learning

In addition to the latest thinking about each of the topics covered, we provide different types of exercises at the end of each chapter that have been tested in the workplace or classroom and evaluated positively by both undergraduate and graduate students as well as working managers. The variety of exercises accomplishes several objectives. First, the instructor can accommodate multiple learning styles by fashioning a subset of exercises appropriate for a particular audience. "One size does not fit all." Second, the combination of experiential and reflective exercises helps give students concrete experience, feedback, and an opportunity to reflect on ways to improve their current skill level. These activities help you create an experiential learning environment that encourages learning through doing. Our experiential focus will allow you to further engage younger learners who tend to prefer and respond more positively to active learning. Finally, in an age when virtual and distance education are increasingly popular, the numerous observational and reflective exercises can facilitate learning even in settings that lack face-to-face interaction.

Why Focus on Interpersonal Skills?

The need to focus on improving interpersonal skills is recognized by more than business school faculty, deans, and executive advisory groups. In a recent survey by the TRACOM Group, more than 80 percent of people identified communication or interpersonal skills training as important for leadership development, and 55 percent said bosses needed to improve these skills.[1] Studies have shown that interpersonal or "soft skills" are extremely important for entry-level success, and the lack of interpersonal skills may be the major reason highly qualified professionals are not promoted.[2] The rise of teamwork in contemporary organizations has increased the need for every employee to work effectively with and through others. Individuals on work teams need to be able to communicate and collaborate effectively with others whose personalities, approaches, and work styles may differ greatly. In addition, as power to make decisions and implement solutions is transferred down the condensed hierarchy to nonsupervisory employees, the ability to marshal needed resources in the absence of power or authority makes interpersonal and managerial skills more critical than ever. Even those in leadership positions need to be skilled on the softer side of management along with having the right knowledge and experience. Recent studies report communication skills, interpersonal skills, and initiative are what corporations seek when hiring MBAs.[3]

Organizations are looking for employees with outstanding interpersonal skills to help them remain flexible and viable in today's competitive workforce. Organizations are profoundly affected by interpersonal interactions within and between employees, customers, suppliers, and other stakeholders. The more effective the relationships and interpersonal communications are, the more productive for the organization and the individuals.[4]

According to Harvard professor Robert Katz, three types of managerial skills are necessary: conceptual, technical, and interpersonal. As one moves through the managerial layers, the need for technological and conceptual skills changes, whereas the need for interpersonal skills remains proportionate for all managerial levels: lower, middle, and top.[5] Improving interpersonal skills goes beyond the classroom and the boardroom; the lessons learned can have broad applications in helping individuals to better deal with problems and conflicts with family and friends.[6] Interpersonal skills help individuals initiate, build, and maintain relationships—in both personal and professional life.

"For things we have to learn before we can do them, we learn by doing them."

Aristotle

A Pedagogical Approach That Works

In today's service-oriented, knowledge- and information-focused, global marketplace, interpersonal skills are essential. However, these skills seldom occur naturally; for most of us they must and can be learned.[7] If these skills are neither learned nor practiced, the good news is that it is never too late to start. Recognizing the need for these skills and acquiring and enhancing them can help workers be continuous learners and remain marketable.[8]

We have designed the text and the supplementary materials to aid students and practicing managers in assessing their level of effectiveness and enhancing their capability in each of 19 skill areas. Each chapter begins with a set of questions that relate to the learning objectives of the chapter. Next, we include a case study that helps the reader understand how the skill (or lack thereof) applies in real-world situations. Then, we lay out the background about the skill—what it is and why it's important. We offer strategies and techniques for learning and using the skill. Key terms are listed at the end of each chapter and highlighted in the margins so students can check their understanding of the terms or phrases. The chapters are written in an easy-to-read style with numerous practical examples in both professional and personal settings. After the chapter summary and list of key terms and concepts, the reader can test his or her understanding of the written material and ability to apply the skills through the many exercises in each chapter. Some exercises are reflective, while others are experiential. Some exercises are designed to be performed in a class environment, while others can be performed outside the classroom. Some exercises allow for feedback from others while some activities encourage self-feedback. Many of the assignments can be used for creating writing assignments, either by reflection on the results of the activity or as a starting point for additional research.

How the Book Is Organized

The book is organized in a practical, experiential learning format that facilitates learning.[9] Each of the 19 chapters can be used as a stand-alone, modular chapter independent of the rest of the book or used in conjunction with other chapters. The chapters are grouped into four units: understanding self (intrapersonal skills), working effectively with others (interpersonal skills), working in teams, and leading individuals and groups.

In the first unit, intrapersonal skills, we begin the process of looking within ourselves to analyze our strengths and weaknesses and gain a better understanding of our personal perceptions, views, beliefs, and work style. Unit I topics include self-awareness, self-disclosure and trust, personal values, goal setting, and ethics, as well as self-management. In the second unit we move to interpersonal skills, or interacting with others, through multiple forms of communication, listening, persuading, and working with diverse others. The third unit focuses on more advanced interpersonal skills for working with teams and groups such as building teams, running meetings, facilitation, and decision making and creative problem solving. In the final unit, we focus on leading groups or individuals through the use of power and politicking, networking, mentoring, coaching, empowerment, and managing projects.

In each chapter, we discuss how a skill or concept can be incorporated into one's self-development, how a skill or concept is used in interactions with others, especially in team settings, and how the skill or concept is applied in the context of managerial roles in organizations.

Note to Instructors

Teaching interpersonal skills using an experiential, learner-centered approach differs greatly from those classes in which a more controlled, lecture-oriented approach may be appropriate. In order to help instructors transition from professor to facilitator—"sage on the stage" to "guide on the side"—we took pains to carefully construct a comprehensive Instructor's Manual and supporting materials that support this goal.

The Online Learning Center (OLC) available at www.mhhe.com/iso5e will enhance instructors' teaching experiences and students' learning experiences. Instructors will have access to the Instructor's Manual, which contains sample syllabi and assignments, chapter-by-chapter explanatory notes, teaching plans, ideas for implementing the material in the classroom, ways to motivate the discussion on a topic, detailed instructions for using the activities and exercises, discussion questions, additional resources, and sample test questions. PowerPoint slides, an electronic test bank with EZ Test, and an Asset Gallery of videos and exercises are also available on the OLC. Students will have access to self-grading quizzes and chapter review materials. Premium content is also available for purchase, including Test Your Knowledge exercises, Self-Assessment exercises, and Manager's Hot Seat videos.

What's New in the Fifth Edition?

Thanks to our students, faculty colleagues, and reviewers, we continue to search for new means to present the material necessary for assessing, learning, and improving interpersonal skills. The emphasis in this edition focuses on making the text more current and enhancing its pedagogic effectiveness for students and instructors. We do this by updating the content as well as enhancing the pedagogical process.

Organization of Material

In this edition, we've added material from the popular press along with results of current research and illustrative current events and company examples to provide depth for skill areas presented in the chapters. We've also added discussion questions at the end of each chapter. Despite these enhancements, the overall map of the book that specifies both the journey and the major stops along the way, including intrapersonal effectiveness (understanding yourself), interpersonal effectiveness (understanding others), understanding and working in teams, and leading individuals and groups, remains intact.

It is always a challenge to determine the exact order for delivering each skill area, so this edition has included more examples to illustrate how these skills are interrelated without reordering the chapters. For instance, effectively coaching others or providing feedback, as discussed in Chapter 17, requires not only well-honed communication skills (Chapter 7), but also listening skills (Chapter 6) and goal-setting skills (Chapter 3) as vital components for success. Dealing with challenging behavior on teams (Chapter 10) is also referenced in Chapters 11 (conflict), 12 (meetings), and 13 (facilitation). In the chapter on project management (Chapter 19), almost every chapter is referenced to reinforce how all of the skill sets are necessary for becoming an overall effective manager. Since Chapter 7 has taken a broader approach in communications beyond just verbal communication, the title was changed to "Communicating Effectively" in this edition to clearly reflect the expansion of material. The content of the chapter was also reworked to emphasize the importance of integrating nonverbal communication and electronic media.

Updating

Updating the material within the chapters was a key focus of this edition. While "landmark" research has been retained, several chapters incorporate new academic and commercial sources to reflect current trends and research on the topics. Several new opening scenarios were added to provide clearer applications of how each interpersonal skill impacts business situations. Greater emphasis is also placed on the importance and challenge of effective interpersonal skills in a global context. The ever-increasing impact of technology on our lives and interpersonal connections is further discussed throughout the text by including more material on virtual communication and social networking. Changes were made to address current implications of how social media, generational differences, and global expansion impact interpersonal skills.

Graphics were added or changed as space permitted to provide visual reinforcement of the content. New shaded boxes were added to illustrate the skill sets in action, and cartoons were included for visual interest and concept illustration.

Topic Expansion

Based on reviewer feedback and our own self-reflection, we've provided clearer explanations, more tips and techniques, and more visuals or examples to enhance several topics. For instance, Chapter 3 clarifies how goal setting and ethical decision making occur in and are affected by different cultures, while Chapter 5 now provides discussions of "global mindset" and generational diversity. Chapter 7 was enhanced with new materials on business writing and public speaking. We continue to update our exploration of virtual communication's impact on negotiation, teams, meetings, and mentoring (Chapters 9, 10, 12, and 16). We've added material on special challenges in Chapter 9, such as negotiating virtually, dealing with defensiveness, and negotiating in a family business. We've added new material in Chapter 11 that covers difficult conversations and how to deal with an abusive boss. Chapter 14 includes new tools and techniques, along with examples and graphic illustrations that use them. And in Chapter 19 a connection to all of the skill sets and chapters has been added to point out the range of interpersonal skills needed to direct a project from start to finish and to illustrate the integration of the skill areas. Overall, chapters have been updated with the latest research and business examples, with the addition of quite a few new exercises; all but a few chapters contain at least one new exercise and many more of the existing exercises were revised and called out in the text. Expansion of ideas for changing many of the activities are also provided in the Instructor's Manual.

The application of concepts through experiential activities has been and continues to be a necessary strength of our approach, and we continuously search for and create exercises that facilitate skill acquisition. We believe the additions and changes to the fifth edition make the text more current, informative, practical, and immediately accessible and applicable. We are excited about these strengths and improvements and hope you find them as valuable as we believe they are.

Endnotes

1. TRACOM, "Creating More Effective Managers through Interpersonal Skills Training," TRACOM Group (August 2008), http://tracomcorp-media.precis5sb.com/Managerial 360 Whitepaper.

2. See L. Glenn, "The 'New' Customer Service Model: Customer Advocate, Company Ambassador," *Business Education Forum* 62, no. 4 (April 2008), p. 17: R. James and M. James, "Teaching Career and Technical Skills in 'Mini' Business World," *Business Education Forum* 59, no. 2 (December 2004), p. 39.

3. Shari Caudron, "The Hard Case for Soft Skills," *Workforce* (July 1999), p. 60; also Karen O. Dowd and Jeanne Liedtka, "What Corporations Seek in MBA Hires: A Survey," *Selections,* Graduate Management Admission Council (Winter 1994), Fairfax, VA; and annual employer survey, National Association of Colleges and Employers, Bethlehem, PA.

4. Zia Ahmed, Frank Shields, Rayondraous White, and Jessica Wilbert, "Managerial Communication: The Link Between Frontline Leadership and Organizational Performance," *Journal of Organizational Culture, Communication and Conflict* 14, no. 1 (2010), p. 107.

5. Robert L. Katz, "Skills of an Effective Administrator," *Harvard Business Review* (September–October 1974), p. 91.

6. See Patrick Lencioni, "The Most Important Leadership Trait You Shun," *Wall Street Journal* (Online), (June 21, 2010); Jennifer Moss and John Barbuto, Jr., "Testing the Relationship Between Interpersonal Political Skills, Altruism, Leadership Success and Effectiveness: A Multilevel Model," *Journal of Behavioral and Applied Management* 11, no. 2 (January 2010), p. 155.

7. Ahmed et al., "Managerial Communication," p. 107.

8. Mary McCarthy, "Experiential Learning Theory: From Theory to Practice," *Journal of Business & Economics Research* 8, no. 5 (May 2010), p. 131.

9. Priscilla Berry, "Redesign of the Undergraduate Business Curriculum: The Way Forward, a Paradigm Shift," *American Journal of Business Education* 2, no. 8 (November 2009), p. 55.

Acknowledgments

As is true of any substantive effort such as writing a book, there are many people to thank—more than can be listed here individually. Many thanks to all our teachers, colleagues, friends, and family members, from whom we learned what interpersonal skills are (and aren't!). Special note needs to be made of several individuals and groups. Among them are our editors and production staff at McGraw-Hill—Michael Ablassmeir, Laura Hurst Spell, Elizabeth Trepkowski, and Mary Jane Lampe—and our colleagues at our respective schools for their support and ideas. Special mention needs to be made of our reviewers, who gave us substantive, honest feedback that strengthened the final product. They include:

Bambi Douma, University of Montana

David J. Hill, Mount Olive College

Deborah Hommer, Penn State Altoona and World Campus

Stanley C. Ross, Bridgewater State University

We also must recognize our many academic friends, especially those in the Organizational Behavior Teaching Society, the Academy of Management, the MBA Career Services Council, and the National Association of Colleges and Employers, who provided a sounding board for our ideas about the book. We thank our families and friends, especially Alex and Gabby de Janasz; Tom Dowd; and Jeff, Andrew, and Nicholas Schneider, for supporting our work. Most importantly, we wish to acknowledge our terrific students—in the United States and abroad—who keep us honest and are a joy to work with.

Introduction

Every journey needs a map . . .

Imagine that you are finally able to take a much-needed vacation. If you're like most people, you will take time to plan your trip—the route you'll take, the places you'll stay, the activities you'll experience. You want to get the most out of this opportunity to relax, refresh, and renew.

What if the journey you were about to take were different? Longer? More meaningful? With more impact? Such is the journey to personal development: an exciting journey with a winding path toward an evolving destination and wonderful sightseeing opportunities. Some of the stops might be short visits, while others are like family and good friends who always leave the light on.

As with any planning for a journey, we first need to take time to consider where we've been and where we want to go. Then we envision all the wonderful places we might want to visit, honing in on a place that would bring us the most happiness. Finally, we'd have to create a plan and devise a route for how we would get there. We can take the scenic route, stopping along many points along the way. We could take a train and observe the passing sights or take a plane and go directly to our destination. Before we leave, we will also need to select from numerous lodging options and make reservations.

This journey of interpersonal skills is no different. In Unit 1, we offer an opportunity for you to assess what (skills, values, traits) you have. By taking inventory, we are better equipped to select where we want to be (clarifying target areas for improving personal and professional effectiveness). The different stops along the way—Units 2, 3, and 4—offer an assortment of options that, individually and collectively, promise to provide an interesting and enlightening journey on your way to personal and professional success.

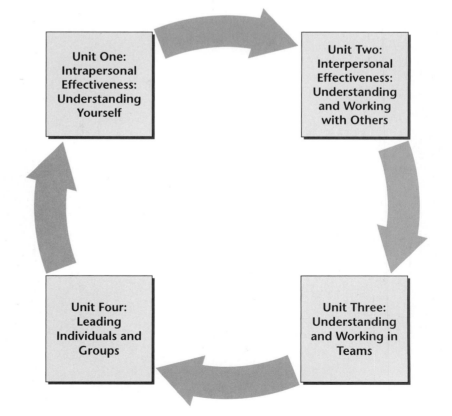

Interpersonal Skills in Organizations

UNIT 1

INTRAPERSONAL EFFECTIVENESS: UNDERSTANDING YOURSELF

1. Journey into Self-awareness
2. Self-disclosure and Trust
3. Establishing Goals Consistent with Your Values and Ethics
4. Self-management

UNIT 2

INTERPERSONAL EFFECTIVENESS: UNDERSTANDING AND WORKING WITH OTHERS

5. Understanding and Working with Diverse Others
6. Listening and Nonverbal Communication
7. Communicating Effectively
8. Persuading Individuals and Audiences

UNIT 3

UNDERSTANDING AND WORKING IN TEAMS

9. Negotiation
10. Building Teams and Work Groups
11. Managing Conflict
12. Achieving Business Results through Effective Meetings
13. Facilitating Team Success
14. Making Decisions and Solving Problems Creatively

UNIT 4

LEADING INDIVIDUALS AND GROUPS

15. Effective and Ethical Use of Power and Influence
16. Networking and Mentoring
17. Coaching and Providing Feedback for Improved Performance
18. Leading and Empowering Self and Others
19. Project Management

Unit 1

The first leg of your journey toward interpersonal skill development begins with an opportunity to take inventory of what you have and what you still need. This first unit is devoted to intrapersonal effectiveness—**understanding yourself** (and your goals, strengths, weaknesses, style, biases) and **improving self-management** skills, such as emotional intelligence, time management, and stress management. As you'll discover, "knowing yourself" may not be as easy as it sounds. However, we give you the tools to facilitate this process. Each of the four chapters in this unit helps you increase the odds of achieving intrapersonal effectiveness, and ultimately, personal and professional success and satisfaction. This first leg provides a solid start to your journey, as well as a strong foundation on which to build interpersonal, team-based, and leadership skills in the units that follow.

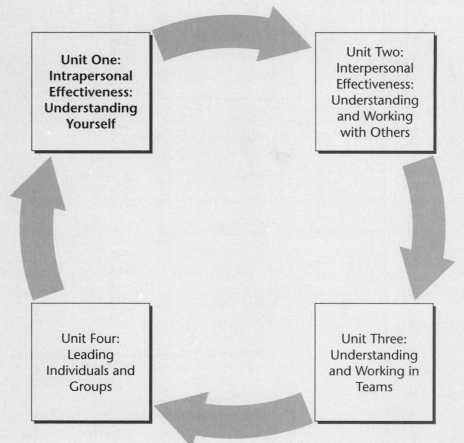

Unit One: Intrapersonal Effectiveness: Understanding Yourself

Unit Two: Interpersonal Effectiveness: Understanding and Working with Others

Unit Three: Understanding and Working in Teams

Unit Four: Leading Individuals and Groups

1 Journey into Self-awareness

Learning Points

How do I:

- Figure out my strengths and understand how they might guide me in personal and professional choices?
- Know what motivates me in order to reach my potential?
- Assess my limitations and develop a plan for improving in these areas?
- Gain understanding and insight into my personality, attitudes, and behaviors?
- Identify the biases I have that affect my understanding and appreciation of others?

James Morgan, age 22, was excited about his first job out of college. He had worked summer jobs and one internship, but never in an environment as professional as the bank for which he'd work upon graduation. After taking some time off in the summer, he began work in August. Eager to show he was worthy of having been hired, he worked hard the first six months on the job. He enjoyed his co-workers, got along well with his manager, and was even involved in a technology project through which he was able to meet people from other departments of the bank.

The project objective was to develop a new system to handle customers. The present system barely met the needs of the bank's customers and was inefficient and costly to run. Over a period of several weeks, James and his project team members worked diligently to study the problem and develop a solution.

The team consisted of James plus five co-workers: two were about his age and the other three were considerably older. Four of the five were college educated and all but one team member had greater tenure than he had. Of the six-person team, four were Caucasian and two were African American. The team did not have an official leader. Things ran smoothly for several weeks, until the time came for decisions to be made. As soon as a deadline was imposed on the group, James became aware of some significant personality differences within the project team. Two members who had always arrived late to meetings were procrastinating on their assignments for the project. Two others who had attended the meetings began to spend more time socializing than working. One person who had been reluctant to state her opinion about the data that had been collected now said she thought the group needed more time before it would be ready to make a decision. James had been very task oriented all along and was eager to finish the project and move on to other projects within the bank. He was very frustrated with the lack of progress being made by the group and was concerned about being part of a team that wasn't going to meet its assigned deadline. Yet he was reluctant to speak up. He felt he was too young and hadn't been at the bank long enough to have credibility with his teammates and take charge of the project. He didn't think he could approach his boss about the situation. He was perplexed about why the group was experiencing so many problems. James thought to himself, "Why can't they get along? Why can't everyone on the team be more like me? I work hard and have pride in how this project is going to turn out. Why don't the others?" He began to wonder if this was the right place for him.

1. Why is James upset?

2. In what ways are the work styles of James's teammates different from his? What causes those differences?

3. Can these differences be resolved? Why or why not?

4. How would you handle the situation if you were James?

"Know thyself."

Socrates

The charge to "know thyself" has commonly been attributed to the ancient philosopher Socrates as well as to Plato, Pythagoras, and Thales. As early as 42 BC, Pubilius Syrus proposed: "It matters not what you are thought to be, but what you are."[1] Understanding yourself—your internal states, preferences, resources, and intuitions—gives you the chance to understand your strengths and shortcomings. This is key not only to your ability to succeed, but also to your ability to work effectively with others. The best managers are keenly aware of their strengths—*and* their weaknesses.[2]

Good managers are able to capitalize on their strengths and either improve their limitations or work with others whose qualities complement theirs. They are able to understand others—their motivation, needs, style, capabilities, and limitations—and use this information to motivate and get results from them. They also keep current and regularly engage in self-assessment exercises and experiences that allow them to learn about and improve themselves continually. This chapter describes self-awareness: what it is, why it's important, and how to improve your level of self-awareness. It also addresses how strong self-knowledge can enhance your ability to manage and work with others and provides a number of exercises that enable you to assess yourself and develop improvement plans.

What Is Self-awareness?

Self-awareness is "the capacity for introspection and the ability to reconcile oneself as an individual separate from the environment and other individuals."[3] It is knowing your motivations, preferences, and personality and understanding how these factors influence your judgment, decisions, and interactions with other people. Internal feelings and thoughts, interests, strengths and limitations, culture, fit within your organization, values, skills, goals, abilities, leadership orientation, career interests, and preferred communication style are just a few of the many elements of self-awareness.

Through self-awareness, you develop the ability to know how you are feeling and why, and the impact your feelings have on your behavior. It also involves a capacity to monitor and control biases that potentially affect your decision making. Self-awareness requires a strong commitment to study and evaluate your behaviors and characteristics and make plans for modification as necessary.[4]

Why Is Self-awareness Important?

Self-awareness is the starting point for effectiveness at work. The astute author and statesman Machiavelli wrote, "To lead or attempt to lead without first having a knowledge of self is foolhardy and sure to bring disaster and defeat." Or as a more contemporary blogger recently wrote: "few skills are as critical for a leader as that of accurate self-knowledge . . . all of us have a view of ourselves but that view is not always accurate. When it is not accurate we often get in the way of ourselves."[5] Self-awareness can help you:

- Understand yourself in relation to others.
- Develop and implement a sound self-improvement program.
- Set meaningful life and career goals.
- Develop relationships with others.
- Understand the value of diversity.
- Manage others effectively.
- Increase productivity.
- Increase your ability to contribute to organizations, your peers, employers, community, and family.

Knowing what you are good at and what you enjoy doing can help you to select a career or job that is professionally, financially, and personally satisfying. By knowing yourself— your strengths, weaknesses, likes, and dislikes—you'll know where you "belong."[6]

Self-awareness is important for managers and organizations. Managers who have heightened self-awareness are superior performers. Awareness of self often leads to a greater understanding of others. Managers who can relate to or empathize with coworkers are more trusted and are perceived as being more competent.[7] Because self-aware managers are in tune with the concerns of others, they are also able to reduce the potential for conflict and are more likely to be open to feedback. Self-aware managers who listen to feedback and make positive modifications to personal behavior are able to create trusting and productive work environments. Working effectively with others will therefore increase managerial and organizational effectiveness.[8]

Self-awareness is key for global leaders. Understanding cross-cultural nuances and differing values, work ethics, and motivations of individuals in countries other than your home country is essential for anyone working in business today. All business is global; enhanced self-awareness gives you an understanding of your abilities and also of how to interact and work effectively with others. In a study of global leadership competencies, Jokinen identified three areas of global leadership competence that must be addressed, and self-awareness is at the top of the list, along with inquisitiveness and personal transformation. The author also stresses the importance of continuous learning, which is key to ongoing self-awareness and change.[9]

In assessing your own levels of self-awareness, be aware that cultural differences may play a part in your own awareness and that of others with whom you interact. While we don't wish to "label" people or groups, some cultures are viewed as more "**individualistic**," meaning that people define themselves independent of group affiliation, and some as more "**collectivist**," meaning that people define themselves in relation to what is acceptable within their group. Typically Westerners are individualists and people from Asian countries are collectivist. In one study it was shown that individualists and collectivists use different strategies to increase self-awareness. Individualists use internal information such as personal emotions when observing themselves, and collectivists assess themselves in relation to group harmony and in relation to group-approved norms.[10] Which are you? What individual and group norms affect your level of self-awareness?

Self-awareness is crucial to understand you and the organization where you are working. Each of us can be thought of as an instrument for assessment and change. By asking ourselves a series of questions, we can diagnose our situation and develop some solutions to problems we or our organizations are experiencing. Doing this requires strong self-awareness of our emotional reactions, initial perceptions, biases, and judgments—and a willingness to learn and change continuously. All of these will be considered in this and subsequent chapters.

Lack of Self-awareness   *"The greatest of faults, I should say, is to be conscious of none."*

Thomas Carlyle—Scottish
author, essayist, and historian
(1795–1881)

Self-awareness enables you to make good decisions: a realistic appraisal of your own and others' needs, objectives, resources, and capabilities can lead to more accurate judgments and more positive outcomes. Lack of self-awareness can lead to poor decisions and to an unrealistic notion of one's competencies. Self-awareness allows you to understand your strengths and core competencies—those core elements that contribute to your success. Lack of self-awareness can result in the opposite—incompetence, because the individual does not realize the gap between his or her perception and the reality of the strengths and competencies in question. Lack of self-awareness has also proven to be correlated with career derailment. In a study by the Center for Creative Leadership, a common factor in derailed careers was "lack of accurate portrait of self." Those who lack self-awareness are less able to see themselves accurately and are therefore less able to "midcourse correct" and make modifications necessary for change and improvement.[11]

"There are three things extremely hard: steel, a diamond, and to know one's self."

Benjamin Franklin

Strategies for Gaining Self-awareness

The first step to becoming self-aware is to recognize your weaknesses, strengths, biases, attitudes, values, and perceptions. There are many ways to enhance self-awareness. Some of these are taking an online assessment; journaling (see Exercise 1–A); watching certain movies and TV shows to identify people to whom you relate; and seeking feedback from trusted role models and mentors throughout your career. Analyzing your own experiences, looking at yourself through the eyes of others, self-disclosing, and acquiring diverse experiences can also increase your self-awareness and improve the way you interact with and come across to others.

Self-analysis   **Self-analysis** requires you to step back and observe (as objectively as possible) the factors that influence your behaviors, attitudes, thoughts, or interactions. Self-analysis is not always easy, yet it is necessary for you to increase your effectiveness personally and professionally.

Self-analysis can begin with reflection and exploring your thoughts and feelings. This helps you to obtain new perspectives based on new insights. You can become more effective by implementing new behavioral and cognitive changes in future situations. For instance, James, from the chapter's opening scenario, has an opportunity to gain self-awareness from his dysfunctional team experience. Through reflection, he could see that his current behavior of remaining silent has not aided the team in its process. Gaining awareness of the impact of his action, or lack of action, could lead to a new perspective regarding teaming and his part in the process and to positive behaviors and attitudes in his current and future team projects. This learning will not only help James in his professional life, but will enhance overall team and organizational effectiveness.

One means to gain insight is through examining your behavior, personality, attitudes, and perceptions. (See Exercise 1–A.)

Behavior   **Behavior** is the way in which we conduct ourselves—the way in which we act. Behavior is influenced by our feelings, judgments, beliefs, motivations, needs, experience, and the

**Figure 1–1
Means for Obtaining
Self-awareness**

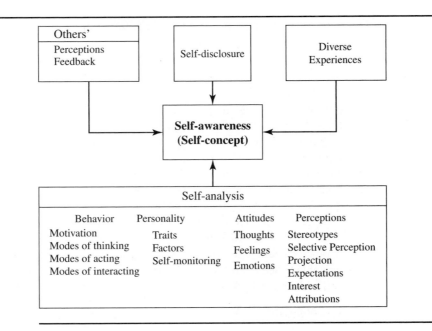

opinions of others. Patterns of behavior develop through reactions to events and actions over a period of time (see Figure 1–1). Behavior consists of four components:[12]

1. **Motivation**—the drive to pursue one action over another. What underlying factors move you to make a particular decision or choice? For example, what drives you to do a good job? The answer might be a competitive nature, strong achievement orientation, or a difficult childhood experience. Being aware of your core drivers, those things that motivate you—positively and negatively—can help you understand the roots of your behavior and make adjustments as necessary to modify your behavior.

2. **Modes of thinking**—the way you process the various inputs your brain receives. How do you analyze information and make judgments about how to use and apply that information? For example, do you process information quietly by reflecting on your own, or do you process information out loud by talking with others? Being aware of how you take in and make sense of information can help you understand how you make judgments and decisions that lead to choosing one behavior or course of action over another.

3. **Modes of acting**—the course of action you apply in a given situation. What approach do you use in response to stimuli, events, and people? For example, when someone does something that offends you, do you react in anger? Or do you react quietly, assessing your options before acting? Being aware of how you express your reaction to things that happen can help you understand the alternatives available when certain events arise.

4. **Modes of interacting**—the way in which you communicate ideas, opinions, and feelings with others. How do you typically share your thoughts with others? For example, are you comfortable in large groups of people? In team situations? Or do you prefer to work on your own? Being aware of how you work with others can help you understand how your preferred style meshes with others.

Personality

Personality describes the relatively stable set of characteristics, tendencies, and temperaments that have been formed by heredity and by social, cultural, and environmental factors.[13] These traits determine how we interact with and react to various people and situations. Some aspects of our personality are believed to be a result of nature—those traits with which we are born and that we possess through heredity. Other characteristics of our personality are thought to be a result of our environment—those factors that we acquire through exposure to people and events in our lives.

Personality traits are enduring characteristics that describe your attitude and behavior. Examples are agreeableness, aggression, dominance, and shyness. Most of these traits have been found to be quite stable over time.[14] This means that if you are cold and uncaring in one situation, you are likely to behave similarly in other situations. The Big Five model[15] is a powerful assessment that organizes numerous concepts into a "short list" of just five factors that are representative of the characteristics that can be linked with satisfaction and success. The Big Five model has five primary components (see Exercise 1–B): extroversion, agreeableness, emotional stability, conscientiousness, and openness to experience. Studies show these factors can be linked to job satisfaction, employee attitudes and behavior, stress, and job performance.[16] The Big Five factors also relate to overall life satisfaction. "Similar to job satisfaction, life satisfaction appears to be dispositionally based. Moreover, it appears the same traits that predict job satisfaction also predict life satisfaction."[17] While some personality characteristics are inherited, some factors can be modified through training, experience, and a conscious attempt to change.

1. **Extroversion** assesses the degree to which you are social or antisocial, outgoing or shy, assertive or passive, active or inactive, and talkative or quiet. A person who rates high for the first traits in these pairs is extroverted, while someone who rates high for the second traits is introverted. Extroversion or introversion, in itself, is not necessarily bad, but extremes at both ends of the spectrum can be equally dysfunctional. A person who is too outgoing could be perceived as overbearing, and a person who is too reserved might be perceived as disinterested.

2. **Agreeableness** measures the degree to which you are friendly or reserved, cooperative or guarded, flexible or inflexible, trusting or cautious, good-natured or moody, soft-hearted or tough, and tolerant or judgmental. Those scoring high on the first element of these paired traits are viewed as agreeable and easy to work with, while those rating low are viewed as more disagreeable and difficult to work with. Being too agreeable could cause a person to be too accommodating, however, and others may take advantage of this weakness.

3. **Emotional stability** measures the degree to which you are consistent in how you react to certain events, weigh options before acting, and look at a situation objectively. Those who rate high on emotional stability are viewed as generally calm, stable, having a positive attitude, able to manage their anger, secure, happy, and objective. Those who rate lower are more likely to be anxious, depressed, angry, insecure, worried, and emotional.

4. **Conscientiousness** represents the degree to which you are dependable, can be counted on, follow through on commitments, and keep promises. Those who rate high on conscientiousness are generally perceived to be careful, thorough, organized, persistent, achievement oriented, hardworking, and persevering. Those who score lower on this dimension are more likely to be viewed as inattentive to detail, uncaring, disrespectful, not interested or motivated, unorganized, apt to give up easily, and lazy.

5. **Openness to experience** considers whether you are interested in broadening your horizons or limiting them, learning new things or sticking with what you already know, meeting new people or associating with current friends and co-workers, going to new places or restricting yourself to known places. Individuals who score high on this factor tend to be highly intellectual, broad-minded, curious, imaginative, and cultured. Those who rate lower tend to be more narrow-minded, less interested in the outside world, and uncomfortable in unfamiliar surroundings and situations. Professionals who are open to experience are more willing to reflect on feedback for personal development.

Your Personality

- What are the characteristics of your personality? How do you know this? (See Exercise 1–B.)

(continued)

- Which aspects of your personality do you like, and which would you like to modify?
- While it's true that some of these factors are ingrained, few of these factors are fixed in stone. You can identify those qualities that are working well for you and worth keeping, as well as those qualities that aren't working well for you that you can change or abandon.

Self-Monitoring

Self-monitoring is the ability to regulate your thinking before speaking or acting. This allows you to quickly assess the needs of others or of a social or business situation and adapt your behavior and interactions accordingly.[18] Monitoring your own personality can help you come to grips with both positive qualities and those you would like to change. By being aware of the role of self-monitoring, you can assess your own attitudes, diagnose which elements you are satisfied with, and identify and develop plans for addressing those aspects you want to change. When self-monitoring, set your standards in accordance with certain accepted norms. High self-monitors are very sensitive to external cues and constantly adapt (and often hide) their true selves to conform to a situation or set of expectations. Low self-monitors display their feelings, attitudes, and behaviors in every situation. In an organizational setting, it is probably best to avoid the extremes. You don't want to be a high self-monitor (solely concerned with what others think) or a low self-monitor (not at all interested in what others think). Always trying to please everyone or conforming to gain everyone's approval—while it might facilitate getting what you want in the short term—can be harmful to you in the long term. Conversely, never adjusting your behavior relative to the audience or situation can be self-defeating. (See Exercise 1–C.)

All of the personality dimensions can have a significant impact on job performance and interpersonal relationships.[19] By understanding the meaning of these factors, you can pinpoint areas for personal and professional development and growth. Knowledge of your ratings on each of these dimensions can also help in selecting a career. Much research in the area of person/job fit demonstrates that individuals who select professions that suit their personality are more likely to be satisfied and productive.[20] Finding work that matches your personal preferences may require a fair amount of investigation; this investment in time and resources pays big dividends—success and happiness. For example, a person who is low on the extroversion and agreeableness factors would probably not be happy (or successful) as a traveling sales representative. The basic nature of the job requires an outgoing, friendly individual in order to contact and build a rapport with clients. A poor fit between one's personality and job can be a recipe for disaster.

Attitudes

Attitudes are evaluative statements or "learned predispositions to respond to an object, person or idea in a favorable or unfavorable way."[21] As human beings, we can choose how we think and feel about a situation or event. Imagine you are on an airplane that has been diverted to another airport due to bad weather. You can choose to become irritated and show your anger to the flight attendant, or you can be patient, acknowledge that nothing can be done to change the situation, and take out a good book to read while waiting for your flight to land. The emotions we choose to act on determine our attitude. This in turn is reflected in our behavior.

Your Attitude

Our attitude can vary from situation to situation. For example, you might have a positive outlook when with friends, feel negatively about your work, and have a neutral attitude toward your academic experience. Attitudes are derived from supervisors, parents, teachers, peers, society, and our own experiences. Attitudes are one of the less stable facets of our personality, which means they are easier to influence and change than our behaviors or values.[22] This is good news because with some effort you can almost always change the way you react to events and people and develop a positive outlook on life even when circumstances change.

Strong attitudes can impact your professional and personal relationships. As a student or manager, it is helpful to remember how much of a role your attitude can play in your success. Your demeanor, whether you are with others or grappling with an issue on your own, can make a significant difference in what behaviors you choose to exercise and in the outcomes of your efforts. Have you heard the saying "She takes lemons and turns them into lemonade?" This is an example of the power of attitude. Your attitude can determine whether you think positively and take control of a situation or think negatively and feel helpless about your ability to change or respond to a situation. Attitude is important to being productive at work or in school.

Attitude can influence those around us. Being aware of your own attitude and making choices about which attitude to display to others is very important. Attitude can affect your job behavior as well as your interactions with others. Friends, significant others, family members, co-workers, and others are definitely influenced by your thoughts and feelings toward situations. As a manager, it is also important to recognize your employees are affected by the attitude you display toward them and toward the work that needs to get done. A manager's attitude is a large factor in how people feel about their jobs. If a manager is upbeat most of the time and supportive of his or her colleagues, employees will generally respond well and work hard to produce the desired results. On the other hand, if a manager is pessimistic and belittling toward his or her employees, staff morale will suffer and, ultimately, so will the expected outcomes.

Perceptions

Perception is the process by which you select, evaluate, and organize information and make sense of it.[23] When you encounter a person or situation, you use your senses to absorb various inputs. Next, your brain selects aspects from stored information in order to process and organize these inputs. Finally, your brain interprets and evaluates the person or situation. Perception is person-specific—no two people will take in, organize, and evaluate inputs the same way. Your perspective on a situation can be entirely different from the way another person looks at the exact same situation. Two friends walking by the window of a crowded restaurant spot a couple engaged in conversation. One friend, taking notice of their mannerisms and gestures, concludes that it "looks like they're breaking off their relationship." The other friend vehemently disagrees. "No, they're probably discussing a plan to spend more time together." Which friend is right?

Individual perception may not always be consistent with reality; it is only the perceiver's interpretation of reality.[24] For example, when you go to a movie with a group, your opinion and those of your friends might differ. You each perceived the same event through a different set of lenses. One might have seen the movie as an action film, another as a romance. There's probably some element of truth in both perspectives. What's reality for you is based on your interpretation of the event. Your reality can be shaped and impacted by learning about others' perceptions of the same incident. For example, checking your perception with others and sharing yours with them might change your opinion of the movie or increase your understanding of it. At work, the best managers are those who augment their own perspective with the views of others. Your perceptions can—and should—change based on new inputs.

It is important to be in touch with your perceptions—what they are and how they're being formed. Equally important is being aware of the perceptions of others. Others' behavior toward you is heavily influenced by their understanding of the situation, and your behavior toward others is equally dependent on your assumptions about them and the situation. It is crucial to understand and disclose your own perspective as well as to solicit information from others about their understanding of the same situation.

Factors from a variety of sources may simultaneously impact your perception (see Figure 1–2). This makes it even more important to be fully aware of the factors that influence your perception. Our past experience, belief system, family background, and personal values heavily influence our perceptions of others. You can check to ensure that your own experience and perspective are not negatively distorting your perceptions of reality.

**Figure 1–2
Factors That Affect
Perceptions**

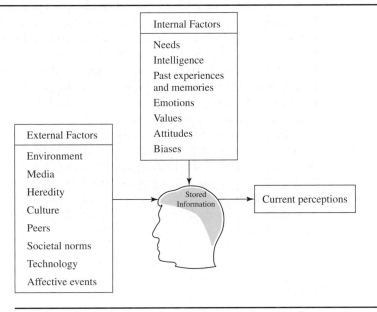

As human beings, we tend to form perceptions based on our biases. If you are not aware of your biases and don't check your understanding with others, you may miss on important information and situations by relying on distorted perceptions. Some of the more common filters that can influence your perceptions are stereotyping, selective perception, projection, expectations, and interest.

■ **Stereotyping:** making assumptions about an individual or a group based on generalized judgments rather than on facts. Many who stereotype others do so on the basis of observable demographic characteristics, such as race or ethnicity, gender, age, disability, religion, and sexual orientation. For example, some companies are reluctant to hire older workers for certain job roles for fear that they lack the energy and stamina to perform at a desired level. Stereotyping is a convenient but faulty way to make assumptions about a person's behavior and abilities. Rather than relying on a stereotype that is probably largely false, it is best to check your own perceptions and come to an event or meet a new person with an open mind. This will allow you to form your own perspective rather than rely on biases that have been shaped by judging and attributing certain behaviors to all members of a group.

■ **Selective perception:** interpreting information for meaning and accuracy, and discarding information that is threatening or not relevant. We are constantly bombarded with stimuli. This has always been true but even more so today, thanks to social media, online newspapers and news feeds, 24-hour cable news channels, mobile devices, instant access to Internet content, texting, and e-mail. In an effort to reduce the breadth and impact of continuous stimuli, our brains attend to information according to our own experiences, interests, attitudes, and background. This means we are constantly "filtering"—absorbing and processing only those inputs we think we can handle, or want to handle, at any given time. For example, people tend to dislike thinking about their own mortality, so they avoid the subject of wills and funeral planning. A college student whose main concern is graduating is probably not likely to be thinking of retirement plans. A graduate student in finance may not pay attention to an excellent speaker who's in marketing. A manager with a project deadline is probably not going to read information for a meeting that's scheduled for next month.

Selective perception serves a useful purpose, but it hinders communication with others. Rather than automatically "tuning out" information with which you disagree, keep an open mind, being open to all new views about a situation before prematurely developing your own opinion. (See Exercise 1–D for more on selective perception.)

■ **Projection:** attributing one's own attitudes, characteristics, or shortcomings to others. For example, someone who cheats and lies might make the assumption that everyone cheats and lies. This validates our own perceptions of the way things are, or at least the way we think things should be. However, projecting our beliefs onto others denies them the opportunity to provide us with a unique and fresh perspective. Rather than transferring your own experience and feelings to another, it is best to consider each new situation and person in your life as unique, paying attention to *their* features and characteristics rather than yours.

■ **Expectations:** forming an opinion about how we would like an event to unfold, a situation to develop, or a person to act, think, or feel. We tend to perceive, select, and interpret information according to how we expect it to appear. For example, when proofreading a paper or report you have written, you may pass over mistakes because you know what you intended to say, so you perceive it to be correct. By understanding what your expectations are and viewing a situation with a clean slate—minus preconceived notions about what to expect—you are better able to approach situations and people and form your own opinions based on actual experience rather than on assumptions.

■ **Interest:** basing our activities and inputs on things that are likeable or appealing to us. We tend to focus our time and attention—consciously or subconsciously—on those things that are enjoyable and meaningful to us. For example, if we are in the market to buy a new home we will notice "For Sale" signs in front of houses that previously would have gone unnoticed. If you have an interest in people, you might focus on a career in teaching or counseling, while ignoring other subjects such as computer science. The tendency to be drawn to things that interest us can be positive, in that it helps conserve our energy for the things that matter to us. However, as you increase your own self-understanding, it is important to reach out to things that go beyond what interests you at the time. By doing this you can broaden yourself and your understanding of the things that are important and meaningful to others.

By understanding yourself, you can begin to change your perceptions that are often affected by the biases described above. Understand and confront your biases. By doing so, you will increase your level of self-understanding and will be more understanding of others and their perspectives. The workplace is increasingly global and diverse. Companies are now involved in developing new business models. You will be better equipped to formulate and embrace these new models by expanding your self- and other-awareness. This step will help you to be a better manager and person.

"There's a changing of the guard, and my weaknesses are suddenly my strengths!"

Source: http://www.cartoonbank.com/1991/theres-a-changing-of-the-guard-and-my-weaknesses-are-suddenly-my-strengths/invt/111066/?.

Attribution Theory

A percentage of your perceptions are derived from what you attribute to the causes of behavior in yourself or others. **Attribution theory** demonstrates that individuals tend to decide that a behavior is caused by a particular characteristic or event.[25] We make these attributions or judgments about what caused the resulting behavior based on our personal observation or evaluation of the situation. For instance, after being fired from a position, you might blame the dismissal on an internal factor or personal characteristic such as being an incompetent worker. Or you might blame the dismissal on an external factor such as a declining economy. Understanding how and why you make these attributions is important because future decisions and behaviors are based more on your perception of why something happened rather than on the actual outcome.[26] Therefore, we tend to reinforce our beliefs about ourselves and others based on the perceptions we gain from these experiences.

It is also important to evaluate whether these judgments are attributed more to internal or external factors. Attributing outcomes to controllable factors tends to be a stronger indicator of future behavior than attributing them to uncontrollable factors.[27] For instance, if you attribute the loss of a job to internal or controllable factors, you might feel shame, which could have one of two effects: hampering attempts to get a new position or pushing you to become a more effective employee in the future. However, if you blame the job loss on an external or uncontrollable factor, it may lead to anger. Perceptions determine behavior in future situations based on the amount of personal control you believe you have over the situation.

Behavior and perception have an impact on your attributions. **Self-serving bias** causes us to overestimate internal factors for successes and blame external factors for failures. This may cause you to evaluate incorrectly your personal strengths and weaknesses. Another bias is **fundamental attribution error**, which causes individuals to overestimate the impact of internal factors and underestimate the influence of external factors when evaluating the behavior of others. We are more likely to judge people who lose their temper as unable to control themselves than to blame the situation. It is important to evaluate both internal and external factors before jumping to conclusions.

Increasing Your Self-Awareness

- Learn from your mistakes.
- Ask for feedback.
- Change your attitude.
- Be aware of your biases.
- Expand your interests and perspective.
- Increase your experience base.

Others' Perceptions

Self-awareness is also gained through understanding how others view us and how we are shaped by others' opinions of us. Stephen Covey refers to this concept as the "**social mirror**,"[28] which has its roots in Cooley's and Mead's work related to the concept of the "looking-glass self."[29] Covey explains that we gain perceptions of ourselves as a result of what other people say about us or how they react to us. We adopt a view of ourselves based on others' views. How do others view us? How do we change our actions as a result of what we think others are thinking about us? These are the questions to ask to get a handle on how we are shaped by others' perceptions. By seeing ourselves through others' eyes, we can learn about our strengths and also about areas in which we can improve. (See Exercise 1–E.)

Learning to read accurately how others see us enhances our "self-maps," our images and judgments of ourselves. For example, you might say to yourself, "I'm not a creative person" or "I'm an athletic person" after hearing comments from others about your artistic or athletic ability. The social mirror is based on our memory of how others have reacted toward us or treated us. Through feedback from others we can gain more insight or perspective into aspects of ourselves and our behaviors. However, our perceptions may not be based accurately on this information. The social mirror can be wrong or only partially correct. For example, an overbearing parent might say something negative such as "You'll never amount to anything." In this case, be very careful to first assess the statement—is it true? If the statement is not a reflection of reality, then work hard to dispel this image of you in your own mind, if not in the mind of the person who said it to you. Negative self-statements can be very damaging to one's self-esteem. The social mirror is designed to help you learn about yourself, but you shouldn't accept everything that others say to you as reality. (See Exercise 1–E for more on the social mirror.)

Self-disclosure

Another means of gaining self-awareness is through **self-disclosure**—sharing your thoughts, feelings, and ideas with others without self-deception, without distortion.[30] Talking with others allows us to share our feelings and responses. Self-disclosing is a key factor in improving our self-awareness; we must disclose information and interact with others to further clarify our perceptions.[31] Through verbalizing our perceptions, we verify our own beliefs, affirm our self-concept, and validate data received from an objective source. For example, if you've received a low grade on an exam, it's helpful to discuss this with others. They can listen to your concerns and give you feedback. They might empathize with the fact that you've received a low grade, then offer to problem-solve—for instance, identifying a test-taking strategy you can use in the future. They might also remind you that in general you do well in school. This helps you to maintain perspective even while going through a hard time about the exam. See more about self-disclosure in chapter 2.

Diverse Experiences

Another way of increasing self-awareness is through acquiring multiple experiences in diverse situations and with diverse others. For example, studying or working in a country other than your home country, working in a multifunctional position at your job, learning a new language, traveling, keeping up with international news outlets, reading books on new subjects, and acquiring broad work experience are ways to broaden our experience base. Even negative situations such as having to face a life-threatening illness, working with a difficult boss, going through your own or your parents' divorce, and overcoming a personal problem such as dyslexia can provide enormous learning and enhance your experience base.

As we acquire more experiences, we have both successes and failures. We can learn just as much if not more from failures. When things go wrong, assess what happened, take responsibility, and most importantly, determine how you can do better the next time. As we encounter new situations, we use skills and acquire new ones, meet people and develop friendships, see new places, and learn firsthand about things we might have only read about. Being open to new experiences broadens our horizons. It helps us to see ourselves in a new light while giving us new information about ourselves and our ability to interact with the world. This boosts our confidence level and encourages us to reach out to further our experiences even more. It makes us more open to new ideas and diverse people with varying ways of living, working, and thinking. Expanding our experience base puts us into situations that test our abilities, values, and goals. This greatly aids in increasing our level of self-awareness.

Summary

Self-awareness is an essential skill for developing personally and professionally. If you have a high degree of self-awareness, you'll be able to capitalize on your strengths and develop plans for improving or compensating for your limitations. Part of being self-aware is being able to monitor and change your behavior. By concentrating on self-improvement, you demonstrate to others your willingness to learn and grow, increasing the likelihood of being able to develop close relationships and success in both your life and career.

Key Terms and Concepts

Agreeableness	Modes of thinking
Attitudes	Motivation
Attribution theory	Openness to experience
Behavior	Perception
Collectivism	Personality
Conscientiousness	Projection
Emotional stability	Selective perception
Expectations	Self-analysis
Extroversion	Self-awareness
Fundamental attribution error	Self-disclosure
Individualism	Self-monitoring
Interest	Self-serving bias
Modes of acting	Social mirror
Modes of interacting	Stereotyping

Discussion Questions

1. What can you do to increase your levels of self-awareness in the coming year?
2. You may have heard the term "personality clash" before. What does this mean and how can this be avoided?
3. How can you respond strategically to others whose styles are different from yours?
4. What effect do you think your country of origin has on your levels of self-awareness?
5. What effect do your current age and state in life have on your levels of self-awareness?
6. How can your self-awareness inform your next career and life decisions?

Endnotes

1. Jayashree, V. "The Starting Point of Change in Individuals—An Empirical Analysis," *Journal of Contemporary Research in Management* 6, no. 3 (July–September 2011), pp. 16–17.

2. Daniel Goleman, "What Makes a Leader?" *Harvard Business Review* 82, no. 1 (January 2004), p. 85.

3. Jayashree, p. 14.

4. Mark Morgan, "Leveraging Self-Awareness," *Strategic Finance* 92, no. 9 (March 2011), p. 23.

5. T. J. Addington, comment on selfknowledge and leadership, "Leading from the Sandbox," http://leadingfromthesandbox.blogspot.com/2012/06/self-knowledge-and-leadership.html, Monday, June 18, 2012.

6. Peter F. Drucker, "Managing Oneself," *Harvard Business Review* 83, no. 1 (2005), pp. 100–109.

7. Craig R. Seal, Stefanie E. Naumann, Amy N. Scott, and Joanna Royce-Davis, "Social Emotional Development: A New Model of Student Learning in Higher Education," *Research in Higher Education Journal* 10 (March 2011), p. 7.

8. John J. Sosik, "Self–Other Agreement on Charismatic Leadership: Relationships with Work Attitudes and Managerial Performance," *Group & Organization Management* 26, no. 4 (2001), p. 484.

9. T. Jokinen, "Global Leadership Competencies: A Review and Discussion (electronic version)," *Journal of European Industrial Training* 29, 199. As cited in James Prewitt, Richard Weil, and Anthony McClure, "Developing Leadership in Global and Multi-Cultural Organizations," *International Journal of Business and Social Science* 2, 13 (July 2011).

10. S. Georgianna, "Self-leadership: A Cross Cultural Perspective," *Journal of Managerial Psychology* 22, no. 6 (2007), p. 573.

11. William D. Macaleer and Jones B. Shannon, "Emotional Intelligence: How Does It Affect Leadership?" *Employment Relations Today* 29, no. 3 (Autumn 2002), p. 13.

12. Patricia A. Hoffman, "The Aura of a Winner: A Guide to Behavioral Hiring," *Journal of Property Management* 61, no. 5 (September–October 1996), pp. 16–20.

13. This definition is adapted from Salvatore R. Maddi, *Personality Theories: A Comparative Analysis* (Chicago, IL: Dorsey Press, 1989).

14. Barry M. Staw, Nancy E. Bell, and John A. Clausen, "The Dispositional Approach to Job Attitudes: A Lifetime Longitudinal Test," *Administrative Science Quarterly* 31 (March 1986), pp. 56–77.

15. Murray Barrick and Michael Mount, "The Big Five Personality Dimensions and Job Performance: A Meta-analysis," *Personnel Psychology* (Spring 1991), p. 11.

16. Margaret Shaffer, David Harrison, Hal Gregersen, J. Stewart Black, and Lori Ferzandi, "You Can Take It with You: Individual Differences and Expatriate Effectiveness," *Journal of Applied Psychology* 91, no. 1 (January 2006), pp. 111–12.

17. Daniel Heller, Timothy A. Judge, and David Watson, "The Confounding Role of Personality and Trait Affectivity in the Relationship between Job and Life Satisfaction," *Journal of Organizational Behavior* 23, no. 7 (November 2002), p. 817.

18. Kindal Shores and David Scott, "The Relationship of Individual Time Perspective and Recreation Experience Preferences," *Journal of Leisure Research* 39, 1 (First Quarter 2007), p. 32.

19. Michael K. Mount, Murray R. Barrick, Steve M. Scullen, and James Rounds, "Higher-Order Dimensions of the Big Five Personality Traits and the Big Six Vocational Interest Types," *Personnel Psychology* 58, no. 2 (Summer 2005), p. 447.

20. Charles A. O'Reilly III, Jennifer Chatman, and David F. Caldwell, "People and Organizational Culture: A Profile Comparison Approach to Assess Person Organization Fit," *Academy of Management Journal* 34, no. 3 (September 1991), pp. 487–516.

21. Abram Poczter, "Attitude Development Hierarchy and Segmentation," *Review of Business* 9, no. 1 (Summer 1987), p. 17.

22. Gregory R. Maio, David W. Bell, and Victoria M. Esses, "Examining Conflict between Components of Attitudes: Ambivalence and Inconsistency Are Distinct Constructs," *Canadian Journal of Behavioural Science* 32 (April 2000), pp. 71–83.

23. Yanhan Zhu, "The Action Mechanism of Social Exchange Relationship Perception on Organizational Citizenship Behavior: An Empirical Study in China," *International Journal of Business Administration* 3, no. 2 (March 2012), p. 84.

24. Zhenzhong Ma, "Negotiating into China: The Impact of Individual Perception on Chinese Negotiation Styles," *International Journal of Emerging Markets* 1, no. 1 (2006), p. 66.

25. Bernard Weiner, "Attributional Thoughts about Consumer Behavior," *Journal of Consumer Research* 27, no. 3 (December 2000), pp. 382–87.

26. Jacquelynne S. Eccles and Allan Wigfield, "Motivational Beliefs, Values, and Goals," *Annual Review of Psychology* 53 (2002), p. 109.

27. B. Weiner, *Human Motivation: Metaphors, Theories, and Research* (Newbury Park, CA: Sage, 1992).

28. Stephen R. Covey, *Seven Habits of Highly Effective People: Powerful Lessons in Personal Change* (New York: Free Press, November 2004).

29. Charles Horton Cooley, *Human Nature and the Social Order* (New York: Scribner's, 1902), and George H. Mead, *Mind, Self, and Society: From the Standpoint of a Social Behaviorist,* ed. Charles W. Morris (Chicago: University of Chicago Press, 1934).

30. C. R. Rogers, *On Becoming a Person: A Therapist's View of Psychotherapy* (Boston: Houghton Mifflin, 1961), p. 103.

31. David W. Johnson, *Reaching Out: Interpersonal Effectiveness and Self-Actualization* (Boston: Allyn & Bacon, 2003), pp. 57–58.

**Exercise 1–A
Journal Writing**

Journal writing has been used by educational disciplines, career coaches, and analysts for years. Developing reflective skills can lead managers and students to increased self-awareness, responsibility, and accountability as well as aid students to relate concepts and theories to practice.

In a separate notebook, keep an ongoing journal to record your thoughts, perceptions, insights, and goals for future interpersonal development. An entry should follow each class session or topic area. Your instructor will select the entry format and inform you of the collection dates.

The length of the entry is up to you. You should not be writing to impress; this is for your own personal learning and development. Write whatever you want, your ideas, feelings, and reactions relevant to the interpersonal skill being discussed. Your entry may be either negative or positive, as long as you try to be genuine and authentic. What you write should represent what you felt, thought, or learned that seemed important to your development. Entries might include such areas as these:

- Insights gained or concepts being explored.
- Reactions to the instructor, course, or other participants.
- Feelings/thoughts about yourself related to the course content, participants, and so on.
- Questions raised, resolutions made, things tried, risks taken.

Begin your first entry by doing a personal analysis based on your current perceptions of your interpersonal skills. Answer the following questions to give yourself a basis against which to compare your future development.

1. How would you describe your overall interpersonal effectiveness?
2. How would you describe your interpersonal relationships? Write about your best and worst relationship.
3. What are your personal strengths regarding interpersonal skills usage?
4. What are your weaknesses regarding interpersonal skills usage?
5. What are your goals for interpersonal development?

Every subsequent journal entry should include the following:

- The date.
- The interpersonal area being covered.
- A reevaluation of your strengths and weaknesses.
- What you have learned regarding the skill area, yourself, or personal improvements obtained.
- Goals and action steps for future growth and development.

Source: From Robert Loo and Karran Thorpe, "Using Reflective Learning Journals to Improve Individual and Team Performance," *Team Performance Management* 8, no. 5/6 (2002), pp. 134–40. Reprinted with permission of Emerald Group Publishing Limited.

**Exercise 1–B
The Big Five Locator
Questionnaire**

1. Participants are to complete the Big Five Locator Questionnaire. On each numerical scale indicate which point is generally more descriptive of you. If the two terms are equally descriptive, mark the midpoint.

2. Complete the scoring sheet, following the instructions.

3. Place the scores on the Big Five Locator Interpretation Sheet.

Source: The Big Five Locator is a quick assessment tool to be used with an instructor and willing learners. Care should be taken to follow up this profile with a more reliable personality assessment instrument. This instrument was developed by P. J. Howard, P. L. Medina, and J. M. Howard. "The Big Five Locator: A Quick Assessment Tool for Consultants and Trainers," from *The Annual, Developing Human Resources*, by J. William Pfeiffer and David Leonard Goodstein, Vol. 1, "Training," 1996, pp. 119–22. Copyright © 1996 by John Wiley & Sons, Inc. Reprinted by permission of John Wiley & Sons, Inc.

The Big Five Locator Questionnaire

Instructions: On each numerical scale that follows, indicate which point is generally more descriptive of you. If the two terms are equally descriptive, mark the midpoint.

1.	Eager	5 4 3 2 1	Calm
2.	Prefer Being with Other People	5 4 3 2 1	Prefer Being Alone
3.	A Dreamer	5 4 3 2 1	No Nonsense
4.	Courteous	5 4 3 2 1	Abrupt
5.	Neat	5 4 3 2 1	Messy
6.	Cautious	5 4 3 2 1	Confident
7.	Optimistic	5 4 3 2 1	Pessimistic
8.	Theoretical	5 4 3 2 1	Practical
9.	Generous	5 4 3 2 1	Selfish
10.	Decisive	5 4 3 2 1	Open Ended
11.	Discouraged	5 4 3 2 1	Upbeat
12.	Exhibitionist	5 4 3 2 1	Private
13.	Follow Imagination	5 4 3 2 1	Follow Authority
14.	Warm	5 4 3 2 1	Cold
15.	Stay Focused	5 4 3 2 1	Easily Distracted
16.	Easily Embarrassed	5 4 3 2 1	Don't Give a Darn
17.	Outgoing	5 4 3 2 1	Cool
18.	Seek Novelty	5 4 3 2 1	Seek Routine
19.	Team Player	5 4 3 2 1	Independent
20.	A Preference for Order	5 4 3 2 1	Comfortable with Chaos
21.	Distractible	5 4 3 2 1	Unflappable
22.	Conversational	5 4 3 2 1	Thoughtful
23.	Comfortable with Ambiguity	5 4 3 2 1	Prefer Things Clear-Cut
24.	Trusting	5 4 3 2 1	Skeptical
25.	On Time	5 4 3 2 1	Procrastinate

Scoring the Big Five Questionnaire

Instructions:

1. Find the sum of the circled numbers on the *first* row of each of the five-line groupings (Row 1 + Row 6 + Row 11 + Row 16 + Row 21 = _____). This is your raw score for "emotional stability." Circle the number in the EMOTIONAL STABILITY column of the Score Conversion Sheet that corresponds to this raw score.

2. Find the sum of the circled numbers on the *second* row of each of the five-line groupings (Row 2 + Row 7 + Row 12 + Row 17 + Row 22 = _____). This is your raw score for "extroversion." Circle the number in the EXTROVERSION column of the Score Conversion Sheet that corresponds to this raw score.

3. Find the sum of the circled numbers on the *third* row of each of the five-line groupings (Row 3 + Row 8 + Row 13 + Row 18 + Row 23 = _____). This is your raw score for "openness to experience." Circle the number in the OPENNESS TO EXPERIENCE column of the Score Conversion Sheet that corresponds to this raw score.

4. Find the sum of the circled numbers on the *fourth* row of each of the five-line groupings (Row 4 + Row 9 + Row 14 + Row 19 + Row 24 = _____). This is your raw score for "agreeableness." Circle the number in the AGREEABLENESS column of the Score Conversion Sheet that corresponds to this raw score.

5. Find the sum of the circled numbers on the *fifth* row of each of the five-line groupings (Row 5 + Row 10 + Row 15 + Row 20 + Row 25 = _____). This is your raw score for "conscientious." Circle the number in the CONSCIENTIOUSNESS column of the Score Conversion Sheet that corresponds to this raw score.

6. Find the number in the far right or far left column that is parallel to your circled raw score. Enter this norm score in the box at the bottom of the appropriate column.

7. Transfer your norm score to the appropriate scale on the Big Five Locator Interpretation Sheet.

Big Five Locator Score Conversion Sheet

Norm Score	Emotional Stability	Extroversion	Openness to Experience	Agreeableness	Conscientiousness	Norm Score
80			25			80
79						79
78						78
77	22					77
76			24			76
75						75
74						74
73	21		23			73
72		25				72
71				25		71
70	20	24	22			70
69					25	69
68				24		68
67		23	21		24	67
66	19					66
65		22		23	23	65
64			20			64
63					22	63
62	18	21	19	22		62
61					21	61
60		20				60
59	17		18	21	20	59
58						58
57		19				57
56			17			56
55	16	18		20	19	55
54		16		19		54
53						53
52		17			18	52
51	15					51
50		16	15	18	17	50
49						49
48	14	15			16	48
47			14	17		47
46		14			15	46
45			13			45
44	13			16	14	44
43		13				43
42			12			42
41				15	13	41
40	12	12	11			40
39						39
38				14	12	38
37		11	10			37
36	11					36
35		10		13	11	35
34			9			34
33	10	9			10	33
32				12		32
31			8			31
30		8			9	30
29	9			11		29
28		7	7		8	28
27				10		27
26		6			7	26
25	8		6			25
24				9	6	24
23						23
22			5		22	22
21	7	5				21
20				8		20

| Enter Norm Scores Here: | Adj = | S = | O = | A = | C = | |

(Norms based on a sample of 161 forms completed in 1993–94.)

Name _____   Date _____

Big Five Locator Interpretation Sheet

Scores:

Emotional Stability   _____

Extroversion   _____

Openness to Experience   _____

Agreeableness   _____

Conscientiousness   _____

Strong Emotional Stability: secure, unflappable, rational, unresponsive, guilt free	Resilient	Responsive		Reactive		Weak Emotional Stability: excitable, worrying, reactive, high-strung, alert
	35	45		55	65	
Low Extroversion: private, independent, works alone, reserved, hard to read	Introvert	Ambivert		Extrovert		High Extroversion: assertive, sociable, warm, optimistic, talkative
	35	45		55	65	
Low Openness to Experience: practical, conservative, depth of knowledge, efficient, expert	Preserver	Moderate		Explorer		High Openness to Experience: broad interests, curious, liberal, impractical, likes novelty
	35	45		55	65	
Low Agreeableness: skeptical, questioning, tough, aggressive, self-interest	Challenger	Negotiator		Adapter		High Agreeableness: trusting, humble, altruistic, team player, conflict averse, frank
	35	45		55	65	
Low Conscientiousness: spontaneous, unconcerned with deadlines, adaptable, fickle, impulsive	Flexible	Balanced		Focused		High Conscientiousness: dependable, organized, disciplined, cautious, stubborn
	35	45		55	65	

Note: The Big Five Locator is intended for use only as a quick assessment for teaching purposes.

Source: The Big Five Locator is a quick assessment tool to be used with an instructor and willing learners. Care should be taken to follow up this profile with a more reliable personality assessment instrument. This instrument was developed by P. J. Howard, P. L. Medina, and J. M. Howard. "The Big Five Locator: A Quick Assessment Tool for Consultants and Trainers," from *The Annual, Developing Human Resources*, by J. William Pfeiffer and David Leonard Goodstein, Vol. 1, "Training," 1996, pp. 119–22. Reprinted by permission of John Wiley & Sons, Inc.

Exercise 1–C
Self-monitoring
Questionnaire

For the following statements, indicate the degree to which you think the following statements are true or false by circling the appropriate number. Use the following key as a guideline for scoring:

5 = Certainly, always true

4 = Generally true

3 = Somewhat true, but with exceptions

2 = Somewhat false, but with exceptions

1 = Generally false

0 = Certainly, always false

1. In social situations, I have the ability to alter my behavior if I feel that something else is called for.   5 4 3 2 1 0

2. I am often able to read people's true emotions correctly through their eyes.   5 4 3 2 1 0

3. I have the ability to control the way I come across to people, depending on the impression I wish to give them.   5 4 3 2 1 0

4. In conversations, I am sensitive to even the slightest change in the facial expression of the person I'm conversing with.   5 4 3 2 1 0

5. My powers of intuition are quite good when it comes to understanding others' emotions and motives.   5 4 3 2 1 0

6. I can usually tell when others consider a joke in bad taste, even though they may laugh convincingly.   5 4 3 2 1 0

7. When I feel that the image I am portraying isn't working, I can readily change it to something that does.   5 4 3 2 1 0

8. I can usually tell when I've said something inappropriate by reading the listener's eyes.   5 4 3 2 1 0

9. I have trouble changing my behavior to suit different people and different situations.   5 4 3 2 1 0

10. I have found that I can adjust my behavior to meet the requirements of any situation I find myself in.   5 4 3 2 1 0

11. If someone is lying to me, I usually know it at once from that person's manner of expression.   5 4 3 2 1 0

12. Even when it might be to my advantage, I have difficulty putting up a good front.   5 4 3 2 1 0

13. Once I know what the situation calls for, it's easy for me to regulate my actions accordingly.   5 4 3 2 1 0

Scoring Key:
Add up the circled numbers, except reverse the scores for questions 9 and 12. On those, a circled 5 becomes a 0, 4 becomes a 1, and so forth. High self-monitors are defined as those with scores of 53 or higher.

Source: Based on R. D. Lennox and R. N. Wolfe, "Revision of the Self-monitoring Scale," *Journal of Personality and Social Psychology,* June 1984, p. 1361. Copyright © 1984 by the American Psychological Association. Adapted with permission.

**Exercise 1–D
Selective Perception**

How does selective perception affect the interpretation of what we see and hear?

_____

_____

_____

Your instructor will read two scenarios. Following the reading of each situation, write in the appropriate column what you see and hear from the description (what picture comes to mind?), what judgments you make or conclusions you draw about the situation, and what (if any) actions you would take.

Scenario One:

_____

_____

_____

Scenario Two:

_____

_____

_____

What I see/hear:	My judgment:	What action I would take:
1.		
2.		

Questions to be considered individually and discussed in small groups:

1. Why do we interpret the same scenario differently from others?
2. What impact does this have on developing relationships?
3. What if in scenario one the person you "met" was a woman? How would your interpretation of the situation change?
4. What if in scenario two, the person with the daughter was her mother instead of her father? Or perhaps the discussion was between a father and his son? How would your interpretation of these situations change?
5. Why is it important to know what our biases are?
6. Let's say it's three years in the future. You've been working for a _Fortune_ 500 firm as a member of a product development team. The meeting is about to start when a man matching the description in scenario one walks in. What's your judgment? Why?
7. As the meeting proceeds, he's about to open his mouth. Before he speaks, do you assume that he is credible or not credible until proven otherwise?
8. How do our biases help/hinder us in the workplace?

Exercise 1–E
The Social Mirror

To recognize the potential inaccuracy or incompleteness of the social mirror, or others' opinions about you as a person, take a moment to reflect on how the social mirror has affected you. Use the questions as a guide. Reflect back on all aspects of your life: personal (dealing with family and friends, roommates, neighbors, significant others), academic (teachers, coaches, classmates), and professional (bosses, co-workers, subordinates, mentors) to examine what influences others have had on your self-image and other areas of importance to you (community, religion, sports, etc.).

1. What would others say about you that is generally positive?

   _____

   _____

   _____

   _____

   _____

2. What "constructive suggestions" would others offer to help you improve or change?

   _____

   _____

   _____

   _____

   _____

3. What do you most like about yourself?

   _____

   _____

   _____

   _____

   _____

4. What do you most dislike in yourself and would like to change?

   _____

   _____

   _____

   _____

   _____

5. What beliefs do you have about yourself that limit you?

   _____

   _____

   _____

   _____

   _____

6. How might these beliefs have been created or influenced by your social mirror?

_____

_____

_____

_____

7. Since it is possible—perhaps even likely—that these weaknesses or limitations are more imagined than real, what could you do to turn them into strengths?

_____

_____

_____

_____

_____

Source: This exercise is adapted from Stephen Covey's _Seven Habits of Highly Effective People,_ Leadership Training Manual.

**Exercise 1–F
Expanding
Self-awareness**

1. Identify a behavior of yours that you would like to change. Practice a different form of that behavior for one week. For example, if you constantly interrupt others, try to go a week without interrupting anyone. Keep a record of every time you change this behavior. Reward yourself at the end of the week for being conscious of the need to change. Attempt a different behavior in week two, and so on.

2. Observe a person you admire at work or in school off and on for several days. How would you describe that person's attitude? What evidence do you have of this? What can you do to emulate his or her positive qualities?

3. Write on a sheet of paper adjectives that you wish could describe your personality. Identify some ways in which you could make changes to incorporate these qualities into your interactions with others.

4. Ask a few close friends for feedback about you as a person, your strong qualities, and areas you could change.

5. Reflect upon the last time you found yourself under a lot of pressure. How did you react? Respond? Behave? Develop a plan to help you think clearly in future situations to have a more controlled and less emotional response. For example, if you usually have a physical response when you get angry, think of an alternative means to handle your anger.

Exercise 1–G
Interpersonal Skills Checklist

Interpersonal skills are vitally important in today's workplace even though you may be an individual contributor. It's critical to communicate effectively with your boss, colleagues, and customers. However, most people do not communicate as effectively as they could. Rate each of the 12 interpersonal skills listed below using a scale of 1 to 5, where 1 means disagree and 5 is agree. Sum your score to see how your interpersonal skills add up. If your score is 60 or lower, develop an action plan to improve your weaker interpersonal skills, which will positively affect your leadership skills and effectiveness.

	Disagree	Neutral			Agree
1. Effective listening skills I always actively listen to both verbal and nonverbal communications of others.	1	2	3	4	5
2. Accepting responsibility I constantly take responsibility and am accountable for my decisions, actions, and behaviors.	1	2	3	4	5
3. Problem-solving ability I am competent at helping others creatively solve tough problems in a calm and soothing manner.	1	2	3	4	5
4. Appropriate expression of feelings and opinions I always clearly articulate my feelings and opinions during meetings without becoming overly emotional.	1	2	3	4	5
5. Self-awareness I am continually aware of my feelings and emotions and take into account how they can affect my actions and behaviors.	1	2	3	4	5
6. Awareness of others I always appreciate others' experiences and contributions from diverse backgrounds as well as being sensitive to how my behaviors affect others.	1	2	3	4	5
7. Acknowledge others' achievements I continually compliment and praise others for their achievements and show appreciation for others' contributions.	1	2	3	4	5
8. Trust and integrity I always follow through on my commitments and demonstrate honesty and integrity in my actions.	1	2	3	4	5
9. Openness to feedback I continually solicit feedback from others and incorporate their suggestions to improve my weaknesses.	1	2	3	4	5
10. Accepting others' perspectives I always empathize with and am sensitive to the needs of others, which enables me to recognize and accept different points of view.	1	2	3	4	5
11. Aligning goals I always manage my behavior during social interactions so I am able to align my goals with the goals of others.	1	2	3	4	5
12. Managing conflict I continually manage conflict effectively and strive to create win–win solutions by constructively influencing the behavior of others and using effective communication and persuasion strategies.	1	2	3	4	5

_____**Total Score**

Evaluation:

    54–60 = Excellent interpersonal skills

    47–53 = Good interpersonal skills

    40–46 = Average interpersonal skills

    33–39 = Weak interpersonal skills

  Below 33 = Poor interpersonal skills

Exercise 1–H
Reflection/Action Plan

This chapter focused on self-awareness—what it is, why it's important, and how to acquire and increase the degree to which you possess it. Other elements that comprise the self, including personality, attitude, and emotional intelligence, were also discussed. Complete the following worksheet upon completing all reading and experiential activities for this chapter.

1. The one or two areas in which I am most strong are:

2. The one or two areas in which I need more improvement are:

3. If I did only one thing to improve in this area, it would be to:

4. Making this change would probably result in:

5. If I did not change or improve in this area, it would probably affect my personal and professional life in the following ways:

2 Self-disclosure and Trust

Learning Points

How do I:
- Improve my personal and professional relationships?
- Learn to trust others, especially when trust has been broken?
- Determine the appropriate amount to disclose to others?
- Use situational cues to guide self-disclosure and trust?
- Share my feelings about and reactions to people and situations, in addition to facts?
- Demonstrate that I can be trusted?

Mary Townsend has been on the fast track at the investment firm for which she has worked for five years. She entered graduate school shortly after graduating with honors from an elite university in the northeast. While in graduate school she interned with an investment firm in New York City that at the time was co-headed by John White, a close friend of the family. During her tenure at the firm, she exceeded all performance expectations and rose to the rank of vice president within three years. Now she is in line for another promotion, but her performance has slacked off. Her record is inconsistent. One minute she appears to be at the top of her game, the next she is preoccupied and unreliable.

Her immediate supervisor, Jane Montgomery, has tried to talk with Mary about her inconsistent performance, to no avail. Jane, a director in the firm, placed a call to John White. John no longer heads the firm, but often serves as a sounding board to senior management on important personnel and client issues in his role as senior partner. Jane has requested that John meet with Mary.

After an initial greeting, John praises Mary for her past performance with the firm and then expresses concern over her current performance. Mary responds by revealing that she feels she is in over her head. "Promise not to tell anyone," she pleads, and begins to discuss numerous personal incidents that are affecting her performance, such as the breakup of a long-standing romance, financial problems brought on by overextending her credit, and a falling out with her family over their concerns about her lack of interest in getting married, having children, and settling down.

While sympathetic, John is dismayed at what he learns from Mary about her troubles. He concludes that Mary's personal problems are detracting from her ability to focus on her job. John recommends to Mary's supervisor that she be let go as soon as a "legitimate" opportunity presents itself. One such opportunity is the upcoming announcement that due to the growth of online investment companies, the firm will be less reliant on the individuals at Mary's level.

1. What could Mary have done to minimize the degree to which her personal problems spilled over into work?

2. Did Mary disclose too much about herself, setting herself up for a negative recommendation from John? How would you have handled this situation?

3. Did John overstep his bounds in his conversation with Mary about her performance? What about the promise he made to her?

"Trust no one. Not your closest advisors, your spouse, your brother, your God. Trust only yourself, or you will face pain every day of your life."

These harsh words were spoken by the Egyptian king portrayed by Yul Brynner in the classic Cecil B. DeMille movie, *The Ten Commandments*. Fortunately, times have changed and we now know better! While it is good advice to not be too trusting early in a relationship, the best relationships—in life and in business—are those that are built on mutual trust. Trust is built through a combination of shared experiences over time and willingness to talk with others about aspects of yourself that are relevant to your relationships. This chapter discusses self-disclosure and trust, their meaning and importance in life and in business.

What Is Self-disclosure?

Self-disclosure means making the self known to others,[1] letting others know what you think, feel, and want. It is revealing personal information to another that results in an enhanced and trusting personal or business relationship.[2] By revealing information about yourself, you allow others to be better able to understand what "makes you tick"—your motivations, fears, work style, strengths, and weaknesses. This knowledge helps others to determine strategies for working effectively with you. In addition, as you self-disclose, others reciprocate, enabling you to better develop strategies for understanding and working effectively with them.

Why Is Self-disclosure Important?

Self-disclosure benefits both individuals and their relationships. Individuals who self-disclose reap psychological and physiological benefits. By self-disclosing and reciprocating others' self-disclosure, we can improve our communication and relationships with others.

■ *Sharing with others about ourselves or problems we are facing often brings an enormous sense of psychological relief.*[3] Think about a time you did poorly on an exam or ended a relationship with a significant other. How did you handle the situation? Some go for a long walk, cry, sleep, or exercise; most will eventually talk to a friend or loved one. Through disclosing to others, we gain an added perspective that helps us see our disappointment or frustration in a different light.

■ *Disclosing to an appropriate person (one who is sympathetic, supportive, trustworthy, and a good listener) can help us validate our perceptions of reality.* By hearing ourselves talk, we process thoughts that are in our heads that help us to better understand the current situation in which we are involved. Often this brings with it a self-validation that tells us either our thoughts are on the right track or our thoughts and perceptions need some tweaking. Imagine you are distraught over a strained customer interaction and fear the customer will cease to do business with your firm. Being new to the firm, you are unsure how management will respond to this "error" and decide to get a co-worker's opinion on the situation. You disclose the situation and your concerns with her; she responds by not only agreeing with how you handled the situation, but also by providing information that this customer has a reputation for "being difficult." You can see how self-disclosure can open us up to new information about ourselves that improves our ability to look at the world through realistic—rather than idealistic—lenses.

■ *Self-disclosure can help reduce stress and tension*. By "getting things off your chest," you feel as if a burden has been lifted. If a customer was verbally abusive toward you or a co-worker took credit for your contributions, you are likely to bottle up your feelings in the interest of appearing professional. However, should these feelings remain unexpressed, you might explode! By sharing your problems or concerns with others, you might find ways to resolve them. Even if you find no resolution, you might feel relieved that you are not alone in your feelings—misery loves company. This intimacy brings us closer to others and increases our comfort in knowing that stress reduction through self-disclosure is available now and in the future in our relationships.

■ *Self-disclosure improves us physiologically*. By sharing ourselves with others, our stress levels go down, lowering anxiety and altering vital signs such as heart rate and blood pressure. Self-disclosure positively affects the mind–body connection and can lead to better physical—and emotional—health.[4] This concept is one of the core tenets of counseling and hotline/crisis-prevention programs.

■ *Self-disclosure can result in clearer lines of communication with others*. By showing our willingness to self-disclose and encouraging others to share self-information with us, we improve our ability to understand diverse perspectives and viewpoints. We become more confident in our ability to clarify others' intentions and meanings, and in giving feedback and having open discussions that minimize uncertainty and confusion.

■ *Self-disclosure can lead to strengthened, enhanced relationships with people in our personal life, colleagues, and clients*. As co-workers get to know each other, disclosure leads to liking, which leads to more disclosure, which leads to more liking—a cyclical effect that also occurs with supervisors and clients. Without self-disclosure, the level of intimacy and trust will be lower than in a group that discloses freely and appropriately. With disclosure comes trust, and with trust comes collaboration.[5] Such collaboration and trust are essential to strong relationships and also to innovation, which is critical for organizations to compete and survive.[6]

■ *Self-disclosure affects team productivity*. The more co-workers enjoy working together, the more productive they can be on projects and in team situations.[7] For example, when working as a team under a tight deadline, knowledge of one another's work styles can help a team pull together and produce a top-quality project even when operating under time pressure. Conversely, a team that has not gotten to know one another will have difficulty pulling together on a tough assignment. This explains why team-building—processes and activities undertaken to help team members identify with one another and the team as a whole—is strongly endorsed by many organizations.

■ *Self-disclosure can create a trusting environment that is conducive to promoting long-term relationships with employees, customers, and suppliers*. Open communication is essential in dealing with and managing conflict, making effective decisions, and enhancing organizational culture. By building relationships through mutual self-disclosure, employees and management will develop open lines of communication. Self-disclosure between customers and suppliers will open the doors to long-term relationships critical for the future viability of an organization.[8]

■ *Self-disclosure also has benefits for people globally*. Culture plays an important role in shaping our personality and communication style, and, like self-awareness in chapter 1, self-disclosure is influenced by cultural rules and norms. Typically, Americans tend to disclose to many people but in less depth, while non-Westerners confide to fewer individuals but in greater depth. Consequently the level of intimacy in friendships may be higher in non-Western cultures than in Western ones.[9] Knowing how and when and to whom to disclose in different cultures is an important skill to master as you carve out a career that has global elements to it.

■ *When used appropriately, self-disclosure can strengthen online communication*. Disclosure is much more common now for many more individuals due to the prominence of interacting with family, friends, co-workers, and even strangers online. Right or wrong, we are becoming more accustomed to sharing information about ourselves in online social network communities. This can be positive when done appropriately—it is an easy way to connect on a regular basis with many individuals in your network—personally and professionally, domestically and globally. Surprisingly, this type of communication can actually enhance trust in relationships over time, as you exchange information that becomes more substantive and mutually beneficial.

Online Self-Disclosure[10]

Trust and control over information play a central role in our online self-disclosure behaviors. In online environments, if we perceive a threat to our privacy, we are more wary about disclosing information about ourselves. But when we trust the source, are assured privacy checks are in place, and have a higher degree of control over what we can choose to share, we disclose more personal information. Internet users, and particularly young people, do not have privacy fears as long as these conditions—trust and control—are met.

■ *Disclosure can improve organizational communication.* Companies are beginning to see some positive outcomes of their employees and customers using self-disclosure in online communities. Innovation, market research, brand ambassador programs, support forums, customer motivation, positive reviews, and increased sales are some of the benefits being cited by organizations that make it possible for their employees and customers to be connected to them through social media.[11]

Strategies for Self-disclosure

Effective self-disclosure includes these elements:[12]

■ **Feelings as well as facts**—When you share your feelings about or reactions to others, let them get to know the real you. Saying you have three co-workers is interesting information, but revealing the kind of relationship you have with them helps others get to know you better.

■ **Transparency**—When you share information either face to face or online, to the extent that you can, prepare in advance, think twice before "speaking," and provide details as appropriate to ensure those with whom you are interacting have the necessary information. Speak openly and transparently without hidden agendas. This will build trust and ensure your comments are taken as genuine. This will in turn encourage a similar tone and openness from others.

■ **Authenticity**—Authenticity is becoming a "currency of exchange" in online communications.[13] Anyone can "google" you or look at your LinkedIn or Facebook account and glean quite a bit of information from you. Make sure that the way you are presenting yourself in meetings and interactions is consistent with what people may already know about you from your online presence.

■ **Greater breadth and depth over time**—Have you ever cared about someone but felt uncomfortable sharing your feelings? In order for self-disclosure to facilitate building a relationship, it has to grow gradually in depth (becoming more revealing about your feelings toward a particular issue or set of issues) and breadth (expanding the discussion to cover more issues, such as work, family, leisure, and core beliefs).[14]

■ **A focus on the present rather than the past**—While sharing about your past might help explain why you behave the way you do, it is not advisable to share all your past skeletons. Doing so might feel cathartic, but it also might leave you feeling vulnerable, especially if this disclosure is not reciprocated. Stay in the present.

■ **Reciprocity**—To the degree possible, try to match the level of self-disclosure offered by people with whom you become acquainted. Be careful not to overdisclose prematurely, before the relationship has had time to build familiarity and trust.[15] Don't be afraid to take the first important step to building a relationship. Lead by example, and others will follow suit. If they don't, pull back.

Self-description

Self-disclosure is different from self-description.

■ **Self-description** is the disclosure of nonthreatening information such as age, address, major, or organization for which you work. Self-disclosure is revealing significant personal information about yourself that exceeds the expectations of the moment[16] and that is not easily apparent to others, such as how you feel about issues that are important to you.

■ **Some amount of risk**—Not surprisingly, self-disclosure has an element of risk. At times, you may share information that might affect others' perceptions and acceptance of you as a person. For every action, there is a reaction, and in the case of self-disclosure, the benefits far outweigh the risks. People who engage in healthy, give-and-take dialogue with others are good managers of other people and of their relationships with others.

■ **Work focus**—We are accustomed to sharing information with people in our lives with whom we are intimate: our parents, loved ones, and close friends. The lesson here is that even in work situations, it is important for project team members and co-workers to get to know each other personally. Naturally there are limits to what is expected and to what is appropriate. There is no need to disclose information of such a personal nature that it becomes awkward or embarrassing for you or your co-worker. And given the prevalence of sexual harassment incidents, we are all well advised to restrict our disclosing to "safe" subjects. A rule of thumb to use is this: If the information would help a co-worker or colleague better understand how to work with you in the present, then the information is probably relevant and should be disclosed. If the information has little or nothing to do with the project you are working on, your ability to do the job, or your work style, it is probably less relevant and does not need to be shared.

Concerns about Self-disclosure

The importance of self-disclosure in business has long been recognized in terms of building client and employee relationships. As organizations become less hierarchical and more team-based, employees have less structure and fewer authority figures to rely on, increasing their need to work collaboratively in making decisions and getting things done. In other words, we can't rely on bosses to issue directives and achieve results based on sheer possession of authority. Collaboration depends to a certain extent on trust. And trust is fostered through self-disclosure.

What does this mean for those who are shy or reserved? Or who come from families or cultures in which self-disclosing is frowned upon? Or who are afraid to disclose themselves to others? Or for people who have been hurt by disclosing information to others who have used it against them?

You may be uncomfortable or hesitate to disclose information about yourself to co-workers for several reasons. First, you may be uncertain about how the information will be received and utilized. Will it be used against you in a performance appraisal? Will it be revealed to others outside the immediate work situation? You may be afraid of being judged harshly by others, concerned that things said in one context might be repeated in an unrelated context. You might have had previous negative experiences with self-disclosure in personal situations, affecting your willingness to be open in work situations. For example, it is quite common early in a close relationship to reveal much about yourself before the other person is willing to open up. If one says "I love you" and the other, now feeling threatened by the implied commitment, says nothing, the original discloser will withhold any further disclosure. Or perhaps you revealed something personal to a co-worker only to have that person violate the trust by disclosing the information to someone else.

There are several other potential concerns about which to be aware. If you have a low self-image, this will inhibit your willingness to self-disclose out of a fear of being judged negatively. However, the very act of appropriate self-disclosure can improve your well-being. Self-disclosure is best when met with responsiveness, caring, understanding, and support.[17] If you can find a friend or colleague that offers this level of support, it is a good first step in the process of learning how to disclose in a safe environment.

Sometimes managers fear self-disclosure because they are concerned that others, especially subordinates, will perceive their willingness to share as a weakness or a shortcoming, leaving them vulnerable. Paradoxically, those managers who are willing to self-disclose in appropriate ways are often viewed very favorably by their co-workers. This happens because subordinates are able to see the manager as more human—complete with strengths and vulnerabilities—than before, allowing subordinates to feel closer to and interested in their manager.

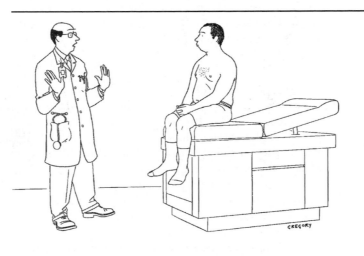

"Whoa—way too much information."

Source: http://www.cartoonbank.com/2002/whoa-way-too-much-information/invt/125155/?

The popularity of the Internet and **computer-mediated communication (CMC)**, as opposed to **face-to-face (FTF) communication**, as a method to meet new people, initiate and carry on meaningful conversations, and build long-term relationships raises interesting issues about the quantity and quality of online self-disclosure. Are online communications more, or less, conducive to self-disclosure? The Internet provides a forum for quick self-disclosure with individuals you don't know well. It can provide an anonymity that can lead to inappropriate self-disclosure. It also has the potential to lead to communication that, because of the lack of verbal and nonverbal cues, can appear to be abrasive, impulsive, and even abusive. Be aware too, that gender can play a role in CMC self-disclosure. An investigation into gender-based patterns of college student self-disclosure on the Internet revealed females were more likely than males to disclose personal information and to be more aware of their self-disclosure behaviors. Males reported they were more likely to disclose negative statements than females.[18]

As with any new development, there are risks in online self-disclosure. Revealing and obtaining personal information on the Web is correlated potentially with legal issues such as defamation, harassment, intellectual property rights, and others. And the promise of "anonymity" seems to be encouraging some people to use the Web as a forum for making controversial and offensive statements.[19] However, by following the guidelines for self-disclosure and building trust in this chapter, CMC has the potential to be as beneficial as FTF interactions.[20]

The benefits of self-disclosure far outweigh the concerns. If you are not used to talking about yourself to others, you will want to start slowly and with people you can trust. As you get to know a person or members of a group, gradually reveal information that helps others understand how to work effectively with you. As they disclose to you, you can increase your level of disclosure accordingly.

By following your instincts about what is appropriate and relevant, you will eventually find that it feels quite natural to talk about yourself with others. Soon you will find your project team members and co-workers will appreciate getting to know you, and that together you will be able to produce results beyond what was possible when you—and they—were more reserved.

Some Guidelines for Self-disclosure

- *Discuss situations as they happen; don't wait until they are old news.*[21] The impact of your disclosure will be greater and more understandable within the context of your relationship when you share your thoughts and reactions to situations at the time instead of days, weeks, or months later. For example, if you are a member of a team evaluating the potential adoption of a new computer system, withholding your concerns about the viability of this new system might prove problematic. On the one hand, you are concerned that others may look at you as too rigid or unable to accept change. However, you may have information or concerns that, if shared, would completely alter the decision-making process—in a way that would benefit your organization.

- *Choose the appropriate time and place.* Just as you may not choose to propose marriage in a crowded bar or noisy restaurant, you wouldn't want to tell your boss of your need for personal time right after he shares news that the department is being downsized.

- *Choose the appropriate level of disclosure.* Match the depth and breadth of your disclosure to the situation. You would be ill-advised to reveal your innermost dreams and fears to your boss on the first day of your new job.

- *Be cautious when sharing personal details* or details regarding your employer online. Share personal information on sites frequented by your friends and family; save information of a more professional nature for LinkedIn or group chats.

- *Share your current feelings to create an emotional connection with others and invite understanding.* You can focus on your feelings without having to act on them. Expressing your feelings, as opposed to focusing strictly on facts, can also stimulate reciprocal disclosure and initiate important conversation.[22]

- *Be sensitive to cultural differences.* Look into the business customs of the home countries of your classmates and co-workers. Understand what is appropriate and effective before attempting disclosure.

The Role of Self-disclosure in Increasing Self-awareness

We have discussed the many benefits of self-disclosure in the business world. While it is important to disclose to others, it is equally important to be honest with ourselves about our strengths and weaknesses. Sometimes this is difficult because we see ourselves differently than others see us or because we're not completely in touch with our inner selves—who we really are, what we believe, and how we come across to others. A concept that explains why this is true is the Johari Window.[23] Created by Joseph Luft and Harry Ingram, the **Johari Window** helps us understand how well we know ourselves and how much of ourselves we let others know. The Johari Window is depicted in Figure 2–1 in a grid that is divided into four regions, which represent the intersection of two axes:

Figure 2–1
The Johari Window

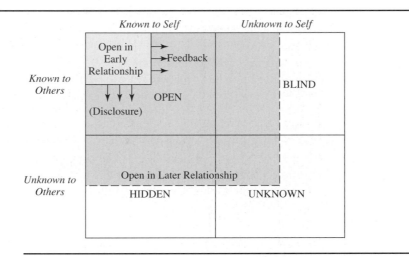

1. Degree to which you know or understand information about yourself (values, attitudes, beliefs).

2. Degree to which others know information about you.

The basic premise of the Johari Window is that our personal and professional relationships can be greatly improved through understanding ourselves in depth and then selecting those aspects of self that are appropriate to share with others. The more we share of ourselves with others, the more we can develop high-quality relationships. In order to complete this exchange, we must be fully aware of those aspects of ourselves that are "hidden" from view and those that we neither see nor know ourselves.

The **open area** consists of information about us that both we and others know, such as our name, job title or role, level in the organization, and possibly something about our personal life such as our marital status or the college from which we graduated. When we first begin a relationship, the open window is relatively small. We begin with safe information, such as the weather, school, and sports. As we build a relationship, we disclose more facts and feelings about ourselves and our beliefs, and the window enlarges vertically, reducing the hidden area. The larger the open area, the more productive and mutually beneficial the interpersonal relationship is likely to be.

The **hidden area** comprises information we know about ourselves but is hidden from others. This information can range from our concerns about a boss or job to financial, family, or health problems. Not sharing hidden information can create a barrier that protects a person in the short term. Over time, this lack of sharing can lead to distrust and miscommunication. In business this can have negative consequences such as reduced trust and morale. As we increase our comfort with and practice disclosing more and more information about ourselves through shared experiences with others, the hidden area shrinks. If we are more reserved, this area will remain rather large, resulting in relationships that aren't likely to develop beyond the acquaintance level.

The **blind area** denotes information others are aware of but we are not. For example, we might have an unknown nervous habit of tapping a pencil or wiggling a foot during meetings when we are feeling stressed or bored. We might see ourselves as patient and helpful, yet our subordinates see us as micromanagers. As we receive feedback from others on their observations of our personalities and behaviors, the blind area will decrease and the open area will become more complete. The more we understand our strengths and weaknesses and are open to others' views of us, the better managers we can be of our personal and work lives.

The **unknown area** contains information that neither we nor others know. This window is unknown due to our lack of experience or exposure to various situations, or due to our inability to process difficult events that occurred earlier in our lives. Until we have experienced certain things in life, we will not fully know how we will react or feel. Until others have seen us in certain situations or we have disclosed to them how we behaved or felt, this information will remain unknown to them. For example, the first time you felt you loved someone other than a family member, you may have found those feelings hard to express. How you express love may be unknown to you and to your significant other. This unknown window can also contain information that is forgotten or purposely suppressed. This window can become smaller over time as we grow, develop, and learn. Personal growth is a process. Self-awareness allows us to assimilate our experiences and move beyond them, rather than being unaware of, or worse, paralyzed by them. It also allows us to move forward in a positive way as we experience life and learn from both our successes and our mistakes.

What Is Trust?

By adding trust to self-disclosure, we are able to complete the relationship equation. The two elements form a circle: The more you trust, the more you disclose, and the more you disclose, the more you trust. How do we define trust? **Trust** is one's faith or belief in the integrity or reliability of another person or thing. Trust means confidence. When you trust people, you believe in them—in their integrity and in their abilities.[24] In business, as in life, trust is an essential building block in developing relationships with customers, colleagues, and business associates. Trust is very difficult to develop, and it is very easy to destroy.[25] Think of a relationship you've had where trust has been broken. Perhaps a promised raise didn't materialize, a client misrepresented his or her financial situation, or a friend informed you that your significant other—who was attending a conference in another state—was seen with someone else. Isn't it difficult to relate to the person who disappointed you now or believe that person's promises? Does the lack of trust make you less inclined to make plans or have anything to do with this person?

Self-disclosure + Trust = Stronger Relationships

Why Is Trust Important?

Trust is essential in the work environment. Research has shown that trust in the workplace promotes cooperation and effective teamwork and can lead to enhanced organizational performance.[26] Clients and customers need to be able to rely on information a company and its employees provide. Subordinates need to be able to trust their managers, managers need to be able to trust senior management, and everyone needs to be able to expect consistent reactions from their co-workers and associates. Trust is a necessary foundation for a healthy work environment. Without trust, employees may focus on self-protection—weakening their willingness to cooperate and collaborate, damaging their motivation, and thwarting innovative and productive work.[27]

■ *Individual impact*—The role of trust in organizations begins at the individual level. Trust is what binds leaders and followers together. In order to build trust, communication and action must be consistent. By demonstrating consistency, integrity, and concern, and by sharing organizational information straightforwardly and accurately, a leader's trustworthy behavior can promote and foster trust.[28]

■ *Organizational impact*—The seemingly endless stream of stories about corporate misbehavior has contributed to a steady erosion of trust in corporate America. When organization members violate trust with stakeholders, organizations lose stakeholder confidence. Losing confidence and integrity can lead to the eventual demise of the institution. Trust is built up on the basis of past experience.[29] In order to regain the trust of employees, stockholders, and the general public, leaders must first prove they are trustworthy, hence regaining integrity and confidence for their organizations.

Concerns About Building Trust

While an essential component of good relationships, trust does not come without some element of risk. Trusting is a two-way street. The person who places confidence in an individual must rely on that person to treat the information that was given in confidence. The element of risk is compounded by the inability of the truster to monitor or control the other party. For this reason trust is best when built up over time. As we gain experience with the judgments and behaviors of others, we can gradually build confidence in their ability to follow through on commitments and keep their word.

The development of trust in relationships may be affected by attribution theory (discussed in chapter 1).[30] As defined, the bias of the fundamental attribution error causes individuals to overestimate the influence of internal factors on the behavior of others. Since trust in relationships is directly impacted by the behaviors of others, we tend to determine that a trustworthy or untrustworthy action by a friend or co-worker was controlled by them rather than the situation. Because this bias greatly impacts individual perception, it is easy to see how quickly trust can be destroyed. Managers must be aware of their judgments and attributions to clearly determine if a perceived untrustworthy behavior warrants the loss of trust in a co-worker. Perhaps it had nothing to do with your relationship and instead simply resulted from the situation.

Strategies for Building Trust

Trust is composed of five elements.[31] (See Figure 2–2.) You are more likely to be seen as trustworthy if you demonstrate these characteristics:

- **Integrity**—honesty and sincerity. In short, you say what you mean and mean what you say. Integrity also relates to your ability to honestly disclose and share your thoughts, beliefs, and feelings.
- **Competence**—knowledge and ability. You are aware of your strengths and limitations, offering help where you can and seeking resources and assistance when needed.
- **Consistency**—conformity with previous practice; good judgment in handling situations. When you are consistent, for example, you do what you say you will do; friends and associates believe in your ability to follow through and do the right thing in a given situation.
- **Loyalty**—faithfulness to your friends and ideals. A trustworthy person supports friends and associates both within and outside their presence. One who sings your praises in front of you, but then spreads rumors behind your back is not only duplicitous but also untrustworthy.
- **Openness**—welcomes new ideas; willing to share ideas with others. This component of trust suggests that you are aware of yourself and comfortable sharing and disclosing with others. In addition, when someone shares with you, you encourage them and offer acceptance and support, as opposed to judgment and ridicule. Openness has been found to be the most important trust factor for employees in an organizational setting.[32]

Figure 2–2
Five Elements of Trust

Competence	Consistency	Loyalty	Openness
Integrity			
(without integrity, all other elements may be meaningless)			

Personal Trust-Builders

We can take some tangible actions to build others' trust in us (see Exercise 2–H). Some of these include the following:

- Follow through on promises and commitments made; and remember the opposite—don't promise what you can't produce.
- Don't reveal confidences told you in private.
- Avoid participating in unnecessary gossip about specific individuals.
- Don't make self-flattering or boasting statements about your capabilities.
- Develop a reputation for loyalty—a willingness to stand by, protect, and save face for others.
- Be consistent: Reliability and predictability help others build faith in your ability to deliver on promises made.
- Be realistic: Don't overcommit to the extent that you break promises.
- Develop personal competence: When you improve your knowledge and skills, people can count on you to hold up your end of the bargain.
- Gain a reputation for honesty and truthfulness: "Say what you mean and mean what you say."
- Make sure your actions are consistent with your spoken words: "Walk the talk."

Organizational Trust-builders

Organizations with low or no trust are susceptible to a range of negative employee responses, including high turnover, reduced job satisfaction, less cooperation, and increased absenteeism.[33] These behaviors often exist in organizations going through a merger or acquisition. As the products, services, employees, and cultures of two or more companies are joined together, clashes inevitably result. The more openly and effectively each company can communicate with its employees about the changes as they occur, the better the employees will be able to adjust and move forward in their work on behalf of the newly merged organization. Those companies that make information available to their employees are more successful at achieving their business goals than are those companies that keep their employees in the dark or misrepresent information to them.[34] Organizational cultures associated with trust emphasize:[35]

- Depth of relationships.
- Understanding of roles and responsibilities.
- Frequent, timely, and forthright communication.
- Member self-esteem and self-awareness.
- High levels of skill competence.
- Clarity of shared purpose, direction, and vision.
- Honoring promises and commitments.

Ten Managerial Tips for Developing Trust[36]

1. Practice what you preach—narrow the gap between your intentions and your behavior.
2. Open lines of communication—declare your intentions to others and invite feedback on your performance.

(continued)

3. Accept disagreements, differences of opinion, and conflict—when things go wrong and problems arise, seek solutions.

4. Keep confidential information confidential.

5. Let others know what you stand for and what you value.

6. Create an open environment—make it safe for others to be with you and to share with you.

7. Maintain a high level of integrity and honesty.

8. Know yourself and how others perceive you and your actions—build on your competencies and accept your limitations.

9. Build credibility with others by being consistent and reliable.

10. Avoid micromanaging—this sends the message that "I don't trust you."

A Note of Caution

Trust is not a right; it is earned. Trust is an aspect of relationships and it varies "within persons and across relationships."[37] That is, we do not automatically trust every individual in every situation. Perhaps we might trust certain but not all aspects of a person. If your co-worker supports you, is to you, and holds sensitive issues in confidence, you will trust her. However, if your co-worker reveals she has been unfaithful in her relationship with her spouse, suddenly her trustworthiness becomes suspect.

Our ability to trust is also situation-dependent. Trust depends on our having the information and experience needed to make good judgments in a given situation or situations. Trust is earned. It evolves over time, based on past successful experiences that build on each other to eventually build a climate of trust. Trust is fragile. It is easier to destroy than it is to build. Consider the couple who have been married for 10, 20, or more years. One untrustworthy act could destroy decades of trusting behaviors, with trust likely never to fully return. By valuing and fostering trust and trustworthiness in your personal and professional relationships, you will be able to build mutually satisfying, long-term relationships in both your work and life.

Summary

Self-disclosure and trust are two mutually reinforcing skills that, when practiced with the appropriate persons at the right time and place, can serve to deepen and improve personal and professional relationships. By letting another person know your values and your beliefs about and reactions to a situation, you not only improve your own understanding and concerns about a situation, but also improve the quality of communication, collaboration, and performance with that person. There are fears and risks associated with disclosure, however; knowing what, when, and how to disclose can serve to mitigate the fears and risks.

By letting others know you, you pave the way for them to develop trust in you. When others trust you, they are more likely to disclose to you. The mutually reinforcing nature of disclosure and trust forms the basis of healthy personal and professional relationships. Organizations that are characterized by a lack of trust, as is the case during times of change (i.e., downsizing and mergers), become primed for employee gossip, absenteeism, and turnover. Those who are characterized by openness and transparency are widely trusted and admired. By practicing the tips and techniques we shared, you can improve your skills in self-disclosure and trust and become more effective as an individual and as a manager.

Key Terms and Concepts

Authenticity

Blind area

Competence

Computer-mediated communication (CMC)

Consistency

Face-to-face communication (FTF)

Hidden area

Integrity

Johari Window

Loyalty

Open area

Openness

Self-description

Self-disclosure

Transparency

Trust

Unknown area

Discussion Questions

1. Self-disclosure has benefits, but it also has risks. Discuss both.
2. Was Mary Townsend's disclosure appropriate in the chapter opening case? Why or why not?
3. With so much work being done by work teams, in what ways can self-disclosure improve team performance?
4. Have you ever worked for a boss you didn't trust? How was this a problem?
5. We might trust certain but not all aspects of a person. Do you agree or disagree?
6. How does trust impact organizations? How can untrustworthy members impact an entire organization? How can organizations ensure members will be trustworthy?
7. Comment on these statements: "Trust is fragile;" "Trust is earned."

Endnotes

1. S. M. Jourard and P. Lasakow, "Some Factors in Self-Disclosure," *Journal of Abnormal and Social Psychology* 56 (1958), p. 91.

2. Yongsoo Kang, Jusik Park, and Jeanny Liu, "A Study of the Online Shopper's Self-Disclosure," *Academy of Marketing Studies Journal* 16, no. 1 (2012). p. 19.

3. Tania Pantchenko, Marie Lawson, and Marie R. Joyce, "Verbal and Non-Verbal Disclosure of Recalled Negative Experiences: Relation to Well-Being," *Psychology and Psychotherapy: Theory, Research and Practice* 76 (September, 2003), p. 260. Also see Georgeta Andreea Maier, Qin Zhang, and Alina Clark, "Self-Disclosure and Emotional Closeness in Intracultural Friendships: A Cross-Cultural Comparison Among U.S. Americans and Romanians," *Journal of Intercultural Communication Research* 42, no. 1 (2013), p. 22.

4. James W. Pennebaker, Cheryl F. Hughes, and Robin C. O'Heeron, "The Psychophysiology of Confession: Linking Inhibitory and Psychosomatic Processes," *Journal of Personality and Social Psychology* 52, no. 4 (April 1987), p. 782.

5. David L. Paul and Reuben R. McDaniel Jr., "A Field Study of the Effect of Interpersonal Trust on Virtual Collaborative Relationship Performance," *MIS Quarterly* 28, no. 2 (June 2004), p. 185.

6. S. L. Brown and K. M. Eisenhardt, "Product Development: Past Research, Present Findings and Future Directions," *Academy of Management Review* 20, no. 2 (April 1995), p. 357.

7. Stephen B. Knouse, "Building Task Cohesion to Bring Teams Together," *Quality Progress* 40, no. 3 (March 2007), p. 49.

8. Richard S. Jacobs, Michael R. Hyman, and Shaun McQuitty, "Exchange-specific Self-disclosure, Social Self-disclosure, and Personal Selling," *Journal of Marketing Theory and Practice* 9, no. 1 (Winter 2001), p. 48.

9. Maier, et al., p. 25.

10. Chyng-Yang Jang and Michael A. Stefanone, "Non-Directed Self-Disclosure in the Blogo-sphere," *Information, Communication and Society* 14, no. 7 (2011), pp. 1040–42. Also see Stefano Taddei and Bastianina Contena, "Privacy, Trust and Control: Which Relationships with On-Line Self-Disclosure?" *Computers in Human Behavior,* 29, no. 3 (May 2013), p. 822.

11. C. Posey, P. B. Lowry, T. L. Roberts, and T. S. Ellis, "Proposing the Online Community Self-Disclosure Model, The Case of Working Professionals in France and the U.K. Who Use Online Communities," *European Journal of Information Systems* 19, 2 (2010), p. 182.

12. David W. Johnson, *Reaching Out: Interpersonal Effectiveness and Self-Actualization* (Boston: Allyn & Bacon, 2003), pp. 46–47.

13. F. J. Perez-Latre, I. Portilla, and C. S. Blanco, "Social Networks, Media and Audiences: A Literature Review," *Comunicacion y Sociedad* 24, no. 1 (2011), p. 66.

14. Irwin Altman and Dalmas A. Taylor, *Social Penetration: The Development of Interpersonal Relationships* (New York: Holt, Rinehart and Winston, 2006).

15. Linda R. Weber and Allison Carter, "On Constructing Trust: Temporality, Self-Disclosure, and Perspective-Taking," *The International Journal of Sociology and Social Policy* 18, no. 1 (1998), pp. 22–23.

16. Charles Antaki, Rebecca Barnes, and Ivan Leudar, "Self-Disclosure as a Situated Interactional Practice," *British Journal of Social Psychology* 44, no. 2 (June 2005), p. 195.

17. Jessica J. Cameron, John G. Holmes, and Jacquie D. Vorauer, "When Self-Disclosure Goes Awry: Negative Consequences of Revealing Personal Failures for Lower Self-Esteem Individuals," *Journal of Experimental Social Psychology* 45, no. 1 (January 2009), p. 217.

18. Narissra Maria Punyanunt-Carter, "An Analysis of College Students' Self-Disclosure Behaviors on the Internet," *College Student Journal* 40, no. 2 (June 2006), pp. 329–31.

19. Taddei and Contena, p. 821.

20. Young-ok Yum and Kazuya Hara, "Mediated Relationship Development: A Cross-Cultural Comparison," *Journal of Computer-Mediated Communication* 11, no. 1 (October 2005), article 7. Accessed at http://jcmc.indiana.edu/vol11/issue1/.

21. Joanne Frattaroli, "Experimental Disclosure and Its Moderators: A Meta-Analysis," *Psychological Bulletin* 132, no. 6 (November 2006), p. 829.

22. S. Alavi, V. Ahuja, and Y. Medury, "ECRM Using Online Communities," *IUP Journal of Marketing Management* 10, no. 1 (2011), p. 39.

23. J. Luft and H. Ingham, "The Johari Window: A Graphic Model for Interpersonal Relation-ships." University of California Western Training Lab, 1955.

24. Stephen M. R. Covey, *The Speed of Trust: The One Thing That Changes Everything* (New York: Free Press, 2006), p. 5.

25. L. Poppo and D. J. Schepker, "Repairing Public Trust in Organizations," *Corporate Reputation Review* 13, 2 (2010), p. 127.

26. Anna-Maija Lämsä and Raminta Pucetaite, "Development of Organizational Trust among Employees from a Contextual Perspective," *Business Ethics* 15, no. 2 (April 2006), p. 130.

27. Risto Harisalo, Heikki Huttunen, and John McInerney, "Trust-Creating Practices for Marketing Managers," *Journal of Change Management* 5, no. 4 (December 2005), p. 468.

28. Melinda J. Moye and Alan B. Henkin, "Exploring Associations between Employee Empower-ment and Interpersonal Trust in Managers," *The Journal of Management Development* 25, no. 2 (2006), p. 113.

29. H. Afzal, M. A. Khan, K. ur Rehman, I. Ali, and S. Wajahat, "Consumer's Trust in the Brand: Can It Be Built through Brand Reputation, Brand Competence and Brand Predictability," *International Business* Research 3, 1 (2010), p. 44.

30. Donald L. Ferrin and Kurt T. Dirks, "The Use of Rewards to Increase and Decrease Trust: Mediating Processes and Differential Effects," *Organization Science* 14, no. 1 (January/February 2003), p. 18.

31. P. L. Schindler and C. C. Thomas, "The Structure of Interpersonal Trust in the Workplace," *Psychological Reports* (October 1993), pp. 563–73.

32. Richard E. Wilmot, "A Commitment to Trust," *Communication World* 24, no. 2 (March/April 2007), p. 36.

33. Stephen J. Deery, Roderick D. Iverson, and Janet T. Walsh, "Toward a Better Understanding of Psychological Contract Breach: A Study of Customer Service Employees," *Journal of Applied Psychology* 91, no. 1 (2006), p. 167.

34. Robert D. Costigan, Selim S. Ilter, and J. Jason Berman, "A Multi-Dimensional Study of Trust in Organizations," *Journal of Managerial Issues* 10, no. 3 (Fall 1998), pp. 303–17.

35. Jeffrey Cufaude, "Creating Organizational Trust," *Association Management* 51, no. 7 (July 1999), pp. 26–35.

36. Robert Glaser, "Paving the Road to TRUST," *HR Focus* 74, no. 1 (January 1997), p. 5.

37. F. David Schoorman, Roger C. Mayer, and James H. Davis, "An Integrative Model of Organizational Trust: Past, Present, and Future," *Academy of Management Review* 32, no. 2 (April 2007), p. 344.

**Exercise 2–A
People Hunt**

Mill around the classroom or training room or participate with your online learning community and identify people who can help you complete the following chart.[1] Write the names of the people you identify in the "match" columns. Try not to use the same person more than three times in your chart. Challenge yourself to meet and talk with as many people as possible.

Information	Match 1	Match 2	Match 3
Same hobby or interest: _____			
Favorite outdoor activity: _____			
Same favorite music: _____			
Same favorite movie: _____			
Same favorite fast food: _____			
Same favorite color: _____			
Same number of siblings: _____			
Same hometown or country: _____			
Same favorite TV show: _____			

After completing the chart, answer the following questions:

1. In what ways did this exercise help you get to know others better?
2. What did you learn about yourself from this exercise?
3. What things do you and don't you have in common with others?
4. What additional questions can be asked to uncover other similarities between you and others?
5. How can you apply this exercise to improving your relationships with others?

[1]If this is a distance learning class, students should use whatever means available to identify people who match your information.

Exercise 2–B
Icebreakers

Name, Face, and Fact

Participants sit in a circle and the first person states his or her name and a fact related to him or her. Facts can include items from the following categories: favorite food, hometown street name, college major, favorite color, favorite book, favorite travel destination, and so on.

Name Repetition

Participants stand in a circle and, taking turns, each person says her or his name. Participants then throw a ball to another member in the circle, each stating her or his name first, followed by the name of the person to whom she or he is throwing the ball. Each time a person receives the ball, his or her name is stated as well as that of the person who threw the ball.

Name Tags

Participants write their name in the center of a piece of paper. In each corner of the paper participants write personal information such as where they are from, their college major, their ideal job, their favorite travel destination, their favorite movie/TV show/book, and so on. Participants mill about the room and introduce themselves to as many others as possible in the time allowed, being sure to listen intently to what each person is disclosing to others.

Show and Share

Participants bring in a personal item—an item that reveals something significant about their personal "essence" or identity. The item can be something the participant enjoys, carries at all times, is of sentimental value, or that holds some personal meaning. Participants show and discuss the meaning behind the object. Others give feedback on what they think the item says about the participant as well as share how they can personally relate to the other's show-and-share item.

Multiple Introductions

Participants stand and mill about the room, introducing themselves to one new person every two minutes. The instructor asks the group to concentrate on one question at a time per person met. After two minutes, the instructor calls time and the participants introduce themselves to a new partner and engage in a two-minute discussion about the next topic on the list. Suggested topics, which can be written in advance on a board, include these:

1. Your college major and why you chose it.
2. Your current job and what you like about it.
3. What you did last summer (and what you wished you had done instead!).
4. Why you chose the college you're attending or attended.
5. Your first job and what you liked, disliked, and learned about it.
6. A favorite hobby or nonschool, nonwork activity.
7. Why you chose the career you're in or are pursuing.
8. What you would do (and in what order) if you won the lottery.
9. Your favorite video game, app, book, TV show, Broadway play, or movie and why.
10. Your favorite travel destination.
11. What you would do if you didn't have to work for a living.
12. What you liked about this exercise—and what you didn't—and why.

Exercise 2–C
Fishbowl

A fishbowl is a clear glass container we can see through and into from every angle. The fishbowl exercise is designed to help participants identify personal things that others can see and that they feel comfortable disclosing to others. This activity may be done in small groups or in front of the class.

Inside the fishbowl is an assortment of small cards, each containing a topic. Participants select a card and present a short (1–2 minutes) impromptu talk regarding an experience they have had relating to the topic. Participants use as many descriptors as possible to allow everyone to be able to understand and relate to the situation. Participants should be as expressive as they can be, telling a story, emphasizing their feelings and those of the other people involved in the story, and including their and others' reactions to what was occurring. Participants should include this information:

- A description of the players—all those involved in the situation.
- Information about the setting, atmosphere, surroundings, and so on.
- Details about the situation as it occurred.
- Thoughts and feelings they had about the experience as it unfolded.
- Outcomes, including lessons learned, awareness gained, and others.

Note: If this exercise is being done outside of the classroom, participants should pair up with a friend at school or work and take turns sharing stories as explained above.

Sample fishbowl questions (your instructor has more):

- Your happiest/saddest holiday memory.
- Your most/least enjoyable travel experience.
- An accomplishment you worked hard to attain.
- A lesson you learned in childhood that remains with you to this day.
- A time when you felt angry/happy/embarrassed/lucky.
- A memorable experience from grade school.
- A time you realized you had made a mistake, how you handled it and what you learned from it.

Exercise 2–D
Johari Window
Questionnaire

Friendship Relations Survey

This questionnaire was written to help you assess your understanding of your behavior in interpersonal relationships. There are no right or wrong answers. The best answer is the one that comes closest to representing your quest for good interpersonal relationships. In each statement, the first sentence gives a situation and the second sentence gives a reaction. For each statement indicate the number that is closest to the way you would handle the situation.

　　5 = You *always* would act this way.
　　4 = You *frequently* would act this way.
　　3 = You *sometimes* would act this way.
　　2 = You *seldom* would act this way.
　　1 = You *never* would act this way.

Try to relate each question to your own personal experience. Take as much time as you need to give a true and accurate answer for yourself. *There is no right or wrong answer. Trying to give the "correct" answer will make your answer meaningless to you. Be honest with yourself.*

	Never				Always
1. You work with a friend, but some of her mannerisms and habits are getting on your nerves and irritating you. More and more you avoid interacting with or even seeing your friend.	1	2	3	4	5

		Never				Always

2. In a moment of weakness, you give away a friend's secret. Your friend finds out and calls you to ask about it. You admit to it and talk with your friend about how to handle secrets better in the future. — 1 2 3 4 5

3. You have a friend who never seems to have time for you. You ask him about it, telling him how you feel. — 1 2 3 4 5

4. Your friend is upset at you because you have inconvenienced him. He tells you how he feels. You tell him he is too sensitive and is overreacting. — 1 2 3 4 5

5. You had a disagreement with a friend and now she ignores you whenever she's around you. You decide to ignore her back. — 1 2 3 4 5

6. A friend has pointed out that you never seem to have time for him. You explain why you have been busy and try for a mutual understanding. — 1 2 3 4 5

7. At great inconvenience, you arrange to take your friend to the doctor's office. When you arrive to pick her up, you find she has decided not to go. You explain to her how you feel and try to reach an understanding about future favors. — 1 2 3 4 5

8. You have argued with a friend and are angry with her, ignoring her when you meet. She tells you how she feels and asks about restoring the friendship. You ignore her and walk away. — 1 2 3 4 5

9. You have a secret that you have told only to your best friend. The next day, an acquaintance asks you about the secret. You deny the secret and decide to break off the relationship with your best friend. — 1 2 3 4 5

10. A friend who works with you tells you about some of your mannerisms and habits that get on his nerves. You discuss these with your friend and look for some possible ways of dealing with the problem. — 1 2 3 4 5

11. Your best friend gets involved in something illegal that you believe will lead to serious trouble. You decide to tell your friend how you disapprove of his involvement in the situation. — 1 2 3 4 5

12. In a moment of weakness, you give away a friend's secret. Your friend finds out and calls you to ask about it. You deny it firmly. — 1 2 3 4 5

13. You have a friend who never seems to have time for you. You decide to forget her and to start looking for new friends. — 1 2 3 4 5

14. You are involved in something illegal, and your friend tells you of her disapproval and fear that you will get in serious trouble. You discuss it with your friend. — 1 2 3 4 5

15. You work with a friend, but some of her mannerisms and habits are getting on your nerves and irritating you. You explain your feelings to your friend, looking for a mutual solution to the problem. — 1 2 3 4 5

16. A friend has pointed out that you never seem to have time for him. You walk away. — 1 2 3 4 5

17. Your best friend gets involved in something illegal that you believe will lead to serious trouble. You decide to mind your own business. — 1 2 3 4 5

18. Your friend is upset because you have inconvenienced him. He tells you how he feels. You try to understand and agree on a way to keep it from happening again. — 1 2 3 4 5

19. You had a disagreement with a friend, and now she ignores you whenever she's around you. You tell her how her actions make you feel and ask about restoring your friendship. — 1 2 3 4 5

	Never				Always

20. A friend who works with you tells you about some of your mannerisms and habits that get on his nerves. You listen and walk away.   1 2 3 4 5

21. At great inconvenience, you arrange to take your friend to the doctor's office. When you arrive to pick her up, you find she has decided not to go. You say nothing but resolve never to do any favors for that person again.   1 2 3 4 5

22. You have argued with a friend and are angry with her, ignoring her when you meet. She tells you how she feels and asks about restoring the friendship. You discuss ways of maintaining your friendship, even when you disagree.   1 2 3 4 5

23. You have a secret that you have told only to your best friend. The next day, an acquaintance asks you about the secret. You call your friend and ask her about it, trying to come to an understanding of how to handle secrets better in the future.   1 2 3 4 5

24. You are involved in something illegal, and your friend tells you of her disapproval and fear that you will get in serious trouble. You tell your friend to mind her own business.   1 2 3 4 5

Friendship Relations Survey Answer Key

In the Friendship Relations Survey there are 12 questions that deal with your willingness to self-disclose and 12 questions that are concerned with your receptivity to feedback. Transfer your scores to this answer key. Reverse the scoring for all questions that are starred; that is, if you answered 5, record the score of 1; if you answered 4, record the score of 2; if you answered 3, record the score of 3; if you answered 2, record the score of 4; and if you answered 1, record the score of 5. Then add the scores in each column.

Willingness to Self-disclose	Receptivity to Feedback
*1. ____	2. ____
3. ____	*4. ____
*5. ____	6. ____
7. ____	*8. ____
*9. ____	10. ____
11. ____	*12. ____
*13. ____	14. ____
15. ____	*16. ____
*17. ____	18. ____
19. ____	*20. ____
*21. ____	22. ____
23. ____	*24. ____
Total ____	Total ____

On the Friendship Relations Survey Summary Sheet, add your score and your group's average score for receptivity to feedback and willingness to self-disclose.

Friendship Relations Survey Summary Sheet

Draw horizontal and vertical lines reflecting your (Part *a*) and the group's (Part *b*) receptivity to feedback and willingness to self-disclose scores. The results should look like the Johari Window.

	Your Score	Group Average Score
Receptivity to Feedback:	_____	_____
Willingness to Self-disclose:	_____	_____

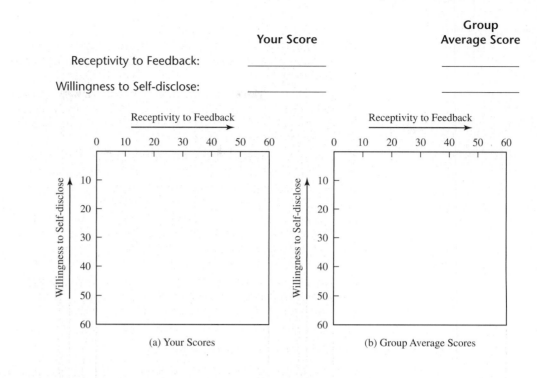

(a) Your Scores   (b) Group Average Scores

**Exercise 2–E
Circle of Friends**

It is important to examine our interpersonal relationships to determine whether the levels of disclosure and trust we have enhance the relationships we value.

1. In the first column, list the people closest to you in different categories: family, friends, and co-workers (include classmates, teammates, or professors), and others (anyone with whom you have a valued relationship and are in frequent contact).

2. In the second column, rate your level of trust with each individual on a scale of 1–5, with 1 having very little trust and 5 having a high degree of trust.

3. In the third column, rate your level of disclosure with the individual on a scale of 1–5 with 1 being very low, dealing with trivial and nonthreatening information, and 5 being a high level of highly personable and sensitive information.

4. In the fourth column, write comments as to the quality of the relationship, such as a comparison on congruency between trust and self-disclosure and notes as to what you want and need to do to improve the relationship.

Name of Individual	Level of Trust (1–5)	Level of Self-disclosure (1–5)	Comments on the Relationship
(Family Members)			
(Friends)			
(Co-workers)			
(Others)			

Look over your completed chart and answer the following questions:

1. Is there a correlation between the level of self-disclosure and the level of trust? Why or why not?
2. How satisfied are you with the level of trust and disclosure in your relationships?
3. In what ways are the relationships progressing the way you want them to?
4. How can you improve the level of disclosure or trust in each of the most important relationships?

Exercise 2–F
Trust-building Activities

The following two activities are designed to expose participants to—and build their comfort level with—trusting others.

Blind Walk

Working in pairs, participants will take turns leading each other around. One member closes his or her eyes, with his or her eyes remaining closed for the entire turn. The other member leads him or her around by the arm. The member should take the participant to as many different places as possible, incorporating other sensory experiences such as touch, smell, and hearing. Participants should then alternate and allow the other member to experience being "blind."

Trust Meal

In pairs, participants share a meal while one member is blindfolded. The sighted member leads the blindfolded partner through the meal, explaining and/or answering any questions or concerns. The blindfolded person may choose to request assistance or attempt to eat without help.

Questions

1. What was comfortable/uncomfortable about each of the above exercises?
2. What were your feelings as you were going through each role in each exercise?
3. What did you learn about yourself and others through each exercise?

Exercise 2–G
Ideal Cards: A Self-disclosure Activity

1. Participants get into groups of five to seven members.
2. The instructor distributes play money and two Ideal Cards to each participant.
3. The instructor explains the following ground rules for buying, selling, or trading Ideal Cards before the exchange phase is begun:
   a. Each individual *must* sell or trade at least one of his/her Ideal Cards sometime during the entire experience.
   b. Each individual *may* buy, sell, or trade Ideal Cards within his/her group. Cards may be bought or sold for any mutually agreed-upon price or traded outright.
4. Participants trade cards within their subgroups.
5. When the trading within subgroups is completed, the instructor announces that participants may exchange cards (in accordance with the rules) with any other person in the room.
6. Following the activity, reflect silently on the following questions:
   a. What were the original Ideal Cards you received? Why did you want to keep/trade them?
   b. How much money did you have at the end of the experience?
   c. Were you more interested in obtaining meaningful Ideal Cards or in accumulating the most money possible?
   d. Which Ideal Cards did you most wish to obtain? Why?
   e. Are you satisfied with the Ideal Cards you now have? Why or why not?

7. Now discuss your reactions to these questions in your original group.

8. The instructor leads a discussion of the entire experience.

Examples of Ideal Cards

1. To persevere in what I am doing.

2. To be honest.

3. Never to be worried about having enough food.

4. To be a member of the opposite sex.

5. To be needed and to be important to others.

6. To have better feelings about myself.

7. To have a better relationship with God.

8. To be a good conversationalist.

9. To have my opinions respected.

10. To develop my potential.

Your instructor has more.

Source: J. Pfeiffer & J. E. Jones, *The 1975 Annual Handbook for Group Facilitators,* University Associates, 1975. Copyright © 1975 by John Wiley & Sons, Inc. Reprinted by permission of John Wiley and Sons, Inc.

| **Exercise 2–H**
Self-disclosure
Poker | The objectives of this activity are to build trust and generally serve as an "ice breaker." |

1. Distribute one pack of playing cards to each team of between four and eight persons.

2. Each team should shuffle the deck and place it in a stack in the center of the team.

3. Team members must, in turn, disclose something interesting about themselves in order to draw a card.

4. Other team members can deny a member a card if their disclosure is not insightful or does not go beyond self-description.

5. The objective is to get as many cards as possible so as to maximize one's poker hand (Note: Members are not allowed to exchange or replace cards in the deck, so they must play the hand they draw.)

6. Only the best five cards are part of the final hand for each member (Note: Hopefully a team member can inform each team of the winning hand.)

7. The winner of the game must do the following:

   a. Describe, without violating anonymity, the most insightful or interesting thing a member of their team said.

   b. Give an example of a purely "self-descriptive" comment from their team (without violating anonymity).

Debriefing can consist of the following discussion questions:

1. How many persons commented, or rounds transpired, before truly insightful comments began to be the norm? (Icebreaker)?

2. How uncomfortable were some of you to hear an insightful or deeply personal comment from a team member?

3. Did an insightful comment from a team member encourage you to be more comfortable sharing a meaningful comment about yourself?

4. How did your level of trust in your teammates change with each round of comments?

Submitted by: Dr. Brian K. Miller, Associate Professor of Management, Texas State University, San Marcos, TX.

Exercise 2–I
Disclosure and Trust
in Action

1. Watch a television show or movie (or read a book) in which trust plays a large part—perhaps trust is broken or is built over time. Describe the role that self-disclosure and trustworthiness played in either the building or destroying of trust. What are some lessons that could be learned and applied in your own life from these depictions? What are behaviors to be avoided?

2. Take someone with whom you would like to enhance your interpersonal relationship to your "special place" (somewhere you feel special, peaceful, content, or comfortable). Discuss with that person what is going on in your life and your feelings and reactions to the situations. Encourage the other person to take you to a special place to discuss what is going on with him or her.

3. Practice "trust-building." Be aware of trust behaviors you are trying to incorporate into your daily interactions with others. Once a week for a month, record the times you have consciously or unconsciously done things that build others' trust in you. Examples can include returning money you've found in a public place to the appropriate office, planning your time so as to be able to follow through on commitments, and keeping a secret told you by a good friend from a mutual acquaintance.

Exercise 2–J
Reflection/Action Plan

This chapter focused on self-disclosure and trust—what they are, why they are important, and how to increase your comfort and skill in using them. Complete the following worksheet upon reading and finishing the experiential activities for this chapter.

1. When do you think it is appropriate to receive feedback from and self-disclose to others? To trust others?

_____

_____

_____

2. How comfortable are you with self-disclosure? With trusting others? What aspects are most difficult for you?

_____

_____

_____

3. How does self-disclosure or trust affect your receptivity to feedback and willingness to give feedback?

_____

_____

_____

4. In what ways is your current use of trust and self-disclosure effective in your relationships with friends and loved ones?

_____

_____

_____

5. What specific changes about your self-disclosure and trusting behaviors would you make that would enhance relationships with your friends?

_____

_____

_____

6. If you made the changes listed above, what impact would this have on your relationships? Explain.

_____

_____

_____

3 Establishing Goals Consistent with Your Values and Ethics

Learning Points

How do I:

- Develop plans that will help me achieve my goals?
- Decide what is really important to me?
- Develop a personal mission statement?
- Make progress toward my goals, especially when I hit a roadblock?
- Evaluate options concerning ethical dilemmas?
- Know if I am making ethical decisions?

Joseph Smith was enjoying his work as an associate at a leading consulting firm in New York. The hours didn't bother him. As the first person from his family to attend college, he was used to working hard for what he wanted in life. He had worked part-time all the way through high school and college to pay for tuition, room, board, and other immediate expenses. Now in his third year, he was contemplating his next career step. Most of Joseph's friends had moved on to graduate business school, but his boss had convinced him to stay on. With all the excitement over "new economy" growth clients, there was plenty of interesting work to go around. He was traveling overseas frequently, had a good set of friends, had a partner, and was enjoying his current situation. So what was troubling him? In the back of his mind Joseph realized he wasn't sure what he should do next. For possibly the first time in his life he didn't have to focus single-mindedly on one goal, such as paying for college. He now had multiple priorities in which he was interested. But he didn't have a clue as to how to start making plans to attain any one of them. Besides, he thought, "I'm always working, anyway. How would I have time to even think of anything else? So it doesn't really matter that I'm not sure where I'm headed." Or does it?

1. What are the issues Joseph is facing?
2. Should Joseph follow the rest of his friends to graduate business school?
3. Why is it difficult for him to set new priorities for himself?
4. What advice would you offer Joseph?

5. How can Joseph set new goals and work toward them while fulfilling his obligations to his present position?

"If you don't know where you are going, you'll probably end up someplace else."

Yogi Berra

A **goal** is a level of proficiency or standard of behavior we wish to attain within a specified period of time.[1] If you don't have a plan to direct your life, where will you end up? Effective goal setting gives you direction and purpose while providing a standard against which to measure your performance. Having goals also allows individuals and organizations to have a clear understanding of what they are trying to accomplish. This chapter describes personal goal setting and values clarification: what goals and values are, the benefits of being aware of your goals and values, and how to improve your ability to set meaningful and ethical goals that are aligned with your core values. We also address the role ethics play in making ethical decisions that are aligned with your personal and organizational goals. At the end of the chapter are a number of exercises that enable you to assess your goal-setting skills and your use of ethical guidelines in decision making, and help you to develop improvement plans.

What Is Goal Setting?

Goal-setting theory is based on the premise that conscious goals affect action.[2] Goal setting is a way of identifying your work/life priorities and developing strategies for attaining personal and professional objectives. Consider the lives of successful people. Do they seem to have a strong commitment to their plans? Are they organized, efficient, confident, well prepared? Most likely you found that most, if not all of these words apply to the successful people you considered. Successful individuals and organizations have learned the key to achieving meaningful results is through effective goal setting.

For example, Jack Welch decided, shortly after graduating from college, that one day he wanted to be the CEO of General Electric (he achieved this goal 20 years after setting it!). Bill Gates, founder of Microsoft, had an early interest in software and began programming computers at the age of thirteen. At nineteen, Gates founded Microsoft with childhood friend Paul Allen to develop software for the newly emerging personal computer market. Jerry Garcia, the lead guitarist and vocalist of the Grateful Dead, said he knew as a youngster he wanted to head a rock band. Early in her career Oprah Winfrey discovered she had a gift for communicating. And many winners on *American Idol* say they knew as a child they wanted to perform on stage.

Contrast these goal setters with those who are unable or unwilling to set goals and achieve them. Consider people you know who seem to set goals frequently but never attain them. Are they realistic about what they can achieve? Do they have the required resources to attain their goals (e.g., time, money, or support from others)? Do they have the necessary capabilities, training, and education? Chances are they may not have one or more of these resources that are so important to success.

Why Is Goal Setting Important?

It has long been recognized that goal setting is an important component within the self-management or self-leadership concept we discuss in chapter 4. Those who are able to monitor their thoughts and actions, being cognizant of their personal and professional goals, are more successful than those who do not exercise this type of strategic approach to their interactions with others, especially in a business setting. This is true globally, not just in certain regional pockets. For example, in a recent study of 15 dimensions across 62 cultures, it was found that Chinese employees had scores higher than average on traits related to goal setting such as performance orientation and uncertainty avoidance.[3] Pursuing achievement goals that agree with one's personal values is important across cultures.[4]

The goal-setting process has several benefits:

- *Results orientation*—Many employees cite being able to use their skills and abilities and achieving results in their job as key factors related to their happiness at work.[5]

- *Purpose/direction*—Establishing written goals can formalize your dreams and wishes. Through the process of careful examination and self-analysis, you can begin to understand what you want to achieve. Goal setting defines the destination point while providing the map to lead you there. Writing goal statements and developing an action plan gives your life purpose and direction. These statements provide you with short-term motivation and long-term vision. Whether or not you are aware of your goals or strategies, they are affecting your life's direction. Once you bring them into consciousness and formalize them, you can guide your life more strategically.

- *Motivation*—Goal setting can help you to build internal momentum. Through goal setting, you can direct your actions toward fulfilling your dreams and ambitions. Usually this process starts by setting incremental steps to achieving a goal. If you want to run a marathon, you start your training by running short distances and increase them over time. Momentum begins to build as soon as you set your goal, and continues as you take steps toward achieving it. To borrow from Sir Isaac Newton's (1642–1727) First Law of Motion, a person who sets goals becomes an object in motion that remains in motion. Directing your life toward fulfilling dreams motivates you to achieve continual success.

- *Productivity*—Goal setting can give you a way to measure your success. Systematically setting goals provides balance and perspective to your decisions about how to allocate your time and resources. Having a clear plan of action greatly focuses the expenditure of time, money, and energy. Goal setting boosts performance to a higher level and helps in overcoming challenges. Up to a point, performance also increases with the level of goal difficulty, provided the individual working to attain the goal is committed to achieving it.[6]

- *Cross-cultural adjustment*—Goal-setting behaviors can assist in acclimating to new cultures.[7] Goals affect the direction, intensity, and persistence of our efforts. In the cross-cultural adjustment process, students who set high goals are more likely to maintain their focus and minimize distractions, giving them a better chance of being successful in their chosen activities.

Key Behaviors for Effective Goal Setting

The approach you use to set goals greatly affects your ability to succeed. A few core behaviors underpin most successful goal-setting efforts:

Be Realistic

Goals should be specific, measurable, and realistic; goals should be compatible with one another to minimize conflict; and realistic prioritizing of goals will lead to success.[8] Be honest with yourself about your skills and abilities and in evaluating all related conditions needed to attain your goals. You can only influence or change things over which you have control. Understand that there will be setbacks. Continually search for means to overcome obstacles and secure all necessary resources.

- *Challenge yourself*—The more you challenge yourself or your team, the more productive you and your team will be. The goals you set should not be out of reach, but more challenging goals can inspire and motivate people, whereas lesser goals that are too easy or mundane may get the job done, but at a lower level than would have occurred with a more compelling set of goals.[9]

- *Be positive*—We face obstacles and challenges in everything we do. The ability to persevere in the face of adversity is a key success factor in goal setting. Adopting an optimistic "can-do" attitude can give you the boost to continue the uphill climb. It is also helpful to describe goals in a positive tone; focus on achieving a positive rather than trying to eliminate a negative. For example, say, "I want to master this new version of a software program" rather than saying, "I need to improve my computer skills."

- *Start small*—Begin with smaller, simpler, more manageable goals. Successfully completing small goals will build confidence and create momentum toward future goal-setting behavior. Setting incremental benchmarks for marking your progress will make broader, long-term goals seem attainable.

- *Take full responsibility*—Even though you may need to solicit the help and support of others, you are in control of your actions. Set your goals with the understanding that you have the power to direct your energy toward personal productivity.

- *Persevere*—Completing a goal requires the ability to maintain strong forward motion. Perseverance is essential for successfully reaching every goal you want to achieve.

Try This

There are a number of online tools for tracking goals. Try one or more of these:

http://www.achievr.biz/

http://www.getgoaling.com/

http://www.43things.com/

http://goalbot.org/

http://weekplan.net

"Success is not measured by those who fought and never fell, but by those who fought, fell, and rose again."

Anonymous

Clarifying Values

To determine what goals you want to achieve, start by clarifying your own values, those things in life that are most meaningful to you. **Values** are concepts or beliefs about desirable outcomes that transcend specific situations and guide your selection or evaluation of behaviors and events.[10] Our individual set of values is a result of learning and personal experiences. Values are influenced by family, friends, peers, religious beliefs, community, and even the organizations with which we are associated. Many of our values are deeply set, and we make decisions or judgments without consciously reflecting on their source. Values can become a matter of habit.

A value is "an enduring belief that a specific mode of conduct or end-state of existence is personally or socially preferable to an opposite or converse mode of conduct or end-state of existence."[11] In other words, we work toward what we value—and our values guide our behavior. There are two types of values: instrumental and terminal.[12]

- **Instrumental values** are the "how's" of goal setting—the standards of behavior by which we achieve desired ends. Courage, honesty, compassion, and loving are examples of instrumental values.

- **Terminal values** are the "what's"—the end states or goals that we would like to achieve during our lifetime. Such values include a happy family life, career success, wisdom, salvation, prosperity, or sense of accomplishment.

Personal values are also tangible and intangible.

■ **Tangible values** are things you can see, feel, or hold, including the kind of car you want to drive, the level of income you want to have, and the size of the house you want to own. Tangible values consist of the material things you want to possess.

■ **Intangible values** are concepts rather than things. Freedom, independence, happiness, friendship, and love are intangible values and can be defined differently for each person. Intangible values consist of ideals you wish to strive toward or pursue.

Identifying your values will help you answer the question, "What do I want to achieve with my life?" How can you begin your career planning process without knowing your lifestyle preferences or having a clear sense of what values provide you with the most motivation? One survey showed over half of the MBAs queried "would not work for a tobacco company for ethical, social, and political reasons."[13] Your values can have a direct effect on your behaviors, attitudes, and decisions. Setting and achieving goals that are congruent with your values will lead to increased satisfaction and positive personal feelings.

Clarifying values is also important for organizations. Positive outcomes result when employees' values are aligned with the values of their organization.[14] Individuals draw from their values to guide their decisions and actions, and organizational value systems provide norms that specify how organizational members should behave and how organizational resources should be allocated. Communication, trust, and job satisfaction are all affected positively when employee and employer values align.

How to Clarify Your Values

■ List the primary experiences you have had to date; what about these experiences was meaningful or important to you?

■ What accomplishments are you the most proud of? What do these represent to you?

■ If you had to evacuate due to a life-threatening tornado, which possessions would you bring with you?

■ What's important for you to have in your current or next professional situation?

■ What qualities do you bring to—and expect in—your relationships with others?

■ What is your personal definition of happiness?

See Exercise 3–A for an activity that will help you to assess your current and projected values.

Once you determine your values and why they are important to you, you can then work on a plan for achieving your goals. For example, Joseph, in our case study, might write down some of the things that are important to him. These might include continued learning, spending time with family and friends, and being secure financially. This might explain why going to graduate school has not been his uppermost priority. He might be concerned about having to borrow money to pay the tuition, or about the time it would cause him to spend away from friends and family.

Try This

Take a minute and write your definition of personal satisfaction. What are the behaviors you'll use to achieve this satisfaction? What will bring you enjoyment or fulfillment? Is this short term or long term? Which values are terminal, the things you must have accomplished? Which aspects of satisfaction are derived from your instrumental values? What aspects are tangible or intangible?

Now write your definition of success. What will you need to accomplish or attain in order to say you are a success in your life? Set these definitions aside for later reflection.

Writing Effective Goals

Developing personal goals based on your personal values begins with creating written goal statements. Written goal statements are the aims or the targets you want to achieve. These goal statements deal with various aspects of your life such as career, social, wellness, community, spirituality, relationships, job/career, family, personal, financial, and so on. Objectives or an action plan should accompany every goal statement. The plan should specify the steps needed or means for reaching your ends. For instance, in our case example Joseph could have as a goal "To achieve the level of vice president within the next two years." His action plan could include talking with his boss about potential career options within the firm, taking extra courses at night to develop the technical skills needed to advance, and networking with several alumni from his college who work at the firm who are in senior positions to gain their support and advice.

One system used successfully by managers and others who wish to incorporate goal-setting principles into their lives is the "SMART" system. **SMART** refers to a goal that is specific, measurable, attainable, realistic, and has a time frame.[15] By ensuring your goal statements are SMART, you create a system for managing action steps and increase the likelihood that these goals will be attained. Use this approach as a checklist for writing your goal statements and action plan.

"SMART" Goal Writing

- *Specific*—Write your goals, including as many details as possible, leaving no room for misinterpretation. Say "I want to lose 10 pounds," or "lower my cholesterol by 20 points," or "increase our sales by 10 percent." Loose, broad, or vague goals are not desirable. When goals are specific, it is much easier to hold someone accountable for their achievement.[16] An employee who establishes career goals is likely to advance his or her career, especially if the goals are specific, challenging, and accompanied by regular feedback on progress toward the goals.[17]

- *Measurable*—Provide a means to measure your progress, a way to measure actual performance against desired performance standards. Set up checkpoints to evaluate your progress from the time you start to the time you expect to attain your goal. Write your goals in quantifiable terms to determine to what extent you completed each goal and fulfilled each objective. For example, "I will write one essay per week to improve my writing skills."

- *Attainable/believable*—Set an actionable, believable goal. In addition to being fully dedicated, you also need the resources and capabilities required for attaining a goal. Goals that are believable have a much higher probability of success. Make sure you have secured all necessary resources and that you anticipate and develop a strategy for dealing with any obstacles that could bar your success. For example, say "I will raise my GPA from 2.5 to 3.0. To do this I will get tested at the Learning Center to see if I have a learning disability."

- *Realistic/achievable*—Write your goals with consideration for your capabilities and limitations. A goal should be challenging enough that you stretch your abilities to gain attainment, but not so difficult that it is impossible to fulfill. Goal-setting theory suggests that specific and challenging goals result in a higher performance than moderate or easily attainable goals, vague goals, or no goals at all.[18] Goals should also have realistic deadlines. Closely tied to the notion of realistic goals is the aspect of control. Only set goals that are within your means to achieve. Say, "I will contact 10 percent more potential clients this week than usual," rather than "I will sell 10 percent more than usual this week." The former statement reflects things that are within your control as well as realistic. The latter reflects a desire about something that may not be totally within your control.

- *Time bound*—Develop a specific deadline for meeting each of your goals; otherwise they will remain dreams and never become reality. Setting a deadline creates a commitment to begin and pursue a goal until it is attained. Saying "I'd like to lose 10 pounds" is specific, measurable, and realistic, but without a target date for completion, you might find yourself continuously repeating "I'll start my diet tomorrow."

(continued)

> Some goals may be unattainable within a compressed time frame, yet possible within a longer time frame. In fact, when setting goals that span a longer time horizon, it is best to establish incremental time frames to make long-term timeliness more manageable and acceptable. Plan a schedule or time frame for goal comple-tion that is sufficient to allow you to achieve the goal, and at the same time not allowing for so much slack time that you lose interest or focus.

Another important criterion that can be added to SMART goals is to make sure the goal is yours. Personal goals are just that, personal. You will be less likely to accept and complete goals that someone else gives you.[19] Goals should be a direct reflection of your values, aspirations, and life mission, not someone else's like your friends', parents', or roommates'. If you are pursuing an accounting degree because a parent believes it's a good solid career, yet you just don't see yourself as an accountant, you may want to reevaluate this goal. You are more likely to stick with and attain goals you desire than goals set for you by others. Likewise, when you are in a position to influence others such as subordinates or children, encourage them, but let them set their own goals. When individuals set their own goals, they have a greater amount of well-being, commitment, job satisfaction, and organizational commitment, resulting in higher performance and productivity.[20]

Overcoming Obstacles

There are several strategic steps you can take to overcome potential pitfalls while ensur-ing progress toward achieving your goals.

1. *Visualize the outcome*—Imagine being at the completion point of your goal. State your goals as if it is definite you will accomplish them. Say things such as, "When I have paid off my car," not "if I have paid off my car." Positive self-talk will reinforce your belief in your ability to achieve your dreams.

2. *Strive for performance, not outcomes*—Throughout the process, you should strive to give 100 percent effort and to perform to the best of your ability. This will allow you to feel confident and proud of your smaller accomplishments. Barry Goldberg, a success-ful TV producer, says he has always focused on creating the best television program possible, seeking first and foremost to produce high-quality entertainment; money and success resulted as a by-product.

3. *Develop a support network*—Determine the resources that will be necessary for you to achieve your goals. Obtain support and commitment from individuals who will be essential in ensuring your success. Associate with people who will support you in at-taining your goals. If someone in your network is hindering your ability to accomplish your goals, reevaluate whether continued association with this person is desirable.

4. *Limit the number*—Focus on a limited number of goals at a time. Having too many goals will only drain your resources and reduce the potency of your efforts. One way to do this is to focus on those goals that relate to your key roles at a point in time. An-other way to do this is to create a master plan—a three- or five-year plan—in which you map out the pursuit of specific goals according to your personal and professional mission.

5. *Allow for setbacks*—We are all human. If you get sidetracked or make a mistake while trying to accomplish your goal, forgive yourself and get back to your plan. If you do not move on, you will never accomplish your goals. When experiencing a setback, it may be an appropriate time to tap into your support network. Let's say you are mid-way in achieving your goal to quit smoking over a three-month period when your favorite uncle is diagnosed with a terminal illness. You might find it difficult to cope with this tragedy without returning to your pack-a-day habit. At this point, you might choose to reevaluate and adjust your goal; you might also seek friends, relatives, or medical or counseling assistance to help you get through this crisis.

6. *Be honest with yourself*—Evaluate objectively how well you accomplish your goals and objectives. The only way you can improve is to understand what you did wrong and focus on how you can change. Ask yourself, "Why did my last semester go so badly?" or "Why did that project go over budget?" You might answer yourself, "Poor study habits, lack of time or discipline, lack of oversight, or lack of priorities."

7. *Reward small accomplishments*—Once you have reached an incremental, objective step or milestone, provide yourself with a reward. Celebrating your continual accomplishments will help to maintain your optimism and belief in your abilities while refueling your commitment and motivation to goal achievement.

8. *Don't lose sight of the big picture*—Make a habit of reviewing your goals on a daily basis. Use positive self-talk to reinforce your beliefs and reiterate the purpose behind your actions. Remain flexible yet diligent. Allow for necessary changes and restructure as needed while still working toward the ultimate end. Understand how everything you do facilitates your ability to complete your goal.

Revisit the Process

Goal setting is not a one-time action; it is an ongoing process. Your values, roles, and dreams may change. Your resources may need to be reevaluated, or you may need to make adjustments to overcome unforeseen obstacles. Goals should remain fluid, enabling you to plan, react, and adapt to changing circumstances as needed.

9. *Consider your ethics*—In developing your goals, consider your and your organization's ethical standards. You will want to have a deep understanding of your personal beliefs and principles. You can do this by clarifying your values as described above and taking these into consideration in all of your personal and job-related activities and interactions. As an employee and manager, be aware of ethical norms as you and your team develop and execute strategic and tactical plans. Involve your employees in corporate planning and goal-setting sessions that include discussions of ethics and social responsibility.[21]

What Are Ethics?

The word **ethics** comes from the Greek word *ethos,* which refers to the moral character of a group or organization.[22] Ethics are moral principles that people use to guide their behavior by separating right from wrong.[23] Business ethics involve issues of morality in the sphere of business organizations, including both normative and behavioral approaches.[24] Many complicating factors make it a challenge to establish, monitor, and maintain ethical behavior in organizations.[25] The difficulty with ethics and the goals we set is that the situations we face as managers are seldom black and white, enabling a clear understanding of which answer is the best for all concerned. Each person has a different worldview (based on life experiences, education, family background, religious and political affiliations, perceptions, and values) that he or she brings into decision making and goal setting. Each person possesses a different **ethical barometer** that stems from his or her experience and background. This diversity affects the ethical decision-making and goal-setting processes, outcomes, and ramifications.

Why Are Ethics Important?

With corporate scandals continuing to surface, the ethics of individuals and organizations are coming under closer scrutiny. Increasingly, people are demanding that organizations and their employees set goals based on high ethical and moral standards. Business ethics has garnered the attention of business school curricula.[26] As we said in chapter 2, maintaining "transparency," or open communication with key stakeholders, has become more than a buzzword, and the general public has high expectations of the political decision-making process and conduct in the business world. Transparency motivates corporations to function based on sound ethics and accountability.

Consider the case of Toyota, the Japanese automaker that has been in the news for the past several years because of a series of recalls.[27] These recalls greatly affected consumers' perceptions of the company: confidence in the company was low, reliability ratings were reduced, the company was thought to show a lack of transparency, and its reputation was badly damaged. Toyota was slow to reveal publicly the extent of the problems it was facing. In one survey, few respondents trusted the statements Toyota was making publicly about the 2010 crisis; half felt that Toyota's decision making was unethical to some degree, and over half expressed little faith in Toyota's transparency during this crisis. While there is some evidence that consumer confidence in Toyota is rising again, the recall crisis greatly affected Toyota's reputation as a trusted, ethical organization and its ability to perform and compete against its rivals.

Ethical guidelines can provide organizations with a set of internal mechanisms to ensure sound decisions are made. This can result in a positive work culture, lower costs, increased reputational value, and consideration for the rights and responsibilities of all stakeholders.[28]

As we saw earlier in the section on values, ethics also help establish a link between an individual's and an organization's values. The more alignment between these two, the stronger the person–organization fit, or congruence.[29]

Lastly, ethics are important in providing consistent guidelines to be implemented across cultures. Managers operating in international markets face significant pressure to act unethically due to bribery and other activities considered standard depending on the country with which they are doing business. Ethical guidelines can address this issue and reduce the variation in managerial judgment that is exercised across cultures.[30] Ethics and character reflect our true inner self; they determine how we respond to managerial dilemmas. Many decisions appear on the surface to be easy, but in reality these actions build up over time and set a foundation for more challenging decisions.[31] It is important to be aware of the guidelines you use for setting goals related to ethical behavior. These guidelines can affect the way you approach larger, more significant decisions in other areas of your life and work.

Ethics play a part in our goal setting and decision making whether we are acting as an individual, a group, an organization, or a member within an organization. **Ethical dilemmas** are situations where we are faced with setting goals or making decisions that will be based largely on judgments and determinations rather than on indisputable facts. Ethical dilemmas can be the result of gross misunderstanding, value conflicts, cultural differences, conflicts of interest, personal differences, or greed. Examples of ethical dilemmas are exchange of inappropriate gifts, making unwanted sexual advances, discovery of unauthorized payments or overpayments, and hiring an untrained person from a "name" family over a more qualified individual.

An ethical dilemma arises when a manager must choose between his or her own interests and the interests of someone else or some other group. Those with an interest in the outcome of the decision are referred to as **stakeholders**. As a manager in an organization, it is up to you to take into consideration the needs and interests of all key stakeholders— the employees, customers, suppliers, and shareholders who are affected by the decision— in addition to yourself. Decisions you make reflect not only your values but also the values of the organization you represent. Decisions you make on behalf of your organization carry consequences for the company's reputation and success in the community.

Ethical Strategies

Three factors influence behaviors and actions: the individual ethics of organizational members, the corporate culture of the organization, and society as a whole. Individuals work within the environment of an organization that reflects the pressures from the external environment.[32]

Individual Ethics

Your personal values, moral reasoning, and personal ideology have a direct impact on your goals and actions. Instrumental values can influence ethical decision making.[33] Your personal level of honesty is strongly related to judgments you make in the workplace. Values reflected in a person's behavior and personality can be the basis for professional behavior.[34] When motivated by selfishness, lack of self-esteem, or envy, the more ambition someone has, the less ethical that person is in their intentions and actions.[35]

Kohlberg's Moral Maturity[36]

To understand personal ethics, we can look at **morality**, or a person's belief about his or her obligations. Building on the work of psychologist Jean Piaget, Lawrence Kohlberg identified six stages of **moral development** and reasoning, which he grouped into three major levels. Each level represents a shift in the social–moral perspective of the individual that explains how judgments affect action. Each level is also comprised of two stages. As an individual advances through each level, the second stage of that level shows greater growth and ethical character. (See Figure 3–1.)

At the first level, the **preconventional level**, a person's moral judgments are characterized by concrete, individual perspectives. Behaviors are guided by self-interest to obey the rules in order to avoid punishment. At this level, organizational members follow rules out of fear and managers tend to be autocratic.

Individuals at the second level, or **conventional level** of reasoning, have a basic understanding of the need to conform to societal standards, realizing that norms and conventions are necessary to uphold society. These members tend to identify with the rules, uphold them consistently, and behave in ways society defines as "right." Within this level, members collaborate and understand the need to fulfill obligations laid out by the organization. Managers at this level tend to encourage cooperation and productive working relationships.

Finally, the **postconventional level** is characterized by reasoning based on personal values and principles. At the final stage, individuals will make ethical decisions based on personal judgments and not on societal norms. When faced with a conflict between a law and a personal core value, the individual's internal beliefs will guide the decision rather than the law. Individuals at this level seek out new solutions and work independently while managers focus on the needs of the employees and empower them to reason for themselves.

Most managers and individuals function at the conventional, or second level, where their thinking about right and wrong is predominantly influenced by significant others and rules and laws. Fewer than 20 percent function at the higher, postconventional level.[37] Since most organizational members function at the level where they take their cue for

**Figure 3–1
Stages of Moral Development**

> **Postconventional Level**
>
> Stage 6: Universal ethical principles—acts are consistent with personal moral principles, seeking the greater good
>
> Stage 5: Social contract—attempt to get social consensus and tolerance

> **Conventional Level**
>
> Stage 4: Social accord and system maintenance—meet expectations of society as expressed in laws
>
> Stage 3: Interpersonal accord, conformity to group norms—act to meet expectations of peers or organization

> **Preconventional Level**
>
> Stage 2: Instrumental purpose and exchange—acting in one's own interest
>
> Stage 1: Obedience and punishment—act to avoid consequences

behavior from the organization, it is critical that organizations examine and reexamine their practices and set ethical standards to guide decision making.

Organizational Ethics

An organization's culture and practices have an impact on the values, attitudes, and behaviors of its members. Ethics codes and training and consistent institutionalized values and guidelines can establish a collective understanding of company ethics. This combination creates an ethical organization that enhances employee ethics, promotes clarity in terms of work expectations, generates positive job attitudes, and reduces turnover.[38] Organizational constraints and pressures, as well as systematic practices, have a strong link to managers' decision making and behaviors. Since it has been shown that most individuals function at the second or conventional level of morality, it is clear members will conform to the standards the organization deems acceptable. Organizational ethics are especially important now because of the different generations that are working in businesses today. Younger managers are more likely to be influenced by organizational ethics than older managers, as more experienced managers are more likely to make ethical decisions independently. Strategies organizations can employ to set the right tone include hiring people who have congruent ethical standards and ethical decision-making skills, ensuring ethical practices are in place across the organization, monitoring ethical performance, and offering training to managers and employees.[39]

When ethical employee behavior at all levels is valued and encouraged, organizations function more smoothly, and perhaps even more successfully.[40]

Ethical Decision Making

Have you ever witnessed someone cheating on a test? Have you ever called in sick when you actually went skiing or to the beach? Have you ever been given too much change and kept it? Every day we face situations where we have to make decisions for which there are no apparent, clear-cut rules. For example, concerns about Internet security fraud are on the rise. Securities firms are constantly on the lookout for employees who are involved in insider trading. Recent surveys suggest increasing numbers of applicants lie about their backgrounds in employment interviews. Employees are creating "intellectual capital" during their day jobs and selling their expertise as consultants after hours. And ordinary employees are being entrusted with valuable financial and strategic information to help them make on-the-spot judgments about how to handle difficult situations. Managers and employees are constantly faced with challenges such as these. An ethical framework for decision making is needed.

Ethical decision making involves recognizing that an issue involves an ethical question, making an ethical judgment, deciding to do the ethical thing, and actually acting ethically.[41] In business transactions, applying principles or standards to moral dilemmas by asking what is right or wrong, good or bad, creates a basic business ethic. Ethics guide people in making decisions that are not completely based on factors that have already been specified. Ethics can present a different perspective and give a new dimension to decision making. For example, it might be obvious—on paper—that opening a new manufacturing center in the remote areas of the Florida wetlands would be profitable due to low cost factors. Yet the detrimental environmental effects on the wetlands would be significant. Should the company open a wetlands-area plant? It's legal, but is it "right"? Who should make this decision? The company? Or the people in the area who are advocates for the wetlands? How should this decision be made? Is profitability the only criterion that should be used in making this decision? What should the decision be? Who will be affected by the decision? Who pulls the plug if it's the wrong decision? These are all ethical considerations that make the decision much more complex than it originally appeared on paper. Your own character and that of the organization for which you work are revealed by the types of decisions you make, how you make them, and to what end. Ethical decision making guides you in making decisions that are right not just for you, but for those who are affected by the decisions.[42] See Figure 3-2 for some applicable guidelines.

**Figure 3–2
Eight Rules of Ethical
Thinking**[43]

1. Consider others' well-being and avoid actions that will hurt others. Before taking action, ask yourself if anyone stands to be hurt by the action, financially, emotionally, or in other ways.
2. Think of yourself as a member of a community, not as an isolated individual. Before taking action, reflect on who will be affected by the decision, positively and negatively.
3. Obey—but don't depend only on—the law. An action may be legal yet unethical.
4. Think of yourself and your organization as part of society. What you do and how you think affect a larger entity beyond you and your immediate circle.
5. Obey moral guidelines by which you have agreed to live. Consider them "categorical imperatives" with no exceptions.
6. Think objectively. Be sure your action is truly ethical and not rationalized self-interest.
7. Ask, "What sort of person would do such a thing?" Or, "Will I be able to look at myself in the morning after doing X?"
8. Respect others' customs—but not at the expense of your own ethics.

Benefits of Ethical Decision Making

Many companies today are providing ethical guidelines or codes of conduct for their employees to use when faced with a situation that is not covered by standard policies and procedures. This practice has several benefits:

- *Customer relations:* Employees in companies with ethical guidelines are better prepared to treat customers fairly if a conflict arises. This helps customers feel that employees respect and understand them, resulting in higher levels of customer satisfaction.

- *Goodwill:* By your company's doing the "right thing" consistently, consumers, suppliers, and others in the community at large see your organization as a desirable one with which to do business. The ethical reputation of a firm can actually increase its opportunities and sales, as shown by The Body Shop. The Body Shop's policy of purchasing natural ingredients that might have gone to waste (good for the environment) from countries that are economically depressed (good for society) has been widely praised. The Body Shop offers a good example of ways a company can be both ethical and humanistic as well as profitable.[44] Employees and customers have noted that decisions like these positively impact their continued association with and patronization of The Body Shop. A company's goodwill also enhances its attractiveness and value to potential employees and acquiring businesses.

- *Employee satisfaction:* Employees in companies with ethical guidelines experience high comfort levels—they are pleased and relieved when they see their organization acting in an ethical way and actively promoting ethical behavior.

- *Employee empowerment:* Employees in companies with ethical guidelines feel empowered to think clearly about dilemmas at hand, to make decisions, to articulate the rationale for their decisions, and to have the support of senior management if their judgment is questioned.[45]

Ethical Decision-Making Strategies

Making ethical decisions is more a matter of having the right values than a set of rules. To help employees cope with the need to make ethical decisions, organizations need to raise the employees' level of ethical consciousness. This starts by first declaring the organization's values and expectations, and then laying out guidelines and a decision framework that employees can use when faced with decisions that require use of judgment in addition to adherence to company guidelines. The following are some tools that companies can use to educate employees about ethical decision making.

- **Code of ethics:** A written statement of values and guidelines for how to treat employees and customers. Codes of ethics provide a tangible description of what the company stands for, what it wants to achieve, and the means for achieving its goals. Codes are a good first step in raising ethical issues but, unless they are part of an organizational culture that values and insists on ethical decision making, they are insufficient to ensure that organizational ethical standards are followed.[46]

*"Have you noticed ethics creeping into
some of these deals lately?"*

Source: http://www.cartoonbank.com/1992/have-you-noticed-ethics-creeping-into-some-of-these-deals-lately/invt/
108626/?

Ethics Test

Ethics test: A series of questions that aids employees in making well-considered judgments about a situation before making a decision. Using this test will not provide one "correct" answer. The test provides criteria to be considered when determining if a course of action is ethical.[47] The test has four components:

- The test of *common sense:* "Does this action I am about to take make sense?"
- The test of *one's best self:* "Is this action or decision I'm getting ready to take compatible with my concept of myself at my best?"
- The *"light of day"* approach or making something public: "How would I feel if others knew I was doing this? Would I be willing to stand in front of my family, friends, and peers and be proud to tell them what I had decided to do?"
- The test of the *purified idea:* "Am I thinking this action or decision is right just because someone with appropriate authority or knowledge says it is right?" For example, if an accountant told you it was okay to claim certain entertainment and travel expenses as business expenses, although you doubt the fairness of this determination, do you abdicate responsibility for this decision since the accountant said it was acceptable?

- **Ethical audit:** A broad-based, agreed-upon system that lets an organization consistently focus and refocus on its values and whether its performance is meeting the standards it professes. An ethical audit analyzes the situational and environmental factors that have a significant impact on ethical behaviors and internal policies. These audits can reduce gaps between an organization's ethical ideals and actual performance, encourage self-reflection across all levels, raise ethical consciousness, and lead to less unethical or corruptive behavior.[48]

- **Decision-making model:** Frameworks that employees can use to help make decisions about ethical actions by following a short, step-by-step list of rules.[49] Models in ethical guidelines, such as those shown in Figure 3–3, aren't a guarantee that employees will

**Figure 3–3
A Sample of an Ethical
Decision-Making Model**[50]

Step 1: Identify the facts and issues.
    a. Who will be affected by my decision?
    b. What will be the short- and long-term consequences of possible courses of actions?
Step 2: Identify applicable values.
    a. How will possible courses of action impact potential stakeholders?
    b. What consideration should I have with regard to:
      The rights of stakeholders?
      Justice among stakeholders?
      The short- and long-term balance of good among stakeholders?
      My gut feeling about what is the "right thing"?
      What I think those whom I respect for their virtue would judge to be the "right thing"?
Step 3: Seek help if needed.
    a. Which course of action might keep me awake at night?
    b. Can my supervisor or human resources department provide guidance?
Step 4: Reach the best decision based on the available information.
    a. Is my decision legal and within organizational policy?
    b. Do organizational values and my personal values support my decision?

always act ethically. They are a means to get employees to think through their actions and consider the ethical standards involved when making decisions that affect them and those around them.

Ethics Training

Companies can offer their employees training about the company's policies and values and how to incorporate an ethical component into their decisions on an everyday basis. This training can be provided via a manual, a workshop, a Web-based self-directed program, or one-on-one mentoring and coaching sessions.

Ethics-enhancing Tools

Unfortunately, workers often accept unethical actions as the consequence of doing business today. Lapses in ethics are viewed as standard—expected in today's diverse, complex, and fast-paced world. One survey reported that 48 percent of workers surveyed said they respond to job pressures by performing unethical or illegal activities, and 58 percent of respondents reported workplace pressures had caused them to at least consider acting unethically or illegally on the job.[51] The most common unethical behaviors cited were these:

- Cutting corners on quality control (16 percent)
- Covering up incidents (14 percent)
- Abusing or lying about sick leave (11 percent)
- Lying to or deceiving customers (9 percent)

It is not easy to raise the ethical consciousness of an organization. Organizations are made up of individuals who may behave in an unethical manner for what they believe are justified reasons. When people are faced with pressures at work and need to make fast decisions, they are not very likely to consult rules, regulations, and policies that often don't apply to the specific situation with which the employee is dealing.[52]

This leads to many of the ethical lapses that occur in business today. In addition, organizations themselves might have policies that encourage employees to make unethical decisions. For example, a company might set unrealistically high sales targets, possibly leading some employees to engage in questionable tactics to increase sales to customers.

Lack of oversight by senior management or even by government agencies, as seen in the 2010 Gulf of Mexico oil spill crisis, compounds the problem.

Summary

This chapter focused on goal setting (why it's important, how to set goals, and how to achieve goals) and the importance of values and ethics in goal setting and decision making. Having an understanding of our values and ethical beliefs is the foundation for the decisions we make in our daily lives. These decisions have an impact on our future as well as an impact on the organizations in which we work. Refer back to your definitions of success and satisfaction. Through the process of writing your goals and action plans, are you now on the right road to securing these values? If not, what changes should you make to get there?

The pioneering management practitioner W. Edward Deming believed that approximately "two of 100 managers and 10 of 100 workers were happy in their work."[53] Since we spend almost a third of our time working, understanding our values and making our goals a reality become essential to living a fulfilled life. Use your goal-setting skills to enhance and guide your life. Consider incorporating goal setting as a fundamental part of your daily life. As the legendary animator and entertainment company founder Walt Disney said, "If you can dream it, you can be it."

Key Terms and Concepts

Code of ethics	Instrumental values
Conventional level	Intangible values
Decision-making model	Moral development
Ethical audit	Morality
Ethical barometer	Postconventional level
Ethical decision making	Preconventional level
Ethical dilemmas	SMART goals
Ethics	Stakeholders
Ethics test	Tangible values
Goal	Terminal values
Goal setting	Values

Discussion Questions

1. While most of us would like to be successful in life, few of us set specific goals as to what success would look like and by when. Why is this so, and how can goal setting help make a difference?

2. How do values relate to goals?

3. We use the example that "getting into shape" is not a SMART goal and offer ways to improve this statement. What if your goal is "to be a better friend"? How can you make this goal SMART?

4. In the 1990s, when asked by a researcher if they had it to do all over again, over half of men aged 50 said they would have taken a different career path. What are your thoughts about this?

5. In large metropolitan cities like Los Angeles, organizations are allowed to pollute up to a certain amount. Beyond that amount, the organization is fined. If they pollute less than the limit, organizations can "sell" their pollution credits to other firms that will

save money by buying the pollution credits rather than paying the fine for exceeding their own limit. Your firm has been paying $25,000 a year in fines. However, it has the option of purchasing pollution-abatement equipment for $200,000 that, if installed, will put it well within the legal limit. Should the organization invest in this equipment, continue paying fines, or . . .? What would you recommend and why?

Endnotes

1. Gary P. Latham and Edwin A. Locke, "Enhancing the Benefits and Overcoming the Pitfalls of Goal Setting," *Organizational Dynamics* 35, no. 4 (November 2006), p. 332.

2. Edwin A. Locke and Gary P. Latham, "Building a Practically Useful Theory of Goal Setting and Task Motivation: A 35-Year Odyssey," *American Psychologist* 57, no. 9 (September 2002), p. 705.

3. M. J. Neubeert and C. Ju-Chien, "An Investigation of the Generalizability of the Houghton and Neck Revised Self-Leadership Questionnaire to a Chinese Context," *Journal of Management Psychology* 21, no. 4 (2006), pp. 360–61.

4. S. Georgianna, "Self-Leadership: A Cross-Cultural Perspective," *Journal of Managerial Psychology* 22, no. 6 (2007), p. 572.

5. Christine Riordan, "The Positive Returns of a Happy Workforce," *Financial Times (On-lineSoapbox),* May 19, 2013.

6. Shawn K. Yearta, Sally Maitlis, and Rob B. Briner, "An Exploratory Study of Goal Setting in Theory and Practice," *Journal of Occupational and Organizational Psychology* 68, no. 3 (September 1995), p. 237.

7. Yaping Gong and Song Chang, "The Relationship of Cross-Cultural Adjustment with Dispositional Learning Orientation and Goal Setting: A Longitudinal Analysis," *Journal of Cross-Cultural Psychology* 38, no. 1 (January 2007), pp. 19, 23.

8. J. J. Donovan, "Goal Setting: How to Create an Action Plan and Achieve Your Goals," *Personnel Psychology* 61, no. 4 (2008), p. 932.

9. Tseng Hsing-Chau and K. Long-Min, "How Does Regulatory Focus Affect Uncertainty Towards Organizational Change?" *Leadership and Organization Development Journal* 29, no. 8 (2008), pp. 713–14.

10. Shalom H. Schwartz and Wolfgang Bilsky, "Toward a Universal Psychological Structure of Human Values," *Journal of Personality and Social Psychology* 53, no. 3 (September 1987), p. 551.

11. Milton Rokeach, *The Nature of Human Values* (New York: Free Press, 1973).

12. Rokeach, *The Nature of Human Values.*

13. Douglas W. Lyon and Eric G. Kirby, "The Career Planning Essay," *Journal of Management Education* 24, no. 2 (April 2000), p. 279, in reference to a study by S. Courter, "Tomorrow's Captains of Industry Rate Gates Almost as High as Dad," *The Wall Street Journal,* May 14, 1998, p. B1.

14. J. R. Edwards and D. M. Cable, "The Value of Value Congruence," *Journal of Applied Psychology* 94 (2009), pp. 654–77.

15. Gary P. Latham, "Goal Setting: A Five-Step Approach to Behavior Change," *Organizational Dynamics* 32, no. 3 (August 2003), p. 311.

16. A. Shahin and Ali Mahbod, "Prioritization of Key Performance Indicators," *International Journal of Productivity and Performance Management* 56, no. 3 (2007), p. 228.

17. T. Kavoo-Linge, V. R. Willie Jansen, and D. Sikalieh, "The Relationship between Goal Setting and Career Advancement: A Case of Women Employees in Kenya," *International Journal of Business and Social Science* 2, no. 17 (2011), p. 235.

18. Shahin and Mahbod, p. 227.

19. Michelle Downie, Richard Koestner, Elizabeth Horberg, and Silje Haga, "Exploring the Relation of Independent and Interdependent Self-Construals to Why and How People Pursue Personal Goals," *Journal of Social Psychology* 146, no. 5 (October 2006), pp. 517–18.

20. M. Huhtala, T. Feldt, K. Hyvonen, and S. Mauno, "Ethical Organisational Culture as a Context for Managers' Personal Work Goals," *Journal of Business Ethics* 114, no. 2 (2013), pp. 266–67.

21. S. Burnaz, M. G. Atakan, Y. I. Topcu, and A. Singhapakdi, "An Exploratory Cross-Cultural Analysis of Marketing Ethics: The Case of Turkish, Thai and American Businesspeople," *Journal of Business Ethics* 90 (2009), p. 381.

22. James O'Toole, "Doing Good Business: Leadership and Sustainable Corporate Cultures." In James O'Toole and Don Mayer (eds.), *Good Business: Exercising Effective and Ethical Leadership* (New York: Routledge: 2010), p. 112.

23. David W. Johnson, *Reaching Out: Interpersonal Effectiveness and Self-Actualization* (Boston: Allyn & Bacon, 2003), p. 378.

24. Dennis Wittmer, "Behavioral Ethics in Business Organizations: What the Research Teaches Us." In James O'Toole and Don Mayer (eds.), *Good Business: Exercising Effective and Ethical Leadership* (New York: Routledge: 2010), p. 59.

25. Betty Velthouse and Yener Kandogan, "Ethics in Practice: What Are Managers Really Doing?" *Journal of Business Ethics* 70, no. 2 (January 2007), pp. 151–63.

26. C. Piotrowski and Roger W. Guyette Jr., "Toyota Recall Crisis: Public Attitudes on Leadership and Ethics," *Organization Development Journal* 28, no. 2 (2010), p. 95.

27. Ibid., pp. 90–92.

28. B. Elango, K. Paul, S. K. Kundu, and S. K. Paudel, "Organizational Ethics, Individual Ethics, and Ethical Intentions in International Decision Making," *Journal of Business Ethics* 97, no. 4 (2010), pp. 543–46.

29. Ibid., p. 544.

30. Ibid., p. 546.

31. Curtis C. Verschoor, "What's Ethical? Here's a Simple Test," *Strategic Finance* (March 2000), p. 24.

32. See Irene Roozen, Patrick DePelsmacker, and Frank Bostyn, "The Ethical Dimensions of Decision Processes of Employees," *Journal of Business Ethics* 33, no. 2 (September 2001), p. 87; and Patrick E. Connor and Boris W. Becker, "Personal Value Systems and Decision-making Styles of Public Managers," *Public Personnel Management* 32, no. 1 (Spring 2003), p. 155.

33. Miao-Ling Fang, "Evaluating Ethical Decision-Making of Individual Employees in Organizations—an Integration Framework," *Journal of American Academy of Business* 8, no. 2 (March 2006), p. 106.

34. Bruce L. Oliver, "Comparing Corporate Managers' Personal Values over Three Decades, 1967–1995," *Journal of Business Ethics* 20, no. 2 (June 1999), p. 147.

35. Glen Pettigrove, "Ambitions," *Ethical Theory & Moral Practice* 10, no. 1 (January 2007), p. 65.

36. L. Kohlberg, "Moral Stages and Moralization: The Cognitive-developmental Approach." In T. Lickona (ed.), *Moral Development and Behavior: Theory, Research and Social Issues* (New York: Holt, Rinehart and Winston: 1976), pp. 31–53; and L. Kohlberg, *Essays on Moral Development,* Vol. 1: *The Philosophy of Moral Development* (San Francisco: Harper and Row, 1981).

37. Linda K. Treviño, Gary R. Weaver, and Scott J. Reynolds, "Behavioral Ethics in Organizations: A Review," *Journal of Management* 32, no. 6 (December 2006), p. 955.

38. Sean Valentine, Martin M. Greller, and Sandra B. Richtermeyer, "Employee Job Response as a Function of Ethical Context and Perceived Organization Support," *Journal of Business Research* 59, no. 5 (May 2006), pp. 583–87.

39. Elango, et al., pp. 553–55.

40. Robert Audi and Patrick E. Murphy, "The Many Faces of Integrity," *Business Ethics Quarterly* 16, no. 1 (January 2006), p. 15.

41. Michael L. Michael, "Business Ethics: The Law of Rules," *Business Ethics Quarterly* 16, no. 4 (2006), p. 481.

42. Danielle S. Beua and M. Ronald Buckley, "Using Accountability to Create a More Ethical Climate," *Human Resource Management Review* 14, no. 1 (March 2004), p. 70.

43. Arthur Gross Schaefer and Anthony J. Zaller, "Why Ethics Tools Don't Work," *Nonprofit World* 17, no. 2 (March/April 1999), pp. 42–44, adapted from Robert C. Solomon and Kristine Hanson, *It's Good Business* (New York: Atheneum, 1985).

44. Y. Dufour and L. Lamothe, "Revisiting a Classic Study," *Journal of Strategy and Management* 2, no. 1 (2009), p. 106.

45. Curtis C. Verschoor, Lawrence A. Ponemon, and Christopher Michaelson, "Values Added: Rules and Values in Ethical Decision Making," *Strategic Finance* (February 2000), p. 24.

46. Shannon Bowen, "Organizational Factors Encouraging Ethical Decision Making: An Exploration into the Case of an Exemplar," *Journal of Business Ethics* 52, no. 4 (July 2004), p. 312.

47. Verschoor, "What's Ethical?"

48. Denis Collins, "Five Levels for Improving Ethical Performance," *Strategic Finance* 88, no. 1 (July 2006), p. 20.

49. Verschoor, "What's Ethical?"

50. Ibid.

51. M. Selart and S. T. Johansen, "Ethical Decision Making in Organizations: The Role of Leadership Stress," *Journal of Business Ethics* 99, no. 2 (2011), p. 130.

52. Verschoor, "What's Ethical?"

53. John Tschohi, "The Qualities of Successful People," *Managing Service Quality* 9, no. 2 (1999), p. 78.

**Exercise 3–A
Values Inventory**

1. From the following list, choose five items that are most important to you. Rank the top five items according to your current values. This is only a partial list; fill in the (other) blanks with items that are of personal value to you. Give the most important item a 1, the next most important a 2, and so on.

Values	Current	3 years	5 years	10 years
Security				
Financial independence				
Having children				
Owning a home				
Free time				
Recognition or fame				
Friendships				
Helping others less fortunate than you				
Family				
Travel				
Having the respect of others				
Playing sports				
Having an interesting job or career				
Having good physical health				
Being a knowledgeable, informed person				
Having a sense of accomplishment				
Spiritual fulfillment				
Doing well in school				
(other)				
(other)				

2. From the same list, indicate in the columns which values would comprise your top five ranking in 3 years, 5 years, and 10 years. Look back over your rankings. Does anything surprise you? Were there any drastic changes from the present through 10 years?

3. In examining your current values, how do these fit in with the way in which you currently allocate your time? Do these values fit in with your dreams, goals, ambitions, and life principles?

4. What major, unanticipated event could cause you to modify your rankings (serious illness, business failure, marriage, etc.)? Discuss how this event would impact your rankings.

Exercise 3–B
"This Is Your Life"

Fast-forward your life video and contemplate a celebration dinner (roast) to honor you. Imagine it is years into the future and we are celebrating your accomplishments at a retirement dinner. Assume that each of the following will deliver a speech: family member, close friend, business or professional associate, community or religious representative.

How would you prefer to have these people think about, see, and perceive you and your actions? Identify the main points each would make in your honor. What would you ideally like to have said concerning your accomplishments, relationships with others, contributions to society, and so on?

Family Member's Speech

_____

_____

_____

Close Friend's Speech

_____

_____

_____

Business or Professional Associate's Speech

_____

_____

_____

Community or Religious Representative's Speech

_____

_____

_____

From reviewing the speeches, is there a common thread or theme? Write a phrase or caption that would summarize your life principle.

_____

_____

_____

Source: Adapted from Stephen Covey, *Seven Habits of Highly Successful People: Powerful Lessons in Personal Change* (New York: Simon & Schuster, 1989).

**Exercise 3–C
Your Personal Mission
Statement**

1. Use the following space to write your personal mission. Your mission statement reflects your personal constitution, set of beliefs, and value system. In it, you should address such questions as these:

   a. What is my purpose? What do I believe?

   b. What do I value?

   c. What do I treasure?

   d. What is really important to me?

   e. How do I want to approach living my life?

   f. How do I want to approach life on a daily basis?

2. Answer these questions by first reviewing the speeches from Exercise 3–B to ensure a multifaceted mission statement. Use the space below to record insights and understandings that you have about yourself and your life plan.

_____

_____

_____

_____

_____

_____

_____

_____

_____

_____

_____

_____

_____

Clarifying your mission is an ongoing process. Revisit and update your mission periodically.

Exercise 3–D
Personal Goal Setting

1. In the space below, brainstorm your goals in the following categories. Write down as many as you wish, including goals that are short-, mid-, and long-term.

Academic, intellectual

Health, fitness

Social, family, friends, significant other, community

Career, job

Financial

Other

2. Of the goals you have listed, select from each of the six categories the two most important goals you would like to pursue in the short term (next 6–12 months). Write these below.

1. _____

2. _____

3. _____

4. _____

5. _____

6. _____

7. _____

8. _____

9. _____

10. _____

11. _____

12. _____

3. From the 12 goals listed above, choose the three that are the most important to you at this time, the three you commit to work on in the next few months. Write a goal statement for each one, using the following guidelines:

- Begin each with the word "To . . ."
- Be specific.
- Quantify the goal if possible.
- Each goal statement should be realistic, attainable, and within your control.
- Each goal statement should reflect your aspirations—not those of others such as parents, roommates, significant others, and the like.

1. _____

   _____

2. _____

   _____

3. _____

   _____

4. On a separate sheet of paper, develop an action plan for each goal statement. For each action plan:

- List the steps you will take to accomplish the goal.
- Include dates (by when) and initials (who's responsible) for each step.
- Visualize completing the goal and, working backwards, specify each step necessary between now and then to reach the goal.
- Identify any potential barriers you might experience in attaining the goal. Problem-solve around these obstacles and convert them into steps in your action plan.
- Identify the resources you will need to accomplish these goals, and build in steps to acquire the necessary information in your action plan.

5. Transfer the dates of each step for each goal in your action plan to a daily calendar.

6. Keep an ongoing daily or weekly record of the positive steps you take toward meeting each goal.

Exercise 3–E
Ethical Stance

Are the following actions ethical or unethical in your opinion? Why or why not? Consider individually and discuss in small groups.

- Calling in sick when you really are not.
- Clicking "Agree to Terms" without reading the fine print before accessing Web content.
- Taking office supplies home for personal use.
- Cheating on a test.
- Turning someone in for cheating on a test or paper.
- Overcharging on your company expense report.
- Trying to flirt your way out of a speeding ticket.
- Splicing cable from your neighbor.
- Surfing the Net on company time.
- Cheating on your income tax.
- Lying (exaggerating) about yourself to influence someone of the opposite sex.
- Looking at pornographic sites on the Web through the company network.
- Lying about your education on a job application.
- Lying about your experience in a job interview.
- Making a copy of a rental video cassette before returning it to the store.

Exercise 3–F
The Gold Watch

The Situation

John is a 35-year-old salesman with Anderson and Sons, Inc., an established wholesaler of office equipment. He lives near Anderson's headquarters in Chicago with his wife and two adopted children.

On a recent sales tour abroad, John met J.R., an office-equipment supplier who was interested in a line of photocopiers worth $500,000. J.R. told John that he would give John an order for the photocopiers in return for a gold Rolex watch worth $13,000. J.R. showed John the watch he wanted in a catalog, and John said that he would see what he could do.

On returning to Chicago, John told Charles, his boss, about the proposition, asking if he could go ahead and buy the Rolex in order to obtain the order. Charles was outraged and said, "This is immoral! It's not decent business practice to offer bribes. We're living in a civilized society. If I find out that you've been bribing customers to get orders, I'll fire you on the spot! Have I made myself clear?"

After the confrontation with Charles, John left the office and drove to the home of Terry, his friend and colleague. He explained his plight and then said, "What can I do, Terry? It's an important order, and there's a chance of repeat business; J.R. is interested in office furniture and typewriters as well as more photocopiers in the future."

Terry thought for a moment and then said, "John, why don't you finance the deal yourself? Buy the stupid watch and land the contract. With your commission and any future business, you'll get a decent return on your investment. Don't even tell Charles; he's so ridiculously old-fashioned—he has no idea how to do business in this day and age."

John left Terry's home, went to his car, thought for a few minutes, and then drove to his bank. Mr. Gray, the bank manager and a close friend of John's father, listened to John's reasons for wanting the $13,000 loan. Despite the fact that John's checking account was overdrawn, he agreed to give John the loan immediately.

The next day John went to a jewelry store near his office and asked a clerk for the specific Rolex watch requested by J.R. While he was waiting for the clerk to bring him the watch, Jane, Charles's secretary, came into the store to buy a birthday present for her mother. Unobserved by John, she watched as the clerk gave the watch to John in exchange for the $13,000 cash. In her astonishment she forgot about finding a present for her mother, hurried back to Anderson and Sons, burst into Charles's office, and asked, "How can a salesman who earns $30,000 a year afford a $13,000 watch?"

Charles was furious. He rushed out of his office and found John just returning from the jewelry store. "You're fired!" he shouted.

"Let me explain . . . " muttered John.

"No excuses! I warned you!"

At that moment a telex came through; it read as follows: "NO LONGER INTERESTED IN THE PHOTOCOPIER DEAL. FOUND ALTERNATIVE SUPPLIER. J.R."

Instructions

Rank order the following characters from 1 (least objectionable) to 6 (most objectionable):

_____ John

_____ J.R.

_____ Charles

_____ Terry

_____ Mr. Gray

_____ Jane

**Exercise 3–G
Evaluating Goals
and Ethics**

1. Watch a current TV show and answer the following questions:

   ■ What are some of the positive goal-setting behaviors exhibited by a primary charac-ter in the show? Describe these behaviors and the outcome achieved in the show.

   ■ Is there a character who offers a negative role model with respect to goal setting? Describe this person's behaviors related to goal setting (or lack thereof) and the outcomes.

2. View a movie in which achievement or goal setting is a theme, such as *The Blind Side*, *Robin Hood*, *An Education*, and answer the following questions:

   ■ Describe the main character's mission, its impact on that person's behaviors, and how he or she dealt with setbacks.

   ■ Identify elements of the character's behavior that you would like to apply to your own life. What would this look like?

3. Choose a TV show or a movie. What ethical dilemmas do the protagonist and antago-nist face? How does each deal with the situation? What decision factors do they use to make decisions? How is the situation resolved to take into consideration the needs of all involved (or is it)?

4. The next time you're in a group situation and an ethical dilemma arises, watch the group to see how the decision is made. What factors are considered? Is an ethics test applied? How is the decision made? Is it the right one? How do you know?

**Exercise 3–H
Company Description**

Write down a description of your life and the company you will work for, five years from now. Include the location (city or rural), your family, your car and house, your job field, your position title, a few of your responsibilities, and a description of your company's size, products or services, culture, people, mission, work environment, as well as your office.

_____

_____

_____

_____

_____

_____

_____

_____

_____

Now, imagine your life except fifteen years from now. Write down the same items and note the changes.

_____

_____

_____

_____

_____

_____

_____

_____

_____

_____

Submitted by: Mr. Bob Eliason, Management Lecturer, James Madison University, Harrisonburg, VA.

**Exercise 3–I
Your Retirement Party**

You are about to retire. At your farewell party, the host wants to list your life's accomplishments. Prepare a list of what you expect to have accomplished over the years. Include personal as well as business successes. What are your most important successes? How will you measure your happiness?

_____

_____

_____

_____

_____

_____

_____

_____

_____

_____

Submitted by: Mr. Bob Eliason, Management Lecturer, James Madison University, Harrisonburg, VA.

Exercise 3–J
Life Goals

Look at your entire life. Set one goal for each life component:

Education

    Yours

    Your children's

Family

    Parents/Stepparents/Biological and adopted

    Marriage/Partner

    Children/Nieces and nephews/Godchildren

    Extended family

Career

    Industry or occupation

    Achievements

    Position at retirement

Income

    Sources

    Financial security

    Investments (short- and long-term)

Housing

    Type

    Location

Recreation

    Hobbies

    Travel

    Interests

    Sports

Health

    Fitness/wellness

    Major health issues

Culture

    Music

    Arts

    Performances

Social involvement

    Community

    Causes

    Charities

    Leadership (or politics)

    Volunteerism

Your emotional state

Other

Submitted by: Mr. Bob Eliason, Management Lecturer, James Madison University, Harrisonburg, VA.

Exercise 3–K **Career Assets**	The following factors are often associated with determining and maintaining a successful career path. Write a brief description of what actions you will take to achieve each career asset.

Education

A plan for your career path

Obtaining a variety of work experiences

Setting high expectations for personal performance

Timely changing of career

Selecting work that energizes you

Being a team player

Selecting career challenges and additional responsibilities

Being assertive or appropriately aggressive

Being flexible

Seeking and accepting feedback

Taking risks

Freeing yourself from the expectations of others

Submitted by: Mr. Bob Eliason, Management Lecturer, James Madison University, Harrisonburg, VA.

Exercise 3–L
Reflection/Action Plan

This chapter focused on goal setting—what it is, why it's important, and how to acquire and increase the degree to which you possess it. We also discussed the role of values and ethics in setting goals that are aligned with your key priorities. Complete the following worksheet upon reading and finishing the experiential activities for this chapter.

1. The one or two areas in which I am most strong are:

_____

_____

_____

_____

2. The one or two areas in which I need more improvement are:

_____

_____

_____

_____

3. If I did only one thing to improve in this area, it would be to:

_____

_____

_____

_____

4. Making this change would probably result in:

_____

_____

_____

_____

5. If I did not change or improve in this area, it would probably affect my personal and professional life in the following ways:

_____

_____

_____

_____

4 Self-management

Learning Points

How do I:
- Evaluate my emotional strengths and identify areas for personal improvement?
- Manage my time to achieve more and be more effective?
- Make better use of my time by working smarter and not harder?
- Identify stressors in my life and find ways to reduce or change my response to them?
- Recognize and overcome barriers to self-improvement?

"It is 8:05 and now I am going to be late!" Janet Smythe screamed, more to herself than anyone else. Just another typical morning of trying to get the kids off to school and get to work on time. "But Mom, I need you to sign my permission slip for the field trip. It needs to be handed in today or I can't go next week," her son yells back. Janet growls back, "Why didn't you have me fill it out last night?"

Somehow she makes it out the door and heads to work. Of course the traffic is backed up, and it doesn't look as if she will be able to make up any lost time on the commute. When she finally gets into her office, her co-worker pops her head through the office door and asks Janet to send an electronic copy of their presentation for the 10:00 sales meeting. Janet then realizes she hadn't completed the final version. With her frustration mounting, she takes her anger out on Mike, her assistant, who unfortunately chose that moment to remind Janet of the 10:00 meeting on her schedule. "I don't need constant reminding, Mike. I do have a schedule and I can read!!" She slumps in her chair, not sure of how she should proceed to get out of this mess. She walks out of her office and finds Mike at his desk. "Sorry, Mike. First I'm yelling at my kids, then you, and I have forgotten my work again. I'm losing my mind. Something has got to change."

1. What problems is Janet facing?
2. What are some strategies Janet could use to better manage the overwhelming situation in which she finds herself?
3. If you were Janet, how would you handle the situation?

"It is not the mountain we conquer, but ourselves."

Sir Edmund Hillary

As many of us have heard before, if you don't take care of yourself, who will? **Self-management** is the effort to exert control over your decision making and behavior by assessing problems and developing specific goals and strategies to structure your environment to address those problems.[1] Because self-management is a learned rather than an innate trait, you have the opportunity to enhance your individual performance through self-management training. As our lives become more complicated and we endlessly juggle multiple priorities, the likelihood of our reacting negatively to unexpected changes or competing demands in our personal and professional lives increases. In this chapter we explore the concept of self-management from these perspectives: management of emotions, or emotional intelligence; time management; and stress management. Being able to manage yourself is a lifelong process. It requires self-awareness and a continued willingness to make changes in your attitudes and behavior. In order to be an effective manager, it is important to be an effective self-manager. In this chapter we discuss how to overcome barriers to interpersonal effectiveness so you can devote your full energies to doing what it takes to succeed, and to be happy in life as well as in business.

What Is Emotional Intelligence?

Effective self-management requires an awareness of our emotional and rational responses, or a strong degree of **emotional intelligence**, commonly referred to as **EQ**. Emotional intelligence has five components:[2]

- *Self-awareness*—emotional awareness, accurate self-assessment, self-confidence, ability to recognize emotions and their effects on you and others.
- *Self-regulation*—self-control, trustworthiness, conscientiousness, adaptability, innovation, ability to manage disruptive emotions and impulses.
- *Motivation*—zeal, achievement drive, commitment, initiative, optimism, and the ability to remain persistent in the face of adversity.
- *Empathy*—understanding others, service orientation, developing others, leveraging diversity, political awareness, the ability to read and respond to others' feelings.
- *Social skills*—interacting smoothly, managing interpersonal relationships, handling emotional responses to others, influence, communication, the ability to build bonds with others.

EQ helps us to use emotions as guiding tools for interpersonal effectiveness in social environments. EQ involves using your mental capabilities to understand your own and others' current emotions correctly and to use those emotions wisely to produce personally and socially desirable outcomes. See Exercise 4–A at the end of this chapter to take the Emotional Intelligence test.

Benefits of EQ

People who successfully apply EQ create win–win relationships and outcomes for themselves and others, and can develop growing networks of healthy social relationships and emotional support structures. In some interesting recent research, EQ is calculated to account for 58 percent of workplace performance in all types of jobs and is the "single biggest predictor of performance in the workplace and the strongest driver of leadership and personal excellence."[3]

As the ancient philosopher Aristotle said,

"Anyone can become angry—that is easy. But to be angry with the right person, to the right degree, at the right time, for the right purpose, and in the right way—this is not easy."

Aristotle was a wise man. He recognized that as human beings we are able to experience a full range of feelings. Learning when, how, where, why, and with whom to share them is more complex than we might think at first glance. Emotional intelligence enables us to do this.

EQ helps us to understand our levels of key emotional responses such as self-control, zeal, and persistence, and the ability to use our emotions, feelings, and moods and those of others to adapt and navigate in society. A guiding principle of emotional intelligence is that having and expressing emotions is a good thing. But expressing emotions, especially in the business world, requires an innate sense of what's appropriate to say, when, where, and with whom. EQ allows you to develop an awareness of your feelings and emotions and use them in appropriate ways. Your level of emotional intelligence—the degree to which you are savvy about the use of emotions when communicating with others—is a huge factor in your ability to be successful. EQ is considered by some to be just as important as or even more important than IQ, one's "intelligence quotient." IQ and EQ involve different parts of the brain. IQ affects our ability to reason, to process information, to think analytically. EQ affects our ability to use emotions in relating to others at work and in our personal lives. Important criteria for professional success in any field are the "people" skills that are derived from understanding our emotions and responses to working with others. This type of self-knowledge is critical to your ability to relate to others and make decisions about your life and work. The good news is that unlike one's IQ, which is determined primarily at birth, EQ is a quality you can actually learn about and improve.

An enhanced EQ is also a positive factor in being able to work cross-culturally. EQ requires a high degree of self-monitoring, which as we learned in chapter 2 is an individual's ability to adjust his or her behavior to external factors. High self-monitors are more willing and able to adapt their behaviors to those of a host country than are low self-monitors.[4]

Understanding your levels of emotional intelligence is essential for self-awareness. By knowing how you presently function when dealing with your emotions in situations with others, you can develop new goals, behaviors, and attitudes toward yourself as well as others. Working to increase your emotional intelligence can help you do this. In the process, you can become a better manager as well as a better person.

What Does EQ Look Like?

High	**Low**
Is self-aware of impact on others	Not aware of how impacts others
Controls emotions	Moody
Concerned about others	Concerned about self
Optimistic	Pessimistic

Improved Workplace Performance

Being able to understand and harness your emotions is just as valuable in the workplace as it is in your personal life. Daniel Goleman, one of the foremost researchers on emotional intelligence, found EQ to be twice as important as IQ and technical skills at all job levels. Without it, a person can have the best training in the world, an incisive, analytical mind, and an endless supply of smart ideas, but he or she still won't make a great leader.[5] Goleman also concludes that EQ plays an even more substantial role in success at higher level positions.

On an individual level, self-regulation, self-awareness, and motivation have been positively associated with concern for quality, problem-solving ability, and ability to manage conflicts. Ranking high on these dimensions suggests an individual will exhibit effective behaviors at work. Being able to interpret the emotions of others, empathy, social skills, and group work skills increase the effectiveness of organizational managers and leaders. In today's organizations, it is important to be flexible, responsive to change, and able to react quickly by sizing up people and situations and being decisive. Developing these skills will result in you becoming an "involved employee"[6]—one who is empowered and equipped to be effective in your role and to help others with theirs.

Improving emotional intelligence allows managers to become leaders who positively influence others with commanding social skills.[7] Some key impacts of EQ in leadership include:[8]

■ *Reduced depression, greater optimism, and less impulsiveness*—These behaviors help managers deal with difficult situations, improve decision making, and positively affect employees' work attitudes.

■ *Increased concern for mastering skills and tasks*—Conscientious leaders strive for personal improvement and facilitate and develop that capability in others, ensuring that people are challenged to develop their own solutions to challenges and that they are supported in doing so.[9]

■ *Improved facilitation of adaptation and change*—Emotional intelligence allows leaders to gain power and become catalysts for change.

■ *Increased influence on positive teaming*—Emotionally intelligent individuals utilize social skills and can moderate their behavior and influence others to collaborate, build bonds, and communicate on team-based efforts.

■ *The development of transformational leadership*—Leaders who have a strong sense of self and strong convictions in their beliefs are able to provide vision and encourage development and motivation in others.

The Manager's Role in EQ[10]

1. *Assess "emotional impact" of jobs*—Managers need to be aware of the emotional pressures associated with particular jobs when designing job assignments.

2. *Create a positive and friendly emotional climate*—Managers need to recognize that workers need a supportive environment; work should not be a cold place devoid of concern for its members.

3. *Properly reward and compensate*—Through appropriately developed reward and compensation systems, managers can encourage a positive emotional climate.

4. *Select appropriate employees and team members*—Managers need to base selection of employees and team members on their record of utilizing a positive emotional attitude.

5. *Provide EQ training*—Managers need to develop training to increase employee EQ and encourage positive emotional responses.

Strategies for Increasing EQ

1. Be candid—assess yourself realistically. Think of situations when you've been at your best—and your worst. What can you do to acknowledge your weaknesses and work on them? How can you place yourself in activities that play to and help foster your strengths?

2. Ask for feedback. At the conclusion of a class or work project, ask a classmate, teammate, or supervisor to let you know what you did well, and what you can improve.

3. Be self-confident. Know your abilities. Stretch—but don't overstretch by taking on tasks for which you lack the necessary skills.

4. Don't overreact when things don't go your way. Objectively look at the situation, gather the facts, and determine rationally the best way to approach the situation or present a solution.

5. Take time to choose an appropriate course of action. Don't react impulsively.

6. Accept and develop skill in coping with ambiguity and change. These are hallmarks of most successful organizations and managers today.

7. Be motivated by a strong internal desire to achieve for the sake of achievement, not (just) for material success.

8. Track your progress. Always be aware of the results you are seeking; don't simply focus on the task itself.

9. Consider others in all of your decisions. "No man is an island." Understand others and take their needs into account when you make decisions.

10. Take time for people. Some of the best managers are known for "walking around" on a regular basis. Take time out from studies or work to develop rapport with your classmates or colleagues. Time spent cultivating friendships with others at schools or work is time well spent.

What Are Time and Stress Management and Why Are They Important?

What distinguishes top performers from those who are just moderately successful? An enhanced EQ, as we've just seen, is key. Naturally our genetic history, cultural background, economic circumstances, family background, education, and work history affect the opportunities that are available to us and our ability to seek and choose among these opportunities. And to be honest, plain luck, "being in the right place at the right time," is a factor in one's success. More and more, however, we are realizing that our ability to manage and allocate time and to handle our response to stress have a lot to do with the extent to which we ultimately succeed, in life as well as in business.

Time Management

Time management is the ability to allocate your time and resources to accomplishing your objectives. Skill in managing how you spend your time allows you to prioritize and accomplish more goals in life, resulting in a sense of well-being because you are able to see the fruits of your labors. It gives you a chance to achieve a balance between work and personal life that can be more satisfying, as opposed to restricting your activities to one arena at the expense of the other. Effective managers find that time management increases productivity. The popular saying "Work smarter, not harder" applies here. By focusing your energy on well-chosen activities, you can actually see your results. This in itself can be motivating, which can then increase your drive to achieve even more.

Managing our time also reduces stress levels. Taking control of your time means taking control of your life. This results in a feeling that you are in charge. "I exercised today, and now I can go back and study for the exam with a clear head" is an example of this, which is better than thinking subconsciously, "I have no time, I have no life. I didn't exercise, and now I don't even have the energy to study for this exam." Time management gives you more time to enjoy the activities that are important to you, such as spending time with family, socializing, reading, exercising, and doing favorite hobbies. This means you are better able to enjoy a varied, textured life. As human beings, we have many dimensions. We are not meant to simply work. Most of us have the need to be many things—a friend, a partner, a family member, part of a community. As you incorporate many elements of life into one, each of those elements is enhanced by your involvement in the others.

"Hold on a second, Bob. I'm putting you on a stickie."

Source: http://www.cartoonbank.com/1997/hold-on-a-second-bob-im-putting-you-on-a-stickie/invt/115106/?

Stress Management

Stress (from the Latin *strictus,* to draw tight)[11] has been a part of daily life since prehistoric times. It plays an important role in how we live our lives and whether or not we succeed in the tasks we undertake. Stress is a fact of personal and organizational life. Stress can be beneficial (eustress) when it generates enthusiasm and productivity or counterproductive (distress) when it dampens your spirits and negatively impacts your mental or physical health.[12] **Stress management** refers to your efforts to change perceptions and behavior when external and internal demands exceed personal resources.[13] Stress, when not understood or managed, can result in a variety of responses, including physiological, psychological, and organizational. A **physiological** response is one in which physical problems develop as a result of mental anguish. Many occupations are high-stress and have negative effects on employees. For example, job stress detracts nurses from qualitative working lives, enhances physical morbidity, and contributes toward physical illness, such as musculoskeletal problems and depression.[14]

Heart disease, high blood pressure, bulimia, anorexia nervosa, migraine headaches, cancer, gastrointestinal disorders, asthma, diabetes, allergies, skin disorders, high cholesterol levels, and weakened body defenses are some examples of physical conditions that are often brought on by mental stress. The National Institute of Occupational Safety and Health (NIOSH) has recognized stress-related physiological disorders as the leading cause of worker disability in the country today. Forty percent say their work load is excessive and they have too much pressure at work.[15] **Psychological** effects are not always as readily identifiable as physiological responses. Depression, sudden bursts of violence or anger, anxiety, chemical dependency, alcohol abuse, overeating, withdrawal, and phobias are examples of psychological reactions to stressful situations.

Organizational stress or work-related stress is the "adverse reaction people have to excessive pressures or other types of demands placed on them."[16] Organizational stress effects include job dissatisfaction, absenteeism, turnover, accidents, low morale, poor interpersonal relations, low productivity, and poor customer service. Stress caused by organizational problems is often difficult to manage, as the factors causing the stress are rarely under our control. Some jobs are highly stressful because of the nature of the work—the jobs of air traffic controllers, dentists, and coal miners are examples. Even businesses that are not commonly viewed as stressful are now prone to high stress levels, especially after so many businesses have experienced drastic downsizing. In addition, employees are working more hours now than they were in the 1960s. High e-mail volume is also a factor. Business e-mail users now send and receive an average of 71 e-mails per day, with some receiving upwards of 200, and these numbers are only expected to rise. Irrelevant e-mails currently waste three and a half years of a manager's work life.[17] These trends, coupled with the desire of many employees, male and female, to lead more balanced lives and spend time with their families and friends, are resulting in increased employee stress levels.[18]

Work-family conflict is another area associated with stress. The belief that we must "do it all" has led to high levels of stress. The changes in the U.S. labor force, with an increase in dual-worker families and single-parent families, have given rise to conflict over balancing the demands of work and the needs of the family. Over half of high-level executives surveyed ranked feeling "overextended" and concern for work–life balance as the top causes of stress.[19] Finding a balance between the roles of family caretaker (which includes taking care of spouse, parents, children, and/or siblings) and worker is necessary to reduce stress and its potential consequences (absenteeism, turnover, job dissatisfaction, family conflict, and life dissatisfaction). Individuals, as well as the managers and organizations for which they work, must address eliminating the potential for role conflict.

These sources of stress can be problematic in personal life and in business. Stress is inevitable, but you can manage how you respond to stress. Managing stress is an important skill for both managers and their employees. Those managers who are able to understand their stressors and manage them—and who can help their employees do the same—will be more productive and successful than those who aren't.

Strategies for Time and Stress Management

"**Time famine**," or feeling we have too much to do and not enough time to do it, is prevalent in a work environment that has increased employee responsibility through empowerment and autonomy.[20] Radical and lightning-quick changes are a permanent feature in today's contemporary business environment. Those managers who are able to stay current with these changes and adopt appropriate response strategies to these changes are more likely to succeed—and to help their employees succeed as well.

Time Management Strategies

There are times in our lives when it feels as if we have no time to think or breathe. This is fine if it only happens periodically. But if you're constantly running from one high-priority task to another, it's likely you'll soon be either suffering from burnout (when you're too fatigued to have an interest in the things on which you're spending time) or doing everything only marginally. It's time to cut back. It's better to do fewer things with quality than many things poorly. See Figure 4-1 on the next page to assess how you're currently using your time.

Time management is an important personal and managerial skill. It is a process of setting or taking on objectives, estimating the time and resources needed to accomplish each objective, and disciplining yourself to stay focused on the objective while completing it. It doesn't mean filling every minute. It means allowing for some "slack" time for the unexpected: those unforeseen circumstances that are inevitable.

We can't change the amount of time we have. There are only 24 hours in a day, 168 in a week. We manage ourselves in order to be more efficient with our time. You can concentrate on the choices you make and be aware of what's motivating you to make them. You can focus on getting things done by being productive—getting the right things done . . . on time, on budget, and through the use of all your resources.

■ *Plan and prioritize.* Planning is essential to effective time management. The minutes you spend organizing your schedule can save you hours of time during your week. Heed the words of Benjamin Franklin: "Failing to plan is planning to fail."

■ *Get in the habit of preparing "to-do" lists.* Make a list of everything you need to do for that day and prioritize the list according to the importance of completing each task. Bear in mind that most people will not complete every item on to-do lists; however, you will accomplish more with a list than without one (see Exercise 4–D).

Figure 4–1
How to Manage Your Time

Use the chart to evaluate your current usage of time, identifying your patterns of behavior and your current time wasters.

Typical Time Wasters	Degree to Which These Affect Me: High		Medium		Low
Procrastination	1	2	3	4	5
Disorganization	1	2	3	4	5
Perfectionism	1	2	3	4	5
Visitors and interruptions	1	2	3	4	5
Telephone, voice-mail, e-mail, Internet	1	2	3	4	5
Daydreaming and distractions	1	2	3	4	5
Lack of focus or interest	1	2	3	4	5
Doing too many tasks at once	1	2	3	4	5
Accepting too much work	1	2	3	4	5
Paperwork and administrative tasks	1	2	3	4	5
Poorly planned meetings	1	2	3	4	5
Lack of necessary resources	1	2	3	4	5
Failure to use technology	1	2	3	4	5

If you score less than 40, you may want to consider ways to reduce your wasted time. To do this, identify what is of value to you by determining what you consider to be important ways to spend your time. By referring to the personal and professional goals you established, you should be able to decide how to spend your time.

- *Follow the "80/20" rule.* An estimated 80 percent of results are achieved from 20 percent of focused time. This includes spending more time doing useful activities, tracking what makes that 20 percent so productive, and making the transition to devoting more time to productive work.[21]
- *Plan for your time-specific activities and non–time-specific activities.* For "time-specific" activities, develop an estimate of the length of time it will take you to complete a certain task, and plan accordingly. This requires self-discipline and allows you to budget your time and accomplish more than you would in a non–time-bound scenario. Also, plan your downtime. Everyone needs a break to rest and recharge. You can actually get more work done if you take several short breaks than if you don't.
- *Find your optimal working time*—referred to as your biological "prime time"—and plan to maximize use of this time by scheduling and doing demanding jobs during these peak periods and less demanding tasks at other times.
- *Control e-mail.* When possible, get key priorities done first, before you check your e-mail. This way you accomplish some important things before being sidetracked with others' priorities.
- *Prioritize tasks by level of importance*: vital, important, should be done today, or can be done tomorrow. Break down complex tasks or projects into manageable steps and set up a time line for completing each step.
- *Organize.* Choose or set up the right environment for the task. This may require you to clear away unnecessary materials, reduce distractions (turn off the phone or close the door), and eliminate environmental interference (heavy traffic or neighbor's music). If all else fails, go to a place such as a library where you can work without distractions.
- *Delegate.* Determine what tasks and activities would be possible to allocate to others. Clearly specify the task and the expected outcomes to ensure they will complete the task without requiring periodic coaching or redoing.

Figure 4–2
Time Management Matrix[22]

	Urgent	Not Urgent
Important	**Quadrant 1** • Dealing with a crisis • Most problem-solving activities • Meeting immediate deadlines • Writing a report due in one hour	**Quadrant 2** • Recreation and relaxation • Preparing for an upcoming event • Spending quality time with friends and family • Exercise
Not Important	**Quadrant 3** • Answering the telephone • Checking e-mail • Dealing with interruptions, such as requests for info or assistance • Many popular activities	**Quadrant 4** • Worrying or being angry • Watching TV beyond time needed to unwind • Surfing the Internet for no reason • Trivia and busywork

■ *Differentiate between what's urgent and what's important.* Most of us *expend* time on what's urgent—those unplanned events that are often thrust on us by others and beg for your immediate attention. Yet not enough of us *invest* time on what's important—those priorities that are meaningful and to which we are committed to spending time. Figure 4–2 illustrates the intersection between task and event importance and urgency. Be careful in deciding here. The interruption from one of your children or a roommate—a quadrant 3 activity—might be an investment if you are committed to spending time with your family and friends. The frequent interruption by a co-worker who likes to chat—also a quadrant 3 activity—is probably an expenditure. Responding to that person every time she or he comes in unannounced takes time from the priority on which you're working and sends the message that it's okay to continue interrupting.

Often when something comes up that was unplanned, it takes away from what is important.[23] The more time spent on important but not urgent activities (quadrant 2), the better you will be able to manage your time. If you devote time to the important, the urgent will often take care of itself. Learn to focus on the important and manage your ability to keep to the deadlines you have set; this will prevent the important from becoming urgent.

■ *Avoid postponing.* Procrastination is one of the biggest time wasters. Unfortunately many times we "put off until tomorrow what we could be doing today." While some people enjoy the adrenaline rush this produces (e.g., waiting until the last minute to write a paper and having to stay up all night to get it done), you will rarely produce your best work operating this way. By waiting until the last minute, many procrastinators find they have been unrealistic about the time required to do the job right. For example, when writing a paper at the last minute, you're likely to have difficulty finding resource materials that are necessary to do a quality job.

Waiting until the last minute also leaves little or no time to review your work, polish it, and ensure it's accurate and of sufficient quality. It's far better to plan ahead, leaving yourself some time toward the end of a project to take care of details that couldn't have been anticipated. Another negative consequence of procrastination is alienating co-workers. For example, your co-workers might think of you as one who always waits until the last minute. This not only causes stress for you but also for your co-workers, many of whom might try to avoid working with you again. Avoid this situation by planning and being realistic about what you can and want to achieve.

Procrastination (intentionally deferring or delaying work that must be completed) can also cause an internal conflict over what a person should do and what he or she wants to do. Although common, with 95 percent of us procrastinating sometimes, for the 25–40 percent of people who routinely procrastinate, the practice of doing so can create serious problems. It is usually associated with avoidance behavior—avoiding necessary action to complete a task—and can be used as a type of coping mechanism to delay an unpleasant task. So how can you overcome procrastination? You must first be aware of your tendency to procrastinate and evaluate the reasons for avoiding the necessary task. You can then work on changing your behavior by making the task more pleasant or less threatening. Planning and directing action to the long-term outcome may redirect your energy.[24]

Commit to evaluating periodically how you use your time. Do time audits—reexamine your goals and whether you allocate time appropriately to achieve them. To keep your schedule organized, reasonable, and attainable, incorporate tasks that are important to you. A balance between discipline and flexibility is key. Stay focused on your overall priorities (remember the 80/20 rule), while continually monitoring your progress and revising your plans as necessary.

Try This

Consult one or more of the following online tools to help build your time management skills:

www.rescuetime.com
http://www.thymer.com
www.toggl.com

Stress Management Issues

Stress is an upset in the body's balance in reaction to an adverse or disturbing event. Hans Selye, a pioneer in stress research, defines **stress** as the nonspecific response of the body to any demand made upon it.[25] Stress comes about not from an event, such as failing an exam or winning the lottery, but from how we respond to it. Stress is found everywhere, in all aspects of life. It is inevitable and unavoidable. The sources of stress vary from person to person. Stress can be derived from external factors such as traffic jams or an ineffective or inefficient work environment. Stress also stems from internal factors such as our emotional state, our perspective on life, or the way we choose to respond to various situations or demands.

Types of Stress

As we stated earlier, there are two types of stress: "good" and "bad." Good stress, or **eustress**, is positive, presents opportunity for personal growth or satisfaction, and pushes people to higher performance. Bad stress, or **distress**, is negative and results in debilitating effects.[26]

Surprisingly, too little stress can be as detrimental as too much stress. As Figure 4–3 demonstrates, when we lack any stress or pressure to perform, we may utilize minimal effort and achieve suboptimal performance. Conversely, too much stress might make it difficult to concentrate or perform effectively or efficiently. Whether a particular stress factor you are experiencing is "good" or "bad" depends largely on how you perceive the stressor and respond to it. In other words, a situation can be termed "stressful" or not—depending on how you choose to look at and handle it.

Figure 4–3
Performance/Stress Graph

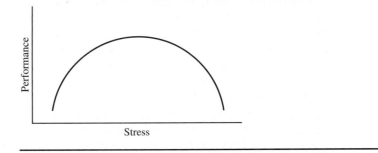

Individual Responses to Stress

Stress, which can be found in all aspects of life, is subjective, and not all individuals respond in the same way to the same stressor. Everyone has a unique level of **stress tolerance**, our ability to cope with changing conditions and unexpected negative events. One person might be elated upon being promoted, while another might be traumatized at the prospect. We might find it impossible to work while children play noisily in the street, whereas our neighbor finds his concentration is actually improved by this external noise. Regardless of level of tolerance, it is important to realize that negative stress can do harm and may manifest itself in physiological, psychological, and social disorders. As mentioned earlier, among the physical disorders to which stress can contribute are high blood pressure, migraine headaches, heartburn, frequent illness, insomnia, persistent fatigue, and binge eating and drinking. Stress can also manifest itself in psychological disorders, including anxiety, depression, anger, feelings of loneliness and inadequacy, chemical dependencies and abuse, and lack of concentration.[27] If the negative stress in your life outpaces your coping skills in stress reduction and weakens your resilience, you should not hesitate to seek professional assistance.

A variety of remedies or techniques are available for different types of stress. *Psychological problems* are much better understood today than in the recent past. Various drugs and other therapies are available for treating a wide variety of problems. Psychological problems are best dealt with by consulting a professional such as a counselor or therapist. These professionals can help individuals suffering psychological effects of stress by helping them understand these situations and manage their response to them more effectively.

Because of the likely connection between emotional or mental concerns and physical ailments, *physiological problems* are best dealt with through consultation with both a health professional and a mental health professional or wellness counselor. Typically an individual experiencing physiological stress will be given a test battery to diagnose the sources of the stress and potential solutions to the problems being experienced. A treatment program will be varied and might include regular exercise, better nutrition, relaxation techniques, and, in some cases, prescription drugs as appropriate.

Job-Related Stress

If you are suffering from job-related stress, evaluate your work style; your level of job satisfaction; and the fit between you, your boss, your co-workers, and your organization. Those who feel the least (bad) stress are those who are in a work environment in which they can thrive, rather than one in which they are drained. Talking with your boss or co-workers about your concerns can help. But if change is not forthcoming, leaving the organization for one better suited to your personality is a good option.

Organizational Responses to Stress

There is an increasing link between work-related stress and negative individual and organizational outcomes. Stress takes a toll on organizations in many ways, including decreased performance, low morale, resistance to teamwork, absenteeism, theft, sabotage, burnout, higher health care costs, and high employee turnover. At the extreme, stress-filled organizations may experience acts of rage and violence.[28] Some studies have tried to assign a dollar value to the impact of organizational stress on the economy, with some estimates at around $300 billion a year.[29] Some organizations have developed stress management programs for their employees. Most stress management programs fall into one of four categories. Employee Assistance Programs (EAPs) generally involve offering professional counseling services to employees. Stress Management Training (SMT) focuses on preventive courses or programs offering employees training in stress reduction skills such as mediation, relaxation procedures, and stress awareness and understanding. Stress Reduction Intervention (SRI) programs attempt to change the intensity and type of stressors impacting employees and may include job rotation, job enrichment, employee empowerment, goal setting, and regular feedback. Health Promotion Programs (HPPs) are generally designed to educate employees about the physical and mental benefits of leading a healthier lifestyle and often include medical screening, exercise and fitness programs, and health club memberships.[30] It is in an organization's best interest to focus on better diagnosis of stress factors and closer examination of stress management practices.[31]

Several factors contribute to an effective organizational response to stress management. Prior to the intervention to assist an individual employee or group, the goals should be made clear to all concerned. The link between the intervention being suggested and the individual's situation should be assessed at the outset. The organization should identify those most at risk, and success should be determined in the context of the organization's environment.

Developing skills and techniques for managing stress will make you more resilient and better able to adapt successfully when confronted with sources of stress. Stress management strategies, whether practiced as treatment or as prevention, fall into two broad categories. **Cognitive strategies** are designed to influence our thinking, emotions, and well-being. This approach can include identification of negative thoughts, positive self-talk, and a focus on beliefs and attitudes.

Behavioral strategies focus on changing behavior to improve one's situation and can include time management, problem solving, goal planning, and healthy lifestyle adjustment.[32] **Self-regulation**, the long-term commitment to control and regulate your impulses, emotions, performance, and other behaviors, is critical to reap the benefits of any stress management approach. Pursuing long-term strategies, as opposed to responding only to the immediate environment, can produce significant benefits.[33]

Strategies for Managing Stress

A number of coping strategies can be used to deal with stress. We'll never eradicate stress, but we can make choices about how we handle it. Several suggestions follow; you'll be able to provide others from your own experience.

■ *Identify your stressors and stress levels.* A **stressor** is a situation, activity, or person that causes you to feel stressed, out of control, or frazzled. **Stress levels** refer to the degree to which you let the source of the stress affect you. It is crucial to understand exactly what your stressors are; in other words, what your "hot buttons" are. What causes you to tense up, feel aggravated, or be angry or resentful? What causes you to get a headache or your blood pressure to rise? What causes you to think no one understands you or that there's no way out of a problem you're facing? It's also important to understand your own unique stress levels. How stressed do you get? What causes a severe versus just a regular headache? You cannot manage stress unless you know what causes stress and how those causes are impacting you psychologically, physiologically, and organizationally. Look at the chart in Figure 4–4 and see if any of these signs of stress look familiar to you. Understanding your stressors—and being able to recognize them *before* they occur—is an essential skill in stress management. Understanding your stress levels—the degree to which you react to certain stressors—can help you manage your response to stress effectively.

■ *Implement time management skills.* For some, feeling a lack of control over a situation causes stress. When this occurs, try to exert some influence over those aspects of a situation that are within your control. Making a change in your environment that reduces the impact of the offending stressor can often do this. For example, if you are feeling

Figure 4–4
Signs of Stress

Physical Signs	Emotional Signs	Mental Signs	Relational Signs	Spiritual Signs	Behavioral Signs
Appetite changes	Bad temper	Lack of humor	Isolation	A feeling of emptiness	Pacing
Headaches	Anxiety	Dull senses	Defensiveness	Apathy	Swearing
Fatigue	Nightmares	Lethargy	Intolerance	Inability to forgive	Substance abuse
Insomnia	Irritability	Boredom	Resentment	Cynicism	Nail biting
Indigestion	Depression	Indecisiveness	Loneliness	Loss of direction	Slumped posture
Colds	Frustration	Forgetfulness	Nagging	Doubt	Restlessness
Weight change	Oversensitivity	Poor concentration	Lower sex drive	Need to prove self	Risk aversion
Teeth grinding	Mood swings	Personality changes	Aggression	Negative outlook	Eating disorders
Tension	Fearfulness	Stuck in past	Abuse	Gloom	Headaches

overwhelmed by a term paper assignment, you could find a quieter place in which to work, organize your work space by using files or piles for the various sections of the paper, or play soft music. These changes can help reduce stress levels.

■ *Learn to share and disclose.* Being open about your thoughts and feelings—with yourself and with others—is a surprisingly effective technique for reducing stress levels. Sometimes just being able to talk out loud about a situation and how it's affecting you can help you process aspects of the situation in such a way that you develop a new attitude about or outlook on it. This changed understanding can result in a more positive perspective on the situation. For example, receiving a bad grade on a paper can be viewed negatively—as a disappointment—or positively—as a chance to get some useful feedback from the instructor that could improve your writing in the future.

■ *Keep a journal.* Journal writing involves setting aside some time on a regular basis to reflect on what's happening in your life. By writing your thoughts and feelings about and reactions to certain events and people, you can air your emotions about something of significance to you, enabling you to acquire a new perspective on the situation.

■ *Talk to a trusted friend, relative, co-worker, or professional helper such as a resident advisor, counselor, physician, or minister.* Talking to someone you respect can be enormously helpful in reducing stress levels. We all get upset at times, making it difficult for us to see things objectively. An empathetic set of ears can help you view things differently and adopt a perspective you might not have imagined on your own. Counseling and advisory services at work can have a positive impact on understanding and dealing with stress. Saying you could use help does not mean you are ineffective at work. Seek ways to improve your stress management, and as a manager, be aware of when others need help.

■ *Use visualization and mental imagery*, increasingly popular techniques for reducing stress. "See yourself making the perfect putt on the green." "Picture where you want to be in five years." "See yourself finishing school and driving a new car." These are all examples of visualization and mental imagery—imagining yourself in a situation, playing out how you ideally see yourself behaving and looking, creating a mental picture of yourself and how you'll feel by achieving a goal you've set. The theory behind visualization is "success breeds success." By thinking positively you can at times will yourself to act and behave in a way that gets you where you want to be.

■ *Try mindfulness-based stress reduction (MBSR)*, a relatively new technique for mitigating the effects of stress. Central to the concept of mindfulness is paying attention, reducing distraction, and holding an intended object in mind.[34] MBSR is a highly structured educational approach that combines meditation and yoga exercises to help people achieve a greater sense of control, reduce their day-to-day stress, make choices with clarity and awareness, and promote healthy living. This process focuses on what is right in your life and aims at reinforcing human capacities for relaxation, awareness, insight, and behavior change.[35]

Try This:

- *Take one or more slow, deep breaths.* Often when we're becoming stressed we begin to take shallower breaths without even being aware of it. This causes you to be short of breath and to have difficulty concentrating. By taking a "time-out" and taking a few deep breaths, you automatically calm the body and the mind and are able to concentrate on the matter at hand. Try this technique before a presentation or during an emotional conversation.

- *Practice yoga or meditation.* Yoga is a form of gentle exercise that positively influences the mind–body connection through the use of deep breathing, stretching, and slow but firm movements in a calm atmosphere. Taking yoga can help you develop effective breathing techniques to manage your stress. In recent years, meditation has gained much recognition as a means of alleviating and coping with stress among employees. In studies it was found that meditation resulted in enhanced openness to challenge, innovation, and organizational performance.[36] Meditation involves setting aside time on a regular basis to clear the mind of details and focus on being alert and calm. Usually meditation involves learning to concentrate on one image or sound, subduing other images and sounds. Practicing meditation for a few minutes each day can help reduce psychological and physical stress levels. Health professionals and even some insurance companies have endorsed both yoga and meditation as proven methods for reducing stress.

- *Try progressive muscle relaxation (PMR) and guided imagery.* In PMR, you isolate various parts or muscle groups in your body, and then tense and relax these muscles several times before moving to the next muscle group. Typically, the pattern begins at one end of the body and concludes at the other. Guided imagery involves engaging our ability to recall a special place or memory (or imagining a fantasy place, such as floating in a cloud) and invite the same positive feelings or sensations to return. Both of these techniques can be done alone or with the use of an in-person or recorded facilitator or guide who can help you focus your thoughts on your body or your imagination in a powerful, stress-reducing way.

- *Consult an online stress resource.* The famed Mayo Clinic in Rochester, Minnesota, has an excellent online site devoted to managing stress: http://www.mayoclinic.com/health/stress-assessment/SR00029. One additional free and reputable site is managed by the Canadian Centre for Occupational Health and Safety: http://www.ccohs.ca/oshanswers/psychosocial/stress.html.

- *Eat healthy food and exercise regularly.* Most scientists and nutritionists agree that proper nutrition and eating habits play a big role in keeping our systems fit. Here are some tips to consider:

  1. *Try to avoid or restrict consumption of alcohol and caffeine*, both of which deplete the system rather than replenish it. Most nutritionists who treat clients for a variety of stress-related ailments agree this is a top recommendation for stress relief.

  2. *Eat for energy throughout the day, rather than simply eating for the sake of eating;* this can also help you cope with stress. Comfort eating involves eating foods that bring immediate pleasant sensations yet yield little value over the long term. Comfort eating is hard to avoid since many of us find the process so, well, comforting! Unfortunately, comfort eating usually results in indulging in unhealthy foods and in undesirable quantities. Eating for energy is an entirely different mindset. It involves asking yourself throughout the day: How am I

doing right now (physically, mentally, and emotionally), and what foods would be helpful? Which foods will help sustain me, and even help me thrive, versus which ones will drain or fatigue me? An example is the midafternoon slump many of us face. Your first choice might be to eat a candy bar, although it would be better to eat a piece of fruit. Not only does fruit supply more energy over a longer period of time, it also provides valuable nutrients and fiber.

3. *Create time for relaxation.* This might seem impossible to the overworked student, the multitasking manager, the harried new parent, or the caregiver of an aging parent or ill significant other. Taking at least some time out for you each day, away from the demands of others and the environment, can be rejuvenating and stimulating.

Overcoming Fear of Failure

No discussion of time and stress management is complete without mentioning a common obstacle to our being effective: **fear of failure**. Fear of failure refers to the disposition to avoid an undertaking because of the anticipation of shame and humiliation upon failing. Current research reveals that fear of failure develops when individuals perceive others as treating them with high levels of criticism, attack, and neglect, and then treat themselves with correspondingly high levels of self-blame and self-neglect and less self-affirmation and self-love. High levels of fear of failure have been linked with health problems including headaches and eating disorders as well as reduced motivation and poor job performance.[37] As you attempt to achieve goals or perform tasks, knowing the right course of action to take isn't always enough. Sometimes you run into obstacles. These obstacles shouldn't stop you. They can be addressed and, in most cases, overcome. See Figure 4-5 below for some tips.

One of the most common barriers to interpersonal effectiveness is fear. **Fear** is one of the most basic of human emotions. It is part of your body's natural alarm system that helps you react physically and mentally to danger and threat or the anticipation of danger and threat. **Anticipatory fear** has two distinct components: **anxiety**, a preoccupation with an anticipated threat, and **worry**, the internal struggle to devise a strategy to escape the threat. The body's reaction to fear, while perfectly normal, can be unpleasant and can include a racing heart, hyperventilation, dry mouth, dizziness, nausea, and a change in blood circulation that can send a chill down the spine. Fear can also weaken our ability to concentrate and cause anxiety disorders. Fear can be good or bad. It can have negative or positive effects on people. **Good fear** maintains your alertness and vigilance. Based on knowledge, reason, and instincts, good fear keeps you from danger or harmful situations. Sometimes good fear can actually "adrenalize" you. For example, in public speaking, a little nervousness is actually good—it can enhance your vitality and enthusiasm. **Bad fear** is a misreading of a situation. It holds you back instead of propelling you forward. It keeps you from applying your full energies to a situation. Some of the reasons for this are

---

**Figure 4–5
Hints for Overcoming
Fear of Failure**

Look at failure as an event, not a reflection on you personally.

Remind yourself that everyone experiences failure.

Look for the "why" and find a solution.

Ask yourself what you learned.

Associate with positive people and abolish fear and failure statements.

Create a new environment.

Access new information; let adversity become advantage.

Create a new perspective or mindset—develop new "self-talk"—for instance, background thoughts.

Take one step at a time; keep moving forward.

concern about rejection, making mistakes, taking risks, and failure. Negative fear stifles learning and interferes with decision making; it also prevents you from being yourself and discovering new talents and interests.

Don't let bad fear stifle creativity or self-expression. Giving in to fear can paralyze you, rendering you passive or unable to act. This can keep you from growing, developing, and ultimately succeeding. At its worst, bad fear can hinder your ability to take chances and be open to new experiences, threaten your existing relationships, and prevent new ones from developing. At its best, good fear can bring out new dimensions of your abilities and personality.

Summary

By understanding and managing yourself intelligently you are more likely to achieve success and satisfaction—in your personal life as well as in business. With practice, managing your emotions, time, and stress will become innate and will help you to feel more in control, enjoy life, and be more productive both personally and professionally.

Key Terms and Concepts

Anticipatory fear

Anxiety

Bad fear

Behavioral strategies

Cognitive strategies

Distress

Emotional intelligence (EQ)

Eustress

Fear

Fear of failure

Good fear

Organizational stress

Physiological stress

Psychological stress

Self-management

Self-regulation

Stress

Stress levels

Stress management

Stress tolerance

Stressor

Time famine

Time management

Worry

Discussion Questions

1. People often say "I need more time" or "I don't have time for (e.g., exercise)." The truth is, we all have 168 hours per week. No more, no less. What's underlying these statements, and what are some potential remedies?

2. Suppose you're in a job where your productivity is measured in billable hours. Does "work smarter, not harder" still apply?

3. Employers are starting to recognize the value of programs geared toward time and stress management, even work–family balance. Is this a worthwhile expenditure?

4. How do you know what your stressors are? What if everything "stresses you out"?

5. We contend that emotional intelligence (EQ) is a better predictor for success than is general intelligence (IQ). Why is this so?

Endnotes

1. Colette A. Frayne and Michael J. Geringer, "Self-management Training for Improving Job Performance: A Field Experiment Involving Salespeople," *Journal of Applied Psychology* 85, no. 3 (June 2000), p. 316.

2. Daniel Goleman, "What Makes a Leader?" *Harvard Business Review* 82, no. 1 (January 2004), pp. 84–91.

3. R. S. Colfax, J. J. Rivera, and K. T. Perez, "Applying Emotional Intelligence in the Workplace: Vital to Global Business Success," *Journal of International Business Research* 9 (2010), p. 91.

4. J. K. Harrison and H. H. Brower, "The Relationship between Cultural Intelligence and the Personality Variables of Self-Monitoring and Core Self-Evaluations," *International Journal of Arts & Sciences* 4, no. 23 (2011), p. 16.

5. Daniel Goleman, *Working with Emotional Intelligence* (New York: Bantam Books, 1998), p. 108.

6. Christine M. Riordan, Robert J. Vandenberg, and Hettie A. Richardson, "Employee Involvement Climate and Organizational Effectiveness," *Human Resource Management* 44, no. 4 (Winter 2005), pp. 471–88.

7. Daniel Goleman, Richard Boyatzis, and Annie McKee, *Primal Leadership: Realizing the Power of Emotional Intelligence* (Boston: Harvard Business School Press, 2002), p. 3.

8. See M. Afzalur Rahim and Patricia Minors, "Effects of Emotional Intelligence on Concern for Quality and Problem Solving," *Managerial Auditing Journal* 18, no. 1/2 (2003), p. 150; and Ceasar Douglas, Dwight D. Frink, and Gerald R. Ferris, "Emotional Intelligence as Moderator of the Relationship between Conscientiousness and Performance," *Journal of Leadership & Organizational Studies* 10, no. 3 (Winter 2004), p. 2.

9. Victor Dulewicz and Malcolm Higgs, "Leadership at the Top: The Need for Emotional Intelligence in Organizations," *International Journal of Organizational Analysis* 11, no. 3 (2003), p. 200.

10. N. M. Ashkanasy and C. S. Daus, "Emotion in the Workplace: The New Challenge for Managers," *Academy of Management Executive* 16, no. 1 (2002), p. 76.

11. "stress, *n.*" *The Oxford English Dictionary.* 2nd ed. 1989. *OED Online.* Oxford University Press. May 5, 2007, http://dictionary.oed.com/cgi/entry/50239243.

12. Victor M. Rojas and Brian H. Kleine, "The Art and Science of Effective Stress Management," *Management Research News* 24, no. 3/4 (2001), p. 86.

13. M. Yu, "Employees' Perceptions of Organizational Change: The Mediating Effects of Stress Management Strategies," *Public Personnel Management* 38, no. 1 (2009), p. 19.

14. M. Jehangir, N. Kareem, A. Khan, M. T. Jan, and S. Soherwardi, "Effects of Job Stress on Job Performance and Satisfaction," *Interdisciplinary Journal of Contemporary Research in Business* 3, no. 7 (2011), p. 454.

15. Ibid., p. 456.

16. Tim Cuthell, "De-stressing the Workplace," *Occupational Health* 56, no. 1 (January 2004), p. 14, quoting definition by the Health and Safety Executive.

17. See Kim Bachman, "Feeling Stressed?" *CMA Management* 73, no. 3 (November 1999), p. 14; and M. Goldstein, "Getting Out from under Successful Meetings," *Bill Communications* 48, no. 11 (October 1999), p. 28, in reference to a survey by Pitney Bowes.

18. Lonnie Golden and Barbara Wiens-Tuers, "To Your Happiness? Extra Hours of Labor Supply and Worker Well-Being," *Journal of Socio-Economics* 35, no. 2 (April 2006), p. 385.

19. Barry Adamson and Murray Axmith, "The CEO Disconnect: Finding Consistency between Personal Values and the Demands of Leadership," *Ivey Business Journal Online* (May/June 2003), p. 1.

20. L. A. Perlow, "The Time Famine: Toward a Sociology of Work Time," *Administrative Science Quarterly* 44 (1999), p. 57.

21. Harry Plack, "Managing Time Can Be Crucial," *Baltimore Business Journal* 17, no. 40 (February 18, 2000), p. 27.

22. Adapted from Steven Covey with A. Roger Merrill and Rebecca R. Merrill, *First Things First* (New York: Simon and Schuster, 1994), p. 37.

23. Stephen R. Covey, *Seven Habits of Highly Effective People: Powerful Lessons in Personal Change* (New York: Free Press, November 2004).

24. Jeanne Farrington, "Procrastination—Not All It's *Put* Off to Be," *Performance Improvement Quarterly* 24, no. 4 (2012), p. 11.

25. Patricia B. Sikora, E. David Beaty, and John Forward, "Updating Theory on Organizational Stress: The Asychronous Multiple Overlapping Change (AMOC) Model of Workplace Stress," *Human Resource Development Review* 3, no. 1 (March 2004), p. 6.

26. Laura M. Little, Bret L. Simmons, and Debra L. Nelson, "Health among Leaders: Positive and Negative Affect, Engagement and Burnout, Forgiveness and Revenge," *The Journal of Management Studies* 44, no. 2 (March 2007), p. 244.

27. Yi-Ping Lee and Brian H. Kleiner, "How to Use Humour for Stress Management," *Management Research News* 28, no. 11/12 (2005), p. 179.

28. Bob Losyk, "Getting a Grip on Stress: What HR Managers Must Do to Prevent Burnout and Turnover," *Employment Relations Today* 33, no. 1 (Spring 2006), p. 9.

29. Ron Ball, "Workplace Stress Sucks $300 Billion Annually from Corporate Profits," *Customer Inter@ction Solutions* 23, no. 5 (November 2004), p. 62.

30. Ahmed Karim, Ali Mir, and Prasad Bingi, "Perceived Usefulness of Stress Management Strategies and Their Implementation: An Empirical Investigation," *Journal of Applied Management and Entrepreneurship* 10, no. 3 (July 2005), p. 23.

31. C. George and M. LeFevre, "Stress Management Practice: Is It Effective?" *New Zealand Journal of Employment Relations (Online)* 35, no. 2 (2010), p. 102.

32. Brenda Gardner, John Rose, Oliver Mason, Patrick Tyler, and Delia Cushway, "Cognitive Therapy and Behavioural Coping in the Management of Work-Related Stress: An Intervention Study," *Work & Stress* 19, no. 2 (April 2005), p. 143.

33. Dianne M. Tice, Ellen Bratslavsky, and Roy F. Baumeister, "Emotional Distress Regulation Takes Precedence over Impulse Control: If You Feel Bad, Do It!" *Journal of Personality and Social Psychology* 80, no. 1 (January 2001), p. 53.

34. Karl E. Weick and Kathleen M. Sutcliffe, "Mindfulness and the Quality of Organizational Attention," *Organization Science* 17, no. 4 (July/August 2006), p. 518.

35. Kathryn Proulx, "Integrating Mindfulness-Based Stress Reduction," *Holistic Nursing Practice* 17, no. 4 (July/August 2003), p. 201.

36. H. Li-An, "Meditation, Learning, Organizational Innovation and Performance," *Industrial Management and Data Systems* 111, no. 1 (2011), pp. 115, 121.

37. David E. Conroy and J. Douglas Coatsworth, "Coaching Behaviors Associated with Changes in Fear of Failure: Changes in Self-Talk and Need Satisfaction as Potential Mechanisms," *Journal of Personality* 75, no. 2 (2007), pp. 384–88.

**Exercise 4–A
Emotional
Intelligence Test**

Answer the following questions by placing a check in the appropriate column; determine your results using the scoring instructions.

	Always	Usually	Sometimes	Rarely	Never
1. I'm aware of even subtle feelings as I have them.					
2. I find myself using my feelings to help make big decisions in life.					
3. Bad moods overwhelm me.					
4. When I'm angry, I blow my top or fume in silence.					
5. I can delay gratification in pursuit of my goals instead of getting carried away by impulse.					
6. When I'm anxious about a challenge, such as a test or public talk, I find it difficult to prepare well.					
7. Instead of giving up in the face of setbacks or disappointments, I stay hopeful and optimistic.					
8. People don't have to tell me what they feel—I can sense it.					
9. My keen sense of others' feelings makes me compassionate about their plight.					
10. I have trouble handling conflict and emotional upsets in relationships.					
11. I can sense the pulse of a group or a relationship and state unspoken feelings.					
12. I can soothe or contain distressing feelings so they don't keep me from doing things I need to do.					

Source: From *Emotional Intelligence,* by Daniel Goleman. Copyright © 1995 by Daniel Goleman. Used by permission of Bantam Books, a division of Random House, Inc.

Figure Your Score

For numbers 1, 2, 5, 7, 8, 9, 11, and 12:

Always = 4
Usually = 3
Sometimes = 2
Rarely = 1
Never = 0

For numbers 3, 4, 6, and 10

Always = 0
Usually = 1
Sometimes = 2
Rarely = 3
Never = 4

Results

36 or above: You probably have superior emotional intelligence.
25–35: Good level of emotional intelligence.
24 or under: Room for improvement.

Questions

1. What is your EQ? How accurately do you feel this score portrays you?
2. What, if anything, about your score surprised you?
3. What, if anything, about your score is most in sync with your view of yourself?
4. Evaluating the five fundamental components of EQ, in which area are you the strongest? Explain, citing a brief example.
5. In which area are you the weakest? Explain, citing a brief example.
6. What implications does your score have for your personal life? Professional life?
7. What steps can you take to increase your EQ?

**Exercise 4–B
Personal Time
Management**

I. "Where Does the Time Go?" Survey

The following survey shows how much time you spend in current activities. When taking the survey, estimate the amount of time spent on each item. Once you have this amount for daily items, you will need to multiply them by seven or five. After each item's weekly time has been calculated, add all these for a grand total. Subtract this amount from 168, the total possible hours per week.

1. Number of hours of sleep each night _____ × 7 = _____
2. Number of hours grooming per day _____ × 7 = _____
3. Number of hours for meals/snacks (including shopping and preparation) _____ × 7 = _____
4. Number of hours' travel each workday _____ × 5 = _____
5. Number of hours' travel time each weekend = _____
6. Number of hours per week for regularly scheduled activities (clubs, church, socializing, etc.) = _____
7. Number of hours per day for chores, errands, extra grooming, and so on _____ × 7 = _____
8. Number of hours of work per week = _____
9. Number of hours in class per week = _____
10. Number of hours per week socializing, dating = _____
11. Add the totals for items 1–10 = _____

Subtract the number on line 11 from 168: 168 − _____ = _____
    These are the remaining hours you have each week for extra activities—studying, family, sports, hobbies, TV, relaxation. Surprised? Where does the time go?

Questions

1. How do you believe you spend your remaining hours?
2. How effectively do you believe you spend these hours?
3. What do you believe are your biggest time wasters?
4. In what areas of your life can you "gain" hours?
5. How can you redistribute your hours to have more time available for the things you want to do?

II. Weekly Tracker

Break down your weekly "extra" activities to identify where you actually spend your extra hours. Use the following time chart to track your activity for one week. Fill in all the hours with the activities you perform. Be honest with yourself to get an accurate picture and pattern of where your time is spent.

	Monday	Tuesday	Wednesday	Thursday	Friday	Saturday	Sunday
5 AM							
6 AM							
7 AM							
8 AM							
9 AM							
10 AM							
11 AM							
12 PM							
1 PM							
2 PM							
3 PM							
4 PM							
5 PM							
6 PM							
7 PM							
8 PM							
9 PM							
10 PM							
11 PM							
12 AM							
1 AM							
2 AM							
3 AM							
4 AM							

Questions

1. Is your actual weekly time consistent with the figures you put in your survey?
2. What are your extra time periods and your time wasters?
3. How can you manage your time more effectively?

Source: Adapted from http://www.gmu.edu/departments/csdc/time.html.

Exercise 4–C
Life Stress Test

The Holmes and Rahe Schedule of Recent Experiences Survey (with some author modifications)

Instructions:

Place a check mark next to each event you experienced within the past year. Then add the life change units associated with the various events to derive your total life stress score.

Life Event	Life Change Unit
_____ Death of partner	100
_____ Divorce	73
_____ Separation from mate	65
_____ Detention in jail or other institution	63
_____ Death of a close family member	63
_____ Major personal injury or illness	53
_____ Marriage	50
_____ Being fired at work	47
_____ Reconciliation with mate	45
_____ Retirement from work	45
_____ Major change in the health or behavior of a family member	44
_____ Pregnancy	40
_____ Sexual difficulties	39
_____ Gaining a new family member (e.g., through birth, adoption, oldster moving in)	39
_____ Major business readjustment (e.g., merger, reorganization, bankruptcy)	39
_____ Major change in financial state (e.g., a lot worse off or a lot better off than usual)	38
_____ Death of a close friend	37
_____ Change to a different line of work	36
_____ Major change in the number of arguments with partner (e.g., either a lot more or a lot less than usual)	35
_____ Taking out a mortgage or loan for a major purchase (e.g., for a home, business)	31
_____ Foreclosure on a mortgage or loan	30
_____ Major change in responsibilities at work (e.g., promotion, demotion, lateral transfer)	29
_____ Son or daughter leaving home (e,g., marriage, attending college)	29
_____ Trouble with in-laws	29
_____ Outstanding personal achievement	28
_____ Partner beginning or ceasing work outside the home	26
_____ Beginning or ceasing formal schooling	26
_____ Major change in living conditions (e.g., building a new home, remodeling, deterioration of home or neighborhood)	25
_____ Revision of personal habits (dress, manners, association)	24
_____ Troubles with the boss	23
_____ Major change in working hours or conditions	20
_____ Change in residence	20
_____ Changing to a new school	20

Life Event	Life Change Unit
_____ Major change in usual type and/or amount of recreation	19
_____ Major change in church, synagogue, or mosque activities (e.g., a lot more or a lot less than usual)	19
_____ Major change in social activities (e.g., clubs, dancing, movies, visiting)	18
_____ Taking out a mortgage or loan for a lesser purchase (e.g., for a car, TV freezer)	17
_____ Major change in sleeping habits (a lot more or a lot less sleep, or change in part of day when asleep)	16
_____ Major change in number of family get-togethers (e.g., a lot more or a lot less than usual)	15
_____ Major change in eating habits (a lot more or a lot less food intake, or very different meal hours or surroundings)	15
_____ Vacation	13
_____ Christmas	12
_____ Minor violations of the law (e.g., traffic tickets, jaywalking, disturbing the peace)	11
Total score =	_____

Source: Reprinted from *Journal of Psychosomatic Research,* August 1967, T.H. Holmes and R.H. Rahe, "The Social Readjustment Rating Scale," p. 216. Copyright © with permission from Elsevier Science.

**Exercise 4–D
Project/Task/Life
Planning**

Part I—Mental Download

1. Do a "mental download" of all of your current "active" projects—school-related, work-related, and personal. Put each on a separate list. This includes work projects (individual and team), classes, part-time jobs, extracurricular activities, hobbies, and so on—anything you consider a "now" project.

2. Circle the most important projects from each list—"school" or "work" and "personal." Build a small outline or plan of "next steps" for each of these active projects. This becomes the basis for a personal/professional daily task list. If you are a student, refer directly to specific course syllabi; if you are an employee or manager, refer to your department's annual or strategic plan; use these as the basis for building your individual task lists.

3. Simultaneously, also map out your calendar for the coming semester or quarter with specific projects, reports, and exams for each course, or work deliverables, as well as other key personal or family/community activities and holidays noted.

4. Once you have these items represented on both your calendar and task lists, then go back to your original list. This is a time to take a deep look at everything on the list and make an agreement with yourself about "tabling" some of these projects/tasks for later. (You can't do it ALL right now!) Put the items that do not truly make the "Active" projects list on a "Possibilities" list, meaning it is something you can possibly pursue later, but you know you do not have time for now. You can also add items to this "Possibilities" list that equate to life goals or dreams—things that may not seem possible or feasible now, but are aspirational for you.

By learning to make critical decisions about what you both can and cannot do right now, you give yourself the opportunity both for excellence in the things you do, AND you reduce the overall stress you feel by not overloading and overwhelming yourself. (This is one of the single hardest things for many people to learn, yet almost always differentiates those who achieve success and those who flounder due to self-imposed distraction and being overwhelmed.) By listing the items you do not have time for now with items in the "life goals and dreams" category, you still provide yourself the opportunity for future growth and accomplishment beyond the means of your current station.

Part II—Morning Regimen

On a daily basis:

1. Look at today's calendar and your calendar for the next several days. This is to get a mental picture at the start of the day of your formal commitments for today, as well as a feel for the time commitments and deliverables for coming days.

2. Look at your "active projects" lists—"school" or "work" and "personal." These lists should include each and every class being taken at this time, as well as any individual course projects, upcoming exams, and key assignments for the class. If you are employed, this should include any specific tasks and deliverables due on or near this day. This is to give yourself a feel for the "bigger picture" view of your active projects. This, of course, leads into . . .

3. Look at your daily task list. With a feel for your calendar and your bigger active projects, your daily task list should accurately reflect these responsibilities with several "next step" actions to take to accomplish those calendar items and projects. Any missing task items should be added—especially those due today. If the task list looks too ambitious for the time available that day, then move either nonurgent or lower importance items to tomorrow's list, to help with making more time for the truly urgent and important items that need to be done today.

4. Now is the time to check your e-mail, voice mail, and text messages, and incorporate any new needed items into your daily task list. NOTE: Do NOT do this step until #4 of your morning process. This is to help you see the bigger, more strategic picture BEFORE getting caught up in the daily urgency that often accompanies e-mail, voice mail, and text messages. Those items very typically exhibit "false urgency," meaning that the sender will try to make them more important or urgent than they truly are. It is important to learn to keep these items in proper perspective when compared to your bigger projects and life goals.

5. After reviewing all of your new inputs (e-mail, voice mail, text) and incorporating items into your daily task list, take one last "big picture" look at that task list. Is it now once again too ambitious for the amount of time available today? Then once again move some of the lower urgency/importance items to tomorrow's task list.

By following this simple five-step regimen at the start of every day, individuals can better balance the struggles of a typical active college student or professional schedule. By looking at your available time AND your active projects list BEFORE looking at your task list and e-mail, it helps you to keep a "bigger picture" and higher priority perspective when it comes to daily task planning, leading to better and more focused long-term accomplishment, as well as reduced personal stress and feeling less overwhelmed. You cannot get it all done—don't even try. You'll do just fine if you instead get the most important items done on a regular daily basis.

And if you are following this regimen and still finding yourself overwhelmed, this is a signal that you are likely trying to do too much. The simple—but not necessarily easy—solution is to take one or two active items and table them so they now are part of your possibilities list. You'll need to learn to say "no" or "later" to yourself, how to juggle and prioritize, and also how to communicate with others (teammates, bosses) if you need to reprioritize your list to get important things accomplished today. This is a critical skill set to develop to live a life of accomplishment and success. By doing the first part of this exercise at the beginning of each academic term or work quarter (and possibly again near midterms if you're a student and before quarterly reports are due if you're employed), and then following the daily routine suggested in part 2 of this exercise, it makes it that much easier to learn to say "no" to yourself and to negotiate with others, as you will clearly and easily know your key priorities and commitments at all times and especially when new projects or commitments come your way.

Source: From David Allen, *Getting Things Done: The Art of Stress-Free Productivity* (New York: Penguin Books, 2001); adapted by Randall Dean, author of *Taming the Email Beast* (Gilbert, AZ: Sortis Publishing, 2009).

Exercise 4–E
Interviews with Three
Business Professionals
(Out-of-Classroom
Activity)

1. Interview three business professionals from companies and industries of your choosing. The purpose is to obtain a real-world perspective on the issues covered in this chapter. This will give you a chance to learn about ways in which different people manage their time, set goals, and make career decisions that have been important in getting them to where they are today. You will also have the chance to explore various careers within different industries and learn what it might take to develop your career within a chosen career path and/or industry.

2. Write a well-crafted essay describing how and why you chose the individuals and their companies to be included in your study, descriptions of what each individual does within his or her company, some background information about each employer and the industry in which it competes, and time management, goal-setting, or career decision-making tips you learned and feel are important to share with others. The latter part is one of the most important aspects of the assignment. Spend the bulk of your time and discussion focusing on this area.

Source: Submitted by Dr. Daniel Connolly, Associate Dean, Daniels College of Business, University of Denver.

Exercise 4–F
Book Review

1. Select a book related to time management, goal setting, or career planning and decision making. Prepare a written review of the book and how it builds on some of the concepts presented in this chapter.

2. Focus on what the book is all about, key lessons learned, and how these lessons can be applied to you.

Source: Submitted by Dr. Daniel Connolly, Associate Dean, Daniels College of Business, University of Denver.

Exercise 4–G
Action Plan

1. Now that you have read this chapter, you might be thinking of how this chapter applies to your own career choices over the next few years.

2. Develop an action plan that will allow you to pick up from where you are presently to where you want to be. The focus should be on what you are going to do next; specifically, what are the next steps you will take to build on what you learned from this chapter? Keep the momentum going and answer the fundamental question: "What do I want to be when I grow up (or now that I've grown up)?"

Source: Submitted by Dr. Daniel Connolly, Associate Dean, Daniels College of Business, University of Denver.

**Exercise 4–H
Reflection/Action Plan**

This chapter focused on emotional intelligence, time management, and stress management—what they are, why they're important, and how to acquire and increase the degree to which you possess them. Complete the following worksheet to reflect on what you have learned on these topics and to develop plans for incorporating that learning into your work and life.

1. The one or two areas in which I am most strong are:

_____

_____

_____

_____

2. The one or two areas in which I need more improvement are:

_____

_____

_____

_____

3. If I did only one thing to improve in this area, it would be to:

_____

_____

_____

_____

4. Making this change would probably result in:

_____

_____

_____

_____

5. If I did not change or improve in this area, it would probably affect my personal and professional life in the following ways:

_____

_____

_____

_____

UNIT 1

INTRAPERSONAL EFFECTIVENESS: UNDERSTANDING YOURSELF

1. Journey into Self-awareness
2. Self-disclosure and Trust
3. Establishing Goals Consistent with Your Values and Ethics
4. Self-management

UNIT 2

INTERPERSONAL EFFECTIVENESS: UNDERSTANDING AND WORKING WITH OTHERS

5. Understanding and Working with Diverse Others
6. Listening and Nonverbal Communication
7. Communicating Effectively
8. Persuading Individuals and Audiences

UNIT 3

UNDERSTANDING AND WORKING IN TEAMS

9. Negotiation
10. Building Teams and Work Groups
11. Managing Conflict
12. Achieving Business Results through Effective Meetings
13. Facilitating Team Success
14. Making Decisions and Solving Problems Creatively

UNIT 4

LEADING INDIVIDUALS AND GROUPS

15. Effective and Ethical Use of Power and Influence
16. Networking and Mentoring
17. Coaching and Providing Feedback for Improved Performance
18. Leading and Empowering Self and Others
19. Project Management

Unit 2

The second leg of your journey features critical skills needed to interact with business associates, classmates, friends, loved ones, and people you don't yet know. You are now ready to sharpen your skills communicating in a variety of situations, overcoming any challenges to effectively achieving common ground. As with any journey, you're likely to come across people of different shapes, colors, and backgrounds. How often have these differences challenged your ability to listen without judging, remain open to diverse viewpoints, or respect others whose beliefs, behaviors, or attitudes seem odd or even wrong? Even when such differences aren't apparent, you've probably experienced situations where you've asked someone to do (or not do) something, but somehow she or he doesn't come through. Or maybe you've been in a situation where you've stopped yourself from speaking up about a situation that's bothering you, choosing instead to drop hints or send telepathic messages. We discuss reasons why these situations may have occurred, and more importantly, provide opportunities to gain valuable knowledge and skills in the art of interpersonal communication.

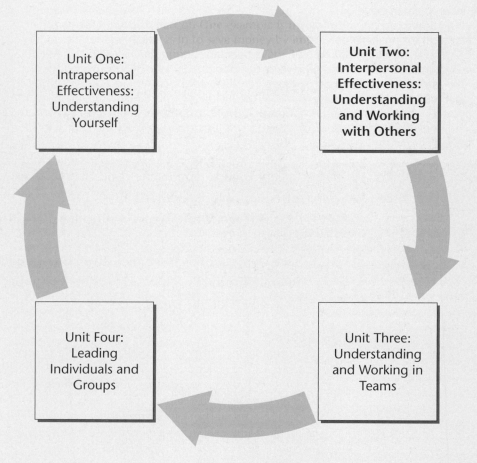

Unit One:
Intrapersonal
Effectiveness:
Understanding
Yourself

Unit Two:
Interpersonal
Effectiveness:
Understanding
and Working
with Others

Unit Four:
Leading
Individuals and
Groups

Unit Three:
Understanding
and Working in
Teams

5 Understanding and Working with Diverse Others

Learning Points

How do I:

- Understand the biases I may have toward others who are different from me?
- Confront those biases by challenging stereotypes perpetuated by society and the media?
- Understand and accept others' biased perceptions of me?
- Accept others' approaches and perspectives when they are completely different from my own?
- Learn to work effectively with others of different races, genders, and ages?
- Seek opportunities to be inclusive both individually and as a member of an organization?
- Help others do the same?

It was the summer before my senior year, and I was about to take part in the internship of a lifetime. I[1] was one of about 20 U.S. college students selected by a Fortune 500 corporation to be part of a very prestigious management internship program. All of us were to be flown into the area's largest airport, picked up by the human resources manager, and taken to housing owned by the corporation. As part of our upcoming orientation, we were given the names of students with whom we'd be living in adjoining suites and encouraged to contact them in advance. After all, we'd be together for 12 weeks!

I remember the first time my suitemate and I spoke. It was about two weeks before we met. I called her to find out what things she was going to bring and, basically, to see what kind of person she was. I said, "Hello, my name is Reza Chamma and you and I are assigned suitemates." She then introduced herself and asked, "What are you?" Bewildered, I replied, "What do you mean?" Did she think I was an alien and she wanted me to assure her that I was a human being? Then she asked, "Are you Chinese or what?" My mouth gaped open in astonishment; I had never before been asked such an odd question. I guess she thought my last name was an Asian name, but still, what person comes out and asks such a direct question? Further, does it really matter where my last name comes from? In answer to her question, I told her that I was Middle Eastern. She replied with a curt and cold "Oh." So far, this girl struck me as stuck-up and politically incorrect.

I was one of the first interns to arrive. I was taken to my room and after unpacking for about an hour, I took a nap. I awakened to noises in the adjoining room. I walked through the bathroom and met my suitemate for the first time. As soon as I saw her, I hugged her. (In the Lebanese culture, we hug and kiss cheeks as opposed to shaking hands as in American culture.) My suitemate immediately pulled away after I hugged her; I was baffled by her reservation toward me. Was she still stuck on the whole "Oh, you are a foreigner" thing? Had she already formed an opinion of me? Would we ever get along? Thoughts raced through my head as I imagined the dreadful relationship we were likely to have while sharing such close quarters. The rest of the day, my suitemate did not even acknowledge my presence.

The next morning, we walked down to breakfast together. We didn't speak until we sat down with our food. Here was my chance to find out a little about her. I had to know why she treated me the way she did. Was she rude to me because I was "different" from her? Or was she rude to everyone? After chatting about "safe" subjects like our majors and hoped-for jobs upon graduation, we talked about our earlier school experiences. I found out she had attended private schools her whole life. All her classmates, teachers, and administrators were white. She had never interacted with anyone from a race other than her own. While she didn't verbalize her feelings about me, I could clearly detect her discomfort with me—as if she wasn't sure what to make of me or whether she could trust me. I was shocked!

After breakfast, we moved into a large conference room and were given activities that helped us learn more about our fellow interns. When we reassembled to talk about our experiences, my suitemate sat on the opposite side of the room. She didn't even make eye contact with me. We took turns sharing how we reacted to the activities; when it was my turn, my suitemate stopped paying attention and began whispering to another woman next to her. It was as if she had no interest in what I had to say. Boy, was this going to be an interesting summer!

1. Why was Reza so taken aback by her suitemate's reaction to her?

2. What could she have done to improve her relationship with her roommate?

3. We see that Reza is upset by her suitemate's reaction. In what ways does she contribute to the problem?

4. While there may be some hurdles that Reza and her suitemate will have to overcome, what are some benefits of living with someone who is "different" from you?

5. At this point, what would you do if you were in Reza's shoes? Why?

"To know one's self is wisdom, but to know one's neighbor is genius."

Minna Antrim (Author)

Successful companies are learning the importance of being inclusive—welcoming people from all types of backgrounds—and leveraging the talents of a diverse workforce. As all business becomes global, technology makes it possible for virtual work teams to be assembled, and the demographics of the world keep changing, valuing and managing diversity and developing an inclusive workplace are at the top of most CEOs' agendas today. In this chapter, we address what diversity is, why it's important in business, and strategies for how to manage diversity effectively and proactively both as an individual and as an organization.

What Is Diversity?

Diversity can be defined as any attribute relevant to an individual that creates or reinforces a perception that he or she is different from another individual.[2] Some differentiating attributes are social-category differences (including race, ethnicity, gender, age, religion, sexual orientation, mental and physical abilities), differences in knowledge or

**Figure 5–1
Primary and Secondary
Dimensions of Diversity**[3]

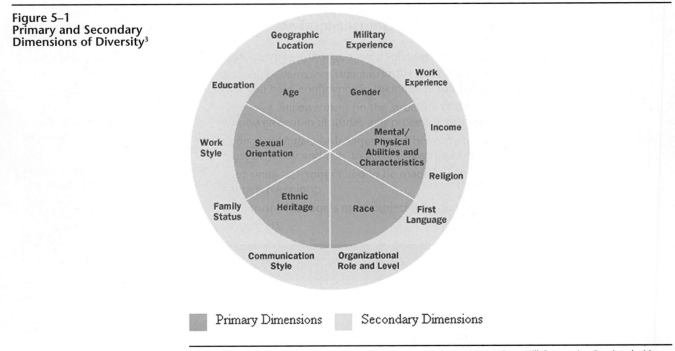

Source: From Marilyn Loden, *Implementing Diversity*. Copyright © 1995 McGraw-Hill Companies. Reprinted with permission.

skills, differences in values or beliefs, personality differences, economic background, organizational- or community-status differences, and differences in social and network ties.[4] As Figure 5–1 depicts, understanding and managing diversity for superior organizational performance presupposes a broad definition, which includes both primary and secondary individual differences. In short, diversity reflects the sum total of individuals' uniqueness.

Valuing and managing diversity are distinctly different phenomena. **Valuing diversity** is passive. Here the importance or significance of someone's difference does not automatically lead to actions or reactions on the part of the individual valuing the diversity or difference. **Managing diversity** is active and involves proactively supervising, coordinating, and directing the diversity or differences individuals bring to the organization to create an environment that will allow employees to achieve their full potential while ensuring that strategic organizational goals are being effectively met.[5] The most productive organizational approach to managing diversity is to adopt the perspective that diversity is an opportunity for everyone in the organization to learn from each other how best to accomplish their work. If this perspective is combined with a supportive organizational culture and effective group leadership focused on facilitating healthy group functioning, it should position the organization to outperform those that fail to take this approach.[6] Diversity is a reality in labor and customer markets in North America today. Organizations must understand the nature, impact, and implications of continuing population and market changes in order to recognize and meet the changing needs and preferences of their employees, clients, and customers in cultures across the globe.

Why Is Diversity Important?

Shifting demographics and market realities have led organizations to reexamine their models of business success. Managing diversity requires developing new ways of measuring how diversity as a business competency aligns with business strategies to achieve growth, profitability, and sustainability. There are a number of benefits to promoting diversity in the workplace:[7]

- Improving corporate culture by unleashing creativity and performance.
- Facilitating recruitment of new employees, who prefer to work where they can expect to advance.
- Improving relationships with clients.

Increasing understanding of cross-cultural work teams and global markets.

- Increasing employee morale, productivity, and retention.
- Expanding the global reach and cross-cultural expertise of the organization.
- Decreasing employee complaints and litigation.

By designing and supporting an organizational culture that maximizes the benefits of diversity, and using that culture to manage various groups of organizational members such as project teams, business startup teams, customer service response teams, the sales force, and top management, businesses can better position themselves to achieve a number of goals:

- Broadening access to the changing marketplace.
- Implementing large-scale business transformation.
- Establishing superior customer service.
- Empowering a company's workforce.
- Pursuing total quality.
- Building stronger alliances with suppliers and customers.
- Creating beneficial global outsourcing partnerships.
- Motivating continuous learning within the organization.

In addition to the examples of the positive outcomes of effectively managing diversity listed above, some compelling statistics should convince all of us of the importance of being inclusive and managing diversity.

- By the year 2050, the U.S. Census Bureau estimates, nearly half of the population will be multicultural. The African American, Hispanic American, and Asian American communities are growing 2.9 times faster than the total U.S. population.[8]
- The Asian and Hispanic populations in the United States are expected to more than double in size between 2000 and 2050, while the Caucasian population will decrease by about 6 percent in the same time period.[9]
- In 1990, 11.9 percent of the labor force was 55 years or older. The Bureau of Labor Statistics projects that the share of the 55-years-and-older labor force will increase to 25.2 percent in 2020.[10]
- The workforce participation rate for women in the United States peaked at 60 percent in 1999, falling to 58.6 percent in 2010. With significant increases of older women in the total population, the overall labor force participation rate for women is projected to slow to 57.1 percent in 2020.[11]
- The Selig Center for Economic Growth at the University of Georgia calculates that by 2013 the combined buying power of African Americans, Hispanics, Asians, and Native Americans will be over $2.6 trillion, up from nearly $700 billion in 1990.[12]

Individual Diversity Strategies

**How to Gain
Awareness**

We all have biases. It's part of being human. We were all brought up with a certain set of values and experiences. We cannot deny who we are; the family, community, and country we come from; or the factors that make up our personality, beliefs, and personal characteristics. We can, however, commit to improving ourselves and our ability to understand and relate to others. You can take some positive steps to be more open to others and their perspectives, including reducing your prejudices and stereotypes, minimizing miscommunication, and building relationships with diverse others.

Reducing Your Prejudices and Use of Stereotypes[13]

- Recognize that diversity exists and learn to value and respect fundamental differences.
- Admit to your own biases and prejudices and commit yourself to reducing them.
- Examine the stereotypes and actions that reflect your views of others, analyze your feelings based on these, and develop plans for changing your biases.
- Dispel myths about diverse others when you are in a group of friends or associates.

Don't engage in any behaviors that could be perceived as bullying—verbal, emotional, or physical. Show respect for others who are different from you, and teach your children and mandate your employees to do the same.

Minimizing Miscommunication with Diverse Others

- Educate yourself about differences by reading, listening, and broadening your experience base.
- Practice effective communication skills (e.g., listening attentively, interpreting nonverbal cues, sending and receiving messages). When conversing with others whose first language is different from yours, pay careful attention to what they say and ask questions about what you don't understand.
- Use words that are inclusive rather than exclusive (for example, refer to "participants" rather than to a group by its primary gender).
- Avoid derogatory comments about particular groups.
- Be aware of current connotations of words; what seemed acceptable yesterday may be offensive to certain groups today. For example, the state of Virginia called its year 2007 founding of Jamestown event a "commemoration" rather than a celebration in deference to concerns raised by Native Americans who felt differently about the coming of "white people" than did Caucasians.
- Avoid forming an opinion about the value of another's communication based on dress, mannerisms, accent, age, or background. Concentrate more on the message than the messenger.

Building Relationships with Diverse Others

- Seek opportunities to interact with a wide variety of peers and associates.
- Form positive relationships with diverse others.
- Seek feedback from diverse others about how well you are communicating respect for them and valuing their diversity.
- Rather than treating diverse others as strangers, treat them as invited guests by showing interest in them. Share information about yourself and invite them to reciprocate.
- Encourage your peers to be candid by openly discussing their personal opinions, feelings, and reactions with you.
- Build trust by being open about yourself and being trustworthy when others share their opinions and reactions with you.

Organizational Diversity Strategies

Companies are finding that utilizing diversity in the workforce and in work teams is a complex undertaking that can cut both ways. A mix of variables, including organizational culture, strategy, and human resource practices determine whether diversity is maximized for the benefit of an organization and its employees.[14] Diversity is best understood and managed within an open organizational culture, one that is inclusive of diverse people and perspectives, values transparency and openness , encourages and rewards learning and change, and controls group processes. Within an open, healthy organizational setting, informed decisions about the creation of diverse or homogeneous work teams can maximize the performance of those teams. A diverse team will almost always have broader cognitive resources, wider vision, and more extensive external contacts than a homogeneous team. High-diversity teams can improve the organization's capabilities to identify new strategic opportunities and new changes in environment. Heterogeneous teams can pool diverse resources and knowledge to develop alternatives in the face of changing environments, leading to innovation and strategic change.[15]

"Let's face it: you and this organization have never been a good fit."

Source: http://www.cartoonbank.com/2000/lets-face-it-you-and-this-organization-have-never-been-a-good-fit/invt/120206/?

Valuing and managing diversity is one of the most important imperatives companies and organizations face today. There are several common approaches to diversity and inclusion policies. **Equal employment opportunity** policies ensure employment decisions are made without regard to legally protected attributes such as race, color, gender, physical disability, or national origin. **Affirmative action** programs seek to remedy past discrimination by implementing proactive steps based on race or gender to prevent current or future discrimination. Diversity management and inclusion programs are more proactive and strategic. They are closely aligned with a company's vision, are holistic and multifunctional, are supported by senior management, and are recognized as a core competence of organizations that are or aim to be competitive in today's environment. It is estimated that organizations spend over $8 billion annually on **diversity training** and other diversity-related initiatives.[16] Just as simply having a diverse workforce does not automatically produce positive outcomes, merely having a diversity training program in place will not by itself automatically yield benefits to an organization. There are several important considerations in designing and delivering effective diversity management and inclusion initiatives:[17]

- Assess situational factors including organizational culture, organization objectives, business strategy, work environment, global niche, customer base, market trends, and senior management, employee commitment, accountability prior to introducing a new program.
- Develop specific and realistic goals based on an honest assessment of the organization. Frame challenges that arise as opportunities. It is critical that the words and actions of management convey strong and positive support for the program.

- Encourage employees to develop team-building skills and expertise in forming diverse and inclusive high-performance teams and work groups. Diversity programs are more likely to succeed when employees develop a rich understanding of their teams and organization and identify strongly with them.

Barriers to Accepting Diversity

Despite a general awareness in business that diversity is a positive factor, some individuals still experience personal barriers to valuing diversity. Those who come from homogeneous backgrounds are especially vulnerable to attitudes that prevent them from being more open to diversity—both in the workplace and in their personal lives. Some common barriers to accepting diversity are:

- **Prejudice**—unjustified negative attitude toward a person based on his or her membership in a particular group, such as not wanting to consider any college students for employment at your business because you believe they are all irresponsible, carefree partyers who will not be reliable workers based on what you have read about them or seen on TV reports, or on one experience you had with a lazy worker who happened to be a college student.

- **Ethnocentrism**—a tendency to regard one's own group, culture, or nation as superior to others,[18] such as sometimes occurs in a selective club, religious sect, or political organization. People who are ethnocentric see their group-related customs or beliefs as "right" and evaluate others' beliefs or practices against this yardstick. Ethnocentrism tends to be consistent with all individuals. It is imperative for managers "to address and monitor work settings so biases don't lead to detrimental behaviors or experiences."[19]

- **Stereotypes**—set of beliefs about a group that is applied universally to all members of that group. While some stereotypes can appear to portray a group in a favorable light, stereotyping, whether positive or negative, is never a good idea because seldom does one statement hold true for all members of a group. Stereotyping is not always bad; it is a means to categorize and simplify a complex world. It is when stereotyping results in negative feelings or actions (such as discrimination or prejudice), leads to inaccurate perceptions, or results in closed-mindedness and myopic viewpoints that stereotyping can be a barrier.

- **Blaming the victim**—making incorrect causal attributions. Sometimes we do this because of a common belief that people generally get what they deserve. However, these beliefs may prevent us from understanding and appreciating others' actions and perspectives. These beliefs may also falsely insulate us from the realities and challenges we all face.

- **Discrimination**—barring an individual from membership in an organization or from a job because of his or her membership in a particular group.

- **Harassment**—consciously shunning or verbally or physically abusing an individual because of membership in a particular group.

- **Backlash**—negative reaction to members of previously underrepresented groups gaining power and influence, which leads to fear, resentment, and reverse discrimination.

Gender Differences

The face of the world's workforce has changed. The female workforce has increased at a slightly faster rate than that of men. While this rate is slowing down now, by 2020, women will account for 57 percent of the workforce.[20] Understanding the potential gender-based differences in communication styles, related traits, and work styles can allow members of both sexes to overcome stereotypes, biases, and behaviors that can hinder individual and organizational effectiveness.

Although men and women are equal, they are different, and they typically communicate differently. Women tend to use communication to connect with others; they express feelings, empathize, and build relationships. In contrast, men tend to use communication to assert their status and request action; in so doing they tend to use more direct, succinct language. Some women, however, tend to be more indirect, vague, and even apologetic when they speak. This language pattern demonstrates not only how women show deference to others, but also why some business associates view women as inferior to men.[21] There are many theories to explain why this is so and how this tendency may evolve and change as more women assume managerial positions in the workplace.

Some surveys have shown women managers are rated higher than their male counterparts in workplace communication, approachability, conducting performance evaluations, being a team player, and empowering others. However, women are perceived to be unclear when giving instructions and also have a tendency to deflect the spotlight, making them appear "unleaderlike." Men may experience fewer task-related problems since their orders tend to be less ambiguous and subtle than those of their female counterparts. However, some employees might find their male co-worker or boss to be competitive and unsympathetic.

These differences between communication purpose and style (see Figure 5–2), along with cultural views on gender roles, have led to stereotypic beliefs about gender (see Figure 5–3), which may limit our ability to work closely and effectively with members of the opposite sex. Understanding these beliefs are generally stereotypes will allow individuals and organizations to move away from discriminating or making false assumptions while managing and working with diverse others. Hopefully, the more exposure and knowledge we gain through working with members of the opposite sex, the better able we will be to evaluate individuals based on all dimensions of their being.

Can We All Just Get Along?

So how can the sexes work more effectively together? Recognize there are strengths in both the "female" and "male" styles. Men can learn from women's managerial style by using appropriate relationship building in the workplace, while women can learn from men's style to be less subtle and more assertive and direct, especially when giving instructions. Learn more about perceived differences between women and men both socially and in the workplace. Be aware that in many situations, gender might play a role in our ability to understand others. Be familiar with cultural gender stereotypes and avoid actions, language, and behaviors that perpetuate negative or hindering views.

Figure 5–2
Male/Female Communication Differences[22]

	Male	Female
Content	Sports, money, business	People, feelings, relationships
Style	To resolve problems and denote status; view conversation as a competition	To seek understanding; use conversation to connect with another individual
Structure	Get to the point without descriptive details	More detailed and descriptive, apologetic, and unclear

**Figure 5–3
Traits Associated with
Gender Stereotypes[23]**

Male Gender Stereotypes	Female Gender Stereotypes
Aggressive	Affectionate
Arrogant	Bitchy
Athletic	Caring
Autocratic	Dependent
Big	Emotional
Competitive	Gentle
Dominant	Graceful
Good at mathematics/science	Helpful
Independent	Indecisive
Insensitive	Jealous
Leaders	Less athletic
Less/not emotional	Loving
Logical/practical	Moody
Loud	Motherly
Macho	Nagging
Pigheaded/stubborn	Not good at mathematics/science
Muscular/strong/stronger	Nurturing
Not aesthetic	Sensitive
Protective	Short/small/thin
Self-centered/selfish	Submissive
Sexist	Superficial
Tough	Talkative
Uncaring	Weak/weaker

Cross-cultural Diversity

In this increasingly global world, it is extremely important to understand the differences among cultures and how these differences can potentially affect communication between members of diverse cultures. Many communication barriers exist even when we speak the same language. Adding cultural and language differences to the mix can compound the potential for miscommunication. By understanding and acknowledging how the following elements vary across cultures, you can improve your ability to understand and be understood by others.

Semantics and Connotations

It is difficult at times to translate meaning perfectly from one language or culture to another. Many companies have found they made mistakes when trying to market a product made in one country to meet the needs of another. For example, Chevrolet had difficulty marketing the Nova in Spanish-speaking countries because in Spanish, the phrase *"no va"* means "won't go!" While a boot is a type of footwear in America, in Australia and England it refers to the trunk of a car.

Social Conventions

Each culture has acceptable social conventions and norms that affect the communication process. What one culture considers rude, another sees as perfectly acceptable. For example, in some cultures it is appropriate to use a stern, direct tone in admonishing strangers or in conducting business deals. Acceptable levels of assertiveness are also an area of difference. And gender status can determine roles and denote status.

Nonverbal Communication

Nonverbal signals and gestures can be a source of embarrassment to an uninformed stranger. Direct eye contact is expected in interactions in some countries, while in others people would experience discomfort with such lengthy, direct stares. Varying cultures view and utilize time differently. Some countries expect business meetings to begin on time—promptness is a virtue—but in others it is not only accepted, but expected that you will be one to two hours late. In some countries, standing close to others and touching are appropriate and expected, whereas in others people like their personal space and prefer not to be touched in business situations.

Cross-cultural Differences

There are many areas of difference between cultures. Language differences are the most pronounced, but other differences can be just as significant. There are five dimensions of cross-cultural differences: power distance, individualism versus collectivism, uncertainty avoidance, masculinity versus femininity, and long-term versus short-term orientation.[24] These differences can play a significant role in our ability to develop professional and personal relationships.

- **Power distance** refers to the acceptance (or lack thereof) of unequal power distribution. In countries where power distance is high, citizens show deep respect for age and seniority and rarely bypass hierarchy in important decisions. Countries with high power distance are characterized by paternalistic management, where a supreme authority maintains tight control over policies and procedures.

  In countries where power distance is low, competence is valued over seniority and status is less important. Countries with low power status are characterized by participative management, where decision making is shared across employee levels, and the opinions of many are considered before taking action.

- **Individualism versus collectivism** (as we noted in Chapter 2) refers to how loosely or tightly integrated the society seems, the degree to which the people of the country prefer to act as individuals rather than as members of groups. In countries with an individualistic approach, individual achievement is emphasized and decision making is open to everyone involved. People in individualistic cultures are valued for their self-motivation and self-interest.

  In countries with a collectivist approach, the emphasis is on group harmony, total involvement in decision making, and a focus on decisions made in the best interest of the group.

- **Uncertainty avoidance** reflects the degree of threat felt when facing ambiguity and risk. In countries that are high in uncertainty avoidance, rules and procedures are preferred and followed, there is a limited display of emotion, and citizens have the expectation of long-term employment.

  In countries with low uncertainty avoidance, risk taking is prevalent, entrepreneurship is encouraged, and citizens change jobs frequently.

- **Masculinity versus femininity** refers to the degree to which emphasis is placed on assertiveness, relationships, and quality of life. In countries that are more "masculine," individuals are encouraged to be assertive. Task orientation and competitiveness are valued qualities, and money and status are valued highly.

  In countries that are more "feminine," individuals are encouraged to work collaboratively and to be less assertive about their own personal needs. Job satisfaction as well as work–family balance are both considered to be very important.

- **Long-term versus short-term orientation** refers to a culture's tendency to focus more on the future or the past, which relates to economic success and values regarding savings and persistence. Long-term orientation implies a focus on the future, with trends toward delaying gratification, thriftiness (saving), and persistence. Long-term–oriented countries typically have higher savings rates and are more economically successful than countries with a short-term orientation.

  In countries where short-term orientation is common, there is a focus on values toward the past and present, with respect for traditions and fulfilling social obligations. These countries' values include the tendency to spend even if this means borrowing money.

Strategies for Addressing Cross-cultural Issues

By implementing the following strategies, you can improve your ability to work with others from cultures different from your own.

For Individuals

- Live and work outside of your home country. Be willing to take an overseas assignment whenever the opportunity arises.
- Travel outside of your home country extensively.
- While away, adapt to the customs of the new country. Get to know the local residents, rather than spending your time with people of your own nationality.
- Develop friendships with people from nationalities other than your own. Make it a point to learn from them about their customs, about the way business is conducted, about the differences and similarities between their country and yours.
- Learn another language or languages.
- Work at developing a perspective on world events that differs from that of your home country. Subscribe to newspapers and periodicals that broaden your understanding of key issues from multinational perspectives.
- When traveling outside your home country on business, learn in advance about cultural differences and customs that will affect the way in which you conduct business outside your home country.

For Companies and Organizations

- Offer language training to your employees.
- Encourage your employees to accept work assignments outside the home country.
- Provide transition counseling to employees and their families both before and after an assignment outside the home country.
- Provide training to help employees learn about and be sensitive to cross-cultural differences.
- Examine your employment practices to ensure that your company is not intentionally or unintentionally discriminating against anyone due to his or her religion or ethnicity. For example, requiring employees to work on Saturdays precludes members of certain religions from joining your organization.

Cross-cultural differences are natural. These differences will be welcomed rather than feared and will not become a source of embarrassment if individuals and organizations accept responsibility for learning about and embracing diverse cultures. Those managers and companies that are knowledgeable about and committed to accepting a diversity of backgrounds and perspectives will be better able to manage cross-cultural differences than those who adopt a narrow, one-culture perspective. This multiple perspective will be useful not only in business, but also in life.

> *"No culture can live if it attempts to be exclusive."*
>
> Mahatma Gandhi

Managing Organizational Diversity

Successful Strategies for Managing Organizational Diversity Effectively

- Communicate diversity goals and expectations clearly to employees, spelling out the benefits for each of them as individuals as well as for the company and industry overall.
- Communicate these goals through a wide variety of means such as in vision, mission, and value statements and written communications such as employee and shareholder newsletters, slogans, speeches, and vendor exhibits.
- Ensure that diversity is a top-down effort. Diversity must have visible support from the top if employees are to view it as real and credible.
- Practice inclusion in as many of the company communications as possible.
- The vital link between successful and unsuccessful diversity initiatives is supervisors: If a supervisor supports and "lives" diversity in the organization, employees are more likely to accept it.

- Take into account generational differences. To establish workplace harmony, avoid labeling, create a common language, build trust, and embrace a collaborative approach.[25]
- Create a management plan that includes assessing diversity, setting objectives, involving employees in generating solutions and initiatives, holding people accountable, and for multinational or global companies, ensuring diversity includes aiding individuals in being successful in cross-cultural settings. Some successful initiatives include:[26]
  - Strengthening leadership and management around diversity.
  - Diversity and international recruiting programs.
  - Education and training, including worldwide diversity conferences.
  - Community relations (domestic and international).
  - Communication.
  - Performance and accountability.
  - Work-life balance.
  - Career development.
  - Marketing plans for international customers.
  - Use of diversity and cross-cultural communications consultants.

Dr. Mansour Javidan and his colleagues at the Thunderbird School of Global Management have been working closely with organizations and corporations to assist individuals and companies in developing more of what he calls a "global mindset."[27] The **global mindset** comprises intellectual capital, psychological capital, and social capital. How strong is your global mindset? Use the suggestions in this book and in Dr. Javidan's work to ensure you are open-minded and embrace diversity of thought and action personally and professionally.

The Attributes That Define Global Leaders
Dr. Mansour Javidan, Thunderbird School of Global Management

INTELLECTUAL CAPITAL: General knowledge and capacity to learn
  Global business savvy
  Cognitive complexity
  Cosmopolitan outlook

PSYCHOLOGICAL CAPITAL: Openness to differences and capacity for change
  Passion for diversity
  Thirst for adventure
  Self-assurance

SOCIAL CAPITAL: Ability to build trusting relationships with and among people who are different from you
  Intercultural empathy
  Interpersonal impact
  Diplomacy

Summary

As you can see, there are many ways individuals and organizations can improve their awareness of the importance of inclusion and diversity. The world is becoming less homogenous and more global—this is evident in our communities, our workplaces, in government and politics, in restaurants, cinema, art, music, residence halls, and places of worship. We live and work in a diverse world. Diversity among our acquaintances, classmates, co-workers, neighbors, and friends is inevitable. How we interact with people who possess characteristics, values, and work styles that differ from ours plays a critical role in our ability to manage ourselves and help others achieve their goals. To work effectively with diverse others, we need to first understand our own uniqueness and that of others. Use this information not to judge others, but as a starting point for building relationships. Seek opportunities to be inclusive of and to interact with diverse others. Share your insights, feelings, and values with them. Encourage them to do the same. The more you do this, the better you will be at interacting with others and building effective relationships.

Key Terms and Concepts

Affirmative action	Individualism versus collectivism
Backlash	Long-term versus short-term orientation
Blaming the victim	Managing diversity
Discrimination	Masculinity versus femininity
Diversity	Power distance
Diversity training	Prejudice
Equal employment opportunity	Stereotypes
Ethnocentrism	Uncertainty avoidance
Global mindset	Valuing diversity
Harassment	

Discussion Questions

1. We discussed the growing diversity of the workforce. However, if you grew up in a fairly homogeneous town and went to a fairly homogeneous school, you may not have had much experience with diversity. How does this (or will it) affect you in the workplace?

2. Witness the growth of popular titles that suggest men and women speak different languages. Do you think this is true? Does this mean communication between genders is doomed from the start?

3. You accept an offer of a position that requires extensive travel abroad. What cross-cultural factors would you need to take into account regarding your communications with others in different cultures?

4. There is continuing debate on the usefulness of affirmative action policies—in organizations' hiring practices, in school admission policies, in preferential treatment in government contracts. Debate this issue. If the mandates didn't exist, would there be sufficient diversity in schools and in the workplace?

Endnotes

1. Case based on real-life experience of James Madison University student in class conducted by one of the authors.

2. Marilyn Loden, *Implementing Diversity* (New York: McGraw-Hill, 1995).

3. K. Williams and C. O'Reilly, "The Complexity of Diversity: A Review of Forty Years of Research." In B. Staw and R. Sutton (Eds.), *Research in Organizational Behavior,* vol. 21 (Greenwich, CT: JAI Press, 1998), p. 81.

4. Elizabeth Mannix and Margaret A. Neale, "What Differences Make a Difference? The Promise and Reality of Diverse Teams in Organizations," *Psychological Science in the Public Interest* 6, no. 2 (October 2005), p. 36.

5. Earnest Friday and Shawnta S. Friday, "Managing Diversity Using a Strategic Planned Change Approach," *The Journal of Management Development* 22, no. 9/10 (2003), p. 365.

6. Thomas Kochan, Katerina Bezrukova, Susan Jackson, and Aparna Joshi, et al., "The Effects of Diversity on Business Performance: Report of the Diversity Research Network," *Human Resource Management* 42, no. 1 (Spring 2003), p. 18.

7. Velma E. McCuiston, Barbara Ross Wooldridge, and Chris K. Pierce, "Leading the Diverse Workforce: Profit, Prospects and Progress," *Leadership & Organization Development Journal* 25, no. 1/2 (2004), pp. 74–75.

8. A. Hanacek, "The Spice of Life," *National Provisioner* 225, no. 2 (2011), p. 33.

9. U.S. Census Bureau, "United States Population Projections: 2000 to 2050" (2009), p. 3. Retrieved May 30, 2013, from http://factfinder.census.gov/population/projections/files/analytical-document09.pdf.

10. Mitra Toossi, M. "Labor Force Projections to 2020: A More Slowly Growing Workforce," *Monthly Labor Review* 135, no. 1 (Winter 2005–2006), p. 49.

11. Ibid., p. 53.

12. A. Hanacek (2011), pp. 32–24.

13. Portions of this are adapted from David W. Johnson, *Reaching Out: Interpersonal Effectiveness and Self-Actualization* (Boston: Allyn and Bacon, 2003).

14. Mary Kwak, "The Paradoxical Effects of Diversity," *MIT Sloan Management Review* 44, no. 3 (Spring 2003), p. 7.

15. Y. Wu, Z. Wei, and Q. Liang, "Top Management Team Diversity and Strategic Change," *Journal of Organizational Change Management* 24, no. 3 (2011), p. 269.

16. Fay Hansen, "Diversity's Business Case: Doesn't Add Up," *Workforce* 82, no. 4 (April 2003), pp. 30–31.

17. Michele E. A. Jayne and Robert L. Dipboye, "Leveraging Diversity to Improve Business Performance: Research Findings and Recommendations for Organizations," *Human Resource Management* 43, no. 4 (Winter 2004), pp. 413–15.

18. David W. Johnson, p. 360.

19. Salma M. Al-Lamki, "Orientation: The Essential Ingredient in Cross-cultural Management," *International Journal of Management* 19, no. 4 (December 2002), p. 568.

20. Mitra Toossi, p. 53.

21. Deborah Tannen, *You Just Don't Understand: Women and Men in Conversation* (New York: HarperCollins, 2001).

22. Judi Brownell, "Communicating with Credibility: The Gender Gap," *Cornell H.R.A. Quarterly* (April 1993), pp. 52–61.

23. Debra L. Oswald and Kara Lindstedt, "The Content and Function of Gender Self-stereotypes: An Exploratory Investigation," *Sex Roles* 54, no. 7/8 (2006), pp. 451–52.

24. Geert Hofstede and Robert R. McCrae, "Personality and Culture Revisited: Linking Traits and Dimensions of Culture," *Cross-Cultural Research* 38, no. 1 (February 2004), pp. 62–65.

25. Gavatorta, Steve, "It's a Millennial Thing," *T + D* 66, no. 3 (March 2012), pp. 61–62 (ABI/Inform-American Society for Training and Development articles, www.astd.org/TD).

26. Rose Mary Wentling and Nilda Palma-Rivas, "Current Status of Diversity Initiatives in Selected Multinational Corporations," *Human Resource Development Quarterly* 11, no. 1 (2000), pp. 41–52.

27. Mansour Javidan, Mary Teagarden, and David Bowen, "Making It Overseas," *Harvard Business Review*, HBS.org (April 2010), pp. 109–13.

**Exercise 5–A
Personal Stereotypes**

Look at the following list of words. What stereotypes come to mind upon first seeing each word? Where did these stereotypes originate? What data or experience can be cited to dispel each of the stereotypes? From the list below, choose 5–10 groups for which you can identify common stereotypes. In the first column write a few adjectives that describe the stereotype (e.g., arrogant, emotional). In the second column list the probable origin of these stereotypes for you (e.g., my parent's beliefs, the media). In the third column, cite a statistic, known fact, or example from your personal experience that dispels the stereotype. Share (depending on your comfort level) your stereotypes, their origins, and ways to dispel the inaccuracies with others in your class or small group.

Group	Stereotypes	Origins	Inaccuracies
Whites/Caucasians			
Native Americans			
African Americans			
Asians			
Women			
Men			
Southerners			
Midwesterners			
Northerners			
Hispanics			
Jews			
Muslims			
Catholics			
Baptists			
Gays/Lesbians			
Elderly persons			
College students			
Teenagers			

Questions

1. What are some of the more common stereotypes?
2. Where do these stereotypes originate?
3. What facts can be cited to dispel the inaccuracies?
4. What, if any, stereotypes are you able to dispel as a result of this exercise?

**Exercise 5–B
Personal Biases
and Stereotypes in
Employee Recruitment**

Four volunteers serving as "candidates" will be given background profiles by the instructor to use while acting as potential employees. A fifth volunteer serving as the "employer" reads a job description for a position to be filled. Individually, on a piece of paper, participants are to rank each of the four, from most likely to be hired (1) to least likely (4), citing reasons each candidate does or does not match the requirements for the job. Participants then vote for the person they think the employer is most likely to hire (out of the four candidates) for this position by going to that candidate. Participants should then explain to the candidate the reasons he or she was selected so candidates can compile a list. Participants are then to go to the candidate they believe would be the least favorable candidate and explain their reasoning for this decision. Candidates are to write on the board the characteristics or issues that made them appear more and less suited for the job.

Questions

1. What are some of the reasons certain candidates appear to be better suited for the position than the others?

2. What stereotypes emerged during the discussion of "fit" between the candidates and the position?

3. What are some of the legitimate factors used to differentiate among candidates, and what are some of the factors used to select one candidate over another that are less legitimate?

Source: This exercise is based on ideas from a JMU class presentation by Kim Aslen.

**Exercise 5–C
Cross-cultural Communication Simulation**

In this simulation, you will play the part of a manager employed by one of three firms—a commercial bank, a construction firm, and a hotel development company—which are planning a joint venture to build a new hotel and retail shopping complex in Perth, Australia. They come from three different cultures: Blue, Green, and Red. Each has specific cultural values, traits, customs, and practices.

You are a manager in the company to which you have been assigned. You will attend the kickoff get-together for the three-day meeting during which the three companies will negotiate the details of the partnership. Your management team consists of a vice president and a number of other managers. Consider the types of topics that the various corporations would discuss at an initial meeting.

Your instructor will provide you with information pertaining to your culture. You will be given about 15 minutes to meet with your fellow corporate members, during which you should:

1. Select a leader.

2. Discuss what your objectives and approaches will be at the opening get-together.

3. Using the description of your assigned culture, practice how you will talk and behave until you are reasonably familiar with your cultural orientation. Be sure to practice conversation distance, greeting rituals, and nonverbal behavior.

You will then return to the kickoff meeting where you will meet with employees from the other firms. As the social proceeds, interact with the managers from the other companies. Maintain the role you have been assigned, but do not discuss it explicitly. Notice how other people react to you and how you react to them. We will discuss the experience after it is over.

Upon completing this activity, answer the following questions:

1. In what ways did your perceptions of others and their differences influence how you interacted with them and your ability to achieve your goals?

_____

_____

_____

_____

_____

_____

_____

2. What did you learn about yourself and others through this activity? Discuss your strengths and weaknesses in cross-cultural interaction.

_____

_____

_____

_____

_____

_____

3. What were things you or others did or said that enabled or hindered you from adjusting to other people and their culture (1) in this activity? (2) In similar real-life situations?

_____

_____

_____

_____

_____

_____

4. What lessons did you learn from this activity? What steps can you take to improve your ability to understand and appreciate differences?

_____

_____

_____

_____

_____

_____

Source: Daphne A. Jameson, "Using a Simulation to Teach Intercultural Communication in Business Communication Courses," *Bulletin of the Association for Business Communication (Business Communication Quarterly)* LV, no. 4, March 1993, pp. 1–20.

**Exercise 5–D
Diversity Squares**

Move about the room and try to find people who can answer yes to your questions. This is just like Bingo in that you are trying to complete a row. Once you have found someone to answer yes to the question, you can cross off the square, placing that person's name or initials in the box. Each person who answers yes to one of your questions can only be used once. Continue to find others until you are able to complete a row.

Have you ever worked with anyone who is 20 or more years older than you?	Have you ever worked on a farm?	Do you speak more than one language?	Have you ever worked with anyone with a physical disability?	Have you ever worked with anyone who is a non-Christian?
Have you ever had a female boss?	Are you of Hispanic or Latin American heritage?	Do you have a family member or friend on welfare?	Have you ever had an African American boss?	Do you have a best friend of a different race?
Do you have a friend who is gay, lesbian, or bisexual?	Have you ever been discriminated against because of race or ethnicity?	Have you ever lived outside of your home country?	Have you ever known a convicted felon?	Did a single parent raise you?
Have you ever been sexually harassed at work?	Has either of your parents been in the military?	Are you of Asian heritage?	Are you a vegetarian?	Have you ever had a doctor whose race or ethnicity differs from yours?
Do you know someone with a chronic disease such as cancer or AIDS?	Have you ever dated someone who was less educated than you?	Have you ever been discriminated against because of gender?	Were your parents or grandparents immigrants?	Have you ever had a boss who was younger than you?

Source: This exercise is adapted from a presentation by Kari Calello, JMU student class presentation; and J. William Pfeiffer and Leonard D. Goodstein (Eds.), *The 1994 Annual: Developing Human Resources,* Pfeiffer & Company, 1994. Copyright © 1994 by John Wiley & Sons, Inc. Reprinted by permission of John Wiley and Sons Inc.

Questions

1. How did you feel asking individuals certain questions? What approach did you use to ask the questions?

2. Were some questions more difficult to ask than others (perceived to be potentially more sensitive or offensive)?

3. Why did you approach certain individuals for certain questions?

4. If you were approached by several people about the same question, how did it make you feel? Why did they select you for certain questions and neglect to ask you about others?

5. Would some of the questions be more difficult to ask or more likely to offend others if worded in the first person? For example, "Are you gay, lesbian, or bisexual?"

6. What did this exercise make you realize about stereotypes and prejudice?

Exercise 5–E
Gender Stereotypes

Part I

Your instructor will divide the group into smaller groups based on gender, resulting in male-only and female-only groups. Groups are to brainstorm a list in response to the following statements. It is not necessary for all members to agree with everything the group generates. Add all inputs to the list.

Female groups complete the following:

All men are . . .

Men think all women are . . .

Male groups complete the following:

All women are . . .

Women think all men are . . .

Part II

After generating your lists, your groups will present a role-play to the class based on the following scenarios by switching gender roles (females portray males, and males portray females):

Two friends (of the same gender) meeting each other back at school for the first time this year.

A person flirting with a member of the opposite sex at a party. (Females play a male flirting with a female; males play a female flirting with a male.)

Questions

1. What aspects of the role-plays were accurate, distorted, or inaccurate?
2. How did you feel portraying the opposite gender and how did it feel to see your gender portrayed?
3. On what stereotypes or experiences were these role-plays based?

Part III

Your group will now write its brainstorm lists on the board for discussion. Remember that these lists are a product of a group effort and are generally based on stereotypes and not necessarily the view of any one individual.

Analyze the lists for positive and negative results in both personal and professional settings. Generate a list of ways to dispel, reduce, or counter negative stereotypes.

Source: Portions of this exercise are adapted from concepts in Susan F. Fritz, William Brown, Joyce Lunde, and Elizabeth Banset, *Interpersonal Skills for Leadership* (Englewood Cliffs, NJ: Prentice Hall, 1999); and A. B. Shani and James B. Lau, *Behavior in Organizations: An Experiential Approach,* 6th ed. (Chicago: Irwin, 1996).

Questions

1. What similarities, patterns, or trends developed from the groups?
2. How do you feel about the thoughts presented about your gender?
3. What implications do these thoughts have on actions and situations in the work environment?
4. What can you do to reduce the negative effects of these stereotypes? What can you do to help dispel these stereotypes? (Brainstorm with your group or class.)

Exercise 5–F
Diversity Awareness

1. Subscribe to a magazine or newspaper that provides you with a perspective that differs from your own (e.g., if you're Caucasian, subscribe to *Black Enterprise;* if you're from the United States, subscribe to the *International Herald Tribune*).

2. Invite someone you know who is from a country other than yours to your next party.

3. Attend a service in a church, synagogue, or mosque that is different from your own.

4. Volunteer to work for a cause that helps children from a country other than your own.

5. Volunteer to work at a nursing home or at a home for physically or mentally challenged children or adults.

6. Watch a movie that deals with diversity. Write a paper addressing these questions: What types and sources of prejudice were in evidence? How did diversity, stereotyping, prejudice, or discrimination affect the characters? What effective and ineffective strategies were employed to handle prejudice? What strategies did you learn to either overcome prejudice or manage diversity?

**Exercise 5–G
Dimensions of
Diversity**

Primary and Secondary Dimensions of Diversity (from Harcourt, Brace, & Company, 1994)

Primary Dimensions

   Age

   Ethnicity

   Sexual orientation

   Race

   Physical ability

   Gender

Secondary Dimensions

   Education

   Religious beliefs

   Military experience

   Geographic location

   Income

   Work background

   Parental status

   Marital status

Activity A

Using the diversity dimensions, create a list of factors that make you diverse from the person sitting next to you.

Activity B

Create a list of factors that make you diverse from anyone else in the classroom, including the instructor.

Activity C

Create a list of factors that make you diverse from anyone else in your school or workplace.

Source: Submitted by Mr. Bob Eliason, Management Lecturer, James Madison University, Harrisonburg, VA.

Exercise 5–H
Empowering Others

Manuel is a 20-year-old man whose family immigrated to the United States when he was very young. Manuel works for you as an administrative assistant in your wholesale electrical supply business. You serve electricians and electrical contractors by providing fixtures, wire, connectors, tools, and parts. Manuel is very good at talking to people on the phone. He is friendly and polite. This is his first job out of high school. He has lived here most of his life, went to the public school, and currently lives with his parents. He is very motivated and a quick learner, but is shy, reserved, and very cautious.

One of your sales staff has quit. You would like to offer Manuel the opportunity to grow professionally and to increase his income. You offered him the sales job. He looked startled, amazed, and then immediately said, "No." How can you empower Manuel to accept the job and to be successful in it?

Source: Submitted by Mr. Bob Eliason, Management Lecturer, James Madison University, Harrisonburg, VA.

Exercise 5–I
Reflection/Action Plan

This chapter discussed the skill of understanding and managing diversity—what it is, why it's important, and how to improve your skill in these areas. Complete the following worksheet upon completing all readings and experiential exercises for this chapter.

1. The one or two areas regarding understanding or managing diversity in which I am most strong are:

_____

_____

_____

_____

2. The one or two areas of understanding or managing diversity in which I need more improvement are:

_____

_____

_____

_____

3. If I did only one thing to improve in this area, it would be to:

_____

_____

_____

_____

4. Making this change would probably result in:

_____

_____

_____

_____

5. If I did not change or improve in this area, it would probably affect my personal and professional life in the following ways:

_____

_____

_____

_____

6 Listening and Nonverbal Communication

Learning Points

How do I:

- Ask a colleague to be a good listener or sounding board for me when I have something important to discuss with him or her?
- Show I'm a good listener or sounding board?
- Differentiate between effective and noneffective listening behaviors?
- Ensure my verbal and nonverbal messages are in sync?
- Accurately interpret others' nonverbal messages?
- Actively listen?

It all started out well. I had been steadily increasing my client base for six months at the investment firm where I work as an analyst. Ron Sanders, the division manager, had recently asked me to handle a dozen accounts of long-established clients previously handled by a retired analyst. I had made a point to meet with all the owners of the transferred accounts to gain perspective on their portfolios.

I remember sitting with Mrs. Crenshaw, a wealthy widow in her late 60s. We discussed her past investments and possible changes for the future. She had the notion that 60 is old, and she didn't believe she had enough money to last her through her final years.

Mrs. Crenshaw stated that she wanted to be more conservative in her investments, no longer willing to risk as much principal. After listening to her family stories and concerns for what I had thought was an acceptable length of time (to me it seemed interminable!), I finally said, "Sixty is young, you have plenty of years ahead of you, and the amount of savings you have is more than sufficient to allow us to combine higher risk investments with some of your more conservative investments." I continued to show her the opportunities she had for making high returns by redistributing her investments. She signed the papers for the new investment instruments and thanked me for my time.

Everything was set. That is why I was so surprised when Ron Sanders informed me that he had just come from a meeting with Mrs. Crenshaw's eldest son and I needed to complete paperwork to delay all changes to her account. I also needed to transfer all of Mrs. Crenshaw's files to Sharon Foster, a senior analyst at the firm. How could I have screwed this up? What was I thinking when I convinced her to make the changes? How could I have missed her discomfort with the changes? All of a sudden I realized I hadn't heard a thing she had been saying—not really heard, anyway.

1. Where did the analyst go wrong?

2. Why did the analyst have a difficult time reading Mrs. Crenshaw?

3. What verbal and nonverbal clues did the analyst miss?

4. What should the analyst do to improve his listening skills with clients?

"If you think you know it all, then you haven't been listening."

La Rochefoucauld

Communication is a two-way street. When done correctly, communication is a fluid, evolving process. Communication is enhanced when all have the opportunity to both speak as well as listen, when all have a chance to check their perceptions of what they're hearing, and when principles of both verbal and nonverbal communication are followed.

Listening, a critical component of the communication process, goes beyond merely hearing what another person is saying to constructing meaning from all the verbal and nonverbal signals the speaker is sending. Words often comprise only a small part of a message being sent. To obtain the complete message you must "listen" with your ears, eyes, and heart. This chapter reviews the basic concepts of effective listening and nonverbal communication and how these principles can be applied in your personal and professional life. Chapter 7 goes into greater detail about communicating effectively and assertively.

What Is Listening?

Listening is the process of hearing someone speak, processing what you're hearing, and demonstrating that you understand the speaker's intent. Effective listening has three dimensions: sensing, processing/evaluating, and responding. **Sensing** involves hearing the words and receiving the nonverbal signals such as body language and facial expressions. Processing/evaluating involves understanding the meaning, interpreting the implications, evaluating the nonverbal cues, and remembering the message. Responding involves the listener sending the speaker verbal or nonverbal signals that he or she is being heard.[1] Listening is an essential skill for those who want to be successful in work and in life. Yet truly effective listeners are hard to find. When was the last time you truly felt listened to? When did you feel someone really made an effort to get to know you—to understand where you were coming from and why, or to help you solve a problem without meddling and without shifting attention to his or her problems and away from yours?

Why Is Listening Important?

"There's a reason why God gave us two ears and only one mouth."

How many of us were fortunate enough to be taught the skill of listening in school or on the job? Listening is critical for effective communication, yet few people have actually acquired training in this essential skill. Most of us have had exposure to the art of talking and presenting, but listening is a skill that is simply overlooked, perhaps because we assume everyone can or will do this. Talking is one of the first skills we practice. Parents can hardly wait for their child to speak for the first time. Yet the most training we typically receive in listening is when someone says those infamous words, "You're not listening to me" or "You had better listen to what I say!"

The act of simply "hearing" is a passive activity. The act of listening—truly listening—demands attention, concentration, and effort. There are several different types of listening:[2]

Passive listening occurs when you are trying to absorb as much of the information presented as possible. You act as a sponge, taking in the information with no or little attempt to process or enhance the messages being sent by the speaker.

Attentive listening occurs when you are genuinely interested in the speaker's point of view. You are aware something can be learned from the interaction. In attentive listening, you make assumptions about the messages being relayed by the speaker and fill in gaps with assumptions based on what you want to hear rather than on what the speaker is actually saying. At this level of listening, you don't check to see whether what you heard is what the speaker intended to say. Many barriers and biases can hinder this form of interaction.

Active or **empathetic listening** is the most powerful level of listening and requires the largest amount of work. In active listening, communication is a vibrant, two-way process that involves high levels of attentiveness, clarification, and message processing. In active listening, you not only hear and react to the words being spoken but also paraphrase, clarify, and give feedback to the speaker about the messages being received.

The 70/30 Principle

Active listening follows the "70/30" principle: When in the role of listener, true active listeners spend almost 70 percent of their time listening and less than 30 percent of their time talking.

Benefits of Active Listening

- *Active listening shows the speaker you are concerned.* By paying full attention to the speaker, you are able to focus on the key elements of the message being sent, ask questions to clarify meanings, and offer statements that enhance both the speaker's and your understanding of what is being said. Active listening leads to getting better information. By asking clarifying questions, you motivate the speaker to be more precise when explaining the nuances of a situation, enabling you to obtain details that otherwise might not have surfaced. Imagine the mother asking her teenage son how his day went. If she accepts his one-word answer ("fine"), she limits her understanding of his situation and might communicate that she really doesn't care to know more.

- *Active listening encourages further communication.* In active listening, the listener is an active participant in the conversation, asking questions and probing for details so the speaker feels both supported and encouraged to share more information about a situation, enhancing both the speaker's and the listener's understanding of what is taking place.

- *Active listening has the potential to enhance relationships.* It takes more time to listen actively to someone else. Just taking this time to focus on a person and his or her issues can improve the relationship. Listening actively also involves offering mutual support and developing common understanding, both of which serve to strengthen trust and enhance interactions between the people involved. Returning to the mother and son example, if she took the time to listen and ask a few thoughtful follow-up questions, her son might begin to open up about his day. For example, he might talk about the fact he failed his geometry exam, won a wrestling match, or that his best friend was arrested for drug possession.

- *When you take the time to truly listen—using your ears and eyes to take in a more complete story—others feel cared for.* These feelings are usually reciprocated, resulting in an enhanced relationship.

- *Active listening can sometimes calm down another person who is feeling very upset about a situation.* Think for a moment about airline ticket agents and how calm most of them are when confronted by an aggressive or just a tired passenger. Most airline ticket agents have received customer service training that emphasizes the importance of listening to the customer. While an agent can seldom do anything that would directly respond to the passenger's needs, such as change the weather or get the flight to leave on time, the best agents are skilled at focusing their attention on passengers in distress, hearing them out, and quietly helping the passengers problem-solve about the situation in which they find themselves. These agents use their training to make the passenger feel heard and understood. They listen, ask clarifying questions, empathize, and offer potential solutions for consideration by the passenger—all in a way that calms passengers.

■ *Active listening invites others to listen to you.* By listening actively you set a good example for others and remind them listening is a valuable skill they can also use. People who have been listened to actively are more likely to reciprocate. This benefit of active listening is echoed in Stephen Covey's best-selling *Seven Habits of Highly Effective People:* seek first to understand and then to be understood.[3] Typically, when two people disagree, one is likely to say something like, "Okay, we don't agree. Let me tell you why you're wrong and how my way is superior." Perhaps that statement is a bit exaggerated, but it demonstrates the need many of us have to be right and have our say—first and foremost. Imagine how this exchange would differ if it sounded like this: "Okay, we don't agree. Why don't you tell me your idea and why you think it will work." When we actively listen to other people, chances are very high they'll do the same in return.

■ *Active listening leads to better cooperation and problem solving.* We're all human and it's easy to make mistakes when we think we understand what someone is trying to say. By listening actively, asking questions, and probing for understanding, together the listener and speaker are generally able to develop more creative solutions than if the listener had remained passive, not offering any insight or support. Team members and employees report that when their team leaders and managers demonstrate real interest in them and their ideas by listening and paying attention to their concerns, their willingness to work collaboratively increases dramatically.

Active Listening and Organizations

Active listening is also important for intraorganizational communication. Employees want and need to be listened to. Addressing employee concerns improves organizational effectiveness, reduces miscommunications and errors, and leads to a responsive work environment. Improving managerial listening skills raises performance levels through responsive and creative problem solving. Employees spend one-third of work time listening while top executives spend two-thirds of their work hours in listening activities.[4] Accurate information sharing in organizations is critical for strategic success. Successful organizations foster active listening in the corporate culture.

**"What do you mean we don't communicate?
I sent you e-mail on Monday."**

Source: http://www.cartoonbank.com/what-do-you-mean-we-dont-communicate-i-sent-you-e-mail-on-monday/invt/105453/?

Active listening can be a powerful competitive tool for organizations. Improving listening skills on an individual level will lead to higher levels of employee responsiveness, clearer understanding of organizational issues, and increased employee commitment to quality. The opening scenario illustrates how the ability of organizational members to listen to the concerns and wants of the customer can have an impact on customer service. By listening to and understanding customers' needs, organizations can better serve these needs, thus providing the organization with a competitive edge.

Barriers to Effective Listening

Despite its importance in promoting effective communication, active listening is often neglected. Many factors contribute to difficulties in listening:[5]

- *Physiological limitations.* Listening can be fatiguing. We are visual beings—about 80 percent of learning occurs though sight. Because the eye is victorious over the ear in the constant process of providing stimulation to the mind, many people don't know how to be effective listeners.

- *Speaking/listening gap.* The average person speaks at a rate of 120–150 words per minute (wpm), while our brains have the capacity to process information at 275–300 wpm. We can think at up to 500 wpm, which is why it is easy to tune in and out of conversations. Optimal speaking rate is about 275–300 wpm even though the other person's thinking rate is higher. One strategy to address this is to develop additional presentation techniques to hold the other person's full attention.[6]

- *Inadequate background information.* Most listeners hate to admit when they haven't heard all of the information necessary to engage in conversation, so they stumble along hoping to catch up. They seldom do.

- *Selective memory.* Some employees treasure every accolade and never hear a single criticism. Others hear only the complaints and never the praise. We have a tendency to hear—and remember—what we want. There's a reason ad agencies run commercials over and over on TV and on the Web. Without reinforcement of key messages, it's easy to forget entirely or to remember only selectively what a company has paid millions for you to remember. Interestingly, steps taken to increase viewers' recall, such as adding an attractive spokesperson or using flashy video, result in viewers remembering the attractive person and not the product or what it can do for them!

- *Selective expectation.* If you expect dishonesty, poor work attitudes, or inattention, you'll probably get them. This is an example of the "self-fulfilling prophecy." Many employees expect not to be listened to. So many managers are preoccupied with immediate tasks and seldom have the time to devote to individual employee concerns that employees become accustomed to not being heard and understood. Often they'll just give up and resign themselves to the short, nonattentive interactions with managers to which they've become accustomed, or withhold information, expecting it wouldn't be attended to anyway.

- *Fear of being influenced or persuaded.* Some managers hold certain beliefs so dear to their hearts that they are biased—unable to entertain another's point of view about a matter. Typically managers who feel this strongly about an issue have a tendency to turn off speakers who dispute their cherished beliefs even before the position is fully explained.

- *Bias and being judgmental.* When you don't like a person, it's hard to hear what he or she says. Sometimes this bias is based on wrong or incomplete information, such as "She's only 17, what could she know?" or "He's a bigot, so why should I listen to him?" When we make a negative judgment about the speaker, we typically stop or severely curtail our desire to listen to the speaker.

- *Boredom.* Thought processes are four to five times the usual speed of speech. When you can guess what an employee is going to say seconds or even minutes before he or she speaks, your thoughts wander. When you return, the speaker may have gone on an unexpected track whose beginnings you lost and whose point you never do understand.

- *Partial listening and distractions.* You may hear the literal words, but miss the connotation, facial expressions, or tone of voice. In essence, you get only part of the message. Perhaps you were trying to remember an important point when an employee interrupts to ask if he or she can leave to deal with an emergency at home. Chances are you didn't give that employee your full attention—even though your empathetic response to the situation would have gone a long way.

- *Rehearsing.* Many of us use the time during another's talking to come up with a bulletproof rebuttal. If you do this, you aren't really listening. Sometimes we are so intent on winning an argument that the conversation veers in a different direction during our "rehearsal," resulting in our losing the segue for and impact of our carefully crafted rebuttal.

- *Selective perception.* Perception is the process by which you take in and process stimuli according to your own experiences or attitudes. As such, you create your own reality, apart from what may actually be occurring. Since communication has a great deal of room for individual interpretation, from the meaning of words to the interpretation of nonverbal signals, your perception can easily distort the true message or its intent. Perception can be influenced by a number of factors such as your needs, opinions, personality, education, or environment. **Selective perception** is a process in which you select or pay attention to only that information that adheres to or reinforces your own beliefs, views, or needs, causing severe distortion of messages.

- *Interference from emotions.* Communication is susceptible to interference by emotions. Though we use communication to express our emotions, not everyone is able to understand, control, or explain his or her feelings adequately or fully. Emotions are neither right nor wrong, but rather an expression of human reactions. By observing nonverbal cues, you are better able to interpret the true level and type of others' emotional states. You can then utilize empathy to neutralize emotional responses, paving the way to begin work on understanding the content of the communication. The emotional state of both the sender and the receiver must be considered in eliminating problems in the communication process.

Online Distractions

Put down your cell phone when interacting with another person! Turn off your mobile device during class, meetings, dinners, and social events. Avoid texting while conversing with someone else. We cannot multitask the way we think we can—plus it's often considered impolite or unprofessional to text or take calls while with others. Show your attentiveness by actively listening to and engaging with people. This will go a long way toward building relationships with people that are genuine and caring.

Selective Perception

Most listeners hear what they want to hear. For example, many a manager has told a new employee that the organization gives "merit" pay increases. That new employee hears these words as "automatic" salary boosts, to which he or she feels entitled. Later, when the employee inevitably complains, the manager protests that the word "merit" means selective, and the employee will insist that to him or her the word "merit" means automatic. Who is right? Technically, the manager is. But in the interest of fostering good communication, it's up to the manager to be more explicit, give examples, and manage expectations by mentioning that only a small percentage of employees actually receive merit increases.

Characteristics of Active Listening

Active listening can be difficult for some people. Fortunately, listening skills can be developed and improved. Just as effective speaking is an acquired skill, so too is good listening. It requires a willingness to constantly practice, utilize various techniques, and evaluate progress.

- *Show interest and be sincere in listening.* Use both verbal and nonverbal cues to demonstrate you truly care about the speaker and his or her message.

- *Ask questions if you don't understand completely.* Ask for clarification on points of contention ("Did he say we would need to lay off employees or just cut costs?") as well as follow-up questions ("When will she have to start this process?").

- *Avoid distractions.* Avoid doing two (or more) things at once. Make the speaker feel that she or he is the most important person in the world.

- *Use direct eye contact.* Look away from the computer, the report, or your calendar while communicating with friends and associates. Also, be sensitive to cultural differences in interpreting the meaning that might be conveyed by making—or avoiding—eye contact with others.

- *Do not interrupt.* To quote the American etiquette expert, Letitia Baldridge, "Good listeners don't interrupt—ever—unless the building's on fire."[7] Pause and count to three to make sure the speaker has completed his or her statements.

- *Read both the verbal and nonverbal messages.* Good listening technique involves good detective work. Take the time and energy needed to understand the whole message and not just what is being spoken.

- *Be empathetic.* Recognize and acknowledge the other person's feelings and emotions. If the person is distressed, cracking a joke or making light of the situation might be interpreted as not caring about the speaker. The earlier example of the airline agent certainly applies here.

- *Paraphrase to correct misinterpretations, reflect the literal message, and improve retention.* Repeat statements for clarification. Say, "If I heard you correctly . . ." or "So what you are saying is. . . ."

- *Evaluate the message after hearing all the facts.* A common habit of listeners is forming a response before the speaker is finished.[8] Avoid judgments by allowing the individual to complete the entire message before assessing the content and merit of the statements.

- *Concentrate on the message as well as the messenger.* Focus on the delivery as well as the content of the message itself, but be sure to check your potential biases about the messenger *before* you start the listening process.

- *Give feedback to check accuracy, express your perspective, and broaden the interaction.* For example, you might say, "So you want me to complete this report by Friday?" or "It sounds like we disagree; are there any elements of the plan on which we can both agree?"

- *Listen with your entire body.* Use direct eye contact, lean forward, nod your head, and use nonverbal communication to denote understanding or to get clarification.

- *Don't talk so much!* If you know you have tendencies toward verbosity, be on guard.

As former U.S. president Calvin Coolidge said, "No one ever listened himself out of a job!"

What Is Nonverbal Communication?

"One can lie with the mouth, but with the accompanying grimace one nevertheless tells the truth."

Friedrich Nietzsche, Beyond Good and Evil

Nonverbal communication is conveying meaning or expressing feelings consciously or subconsciously through means other than words. Since most of us are visually oriented and live in an environment dominated by visual images, it is not surprising that research indicates that over 55 percent of interpersonal communication is conveyed nonverbally.[9]

Nonverbal communication cues fall into two broad classes. Nonverbal visual cues include facial expressions, eye blinks, eye contact, gaze aversion, nodding, smiles, postural shifts, physical positioning, and other bodily behaviors. Paraverbal communication cues include aspects related to speech, such as pitch, pauses, tone of voice, inflection, and voice volume.[10]

How often have you experienced talking with someone who says he or she is listening even though the person is watching television or texting? Or having someone say they agree to something while shaking their head in disagreement? Conversely, have you experienced empathy from someone as evidenced by the person nodding in support rather than sharing their agreement with you verbally? We often communicate nonverbally in ways that contradict what we're saying verbally. Nonverbal messages are often sent subconsciously, leading others to believe they hold more of the true meaning than the verbal message.

Why Is Nonverbal Communication Important?

Most of us trust nonverbal cues far more than we trust another's words. Fifty-five percent of communication is comprised of body language, 38 percent of audio codes, and 7 percent of words.[11] Nonverbal communication includes many components such as silence, body posture, touching, place and time, position of the eyes (for example, rolling of the eyes), hand or foot moves (such as wringing hands or shaking a leg/foot), attire, eye contact, and so on. Nonverbal communication indicates feelings, whereas ideas are expressed verbally. People will almost always disbelieve the spoken word if an opposite message is being delivered with tone of voice, posture, and facial expression. Given the importance of nonverbal cues in communication, relying primarily on the spoken word to convey your ideas in face-to-face interactions neglects essential communication tools.

Nonverbal communication is powerful and is most effective in reinforcing your message when a combination of consistent nonverbal behavior cues is used, such as maintaining eye contact while using an appropriate voice volume and maintaining an erect posture. It is important to understand first how we communicate nonverbally, and then how to interpret correctly nonverbal messages that others send us.

Benefits of Nonverbal Communication[12]

- Nonverbal communication covers items that cannot be expressed with words.
- Nonverbal communication is very effective at sending accurate messages.
- It is usually easy to get almost immediate feedback on how nonverbal communication is being interpreted by the receiver.
- Paying attention to your nonverbal communication skills makes you more aware of both your unconscious as well as your conscious thoughts. By getting these two into greater alignment, your overall communication and listening skills improve, resulting in enhanced understanding and decision making.
- Trust improves when your nonverbal and verbal communication are in alignment.
- Awareness of cross-cultural differences in nonverbal communication increases your understanding of ways to interact effectively in business and social settings with individuals from diverse backgrounds.

Nonverbal Communication Components

There are several components of nonverbal communication. **Kinesics** involves body movement, gestures, and posture. This includes eye contact, leaning, and body positioning. For example, we tend to use eye contact to provide information, express interest or intimacy, or facilitate the accomplishment of tasks. Many gestures are passed from one generation to the next without conscious effort. The way your dad looked at you when you did something wrong may be echoed in your behavior toward others. Check yourself and ask for feedback if you think others may find your gestures offensive. In addition, there are differences—some small, some vast—in the use, acceptability, and interpretation of gestures in other cultures. As we said before, it is important to know your audience.

Para-language refers to the tone of voice, volume, pitch, or speech rate. Is the sender using a strong, loud tone of voice, or is he or she soft-spoken or timid in making an announcement? It is important to check both your message and how you deliver it to ensure that the receiver will interpret and respond to it as intended. The same message can have very different meanings depending on which words are emphasized. For example,

- *Where* is your mother? might be used when another adult is helping a child locate his or her mother.
- Where is *your* mother? might be said by a child's classmate at the start of the annual May Day parade.
- *Where is your mother?* might be said by a neighbor staring alternatively between her newly broken window and a child wearing a baseball glove.

Environment refers to the layout of the space or room, lighting, color scheme, noise, decorations, and so on. The way in which you arrange your office may send a message to subordinates that may denote invitation or seclusion. For example, arranging your desk with your back to the door sends a very different message than arranging your desk facing the door. Also, placing chairs on the other side of your desk, facing you, places a barrier—figuratively and literally—between you and your co-workers. If you want to send a more egalitarian message, arrange your chairs next to your desk, or sit around a table with chairs when speaking with your employees or associates.

Chronemics is the study of how human beings use and structure time. Are you always late, early, right on time? What is the message you're sending, and how do your superiors, peers, or subordinates perceive it? If you are always late to meetings, what do others interpret about this behavior? What if you're always early? Is what your actions are communicating the message you intended to send? Again, there are cultural differences in how chronemics plays out in communication. Be aware of these differences to ensure mutual understanding.

Proxemics is a term to describe the way we use space in communication. The amount of personal space you need often depends on your gender, age and culture.[13] You may notice that when talking to a close friend, you stand very near—perhaps a foot or less away. Conversely, when you go to the beach, you are more likely to look for a spot that is 10 or more feet from the next occupied space. How closely we stand to others with whom we communicate has a powerful effect on how we regard others and how we respond to them. For example, Americans prefer a "safe zone" when interacting with others, a space of a couple of feet or more. By contrast, many people in Latin American countries stand quite close and often touch those with whom they speak—in personal and even business conversations.

Haptics (tactile communication) refers to the use of touch. Touch can provide a strong nonverbal cue. Individuals tend to touch those they like or those with whom they have a close association, such as when a friend puts her arm over her friend's shoulder to express warmth and encouragement. Other types of touch can indicate varying degrees of aggression, such as pointing a finger or smacking another's hand. Touch-based communication

Figure 6–1
Common Nonverbal
Behavior and Interpretations
(in Western Industrialized
Countries)

Nonverbal Behavior	Common Interpretation
Darting eyes	Lying, bored, distracted, uninterested
Crossed arms	Closed to other's opinion, defensive
Tapping fingers	Impatient, nervous
Body lean (forward)	Interest, paying attention
Rubbing hands	Anticipation
Chin rub	Disbelief
Hands on hips	Anger, frustration
Steepling fingers	Authority, superiority
Rubbing nose	Lying, doubt
Quiet voice	Uncertainty, shyness, scared
Raised eyebrow	Amazement, disbelief

varies depending upon the type of relationships, including functional/professional (dental examination, haircut), social/polite (handshake), friendship/warmth (clap on the back), and love/intimacy (kisses and hugs).

The old saying, "Actions speak louder than words" holds true. Figure 6–1 illustrates some common examples of nonverbal communication. Nonverbal messages tend to be ambiguous, so they may still need verbal clarification. Silence is probably one of the most misunderstood forms of nonverbal communication. Imagine you are at a team meeting and a major decision is about to be ratified. Some members vocalize their agreement while others remain silent. Are they in agreement, still thinking, bored, angry, tired, uninterested, or daydreaming? Interpreting nonverbal messages is a complex task; there is not one universal interpretation for each gesture or response. Before you interpret a nonverbal message, ask clarifying questions or get a verbal response to ensure a correct interpretation.

Barriers to Effective Nonverbal Communication

- *A number of nonverbal communication behaviors are culturally specific*—the way they are perceived in one culture may not be the way they are perceived in another culture. For example, short handshakes may be perceived positively in one country, while handshakes of a longer duration may be the norm in another.[14]

- *A number of behaviors that prevent us from communicating effectively are in our "blind area."* Tapping a foot may signal unconsciously impatience; reading a sign while someone is talking may signal lack of interest in the person speaking; twirling a pencil may unwittingly signal nervousness.

- *We may be misinterpreted.* By concentrating on what we are saying we often lose sight of other mannerisms that could be signaling a different reaction or emotion from what is stated.

- *Our reliance on constant use of mobile devices* even when talking or in meetings may reduce our ability to be attentive to both verbal and nonverbal messages when interacting with others.

- *Many are now experiencing what they perceive to be "short attention spans."* The constant barrage of ads, social media, face-to-face and virtual interactions may make it difficult for us to concentrate fully on the person or persons with whom we are speaking in the present moment, resulting in incorrect or poor understanding of messages received verbally or nonverbally during increasingly brief interactions.

- *Be aware of the limitations of e-mail*—as we stated earlier, e-mail is a form of communication to use for brief, noncontroversial messages—precisely because the receiver cannot see your nonverbal messages, speak with you in person, or read "tone" into the content of your message.

Try This

- Spend a day at the office without your computer. Well, if you're a telemarketer, this won't be possible. But if you are a manager who works at a desk, "forget" your computer at home for a day, or don't turn it on in the morning. Walk around. Meet people face to face. At the end of the day, evaluate how things went—were you more energized, more connected without multitasking throughout the day, handling incoming e-mails along with meetings and face-to-face interactions? Did you feel more, or less, productive?

- Leave your mobile device home (or locked away in your purse or briefcase) for one dinner or meeting. How did it feel not to be constantly checking for messages while you were in a meeting or having dinner? Were you more present with your meeting host or dinner guests? Were you anxious—or did you feel liberated—by not multitasking during your meeting?

Nonverbal Communication Strategies

- *Be self-aware of those mannerisms* that may signal distraction or boredom. Be aware of the need for congruence between your spoken words and nonverbal behaviors. Do your nonverbal signals reinforce the verbal message? Or do they contradict the intended message, confuse the receiver, and result in a communication failure? For example, a boss who says he or she loves your ideas while rolling his or her eyes would lead you to believe that the boss might lack confidence in your suggestions.

- *Be "in the moment"* and show respect by paying attention. If you are rushed and can't pay sufficient attention to someone who needs to meet with you, disclose that another time would be better when you can pay full attention.

- *Research cross-cultural mores* in advance so you do not inadvertently use a mannerism that could be viewed as offensive.

- *Make a rule not to e-mail, text, or take phone calls during meetings* and social events unless absolutely necessary.

- While this may sound preposterous, *limit your use of e-mail in business settings*, or at least be aware of how important it is NOT to use e-mail to convey negative feedback or make announcements that could be viewed as negative.

- *Arrange to watch yourself on tape*—this will help you to be aware of mannerisms that may be affecting the way you are perceived when you interact with others.

- *Take a class* on presentation skills, debate, voice enhancement, breathing, improv, or drama—all of these help you to be more aware of how you come across to others and how you can improve your ability to relate to and interact with others.

- *Think before you speak.* Slowing down even just for a moment will give you the time needed to concentrate on speaking while sending nonverbal cues that support what you are saying.

- If you are generally impatient, have a short attention span, or are time-challenged, be aware of the impact this might have on others and arrange, when possible, to *set blocks of time to meet with people* on issues of importance to them.

- *Be aware of some behaviors, like being late on a regular basis, that may be perceived as lack of interest or respect* on your part, and make a commitment to change these behaviors.

- *Be aware of always nodding in agreement*—don't nod automatically, which may signal 100 percent agreement with what the speaker is saying; nod to show understanding, then communicate verbally by asking probing and clarifying questions to ensure the speaker is clear about where you stand on the issue being discussed.

- *Develop a genuine interest in others* and in their perspective. Your ability to serve others is enhanced when you allow yourself to be at least as focused on others—showing this verbally and nonverbally—as you are on yourself.[15]

Summary

Listening is an essential skill for establishing and enhancing personal and professional relationships. If you are a good listener, you'll notice others are drawn to you. Friends and associates confide in you and relationships thrive.

Listening also involves observing and interpreting nonverbal messages—yours and those of others. By concentrating on sending and receiving the whole message, verbal and nonverbal, we increase the likelihood for professional success and personal satisfaction.

The communication process involves much more than the spoken word and is optimized when verbal and nonverbal elements are integrated. Sending nonverbal signals congruent with our verbal messages is key.

We communicate nonverbally in several ways. By being a better listener and increasing awareness of your own tendencies to communicate nonverbally, as well as the potential meaning of others' nonverbal communication, you can increase confidence in your ability to communicate effectively.

Key Terms and Concepts

Active (or empathetic) listening

Attentive listening

Chronemics

Environment

Haptics

Kinesics

Listening

Nonverbal communication

Para-language perception

Passive listening

Proxemics

Selective perception

Sensing

Discussion Questions

1. Why is active or empathic listening so hard to do?

2. Few would argue the importance of active or empathic listening. However, there may be times when you aren't in the mood. Should a friend or loved one catch you at this time and begin sharing a problem with you, what would you do? What should you do?

3. One element of active listening is maintaining eye contact with the speaker. For various reasons, some people don't or can't do this. Why is this so and what impact might this have on communication?

4. The text discusses proxemics or the way in which we use space in communicating and how one's "safe zone" may be larger or smaller depending on the context (business or personal) and the culture. If someone were too close, how would you respond?

5. Tell us about a time when your nonverbal cues were inconsistent with what you were saying verbally. How did this affect the conversation?

6. What are some positive and negative nonverbal behaviors you've seen in other people? In yourself?

Endnotes

1. Tanya Drollinger, Lucette B. Comer, and Patricia T. Warrington, "Development and Validation of the Active Empathetic Listening Scale," *Psychology & Marketing* 23, no. 2 (February 2006), pp. 163–64.

2. Stephen Robbins and Phil Hunsaker, *Training in Interpersonal Skills* (Upper Saddle River, NJ: Prentice Hall, 2005).

3. Stephen R. Covey, *Seven Habits of Highly Effective People* (New York: Simon and Schuster, 2004).

4. See J. D. Weinrauch and J. R. Swanda Jr., "Examining the Significance of Listening: An Exploratory Study of Contemporary Management," *Journal of Business Communication* (February 1975), p. 25; and J. P. Kotter, "What Effective General Managers Really Do," *Harvard Business Review* (November–December 1982), p. 156.

5. John S. Morgan, *Interpersonal Skills for the Manager, 5th Edition, Participant's Manual* (Harrisonburg, VA: Institute of Certified Professional Managers, September 1999). Revised by Beth Z. Schneider, January 2000.

6. D. R. Haas, "Is Anybody Listening?" *Advisor Today* 97, no. 5 (2002), p. 86.

7. Winston Fletcher, "Good Listener, Better Manager," *Management Today* (January 2000), p. 30.

8. Ibid.

9. Ian Lavan, "NLP in Business—or More Than a Trip to the Zoo," *Industrial and Commercial Training* 34, no. 4/5 (2002), p. 182.

10. Siegfried L. Sporer and Barbara Schwandt, "Moderators of Nonverbal Indicators of Deception: A Meta-Analytic Synthesis," *Psychology, Public Policy, and Law* 13, no. 1 (February 2007), p. 2.

11. M. Demir, "Using Nonverbal Communication in Politics/Utilisation de la communication non-verbale dans la politique," *Canadian Social Science,* 7(5), 2011, pp. 1–4.

12. M. Demir, pp. 1–4.

13. L. Hills, "Reading and Using Body Language in Your Medical Practice: 25 Research Findings," *The Journal of Medical Practice Management (MPM)* 26, no. 6 (2011), p. 362.

14. Robin T. Peterson, "An Examination of the Relative Effectiveness of Training in Nonverbal Communication: Personal Selling Implications," *Journal of Marketing Education* 27, no. 2 (August 2005), p. 144.

15. S. Roth and T. Goss, "The Art of Listening," *Dental Economics* 90, no. 3 (2000), pp. 70–72.

Exercise 6–A
Listening via the Rumor Mill

Five volunteers will be listeners. Four of the volunteers leave the room. All others in the room serve as observers, taking note of effective or ineffective listener behaviors (i.e., paraphrasing, eye contact, interrupting the speaker). The instructor tells the first listener (A) a brief story or reads a short passage. Another volunteer (B) returns to the room. The first volunteer (A) relates the story to (B). They then have a conversation. Another volunteer (C) returns and (B) relates the story to (C). This process continues through five volunteers. The final listening volunteer (E) writes on the board what (E) recalls of the story. The volunteers compare notes—and laugh at the distortions between the first version of the story and the last!

Questions

1. How much of the original story was retained? What implications does this have for our ability to communicate effectively?

2. What types of information were easiest to remember? Why?

3. What active listening techniques were used in helping to absorb the information?

4. Which techniques that weren't used could have helped in recalling information? Give examples of how you would have used these techniques.

5. What could the senders have done to encourage active listening?

6. In what ways did the listeners change the context of the information to make it more personal or memorable according to their own needs?

Exercise 6–B
Active Listening

This exercise involves triads. Each triad counts off into threes: 1, 2, 3, 1, 2, 3, and so on. In the first round, all the 1s in their respective triads take the pro position (see topics below), all the 2s take the con position, and all the 3s act as observers. After a topic is given, two individuals representing opposing viewpoints have one minute to collect their thoughts, and then five–seven minutes to arrive at a *mutually agreeable position* on that topic.

The observer should use the form below to capture *actual examples* of what the individuals said or did that indicated active and less-than-active listening. When time is called, the pro individuals share their opinion of which listening behaviors they performed well and which ones they'd like to improve. Then the con individuals do the same. Finally, the observers share their observations and insights, using examples to reinforce their feedback.

If additional rounds are used, rotate the roles so that each person plays a speaking role, and if possible an observing role.

Round 1:

Topic selected: _____

Notes:

Round 2:

Topic selected: _____

Notes:

Listening Feedback Form

Indicators of Active Listening	Pro	Con
1. Asked questions for clarification		
2. Paraphrased the opposing view		
3. Responded to nonverbal cues (e.g., body posture, tone of voice)		
4. Appeared to move toward a mutually satisfying solution		
Indicators of Less-than-Active Listening		
5. Interrupted before allowing the other person to finish		
6. Was defensive about their position		
7. Appeared to dominate the conversation		
8. Ignored nonverbal cues		

Potential topics to be used:

1. Gun control
2. Capital punishment
3. Race as a criterion for college admission
4. Health care reform
5. U.S. intervention in wars outside of the United States
6. Legalization of marijuana
7. Mandatory armed forces draft
8. Texting while driving
9. Gay marriage
10. Work ethic differences among generations
11. Bailing out big banks
12. Allowing illegal immigrants to work in the United States

Questions

1. Did you arrive at a mutually agreeable solution? What helped you get there?
2. What were some factors that hindered this process?

3. How comfortable did you feel "arguing" the position you were given? How did this influence your ability to actively listen?

4. If the position you were given was exactly opposite your values or beliefs, do you see this topic differently now than before the exercise?

5. What steps can you take to improve your ability to listen actively to friends or associates, especially when you don't agree with their viewpoint?

**Exercise 6–C
Tools of Active
Listening**

Instructions

A. For each of the following active listening tools, write examples in the appropriate blanks.

1. Empathetic Responses

Empathy is the ability to understand things from the other person's point of view. Empathetic responses communicate acceptance and your willingness to listen to the speaker.

Use empathetic responses when

■ You want to convey acceptance and establish rapport.

■ You want to encourage the speaker to continue talking.

Example   Speaker: I am really tired of being told I am empowered to do my job when the truth of the matter is what and how I work is still highly controlled.

Listener: _____

_____

2. Restatement

Restatement is a repetition of part of the speaker's own words, to show the speaker you have received the information being communicated.

Use restatement when

■ You want to "check out" the meaning of something the speaker has said.

■ You want to encourage the speaker to explore other aspects of the matter at hand and discuss these with you.

Example   Speaker: With these changes the report will have to be redone. It's going to take at least two or three days to do it.

Listener: _____

_____

3. Paraphrasing

Paraphrasing involves stating, in your own words, your interpretation of the speaker's message.

Use paraphrasing when

■ You want to confirm that you understand the speaker's feelings and their relation to the content of the communication.

■ You want to help the speaker evaluate his or her feelings about the matter at hand.

■ You want to help the speaker reach a solution to a problem.

Example   Speaker: I'll be working on this project with Blackwell, and he's sharp technically, but he's not the easiest person in the world to work with.

Listener: _____

_____

4. Summative Statements

Summative statements condense large portions of what has been said, highlighting the key ideas.

Use summative statements when

- You want to focus the discussion.
- You want to confirm mutual understanding at a particular point in the discussion.
- You want to get agreement on certain points that have been raised in order to close the conversation.

Example   Speaker: I have some problems with this team effort. Few of us have been at every meeting, fewer still complete their action items, and we seem to be going nowhere.

Listener: _____

_____

5. Questioning Techniques

Questioning techniques are key tools in active listening. In particular, when the listener uses *open-ended* and *specifier* questions in combination, it can help the speaker express feelings and thoughts about a problem. Asking questions sends the message that you are willing to work at understanding.

Example   Speaker: The other day I heard that one of my major clients dropped us for another company.

Listener: Open-ended: _____

Specifier: _____

6. Nonverbal Behavior

Use eye contact and a shift in posture to tell the speaker that you are listening. Anticipate and block interruptions/distractions. Observe the speaker's nonverbal behavior and mentally note its message.

Example   Speaker: (Sitting a few feet from the conference table with his or her body facing away from the others, the speaker gives input only when solicited and in short, one- or two-word phrases.)

Listener: _____

_____

B. Match the following examples to their respective active listening tools.

Examples	*Active Listening Tools*
1. "As I understand it you feel . . ." "So the key ideas you expressed are . . ." "What we have agreed on is . . ."	**a.** Restatement
2. Face squarely, lean forward, uncross arms/legs, nod head, eye contact, facial expression	**b.** Summative statements
3. "Two or three days?"	**c.** Empathetic responses
4. "How did you feel about it?" "Which one?"	**d.** Paraphrasing
5. "You feel it would be difficult to get along."	**e.** Questioning techniques
6. "Uh-huh," "I see," "I understand."	**f.** Nonverbal behavior

Source: S. de Janasz, L. Johnson, M. McQuaid, A. Paulson, D. Roccia, S. Stubblefield, P. Wahl, and C. Wojick, *Fundamentals of Facilitation*, Training Manual created for Hughes Aircraft Company, 1992, pp. 4–28.

Exercise 6–D
Improving Nonverbal Observation Skills

1. Observe a TV talk show with interviews or watch a debate or speech to evaluate listening skills and nonverbal messages.

   - Facial gestures—look at their eyes, eyebrows, mouths.
   - Arm and hand gestures.
   - Feet, balance, and posture.
   - Breathing.
   - How can you tell if the moderator/facilitator is using active listening?
   - What nonverbal messages are they sending?

2. Go to a public place (shopping center, stores, fast-food restaurant) and watch how employees (salespeople, cashiers) of certain establishments interact with the customers. Observe for approximately 15 minutes and make note of the nonverbal signals they send to the customers.

   - What nonverbal messages do the customers send?
   - Do the employees read the nonverbal messages?
   - How can you tell if the customers or employees are using active listening?

3. Stand in the middle of a room or empty space and have someone walk slowly toward you. Ask that person to stop walking as soon as you begin to feel uncomfortable. Instruct him or her to move closer and further away until you are at a comfortable distance. This is your personal buffer zone.

   - Does this zone change when different people walk toward you? Explain.
   - Compare your notes with one or two others who have done this exercise. Were there differences? To what can you attribute these differences?
   - Experiment with others' buffer zones. For example, stand "too close" while waiting in line, on an elevator, or in a bus. Observe that person's response to you. (Proceed carefully . . . possibly with members of your own gender.)

Source: Adapted from Matthew McKay, Martha Davis, and Patrick Fanning, *Messages: The Communication Skills Book,* 2nd ed., Oakland, CA: New Harbinger Publications, 1995, p. 58.

Exercise 6–E
Nonverbal Role-Play

In small groups, create a role-play involving only body language with no talking. Pick a scene and characters and let the members improvise the rest. Do not overplay the scene; allow the audience to guess and make assumptions based on use of everyday nonverbal cues.

The group will present its role-play in front of the class. You may or may not set up the scene for the audience. Play out the scene for a few minutes.

Questions

1. Based on the body language, what was the scene depicting?
2. What was the relationship of the members to each other?
3. What were the personalities of the members?
4. What issues were affecting the group?
5. What emotions, behaviors, or feelings would you assume from the body language?

Source: Adapted from John Suler, Department of Psychology, Rider University, www.rider.edu/users/suler, 2000.

Exercise 6–F
Reflection/Action Plan

This chapter focused on listening and nonverbal communication—what they are, why they're important, and how to improve your skills in these areas. Complete the following worksheet upon completing all the reading and experiential activities for this chapter.

1. The one or two areas in which I am most strong are:

_____

_____

_____

_____

2. The one or two areas in which I need more improvement are:

_____

_____

_____

_____

3. If I did only one thing to improve in this area, it would be to:

_____

_____

_____

_____

4. Making this change would probably result in:

_____

_____

_____

_____

5. If I did not change or improve in this area, it would probably affect my personal and professional life in the following ways:

_____

_____

_____

_____

7 Communicating Effectively

Learning Points

How do I:

- Improve my ability to send clear messages?
- Reduce ineffective communication?
- Determine which communication medium will best serve my needs in varying situations?
- Send messages that express and address my thoughts directly?
- Get my message across in a way that doesn't cause defensiveness on the part of the receiver?

David Jameson was in a bind. After years working as a technical specialist, he was promoted to supervisor in his department. This required him to be responsible for people who at one time had been his co-workers, which created a good deal of resentment on the part of his co-workers. Yet he had business objectives to meet. Much was expected of him, and senior management was eyeing Dave for another promotion soon if all went well. After several weeks Dave discovered an unsettling communication pattern. Whenever he asked that something be done, his co-workers would nod in agreement. But when the time for the deadline came, the expected outcome hadn't happened. Just last Monday he met with Ann and Frank, telling them they needed to complete the computer drafts for the Winston project by the end of the business day on Thursday. However, the reports were still not on his desk on Friday morning. When he had finished talking to them on Monday, they had given him no response or indication that the project would not be completed on time. Dave thought he was communicating clearly. He had informed them of the deadline and simply left it at that when neither of them gave him a response. What was their problem? Dave didn't want to condescend to his subordinates by looking over their shoulders and checking on their progress, but he was afraid he might have to do this if things didn't change soon.

1. What issues are involved here? What's going on?
2. If you were one of Dave's co-workers, what would you think and how would you feel about the situation?
3. What ideas or suggestions do you have for Dave?

"The medium is the message."

Marshall McLuhan

Master communicator Marshall McLuhan said it best when he said that the medium used to send a message is just as important as the actual message, if not more so. Another way to say the same thing is "It's not just the message, it's the messenger." Both form and substance are important in the communication process. Everything you do or don't do, say or don't say, communicates something, and so does the way in which you send messages to others. As discussed in Chapter 6, communicating effectively consists of both sending and receiving messages in ways that are both verbal and nonverbal. In contemporary organizations, more than 75 percent of knowledge workers' time is spent on communication.[1] We looked at listening skills and nonverbal communication in the previous chapter; in this chapter we look at communication in greater depth—especially verbal communication: what it is, why it's important, and how to both send and receive messages effectively.

What Is Communication?

Communication is the act of exchanging thoughts, messages, or information.[2] Communication facilitates collaboration and cooperation. You communicate because you want something to happen or want to satisfy a need. In fact, the majority of your work and life is devoted to communicating with others, whether writing, reading, speaking, interacting nonverbally, or listening.

Why Is Communication Important?

The proliferation of ways to communicate has made communicating effectively more complex. Oral, written, electronic, and nonverbal communication all contribute to the way we are perceived and to our ability to relate to and work with others. Communication skills are consistently rated year after year as the most important by employers in both performance reviews and during the hiring process. In a recent survey,[3] 80 percent of companies said their employees (or prospective hires) are evaluated on their communication skills; 72 percent said critical thinking, 71 percent said collaboration, and 57 percent said creativity. Seventy-six percent said these skills and competencies—or "Four Cs"— will be very important in the next several years as the economy shifts and organizations look to expand.

The quality of an organization's communication directly impacts its bottom line. In a survey of nearly 300 respondents from numerous industries,[4] 85 percent say they believe their organization lost business due to an ineffective proposal, presentation, memo, or e-mail. On the other hand, appropriate communications can improve performance issues, reduce errors, decrease stress, improve morale, and reduce turnover.

Strategies for Effective Communication

The Communication Channel

Because most of us communicate constantly, we need to communicate effectively—to do it right. It's not easy to communicate effectively all the time. To do this takes work, effort, and practice.

As you communicate to meet your needs and goals, others form perceptions about your competence, accuracy, and sincerity. In verbal communication, your effectiveness is enhanced when the goals you set for the communication interaction are fulfilled.[5] Your communication competence can be improved by choosing the most appropriate **communication channel** to speak appropriately and effectively.

**Figure 7–1
The Communication
Channel[6]**

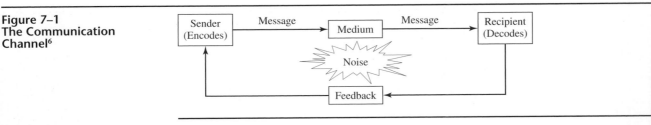

When a message needs to be sent, a communicator (the *sender*) **encodes** a message according to her or his own perceptions, experiences, and abilities. The sender then determines which communication medium is most appropriate to convey the message. The message travels across the communication channel and is then decoded by the *receiver,* who interprets (**decodes**) the message according to his or her own perceptions, abilities, and experiences.

Sending a message to a receiver is one-way communication. Two-way communication occurs when the recipient sends a message, or gives **feedback** to the sender (see Figure 7–1). Feedback is a response to a sender's behavior, and it influences the manner in which that behavior will continue or not.[7] During the feedback process the receiver puts the message back into a channel to seek clarification, confirm what the receiver thought the sender said, or check for understanding and possible misinterpretation. Feedback can be verbal or nonverbal through the use of paraphrasing, questioning, nodding, gesturing, or even eye movement.

Feedback is an essential component of two-way communication. It allows the receiver to show the sender she or he is paying attention and clearly understands the messages being sent. By listening, repeating, reaffirming, and asking questions, it is more likely the sender and receiver can understand fully what each is saying. This process doesn't guarantee agreement, but it does contribute to understanding. Two-way communication is so essential that you should consider all your business communications to be two-way, unless you are simply making an announcement or issuing an important directive that can't be challenged.

Generational Differences

Want to get your message across? Pay attention to generational differences.[8] There is a possibility you could be working in a workplace with members of up to four generations: Generation Y, born 1981–2000; Gen X, 1965–1980; Boomers, 1946–1964; and Veterans, 1922–1945. As a skilled communicator, you will want to be aware of the best ways to communicate successfully with members of each of these groups. There are some substantive differences in things like work ethic, expectations, change management, motivation to work, productivity, and work and communication styles. While it is important not to stereotype, understanding these potential differences and adapting your communication style as appropriate, will go a long way to improving your interactions with your co-workers.

Effective Media Selection

As the quote at the beginning of this chapter implies, the medium you choose to convey your message is just as important as the content of the message itself. The advertising world has long understood this principle. In the business world it is just as true that "it's not just what you say, but how you say it that counts." This saying has survived because it is so practical, so true. The medium (or media, if more than one medium is needed) selected to transmit a message can enhance or reduce the effectiveness of the message being sent. Several choices are available for communicating directly with others; they include oral, written, and electronic forms. Choosing among these forms of communication requires you to assess the message you need to send, your intended audience (from one to a hundred or more), and the response you hope to receive from the audience. Each method has its advantages and disadvantages.

- *Oral or spoken communication* tends to be the most preferred form of communication for managers. Oral communication is used when it is important to engage in discussion and come to a consensus with one or more persons, or when we are trying to communicate an explanation as well as an emotion.[9] One prominent benefit of oral communication (in person or via telephone, Skype or videoconference) is that it provides an automatic two-way exchange—both the sender(s) and receiver(s) can share information and obtain immediate feedback. This helps the sender shape the message as soon as a response is received on numerous points. Face-to-face contact is typically more effective than other types of oral communication, as both verbal and nonverbal signals are readily and simultaneously available. Since it is estimated that as much as 90 percent of communication is likely nonverbal, and impressions about the people we are communicating with are formed within minutes—or less[10]—communicating face-to-face may allow you to avoid various communication pitfalls. Through oral communication we are able to obtain immediate feedback, communicate through multiple channels (eye contact, gestures, tone of voice, etc.), speak personally rather than just organizationally, and use a more natural style of language.[11]

  On the other hand, oral communication does have its drawbacks. Communicating orally via a phone call, video conference, or meeting often results in people arriving at the exchange less prepared than if they were communicating in writing. With oral communication, it is easy for the participants to forget the major points that were made soon after the meeting concludes. Without a common written record it is likely some of the promises made won't be followed up. Oral communication activities also tend to cause the participants to experience "information overload." Communicating orally is not the best choice when a large amount of complex information must be delivered. One way to improve oral communication as a medium is to add a written component. Taking minutes during a meeting, entering personal notes about follow-up actions in a day planner, and issuing a short e-mail summarizing agreed-upon action steps and deadlines, are some of the ways oral contact can be strengthened as a medium of communication.

- *Written communication* is the most effective method for sending precise or complex information. It is also appropriate when making an announcement that does not require two-way dialogue. Written communication should not be used when the subject is controversial and requires further input from others and decisions to be made. The written document, such as a letter, contract, memo, report, or presentation, has several benefits. Written communication is an effective way to get a message to a large number of individuals in a time- and cost-efficient manner. A written document or set of documents also ensures a "paper trail"—a record of exchanges made between individuals and groups. Written communication provides a formal or official document. Most of us prefer a legal, binding contract to be in written rather than in oral form. Written evidence is far more binding than is oral recall of events. Written information can also provide a reference for later use. For example, a work team that regularly records minutes for meetings will save time at each meeting by not having to recall what was said and agreed upon in previous meetings.

  Written communication also has its drawbacks. It is too easy for us to write a long letter when a short memo would be sufficient. Written communication prevents a two-way dialogue, or results in a lengthier exchange if two-way communication is desired. In written communication it is nearly impossible to decode the nonverbals—those nuances, movements, and gestures that serve to reinforce and clarify a sender's message and intent. Written communication is also prone to misinterpretation and inaccuracy. Just because something is written doesn't mean it's necessarily true or will be correctly interpreted! To improve the effectiveness of written communication, carefully evaluate messages sent or received to determine bias, misinterpreted connotations, and hidden agendas, and seek verbal or written clarification to accurately encode or decode messages.

- *Electronic communication* is effective for sending brief messages quickly to one or more persons. It is useful for clarifying agreements that have already been reached, when fast turnaround time is needed, and when members of a team are working "virtually" (meaning they're not all in the same location). Electronic communication should not be the primary medium when the message that needs to be sent is negative, controversial, or requires additional dialogue.

Much electronic communication in the workplace now takes place via e-mail, instant messaging, texting, video conferencing, cell phones, Skype, voice-mail, social media, websites, and other Internet-reliant technology. The global person-to-person e-mail load has reached over 97 billion messages per day[12] and the number of electronic mailboxes worldwide will increase 136 percent per year for the near future.[13] Electronic communication should carry the same amount of professionalism as traditional communication forms, including proper spelling, punctuation, capitalization, and grammar.[14]

While some of these avenues can be extremely fast, accurate, and efficient, they still require judgment, discretion, and "people skills" to be used correctly. New technology presents unique challenges in communication not only in speed and distance, but in evaluating the audience, which can comprise one or hundreds of individuals, with virtually little knowledge or understanding of the receiver(s). Due to the relative ease of sending a message, many senders neglect the need for careful execution of their communication. How many of us have read about the guy who jilted his girlfriend in favor of another via e-mail—only to find he had sent the "jilt" e-mail to the new girlfriend and the "amorous" e-mail to his old girlfriend! Or the CEO of a prominent entertainment company who confessed in a commencement speech that he had unintentionally sent the company's disappointing quarterly earnings report to representatives of the media rather than to his board.

(Office sign reads, "14 Days Since the Last Inappropriate E-mail".)

Source: http://www.cartoonbank.com/2003/office-sign-reads-14-days-since-the-last-inappropriate-e-mail/invt/126817/?

The use of social media such as blogs, Facebook, Renren, Weibo, Twitter, and so on is growing at rapid speed. People are sharing personal information about themselves with more people in greater detail than ever before. From a personal and professional perspective, it is highly important to "think" before you text or post information about yourself or others on the Web. The old adage "Don't say anything you wouldn't want to see in the newspaper tomorrow" holds true for social media. Social media channels encourage spur-of-the-moment, "stream-of-consciousness" communication and provide no "brake" to give the sender time to reflect on how his or her comments might be interpreted by those who read them. Rapid messaging also opens the door for people to say things about others that can be offensive or hurtful. In using social media, as in all forms of communication, take time to reflect on how what you say will be interpreted by others. Don't put anything—words or photos—on the Web that can come back to haunt you later when you are in interviews or working for a company or organization. Once it's online, it's there forever.

Managing Workflow

A word of caution: On average, knowledge workers spend three hours or more per day handling incoming information. Approximately half (or more) of this time is spent handling e-mail. How much time do you spend per day on e-mail? Managers are averaging at least one and a half hours per day simply responding to simple e-mails, not to mention the time needed to answer more complex e-mails, deal with attachments, set up meetings, gather data, and so on.[15] Eighty-five percent of respondents to one survey said managing daily information workflow was a challenge, and the vast majority said it is tougher than ten years ago.[16] Individuals and companies can help by using face-to-face communications when possible, deleting or giving lower priority to e-mails that don't require attention, and limiting work time to dealing with work-related information, saving personal communications for post–work time.

Thoughtful use of electronic forms of communication will help you develop effective communication skills. One of the first rules of using electronic communication is to "remember the human." Do not forget that on the other end of the quick response to an e-mail is another human being who will interpret the message. Our online actions and messages affect people. Electronic messages can lose the emotional aspect of the message in both content and tone, opening the door to miscommunications. Electronic communication also has the potential downside of reducing the quality and amount of human interaction. E-mail can reduce the amount of interaction between organizational members and promote nonpersonal communication. Figure 7–2 provides some tips for using—and not using—electronic communication.

Figure 7–2
Professional Communication: DOs and DON'Ts

- DO keep your address list up-to-date. DON'T set aside until "later" letters and messages you receive from colleagues giving you their new contact information.
- DO send business-related messages during work hours. DON'T send or receive personal text or e-mail messages during work hours.
- DO write concisely, stick to a single topic, use a clear subject line, and identify goals in the first paragraph.
- DON'T mix personal matters with business-focused content.[17]
- DON'T send lengthy e-mails or e-mails covering more than just one or two topics.
- DO remember that anything you "say" in an e-mail or on a social media site can potentially be "seen" by many others. DON'T say anything that is personally negative about or potentially damaging to another person in an e-mail, text, or post.
- DO have a personal e-mail account separate from your account at work or school. DON'T use your work account for both business and personal purposes.
- DO send brief messages to announce noncontroversial information or to confirm something that's already been agreed to. DON'T send lengthy announcements or messages about something that is best handled through face-to-face discussion or debate.
- DO send appreciative notes to people with copies to their supervisors. DON'T give negative feedback via e-mail.
- DO copy your boss on important messages that are relevant to him or her. DON'T leave your boss and significant members of your team out of the loop. DON'T go over your boss's head, even though you have access to the personal e-mail address of her or his boss.
- DO keep a hard copy of important documents for the record. DON'T keep paper copies of all e-mails sent and received (archive electronically).
- DO clarify important details verbally. DON'T rely on e-mail communication for important matters (the person you're writing to might be out of town).
- DO send personalized e-mails. DON'T send mass e-mails, or if you do, don't include everyone's address at the top—that's giving away sensitive information. Send your message to yourself and blind copy it to the others.
- DO use proper grammar and syntax, and use capitalization and punctuation appropriately. DON'T substitute casual language for specific business vocabulary in professional e-mails.
- DON'T type in all caps—this is the equivalent of yelling.
- DO use a polite tone—remember the reader can't hear your voice or see your nonverbal meaning.

Improving Public Speaking[18]

- Prioritize preparation.
  - Calm your nerves by showing up prepared.
- Alter your outlook.
  - Think positively about the message you believe in passionately and that you get to share with your audience.
- Make peace with quiet.
  - Calm your nerves by realizing you can pause to take a breath during presentations.
- Embrace the short and sweet.
  - The average listening span is 20 minutes—don't talk too long, as many speakers do.
- Embody energy.
  - Show up with high energy to deliver a presentation that will engage your audience.
- Engage in eye contact.
  - Make a connection with the audience rather than just speaking to them.
- Turn to TED.
  - Watch some of the highest rated "TED" talks to observe dynamic, high-quality speakers in action.
- Rinse and repeat.
  - The more you speak publicly, the better you will get.

Information Richness and Media Selection

We make media choices based on our perception of which choice will result in effective communication. Higher performing managers are more sensitive to communication situations than lower performing colleagues.[19]

Take into consideration the complexity of the message to determine which medium will be appropriate for disseminating your message. One means to evaluate which medium to select is **information richness**, the potential information-carrying capacity of data. Data that provide substantial new understanding would be considered rich. On the other hand, if the data provide relatively little understanding or common information, they would be considered low in richness.[20]

When you need to convey more complicated or nonroutine information, a richer channel of media will be more effective. Face-to-face communication is the richest form of communication. It allows for immediate, two-way feedback and includes visual and audio cues. Face-to-face communication also is highly personal and its source is directly from the individual or natural source. Written announcements or reports are some of the lowest channels of richness. They tend to discourage or slow the feedback process, are very impersonal, are sourced from pure data and information, and are limited to visual cues. Leaner channels are more appropriate when the information is routine or straightforward.

As you consider what you intend to communicate and the amount of richness or information to be transmitted in the message, evaluate potential media choices by using these factors:

- *Feedback:* Does the medium allow for two-way communication and contain the ability and speed necessary to provide the requisite feedback?
- *Channel:* Does the medium allow for multiple cues ranging from combined visual and audio to limited visual?
- *Type of communication:* Does the medium allow for emotional or personal connection; is it personal or impersonal?
- *Language source:* Is the information from a natural source or body source (an individual) or is it from a purely data or numeric source?

These selection factors will help you choose the appropriate medium. One survey of executives has shown the most effective communication is personalized, evokes an emotional response, comes from a trustworthy or respected source, and is concise.[21] Depending on the content of the message, multiple media may be necessary to ensure effective communication.

Effective Writing[22]

- Gather the information that will help you to have a deep understanding of the topic(s) about which you are writing, using the Internet, articles, research, personal notes, and so on.
- Organize your thoughts, grouping similar ideas together.
- Focus the message to ensure you are capturing the priority concepts.
- Draft the document without taking time to edit—let your ideas flow (you can edit and refine later).
- Edit the document, preferably from a printed version so you can see the overall strategy and flow.

Barriers to Effective Communication

As anyone who has ever been in an argument or had difficulty getting a message across knows, communicating is a complex skill, and there are many obstacles to getting it right. One of the reasons for this is that in communication, "noise" and potential barriers exist. **Noise** is any distortion factor that blocks, disrupts, or distorts the message sent to the receiver, interfering with the communication process.[23] These distortion factors can range from emotional states or language differences to telephone static or an inaccessible e-mail system. Using American slang when discussing the results of a new product design with an international colleague could lead to a distortion of meaning, which would constitute noise. Barriers to effective communication may be interpersonal or organizational. Interpersonal barriers can include perceptions, semantics, media selection, and inconsistent verbal/nonverbal cues. Organizational barriers include physical distraction, information overload, time pressure, overly technical language, or the absence of established communication channels.[24]

Even good communication processes contain noise; it is inherent in all forms of communication. One way to improve your communication skills is to become aware of these barriers to communication and learn how to minimize or reduce their adverse effects.

Information Overload

As human beings, most of us have the ability to process only so much information. The sheer volume of incoming information from various electronic media is increasing faster than we can reasonably absorb it. **Information overload** occurs when the volume of information a person receives exceeds his or her capacity to process it.[25] A recent survey revealed that information overload was a leading cause of computer-related stress (technostress).[26] Some of the behaviors that can cause information overload for the receiver of your messages are listed below.

- *Presenting too much material:* Keep the information to an amount that the person or persons with whom you are speaking can easily absorb. Check for understanding and pause frequently, giving the person time to formulate clarifying questions and indicate to you that he or she understands what you are saying.
- *Presenting information that is overly complex:* When feasible, practice your main message or messages ahead of time, ensuring you will deliver the message succinctly and coherently. If necessary, back up your words with visuals, or send data or a summary report ahead of time.

- *Presenting information too quickly:* Deliver your message slowly, in an organized fashion, focusing on just a couple of points at a time.

- *Presenting at a level of difficulty that goes beyond the person's understanding:* Always know your audience. If you don't, begin your message with a few overview comments and perhaps some questions to determine how much information the receiver already has on the subject.

- *Not giving the person sufficient time to process the information:* Give your listeners an opportunity to ask questions and to provide their perspective before asking for a decision. When possible, try to hold off on a decision until all the necessary information is available, perhaps at another time.

Emotions

Another factor that can hinder effective communication is **emotions** or emotional states. Emotions are strong feelings such as fear, love, hate, happiness, and anger. Because emotion is the opposite of reason, it is difficult to anticipate, predict, control, or read emotion in yourself and in others. Emotions are neither right nor wrong, but rather an expression of human reactions. However, communicating emotionally can prevent you from being objective about a situation. To reduce the potential for miscommunication, consider the emotional state of both the sender and the receiver in all interactions with others. In most business situations, it's best if both parties can remain as open and objective as possible. This is not to say emotions will be nonexistent. However, it is wise to understand the potential effects emotional states can have on the communication process. A good rule of thumb is to stop and think. This might seem simple, but it requires an amount of self-discipline. Assess the impact of what you are about to say on the other person. Say things that won't offend others to avoid diverting their attention, which interferes with your ability to make a point. It is a good idea to leave a discussion and return to it later if you find yourself so emotional about the subject that your feelings are getting in the way of your being able to communicate. Similarly, if a person is reacting emotionally to something you are saying, it's a good idea to part and regroup later if possible (note: this only works with colleagues, not your boss).

Trust and Credibility

As we noted in chapter 2, *lack of trust* is a huge barrier to effective communication. For example, if a company begins to lay off workers after having told them layoffs would not occur, those employees will be less likely to believe anything else their managers tell them. If you need to communicate with someone with whom trust has been broken, take the time to talk with the person, listening to his or her concerns and emphasizing the importance of the long-term relationship. If possible, wait until trust has been rebuilt before asking for a decision or insisting on the person's cooperation.

Lack of credibility prevents the listener from fully receiving your message. The receiver can hear your words, but won't believe you or acknowledge your perspective because he or she questions your knowledge base. New entrants into the workforce often experience this problem with more senior workers who may question their expertise. The best way to build credibility is to prepare, prepare, prepare. The more thoroughly you have done your homework before approaching someone with an issue or solution, the more likely you are to be well received.

Know Your Audience's Culture

In chapter 5, we looked at cross-cultural differences in terms of things like power distance, uncertainty avoidance, collectivism, gender, and short-term orientation. Take these factors into account as you assess whether e-mail is appropriate or not for your audience and goals. For example, depending on one's culture:[27]

- Some individuals rely on interpersonal relationships and are less likely to trust business partners with whom they have only an electronic relationship.
- Some individuals may hesitate to request clarification for fear of losing face.

- Some individuals may assume a communication is just a suggestion, not a final decision.
- Some people may expect a high level of formality in e-mail "**netiquette**" (Internet etiquette).
- Spamming (advertising), dissing (speaking ill of someone), flaming (insulting), or shouting (using all capital letters) may be unacceptable in some cultural contexts.
- Humor and sarcasm, acceptable in some cultures, may be offensive to others.

Time

Lack of time is a major concern for practically all of us, whether you're a student, home-maker, parent, or manager (or all of the above!). Poor communication often results from lack of time. Being in a hurry does not lend itself to thorough responses or decision making. Rushing to communicate often leads to making errors, leaving out important details, or saying things you later regret. The best way to approach this problem is to develop a habit of focusing on just one communication at a time. This flies in the face of the "multitasking" environment so favored in many industries today, wherein employees are encouraged and expected to perform multiple tasks simultaneously. While not everyone can or prefers to multitask, studies suggest that multitasking causes a good deal of stress. Focusing your attention on one communication at a time will reduce errors and improve the quality of your communication. For example, when sending an e-mail message, take time to proofread it before sending it. When on the telephone, devote full attention to your listener and resist putting him or her on hold or call waiting (except in an emergency). When conducting a meeting, close the door to the meeting room to reduce distractions. You can't always adhere to these principles, especially if you work in an "open" office environment. But when what's being said or who's saying it is very important to you, it's worth doing it right.

Another communication problem related to time is today's increased expectation of speedy response. The use of texting and 24/7 access to e-mail due to mobile devices have resulted in a "just in time" mentality in the workplace. It used to take first-class mail three to four days to arrive at a destination. It wasn't uncommon for a manager to answer a letter within the next week or even two. Today, that's hardly practical. Generally an e-mail message, phone message, or drop-by conversation in the office hallway carries with it the expectation of an almost immediate response. This can pose problems for you as the number of messages that need handling simultaneously mounts. Many successful managers are finding it helps to batch their communications or group their responses by category. For example, you can attempt to set aside time each day for responding to and sending e-mail messages, a different time for responding to and making phone calls, and yet a different time of day for quick hallway conversations with co-workers. Of course this won't always be possible, but by setting some limits on the way you respond to these inquiries, you'll have a better chance of responding to each contact appropriately, accurately, and within a reasonable period of time.

Filtering

Filtering is the intentional manipulation of information to make it more favorable to the receiver. The way information is sent, the tone, and the framing of the material can greatly distort a message to serve an individual's or a group's needs. Filtering can make objective decision making difficult because the true message is never accurately sent or received. For example, a manager afraid of offending his subordinates may sugarcoat a message about the need to work overtime by leaving out information that clarifies why the work can't wait. Or an employee might inform a manager of errors, but leave out details on the extensive amount of damage that occurred. To resist filtering when you speak, present information based on the relevant facts. Deliver information sensitively but firmly and honestly. To prevent receiving filtered information, ask probing questions about a situation that's being presented to you. Ask follow-up questions about each detail that is of interest to you, focusing on results and outcomes, not just the facts that have been presented.

Message Incongruency   As stated earlier, the communication process is much more than just the spoken word. In our interactions, we form our impressions about others based on many factors, including the various forms of direct and indirect information available to us. This reinforces the need for you to send verbal and nonverbal messages congruently.

Eye Contact

Want to improve your overall communication effectiveness? Work on your eye contact. Adults make eye contact between 30 percent and 60 percent of the time. But people should be making eye contact 60–70 percent of the time. One barrier to doing this is the use of mobile devices—which, among twentysomethings, has become culturally acceptable. Yet eye contact can be a tool for influencing others. People who are high-status tend to look longer at people they're talking to. People who avert their gaze too soon may be missing out because they are possibly perceived as untrustworthy or nervous.[28]

Assertive Communication

One way to increase your communications skills is to practice the art of assertive communication. **Assertive communication** is a form of communication in which you both speak up for your rights *and* take into account the rights and feelings of others.[29] Assertive communication includes:

- Fairness
- Directness
- Tact and sensitivity
- Honesty

The purpose of assertive communication is to keep contact lines open and show respect for others while affirming your beliefs and preferences. Unfortunately, many of us feel uncomfortable being assertive; some falsely equate assertiveness with aggressiveness and instead use passive styles of communication.[30]

Passive communication includes indirectness, avoiding conflict, being easily persuaded/bullied, being overly concerned about pleasing others, and screening or withholding your thoughts and feelings to the extent that the person with whom you're communicating has no idea of your real opinion on the matter being addressed. We use passive communication when we are fearful of losing someone's affection or have low self-esteem, when we are in a situation where we have little control, or when we have decided the issue isn't worth taking a stand. Frowning, crying, whispering under your breath, or simply saying nothing are all ways you demonstrate passive communication. Usually the primary purpose of responding passively to a person or situation is to avoid confrontation at all costs. Passive communication is usually not recommended, as it seldom results in getting what you really want. It can be useful, however, if avoidance is truly desirable, such as when you're in an organization where you have chosen not to speak up about everything with which you disagree.

Aggressive communication includes exerting control over others, humiliating others, dominating, being pushy, always needing to be right, using absolute terms, and blaming others.[31] Aggressive communication is often unclear because it is emotionally charged, reactive, and sometimes irrational.[32] We respond aggressively when we want to be in control, are insecure, are afraid, don't value the opinions of others, or have unresolved anger. The purpose of aggressive behavior is to win or dominate—to prove one is right and others are wrong. Aggressive communication is usually not recommended, as it results in a win–lose situation where you get your way at the expense of someone else. It can be appropriate, however, if you are in an extreme situation that dictates the need for an aggressive response, such as directions in crisis management or a physical attack.

Assertive communication is usually the most appropriate communication style. There are times when we all feel somewhat passive or even aggressive. But for the most part, it's a good idea to learn to be firm about your needs and to insist on those needs being met. Have you ever had a roommate who ate your food or wore your clothes without asking? A boss who wouldn't give you a much-deserved raise? A family member who consistently lied? How did you handle this? Assertive communication will provide you with the ability to pass on information accurately and intelligently and to accomplish objectives while still having respect for others and not making them feel "put down."

Nearly all of us have been involved in group projects, whether in school, business, or community organizations. Many of us have also been in groups where one member (or more) contributes little or nothing to the task. What do you do? Do you ignore the situation, hoping that (1) it will improve, or (2) someone else will deal with the nonperformer? Using assertive communication may help you to remedy these and similar situations.

How to Communicate Assertively

There are three parts to developing an assertive statement:[33]

- Your *perspective/perception* of the situation: In your own words, what is the issue or situation as you see it? For example, "I've noticed that the common areas are frequently messy and dirty."

- Your *feelings* about the situation: Describe how the situation makes you feel without placing blame on others. For example, "I feel frustrated since I am holding up my end of the deal, yet others don't seem to do theirs."

- Your *wants* regarding the situation or outcome: Own your request for a resolution by using "I" instead of "you." "I would like to revisit our roommate agreement and come up with a plan that we all can live with regarding the cleanliness of our apartment."

Taking Responsibility and "I" Messages

An element of assertive communicating involves "taking responsibility." It is human nature to try to assess or make sense of our and others' behavior. However, the assumptions we make about the behavior of others are not necessarily consistent with reality; instead, your assumptions reflect your own values and beliefs. When conversing with another person, remember to clarify assumptions, and be willing to accept at least some of the responsibility for any ambiguity in the communication. Ways to take responsibility and clarify assumptions are:[34]

- *Specify the behavior(s)* on which the assumption is based: "Your facial expression suggests to me that I may not have made my point very clearly," rather than "Are you following what I'm saying?"

- If your assumption is based on your own expectation of the listener's behavior, *state that expectation specifically*; do not assume the listener knows the details of your expectation: "I'm expecting that report next Monday at 4:00. Can we agree on that?" rather than "Is that report going to be done on time?"

- If your assumption compares the listener's behavior with that of other members of a reference group, *clarify that group and exactly how the behavior compares*: "The other members of the department always submit their weekly production reports on Monday, and each of your last four reports wasn't submitted until Thursday," rather than "You didn't submit your weekly production reports promptly."

- *Elicit feedback about your assumptions*. Ask the listener to tell you whether the assumption is accurate: "Am I correct in assuming that you've already begun writing the report that's due next Monday?"

Another element of assertive communication is the use of "I statements."[35] Most of the messages we send to people about their behavior are "you" messages—messages that are directed at the other person and have a high probability of putting them down, making them feel guilty, making them feel their needs are not important, making them defensive, and generally making them resist change. Examples of "you" messages are usually orders or commands ("Stop doing that! Get in the car!"), blaming or name-calling statements ("You are acting like a baby! You are driving me crazy!"), or statements that give solutions ("You should forget that idea. You better reconsider your plan"). Statements like these tend to remove the responsibility for behavior change from the other person. Some call this being "should on."[36] Perhaps the worst example of a "you" message is the "if . . . then" threat: for example, "If you don't . . . then I will . . ."

Conversely, an "I" message allows a person who is affected by the behavior of another to express the impact it has on him or her and leave the responsibility for modifying the behavior with the person who demonstrated that particular behavior. An "I" message consists of three parts:

- The specific behavior.
- The resulting feeling you experienced because of the behavior.
- The tangible effect on you.

Thus, a teacher might say to a student: "When you tap on your desk with your pencil, I get distracted and have difficulty teaching," rather than "You had better stop tapping your pencil!" Or a wife might say to her husband: "When I try to talk and you don't say anything, I don't know how you feel about helping me," rather than "You never talk to me!" In effect, the "I" message removes the possibility of defensiveness and allows the sender to project, "I trust you to decide what change in behavior is necessary." "I" messages build relationships and don't place the sender in the position of enforcing a new behavior, as is frequently the case with "you" messages.

"Mend your speech a little, lest it may mar your fortunes."

William Shakespeare, *King Lear*

Sending Messages Effectively

The better your communication, the better your performance, interactions with co-workers, and relationships with others in your personal life. Sixty percent or more of business communication is ineffective in achieving its intended purpose.[37] Figure 7–3 provides some suggestions for increasing your skills in communicating effectively.

Figure 7–3
Tips for Sending Effective Verbal Messages

- *Be direct:* others may not pick up on your hints or may misinterpret them.
- *Consider your audience:* communicate with them in terms of their interests, values, and backgrounds.
- *Be clear:* don't ask questions when you need to make a statement. Focus on one thing at a time; know your purpose and have an objective; think and organize your thoughts before speaking.
- *Watch the nonverbal aspects of communicating:* make your facial expression and gestures congruent with your verbal statements.
- *Pay attention to the receivers:* watch for their nonverbal clues, not just what they're saying.
- As necessary, *be redundant:* repeat when needed or restate something to make it clearer to the receiver.
- *Communicate bit by bit:* make the pieces sufficiently understandable individually and as a whole.
- *Use varying techniques to send your message;* we all process information differently and have varying learning styles.
  - Some are *auditory*—they have to hear it to learn it.
  - Some are *visual*—they need to read it or see it on paper.
  - Some are *kinesthetic*—they need to have hands-on use or personal practice to learn.
  - Some are *didactic*—they ask questions and get full background info before processing what others are saying.
- *Cover your bases:* write it, review it, demonstrate it, and defend it.
- *Build in feedback and check for understanding:* encourage and incorporate means that allow others to know you want feedback. They are unlikely to do it automatically. Ask for feedback and clarification.
- *Be straightforward* with no hidden agenda or lies: deal with issues straight-on and in a timely manner, often, and openly.
- *Be supportive:* avoid labels, sarcasm, dragging up the past, negative comparisons, and "you" messages and threats.

Summary

What and how you communicate affects your behavior as well as that of others. Through effective communication, you develop better relationships and ultimately better organizational performance.

Communication is not as easy as it might seem. Developing skills in communicating with others is important for managerial success as well as success in your personal relationships. If you have a high degree of proficiency in communicating, people will be able to interpret your messages clearly. Part of communicating is being able to communicate assertively. By sending messages clearly, seeking and giving feedback fairly, and working to overcome obstacles to effective communication, you increase the likelihood of personal and professional success.

Key Terms and Concepts

Aggressive communication	Feedback
Assertive communication	Filtering
Communication	Information overload
Communication channel	Information richness
Decode	Netiquette
Emotions	Noise
Encode	Passive communication

Discussion Questions

1. With so much communication occurring online today—in fact, it's not unusual to find people in adjacent offices using e-mail to communicate to one another—what are some ways to ensure your message is received as it was intended?

2. Which of the common barriers to communication have you experienced? Discuss how they impact the communication process and ways to overcome them.

3. Picture this. It's Sunday morning, a few hours before the annual company picnic. The wife, while ironing her dress, asks her husband, "Do we *really* have to go to the picnic today?" The husband responds, "Yes." Is there a communication breakdown, and if so, who is responsible?

4. Picture this. Your roommate is a total slob. Today, you've decided you've had enough and piled all his or her dirty clothes on his or her bed and vacuumed the room you share. What message did your roommate receive from this gesture? Was this effective? Why or why not?

Endnotes

1. Younghwa Lee, Kenneth A. Kozar, and Kai R. Larsen, "Does Avatar Email Improve Communication?" *Communications of the ACM* 48, no. 12 (December 2005), p. 92.

2. Vickie Wickhorst and Gary Geroy, "Physical Communication and Organization Development," *Organization Development Journal* 24, no. 3 (Fall 2006), p. 56.

3. S. Peckham, "Technically Speaking," *Tech Directions* 70, no. 1 (2010), p. 4.

4. "Information Mapping, Inc. Survey Reveals the True Impact of Ineffective Business Communications, *Business Wire* (press release), December 7, 2006. http://www.businesswire.com/news/home/20061207005429/en/Information-Mapping-Survey-Reveals-True-Impact-Ineffective.

5. Stephanie A. Westmyer, Rachel L. DiCioccio, and Rebecca B. Rubin, "Appropriateness and Effectiveness of Communication Channels in Competent Interpersonal Communication," *Journal of Communication* 48, no. 3 (Summer 1998), pp. 27–30.

6. D. K. Berlo, *The Process of Communication* (New York: Holt, Rinehart and Winston, 1960), pp. 30–32.

7. Stephanie A. Watts, "Evaluative Feedback: Perspectives on Media Effects," *Journal of Computer-Mediated Communication* 12, no. 2 (January 2007), p. 385.

8. Barry P. Haynes, "The Impact of Generational Differences on the Workplace," *Journal of Corporate Real Estate* 13, no. 2 (2011), pp. 99–104.

9. Marek P. Pfeil, Alison B. Setterberg, and James S. O'Rourke IV, "The Art of Downsizing: Communicating Lay-Offs to Key Stakeholders," *Journal of Communication Management* 8, no. 2 (2003), p. 135.

10. M. Demir, "Using Nonverbal Communication in Politics/Utilisation de la communication non-verbale dans la politique," *Canadian Social Science* 7, no. 5 (2011), p. 1.

11. D. Turner, "Orally-Based Information," *Journal of Documentation* 66, no. 3 (2010), p. 373.

12. E. Y. Huang and S. W. Lin, "Do Knowledge Workers Use E-mail Wisely?," *The Journal of Computer Information Systems* 50, no. 1 (2009), p. 65.

13. Ibid., p. 65.

14. Nelda Spinks, Barron Wells, and Melanie Meche, "Netiquette: A Behavioral Guide to Electronic Business Communication," *Corporate Communications* 4, no. 3 (1999), p. 145.

15. Huang and Lin, p. 66.

16. R. Orlik, "Technology Feeds Client Demands but Overload Affects Partner Productivity," *Legal Week* 14, no. 5 (2012), p. 8.

17. Thomas Clark, "Teaching Students to Write Effective Email," *The Business Review* 5, no. 1 (September 2006), pp. 141–42.

18. Brooke Howell, "Eight Ways to Improve Public Speaking," *Monster Worldwide, Inc.,* as seen in *The Denver Post,* Sunday, May 26, 2013, p. 7K.

19. Jeanine Warisse Turner, Jean A. Grube, Catherine H. Tinsley, Cynthia Lee, and Cheryl O'Pell, "Exploring the Dominant Media: How Does Media Use Reflect Organizational Norms and Affect Performance?" *The Journal of Business Communication* 43, no. 3 (July 2006), p. 226.

20. R. L. Daft and R. H. Lengel, "Information Richness: A New Approach to Managerial Behavior and Organizational Design," *Research in Organizational Behavior* (Greenwich, CT: JAI Press, 1984), p. 196.

21. Stuart Crainer and Des Dearlove, "The Write Stuff," *Business Strategy Review* 15, no. 4 (Winter 2004), p. 20.

22. Mary Munter, *Guide to Managerial Communication,* 5th ed. (Upper Saddle River, NJ: Prentice Hall, 2000), pp. 37–42.

23. Dawn Kelly, "Using Vision to Improve Organisational Communication," *Leadership & Organization Development Journal* 21, no. 1/2 (2000), p. 93.

24. Ibid., pp. 93–94.

25. Gail Fann Thomas and Cynthia L. King, "Reconceptualizing E-Mail Overload," *Journal of Business and Technical Communication* 20, no. 3 (July 2006), p. 255.

26. Richard Gendreau, "The New Techno Culture in the Workplace and at Home," *Journal of American Academy of Business, Cambridge* 11, no. 2 (September 2007), p. 193.

27. Anne S. Davis, Penny A. Leas, and John A. Dobelman, "Did You Get My E-mail? An Exploratory Look at Intercultural Business Communication by E-mail," *Multinational Business Review* 17, no. 1 (2009), pp. 76–77.

28. Sue Shellenbarger, "The Workplace Perils of Staring at Our Phones and Elsewhere; the Ideal Gaze Lasts 7–10 Seconds," *Wall Street Journal,* Wednesday, May 29, 2013, p. D1.

29. Matthew McKay, Martha Davis, and Patrick Fanning, *Messages: The Communication Skills Book,* 2nd ed. (Oakland, CA: Harbinger Publications, 1995).

30. R. E. Alberti and M. L. Emmons, *Your Perfect Right: A Guide to Assertive Behavior* (San Luis Obispo, CA: Impact Publishers, 1995).

31. Stephen Robbins and Phil Hunsaker, *Training in Interpersonal Skills* (Upper Saddle River, NJ: Prentice Hall, 1996).

32. Suzanne Updegraff, "Maximizing Human Potential: Tips to Foster Personal Effectiveness," *Employment Relations Today* 31, no. 1 (2004), p. 48.

33. McKay et al., *Messages,* p. 128.

34. This is adapted from an exercise in J. William Pfeiffer and John E. Jones, *Structured Experiences Kit,* entitled "Taking Responsibility," C-CAE/0-15 (San Francisco, CA: Jossey-Bass Pfeiffer, 1980).

35. Ibid.

36. Morris E. Massey, *The People Puzzle: Understanding Yourself and Others* (Reston, VA: Reston/ Prentice Hall, 1979).

37. J. Hoia, "Internal Communication in the Small and Medium Sized Enterprises," *E+M Economie a Management* 3 (2012), p. 34.

Exercise 7–A
Completing the
Channel—Two-way
Communication

The sender will sit or stand facing away from the group. (If the sender can be hidden from sight, this would be helpful.) The sender will then proceed to describe a series of objects to the class. The participants are to draw what they believe is being described to them as accurately as possible. Participants are not allowed to ask questions or have any discussion with the sender. They are to work on their own and make no audible responses. (The instructor will record how long the first activity took, and participants are to write down how many objects they think they have drawn correctly.)

The sender will now face the group and proceed to describe another series of objects. The participants are to draw the objects as best they can from the description. This time participants are allowed to ask questions and discuss the objects with the sender. The instructor will write down the length of time the second activity took.

Questions

1. What happened during the drawing of the first objects? How did you respond? How did you feel doing the task? How many of the objects did you actually get right?

2. What happened during the drawing of the second objects? How did you respond? Did you ask for any clarifications? How did you feel doing the task? How many did you actually get right?

3. From the class results, what assumptions can be made in comparing one-way versus two-way communication? Does it take more time to communicate effectively?

Source: Exercise is adapted from Harold J. Leavitt, *Managerial Psychology* (Chicago: University of Chicago Press, 1958), pp. 118–28.

Exercise 7–B
The Assertion
Inventory

Many people experience difficulty in handling interpersonal situations requiring them to assert themselves in some way; for example, turning down a request, asking a favor, giving someone a compliment, expressing disapproval or approval, and so on. Please indicate your degree of discomfort or anxiety in the space provided *before* each situation listed below. Utilize the following scale to indicate degree of discomfort:

1 = none

2 = a little

3 = a fair amount

4 = much

5 = very much

Then, go over the list a second time and indicate *after* each item the probability or likelihood of your displaying the behavior if actually presented with the situation.* For example, if you rarely apologize when you are at fault, you would mark a "4" after that item. Utilize the following scale to indicate response probability:

1 = always do it

2 = usually do it

3 = do it about half the time

4 = rarely do it

5 = never do it

*Note: It is important to cover your discomfort ratings (located in front of the items) while indicating response probability. Otherwise, one rating may contaminate the other and a realistic assessment of your behavior is unlikely. To correct for this, place a piece of paper over your discomfort ratings while responding to the situations a second time for response probability.

Degree of Discomfort	SITUATION	Response Probability
_____	1. Turn down a request to borrow your car	_____
_____	2. Compliment a friend	_____
_____	3. Ask a favor of someone	_____
_____	4. Resist sales pressure	_____
_____	5. Apologize when you are at fault	_____
_____	6. Turn down a request for a meeting or date	_____
_____	7. Admit fear and request consideration	_____
_____	8. Tell a person you are intimately involved with when he/she says or does something that bothers you	_____
_____	9. Ask for a raise	_____
_____	10. Admit ignorance in some areas	_____
_____	11. Turn down a request to borrow money	_____
_____	12. Ask personal questions	_____
_____	13. Turn off a talkative friend	_____
_____	14. Ask for constructive criticism	_____
_____	15. Initiate a conversation with a stranger	_____
_____	16. Compliment a person you are romantically involved with or interested in	_____
_____	17. Request a meeting or a date with a person	_____
_____	18. Ask for a meeting when your initial request was turned down	_____
_____	19. Admit confusion about a point under discussion and ask for clarification	_____
_____	20. Apply for a job	_____
_____	21. Ask whether you have offended someone	_____
_____	22. Tell someone that you like them	_____
_____	23. Request expected service when such is not forthcoming, e.g., in a restaurant	_____
_____	24. Discuss openly with the person his/her criticism of your behavior	_____
_____	25. Return defective items, e.g., store or restaurant	_____
_____	26. Express an opinion that differs from that of the person you are talking to	_____
_____	27. Resist sexual overtures when you are not interested	_____
_____	28. Tell the person when you feel he/she has done something that is unfair to you	_____
_____	29. Accept a date	_____
_____	30. Tell someone good news about yourself	_____
_____	31. Resist pressure to drink	_____
_____	32. Resist a significant person's unfair demands	_____
_____	33. Quit a job	_____
_____	34. Resist pressure to do drugs	_____
_____	35. Discuss openly with the person his/her criticism of your work	_____
_____	36. Request the return of a borrowed item	_____
_____	37. Receive compliments	_____
_____	38. Continue to converse with someone who disagrees with you	_____
_____	39. Tell a friend or someone with whom you work when he/she says or does something that bothers you	_____
_____	40. Ask a person who is annoying you in a public situation to stop	_____

Lastly, please indicate the situations you would like to handle more assertively by placing a circle around the item number.

Add the total scores for each column.

Degree of Discomfort _____   Response Probability _____

Source: From Gambrill, E. D. and Richey, C. A., in *Behavior Therapy,* 1975, vol. 6, pp. 550–61. All Rights Reserved.

Assertiveness
Inventory Scoring Grid

Response Probability

		Low (105+)	High (40–104)
High (96+)		UNASSERTIVE	ANXIOUS PERFORMER
Degree of Discomfort			
Low (40–95)		??? DON'T CARE	ASSERTIVE

Exercise 7–C
Communication Styles

For the following situations describe a passive, aggressive, and assertive statement or response. Discuss the potential consequences for each.

I. You've been standing in line at the bookstore for over an hour and someone cuts in front of you.

Passive response

_____

_____

Aggressive response

_____

_____

Assertive response

_____

_____

II. You live in an apartment with three other people. One person is very messy and sloppy, leaving dishes on the table and in the sink, eating your food, leaving garbage in all rooms of the apartment.

Passive response

_____

_____

Aggressive response

_____

_____

Assertive response

_____

_____

III. A telemarketer calls you on the phone when you are in the middle of completing work for a deadline. She or he is going through the sales pitch for buying magazines.

Passive response

_____

_____

Aggressive response

_____

_____

Assertive response

_____

_____

IV. You go to an expensive steakhouse and order your steak medium rare, but it is served to you well done.

Passive response

_____

_____

Aggressive response

_____

_____

Assertive response

_____

_____

Questions

1. From the above situations, which responses would you most likely give? What is your rationale?

2. Is there a pattern for your behavior? Describe.

3. If your approach to these situations is primarily passive, why is this so? Are your needs being met?

4. If your approach to these situations is primarily aggressive, why is this so? What impact might this have on others?

5. Which responses are the most effective and why?

6. What are some alternate responses that would work effectively in these situations?

Exercise 7–D
Taking Responsibility

For each of the following comments:

1. Write the underlying assumption(s) about the speaker's intent in making the statement.

2. Rewrite the comment to reflect efforts to take responsibility and to communicate assumptions clearly. Utilize the strategies discussed in the chapter.

1. "Can't you work under pressure?"

   Assumption: _____

   Rewritten statement: _____

   _____

2. "You're not listening to me."

   Assumption: _____

   Rewritten statement: _____

   _____

3. "Will you work overtime on Friday?"

Assumption: _____

Rewritten statement: _____

_____

4. "Joyce, what have you done with the production figures?"

Assumption: _____

Rewritten statement: _____

_____

5. "Are you getting all this down in writing?"

Assumption: _____

Rewritten statement: _____

_____

6. "Why are you mad at me?"

Assumption: _____

Rewritten statement: _____

_____

7. "You've never appreciated my work."

Assumption: _____

Rewritten statement: _____

_____

Source: Exercise adapted from an exercise in J. William Pfeiffer and John E. Jones, *Structured Experiences Kit,* entitled "Taking Responsibility," C-CAE/0-15 (San Francisco: Jossey-Bass Pfeiffer, 1980).

**Exercise 7–E
Aristotle**

Aristotle once said, "Anyone can become angry—that is easy. But to be angry with the right person, to the right degree, at the right time, for the right purpose, and in the right way—this is not easy."

Answer these questions:

1. When is it appropriate, in business, to get angry?

_____

_____

2. What is the right purpose for using personal anger?

_____

_____

3. What is the right way to be angry?

_____

_____

Source: Submitted by Mr. Bob Eliason, Management Lecturer, James Madison University, Harrisonburg, VA.

Exercise 7–F
Reflection/Action Plan

This chapter focused on the skill of verbal communication—what it is, why it is important, and how to improve your skills in this area. Complete the following worksheet upon completing all readings and experiential activities for this chapter.

1. The one or two communication areas in which I am most strong are:

_____

_____

_____

2. The one or two communication areas in which I need more improvement are:

_____

_____

_____

3. If I did only one thing to improve in this area, it would be to:

_____

_____

_____

4. Making this change would probably result in:

_____

_____

_____

5. If I did not change or improve in this area, it would probably affect my personal and professional life in the following ways:

_____

_____

_____

_____

8 Persuading Individuals and Audiences

Learning Points

How do I:

- Influence others to adopt beliefs or behaviors different from current beliefs or behaviors?
- Get co-workers or team members to perform tasks even when I have no direct authority?
- Incorporate tactics and strategies to improve my influence and persuasion skills?
- Use elements of persuasion to give an effective presentation?

When she was hired, Monica accepted a salary that was 5 percent lower than in her previous job. She rationalized accepting a lower salary for two reasons. First, the 20-minute commute was about half that of her previous job, saving her time and money. Second, her boss told her that in 90 days, her performance would be evaluated and "an adjustment to her salary would be made." Over the last four months, Monica's performance has been excellent. Even her boss, Alan, has told her so on several occasions. The problem is that it's been more than a month past the promised performance evaluation, and Monica has yet to sit down with Alan beyond a couple minutes here and there. He's been traveling quite a bit and under great pressure to "make the numbers," especially since the company was acquired by a larger firm four months ago. Monica knows she deserves that salary adjustment, and she has gently—and sometimes jokingly—reminded Alan of his promise. Unfortunately, it seems as if everything else has a higher priority for him. Monica fears that the more time that passes, the more unmotivated she will feel about working for less than she's worth. The time never seems to be right, as all her hints and reminders go unheeded.

1. What is the nature of Monica's dilemma?

2. Why has Monica been unsuccessful at persuading her boss to provide the promised performance evaluation?

3. Why do you suppose that when asking for a raise, Monica utilized strategies such as "joking" and hint dropping? What do you think was her intent in using these approaches, and why were they unsuccessful?

173

4. If you were Monica, what steps would you take and why?

5. If in fact there is pressure to "make the numbers," how would you make your request more persuasive?

"Persuasion is a governing power. Those who have it use it to their advantage. Those who don't have it let it run their lives."[1]

Paul Messaris (Author)

The way we conduct business is changing as fast as the environment in which organizations operate. Organizations are becoming less hierarchical. Managerial levels have been flattened. Organizations are more diverse. Communication is increasingly electronic. Decision making is spread throughout all employee levels. What does this mean for you? As the power base has shifted to employees and they make decisions that affect their work environment, they need to convince others of the soundness of their decisions, often without any direct authority. Such is the case in work teams where members, not managers, make decisions about who does what, when, and how. This chapter is about persuasion—the ability to influence people through means other than issuing direct orders. We discuss the importance of persuasion in today's business world, provide an overview of persuasion theories, offer strategies for persuasion, and provide some tips for persuading audiences through effective presentations.

What Is Persuasion?

Persuasion is a form of influence. It is a process of guiding people toward the adoption of a behavior, belief, or attitude that the persuader prefers.[2] It can take place in a single meeting or over a series of discussions.[3] It involves careful preparation and proper presentation of arguments and supporting evidence in an appropriate and compelling emotional climate. Unlike manipulation or coercion, persuasion does not rely on deceit or force, nor does it involve directly giving orders. As Allied Signal CEO Lawrence Bossidy explains:

The day when you could yell and scream and beat people into good performance is over. Today you have to appeal to them by helping them see how they can get from here to there, by establishing some credibility, and by giving them some reason and help to get there. Do all those things, and they'll knock down doors.[4]

Persuasion is an essential component of doing business. Organizational leaders are most effective in getting others to buy into their ideas when they are democratic in their approach and show that they respect and care about others' beliefs and needs, regardless of their position or status.[5] Increasingly, employees without positional authority are tasked with getting work done with and by others who expect to be treated with respect and involved in decisions that affect them. To be an effective persuader, you cannot tell others what to do; you must engage them in a dialogue about the situation or problem and collaboratively agree on how to approach or solve it. In so doing, employees and teammates cooperate with an effective persuader because they want to, not because they have to.

Why Persuasion Is Important

To be an effective manager, you must be an able persuader. Gone are the days when managers could delegate to others and have their decisions implemented without question. Employees today show little tolerance for unquestioned authority.[6] Even the military, where unquestioned authority has been a core value, is making changes that include giving officers and nonofficers alike input into key decisions about the way the organization should be run. More and more companies are adopting a participative work style where employees at all levels are involved in formulating strategy, discussing business needs, making bottom-line decisions, and implementing workplace changes. In this nonhierarchical environment, the skill of persuasion is invaluable.

Another trend that makes persuasion a necessary skill in today's business world is the increasing amount of work being done by teams and virtual employees. In a team-based or team-supported workplace, seldom does a higher authority mandate decisions. More likely the work is divided between the work group members and overseen by the members of a self-managing team rather than by a higher level manager. In this new business world, persuasion is now the way to get your—and others'—tasks accomplished. Employees and teammates cooperate with you because they want to, not because they have to. More often than not, you'll be working with others who are your peers rather than your subordinates. In this situation the skill of persuasion is not simply the best alternative, it's the only one!

The primary focus of this chapter is on persuasion as it is experienced in the business world, where in addition to discussing a starting salary or salary increase with your boss, you might be asked to sell your company's services to a client or negotiate advantageous terms on a lease with an equipment supplier. Persuasion skills and strategies can also be applied in your personal life as well, for example, convincing your parents to let you have a car at school, deciding with your spouse or partner what movie to see or where to vacation, or ending roommate conflicts by finding agreement in dividing household responsibilities in a way that restores or improves relations. More than ever before, your ability to influence and persuade may determine whether and how effectively you achieve your objectives.

Overview of Theories of Persuasion

Some of the skills and techniques of persuasion are rooted in research in traditional and cognitive psychology. Back in the 1950s, psychologist Leon Festinger coined the term **cognitive dissonance** to explain the tension that exists when individuals' beliefs do not align with their behaviors. The dissonance results in tension or discomfort.[7] An effective persuader will be aware of this dissonance and employ a variety of tactics to help restore consonance or alignment between espoused values or beliefs of those to be persuaded and their behaviors or actions.[8] To illustrate, let's say that you were recently hired by a company that touts itself as "family-friendly," a fact that weighed heavily in your decision to accept the job. Several weeks into the job, your supervisor asks you to work on Saturday in order to get ready for an upcoming client meeting. Unfortunately, you already have plans to attend your child's school play. Your supervisor seems pretty intent on having you come in, and being new on the job, you want to make a favorable impression. However, the commitment to your child is important to you, and, as you thought and hoped, consistent with the company's philosophy. How would you persuade your supervisor to happily accept your declining to work on Saturday? We've created an exercise (Exercise 8–A) to let you develop your approach to this situation.

Another theory that underpins the concept of persuasion is **inoculation theory**. Borrowing from the medical field, McGuire suggested that in the same way individuals receive a small injection of a disease-producing substance to increase their immunity against that disease, persuaders can be effective when they anticipate the objections of the persuadee and address those objections before they arise.[9] For example, a firm could send information showing lower-than-expected profits prior to announcing a decreased merit pool. Other strategies for countering objections include presenting all points (for and against) and demonstrating how what's being proposed is the right solution, or broaching controversial subjects gently and early, before your audience has the chance to raise an issue that could become contentious or divisive.

Returning to Monica's dilemma, she might employ the inoculation theory by starting her conversation with her boss this way: "Alan, I realize you have been extremely busy trying to meet the financial goals set by the new management team. Since your time is limited, I propose we meet over lunch to discuss my overdue performance evaluation. You have to eat. . . ." By reminding Alan that he has to eat, Monica is trying to overcome this objection before Alan can use the "I don't have time" excuse. Moreover, the first part of her request demonstrates awareness of and empathy toward Alan's current challenges.

A more recent model of persuasion effectiveness is Reardon's **ACE Theory**. She suggests that people use three criteria to determine whether to respond to a persuader's arguments: *appropriateness, consistency,* and *effectiveness.*[10] Therefore, most successful persuasion attempts employ one or more of these characteristics:

- **Appropriateness**—the right thing to do, based on generally accepted standards or norms, or in some cases, rules of law or morality. Appropriateness appeals are geared to the persuadee's or audience's belief system and interests.

- **Consistency**—the degree to which the action or belief proposed compares to that of similar others or to their own past behaviors or espoused beliefs. Appeals to consistency demonstrate that the persuader understands the beliefs or past behaviors of similar others and presents arguments that make sense or track with these beliefs or behaviors.

- **Effectiveness**—the degree to which an action or idea leads to a desirable state or outcome. By knowing what the persuadee or audience wants or needs, a persuader can demonstrate how adoption of the proposed idea or action will help meet those needs.

For example, let's say you have been working for the last six months for a financial services firm doing research on market trends. The job is great, but the commute is a hassle . . . and getting worse. Not only has there been an increase in the traffic and commute time, but also in the cost of gas and parking. You would like to convince your department head that telecommuting is a viable option—particularly since you could do your research job anywhere there is a computer and high-speed access—and that allowing you to work from home two days a week is in everyone's best interest. So, you construct your three-pronged appeal:

Appropriateness: *"You know, our two biggest competitors—Company X and Company Y—have been allowing their employees to telecommute for two years now. By implementing a similar program, we can increase our competitiveness in recruiting while also showing that we care about the environment."*

Consistency: *"You've always said that it's important that we're on the leading edge of technology . . . well, here's a way that we can capitalize on the technology available and assert our position as a technology leader."*

Effectiveness: *"If employees are allowed to work at home, they will be less stressed and more productive because they didn't have to fight traffic or worry about picking kids up from daycare on time. They can even work on days they would otherwise be absent due to illness—theirs or a family member's. Moreover, the ability to telecommute may help us attract even more desirable employees."*

The Persuasion Process

Whether you use one, two or all of these prongs in your persuasion attempt will depend on your preferences for—and the actual effectiveness of—each prong.

We all know people who are natural persuaders. What makes them successful depends on a number of factors; however, our review of research in psychology, sociology, communication, and business suggests six components or steps in the process. They are listed in Figure 8–1 and then described in detail.

Figure 8–1
The Persuasion Process

Understand others' motivations and needs.
Establish credibility.
Frame for common ground.
Engage in joint problem solving.
Support preferred outcome with logic and reasoning.
Reinforce with appeal to emotions and basic instincts.

Understand Others' Motivations and Needs

In his best-selling book, *Seven Habits of Highly Effective People,* Stephen Covey tells us that if we want others to listen to us, we must first listen to them.[11] It may seem counterintuitive, but the most effective persuaders start by extending an invitation to the persuadee to share his or her views. After listening to what the persuadee wants or needs, you will be better equipped to frame what you want in those terms. To understand others' needs, you will need to be able to do all of the following:

- **Actively listen**—Listen not only to the specific words said, but also to the feelings behind them. To do this, you'll need to listen carefully to the speaker's verbal and nonverbal communication (e.g., tone, inflection, gestures). Someone who offers a meek "Okay" but doesn't make eye contact with you is not likely to fully support the proposal under discussion. Accepting the "Okay" response may be efficient, but it will be ineffective in the long run. That conclusion is equally true when the persuadee responds with silence. "So, we're all in agreement" may seem like a great way to check if there's consensus, but statements like these may result in little or no response. For the speaker who believes that silence means agreement, this result may be a welcomed and efficient end to a long discussion. Accepting silence as agreement in this case may produce undesirable results in the long run.

- **Check for understanding**—Checking involves sharing your perceptions and soliciting feedback. For example, "When I asked if we were all in agreement, no one spoke up. Does this mean everyone supports the proposal and will do their part? What do you think, Bob?" Directing a question to a specific person is particularly important when there are more than two people involved in the interaction, due to the dynamics at play in group settings. Doing so will communicate to Bob, for example, that his opinion is being specifically solicited.

- **Read people**—Learning what makes others tick may involve direct and indirect means. Asking open-ended questions is a fairly direct approach, and will often bring about the information you need. You might also learn this through your interactions with this person on and off the job. How does she dress (e.g., to impress, for comfort)? How does he spend his free time? What sort of personal items (e.g., photos, knick-knacks, a mug with the company logo) are in her office? How well organized is his office? Where did she go to school? No one clue will tell you everything, but the more you understand, and the more you ask, the more you'll know.

Establish Credibility

Imagine you are walking down a busy street and you notice a disheveled, dirty man running around proclaiming that, "a spaceship has landed and aliens have come to take us away." Chances are, you'll laugh to yourself and think "what a crazy man!" Because of his appearance and the words he is speaking, you will not take him seriously, as neither he nor his speech is credible. An exaggerated example, perhaps, but it is illustrative. Management guru Jay Conger believes that for persuaders to be effective, they must be perceived as credible, as the quality of the message received is judged not only by its content but also by the character of the person delivering it.[12] **Credibility** relates to the believability of the message deliverer.[13] You will be considered credible to the degree you demonstrate a positive appearance, expertise, trustworthiness, and composure.[14]

- **Positive Impression or Appearance**—How we look and dress communicates how we feel about ourselves and our situation and influences how others see us. Have you ever been in court (remember that speeding ticket you tried to fight?) and noticed that the attire of those in attendance (lawyers excluded) varies widely, from crumpled, dirty, and ill-fitting to clean, pressed, tailored suits? Have you also noticed that the judge is more lenient to the latter group? The plaintiff who doesn't bother to shave or wear clean, conservative clothing is telling the court that he doesn't respect himself or the judge, so why should the judge respect him? The same is true when dressing for a job interview, yet we've all heard of (or seen) examples of outlandish or inappropriate attire in those situations, usually resulting in quick, dismissive interviews. If you want to persuade others that what you have to say is important, you have to dress the part. You have to act the part as well, and this includes displaying appropriate gestures (handshake, posture) and behaviors (manners, business etiquette, remembering others' names), and may also include the possession of credentials (appropriate title, education).

While first impressions are important—and formed within seconds, so too are the sum total of your interactions with others.[15] Others' historical impressions of you (and your reputation) can work to your advantage or disadvantage. A history of positive interactions and appropriate appearance will likely overshadow one atypical moment. In the 2007 movie *The Pursuit of Happyness,* actor Will Smith plays a tenacious single father trying desperately to succeed despite the many challenges he faces. After several well-presented and well-groomed meetings with the HR director of a stock brokerage, Smith finally gets the interview he covets. Unfortunately, due to circumstances, he shows up at the designated time wearing only a paint-splattered undershirt and pull-on pants, along with a casual zippered jacket. Knowing how bad he looks, Smith's character earnestly explains the situation (before being asked . . . inoculation theory in action!) in a way that evokes both humor and empathy. Because all of his previous interactions were positive and professional, the interviewers overlook the momentary lapse of credibility and offer him the job. Conversely, if your previous encounters have been negative or inconsistent, others are likely to question and search for faults in your reasoning, creating an uphill battle for your persuasion attempts.

Make Positive Impressions, and Make Them Early

You're heard the saying "you never get a second chance to make a first impression." This adage is backed by research suggesting that first impressions are in fact persistent. New information or behaviors presented are unlikely to change others' initial impressions of a person. More specifically, according to recent research by a team of psychologists, when new experiences contradict a first impression, they can only influence the impression in the context in which they were made, while the initial impression will persist in other contexts.[16]

For this reason, it's important to think about the impression you want others to have of you before they even meet you. Job interviews are a great example. Recruiters today have many ways to learn about you before the interview begins. Your résumé, dress, and handshake are important, but remember that information about your non–work life precedes you and is available via social networks. Fair or not, this information has cost many a promising recruit a job opportunity.

There are many ways that you can positively influence people in your professional and personal circles, according to Stephen Covey.[17] Among those that fall into the "model by example" category are:

- Refrain from speaking negatively about others, even when you're stressed or provoked. Exercise restraint and courage to not let your emotions get the better of you.
- Be patient with others, and accept that processes (learning, growth) require time. Take the time to wait for a late person or listen to a too-long explanation. Their response might surprise you.
- Perform anonymous acts of service without expecting anything in return.

He also suggests that we can positively influence others by building caring relationships, and suggests the following:

- Assume the best of others. By appealing to the good in others, you can bring out the best in them.
- Reward open and honest questions by not judging or criticizing—which would only serve to curtail future openness.
- Admit your mistakes and apologize, rather than being defensive or offering excuses. Related to this, if you are offended, take the initiative to clear it up.

- **Expertise**—To be perceived as credible, you must be very knowledgeable about the subject matter (e.g., product or service you offer) and be able to present your knowledge in a way that compels the listener to adopt a certain point of view. You demonstrate this knowledge by presenting appropriate information (e.g., product specifications) and reliable data (e.g., independent studies, verifiable outcomes) and by being passionate about the subject. While you should be able to provide nondefensive responses to questions or criticism, it is important not to exaggerate claims, misrepresent facts, or invent answers to questions for which you were unprepared.

- **Trustworthiness**—This component carries more weight in an established relationship, but it is important nonetheless. Trustworthiness is acquired over time through personal and professional relationships in which others perceive you as consistent, reliable, and conscientious. People who keep their promises, say what they mean and mean what they say, and display strong emotional and moral character tend to be seen as worthy of others' trust. Typically, this trust is then reciprocated, enabling an open, honest dialogue that can facilitate the building of mutually beneficial solutions. In new relationships, trustworthiness can be demonstrated by actively and empathically listening to others, communicating directly and unambiguously (e.g., your body language is in sync with your verbal language), being humble (e.g., willing to admit you are wrong or don't have an answer), and looking out for the other's best interest. But be careful, especially in this age of social connectedness. A recent study by Anderson and Shirako suggests that actual interactions are not the only means by which opinions about one's trustworthiness and cooperativeness are formed. Individuals who are socially connected—share common networks—and are talked or gossiped about have reputations that precede them.[18] Anderson and Shirako's study suggested that the reputations of such individuals are not necessarily positive; in fact, social connectedness is a double-edged sword due to its effect of increasing scrutiny on individuals' positive qualities and achievements, as well as their negative qualities and failures.[19] When parties enter into an interaction, actual and perceived (i.e., reputational) behaviors will lead to expectations of behaviors such as cooperativeness, trustworthiness, and even competitiveness and dishonesty. Our reputations, or worse, others' beliefs about our reputations gleaned from pictures and postings on MySpace and Facebook may impede the persuasion process and even your candidacy for a job.[20]

- **Composure**—When you are composed, you are solid and sure, even under pressure. "Never let them see you sweat" alludes to the contribution that composure makes to credibility. How do you appear composed? First, you must have a plan, which means knowing what to say and when. This requires outlining key points—even writing them on note cards—and doing a dry run of your pitch in front of a mirror or someone who will give you honest feedback. These steps will help you feel ready to answer any questions and ensure that you are perceived as confident, composed, and credible.

Frame for Common Ground

Once effective persuaders understand others and can project credibility, they develop a framework or plan for how to proceed. **Framing** involves describing one's position in ways that identify common ground and establish a collaborative tone. Framing for common ground attains three interrelated objectives:[21]

- It provides a perspective we would like the other party to consider. Sometimes, it's all in the packaging of the message. For example, if you need to introduce a new computer system to your company, you could present the technology as something new and exciting versus something that can free up time to be spent on more important tasks. Chances are the latter approach will be more effective. This relates to knowing what makes the persuadee tick.

  Do you remember Monica's unsuccessful attempts at persuading Alan to sit with her to review her performance? Employing this component, Monica might say: "Alan, I have been fleshing out a few ideas that, if implemented, will help our division meet the goals set by the new management team. Can we set aside 20 minutes to discuss this tomorrow morning?" Alan would most likely agree as it is in his best interest to do so; and, in that meeting, Monica can frame her desire to be evaluated in terms of taking on the greater challenge and responsibility inherent in her ideas for change.

■ It provides an open-minded way for alternatives and ideas to be compared and contrasted. For example, "We need a solution for this problem. I've jotted down some benefits these improvements will likely bring and a few ideas for consideration. How do you think we can arrive at a solution?" With this common ground, the speakers can unite and work together to compete against or resolve the shared problem as opposed to competing against one another.

■ It creates a logical structure and establishes constraints for decision making. Clarifying the rules upfront reduces the appearance of arbitrariness and manipulation—one day this, the next day that—down the line.[22] By planning and creating a framework ahead of time, you provide a manner in which you and others can collaborate in the problem-solving process.

Engage in Joint Problem Solving

Involving the other party in the search for a solution is one of the best ways to get his or her buy-in to the solution. Collaborating with persuadees in the search for solutions demonstrates that you are open to and interested in their ideas, and increases the likelihood that they will fully support those solutions that were jointly developed, compared, and contrasted. Furthermore, since two heads are better than one, collaborating may result in the development of new and different ideas, which, when considered collectively, may bring about a more innovative and mutually beneficial solution than either party had previously conceived prior to the discussion. Not all persuasion attempts come with the opportunity to create an entirely new solution. However, involvement can come in other forms. Even something as small as having the purchaser complete all or part of her own order or sales agreement can increase her commitment to complete the sale. Putting your commitment on a piece of paper ups the ante—most will do what they've agreed in writing to do. This public commitment/consistency principle has been applied successfully in the goal-setting arena and has been shown to be especially effective when used with people with a high level of pride or public self-consciousness.[23]

Support Preferred Outcome with Logic and Reasoning

Presenting compelling evidence is extremely effective as a persuasion technique. Passion and emotion are important, but facts and data can make the difference between your audience supporting your argument or not.[24] Know the sources for your data; others might ask. Any errors in your reasoning can give the listener reason to doubt you. This does not imply that you must say everything you know about the subject. You must judiciously select the information regarding the subject that will have the most impact on your audience.[25] For most people, this information will include a compelling and logically supported review of

"I hired a musician to play a sad melody while I give you a sob story about why I didn't do my homework. It's actually quite effective."

the projected benefits the persuadee can expect to receive by adopting the preferred view. This is consistent with the advertising approach to demonstrating the features, advantages, and benefits of the products and services being promoted. Most people want to save time, money, and hassle and can be effectively persuaded by clear and compelling explanations and demonstrations that show these outcomes. Think about most infomercials. The benefits are shown and explained—multiple times—by a persuasive pitchman. Wouldn't you want to save time and money (apparently the average consumer spends $20 a month on paper towels)? Apparently so, as the millions of "Shamwows" sold will attest.

Reinforce with an Appeal to Emotions and Basic Instincts

While logic is essential, so too is appealing to people's feelings, fears, values, dreams, frustrations, egos, vanities, or desires. Many charismatic leaders, such as John F. Kennedy, Martin Luther King, Jr., and Mother Teresa, inspired others to support or join their cause not only because of its importance, but also because of their contagious passion and conviction for the cause. By engaging yourself and your audience in the subject matter, everyone is vested in working together to find solutions to the problem at hand. We see this appeal to emotions in print and TV commercials that ask the public to donate to organizations whose mission is to feed the homeless, nurse the sick, and bring hope to those hit by tragic events. Within hours of the 7.0 earthquake that hit Haiti on January 12, 2010, pictures of devastation were all over the media. Not long after, several organizations put out calls for donations of food, medical supplies, and money. Donations started pouring in, and even doctors and nurses were getting on small planes en route to help this nation that had been struggling economically before the earthquake hit. The earthquake exponentially amplified Haiti's struggles, and footage depicting this devastation tugged at heartstrings and engaged people from all over the world to come together and help. On a smaller scale, you can be persuasive when you inspire others to "join the crusade" by appealing to others' emotions and values.

Sociologist and scholar Robert Cialdini has written extensively on influence. In his book, *Influence: Science and Practice,* Cialdini talks about certain triggers that evoke an automatic response in humans. These "click-whirr" responses are instinctual short-cuts that save us time and effort when we need to make decisions.[26] When you reinforce your persuasive appeal with words or actions that trigger a "yes" response, you will be more likely to be influential. Three of these universal forms of influence follow:

Reciprocity/Obligation: In general, people want to, or feel obligated to, repay favors and kindness. If you buy me a gift, however small, I feel obligated to respond in kind, lest I seem thoughtless, cheap, or ungrateful. Moreover, when I am given something, I'm anxious to restore the balance to the point where I don't owe you and you don't owe me. Advertisers use this principal when they give away free samples. Of course, one goal is to get consumers to try the new product. However, another is the hope that after receiving some of the product for free, you will feel obliged to purchase the next "batch." Consider also the packaging—"buy two, get one free." Not only are we getting a good deal, we are getting something for nothing.

There are several ways to use the reciprocity/obligation rule in persuasion:

- Give information, support, concessions, even gifts, and give first. While our tendency may be to hold our cards close to the vest, sharing information freely leads to others doing the same.

- Practice giving regularly and genuinely. If you give only when you want something from someone, your request will be seen as manipulative rather than consistent with your generous spirit.

- Consider the rejection-then-retreat approach. Ask someone to agree to a more costly proposal, but be ready to present a lower cost alternative. Because he turned down your first offer, he will view your second offer as a concession and may feel inclined to respond with a concession of his own . . . complying with your second request.[27]
A recent comic strip illustrates this point. A man asks his wife if he can have an affair. When she says "no," he responds with, "Then would you mind if I played golf with the guys on Saturday?"

A few words of wisdom about the reciprocity rule. When giving, be careful not to respond to others' acknowledgements with phrases like "it was nothing," or "no problem." Such phrases negate your contribution and thus the reciprocity norm. Also, remember that you get what you give. If you give help, you'll get help; but, if you give trouble, you'll get trouble.

Scarcity: People are more motivated to go after that which they perceive is scarce. Lines of people waiting all night outside stores selling the Wii® (Sony) and iPhone® (Apple) fueled even greater demand for these products, despite the frustration of obtaining them from a low and diminishing supply. Consider also the tactics of infomercials and television shopping programs. In addition to the "Today, and today only, we have a limited supply . . ." introduction, viewers are able to see a continuously updated counter showing how many of the items are remaining. If you watch carefully during the typical two-minute segment, you'll notice that the greatest volume is sold in the last 30–45 seconds. This is, when buyers fear they may be shut out of this once-in-a-lifetime opportunity. While it may be tempting to use the scarcity principle to entice consumers to buy a product or service, the information must be accurate. If customers later find out that there was in fact no shortage, they will feel manipulated and will lose trust in the persuader.

Consensus/Social Proof: People often decide what to do based on what they see others doing. Why else would most drivers drive at 5 or 10 miles over the posted speed limit on a busy freeway, even when a traffic ticket could have multiple negative consequences? Or why would all drivers stop to view an accident, further tying up an already stalled road? Cialdini explains that we "view a behavior as correct in a given situation to the degree that we see others performing it."[28] Advertisers are aware of this and persuade us to buy their products by telling us not necessarily how good a product is, but how strongly others think so (e.g., "number one selling," or "most popular model").

Conversely, we see no problem with what could be considered deviant behavior if everyone does it, as is the case in a parking garage that has been littered with unwanted flyers posted on unsuspecting drivers' cars.

An effective persuader can use consensus/social proof in several ways:

- To show the persuadee that similar others (those the persuadee would identify with) are doing what you are asking them to do.
- To show that others have benefited as a result of saying "yes" to your request.
- To share testimonials of similar others and experts.

A Word of Caution

By adhering to many of the principles we've discussed, persuasion efforts are likely to be effective, resulting in positive outcomes for both the persuader and persuadee. Used incorrectly or for the wrong reasons, persuasion has the potential to be viewed as **manipulation**—convincing people to believe or adhere to something that is neither in their best interest nor something they would believe or do without the presence of the persuader. There can be a fine line between effective persuasion and manipulation. For example, imagine a boss telling a new hire that "everyone who wants to advance works for at least an hour after they punch out." It doesn't seem fair, and in fact, such an act is illegal, though not all companies comply with the law. The boss's comments come across as a threat, that is, if you don't work "off the clock"—in essence, provide free labor—your chances of advancing are slim. Because you want to make a positive impression, perhaps you adhere to this practice. However, you probably feel you have no choice, and therefore comply out of fear. Clearly, from your perspective, this situation doesn't feel good, nor does it engender positive feelings toward your boss or organization. From the boss's perspective, your compliance means success—even if it means ignoring employees' occasional grumbling over this practice—and perhaps reason to use this tactic more frequently, especially when the department's "numbers" look good to upper management. However, over time, employee discontent and resistance increases. In the long run, coercive tactics like these do not work or bring about the desired change in behavior or belief. Some may result in significant negative consequences;[29] at a minimum, they damage the relationship.[30]

To determine whether a speaker is positively persuading or negatively manipulating, ask these questions:

- Who is really benefiting as a result of this act?
- Is the information being presented accurately?
- Does this interaction feel like a test of wills—a competitive game—or is it a healthy and positive debate—a two-way interchange?

Warning signals of manipulation include the persuader having more to gain from the exchange than the persuadee, discrepancies in the facts being presented as part of the argument, a war of words that heavily favors just one side, and a larger role for self-interest than public interest. If any or all of these conditions are present in an interaction, it's best to disengage and either discontinue or agree to résumé the interaction when you can gain a more equal footing. To defend yourself against manipulation:

- *Be clear on your convictions and why you hold them.* Avoid being a victim of unscrupulous manipulators by being smart when interacting with them. Ask plenty of questions to ensure you understand clearly all sides of an issue. Analyze their intent and evaluate their argument before accepting what's being said, especially if your opinion is based primarily on the person's likeability or reputation.

- *Think substance, not appearance.* Base your acceptance of a persuader on the strength of his reasoning, not simply because he has connected with you or the audience emotionally.

- *Doubt the trust of what's being said.* Do ask questions of speakers before being convinced by the power of their words that they are right. Most of the time you will encounter presenters and persuaders who are truthful and honest. But it's a good strategy to be aware of the tactics that can be utilized by some whose self-interests override their interest in others.

- *Know the source.* Increasingly, people rely on the Internet for information and expertise. Yet much of the material readily available can't be attributed to a specific author, organization, or date. Out-of-context information is unreliable. Know the source before using content in personal or professional decision making. Otherwise, as Bostrom notes in an article on future risk communication, "we may cross the divide from informal decision making to persuasion without reason."[31]

- *Consider the needs of others besides yourself.* When being courted by a persuader, consider not just your interests but those of others who may be affected by the action or perspective being advocated.[32] Is the action of benefit to the greater common good? Or will it benefit only a select few?

Making Effective Presentations

As persuaders, we often find ourselves making a formal presentation to others. Knowing how to create a persuasive presentation can increase sales, advance your career, enhance your reputation, and create both professional opportunities and personal satisfaction.[33]

Being able to present, defend, and gain acceptance for your ideas is a critical skill in today's business environment. Persuasive presentations require the presenter not only to give information, but also to get the audience to accept, believe, and act on the ideas presented.[34] Many individuals spend great amounts of time and energy creating and developing their ideas, but forget to learn the techniques necessary to sell the ideas. Selling the ideas is a critical component. A lack of "show and tell" ability can compromise a person's productivity, effectiveness, and opportunity to advance within an organization. Mastering these skills allows an audience to trust your expertise and your message, allowing you to sell your ideas and display your leadership ability.[35]

When creating persuasive presentations, it is crucial to determine your reason for giving the presentation and find the need behind your idea. This will provide the basis for your presentation. Once you have determined the information, shape the message to your audience. Your efforts will be more successful if you deliver the speech around the information needs of your audience. Imagine you need to make a presentation for a new product idea. You must first begin with the reason for the new product, the data and information necessary to show the projected demand for the new product. However, you will not get the rest of the team to buy into your product idea unless they have been shown the benefit it can provide to the organization. You must understand the group's concerns and its motivation for the new product development in order to create a persuasive pitch.

Elements of persuasion can be useful tactics when developing effective presentations. Figure 8–2 provides pointers for making persuasive business presentations successfully.

Figure 8–2
Tips for Effective Presentations

Before the Presentation

- *Research your intended audience.* What are their interests? Their beliefs? To what kind of presentation are they accustomed (i.e., length, format, and type of technology used)? Will they want to see your materials in advance? Will a handout or copy of the report being presented be expected?

- *Determine appropriate dress.* Many businesses are "business casual" every day of the week, while others reserve this for Fridays only or not at all. Find out what's appropriate in the environment in which you'll be speaking.

- *Prepare your remarks.* There are two kinds of presenters: those who are best when they have not prepared in advance, and those who are not. Those few who are blessed with the skill of relating to others extemporaneously, or "on the spot," can get away with minimal preparation. All the rest of us need to prepare, prepare, prepare!

- *Practice.* You don't have to write out the whole speech. Make a list of the key concepts you want to address and develop "talking points" that support each of these concepts. Practice saying these points in sequence, using a natural conversational tone.

- *Relax.* Just before the presentation, clear your head and focus on the task at hand.

During the Presentation

- *Begin with an anecdote or quote.* This ensures you begin with an attention-grabber that helps the audience focus on your presentation. Avoid the use of a joke—jokes can be offensive to members of a particular group. It's better to start with something of substance that relates to the subject matter or the audience.

- *Give your audience an organizing framework.* Begin your presentation by telling your audience the key concepts you'll be addressing. You could also present an agenda as a visual aid and means to reinforce key points throughout your remarks.

- *Present the core of your argument at the beginning.* This gives the audience a road map—they know where you're heading and why. "Tell them what you're going to tell them, then tell them." This also gives you a platform for demonstrating your enthusiasm about your subject, and for engaging them in that enthusiasm. Then build your case by presenting data or facts that support your argument.

- *Make your session interactive.* Take questions throughout. If there's no time for audience interaction, ask one or two rhetorical questions, or begin your presentation with a question that can focus their thinking, even if a response is not expected. The more engaged they are, the greater the likelihood that they'll buy in to your arguments.

- *Use technology, but sparingly.* You want to be up on the latest cutting-edge methods—as appropriate for the message and audience—but you don't want to lose the personal connection with the audience or give the impression that you're more style than substance.

- *Be interesting but not necessarily entertaining.* It's important to engage your audience. Making people laugh can do this. Even more effective is making them think.

- *Summarize.* "Tell them what you told them." This helps focus the audience's attention on the essence of your presentation—the key take-aways or lessons of your message.

After the Presentation

- *Evaluate.* Ask yourself, and others who were present, what went well and what you can do differently in the future. It helps to debrief while your presentation is still fresh in your—and others'—minds. Debriefing is also helpful when recycling your presentation. If planned correctly, your presentation can serve as a "template" for your next one. The content will likely change but the format—opening, main concepts, key points that support your case, summary, and close—can stay the same.

- *Follow up.* Prepare and send any materials or data you promised to the audience, and send a formal thanks to the organizer of the event at which you spoke.

Strategies for Dealing with "Stage Fright"

Many people, when asked, would say they dislike giving presentations. It's been suggested that public speaking is at or near the top of lists of people's greatest fears, even higher than death. Unless you're a natural salesperson or an expert on a topic, the prospect of giving a presentation can be a bit daunting. If you suffer from "stage fright" or find speaking in front of an audience difficult, consider the following pointers:

- *Prepare.* Begin preparation as soon as you find out about your presentation. Set aside 10–15 minutes a day, outlining what you will cover so it feels natural. Determine and practice your opening story or remarks in order to get through the time of your presentation that provokes the highest anxiety—the very beginning.

- *Visit the site.* Familiarize yourself with the speaking environment. Before the event, go to the place where you will be speaking so the setting won't surprise you and increase your anxiety. Find out who your audience is (their background, education, reason for attending) and how many will attend.

- *Visualize success.* Picture yourself in front of your audience in the place where you will be speaking. See yourself being totally confident and in control of the situation, and see your audience enjoying your speech. Avoid all negative thoughts during the visualization. This helps to reduce damaging self-thinking and substitutes a positive image for a negative one.

- *Maintain realistic expectations.* You don't have to be perfect. Just be the best you can be. Remember that you appear much more confident than you feel. You probably know as much or more about the topic than your audience does. They're there to learn from you, not to see you fail.

- *Gain experience.* The more you rehearse your speech, the better you feel about it. Present your speech to a group of friends to become more comfortable and get feedback on what you did well and what you can do to improve. "Rehearsal and preparation can reduce a speaker's fear by 75 percent."[36]

- *Talk about something that interests you.* You will feel more positive delivering your message if it is something that you believe and that is familiar to you.

- *Develop a relaxation routine.* Relaxing the body can eliminate or reduce physical discomfort that can add to levels of anxiety. Relieve the built-up tensions in your body in advance by exercising, meditating, or doing deep-breathing exercises.

- *Breathe deeply before a presentation to relax the body and vent tension.* Remembering to take breaths between sentences *during* a presentation can help you stay at a conversational level with the audience rather than quickening to a jittery "let's get this thing over" pace. Deep breathing can reduce stage fright by 15 percent.[37]

- *Reduce tension, which restricts breathing and creates discomfort.* Stand in a relaxed rather than a rigid position. Don't tense your muscles or shoulders. Keep your shoulders low and relaxed, and your knees slightly bent. Before your presentation, stand in front of a mirror to get a visual and physical image of what a relaxed posture looks and feels like. Remember this image should tension creep in during your presentation.

- *Use visual aids.* They divert attention away from you so you can feel more relaxed and less like the center of attention. It's best to use them at the beginning of your presentation when the level of your anxiety is probably the highest.

- *Use gestures.* Don't be afraid to move. Be natural. When presenting, use the same gestures you would during a casual conversations. These movements will keep your body loose and relax your muscles. Smiles and other facial gestures convey confidence as well as engage the audience.

Summary

Persuasion is a skill that can benefit you in your personal and professional endeavors in many ways. Whether asking for an increase in salary, bidding on a project, or advocating for a significant organizational change, your ability to get what you want is influenced by your knowledge and application of persuasion theory and techniques. Knowing what influences your persuasiveness—including characteristics of you, your message, and those you hope to persuade—will enable you to influence others to act or believe in something that benefits them as well as you. These principles can be applied to making persuasive presentations, something you will probably be called upon to do many times in your work and life.

Key Terms and Concepts

ACE Theory

Appropriateness (ACE)

Cognitive dissonance

Composure

Consensus/social proof

Consistency (ACE)

Credibility

Effectiveness (ACE)

Expertise

Framing

Inoculation theory

Manipulation

Persuasion

Positive impression or appearance

Reciprocity/obligation

Scarcity

Trustworthiness

Discussion Questions

1. People who sell security systems—to be used in our homes, cars, and even computer systems—often play on our fears (about safety, privacy, concern for our loved ones) to persuade us to buy their products. Does this constitute persuasion as defined in the text?

2. We suggest that in an era of empowerment, team-based structures, and reduced layers of management, one's ability to persuade has become increasingly important. Why is this so?

3. If you were the human resources manager and wanted to convince the CEO to implement a flextime policy (e.g., can work any 8 hours between 6 am and 6 pm) to assist employees with children (and others) to care for, what might you say/do, taking into account Conger's four suggestions?

4. Imagine you are the operations manager of a mid-sized firm. In an effort to cut costs, the CEO is suggesting that it might be more cost-effective to move all manufacturing overseas. Using inoculation theory, develop an approach to address this suggestion.

5. Making presentations is a skill that is expected of all managers in organizations today. Whether you'll be presenting an organization's quarterly earnings to a board, arguing on behalf of a new product development cycle, or convincing senior management to invest more in training and development programs for employees, professional presentation skills are a must. Yet we know that making presentations is something that very few people actually enjoy doing. What advice would you give someone who gets extremely nervous before presentations and would prefer to avoid making presentations?

Endnotes

1. Paul Messaris, *Visual Persuasion: The Role of Images in Advertising* (Thousand Oaks, CA: Sage Publications, 1997).

2. Kathleen K. Reardon, *Persuasion in Practice* (Newbury Park, CA: Sage Publications, 1991), p. 2.

3. *Power, Influence, and Persuasion: Sell Your Ideas and Make Things Happen* (Boston, MA: Harvard Business School Press, 2006).

4. Jay Conger, *The Necessary Art of Persuasion* (Boston, MA: Harvard Business School Press, 2008).

5. Daniel Goleman, *Emotional Intelligence: Why It Can Matter More Than IQ* (New York: Bantam Dell, 2006, 10th Anniversary Edition).

6. Conger, "Necessary Art."

7. Leon Festinger, *A Theory of Cognitive Dissonance* (Stanford, CA: Stanford University Press, 1957).

8. These tactics include increasing the attractiveness of the chosen alternative, decreasing the attractiveness of the unchosen alternative, creating cognitive overlap, or revoking the decision. See Festinger, *A Theory of Cognitive Dissonance,* for more information.

9. W. J. McGuire, "The Effectiveness of Supportive and Refutational Defenses in Immunizing and Restoring Beliefs against Persuasion," *Sociometry* 24 (1961), pp. 184–97.

10. Reardon, *Persuasion in Practice,* p. 70.

11. Stephen R. Covey, *Seven Habits of Highly Effective People,* rev. ed. (New York: Free Press, 2004) Revised edition.

12. Conger, "Necessary Art," p. 84.

13. James M. Kouzes and Barry Z. Posner, *Credibility: How Leaders Gain and Lose It, Why People Demand It* (San Francisco, CA: Jossey-Bass, 2011).

14. Reardon, *Persuasion in Practice.*

15. http://blogs.hbr.org/cs/2013/05/twelve_rules_for_new_grads.html, accessed 31 May 2013.

16. http://communications.uwo.ca/com/media_newsroom/media_newsroom_stories/research_discovers_why_first_impressions_are_so_persistent_20110118447277/ accessed 31 May 2013.

17. Adapted from Stephen R. Covey, *Principle-Centered Leadership* (New York: Simon & Schuster, 1999), pp. 119–28.

18. C. Anderson and A. Shirako, "Are Individuals' Reputations Related to Their History of Behavior?" *Journal of Personality and Social Psychology* 94, no. 2 (2008), pp. 320–333.

19. Ibid.

20. For a fictionalized case study depicting this phenomenon, please see Diane Coutu, "We Googled You," *Harvard Business Revew Case Study,* Product # R0706X (June 2007).

21. Lyle Sussman, "How to Frame a Message: The Art of Persuasion and Negotiation," *Business Horizons* (July–August 1999), p. 2.

22. Stephen R. Covey, "30 Methods of Influence," *Executive Excellence* (April 1991).

23. A. Fenigstein, M. F. Scheier, and A. H. Buss, "Public and Private Self-consciousness: Assessment and Theory," *Journal of Consulting and Clinical Psychology* 43 (1975), pp. 522–27.

24. Deborah C. Andrew, *Technical Communication in the Global Community,* 2nd ed. (Upper Saddle River, NJ; Prentice Hall, 2001).

25. James P. T. Fatt, "The Anatomy of Persuasion," *Communication World* (December 1997), p. 21.

26. Robert B. Cialdini, *Influence: Science and Practice* (Boston: Allyn & Bacon, 2001).

27. Cialdini, *Influence,* p. 38.

28. Cialdini, *Influence,* p. 100.

29. Thus was the case for Wal-Mart, which was held liable for forcing employees to work off the clock. Some of the 40 class-action lawsuits have been settled, with many millions of dollars expected to be paid. See, for example, Francie Grace, "Wal-Mart Loses Unpaid Overtime Case," CBSNEWS (December 20, 2002) (http://cbsnews.com/stories/2002/12/10/national/main533818.shtml; accessed December 10, 2010).

30. Roger Fisher and Scott Brown, *Getting Together: Building Relationships as We Negotiate* (New York: Penguin Books, 1988).

31. A. Bostrom, "Future Risk Communication," *Futures* 35, no. 6 (August 2003), p. 553.

32. Richard Alan Nelson, "Ethics and Social Issues in Business: An Updated Communication Perspective," *Competitiveness Review* 13, no. 1 (2003), p. 66.

33. Bernard Rosenbaum, "Making Presentations: How to Persuade Others to Accept Your Ideas," *American Salesman* (February 1992), p. 16.

34. Robert W. Rasberry and Laura Lemoine Lindsay, *Effective Managerial Communication,* 2nd ed. (Belmont, CA: Wadsworth, 1994), p. 256.

35. Robert E. Kelley, *How to Be a Star at Work: Nine Breakthrough Strategies You Need to Succeed* (New York: Times Business, 1998), p. 225.

36. Debra Hamilton, "Prepare and Practice," *Officepro* (March 2000), p. 14.

37. Ibid.

Exercise 8–A **Creating Consonance** **out of Dissonance**	Earlier in the chapter, we shared the example of a newly hired employee (of a family-friendly company) who is being asked by her boss to work Saturday to get ready for an upcoming client meeting when she already has plans to attend her child's school play.

1. Knowing of the company's family-friendly philosophy and the dissonance involved in this request, how would you advise her to persuade her supervisor to accept her declining to work on Saturday?

   _____

   _____

   _____

2. Why is there dissonance? Explain.

   _____

   _____

   _____

3. How can she restore consonance? For example, Festinger advises that the persuader can show the attractiveness of the chosen alternative, increasing it in the eyes of the persuadee. The persuader can also decrease the attractiveness of the unchosen alternative. Use the space below to create a script that demonstrates your application of Festinger's advice in this situation.

   _____

   _____

   _____

   _____

Exercise 8–B **Online Assessment:** **What is Your Influence** **Quotient?**	Earlier in the chapter, we referenced the influence research of Cialdini. On his website, www.influenceatwork.com, there is a wonderful (and challenging!) scenario-based quiz. Visitors to this website can register and take this 10-question quiz for free; we recommend you do so. Two sample questions are listed below:

Questions

- If you want to influence someone to agree to a costly proposal (e.g., time, effort, money), should you present the most or least costly option first?
- Is it better to tell someone what she or he will gain from complying with your request or what they will lose if they do not?

Answers

- More (reciprocity principle: rejection [now you owe me] then retreat [so buy/do this for me]).
- Lose (scarcity principle: People are more motivated to go after what's scarce).

Debrief

1. How did you do?
2. Did any of the answers surprise you? Which ones? Why?
3. What was the most important thing you learned from this quiz?
4. How will you apply this learning to a future opportunity that requires your persuasion skills?

**Exercise 8–C
Debate Persuasions**

Watch one political debate for the upcoming elections. The debate you choose to watch should be one for which you are already aware of the candidates and issues.

After watching the debate, please answer the following questions.

Debate watched _____   Date of debate _____

1. Discuss the nonverbals used by the candidates. Did these support their verbal statements/positions?

   _____

   _____

   _____

2. Was one candidate more credible than the other? Considering the four dimensions offered by Jay Conger and as discussed in the chapter, what made this candidate more credible? If both were equally credible, discuss why you thought this was the case.

   _____

   _____

   _____

3. What other forms of persuasion did the candidates utilize in the debate?

   _____

   _____

   _____

4. Choosing one of the candidates, what could he or she have done differently to make his or her debate performance more persuasive and effective? Explain.

   _____

   _____

   _____

5. How important was your own political ideology in assessing the relative performance of each candidate? How did your belief system affect your interpretation of the debate?

   _____

   _____

   _____

Source: Contributed by Dr. David Kaplan, College of Business, St. Louis University.

**Exercise 8–D
Persuasive PSA**

The vice president of student affairs has asked your class to participate in a statewide competition that involves developing a PSA (public service announcement) aimed at getting teenagers and twenty-somethings to quit (or refrain from starting) smoking. Each team will have 10–15 minutes to develop a two-minute persuasive PSA to present to the instructor and class. After all groups present their PSAs, the class will vote on which team should represent your school in the statewide competition.

Questions

1. How successful was your team in devising and presenting solid, persuasive arguments?
2. What were the strongest arguments in your team's PSA? Explain.
3. What were the weakest areas of your team's PSA? Why were they weak?
4. Thinking about the persuasion process and specific strategies mentioned in the chapter, what could your team have done or said differently to ensure greater success?

**Exercise 8–E
"I Deserve a Raise"
Role-Play**

You have been employed in your first job after college for a little more than one year. When you were hired, you were promised a raise after the first year. However, at your recent performance appraisal, there was no mention of a raise despite the fact that you received above-average ratings on most performance criteria. You are considering leaving your employer to go to graduate school if you don't get a raise.

In your triad or small group, devise a persuasive argument to present to your boss to convince her or him you should get a raise. In each round, two of you play the roles of employee and boss, while the third and other persons are observers. In round one, person A is the employee, B is the boss, and C is the observer. In round two, person A is the boss, B the observer, and C the employee, and so on. Each round should last about 10 minutes and should include first the persuasion role-play and then a round of feedback in which the observer(s) gives feedback to the employee about his or her persuasion skills.

Questions for the Observer(s)

1. How successful was the employee in devising and presenting a solid, persuasive argument?

2. What areas of the employee's argument were weak or lacking support? Which were positive and supportable?

3. What did the employee do that contributed to her or his success? What could the employee have done to ensure greater success?

4. What, if any, objections did the boss present for which the employee was not prepared? What was the impact on the outcome?

**Exercise 8–F
Back to the Future**

Your parents own a small print shop, one that had been passed down from one of their parents during the B.C. (before computers) period. Inventory and sales records are kept in notebooks or on cards filed in shoeboxes. Customers' names and numbers are listed on a Rolodex file. To send the annual Christmas card, one of the employees hand-addresses about 350 envelopes. While technology has changed, things in the print shop have not.

You are home over winter break and wish to apply some of your technology-based knowledge and skills to improve things in the print shop. You know of several computer systems and software applications that can keep track of customers, sales, and inventory, all at the touch of a button. Send a letter to only those customers in a particular city? Piece of cake most anywhere else, but not at your parents' shop. You explain the value of computers to them, but they insist that all is well in the print shop. Besides, they tell you, "If it ain't broke, why fix it?" To convince them to adopt (and use!) the kind of computer system you know will benefit them, you decide to apply the six steps of persuasion. Use the worksheet below to develop a script for what you'll say and do to address each of these prongs:

Understand others' motivations and needs

_____

_____

_____

Establish credibility

_____

_____

_____

Frame for common ground

_____

_____

Engage in joint problem solving

_____

_____

_____

Support preferred outcome with logic and reasoning (and benefits)

_____

_____

_____

Reinforce with appeal to emotions and basic instincts

_____

_____

_____

**Exercise 8–G
Applying the Six
Persuasion Steps to
Your Own Situation**

Jot down a current situation in which you would like to persuade someone to do something that you think she or he is not likely to do in the absence of your persuasion attempt.

Current situation:

_____

_____

_____

What I would like to see (ideal situation):

_____

_____

_____

Now, complete the following worksheet as if you were preparing a script to use in this persuasion attempt:

Understand others' motivations and needs

_____

_____

_____

Establish credibility

_____

_____

_____

Frame for common ground

_____

_____

_____

Engage in joint problem solving

_____

_____

_____

Support preferred outcome with logic and reasoning (and benefits)

_____

_____

_____

Reinforce with appeal to emotions and basic instincts

_____

_____

_____

Exercise 8–H
Understanding the Power of Leveraging Basic Instincts

This chapter discussed three ways to use Cialdini's basic instincts to persuade others. They are listed below. Research current events in the workplace or the world to provide examples of each. Then explain why the persuasion attempt was successful.

	Example	Why It Worked
Reciprocity/obligation		
Scarcity		
Consensus/social proof		

Pick one of the above instincts and apply it to an upcoming persuasion attempt in the space below. Describe which approach you would use and how you would use it. Be specific in describing exactly what you would do or say in employing this approach.

_____

_____

_____

Exercise 8–I
Successful and Unsuccessful Influence: Mel Gibson, Jack Nicholson, and me

In *Braveheart* (1995, directed by Gibson), we find William Wallace attempting to influence a group of ragtag Scottish soldiers to fight against the larger, more powerful English army. Wallace stands alone; after all, the odds of losing (i.e., dying) are great, but he argues, the risks of fighting are worth it. Please watch the entire clip: http://www.youtube.com/watch?v=WLrrBs8JBQo&feature=related.

1. Why was Wallace successful? Discuss the influence tactics or approaches he employed. If you were the target of his influence, would you have been influenced? Explain.

_____

_____

_____

_____

2. Discuss a time when you challenged the status quo and influenced others successfully. Why were you successful? What did (or didn't) you do or say that prevented you or your organization from reaping the benefits of a new or improved process?

_____

_____

_____

_____

Not all influence attempts will be successful. In this diner scene from *Five Easy Pieces* (1970, directed by Bob Rafelson), Nicholson's character makes multiple attempts to influence the waitress to get what he wants. Watch this clip: http://www.youtube.com/watch?v=6wtfNE4z6a8.

3. What tactics did he use? Why was he unsuccessful (or, put another way, what could he have done to get what he wanted)?

_____

_____

_____

4. Think about a time when you were unable to challenge a process or influence others. Why were you unsuccessful? What did (or didn't) you do or say that prevented you or your organization from reaping the benefits of a new or improved process? If you could redo this attempt, what one or two key things would you have done differently and how would the outcome have changed?

_____

_____

_____

_____

**Exercise 8–J
Applying the ACE
Theory**

Scenario One

You learn that your college roommate will be spending a semester abroad. Just as you begin planning a new and better arrangement of your room, your RA knocks on your door. Standing beside him is someone who is, from the looks of it, not going to be a lot of fun: the thick-rimmed glasses, the pocket protector, the skin color suggesting little if any time spent outdoors. You keep your stereotypes to yourself and hope for the best. Unfortunately, your expectations are met. Pat rarely talks, leaves the room, or spends time with anyone or anything besides the books and computer. You'd like to see Pat have a little bit of fun, but you're afraid that your offer will be declined, only adding to the tension in the room. Tomorrow night is movie night at your college, when a relatively recent film is shown for free in the main auditorium on campus. Perhaps, if your persuasion attempt follows the ACE Theory, you might be successful. Use the following worksheet to prepare a script for what you would say or do to convince Pat to take a break from the books and join you in a movie.

Appropriateness (What is typical, common, or accepted practice for similar others?)

_____

_____

Consistency (In what ways might going to the movies align with Pat's behaviors or beliefs?)

_____

_____

Effectiveness (How would going to the movie result in a positive outcome for Pat?)

_____

_____

_____

_____

Scenario Two

You just received a fabulous invitation to study and work abroad for one year. This opportunity couldn't be more perfect. Your parents support the idea (especially considering one of your uncles lives in the same European town) and have agreed to pay the costs associated with it. It's what you've always wanted to do, and it supports your goal of appearing more worldly to potential employers. And you'll even get paid—however modestly—for part-time work you'll perform while there. Everything about the situation is ideal . . . except that one of the employees in the advising office lets you know that only about half of the credits will transfer and count toward your degree, partly because your school doesn't currently have an official study abroad program.

Use the ACE model to plan how you will try to persuade the advising office to agree to award you the maximum credit possible for successfully completing your study/work abroad opportunity.

Appropriateness (What is typical, common, or accepted practice for similar schools?)

_____

_____

_____

Consistency (In what ways might granting the credit align with the school's goals or objectives?)

_____

_____

_____

Effectiveness (How would approving your request result in a positive outcome for the advising office and/or school?)

_____

_____

_____

Scenario Three

You work at an insurance firm consisting of approximately 150 employees, with most involved in desk work. You would like to convince the owner that an exercise/wellness program should be added to the workplace. The owner is a man in his mid-50s and is highly concerned with attendance and productivity. Use the worksheet to script out how the ACE Theory could help you in being successful in your persuasion attempt.

Appropriateness (What is typical, common, or accepted practice for similar others?)

_____

_____

_____

Consistency (In what ways might developing an exercise/wellness program align with the owner's behaviors or beliefs?)

_____

_____

_____

Effectiveness (How would developing an exercise/wellness program result in a positive outcome for the owner?)

_____

_____

_____

**Exercise 8–K
Reflection/Action Plan**

This chapter focused on persuasion—what it is, why it is important, and how to improve your skills in this area. Complete the following worksheet upon completing all reading and experiential activities for this chapter.

1. The one or two areas in which I am most strong are:

_____

_____

_____

2. The one or two areas in which I need more improvement are:

_____

_____

_____

3. If I did only one thing to improve in this area, it would be to:

_____

_____

_____

4. Making this change would probably result in:

_____

_____

_____

5. If I did not change or improve in this area, it would probably affect my personal and professional life in the following ways:

_____

_____

_____

UNIT 1

INTRAPERSONAL EFFECTIVENESS: UNDERSTANDING YOURSELF

1. Journey into Self-awareness
2. Self-disclosure and Trust
3. Establishing Goals Consistent with Your Values and Ethics
4. Self-management

UNIT 2

INTERPERSONAL EFFECTIVENESS: UNDERSTANDING AND WORKING WITH OTHERS

5. Understanding and Working with Diverse Others
6. Listening and Nonverbal Communication
7. Communicating Effectively
8. Persuading Individuals and Audiences

UNIT 3

UNDERSTANDING AND WORKING IN TEAMS

9. Negotiation
10. Building Teams and Work Groups
11. Managing Conflict
12. Achieving Business Results through Effective Meetings
13. Facilitating Team Success
14. Making Decisions and Solving Problems Creatively

UNIT 4

LEADING INDIVIDUALS AND GROUPS

15. Effective and Ethical Use of Power and Influence
16. Networking and Mentoring
17. Coaching and Providing Feedback for Improved Performance
18. Leading and Empowering Self and Others
19. Project Management

Unit 3

A trip to Disneyworld would be fun, for sure, but the experience would be even more memorable if you shared it with others. Today's organizations are cognizant of the value of teams and use them extensively in delivering and improving their products and services. In the same way you find value in sharing and comparing experiences with friends, organizations use work teams to support collaboration that often results in greater productivity, creativity, and innovation and fosters increased employee satisfaction and commitment. Along with these benefits, teams often face challenges, as many of you who have participated on teams—whether in school, sports, work, or other organizations—have found. In this unit, we discuss the team phenomenon and offer opportunities for you to improve your skills in managing conflict, negotiating, persuading, and facilitating the team process. Mastering these skills will help your team "accentuate the positive and eliminate the negative" aspects of team functioning.

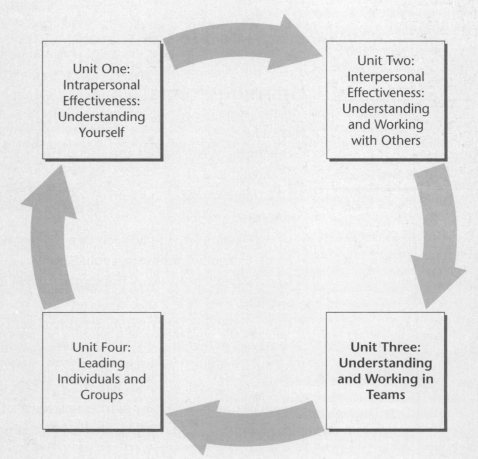

9

Negotiation

Learning Points

How do I:
- Determine what I want in a negotiation and make a plan to facilitate achieving it?
- Determine my best alternative to that goal if I don't get all that I want in a negotiation?
- Understand the other party's wants and needs in a negotiation?
- Involve the other person in a collaborative and interest-based negotiation?
- Know when to walk away from a negotiation if a resolution doesn't appear possible?
- Utilize agendas, questioning, framing, scripting, and other negotiation strategies to increase my effectiveness as a negotiator?
- Identify unethical negotiation behaviors and determine the motivation for engaging in such behavior and strategies for dealing with it?
- Increase my comfort and skill with special situations in negotiation, such as multiparty, virtual, and global negotiations?

John Monroe is a senior vice president for one of the country's largest hotel chains. Given his well-earned reputation as an industry leader in improving customer focus and satisfaction, it's not surprising to learn that a competitor based in the United Kingdom is attempting to lure John away from his company. In fact, the initial contact with Rupert Kingston, the CEO, progressed to two additional phone conversations, and most recently, a face-to-face visit where Rupert and members of the senior management team wined and dined John and ended with "an offer he can't refuse." While John has had some concerns about his present employer, he hadn't been actively looking for another position. In addition, he is concerned about how his wife and 14-year-old daughter would react to a move. They moved 800 miles away from their home when he took his current position five years ago, and both ladies had a tough time making new friends and adjusting to a town that was substantially larger (in size and population) than what they were used to. After his visit, John found himself sitting on the plane, contemplating whether he should accept the offer.

1. At this point, what should John do? What, if anything, should he refrain from doing?

2. What kind of preparation should John do prior to his negotiation about the terms of the offer? What kind of data should he gather, what people should he talk to, and what decisions should he make?

3. What are some specific arguments he could use to improve his chances of getting the opportunity package in which he is interested?

4. Even if he decides not to take the offer from the UK, how can John use this situation to address and improve the "concerns" he has with his present employer?

"You often get not what you deserve, but what you negotiate."[1]

John Mariotti

E veryone negotiates. Children negotiate to decide which games to play or which television show to watch. Students try to negotiate a higher grade from their professor. Employees negotiate for a certain salary, benefits, or perquisites. Corporations negotiate with other organizations on the sale or purchase of assets, materials, or operating units. Negotiations occur globally as in the case of the Mideast, the NATO treaty, and NAFTA. Whether you're a diplomat or dignitary, spouse or salesperson, student or teacher, you negotiate almost daily. Sometimes the stakes are high, as in the case of a buyout of a firm; sometimes the stakes are low, as in the case of which movie you and your friends choose to see. In this chapter, we discuss the fundamentals of negotiation, benefits of doing it well, types and stages of negotiation, and principles and strategies for enhancing your skill in this arena. At the end of the chapter are several exercises to help you build your negotiating skills, as well as a list of references that will help you pursue this important topic further.

What Is Negotiation and Why Is It Important?

Negotiation is a process in which two or more people or groups share their concerns and interests to reach an agreement of mutual benefit.[2] It occurs when all parties have both shared interests (meaning they're committed to a resolution) and opposed interests (meaning they don't agree on everything). This definition implies that both parties have an incentive for devoting energy to the negotiation and that they are willing to collaborate on reaching a shared agreement.[3] Sometimes we use the terms *bargaining* and *negotiating* interchangeably, although most associate bargaining with the type of haggling that occurs over items in a yard sale and negotiating with a more formal process in which parties attempt to find a mutually agreeable solution to a conflict situation.

Why Do We Negotiate?

We negotiate when what one party wants is not necessarily what the other party wants. The conflict of interests may be clear and simple. If the competitor offers John a significant increase plus a package that is attractive to John's wife and daughter, John may accept the offer. If the competitor doesn't have the latitude to offer a significant increase, or doesn't show an interest in the family's overall needs, John may turn down the offer. At other times, the conflict is more complex, consisting of multiple issues, competing interests, and unlimited potential solutions. Examples of this type of conflict include the merger or takeover of a company, a rift between a company's management and its unionized employees, or a divorce. While some conflicts wind up in court, most conflicts of this type, even those that appear to be quite complicated, can be negotiated and settled before trial.

Complex negotiation is a fact of life for anyone in business. Managers ensure work gets done on time and within a budget. To do this successfully, managers negotiate for the necessary resources. As long as resources are scarce, negotiation will always be an

Source: www.CartoonStock.com. EA: Reprinted with permission.

essential skill for businesspeople. Another factor driving the need for negotiation skills in business is the increased use of teams in the workplace. As individuals from "competing" business units are brought together on projects, the ability to negotiate with others—both inside and outside the team—is critical for the ultimate success of the project team. Global diversity is another factor motivating the need for acquiring skills in negotiation. As employees from a variety of countries and cultures are brought together to work on projects and joint ventures, an inevitable clash of customs and business practices results in almost constant negotiating that involves developing and modifying relationships and expectations over time. A backlash against the litigious tendency of our modern society is another reason why it is important for managers to develop skill in negotiating. As the court dockets fill with numerous (and often frivolous) lawsuits, the negotiation of differences has become accepted and valued as a cost-effective alternative to litigation. Witness the growth of the number of organizations dedicated to helping individuals and companies improve their negotiating skills. The increasing number and availability of books, audio and videotapes, and Internet sites devoted to this topic provide further testimonial to the importance of effective negotiating in today's world. All these factors build a compelling case for acquiring and enhancing your negotiating skills.

Benefits of Honing Negotiation Skills

Individuals who master the skill of negotiation can gain many benefits, among which are these:

- **Increase your salary, profits, and marketability.** Good negotiation skills lead to better deals in everything from your salary and benefits to anything you purchase or sell. Near the end of a positive job interview, a recruiter may offer a particular salary/ compensation package. An inexperienced or unskilled person will see this offer as fixed—one to accept or decline. However, a good negotiator knows that this typically is an opening bid, and not a final figure. She or he has the experience and confidence to ask relevant questions, present compelling evidence, and request a better deal. The same is true when negotiating on behalf of your employer (or yourself, if you are an independent contractor). Good negotiation skills breed confidence, which breeds successful outcomes, which leads to even greater confidence in yourself and your ability to succeed—in your current and future endeavors.

- **Save time, money, and grief, while ensuring needs are met.** Negotiation is a more efficient and effective way to reach a solution than either a lawsuit or arbitration.[4] In a lawsuit, the adversarial nature of the environment pits one set of interests against the other. The goal is a "win–lose" situation, where one of the parties is clearly victorious over the other. In arbitration, both parties agree to a settlement reached by a third party, which may or may not reflect the interests of the conflicting parties. Arbitration occurs outside of the courtroom; however, the parties involved are bound by the verdict—one that may or may not bring satisfaction. Verdicts resulting from arbitration often resemble "win–lose" or even "lose–lose" resolutions, where either one party is victorious or both parties must compromise so severely that the final agreement is perceived as losing by both parties. In contrast, negotiation, when handled properly, typically results in identifying the primary interests of both parties and generating an agreement that addresses key issues of both parties. This can result in a "win–win" solution where both parties feel their primary interests have been listened to, if not addressed.

If a resolution can't be reached, arbitration or litigation may be necessary. However, these options tend to require more time and effort than negotiation. In a lawsuit, attorneys spend many hours doing research and preparing. In arbitration, an outside third party (an arbitrator) spends numerous hours getting up to speed on a case before being able to rule on it. All of this time is costly—hundreds of dollars per hour—to the parties involved. In negotiation, both parties are involved from the outset. Each party serves as the chief spokesperson for her or his point of view. Naturally others are involved, principally the negotiator or negotiators. But they work in partnership with the two parties, not as surrogates. The principal work is performed by the two parties themselves, resulting in a saving of time and energy spent on the negotiation process.

- **Improve relationships.** Even something as simple as a disagreement or misunderstanding with a friend or neighbor can escalate to an ugly and consuming battle if the parties are unable or unwilling to negotiate to resolve their differences. Working or living alongside an "enemy" can be anything but enjoyable. Another benefit of negotiation is that when it works, it helps both parties not only to achieve a workable resolution, but also to help preserve and improve their relationship, reputations, and sense of professional achievement. Conversely, after an arbitration or lawsuit has concluded, the parties involved often experience lingering feelings of resentment and anger that preclude them from being able to continue working together.

- **Reduce the number and severity of conflicts, thereby reducing stress.** Studies show that those who have sound negotiating skills are able to maintain better control in business and personal situations.[5] Good negotiators can focus on identifying each other's key interests and viewing the situation objectively, while putting their emotions aside. Over time, those who practice negotiating find they are better able to resist responding emotionally to a potential conflict, and tend to experience a reduction in the number of potential future conflicts. Being able to surface issues, clear the air, and deal directly with all legitimate concerns during a negotiation results in a clean slate—a feeling that both parties have been fully listened to and understood. This reduces frustration and the chance that these issues will resurface and generate additional conflict.

How to Negotiate Advancement in a Troubled Economic Market[6]

You don't get what you don't ask for. This adage is especially relevant in the tough economic times that find individuals and organizations struggling to keep pace. Are employees so grateful to have a job that they choose not to seek a raise? Does knowing that the organization is struggling keep employees from asking . . . assuming they wouldn't be successful and choosing to avoid hearing "no"?

Asking for a raise, especially at a time when many employers are cutting costs, often by workforce reductions, may seem counterintuitive. Despite widespread pessimism, savvy employees recognize that tough economic times may offer unique opportunities to improve their employment situation by helping their employer reduce costs, increase revenues, or improve competitiveness. Your ideas and innovations will provide invaluable rewards to the company; a small share of those rewards in the form of a raise is realistic and a way to make you feel appreciated.

(continued)

Know What You Want and Why

To increase the likelihood of a successful negotiation, start by clarifying exactly what you want and why. You need to articulate the amount you expect and a compelling reason for it (NOT that the rent on your apartment was just increased). Research salaries for someone with your responsibilities, education, and experience . . . and in your geographical region. Salaries in London are higher than they are in Warsaw. If you believe you are underpaid, demonstrate this with reliable data. Better still, demonstrate your worth by pointing out inefficiencies that your ideas have reduced or new clients you've brought in. Who could argue with a $10,000 raise for someone who has increased revenues by $175,000 last year?

Also, consider the other party's goals in your preparation. Would your promotion enable your boss to offload tasks that would free his or her time for more strategic activities? Look for voids that you might fill or problems you might alleviate. And always, remember that when dealing with an employer, maintaining a good relationship is a key interest regardless of the substantive outcome of the negotiation.

What If the Boss Says "No"?

When you know what you want and why, you're better equipped to consider multiple satisfactory alternatives. Going in with an ultimatum is unwise; such threats can harm the working relationship. In times of budget crises, a higher salary might be difficult to obtain, but there are other ways to "win." Working from home one or two days a week would save you several hours of commuting, as well as gas and wear and tear on your car (and your nerves!). Having alternatives to your goals gives you more confidence in the negotiation process since you aren't in the position of having to accept whatever is—or isn't—offered. It also gives you the ability to be persistent without alienating the other party. By suggesting other possible solutions, you help reframe the negotiation into a collaborative problem-solving session.

Finding a "Yes"

Sometimes, negotiation ends in a stalemate. The employee leaves unhappy, and, as is often the case when a boss's hands are tied by rules or other constraints, the boss leaves frustrated. Friction remains, along with the employee's declining motivation and commitment to the organization. The economy may be tough, but talented employees with in-demand skills will find other options. The unhappy, talented employee is attractive to other employers, and if he or she leaves, the losses will be great (recruiting and training costs, learning curves, lowered morale among remaining employees, loss of employee's clients). Research suggests it costs as much as 2.5 times the annual salary to replace a professional/managerial employee.

To avoid this situation, prepare to present a yes-able alternative. For example, you might negotiate an increase (or bonus) that is tied to the accomplishment of a specific goal.

> "If my plan for decreasing production costs succeeds and I can demonstrate a 5 percent reduction by December 31, I think it's fair to receive a bonus equivalent to 10 percent of that overall savings, with another 10 percent of that savings distributed among the team I'm leading. Compared to this time last year, that would mean a $150,000 savings: $15,000 to me, $15,000 split among the team of six, and $120,000 savings to the company. How can we get senior management's approval on this?"
>
> Or, "How about we make the raise (or bonus) contingent on exceeding my sales targets? That is, if I exceed my target by 10 percent, I get a 5 percent bonus, and if I exceed my target by 20 percent, I get a 10 percent bonus?"

Another yes-able alternative would be a phased-in agreement.

> "Considering the data I presented, which shows I am underpaid by 20 percent compared to all the recent new hires, how about we increase my salary by 5 percent in June, with an additional increase of 5 percent at year-end, if I bring my project in on time and on budget?"

Or, at the very least, you might agree to revisit the conversation at a specific time, for example, in three months.

Closing the Deal

Whatever is decided in the negotiation, be sure you nail down the specifics of your agreement (verbally and in a follow-up e-mail), including the measures to be used and time lines for a phased agreement. Thank your boss for taking the time to discuss this important issue, and remind her of the benefits she and the company will reap.

In tough economic times, your good performance is more valuable than ever. There may be cheaper employees available, but no one knows the job—or is as committed to seeing the company succeed—as much as you do. Remind yourself of that, and prepare yourself thoroughly to remind your boss what you deserve and why. You might not get everything you ask for, but you will certainly get none of what you don't ask for.

Integrative and Distributive Bargaining Strategies

Once we decide to negotiate,[7] our approach to negotiation or bargaining will generally fall into one of two categories or strategies: integrative, or "win–win," and distributive, or "win–lose."[8] Both strategies have their benefits and disadvantages and can be used depending on the needs inherent in a specific situation.[9]

Negotiators use an **integrative bargaining strategy** when they believe that a win–win situation exists and can be reached. This means that there's a chance both parties can achieve their primary objectives, without either feeling they lost. In integrative bargaining, the goal is to collaborate and generate one or more creative solutions that are acceptable to both parties. A simple example would be a couple trying to decide on a movie to rent. Taking an integrative approach, they would begin their discussion by drawing up a list of only those movies that were acceptable to both parties. They would discuss the available choices and choose a movie to see from that list, rather than arguing in favor of a movie that only one of the two parties wants to see.

A more complex example involves the creation of a "preferred supplier" agreement. Many firms seek to formalize the arrangements they may have with a particular supplier or vendor in order to reduce the uncertainty of changes in price and other market conditions. Should both organizations take an interactive approach to this solution, they would look beyond price—after all, the supplier's likely interest to maximize price is at odds with the organization's need to minimize it—to understand both the short- and long-term needs of both organizations. Issues of availability, reliability, quality, and prompt delivery and payment all enter into the equation in which price is but one factor. It's in both parties' best interests to find a workable solution, one that meets these multiple criteria. The supplier wins because it has a consistent customer for its product, ensuring a positive cash flow, steady employment, and predictable operations. The organization wins because it can rely on receiving the supplier's product consistently, when it's needed, at a fair price, and in the requested quantity. It doesn't need to search for additional options to save a few pennies; when all factors are considered, a preferred supplier arrangement benefits both parties.

Integrative bargaining only works when both parties are committed to preserving the relationship that exists between them. Integrative bargaining requires a great deal of creativity, problem-solving ability, and time, as well as a set of ultimate goals on which both parties can agree. Arriving at a truly integrative or collaborative solution to a conflict requires that those involved gain and use the necessary skills, knowledge, and attitude (including patience). Another requirement for integrative bargaining to work is a climate that supports and promotes open communication. Both parties need to be willing to change and to confront their conflict directly rather than run from it, resolve it through brute force, or pretend it will go away. The parties must be open to establishing longer-term goals on which they can both agree. For example, the couple choosing a movie must recognize that their relationship is more important than the choice of a movie and must be willing to collaborate or, if necessary, compromise for the sake of the overall relationship.

A **distributive bargaining strategy** is based on an attempt to divide up a fixed "pie" or amount of resources, resulting in a win–lose situation.[10] Negotiators taking a distributive approach typically take an adversarial or competitive posture to dividing a fixed amount of resources. One improves its lot at the expense of the other. This scarcity mentality implies that only one of the two parties can have the conflict resolved to its

**Figure 9–1
Comparing Bargaining
Approaches**

Considerations	Integrative Bargaining	Distributive Bargaining
Likely solution or end result	Win–win	Win–lose or lose–lose
Importance of continued relationship with bargaining partner	High	Low
Goal	Collaborate and generate multiple options or solutions; expand the pie	Winner takes all (scarcity mentality); distribute a fixed pie
Bargaining climate	Open, communicative, creative, willing to change	Determination to win, willingness to walk away, cards held close to the chest, ends justify the means
Amount of time needed	More	Less
Time horizon in consideration	Current and future	Immediate only

satisfaction. In distributive bargaining, the focus is on achieving immediate goals, with little or no regard for building future relationships. Little time or energy is expended in resolving the conflict in a distributive negotiation, resulting in the generation of few if any creative solutions. Generally, one or two fixed solutions are presented and a decision or choice is expected almost immediately, with possibly some consequence if a choice is not made soon. If distributive bargaining were used to resolve the movie decision mentioned earlier, the couple would likely not be very close, and one or both parties would not care whether the relationship was a good one or lasted much longer. In this example, one member of the couple would say something like, "This is the movie I want to see. Take it or leave it." There would be no real discussion of the wants and interests of both parties. The "agreement" would be reached either by dictate or after some fierce arguing. While win–lose is not a recommended strategy for resolving issues, it can be used in situations where achieving short-term goals is more important than maintaining or building longer-term relationships. Distributive bargaining is also appropriate to use in situations that are so contentious there is no possibility of a win–win solution, when there's a sense of urgency and time is short, and when the relationships involved are relatively unimportant compared to the issue at hand. Forcing children to wear protective gear when bicycling is an example of this. "Aw, Mom, do I have to wear my helmet? What if I promise to be really careful?" Allowing the child to negotiate on this issue is a waste of time, as his or her safety is paramount in this situation. Despite the intuitive appeal and apparent societal acceptance of the "winner take all" or "ends justify the means" approach to negotiation, distributive bargaining generally tends to be ineffective and counterproductive and should be used only in certain circumstances. Figure 9–1 summarizes these two approaches.

Five Stages of Negotiating

We've discussed why people negotiate and the types of negotiation. Now we turn to the how, or the process of negotiating. Keep in mind that all negotiations are different. Simple negotiations, such as choosing which movie to rent, need not require an extensive negotiation process. However, when negotiations involve significant or complex issues, you should consider using the five-stage process model depicted in Figure 9–2. As illustrated, negotiating consists of five stages: (1) preparation and planning, (2) defining ground rules, (3) clarifying and justifying your case, (4) bargaining and problem solving, and (5) closure and implementation.[11] These stages are described below.

1. *Preparation and planning.* Without question, preparation and planning are the keys to successful deal making. While some may think they can negotiate effectively "on the fly," all negotiators benefit from thorough advance thought and preparation. Be clear about what you want and why. Gather data to support your position. Consider ways to present your arguments persuasively. Consider what the other party wants and why. What

Figure 9–2
The Five Stages of Negotiation

1. Preparation and planning	2. Defining ground rules	3. Clarifying and justifying your case	4. Bargaining and problem solving	5. Closure and implementation
• Clarify what you want and why • Establish a BATNA • Develop a frame • Create a strategy/script	• Set an agenda • Agree on objective criteria • Agree on what to do if an agreement is not reached • Discuss what is, is not acceptable, e.g., yelling	• Clarify your interests • Use a frame to make your case persuasive • Use questions to understand others' interests • Share relevant information that supports your case	• Focus on problems, not people • Focus on interests, not positions • Look forward, not backward • Create options for mutual gain; adapt win–win attitude • Select from options using principles, or objective criteria	• Verbally summarize what both parties agreed to • Review key points to ensure understanding • Draft agreement in writing • Have both parties sign agreement

Many of the strategies or tips discussed in the chapter that should be considered during each phase are listed under the corresponding stage.

data or tactics might they use? How will you counter? Answer these questions when preparing your negotiation strategy. Understand your and the other party's strengths and weaknesses, and take these similarities and differences into account in your strategy. If negotiating is new to you, learn and practice the basics of negotiating well in advance of a planned negotiation. Build new skills that are appropriate to this particular situation.

Another important component in preparing for negotiations is determining your **BATNA**, which, according to negotiation experts Fisher and Ury, is the best alternative to a negotiated agreement or the best outcome one party to a negotiation could get should the negotiation neither occur nor conclude.[12] By identifying your BATNA, you strengthen your bargaining position and chances for a positive outcome. For example, if you want to secure a position with a well-regarded firm in a particular industry by June, what will you do if that hasn't happened by then? Will you accept a lower salary at a lesser firm? Will you choose to go to law school? Would you accept a low-paying or nonpaying internship that provides marketable experience? The BATNA is not your bottom line, or the minimum you'd accept; instead, it's a desirable outcome that you've considered or arranged prior to the negotiation should the negotiation not take place. This alternative gives you flexibility and a sense that you don't have to take whatever is offered.[13] Lastly, prepare for a negotiation by learning as much as you can about the other party prior to the negotiation. In addition to the questions above, see what you can uncover about their negotiating style by talking with others with whom they've negotiated. If possible, try to become acquainted with the other party before the planned meeting. By establishing your willingness to get to know the other party, you will be better able to begin the negotiation with a positive, relationship-based tone rather than on an adversarial note.[14] We discuss framing and scripting later in the chapter.

2. *Definition of ground rules.* Determining your own guidelines or rules for the negotiation helps you plan a strategy that can be successful.[15] Establish who will or should be present and at what part of the negotiation. Decide where the meeting will be held and offer a possible agenda for how the time will be allocated and for which issues. The location has implications in terms of who's in charge. While there may be a benefit to having the negotiation at your office—the home court advantage—agreeing to have the negotiation at the other party's office might show flexibility and willingness to negotiate on your part. When the topic covered is potentially divisive or difficult, a neutral location might help level the playing field for both parties—an important consideration when an integrative solution is desired.

Set enough time in the negotiation to deal with the critical issues that are involved. Getting two opposing parties to agree, especially when multiple issues are being simultaneously considered, requires more time than you might imagine. Shortening the time available for the discussion serves as a conversation stopper and is counterproductive. Prior to the negotiation, establish a flexible, reasonable plan that outlines what you hope to accomplish, how you intend to talk about the topic, how you plan to introduce the topic, and how you will handle any responses from the other party. Set clear parameters for the discussion and the process, such as: no name calling, it's okay for either party to call a time-out, additional issues may be set aside for a later discussion, and you both must agree. Finally, seek agreement on standards and criteria to use when discussing the various alternatives that the discussion generates.[16]

3. *Clarification and justification.* As the negotiation begins, state what you want and why. A key issue here is the difference between positions and interests. A **position** is a stance—typically a firm one—taken by a negotiator. "I'll give you $4,500 and that's my final offer." An **interest** is the explanation behind the position, need, or desire that expresses why a negotiator wants what he or she wants. "I'm asking for $5,000 because the car has low miles, an upgraded stereo system, and brand-new, all-weather tires." It's important for both parties to learn the interests behind the stated position. When you share your interests and expectations, you set the stage for the other party to be similarly open about their desires and reasons behind them. Doing so also allows them to become fully engaged in the process. Clarifying to one another your proposals and the rationale behind them requires excellent communication skills and enhances both parties' understanding of the key issues that are involved and the ability to collaboratively discover common interests. The first three verbal tactics included in Figure 9–3 will facilitate this negotiation stage, and Figure 9–5 expands on the use of questions.

Figure 9–3
Verbal Negotiation Tactics[17]

Tactic	Description	Example
Self-disclosure	I will tell you something about myself or important information.	We have had to lay off 100 employees this month. We really need to sign a major contract by the end of the year.
Question	I will ask you something about yourself.	Can you tell me more about your foreign operations?
Reward (unconditional, positive)	I will give you something positive now, on the spot.	Let's make it easier on you tomorrow and meet closer to your office. I have appreciated your meeting at my building.
Threat (conditional, negative)	I will do something you do not want me to do, if you do something I don't want you to do.	If you don't give me a good price, I'll take my business elsewhere.
Recommendation	If you do something I want you to do, a third party will do something you want.	If you give me a good deal on this item, I will get my friend to buy one too.
Warning	If you do something I don't want you to, a third party will do something you do not want.	If you do not replace this item, the government will investigate your operation.
Promise (conditional, positive)	I will do something if you will do something I want you to.	I will lower the price by $5 if you will order in bulk.
Punishment (unconditional, negative)	I will give you something negative now, on the spot.	I refuse to listen to your screaming. I am leaving.
Normative appeal	I will appeal to a societal norm.	Everybody else buys our product for $5 per unit.
Commitment	I will do something you want.	I will deliver 100 units by June 15.
Command	I will order you to do something.	Lower your price.

4. *Bargaining and problem solving.* In the fourth stage, both parties are actively and constructively engaged in working toward solutions. Once the interests and criteria are clearly communicated, it is time for a creative, idea-generating process. This requires skill in finding solutions that might address one or more of the parties' collective needs, as well as "expanding the pie" and generating even more creative solutions that may not be readily apparent. At this stage, it is best to remain open-minded, considering options without making value judgments or critiquing them. Judgment curtails creativity. By exploring all possibilities for solutions, rather than trying to focus too quickly on one fixed solution, interesting ideas and combinations of ideas may emerge.

Consider, for example, the aging patriarch who is looking for a potential suitor to buy his company. It would be easy to argue over dollars and cents—what the company is worth—and never arrive at a mutually agreeable solution. First, the assumptions or models both parties used to estimate the company's value are likely different. Second, there is a great deal of hidden "value." The business is not just a collection of assets, employees, customers, patented processes, and accounts receivable; it is, in the founder's mind, a child he nurtured for years and years. Putting yourself in the shoes of the founder, think about what he really might want, besides money. Recognition for his business acumen? A position as chairman emeritus and consultant? A monthly stipend and benefit package? An opportunity to share in the profits for the years he remains as a consultant to the new owner? When you look outside the box of the calculable solution, you might find something even better.

Negotiation in a Family Business[18]

Families in business are exposed to many types of conflicts. This is inherent to the structure. The shared history and emotional connections are not always sufficient to bring a solution, and can exacerbate the conflict.

Not all members of a family business are created equal. Not just in their power positions, but also in their motivations for being involved in the business. Some become de facto leaders—no choice but to take over the business, others campaign vigorously only to be overlooked in favor of a less talented or deserving sibling, and still others work just hard enough to justify their salary. Depending on the motivation, one family member may approach negotiations (with other family members or with external negotiators) very differently from another. Those family members who want to continue the family business for generations are more likely to adopt an integrative approach—focusing on the long-term relationship and creating value for both parties, while those who want to cash out as quickly as possible will likely adopt a distributive approach—grab the biggest piece of the pie without concern for the relationship. These different dynamics have the potential to tear a family apart, as negotiations within a family-owned business are not book-ended, but are ongoing, spillover-prone negotiations. Take the case of four brothers of a Dutch shipping company. When their father, a 20 percent owner, considered selling his stake, he only offered it to one son—the one he thought was best equipped. Or the case of a Chinese family business that automatically excluded the daughters from ownership. When power is unequally shared among family members, it becomes difficult to make decisions for the good of the family, especially for those who feel they've been slighted.

Another issue affecting family negotiations is the untested and faulty assumption that sharing the same last name means sharing the same views. If I "know" that all members of the family (like me) want to keep operations in the small town where the business began—even if regulations or labor supply would be more favorable elsewhere—I'm not going to ask what I already know. This type of self-censoring may preclude a family member from suggesting an alliance with another firm when previous suggestions were dismissed because "we're a family business." Moreover, even if one or more family members were willing to challenge their assumptions and propose a new way of operating, they may find strong opposition from members unwilling to accept a solution that conflicts with family history, traditions, and the "way we do things."

(continued)

A prerequisite to creating win–win opportunities is keeping an open mind, which means being willing to set aside preconceived "solutions" and consider new and creative possibilities. When someone negotiates on behalf of her family-owned business, her ego and identity is intertwined with the business. A challenge to an offer may be perceived as a personal attack, as was the case of a CEO who had been running his niche automotive parts business for the last 40 years. As he was nearing retirement, he considered his options, including selling the business. He hired a professional valuation firm, confident of the value of the empire he built. When the professionals shared their results—valuing the business at about 30 percent of what the CEO thought it was worth—the CEO insulted them, kicked them out of his office, and demanded a refund. If negotiators can't see the business and its offerings objectively because of their psychological attachment to the business, they'll be unable to engage effectively in collaboratively generating creative solutions.

In family businesses, typically the major conflicts, confrontations, and negotiations arise around the issue of generational transition of ownership and management control. These are the times when creativity—and rationality—are needed to imagine new opportunities and role changes for the individuals involved. Rather than looking back and disagreeing about splitting roles and responsibilities, the better way is to imagine an engaging new growth project, jointly developed and shared by members of different generations. A yes-able and win–win proposition might sound like this: "Why don't we open a new office in China and explore new possibilities for new markets and new products? This would be an exciting learning and development opportunity for us as a family, and could offer diverse roles for interested family members."

Have you ever been involved in a family business? What strategies might you use to overcome these special challenges? You can also experience a conflict in a family business in Exercise 9-K.

Once a number of alternatives have been put forth, analysis and discussion of each can begin. Take the time to assess carefully how well each alternative meets the interests of both parties, the benefits and disadvantages, and its relation to the key issues involved in the negotiation. At this stage, it is appropriate to begin narrowing the options to the one or few that appear to best solve the initial problem in a way that is satisfactory to both parties. Don't worry about "dotting all the i's and crossing all the t's" at this point. Details like the exact percentage of the profit-sharing plan described above can be worked out later. Structure a deal on which you can both agree by recording key terms of the agreement and the steps necessary to complete the details and maintain the agreement.

Sometimes, you don't have all the data available to finalize a decision. For example, you might agree to provide a benefits package to the founder of the company for a period of no longer than three years and at a price no greater than 30 percent of his monthly draw. Determining which insurance company and whether it covers monthly chiropractic visits is more detail than is necessary at this point. Other times, you might have to end the discussion with some terms still up in the air. Perhaps a key piece of information will only be available at year-end. Record the terms to which you've reached agreement, and agree to postpone deciding on the remaining issues until a specified future date. This approach is generally preferable to one in which the last few details are quickly and perhaps forcibly pushed through. If the deal is likely to stipulate how two parties will work together over the next 5, 10, or more years, isn't it worthwhile to invest a proportionately similar amount of time and energy to ensure that the partnership will be successful?

5. *Closure and implementation.* In this final stage, the terms of the agreement that has been reached are formalized. Unfortunately, many overlook or ignore this step, thinking that once an agreement is reached it will be implemented automatically. Leaving out this step can lead to future misunderstandings. No two people will leave a communication with the same perceptions. The only way to ensure that both parties know what they're agreeing to is to take specific steps:

- Document what you agreed on.
- Review the key points to avoid misunderstanding.

- Discuss issues that the parties hedged on, describing clearly all stipulations of the agreement.

- Get it in writing.

- Read the written agreement before signing to ensure clarity and commitment to what was negotiated.[19]

Every negotiation is likely to present you with different challenges and opportunities. By following these five steps and the advice contained therein, you can increase the likelihood of arriving at an agreement that meets the needs of all parties involved in the negotiation.

Strategies for Negotiating Effectively

The process model we described provides a helpful template for preparing for and participating in a negotiation. Within these stages, and as depicted in Figure 9–2, a number of tips and techniques can improve the likelihood of achieving success. Because of their importance in the negotiation process, three of these concepts—scripting, framing, and managing—are discussed in greater detail below.

Scripting

There is no substitute for adequate preparation in negotiation. Unlike other business interactions that can be handled simultaneously, negotiation is a serious enterprise that requires focus, attention, time, research, and planning. The more prepared you are, the greater the chances that you'll get what you deserve and bargain for.

One of the best ways to ensure adequate preparation time is to develop a **script** or **strategy outline** (see Figure 9–4). Take some time to think about the negotiation situation in which you find yourself. What are your interests and those of the other party? What would you each ideally like to see come out of the negotiation? How would you each like

---

**Figure 9–4
Negotiation Script/Strategy
Outline**

Goals:

- Develop an interest-based strategy/approach prior to a face-to-face negotiation.
- Identify potential options/plans that can be proposed.

Topics to Consider:

1. The other person's probable strategy. What do they want (goals) and why (interests)?
2. My strategy. What do I want and why? What am I willing to accept (my BATNA—best alternative to a negotiated agreement)?
3. How I'll begin the negotiation. What can I say to position the negotiation positively and to express my desire to arrive at a solution that is mutually rewarding and satisfactory?
4. The core issues, and any assumptions about those issues, include the following (remember to focus on the problem and not the person):
5. The primary focus or the real problem(s) to be resolved is:
6. What might get in the way of achieving the desired outcome? How can I overcome this?
7. How I'll react to . . . (list several potential proposals that may emerge during the negotiation and how you feel about those proposals):
   (a)
   (b)
   (c)
8. Potential creative options or integrative, win–win solutions that I might suggest:
   (a)
   (b)
   (c)
9. Components of a plan and/or objective criteria on which we can both agree:

things to end up? What are some ways in which that might be possible? What can you do to make this happen? By thinking through the issues, objectives, options, and solutions from both your and the other's perspective, you are better able to handle almost anything that develops during the negotiation. Preparing ahead doesn't prevent surprises. But it can certainly lessen the number of surprises and make it more likely you can handle the unexpected if and when it happens.

Framing

Another important element to consider when preparing for or managing a negotiation is a **frame**. A frame is a point of view or perspective we bring to an interaction such as a negotiation. How we view a situation can affect how willing we are to engage in a negotiation and even our goals. Negotiation experts Margaret Neale and Max Bazerman offer the following example.[20] You and a friend go to the beach. After a few hours, your throat becomes dry and you'd like a sparkling water—if the price is right. Your friend offers to investigate the options, and you consider your limits. In one scenario, you're about a mile from town and notice a small, run-down market about a block away. How much are you willing to pay for a bottle of water? In another scenario, you and your friend are lying on the beach owned by a four-star resort. The waiter is about to approach and ask if he can get you anything. Now, how much are you willing to pay for that sparkling water? Chances are, you'll pay more in the second scenario—for the same bottle of water. Similarly, if people are convinced they are getting a good deal, they are more likely to accept the offer presented. On the other hand, if they think they are being taken advantage of, they are much less likely to accept the offer even if it means they end up worse off. Indeed, the more negatively you frame a situation, the more risk you are likely to take, because you believe you have less to lose. Imagine you were working at General Motors in the summer of 2006 when the company offered a buyout—paying you to leave your job—to a large number of employees. If you hated your job or believed you would be laid off permanently, you would be more likely to accept the buyout, even if you didn't have another job lined up, than if you liked your job and believed you were unlikely to be laid off.[21]

When we use frames in negotiation, we provide a perspective that helps others understand where we are coming from and manages expectations. When proposing a plan for downsizing an organization to shareholders, one possibility is to frame this move as a means to minimize costs or losses. Another possibility is to frame this move as a means to maximize competitiveness. While both frames explain downsizing, the frames—posed as either losses or gains—will likely have differing effects on the perceivers. Similar to framing a picture, the frame highlights the points you want to make in negotiation and provides a filter for the other party to assess your position and supporting evidence. This is done by selecting a perspective believed to be credible, compelling, and appropriate to your intent. Frames can also provide a rationale for the evidence presented and a sequential pattern for presenting the evidence. This is done by creating a structure for organizing and presenting the evidence.[22]

Framing is beneficial in negotiation because it helps focus attention on the priorities you want to emphasize—the data and premises within the frame. It also establishes a "big picture" context for the listener to use in perceiving and sorting through various options.

Framing can also save time and words. Extending the picture analogy, because a picture is worth a thousand words, a frame that paints a picture can efficiently and effectively enliven the goals you are pursuing. Imagine two CEOs discussing a potential merger of their companies. One uses a metaphorical frame and alludes to a "melting pot of employees" in describing his hoped-for outcome for the merger. This frame paints a picture that both parties understand. The second CEO is a bit more creative. She recasts the frame and refers to the "mixed salad of employees" her plan is designed to create. Both plans highlight employee diversity, but the second frame recognizes the individual talents and skills of employees who can collaborate and work together while the first plan may be interpreted as a homogenization of all employees. As negotiators we can use frames to recast the other party's notion of what is desired in a negotiation. We do this by reframing the discussion—describing it differently to ourselves.

By reframing we're able to see it in a new light and approach the negotiation in a different way. A frame can be used to sell a proposal and overcome objectives others might raise. To do this,

- Develop a frame based on *both* your needs and those of the other party.
- Construct a set of messages that influence the other party's perception of these needs.
- Provide the other party with a filter to interpret your message—such as "half-empty or half-full," "good or bad," "profit or loss," "cost or benefit."
- Think ahead about possible misinterpretations or negative twists on your frame, and be prepared to reframe as needed.

Managing

The last strategy to consider when preparing for and in the thick of the negotiation is *managing*. Every negotiation is an opportunity for you to manage: yourself and the impression others have of you (see shaded box), your expectations, the timing of the event, the way in which you approach the situation, your feelings toward the other person. The more you respond to a negotiation as a management challenge, the more proactive you can be in looking at it positively. A negotiation can be a learning experience, a chance to acquire some new skills, and maybe even a way to get what you want! Or it can be something you dread, fear, and avoid if possible.

The adage "practice makes perfect" really applies here. Negotiation doesn't come naturally to most people. Practicing negotiation greatly improves your ability to manage a negotiation situation successfully. Start small, with minor events day-to-day, such as negotiating an earlier lunchtime with co-workers. The more you negotiate—paying attention to your needs and speaking up for them—the better prepared you will be for significant negotiations in business and in life. Only negotiate when you're ready—when you have the time, have had the time to prepare, and are in an appropriate state of mind. Thorough negotiations can be exhausting; you have to be ready to persist. You can ensure you're ready by managing the circumstances under which you'll negotiate. Only agree to terms that are acceptable to you. For example, where, when, and with whom you'll negotiate are all things that make a difference and things over which you have some control. Assert that control so that you are at your best at the time of the negotiation. For example, if your boss asks you if you would delay your vacation by two weeks, and your plans involve others, respond with, "I'll have to get back to you in a day or two after I discuss this with my spouse."

Managing Impressions in Negotiation[23]

Impressions emerge from a process where numerous pieces of information are communicated, not only verbal but also nonverbal, through behavior and emotional expressions. To persuade someone to act in a desired way, it is in our interest to manage the impression the person forms of us or a situation.

One example is a Danish negotiator entering the last negotiation round in a sale to an Asian buyer of factory equipment for the food industry. Before giving the last concession, he attempts to create the impression that this is almost impossible. He does this by recalculating, calling his boss one extra time to see if he is able to give the last concession, and he appears to be under pressure and stressed. All along, the negotiator knows that he will end up by giving the concession to reach an agreement, but he attempts to create an impression that justifies the concession and supports his claim that this is the best price he can offer.

By presenting a coherent performance supported by several pieces of information, not only objective features but also in how he expresses emotions of stress, the negotiator can influence his counterpart's impression. The negotiator ended up giving the final concession he was prepared to give and without further negotiation of the price, the parties reached an amicable agreement.

Don't let your emotions destroy the negotiation and relationships within it. Demonstrate exceptional listening and clarifying (communication) skills. This helps you focus on the issues at hand, not on your fears and anxieties. Plan to engage only in discussions or arguments that are constructive. Be prepared to walk away or take a "time-out" if necessary. Sometimes called a **caucus**, this time-out could be used alone (or with a negotiating partner in a team negotiation) to gather your thoughts, adjust your strategy, and discover new frames or solutions.

Agree to disagree. Sometimes issues are unsolvable at that moment. It's better to quit while you're ahead and set another time to continue discussing remaining issues. Don't put anyone on the defensive. When we're upset, we often blame or label others, causing them to strike back in kind. This kind of negotiation will go nowhere. Make statements that are factual and "I" based rather than "you" based. For example say, "I am upset about the amount of raise I got," rather than "You're unfair for giving me such a low increase." Other techniques for managing negotiations include the use of agendas, questions, and summarizing techniques. A negotiation is a meeting and should be treated as such. If an agenda was not created in advance, and the negotiation is getting off-track, spend a few minutes establishing an agenda. Decide key issues to discuss, and allocate time accordingly. Post the agenda and refer back to it to keep the discussion on track. Periodically summarizing what's been discussed and agreed upon not only helps to keep the discussion focused, but can also help reduce redundancy (i.e., beating a dead horse). Sometimes, negotiators revisit issues that have already been resolved because they forget or are unsure whether a point was resolved or deferred for later discussion. By saying, "Okay, let's review. We agreed to points *a*, *b*, and *d*, but are still working out the details on points *c* and *e*. Does that track with how you see it?" you can manage time and stay focused on the negotiation.

Finally, questions can be useful in many ways. Aside from helping you understand others' viewpoints and needs, questions can help steer the discussion toward desirable issues in a more subtle way. Depending on the goals of the negotiation, consider using various types of questions as appropriate from the list shown in Figure 9–5.

Electronic Negotiation Systems[24]

Information systems that help negotiators to better perform are often called electronic negotiation systems (ENS). In the last decades, researchers have identified several ways in which ENS might support negotiators. At the most basic level, communication technology enables parties to negotiate across large distances, and also to bridge the gap across different time zones, enabling parties to respond to messages at a time that is convenient for them. However, communication support in ENS can go far beyond the capabilities of e-mail. ENS can help to structure the negotiation process (for instance, by imposing a certain protocol that requires parties to respond to offers with offers of their own) and by providing clear message types that reduce the risk of misunderstandings when negotiating in an international context. For example, the Negoisst system (www.negoisst.de) not only provides structured message types for offers, counteroffers, queries, responses, and so on, but also provides an informal meeting space in which parties can exchange noncommitting messages in addition to their (binding) offers.

Going beyond communication support, most ENS contain decision support components, which help parties to evaluate offers in complex, multi-issue negotiations, and behavioral support components, which evaluate negotiation strategies and tactics and provide advice, for example, on how to overcome an impasse during the negotiation. Decision support components can be used not only to evaluate current offers on the "electronic bargaining table," but also provide users with a history of the negotiation, so they can trace the concessions made by themselves, as well as the opponent.

This type of support is still quite passive; negotiators must find suitable offers themselves, as the system provides only an evaluation. More recent approaches also try to support users in formulating their offers. Active facilitation-mediation systems provide such support if requested by the user. For example, the system Negoisst already mentioned contains a component that will propose different offers according to a bargaining strategy that can be selected by the user. Similar concepts are also available in the system eAgora. These systems utilize mathematical programming models to find possible offers (combination of values for all the issues being negotiated) that not only provide a certain value to the supported party, but also have other desirable properties, such as being similar to whatever offer the opponent recently made (thus increasing the chance that the offer is also attractive for the opponent).

Taking this idea one step further, the system could actively monitor the negotiation process and, for example, alert the user if he or she is going to make a disadvantageous offer or is destroying value. Such proactive systems are still mostly only a vision, but could be the next step in electronic negotiation support.

Figure 9–5
Questioning[25]

Questioning is recommended in negotiation when it is necessary to clarify communication. **Manageable questions** start thinking, get information, and prepare the other person for additional questions. **Unmanageable questions** cause difficulty by bringing the discussion to a false conclusion. Manageable questions can produce dialogue and creative approaches, while unmanageable questions may produce defensiveness and/or anger.

Manageable Questions

Type of question	Example
Open-ended	Could you explain the reasons for your decision?
Open (to get the other person thinking)	What is your feeling on the matter?
Leading (point toward an answer to the question)	Do you feel our proposal is fair?
Cool (without emotion)	How much would be charged for the additional work?
Planned (follows an overall sequence of questions)	After the additional work is completed, may we begin our phase?
Treat (flatters the opponent while soliciting information)	You are an expert in this area; what is your opinion?
Window (assists in seeing what the other person is thinking)	What brought you to that conclusion?
Directive (focus on a specific point)	How long will it take to complete the job?
Gauging (assists in determining how the other person feels)	What do you think about our proposal?

Unmanageable Questions

Type of question	Example
Close-out (forces your opinion on the opponent)	You wouldn't want to make us look bad, would you?
Loaded (puts opponents on the spot regardless of answer)	So, you are not willing to negotiate further?
Heated (triggers an emotional response)	Haven't we spent enough time on this crazy idea?
Impulse (tends to get the conversation off track)	While we are on the subject, is there anyone else who might care about this?
Trick (appear straightforward, but are actually "loaded")	What are you going to do—agree to our position, or go to court?
Reflective "trick" question (directs the opponent into agreeing with your point of view)	Here is the way I see it, don't you agree?

Additional Tips for Effective Negotiating

What else can you do to ensure that you not only reach an agreement but also maintain or enhance your relationship with the other party? The following principles of successful negotiation should help ensure that negotiations are integrative, objective, and potentially relationship enhancing.

- *Determine the importance of the outcome for you.* What do you want and why? Only negotiate when the matter is something you truly care about and when you have a chance of succeeding. Identify what you really need from the deal, not what you assume you need. Identify several items of interest to you and rank them in descending order of importance.[26] Do your homework. If the negotiation includes a financial outcome, consider several options or scenarios and the economic implications of each. This information will serve to eliminate the guesswork and strengthen the rationale of your proposal during the negotiation. Will you lease or buy the car? What if you put 10 percent, 20 percent, or nothing down? How does the financing rate change when the loan period changes or if you decide to buy a used instead of a new car? Calculating the implications in advance can also increase your confidence and strengthen your position in the negotiation.

- *Look forward, not backward.* It's easy to get caught up in who did what and who is to blame. We sometimes do this to avoid having to resolve the problem or just out of habit. While it may be easy to get into long discussions about the past, it is clearly unproductive. Focus on where you want to be and not where you've been. There's no harm in brief discussions of the conditions that led to the current problem, but move on to what to do now and in the future.[27]

- *Separate people from problems.* To negotiate effectively, separate the people involved in the discussion from the issues that are being addressed. Remain objective. Avoid personalizing issues, and don't allow yourself to be drawn into an emotional debate.[28] If the negotiation veers in this direction, request a time-out. After you reconvene, remind the negotiators of the ultimate goal and the ground rules previously set. If emotions are still running high, consider deferring the remainder of the negotiation to another time. Focus on the problem, the issue at hand. Avoid making personal attacks, criticizing style or personality traits, and placing blame. Negotiate in such a way that the people on the other side know they will not lose face if they have to back down on something. For example, match the other's concession with one of your own. A good rule of thumb is to be hard on the problem, soft on the people. Throughout the negotiation constantly ask, "Am I dealing with the person or the problem?" Entangling people, issues, and relationships with the problem dooms the negotiation to failure.[29]

- *Adopt a win–win attitude.* Negotiation is a collaboration between parties with common interests and objectives. Think in terms of helping, not hindering; of listening, not ramming something down someone's throat; of a team and partnership, not competition. Take the perspective that both parties can win and it's in your best interest to want the other side to thrive, as future cooperative ventures may be possible.[30]

- *Be clear about your best alternative to a negotiated agreement* (BATNA). Fisher and Ury explain that results from a negotiation can be improved by identifying your best alternative for each of your goals. Don't set your BATNA too low. When you go to a job interview with no other offers or prospects, you go in with a low BATNA—this job or nothing. Sometimes you have to do this. But whenever possible, it's better to have options in mind to avoid being or appearing desperate. For example, in the absence of job offers, you could consider living with family for a while rather than taking a job you don't want. This alternative gives you flexibility and a sense that you don't have to take whatever is offered.[31]

    Fisher and Ury argue that negotiators ought to be problem solvers who explore interests as opposed to refusing to change or compromising only slightly on their positions. In fact, when you carefully listen to and help the other side get what it wants, you increase the chances of getting what you want.[32] When a negotiation is a test of wills, it is destined to fail. By identifying compatible interests, you can build a bridge from your goals to the others.[33]

■ *Go into the negotiation with* **objective criteria**. This leads to principled negotiation—negotiations based on principles, or objective criteria on which both parties agree. Bringing standards of efficiency, fairness, and scientific merit, for example, can facilitate agreement and final satisfaction with an agreement. Rather than struggling for dominance, locate objective criteria both of you can agree to apply in determining goals and actions. Sometimes objective criteria are readily available. Other times, the negotiators will have to research, present, and jointly decide on these criteria.

Objective criteria should be independent of each side's will and should be legitimate and practical. For example, you can find published data on industry salaries, comparable house sale prices, and area bank or finance company mortgage rates. Once you have determined objective criteria, you can frame each issue as a joint search for the solution that best fits the criteria.[34]

■ *Respond, don't react.* When other parties throw their power around, don't react negatively or emotionally. When this happens, Fisher and Ury recommend you invite feedback and input with regard to the problem. Ask them their opinion. You can also reframe or recast their objections as attacks on the problem, not on you—attacks that are understandable given the circumstances or pressure they might be experiencing. When the other party attacks, ask questions. Avoid getting bullied into battle.

■ *Use a* **third party**—someone who is objective and has no vested interest in the outcome of the discussions. When two parties can't arrive at a mutually agreeable resolution, it can be helpful to involve a third party. Consider using the one-text procedure. Let someone draw up a plan that considers your interests and those of the other party. Then each of you does some editing. The third party redrafts it and perhaps requests additional feedback from both of you. By involving everyone in the development of a single text and having the parties involved edit it several times, at the end both parties feel they have been included in the solution. At the end, all that is left to do is make a simple yes–no decision, not enter into a long discussion or argument over details.[35]

Emotions and Defensiveness in Negotiation

Our behavior is strongly influenced by our emotions, and particularly our emotional state as we enter the negotiation room, which in turn could be affected by our mood that day or recent experienced events. Emotions are important in the negotiation room: they motivate us, and they tell us something about ourselves, our negotiating partners, and the negotiation itself. In the negotiation, if we are able to consciously override the defensiveness that accompanies emotion—through self-awareness, motivation, and attentional capacity[36]—we can use our emotions strategically, acting as incentives or deterrents to the other side.[37]

Emotions are at the core of conflict interactions; they might hinder negotiators from behaving rationally.[38] Research demonstrates that negative emotions increase competitiveness, while positive emotions increase cooperation in negotiation.[39] However, negative emotions can also have positive effects; when expressed pain or distress induces cooperative behavior, anger and fear can motivate the parties to overcome a crisis.[40] Should a negotiator start the negotiation with feelings of anxiety and fear that are expressed as negative emotions, because of emotional reciprocity and contagion, the same behavior is often unconsciously and automatically mimicked by the counterparts.[41] Simply put, our emotional response to a conflict situation can actually exacerbate the conflict. Once in this cycle, our emotions can create defensiveness, blinding us to the possibility of changing our style of negotiation beyond our habitual response, even when our negotiation style is inappropriate or not having the desired effect.[42]

Defensiveness is an emotion that is particularly associated with conflict situations and leads us to use protective strategies when negotiating. When we are anxious, fearful, or feel threatened, in the same way as in situations of danger, defensive behavior is automatically triggered.[43] Conflict and defensiveness are self-reinforcing; the more difficult the conflict is, the greater our defensive behavior becomes.[44] This provokes a reaction where the distance between the two parties widens and the negotiation is viewed as a contest.[45]

When we are defensive, we focus more on avoiding potential threats and protecting ourselves than on rationally discussing key issues. Effectively, we become trapped and are unable to move forward in the negotiation.

In these situations, it's best to stop the negotiation, or at the minimum, take a time-out or caucus to step outside of ourselves, calm our emotions, and try to identify why we are feeling defensive. In doing so, we can evaluate whether the conflict is real or perceived and consider adjusting our negotiation strategy. To continue to act defensively during a negotiation is unlikely to result in a satisfactory conclusion. It might actually become a self-fulfilling prophecy and result in exactly the thing we feared most—a failure in the negotiation.[46]

Integrity and Ethics in Negotiation

So far, we've discussed the process of, benefits of, and strategies for negotiating effectively. It all sounds straightforward, and with practice, negotiation is a skill that will bring personal and professional success. However, there are times when others—or perhaps even you—knowingly or unknowingly use tactics that are questionable or unethical. Perhaps this has happened in the past, as in a time when you didn't tell the "whole truth,"[47] but managed to get what you wanted. Or maybe you were in a situation where you sensed your negotiating partner was lying,[48] but you weren't sure, nor were you sure how best to deal with such behavior. The use of deceptive tactics negotiation, which can include withholding information, stretching the truth, and bluffing, is risky, to say the least. In some cases, it may be illegal.[49] While some negotiators engage in these activities and "get away with it," they do so at the risk of bungling the present deal and damaging others' trust in and cooperation with the negotiator and his or her organization. Let's start by clarifying what we mean by unethical behavior with some examples:[50]

- Withholding information that would alter decision choices.
- Disguising information so that it is more acceptable to the other party.
- Manipulating the other party through emphasis on false deadlines.
- Making false statements about expertise or understanding about issues.
- Lying to mislead the other party.
- Using information gained through covert methods to create unfair advantage.
- Using bribes or kickbacks that are unknown to some of the negotiators involved.
- Insulting or demeaning the other party to inhibit confidence or judgment.
- Making promises that can't be fulfilled.

The two questions these examples raise are why negotiators use such tactics, and more importantly, what we should do when we become aware of such behavior. Let's start with the first one. By knowing what motivates such behavior—ours and others—we may be better able to behave ethically and identify when others aren't doing so in negotiation situations. Why do people intentionally lie or deceive in negotiations? Two reasons seem especially important:

- *Expected norms.* In some situations, negotiators use a tactic because they believe "everyone does it."[51] For example, the use of puffery or exaggeration in résumés and during interviews is widespread. In 2004, the outplacement firm, Challenger, Gray & Christmas, reviewed 249,000 résumés and found 52 percent had discrepancies.[52] You might also recall that Michael Brown, the infamous ex-FEMA director whose performance during the Hurricane Katrina disaster was publicly criticized, was found to have lied on his résumé and in his interviews about positions he'd held, degrees awarded, and awards he supposedly received.[53]

- *Pressure from management or others.* As we've discussed in an earlier chapter, performance expectations from stakeholders, combined with the behaviors of top management, can set the tone for ends expected and means necessary to achieve those ends.

Related to this issue, some negotiators use deceptive behaviors to gain an advantage[54] and thus, "win" in the negotiation. Businesses reward the achievement of goals, and negotiators base their sense of self-worth on "winning" and achieving these goals and the rewards that go with them.[55]

How do we deal with others' potentially unethical behavior? The first rule of thumb is to know as much as possible about the other party's situation, goals, and approach. Is she under pressure to win, and to do so within a tight time frame? Is she, and does she view you as, trustworthy? Will we negotiate again in the future?[56] If you have done your homework, you'll know what to expect and be ready to prevent unethical behavior from creeping into the negotiation. However, despite your best efforts in preparing, you might face another party's use of unethical tactics. These suggestions can help you deal with such behavior:

- *Ask direct questions to reveal the truth or missing information.*[57] This may include asking specific questions about things that might be presumed to be "understood" but not communicated. For example, you might ask, "Is this piece of equipment covered under warranty . . . and under what circumstances?" even when you've purchased other equipment from the same vendor.

- *Inform the other party about the tactic being used.* Describe it using specific examples of what was said or done and the impact it is having on you (e.g., "I'm having a hard time trusting what you're saying is true and it's making me hesitant to continue"), and explain that such behaviors will not be tolerated. By discussing the tactic you remove its strength and cause its user to worry about alienating you further.[58]

- *Request a different party with whom to continue negotiations.*[59] If your attempts to curb others' questionable tactics aren't successful, consider asking, "I'm concerned that continuing our conversation won't get us sufficiently closer to an agreement. Is there anyone else that I can speak to?"

- *End the negotiations immediately.* It's better to end the negotiation without a resolution or contract than participate in a negotiation that compromises your values or reputation, or causes you to be a victim.[60]

Resisting the Temptation to Lie or Deceive: Three Suggestions[61]

1. If you're asked about your bottom line and you're hesitant to reveal it, ask your opponents for their bottom line, or say that you are not ready to reveal yours at this point . . . but you will in due time.

2. If you don't want to offer up other options or alternatives when asked to do so (because you feel that you'd be giving away too much), don't say that there aren't any. Instead, ask your opponent to suggest options to which you could respond, or engage your opponent in collaborative brainstorming or problem solving.

3. Don't lie about your intentions and only make promises you can keep. You could say, for example, "I'm sorry, but that's not something I'm able to implement. We could consider . . . ." Related to this alternative, don't check with your management or other authority figure prior to a negotiation. This way, if you are asked, you can honestly say that you do not have the authority but will pursue it if an agreement on the issue can be reached.

In sum, behaving unethically in negotiations is a risky move. The ends do not justify the means, and there's a good chance the behavior will be discovered and the relationship will be irreparably damaged. Even though you may view your negotiating partner as an opponent or even competitor, your goal—much of the time—should be about cooperating to find mutually beneficial resolutions and not about winning at all costs. Don't underestimate the role of the relationship—and thus, trust—in a negotiation. As we've said earlier in the text, while it takes a long time to build trust in a relationship, that trust can be broken in the blink of an eye. And once broken, trust is difficult if not impossible to restore. It's best to put your efforts into preparing thoroughly and negotiating with integrity.

Special Situations in Negotiations

Not all negotiations involve two individuals who meet face to face in an effort to reach a resolution or sign a contract. Some negotiations involve a third party, teams of individuals (called multiparty negotiations), virtual communication (using teleconferencing, telephones, e-mails, and faxes), or global negotiating partners.

Third-Party Negotiations

Serious negotiations—such as high-stakes strike threats—often require the use of a third party to gain an agreement. Other times, it is simply a wise idea to bring in an objective third party to help two opposing sides develop a shared agreement. Bringing in a third party has several advantages. A third party offers each party a chance to "vent" in a non-threatening environment. By venting out of earshot of the other party, you have a chance to disclose your feelings about the situation. By sorting through your emotions with a third party, you can then begin to uncover what's really important and why, and address these issues in the negotiation. Another advantage of bringing in a third party is that you and the other party can both benefit from the third party's expertise and experience. Assuming they have helped others negotiate before you, they have models and templates to offer—ways to structure the negotiation—that can help you arrive at an agreement faster than if you were starting from scratch on your own. They won't have had the exact same situation presented to them in the past. But their experience with other cases can help them advise you on a strategy for which there is probably a successful precedent.

Negotiation in the News

In March 2013, the merger between American Airlines and US Airways was approved, creating the world's largest airline. The judge did not approve of the $19.9 million severance package for the outgoing CEO of AMR (American Airlines' bankrupt parent).[62] US Airways is a much smaller company than American but it is, effectively, taking over rather than merging with American. Ownership of the new company will be a combination of US Airways shareholders and American Airlines creditors.

Reduction in "excess capacity" was the stated goal of the merger. Critics have translated this as "less competition and less service"; and with 70 percent of the U.S. domestic flights now controlled by four giant airlines, this could mean increases in passenger fares even on popular routes as the "excess capacity" is reduced, leaving passengers fighting over fewer seats.

Experts believe other changes resulted in the merger and had to be negotiated:[63]

Miles and Upgrades—The two carriers' policies on free upgrades are different. Like most U.S.-based carriers, US Airways' top-tier members received unlimited free upgrades based on status and upgrade request. American's policy enabled top-tier members to receive free upgrades on any published fare, a benefit not offered to other tier members who instead received 4 reduced upgrades for every 10,000 miles they earned. This system essentially regulated how many people requested upgrades as they tended to keep their upgrades for longer trips rather than shorter ones.

Credit Cards—American and US Airways both had a credit card linked to building up frequent flyer miles.

In-Flight Products—US Airways business passengers only got a meal if the flight was over 3 hours and 15 minutes, while on American, passengers received meals on flights longer than 2 hours.

Routes—Both companies said the new airline would keep all of its hubs (more than 6,700 daily flights to 336 destinations); critics believe this might not make sense.

What would you do if you were called in to mediate this negotiation?

Lastly, bringing in a third party helps the negotiating parties organize their thoughts and develop options that may be acceptable to both parties. The negotiator won't take sides, but will offer wise counsel about the potential benefits and pitfalls of each of the alternatives being considered. Part of what enables third parties to do this successfully is that they are just that, a third party. Third parties are able to help the negotiating parties develop criteria and solutions from an untainted, and therefore unemotional, perspective. This can be invaluable when it comes time to develop an agreement that is satisfactory to both parties. There are several types of third-party negotiators.[64]

- A **mediator** is a neutral third party who has no stake in the outcome of the agreement. Many private training programs are now available for ordinary citizens to become mediators. Mediation is a very popular, low-cost option that is being used more and more as an alternative to costly litigation.[65] In schools, mediators are used to help children (and faculty) resolve conflicts with each other, and in many businesses, employees are encouraged to work out conflicts (e.g., grievances) with a trained mediator when possible.

- An **arbitrator** is a neutral third party who has the legal power to bind both parties to an agreement determined by the arbitrator. Both parties submit information to arbitration and then are subject to whatever decision is made. Arbitration is mandated frequently as a cost-effective and time-effective alternative to litigation. One disadvantage is that neither party is involved in generating the solution that the arbitrator ultimately provides.

- A **conciliator** is a trusted third party whose role is to ensure that a steady flow of accurate information exists between the negotiating parties. A conciliator does not rule on an agreement but merely counsels the parties about ways to approach the agreement and ways to view the information that is being presented as part of the negotiation.

- A **consultant** is a neutral third party who teaches and advises the negotiating parties on skills and techniques of negotiation. The consultant hears both parties, suggests an operating plan and strategy, assists both sides in identifying their chief concerns, aids the parties in arriving at a mutually satisfying resolution or agreement, and assists the parties in writing up this agreement.

Multiparty and Team-Based Negotiations

Multiparty negotiations are those where "more than two parties are working together to achieve a collective objective."[66] One type of **multiparty negotiation** involves three or more "sides" represented by one or more individuals. This is the situation represented in the opening scenario, where each party (i.e., family member) attempts to maximize his or her goals and interests while working toward a solution that all can accept. Another type of multiparty negotiation is the **team-based negotiation**, where each side is represented by at least two individuals who work together as a team to achieve the goals and interests within a negotiation.[67] For example, you might have multiple homeowners in a subdivision working together to negotiate with a construction company to reduce the noise, mess, and traffic that have increased as a result of a building project in the neighborhood. Or employees of a university—who belong to different unions or organizations (e.g., faculty, administrative staff)—may be involved in bargaining with the goal of increasing salaries and benefits across the university. While multiparty negotiations share many similarities with traditional, two-party negotiations, the fact that more people are involved makes such negotiations more complex and therefore more difficult to manage. First, with more people comes a greater variety of perspectives, information shared, and goals and approaches, not to mention increased competition for airtime. This makes the conversation more difficult to navigate and manage. It also increases the likelihood that group dynamics (see Chapter 10) will affect the negotiation.[68] Finally, whereas a one-on-one negotiation involves each side taking turns, the procedural rules in a multiparty negotiation become less clear,[69] making it more important for the parties to establish an agenda, allow sufficient time to get through it, and establish ground rules for interaction. Let's return to our opening scenario. We learn that John is concerned about his wife and daughter, as well he should be. Assuming he is not an all-powerful dictator in his family, John will find himself in a multiparty negotiation. Gina, John's wife, feels that she will not only have to assimilate to a new country, but will also have to bear the brunt of Rebecca's anger and concerns while John concerns himself with his new job. As difficult as it is for two parties to find agreement, imagine the challenge facing these three individuals. Preparing for such a negotiation requires considering three sets of goals and objectives—yours and those of the other two parties; Exercise 9–I gives you a chance to do just that.

Virtual Negotiations

Each year well over 4 trillion e-mails are sent worldwide from more than half a trillion mailboxes,[70] and the number of mailboxes worldwide is expected to increase by 138 percent each year.[71] As opportunities for virtual communication have increased, so too have opportunities for **virtual negotiations**—carrying out all or part of a negotiation electronically. The ability to negotiate virtually—via phone, fax, e-mail, synchronous chat, and teleconferencing—brings with it benefits and challenges. One of the obvious benefits of utilizing electronic methods of communicating is the cost savings. For example, Lockheed Martin has assembled a team of engineers and designers from around the world to design and build a new stealth fighter plane to be used in military operations.[72] Over the course of the 10-year, $225 billion project, the company expects that meeting virtually instead of in person will save over $250 million.[73] Such benefits don't come without a cost. Reductions in communication bandwidth—varied by the particular electronic communication channel chosen—will impact both the process (e.g., norms of behavior, accuracy of communication interpretation) and outcomes of a virtual negotiation.[74]

Of course, the particular communication channel chosen provides unique implications for a virtual negotiation. Research on interacting negotiating parties suggests that personal rapport is more easily developed in face-to-face communication than with other channels.[75] This finding is consistent with the finding that virtual communication has the effect of equalizing social interactions, effectively removing status issues from the negotiation.[76] In addition, because it is easier to hide behind one's computer, parties in face-to-face negotiations are more likely to disclose information truthfully.[77] These issues are less problematic in teleconferenced negotiations; however, managing and keeping the conversation on track will be more difficult than in a face-to-face negotiation. Because building rapport and trust is so important to the success of negotiations, parties about to engage in a virtual negotiation should insist on an initial face-to-face or even teleconference or videoconference meeting. Doing so helps improve trust, cooperation, and optimism about negotiating a resolution now and in the future among the parties.[78] Additional advice for negotiating virtually is included in Figure 9–6.

Some negotiations begin face-to-face and progress to virtual channels. In such negotiations, the parties benefit from the ability to take the time to gather necessary data and think through their responses, unlike the irresistible urge to respond immediately in a face-to-face negotiation to avoid silence.[79] While the asynchronicity of communication likely lengthens the time that elapses over the course of a negotiation, the quality and quantity of information shared appears to be greater in a virtual setting.[80] Communicating virtually reduces the impact of nonverbal behavior, which can be an advantage as well as a disadvantage. Virtual negotiators may miss the inflection and emphasis that comes

Figure 9–6
Top 10 Rules for Virtual Negotiations[81]

1. Try to meet face-to-face at least once before or early in the negotiation.
2. Be explicit about the process or procedure to be followed in the negotiation.
3. Ensure that everyone is introduced and his or her roles are clarified.
4. Pick the communication channel most appropriate for the goals of both sides.
5. Don't use computer jargon, acronyms, or emoticons that may not be universally understood.
6. Ensure that everyone has a turn and speak up if someone is being left out.
7. Check assumptions and ask questions about what is and isn't said.
8. In an e-mail or chat negotiation, what's discussed is retained in written form. Remember not to make promises you don't intend to or can't keep.
9. Where nonverbal communication is limited, the temptation to engage in unethical behavior may increase. Be wary of this.
10. As with any new tool, your comfort and ability using communications technology may be limited at first. Realize this, and allow yourself more time (and patience) with the process and your role in it.

from tone and gestures; however, this can be helpful when one party perceives a power difference or maintains a bias against some observable characteristic of the other party. One example is the case of a divorced mother and father who were finally able to communicate effectively via teleconference because the mother was no longer intimidated by the father's nonverbal cues.[82]

Virtual negotiations can be facilitated by the use of Google Docs and other cloud services. Google Docs (and most recently Microsoft 365) allows individuals to collaborate on producing shared documents—anything from project manuals to legal contracts—that all users can edit and update in their own time zone. One company, kiiac (www.kiiac.com), offers customizable Non-Disclosure Agreements (NDAs). Customers answer seven questions and give their e-mail address. Using Google Docs and standard legal clauses, kiiac creates a customized NDA, which is then e-mailed to the customer.

Within a negotiation, each side could use Google Docs or Microsoft 365 to develop a mutually agreed-upon contract. Updates and edits are seen by both parties and can be amended as part of the virtual negotiation. Further, while the virtual negotiation takes place, agreed articles, clauses, and other negotiated points can be created simultaneously during the negotiation and wording edited by both parties. This also saves time and diminishes the possibility that the negotiators would add "extra" clauses into the document after the negotiation.

Global Negotiations

No longer are geographic boundaries impediments to doing business. In fact, in the global marketplace, organizations large and small buy from, sell to, merge with, network among, and in general do business with other organizations around the world. With negotiations between domestic and foreign firms (**global negotiations**) becoming more prevalent, it has become more important than ever that in addition to basic negotiation skills, individuals involved in global business have a solid understanding of how different cultures, practices, and customs affect negotiations.[83] Achieving that understanding, according to negotiation expert Kathleen Reardon, requires a look inward, as understanding another's culture is impossible without understanding one's own.[84] Knowing how we think and act gives us a reference point for understanding how and why diverse others think and act the way they do.[85] For example, Americans are known to be impatient and individualistic; representatives tend to work alone (granted the authority to do so on behalf of the organization) and strive to make decisions quickly. The Japanese take as much time as needed—away from the negotiating table—to arrive at a consensus among multiple representatives of the organization.[86]

The silence and waiting causes many Americans to offer an even better deal before waiting to hear if the original proposal is accepted. Or, Americans might offer to compromise and "split the difference," which, while expedient, may be viewed by French negotiators as "an insult to their carefully crafted logic."[87]

To be effective when negotiating across borders, you must prepare carefully and be familiar with—and open-minded toward—others' cultural differences and expectations.[88] This is easier said than done. While we may be aware of others' cultural and style differences, our tendency is to fall back on our predispositions and become frustrated with others who think and act differently from us.[89] Businesspeople in many parts of South America will take much time to build an emotional bond—through dinners and other social gatherings—before "getting down to business." Of course, this description is American; the "business" of negotiation to a South American is first and foremost the building of the relationship. Another potentially frustrating difference is the issue of eye contact. Americans place great importance in eye contact, as eyes are "the window to the soul," and the means by which we judge the trustworthiness and veracity of a negotiator and his or her claims. The Japanese, who avoid direct eye contact to show respect, report discomfort at the "aggressive staring" of Americans, who in turn report frustration in not knowing where they stand in a negotiation with Japanese counterparts.[90]

When negotiating abroad, preparation—the first and most important stage of negotiation—is key. As in domestic negotiation, you need to clarify what you want and why, determine your BATNA, gather data to present and compare (i.e., objective criteria) your arguments/proposals, consider ways to learn your opponents' wants and needs, and identify means for collaborating to discover mutual benefits. However, your strategy and the way in which you implement it will likely vary based on what you know about the

Figure 9–7
Ten Ways That Culture Can Influence Negotiation[91]

Negotiation Factors	Range of Cultural Responses	
	From	To
Nature of agreements	Specific	General
Definition of negotiation	Contract	Relationship
Negotiating attitude	Distributive	Integrative
Selection of negotiations	Experts	Trusted associates
Personal style	Informal	Formal
Communication style	Direct	Indirect
Time sensitivity	High	Low
Risk propensity	High	Low
Groups versus individuals	Collectivism	Individualism
Emotionalism	High	Low

practices and customs of your global negotiating partner. Because the process of the negotiation may look and feel very different from that to which you are accustomed, preparation is key. Start by doing background research on the organization's culture, practices, and business. Some information can be found on the Internet by searching government pages from the State Department (go to http://www.state.gov/r/pa/ei/bgn/, and then click on the region of interest). Other information can be obtained by identifying other firms who have done business with this organization or individuals who were born or spent time in the country. In addition to basic information, it is a good idea to learn about the ways that a particular culture influences negotiation—from the way it is viewed, to the process, and the ultimate goal or purpose. Figure 9–7 provides a framework for viewing the range of responses countries have in how they approach and behave in negotiations.

For example, whereas Americans expect to develop detailed multipage contracts filled with legal terminology and clarifying all possible circumstances, the Chinese prefer a contract that establishes general principles versus detailed rules.[92] Americans negotiate a contract while Japanese negotiate a personal relationship. A negotiator's style—which includes how she or he dresses, interacts with, and speaks to others—can be seen as formal or informal. Informal negotiators, such as Australians and Americans, try to set a personal, friendly tone by using first names, removing their jacket, rolling up their sleeves, and sharing personal anecdotes. To an Egyptian, Japanese, or French negotiator, these informal actions are seen as a sign of disrespect.[93] We've discussed some communication differences already, but another nonverbal communication difference is the use of the smile. While in many cultures, a smile indicates friendliness and perhaps agreement, Japanese use smiles to show happiness as well as to mask shame, disappointment, and discontent.[94] Finally, while Germans are known—and expect others—to be punctual, negotiators from Spanish-speaking cultures tend to view start times as approximate.

Aside from these differences, it is important to know about customs and laws specific to each country. For example, while the handshake is common in American business, in other countries, negotiators greet one another with an exchange of kisses and bows. Offering gifts to a negotiating partner is expected and considered common courtesy in some countries (and as bribery in others!). The Chinese often engage in gift giving, but you would be wise not to present your Chinese counterpart with a clock—it symbolizes death.[95] Even how you present and where you open a gift is no small detail.[96] You would also do well to know whether certain foods (e.g., pork, artificial sweetener) and drinks (e.g., alcohol) are forbidden in a particular country. In fact, an American firm sent a business proposal bound in pigskin to a country in which pigs were considered unclean. The proposal was never opened.[97] Understanding the laws and regulations of another's country is even more complicated. The degree to which the government regulates industries and organizations varies widely.[98] Except for highly regulated industries (e.g., defense, airlines), American businesses enjoy a fairly laissez-faire approach; the opposite is the case in some developing and communist countries.[99] Depending on the nature and goal of a particular negotiation, it might be wise to hire a local intermediary to facilitate negotiations in heavily regulated countries.

Global negotiations are admittedly complex and uncertain. Planning is crucial to the process. Gathering information about a country and its practices and customs is a necessary step to understanding how to approach your negotiating partner. Understanding differences (and similarities) between your and your foreign counterpart's communication style, behaviors, and practices can help you manage the negotiations and increase the likelihood that both parties leave the global negotiating table with satisfactory outcomes and a desire to continue the business relationship.

Summary

In this chapter we discussed the definition, importance, and benefits of negotiating. We reviewed the different types of negotiation strategies and the stages of negotiating. In addition, we provided strategies for negotiating effectively and tips for negotiating successfully. Lastly, we covered special situations in negotiating. Negotiating is a fact of life for all of us—in personal as well as business situations. Following the suggestions in this chapter will help you be effective in developing negotiation strategies that meet your and others' needs.

Key Terms and Concepts

Arbitrator	Mediator
BATNA	Multiparty negotiation
Caucus	Negotiation
Conciliator	Objective criteria
Consultant	Position
Distributive bargaining strategy	Script or strategy outline
Frame	Team-based negotiation
Global negotiations	Third party
Integrative bargaining strategy	Unmanageable questions
Interest	Virtual negotiation
Manageable questions	

Discussion Questions

1. In what ways do distributive and integrative approaches to negotiation differ? In what situations would you use one approach over another?

2. Describe the negotiation process or the five stages. Why is the first stage most important?

3. You are preparing to negotiate your compensation package for a job you've just been offered. What techniques or strategies could you use to improve the likelihood that you'll get what you want in this negotiation?

4. Why is managing important in negotiations? What are some ways to do this?

5. Your boss informs you that s/he will be sending you overseas to negotiate a deal with a new European supplier. How will you prepare for this negotiation?

Endnotes

1. John Mariotti, "Are You an Effective Negotiator?" *Industry Week* (September 7, 1998), p. 70.

2. Roger Fisher, William Ury, and Bruce Patton, *Getting to Yes,* 2nd ed. (New York: Penguin Books, 1991).

3. Ibid.

4. Danny Ertel, "How to Design a Conflict Management Procedure That Fits Your Dispute," *Sloan Management Review* (Summer 1991), pp. 29–42.

5. Darl G. Williams, "Negotiating Skills—Part I," *Professional Builder* (Jan. 2000), p. 155.

6. Adapted from Suzanne de Janasz and Beverly de Marr, "How to Negotiate a Salary Hike in Tough Times," *BusinessWorld*, India, September 17, 2012. http://www.businessworld.in/en/storypage/-/bw/how-to-negotiate-salary-hike-in-tough-times/538392.37479/page/0,. Accessed June 3, 2013.

7. It is important to note, however, that one or both parties may choose to avoid negotiations or defer them until a future date. Doing so may serve a number of purposes. For more information on deferral, see Roy Lewicki, David Saunders, and John Minton, *Negotiation: Readings, Exercises, and Cases,* 3rd ed. (Burr Ridge; IL: Irwin McGraw-Hill, 1999), pp. 45–46.

8. R. E. Walton and R. B. McKersie, *A Behavioral Theory of Labor Negotiations: An Analysis of a Social Interaction System* (New York: McGraw-Hill, 1965).

9. Stephen Robbins, *Organizational Behavior,* 8th ed. (Upper Saddle, NJ: Prentice Hall, 1998).

10. Max Bazerman and Margaret Neale, *Negotiating Rationally* (New York: Free Press, 1992).

11. R. J. Lewicki, "Bargaining and Negotiation," *Exchange: The Organizational Behavior Teaching Journal* 6, no. 2 (1981); and Robbins, *Organizational Behavior.*

12. Fisher et al., *Getting to Yes.*

13. Danny Ertel, "Turning Negotiation into a Corporate Capability," *Harvard Business Review* (May 1999), pp. 55–70.

14. Janine S. Pouliot, "Eight Steps to Success in Negotiating," *Nation's Business* (April 1999), p. 40.

15. Ertel, "How to Design."

16. Pouliot, "Eight Steps to Success."

17. Nancy J. Adler, *International Dimensions of Organizational Behavior,* 3rd ed. (Cincinnati, OH: Southwestern College Publishing, 1997), p. 214.

18. Suzanne de Janasz and Joachim Schwas, *The Business Times*—Singapore, April 13, 2012.

19. Mariotti, "Are You an Effective Negotiator?"

20. Margaret A. Neale and Max H. Bazerman, "Negotiating Rationally: The Power and Impact of a Negotiator's Frame," *Academy of Management Executive* 6, no. 3 (1992), pp. 42–51.

21. B. DeMarr and S. de Janasz, *Negotiation and Dispute Resolution* (Upper Saddle River, NJ: Prentice Hall, 2012).

22. Lyle Sussman, "How to Frame a Message: The Art of Persuasion and Negotiation," *Business Horizons* (July–August 1999), p. 2.

23. We thank Ditte Mølgaard Mathiasen, PhD student at Aarhus University School of Business and Social Sciences, for contributing this example.

24. We thank Rudolf Vetschera, University of Vienna Faculty of Business, for contributing this update on ENS (June 2013).

25. Adapted from R. J. Lewicki and J. A. Litterer, *Negotiation* (Homewood, IL: Richard D. Irwin, 1985).

26. Ron Shapiro, Mark Jankowski, Leigh Steinberg, and Michael D'Orso, "Powers of Persuasion," *Fortune,* Oct. 12, 1998, p. 160.

27. Fisher et al., *Getting to Yes.*

28. Terry Neese, "Negotiations Should Not Be a Contest of Wills," *LI Business News* (August 13, 1999), p. 30A.

29. Fisher et al., *Getting to Yes.*

30. Shapiro et al., "Powers of Persuasion."

31. Danny Ertel, "Turning Negotiation into a Corporate Capability," *Harvard Business Review* (May 1999), p. 55.

32. Shapiro et al., "Powers of Persuasion."

33. Harvey Mackay, "Flexibility Is a Word for the Wise," *Providence Business News* (August 9, 1999), p. 30.

34. Fisher et al., *Getting to Yes.*

35. Fisher et al., *Getting to Yes.*

36. J. A. Bargh, M. Chen, and L. Burrows, "Automaticity of Social Behavior: Direct Effects of Trait Construct and Stereotype Activation on Action," *Journal of Personality and Social Psychology* 71, no. 2 (1996), pp. 230–44.

37. D. Fromm, "Emotion in Negotiation," *The Theory and Practice of Representative Negotiation* (Toronto, Canada: Emond Montgomery Publications, 2008).

38. B. Barry and R. L. Oliver, "Affect in Dyadic Negotiation: A Model and Propositions," *Organizational Behavior and Human Decision Processes* 67, no. 2 (1996), pp. 127–43.

39. G. A. Van Kleef, C. K. W. De Dreu, and A. S. R. Manstead, "The Interpersonal Effects of Emotions in Negotiations: A Motivated Information Processing Approach," *Journal of Personality and Social Psychology* 87, no. 4 (2004), pp. 510–28.

40. R. A. Friedman, C. Anderson, J. Brett, M. Olekalns, N. Goates, and Lisco, "The Positive and Negative Effects of Anger on Dispute Resolution: Evidence from Electronically Mediated Disputes," *Journal of Applied Psychology* 89, no. 2 (2004), pp. 369–76.

41. R. Vetschera, S. Koeszegi, and M. Schoop, "Electronic Negotiation Systems" in *Wiley Encyclopedia of Operations Research and Management Science* (2013).

42. A. Mazen, "Transforming the Negotiator: The Impact of Critical Learning on Teaching and Practicing Negotiation," *Management Learning* 43, no. 1 (2012), pp. 113–28.

43. M. Kets de Vries and K. Korotov, "Creating Transformational Executive Education Programs," *Academy of Management Learning and Education* 6, no. 3 (2007), pp. 375–87.

44. Mazen, 2013.

45. M. Kets de Vries, "Organizations on the Couch: A Clinical Perspective on Organizational Dynamics," *European Management Journal* 22, no. 2 (2004), pp. 183–200.

46. Mazen, 2013.

47. In their book *Negotiation,* 5th ed., R. J. Lewicki, D. M. Saunders, and B. Barry call this behavior—failing to disclose information that would benefit the other—the "sin of omission" (Burr Ridge, IL: McGraw-Hill Irwin, 2006), p. 251.

48. Lewicki et al. call this behavior—actually lying—the "sin of commission" in *Negotiation,* p. 251.

49. M. L. Spangle and M. W. Isenhart, *Negotiation: Communication for Diverse Settings* (Thousand Oaks, CA: Sage, 2003), p. 171.

50. Ibid., p. 172.

51. Ibid., p. 172.

52. Ira S. Wolfe, "Resume Lies Leave a Paper Tale," *Business 2 Business* (December 2005) (http://www.super-solutions.com/EmployeesLies_Resumes.asp; accessed July 20, 2007).

53. Ibid.

54. M. R. Carrell and C. Heavrin, *Negotiating Essentials: Theory, Skills, and Practices* (Upper Saddle River, NJ: Pearson Prentice Hall, 2008), p. 192.

55. R. J. Lewicki, A. Hiam, and K. W. Olander, *Think before You Speak: The Complete Guide to Strategic Negotiation* (New York: John Wiley, 1996).

56. Carrell and Heavrin, *Negotiating Essentials,* p. 214.

57. Spangle and Isenhart, *Negotiation,* p. 173.

58. Fisher et al., *Getting to Yes.*

59. Spangle and Isenhart, *Negotiation,* p. 174.

60. For supplementary reading on this topic, see George Kohlrieser, *Hostage at the Table: How Leaders Can Overcome Conflict, Influence Others, and Raise Performance* (New York: John Wiley, 2006).

61. G. Richard Shell, "Bargaining with the Devil without Losing Your Soul: Ethics in Negotiation," in C. Menkel-Meadow and M. Wheeler, Eds., *What's Fair: Ethics for Negotiators* (San Francisco: Jossey-Bass, 2004), pp. 57–78.

62. N. Brown, "American Airlines–US Airways Merger Approved by Court; World's Largest Airline Created," *The Huffington Post*, March 27, 2013. Accessed June 2, 2013.

63. S. Rosenbloom, "If American and US Airways Merge, What Should Fliers Expect?", *The New York Times*, April 10, 2013. Accessed June 2, 2013.

64. J. A. Wall Jr. and M. W. Blum, "Negotiations," *Journal of Management* (June 1991), pp. 283–87.

65. Robert D. Benjamin, "Mediation: Taming of the Shrewd," *Commercial Law Bulletin* (January–February 2000), pp. 8–10.

66. Lewicki et al., *Negotiation,* 2006, p. 349.

67. DeMarr and de Janasz, *Negotiation and Dispute Resolution.*

68. Ibid., p. 352.

69. Ibid., p. 352.

70. Aysar Philip Sussan and Anthony Recascino, "The Impact of E-Mail Utilization on Job Satisfaction: The Case of Multi Locations," *The Business Review* 6, no. 1 (December 2006), p. 25.

71. Paul Hewitt, "Electronic Mail and Internal Communication: A Three-Factor Model," *Corporate Communications* 11, no. 1 (2006), p. 79.

72. S. P. Robbins and T. A. Judge, *Essentials of Organizational Behavior,* 9th ed. (Upper Saddle River, NJ: Pearson Prentice Hall, 2008), p. 145.

73. S. Crock, "Collaboration: Lockheed Martin," *BusinessWeek* (November 24), 2003, p. 85.

74. M. H. Bazerman, J. R. Curhan, D. A. Moore, and K. L. Valley, "Negotiation," *Annual Review of Psychology* 51 (2000), pp. 279–314; and R. J. Lewicki and B. R. Dineen, "Negotiation in Virtual Organizations." In R. Heneman and D. Greenberger, *Human Resource Management in Virtual Organizations* (New York: John Wiley & Sons, 2003).

75. A. L. Drolet and M. W. Morris, "Rapport in Conflict Resolution: Accounting for How Face-to-Face Contact Fosters Mutual Cooperation in Mixed-Motive Conflicts," *Journal of Experimental Social Psychology* 36 (2000), pp. 26–50.

76. Alice F. Stuhlmacher, Maryalice Citera, and Toni Willis, "Gender Differences in Virtual Negotiation: Theory & Research," *Sex Roles: A Journal of Research* 57, no. 5/6 (September 2007), pp. 329–39.

77. K. L. Valley, J. Moag, and M. H. Bazerman, "A Matter of Trust: Effects of Communication on the Efficiency and Distribution of Outcomes," *Journal of Economic Behavior and Organization* 34 (1998), pp. 211–38.

78. M. Morris, J. Nadler, T. Kurtzburg, and L. Thompson, "Schmooze or Lose: Social Friction and Lubrication in Email Negotiations," *Group Dynamics Theory, Research, and Practice* 6 (2000), pp. 89–100.

79. Laurie Coltri, *Alternative Dispute Resolution: A Conflict Diagnosis Approach* (Upper Saddle River, NJ: Prentice Hall, 2010), p. 223.

80. Coltrie, *Alternative Dispute Resolution,* p. 223.

81. Adapted from Lewicki et al., *Negotiation,* p. 175.

82. Springer, 1991, as quoted in Coltri, *Alternative Dispute Resolution,* p. 223.

83. Anthony Wanis-St. John, "Thinking Globally and Acting Locally," *Negotiation Journal* 19, no. 4 (October 2003), p. 389.

84. Kathleen Reardon, *Becoming a Skilled Negotiator* (Hoboken, NJ: Wiley, 2005).

85. Dean Allen Foster, *Bargaining across Borders: How to Negotiate Business Successfully Anywhere in the World* (Burr Ridge, IL: McGraw-Hill, 1995).

86. J. L. Graham and Y. Sano, *Smart Bargaining: Doing Business with the Japanese* (Los Angeles, CA: Sano Management Corporation, 1989).

87. Reardon, *Skilled Negotiator,* p. 167.

88. Robert Rosen, Patricia Digh, Marshall Singer, and Carl Phillips, *Global Literacies: Lessons on Business Leadership and National Cultures: A Landmark Study of CEOs from 28 Countries* (New York: Simon and Schuster, 2000).

89. Reardon, *Skilled Negotiator,* p. 165.

90. Graham and Sano, *Smart Bargaining,* p. 90

91. Adapted from Lewicki et al., *Negotiation,* p. 420.

92. Jeswald W. Salacuse, *Making Global Deals: What Every Executive Should Know about Negotiating Abroad* (New York: Times Books, 1991), p. 66.

93. Salacuse, *Making Global Deals,* p. 63.

94. Salacuse, *Making Global Deals,* p. 63.

95. Foster, *Bargaining across Borders.*

96. See Reardon, *Skilled Negotiator,* p. 170, and K. K. Reardon, *Gift Giving around the World* (Stanford, CA: Passepartout, 1986) for more details.

97. Rosen et al., *Global Literacies,* p. 176.

98. Lewicki et al., *Negotiation,* p. 408.

99. Ibid., pp. 408–409.

**Exercise 9–A
A Trip Down Memory Lane**

Think back on occasions when you have negotiated the sale or purchase of a product or service or attempted to get what you wanted from a colleague, classmate, friend, or family member. These negotiations could have been successful or unsuccessful. For each example try to remember as much detail as possible—the who, what, where, and when of the situation. What, if anything, did you do to prepare or get yourself psyched up? What was the substantive outcome? What was the effect on your relationship with the other party?

Using the following worksheet, record the details of a successful and unsuccessful example of your attempts to negotiate a purchase or sale.

1. Examples of when you were **buying** or **trying to buy** something and wanted to get a good deal on it.

Successful	Unsuccessful
Who: _____	Who: _____
What: _____	What: _____
Where: _____	Where: _____
When: _____	When: _____
Preparation: _____	Preparation: _____
_____	_____
_____	_____
Outcome: _____	Outcome: _____
_____	_____
_____	_____
Comments: _____	Comments: _____
_____	_____

2. Examples of when you were **selling** or **trying to sell something** and wanted to maximize your "return."

Successful	Unsuccessful
Who: _____	Who: _____
What: _____	What: _____
Where: _____	Where: _____
When: _____	When: _____
Preparation: _____	Preparation: _____
_____	_____
_____	_____
Outcome: _____	Outcome: _____
_____	_____
_____	_____
Comments: _____	Comments: _____
_____	_____

Looking over the details of each example, identify commonalities in the situations where you have been successful and in the situations where you were unsuccessful. For example, are you generally more or less successful when dealing with family members or strangers? Are you more or less successful when buying or selling? Big-ticket versus small-ticket items? Things versus tasks? Is there anything you do to prepare that seems to help?

Considering the examples you have identified, complete the following paragraphs.

In general, I am more successful negotiating when: _____

_____

_____

_____

In general, I am less successful negotiating when: _____

_____

_____

_____

Source: Adapted from B. J. DeMarr and S. C. de Janasz, *Negotiation and Dispute Resolution* (Upper Saddle River, NJ: Prentice Hall, 2012).

Exercise 9–B
Case Study—Keeping Up Appearances

Bill and Rachael are both analysts in the market research department at Bravo Inc. Bill is generally viewed as a top performer. Objectively, his work is good, but he really excels at self-promotion. When dealing with others, he is a tough negotiator, confident to the point of being cocky. He likes to win and win big. He is unafraid of stepping on anyone's toes and lives by the motto that it is easier to beg forgiveness than to ask permission.

Rachael is bright and hard-working; however, she is also timid and generally has low self-esteem. She doesn't promote or publicize her accomplishments and instead relies on others to notice the good work she does. She has a very difficult time standing up for herself, which often results in others taking advantage of her.

Bill and Rachael have recently been assigned to work together on what has the potential to be a highly visible project. The project involves doing a lot of research, writing a report, and presenting the findings to the senior executives. They just finished meeting to lay out the tasks involved and establish a plan for the project. In their meeting Bill told Rachael that she can do the research and draft the report, and he will make the presentation. When Rachael suggested they work together on the research and jointly make the presentation, Bill told her that she needs to do the research and draft the report because she is better at "that sort of thing" while he needs to make the presentation because of his superior presentation skills.

Bill left the meeting satisfied that he has won yet again and believes that since he will be making the presentation, he will get the majority of the credit for the project. This is important to him because he has heard there will be an opening in the near future for a senior analyst. He wants the promotion and thinks the visibility of this project will make him a shoo-in for the job.

Rachael left their meeting feeling resentful and put upon but doesn't know what she can do about it. While this sort of thing has happened to her in the past, she is especially upset this time because she has heard there will soon be an opening for a senior analyst and she is very interested in the position. She needs to revisit and negotiate her and Bill's roles and responsibilities, but isn't sure what to do or say.

Questions

1. If you were Rachael, how would you prepare for this negotiation? What kind of approach—distributive or integrative—would you take? What kind of outcome do you want? What would your BATNA be? What questions would you ask Bill and why? How would you go about appearing credible?

2. Is Bill behaving ethically? Explain. How will this behavior affect Rachael's preparation for—and behavior during—the negotiation? What would you do in this situation if you were Rachael?

3. Should Rachael inform Bill that they "need to discuss the presentation," what do you think he should do to prepare for this discussion? Explain.

Source: Adapted from B. J. DeMarr and S. C. de Janasz, *Negotiation and Dispute Resolution* (Upper Saddle River, NJ: Prentice Hall, 2012).

Exercise 9–C
Thawing the Salary Freeze
(Video Case)

Your instructor will show a short video depicting a negotiation interaction, which we summarize below. After viewing the video, answer the following questions. Your instructor might ask you to discuss your answers with your small group.

Katherine Knudsen, vice president of production at JBL Publishing, is meeting with Alisa Jackson, a union representative, to renegotiate the production workers' contract. The main issues are salary increases (the union requested a 7 percent increase), health benefits (the union requested an improved benefits package), and flexible work schedules. Alisa is irate because she just found out, prior to this meeting, that the executive board has received enormous bonuses for the year, at the same time as JBL is refusing to budge on the requested salary increases for the production workers.

Questions

1. In what ways was this negotiation distributive and integrative? Explain, using specific behaviors to demonstrate Alisa's and Katherine's use of one or both approaches.

2. Do you agree with their approaches? Explain, and tie your answer to your beliefs about each party's goal in the negotiation.

3. To what degree did Katherine and Alisa demonstrate credibility? Explain, using examples of what the negotiators did or said before (presumably) or during the negotiation.

4. What did you think of Alisa's threat to inform the press? What effect do you think this has on the negotiation outcome? Her relationship with Katherine?

5. When Alisa implies that Katherine has been lying, Katherine appears defensive. How would you have responded to this accusation if you were Katherine? Why?

6. Despite strong attempts to get Katherine to budge, Alisa is unsuccessful in unfreezing the salary freeze. What would you have done at this point if you were Alisa? Why?

7. Near the end, Katherine suggests a potential solution (bonus sharing). Why didn't she offer this earlier in the negotiation?

8. How would you evaluate the negotiation? Did either party "win"? If so, which? If not, why not?

Exercise 9–D
The Car Swap

This exercise consists of three parts: (1) researching market values, (2) preparing to "sell" your car, and (3) the "swap."

Part 1: Researching Market Values

Imagine you were going to sell your (or a family member's) car to a private party. You will have to know the year, make, and specific model of the car, as well as the current odometer rating and an inventory of the car's features.

Go to at least one national site (e.g., Edmonds, Kelly Blue Book), and one local site (the classifieds for your local or near-local newspaper). Starting with the national site, research the value of your car, and then temper that estimate based on values for similar cars advertised in the local market and how quickly you need to "sell" your car. Keep a record of the total estimate, as well as how you arrived at that estimate (e.g., bonuses/reductions for extra/missing or poor elements of your car).

Part 2: Preparing to Sell Your Car

Using the information you gathered in Part 1, create an advertisement that could be included in the classifieds section of your local newspaper. The ad must be factual (not falsely embellished) and should indicate the year, make, model, and price of the car. In addition, you may include any or all pertinent features and benefits and contact information (e.g., phone number, e-mail address). Note that there is a 40-word limit for your ad.

Next, prepare a strategy outline for selling your car by answering the following questions:

1. How much do you want for your car?

2. Why? What elements of your research suggest this price?

3. What are you willing to accept? Why (what is this figure based on)?

4. What is your BATNA? If you don't receive a satisfactory offer for your car, what is your best alternative?

5. How is this price a good value? Be prepared to explain key elements of your research.

6. What persuasive arguments will you make to convince the buyer that your price is fair and the deal is a good one? Consider using the ACE and inoculation theories, as well as arguments that are logical and/or appeal to the buyer's basic instincts.

Part 3: The Car Swap

This activity may be completed using an in-class bulletin board or an electronic discussion board (e.g., WebCT, Blackboard).

Stage 1: Selling your car:

1. You will need to have completed initial research (Part 1) and have composed an ad (Part 2) to "sell" your car.
2. In the designated area, you will post your ad (additional information is available from your instructor) by a given deadline. In an electronic environment, you will post a new thread with the title that includes the year, make, and model of your car.

Stage 2: Buying a car:

1. By another deadline, you must indicate the used car (of one of your classmates) that you want to "buy." This may be done by sticking a Post-it note (e.g., "I want this") with your name on it, or in an electronic environment, by clicking on the thread representing the car of your choice, clicking Reply, and typing "I want this." If your desired car has already been selected, you must choose another car. All participants must choose a car (NOT their own!), and all cars must be chosen, that is, a single car cannot have multiple buyers. Clearly, the earlier you respond after the "ads" are placed, the better selection you'll have.
2. Now that you know the car in which you're interested, it's time to do some research. Before the class session that features the car swap negotiation, gather whatever pertinent data you'll need to successfully negotiate the purchase of your new used car.
3. Your instructor has more information about the timing and sequence of the remaining activities.

Discussion Questions

1. Regarding the sale of your car:
   a. How well prepared were you for this negotiation? Explain.
   b. Did you use distributive or integrative bargaining? Give examples. Was this effective, given your goals? Explain.
   c. Was your negotiation a success? Why or why not? If you could redo the negotiation, what would you do differently and why?
2. Regarding the purchase of another's car:
   a. How well prepared were you for this negotiation? Explain.
   b. Did you use distributive or integrative bargaining? Give examples. Was this effective, given your goals? Explain.
   c. Was your negotiation a success? Why or why not? If you could redo the negotiation, what would you do differently and why?
3. Which negotiation felt more comfortable for you, buying or selling? Why?
4. What did you learn about yourself as a negotiator (your strengths and weaknesses) through this process? Explain.

Source: Adapted from S. C. de Janasz and B. J. DeMarr, "Can You Negotiate Anything? Identifying and Sharing Best Practices in Teaching Negotiation," presented at the 2006 Organizational Behavior Teaching Conference, Rochester, NY.

**Exercise 9–E
Negotiation Role-Play**

Working in groups of four or five, choose one of the following scenarios and develop a script to prepare for a negotiation you are about to enter. Role-play the script with another member of your group and get feedback from the other members on your skill as a negotiator. When all in the small group have taken a turn as a negotiator, discuss the activity with the class or group as a whole, using the discussion questions below.

Negotiation Scenario 1

You have worked in your current assignment for two years. During that time, your company initiated a new bonus system. However, neither you nor other employees know very much about the new system. Your employer cautioned everyone to keep their salaries and bonuses confidential, so you have little information about how others in your company are compensated. At year-end, you received a bonus, but it's significantly smaller than you anticipated. You want to approach your boss to ask for a larger bonus, but without information on what everyone else got, you have little information on which to base your argument. How do you prepare to negotiate with your boss?

Negotiation Scenario 2

You have been working hard on the job for five years. Your wife recently gave birth to your first child. She has an opportunity for a promotion at work and has asked if you would be willing to work part-time briefly while she pursues her career. You support the idea and agree to switch to part-time status on your job, pending your boss's approval. How do you prepare to negotiate with your boss to get his approval on this request?

Negotiation Scenario 3

Your parents have told you that you cannot have a car at school. They are concerned about your safety (you have already been in one car accident that was your fault), your grades (you have a C+ average), and your ability to keep up with the payments financially (you earn just enough at your part-time job to cover your expenses while at school). How do you prepare to negotiate with your parents?

Questions

1. What was your strategy going into the negotiation? Was it effective? What worked? What didn't?
2. What ideas did you get from other group members about how you could improve your negotiating skill?
3. What was difficult about negotiating (other than having to role-play!)?
4. What did you learn about yourself as a negotiator (your strengths and weaknesses) from this exercise?

**Exercise 9–F
Negotiation Scripts**

1. Think of a situation you've been involved in recently where you wish you had negotiated. Using the script outline (see Figure 9–4), develop a script for how you would approach the situation if you had a second chance. Comparing this script to what actually happened, what aspects of your actual negotiation were positive? In need of improvement? What impact would the changes alluded to in your script have had on the actual outcome? Explain. Discuss this situation with a partner.
2. Use the script outline (see Figure 9–4) to prepare for an upcoming negotiation—with a friend, relative, significant other, current or prospective boss, or co-worker. Role-play with a partner who will play the person with whom you'll negotiate. Request your partner's feedback on what worked well and what you could do differently in the future. Make adjustments to your script outline.

**Exercise 9–G
Negotiating a Home
Purchase**

The Situation

You and your family have been renting a house for the last eight months. During a recent visit from your landlord, he mentioned his desire to sell some of his properties. "Not this one," he tells you, "but I have another house a few miles away." Hmmmm. You love the area, the school district is great, and you've been thinking about buying, although there have been few if any properties available in your price range. Your landlord, who lives in another state, gives you the address and his phone number. "Call me if you're interested and we'll talk," he says. You and your spouse drive by the house the next day. Not your dream home, but it is a possibility—if the price is right.

The Players

The landlord (additional information available from your instructor)
The renter (additional information available from your instructor)
An observer

The Process

Decide who will play which role in your triad. Read the situation and additional information, create a plan, and then negotiate. The observer should take notes on effective and less-than-effective negotiating behaviors. The observer will then lead a feedback discussion after the negotiation is complete.

Exercise 9–H
Negotiating a Raise

The Situation

You have worked hard at your job for three years. During that time, you also went to school at night and completed your MBA degree. You have discovered that your company is bringing in newly minted MBAs at a salary that is 25 percent higher than yours. You want to ask your boss for a raise. How do you prepare to negotiate with your boss?

The Players

The boss (additional information available from your instructor)

The subordinate (additional information available from your instructor)

An observer

The Process

Decide who will play which role in your triad. Read the situation and additional information, create a plan, and then negotiate. The observer should take notes on effective and less-than-effective negotiating behaviors. The observer will then lead a feedback discussion after the negotiation is complete.

Exercise 9–I
Going Across the Pond

You've read the opening scenario. Now you have an opportunity to negotiate one of the three roles: John, Gina (his wife), or Rebecca (his daughter). Your instructor will provide role information to you.

Step 1: After roles are selected/assigned, each person should read the additional information and plan his or her goals, BATNAs, and other components of his or her negotiation strategy. Consider using the strategy outline discussed in the chapter.

Step 2: Have the negotiation. Each person present should introduce him- or herself (and the role she or he is playing) and share any relevant information. Consider collaboratively developing an agenda.

Step 3: Debrief/self-assessment

1. Discuss your opinion about the negotiation outcome (what you "got") relative to what you strategized for. What explains the discrepancy (if any) or similarity between the planned and actual outcome? (This discussion might include reference to what might have been done differently to achieve the desired outcome . . . or more, if you got what you wanted too easily.)

_____

_____

_____

2. Discuss the dynamics of the negotiation. Specifically explain two dynamics or issues that arose that threatened to undermine the effectiveness of the negotiation. What actions were taken to overcome or manage these issues? In what ways were the actions successful? What other actions might have been taken, and toward what likely effect?

_____

_____

_____

3. To what degree were all sides' key interests satisfied? Describe elements of the negotiation process that helped all parties get there (or not!), as well as evidence to support your opinion that key interests were satisfied (or not).

Exercise 9–J
The Right Team to Work With

As is often the case, the management of Turgot Optics, a successful traditional French producer of optical instruments, wants to optimize the company's capital structure. Capital needs and market conditions frequently change, and a company's capital structure has to be adapted to these changes from time to time. At its last board meeting, Turgot's management decided to go for a hybrid private equity placement, a type of financial transaction that is completely new to France (to negotiate this role-play, no specific knowledge in finance is needed, though). Turgot's management has decided to place a volume of €100 million on the market. The management subsequently discussed the deal with Turgot's main bank partner, CRI, but these talks were not very satisfactory. Hybrid capital is already very popular in some European countries, but so far no French company or bank, including CRI, has had any experience with it. Turgot's management therefore looked for alternatives and found Silverman Brothers, a leading German investment bank. Silverman Brothers has a good reputation and is also very experienced in hybrid financing. But they are also much more expensive. Moreover, Turgot has already been collaborating with CRI for several decades and CRI has always been generous when Turgot was facing problems. Can an important and reliable partner just be ignored for such an important deal? What about including both financial institutions in the transaction? Which is the right team to work with?

Read the role information (three teams; confidential role information for each team will be provided by your instructor) and prepare, as a team, for the negotiation.

After the negotiation, please discuss the following questions in your team:

1. What do you think were the goals and aspirations of the other parties? Did the parties have any restrictions, limitations, or hidden agendas?
2. What were your own goals and aspirations? How well did your team perform? Identify one strength and one weakness in the negotiation and explain why you thought these were strengths/weaknesses.
3. What were the key business challenges to reaching a resolution in the negotiation? How did you overcome them? What could have been done differently?
4. What were the key process challenges (i.e., how you went about generating a resolution) in the negotiation? Please explain.
5. How was your relationship with the other parties? Did you try to form a coalition? If yes, with which party and why? Which parties could gain from a coalition?
6. What did the power game look like? Was one party more powerful than the others? Was there a possibility of influencing the power constellation?

Source: We thank Peter Kesting, Associate Professor in the Department of Management at Aarhus University Business and Social Sciences in Denmark, for contributing this case and related materials.

Exercise 9–K
Negotiating in the Family Business

Your instructor will show you a clip from the movie *Arven* (Danish for *The Inheritance*; 2003, directed by P. Fly), which is a story of a Danish man named Christoffer who is forced into taking over the family business after his father commits suicide. When the movie opens, we meet Christoffer, a 30-something restaurant owner living in nearby Sweden where he is happily married to Maria, an aspiring actress. Shortly after an unexpected visit from his father, we learn that the father has killed himself. Christoffer flies to Denmark to comfort his mother, Annelise, and attend his father's funeral, when he:

- Learns that his father's steel business is floundering and will only survive if workers are laid off and the business merges with a French steel company.
- Is pressured by his mother to take over the business—despite his brother-in-law Ulrik's clear succession to CEO, and even though Christoffer is adamantly against it. This also puts him at odds with his sister, Benedikte, a stay-at-home mom.

- Reluctantly agrees, feeling obligated to take up the task but limiting his involvement to one year. The decision is met with frustration and anger from his wife Maria, who eventually accepts his decision and moves back to Denmark along with him.
- Gets absorbed by the enormity of the situation, which begins to take over his life and marriage.

In groups of six, decide who will play which role:

Christoffer—the son who reluctantly takes over the business, a steelworks factory that is in trouble with its creditors, who are asking for drastic changes (e.g., layoffs, merger with another company).

Annelise—the mother (and now widow) who puts pressure on him to take over the family business.

Maria—Christoffer's wife and a free-spirited actress who fears that Christoffer's decision will create problems for him as well as their relationship.

Benedikte—Christoffer's sister, who is not involved in the business but whose livelihood depends on her husband's continued employment at the family firm.

Ulrik—Benedikte's husband, who fully expected to take over the business when his father-in-law committed suicide.

Niels—The long-serving CFO and only non–family member involved in managing the business.

For the negotiation, each person should prepare relative to the current situation:

It's now nine months after Christoffer has taken over the business. Responding to internal and external pressures, he announces layoffs of 200 employees and meets regularly with a French steel company in merger discussions.

Christoffer's wife becomes increasingly unhappy and makes regular trips between Sweden and Denmark. She's unhappy with how Christoffer shuts her out of "business issues" but would like to patch up their relationship if possible.

The long-serving CFO (Niels) seems to want to exert more influence, but as a non–family member, he's constrained. He's also informed Christoffer that Ulrik (his brother-in-law) might have spread a rumor that negatively impacts the reputations of both Christoffer and the family business.

The six of you find yourselves together in the boardroom . . . a somewhat surprise finding undoubtedly organized by Annelise (the mother) to agree on the long-term goals of the company, clarify roles/responsibilities, and reduce the growing conflicts between some of you.

After the negotiation, the six players should:

1. Discuss your opinion about the negotiation outcome (what you "got") relative to what you strategized for. What explains the discrepancy (if any) or similarity between the planned and actual outcome? (This discussion might include reference to what might have been done differently to achieve the desired outcome . . . or more, if you got what you wanted too easily.)

_____

_____

_____

2. Discuss the dynamics of the negotiation. Specifically explain two dynamics or issues that arose that threatened to undermine the effectiveness of the negotiation. What actions were taken to overcome or manage these issues? In what ways were the actions successful? What other actions might have been taken, and toward what likely effect?

_____

_____

_____

3. Describe your emotions and how they affected you, your relationship with the other players, and the negotiation itself. What could you have done before, during, or after the negotiation to improve in this area?

_____

_____

_____

**Exercise 9–L
Reflection/Action Plan**

This chapter focused on negotiation—what it is, why it is important, and how to improve your skills in this area. Complete the following worksheet upon completing all reading and experiential activities for this chapter.

1. The one or two areas in which I am strongest:

_____

_____

_____

2. The one or two areas in which I need to improve:

_____

_____

_____

3. If I did only one thing to improve in this area, it would be to:

_____

_____

_____

4. Making these changes would probably result in:

_____

_____

_____

5. If I did not change or improve in these areas, it would probably affect my personal and professional life in the following ways:

_____

_____

_____

10 Building Teams and Work Groups

Learning Points

How do I:

- Recognize developmental stages and help a team progress through them?
- Distinguish high-performance teams from other types of work teams?
- Ensure that all members of a team understand their roles and responsibilities and contribute equitably to meeting team objectives?
- Effectively manage differences in values and work styles in a team setting?
- Ensure team success while minimizing the impact of potential limitations?

Angela Higgins was pleasantly surprised when she was selected for the company's task force charged with developing criteria for a new, high-end product line to complement the company's existing mid-range offerings. Yet after only a few short meetings, Angela was starting to wonder about her project work team even though the team consisted of some of the top talent in the company. She was sensing that no one was overly committed to finding innovative options, except for Ryan. However, Angela felt Ryan had an ulterior motive and simply wanted the team to come up with a good plan because, as he put it, "This could be my ticket to the top," and while he pushed the team to be productive, he personally never had anything to offer. And then there was Kim, who couldn't get past her negativity to even try to be creative, as she was convinced that a high-end line was a bad business move and doomed to fail in this poor economy. Sarah and Andrew were great to work with but they seemed to be stretched thin with their main job duties and never able to devote the full time to any of the meetings. In the last meeting, Sarah also informed the team that she would be in China for the next month working on her new expansion line and would try to participate when she could, but feared she would be limited in her contributions. And who knew about Chase; he only rarely raised his head from his Black-Berry just long enough to mutter, "Sounds good to me." With all this talent they should be able to put together a sound proposal, but with the way things had progressed so far, Angela was starting to wonder how.

1. What is the situation Angela faces? What are the core issues impacting the team's process?

2. How did this situation develop? What could have been done to achieve a different outcome?

3. How would you feel if you were Angela? Has a similar situation happened to you?

4. What would you do if you were Angela?

5. What should Angela do?

"We are a pack animal. From earliest times we have used the strength of the group to overcome the weakness of the individual. And that applies as much to business as to sport."[1]

Tracey Edwards
(skippered the first women's crew
to circumnavigate the globe)

From the popular NBC reality show *The Apprentice* to most of the *Fortune* 500 and many high-tech startup firms to competitive sports, teams are an everyday occurrence in our personal and work lives. As the nature of work progresses from individually based work to group settings, understanding teams and how to work in team settings and in work groups has become a crucial interpersonal skill. Not everyone is convinced that teams are more effective than individuals working on their own. But the reality is that many organizations are attempting to set up a team-based structure when tackling particular issues or processes, and the ability to work as a team is one of the most commonly required skills in the work environment.[2] For example, Frits van Paasschen, CEO and president of Starwood Hotels & Resorts Worldwide, attributes his success to his teaming skills, whether in his current position or as a former executive with Nike Inc. and Coors Brewing Co. He believes that the variation in industries (hotels, shoes, beer) is not the issue; it is to recognize that business has evolved, it is multicultural, and change is rapid. To be successful, you need to build teams that are agile to adapt to what is going on today. For him, the important skill is the ability to influence and motivate teams by creating an environment where other people come up with the answers.[3]

This chapter covers the basics of teamwork. We define teams and detail their importance in business today. We discuss strategies for forming teams and tips for making teams effective and successful. We also include several exercises at the end of the chapter for you to further enhance your team skills, and we list resources available for further exploration.

What Is Teamwork?

A team is a formal work group consisting of people who work together to achieve a common group goal.[4] The word *team* is not synonymous with *group*. A **group** is a collection of people who work together but aren't necessarily working collectively toward the same goal. A **team** is composed of three or more interdependent individuals who are consciously working together to achieve a common objective, such as product development, service delivery, or process improvement. A group becomes a team when members demonstrate a commitment to one another and to the end goal toward which they are working. A team has a higher degree of cohesiveness and accomplishment than a group.[5]

From earliest times, human beings have used teams or groups to overcome the limitations of individuals. Collections of nomads in search of food and land, kingdoms composed of villagers and their leaders, native settlements, wagon trains and pioneers, the crews of ships—all were formed with the idea that more could be accomplished together than by an individual.[6] Even the U.S. president puts together teams to create public policy for the country, as do the quasi-"alliances" on the CBS television show *Survivor* and other reality shows that follow similar formats, such as *The Apprentice* (NBC) and *Hell's Kitchen* (FOX). Aside from gains in sheer horsepower, as in the case of a ship's crew, teams exist because few individuals possess all the knowledge, skills, and abilities needed to accomplish all tasks. Simply put, two heads are often better than one.

Within many professional sports teams, we can find shining examples of teamwork. Michael Jordan, one of the world's greatest basketball players and author of the book *I Can't Accept Not Trying,* writes, "One thing I believe to the fullest is that if you think and achieve as a team, the individual accolades will take care of themselves. Talent wins games, but teamwork and intelligence win championships." He says he never forgot that he was only one-fifth of the effort at any time.[7] Staying with sports for a moment, consider the differences between a tennis team and a football team. In tennis, the members of a team may work together, but the ultimate achievement of a team is based on the collective efforts of the individual tennis player. A winning team has the highest combined score for matches won. In football, a great quarterback is nothing without a great wide receiver, tight end, or offensive line that can keep him or her from getting sacked. The football team wins when all members work interdependently toward the same goal—passing and rushing their way toward touchdowns.

Returning to the workplace, it is estimated that between 70 and 82 percent of U.S. companies use the team concept, making teamwork skills one of the most commonly required skills in the work environment.[8] Many businesses are adopting a collaborative management approach that encourages sharing ideas and strategies throughout the organization. This collaboration provides many benefits to the organization as well as to the individuals who make up the teams.[9]

Types of Teams

In the same way sports teams differ in function, makeup, and ultimate goal or purpose, so do teams in the workplace. Because different types of teams will require varying levels of skills, participation, and leadership, organizations and managers need to consider the type of tasks to be completed, the level of autonomy needed, and the potential for synergy before creating a team.[10] The more commonly used team types are described below. These include members from various departments or business specialties such as marketing, information systems, communications, public relations, operations, human resources, accounting, finance, planning, research and development, and legal.

Cross-functional Teams

Cross-functional teams are usually charged with developing new products or investigating and improving a companywide problem such as the need to increase speed and efficiency across departmental lines or the need to adopt a new companywide computer system. Cross-functional teams derive their strength from diversity. By including representatives from all or most of an organization's primary functional areas, the team can diagnose a problem from multiple perspectives simultaneously, ensuring that all relevant points of view are taken into account. This can speed up the problem-solving process and result in an outcome that the various departments affected by the change more readily accept.

Case in point: Prior to producing its LH line of cars, Chrysler followed what most would call a serial design process. Engineering would design a car and throw it over the wall to manufacturing. "We can't build this," manufacturing would reply, sending it back over the wall to engineering. This would continue for months or years until marketing was charged with marketing a car that no one wanted. From product inception to market, this process could take as long as six years or more. By that time, technologies were obsolete and other companies easily stole market share. Realizing this, Chrysler moved to a simultaneous, cross-functional, team-based design process. Everyone who had a stake in or was affected by the design of a new product was on a team that hashed it out—together. This included people from marketing, sales, engineering, design, and many others. These meetings had conflict, but the conflict was actually helpful. Chrysler was able to reduce the cycle time from over six years to less than 18 months!

Another example of a cross-functional team is a top management team. In many large organizations, the CEO typically makes strategic decisions in collaboration with the leaders of the major functional areas. Even at this level in the organization, top management recognizes their individual strengths and weaknesses and the value that diverse perspectives can add when making key organizational decisions. For example, Walt Disney, after a few failed business attempts, used his vision for turning cartoons into a franchise as a draw to put together a top management team. His base team, which was comprised of people with varying skills and a reputation for excellence, allowed him to then attract the top talent in the animation industry (known as his "Nine Old Men") in order to fulfill his dreams.[11]

Self-managed Teams

Self-managed teams are "groups of employees who are responsible for a complete, self-contained package of responsibilities that relate either to a final product or an ongoing process."[12] Also known as self-directed, self-maintained, or self-regulating, **self-managed teams** are typically given a charge by senior management and then are given virtually complete discretion over how, when, and what to do to attain their objective. Self-managed teams are expected to coordinate their work without ongoing direction from a supervisor or manager. Self-managed teams set their own norms, make their own planning schedules, set up ways to keep relevant members and others informed of their progress, determine how the work is going to be accomplished, and are held accountable for their end product or "deliverable." Many of these teams are responsible for hiring, training, and firing team members. The flattening of organizational structures, resulting in less hierarchy and fewer managers, makes self-directed teams a popular concept in business today. Of course, it's not as if management flips a switch and a team becomes self-managing. It's a long process of team building and teamwork combined with sufficiently greater responsibility and accountability gained through the team's demonstrated capabilities and performance. At Consolidated Diesel, a manufacturing company in Whitakers, North Carolina, a brand-new (nonautomobile) diesel engine rolls off the assembly line every 72 seconds. Thanks to self-managed teams that have complete responsibility over what they do and whom they hire/fire, the company is a leader in the industry, has never had a major layoff, maintains a huge span of control (one manager per 100 employees—four times the industry average), and boasts an injury rate that is one-fifth the national average. The employees, who are extensively cross-trained and often fill in for one another—which increases their respect for one another's skills and challenges—cooperate fully to achieve superior results.[13]

Task Force

A **task force** is an ad hoc, temporary project team assembled to develop a product, service, or system or to solve a specific problem or set of problems. Companies are always faced with the challenge of getting ongoing, day-to-day work done while utilizing available resources to work on various change processes or product innovations. For example, a technology company might designate a group to study the next wave in software development while others are maintaining and servicing existing software programs. Or a company looking to lease additional space may ask a team to study available buildings and land in the area and recommend whether to lease or build based on its cost/benefit analysis. Often task force members are individuals who have demonstrated interest or skill in the area being examined by the task force, so the members are enthusiastic about the project and its potential. The task force process is very common in business today. It is lower in cost than hiring an outside consultant or group of contract workers and allows for management to allocate resources at will to various projects as the needs of the company and the interests of its employees change.

Process Improvement Teams

Process improvement teams focus on specific methods, operations, or procedures and are assembled with the specific goal of enhancing the particular component being studied. Process improvement teams are typically composed of individuals with expertise and experience in the process being reviewed. They are assigned the tasks of eliminating redundant steps, looking for ways to reduce costs, identifying ways to improve quality, or finding means for providing quicker, better customer service.[14]

Process improvement teams are often given training on problem-solving tools and techniques to help them map processes, identify root causes of problems, and prioritize potential solutions. To analyze a system and make recommendations for changes, process improvement team members diagnose the current state of a process and chart how it occurs step by step. They review customer or internal data and collect data from other sources such as managers, competitors, and others as needed. They identify ways the process can be enhanced, make their recommendations, and sometimes assist the operating units involved in implementing the changes. Process improvement teams are usually temporary and disband once the process being studied has been changed to the satisfaction of management.

Sun Microsystems' highly successful Java programming language was the result of a process improvement team. After programmer Patrick Naughton presented a document criticizing Sun's lack of innovation and customer focus, he was allowed to put together a team to work on the assignment, dubbed the "Stealth Project." This team, which evolved and attracted other talented individuals such as James Gosling, worked 100-hour weeks at a remote office and eventually developed the money-making technology for the company.[15]

Virtual Teams

The team types described above are generally assumed to be ones that consist of employees who physically meet together to develop or deliver products and services, improve processes, manage work, or solve ad hoc issues. As more employees have access to Internet and other virtual communication technologies, and as organizations expand operations beyond a single location, state, or country, **virtual teams**—those that operate across time, space, and organizational boundaries using means other than face-to-face meetings—have become more common.[16] For example, Lockheed Martin has assembled a team of engineers and designers from around the world to design and build a new stealth fighter plane to be used in military operations.[17] Over the course of the 10-year, $225 billion project, the company expects that meeting virtually instead of in person will save over $250 million.[18] SNL Financial, a Virginia-based research firm in the financial information marketplace, has offices in India, Pakistan, and the United Kingdom, as well as in New Jersey and California. As the number of virtual teams working together across these locations has increased, the company put together training modules on how teams can meet and work effectively, despite geographic, time, and cultural differences, using teleconferencing and videoconferencing. It hasn't always been easy, but the training modules—partly comprised of lessons learned since SNL's early implementation of virtual teams—have shortened the learning curve and increased team effectiveness.[19]

Medtronics, a *Fortune* 500 medical devices company headquartered in Minnesota with 250 facilities worldwide, uses international teams so employees can strategically collaborate with virtual peers for continuous improvement. They believe so much in teaming that they sponsor the Twin Cities Marathon with an "All for Run—Run for All" challenge to encourage all levels of corporate teamwork.[20]

Why Teams?

Teaming is more than a phase or a buzzword. If it didn't work, organizations would abandon this strategy for getting work done. But there is substantial evidence that teams can be effective, especially when tasks are complex and task interdependence is high. It is not always appropriate, of course, for work to be done in teams. But when a team structure is employed, and those teams work effectively, many benefits accrue to the organization and to the team members themselves.

Benefits of Teams

- Increased creativity, problem solving, and innovation.
- Higher-quality decisions.
- Improved processes.
- Global competitiveness.
- Increased quality.
- Improved communication.
- Reduced turnover and absenteeism and increased employee morale.

- *Increased creativity, problem solving, and innovation:* Bringing together a group of individuals who possess a wealth of ideas, perspectives, knowledge, and skills can result in a synergy through which new ideas can be entertained. We each have a unique set of skills. Working with others allows us to combine our skills and talents to create new approaches to solving problems.[21] An example is a team of marketers where each person applies his or her strengths to the issue at hand. One person who is very creative can lead the process of coming up with ideas; another who is detail-oriented can do the initial research; a third person who is skilled in graphic applications can put together a great sales presentation. Harley-Davidson relies heavily on cross-functional teams to design new products using a "creative friction" process that ensures that multiple conflicting viewpoints are heard at every stage of development; this approach has resulted in the company's ability to offer highly desirable, profitable bikes.[22]

- *Higher-quality decisions:* Teamwork enhances the quality of the outcomes. Teamwork involves the collective effort of a group of people who represent diverse backgrounds and experiences. As more ideas are produced and alternatives are considered, the team gets closer to optimal decisions—decisions that are stronger because they have been made with various perspectives and interests in mind.

- *Improved processes:* Teamwork results in a systematic approach to problem solving. Because of the necessary coordination between and transfer of learning among team members, teamwork results in organized approaches to the situation at hand. For example, a team is more likely than an individual to set up project checkpoints and planning systems to enable all team members to contribute to the project as it unfolds. Teamwork also permits distribution of workloads for faster and more efficient handling of large tasks or problems.[23] The use of self-managed teams can be a potent means for increasing employee involvement when transforming and developing organizational processes. They tend to value the need for ongoing improvements, resulting in higher productivity as teams tend to set higher production goals for themselves than those dictated by the organization.[24]

  When members representing different organizations work together to improve a process that cuts across multiple organizational functions, more glitches and interdependencies will be uncovered and addressed than would be by individuals working independently. Fed up with being blamed for the inconsistent delivery of materials needed for production on an upcoming project, a group of defense contracting employees decided to take a closer look at the entire procurement process, from the initial request to the actual delivery of ordered goods. They found several problems, including cumbersome authorization policies (e.g., requests for required signatures from those higher up in the hierarchy could sit on desks for days, weeks, even months!) and difficulty tracking where in the process an ordered part was. While the team came up with excellent suggestions for improvement, members knew they would not be able to implement the solutions on their own. They presented the process, problems, and solutions to a group of employees representing all departments that would be impacted by the potential changes to the process.

A Healthy Dose of Teaming[25]

Health care management is steadily moving away from the hierarchical structure and traditionally independent practices of the past toward a culture of teamwork. In keeping with a patient-centered approach to patient care, two of the most high-quality and cost-effective health care institutes have embraced collaboration by creating teams of specialists to treat each patient.

The Mayo Clinic, where "teamwork is not optional," is described as a "culture that attracts individuals who see and practice medicine best delivered when there is an integration of medical specialties functioning as a team." Patients don't just get a doctor but rather a whole team to quickly and efficiently handle their treatment through a holistic approach. The world-renowned Cleveland Clinic has also created eighteen "institutes" that use multidisciplinary teams to diagnose, problem solve, and treat diseases at a cost of nearly 50 percent less than the most expensive medical care provided to patients in the United States.

In so doing, they learned of additional challenges and ways to overcome those challenges. More importantly, by involving those who would be implementing the changes, the team came up with an optimum decision and employees were only too happy to implement the decision. The procurement process went from as long as 18 months to an average of 10 to 12 days.

- *Global competitiveness:* Teamwork enables companies to compete globally. Firms in the United States are relying increasingly on diverse teams to compete in the global economy.[26] Diverse teams have skill sets and perspectives that are superior to what a single individual can bring to the table. For example, when Clairol marketed its popular Mist Stick in parts of Germany, it flopped. Had the Clairol marketing team included someone of German origin, they could have informed the group that *mist* was a slang word for *manure*. As we continue developing and marketing our products in a global marketplace, combining diverse perspectives is essential.

- *Increased quality:* Studies show that those large, complex, global companies that have moved to teams show increases in productivity, employee ownership of and accountability for their work, timeliness, efficiency, and customer service.[27] This results in higher-quality standards than are possible when individuals or groups of individuals, who lack a common goal, are doing the work.

- *Improved communication:* The use of teams in the workplace enhances employee communication. In a traditional, hierarchical organization, communication tends to flow primarily in one direction—downward. In a team-based organization, communication flows laterally, upward, downward, and even outside the organization's boundaries (e.g., customers and suppliers). Teamwork requires collective action that is grounded in words and actions. It's not sufficient for one person to determine how he or she wants to work. Each person must get others on board before proceeding. In effective teams, there is rich sharing of information and ideas that improve communication within the team and between the team and the organization.[28]

- *Reduced turnover and absenteeism and increased employee morale:* Teamwork results in changes in employee behaviors and attitudes. Teamwork fosters a camaraderie that helps many employees feel more a part of the organization than when working independently. They feel ownership of the problems on which they work, get immediate feedback from teammates, see the fruits of their labors, and feel they have an impact on their job and the organization. Compared with the alienation employees often experience in traditional firms, employees in team-based organizations are happier, more committed, and more loyal to their organization. For example, management at John Deere decided to add assembly-line workers to teams of company representatives making sales calls.[29] Not only did the salespeople learn more about the products from working alongside those who actually built them, but also the assembly-line workers learned new skills and felt more involved in and motivated by their job.[30]

The accompanying box contains examples of the positive outcomes that resulted when organizations embraced and encouraged team-based work.

Examples of Team-Based Successes[31]

Organization	Reported Successes
Harley-Davidson	Returned to profitability in six years.
Hallmark	200 percent reduction in design time. Introducing 23,000 new card lines each year.
Liberty Mutual	50 percent reduction in contract process time. Saving of more than $50 million per year.

Organization	Reported Successes
Johns Hopkins Hospital	Patient volume increased by 21 percent. Turnover reduced, absenteeism reduced by 20 percent.
Monsanto	Quality and productivity improved by 47 percent in four years.
Saab and Volvo	4 percent increase in production output. Inventory turnover increased from 9 to 21 times a year.
Wilson Sporting Goods	Average annual costs savings of $5 million.
Corning	Defects dropped from 1,800 ppm to 3 ppm.
Exxon	Saved $10 million in six months.
IDS (subsidiary of American Express)	Improved response time by 96 percent—from several minutes to only a few seconds.

Potential Limitations of Teams

While this chapter focuses primarily on the effectiveness of teams and work groups and how to be a productive team member, there are times when teams fail or fall short of their potential. Several phenomena may explain these shortfalls. We describe several key self-limiting behaviors in the accompanying box.

Self-Limiting Team Behaviors

- *Groupthink.* **Groupthink**[32]—or individuals agreeing reluctantly with a group's decision because they are more concerned about maintaining harmony and cohesiveness than critically thinking about problems or alternative approaches—is a potential problem for teams. More specifically, in groupthink, "members of the group avoid promoting viewpoints outside the comfort zone of consensus thinking . . . to avoid being seen as foolish or . . . to avoid embarrassing or angering other members of the group."[33] Recently, the city council of East Grand Forks signed a mall lease agreement without clearing it first with the U.S. Economic Development Administration, despite being warned by one of the members of the team. Apparently, the city was not allowed to sell an important property, which it did, despite knowing about a condition placed upon the city by the federal agency. A consultant hired because of his expertise—who warned the city council about the condition and the need to clear their decision with the agency—resigned prior to the team's "mistake" after complaining that his advice wasn't being listened to. This mistake may cost the city $1.3 million.[34] Groupthink is more likely to occur when the group feels pressure to perform—especially when a deadline is approaching (as was the case with NASA's pressure to stay on schedule for the *Columbia* flight of 2003 in which all crew members died upon reentry[35]), when one or a few members are extremely dominant in a group setting, or when one or more members believe they haven't had a chance to air their concerns before an action is taken.
- *Group-hate.* According to Sorensen, **group-hate** is the negative view that some people have of working in groups that can influence their active participation in group socialization and group work activities. In other words, one (or more) bad experience on a team causes that individual to believe that all teams are bad or a waste of time. Because they distrust the team concept, individuals harboring group-hate would resist membership on a team and contribute little toward a team's goals

(continued)

and objectives.[36] Even just one individual who feels this way can contaminate the morale and productivity of a team. Research has shown that a bad classroom team experience can sour a student's perception regarding teamwork. This attitude can impact students' performance not only in future school assignments, but may even affect their performance in future employment.[37]

■ *Social loafing/Free riding.* By definition a team is a collection of three or more people. As the number of people working on a task increases, so does the likelihood that one or more members slack off, hoping that others will pick up the slack. One reason **social loafing** or **free riding** occurs is the lack of individual accountability, meaning that when "everyone" is responsible, "anyone" expects the work will be done by "someone" in the team and "no one" will know whether "everyone" did his or her equal share. Greenberg notes that the tendency for people to reduce their effort when working with others on an organizational project is problematic and also analogous to the research demonstrating that people dining alone leave bigger tips than when sharing the bill of a larger party.[38] It is for this reason that many restaurants automatically add the tip or a service charge for large (i.e., six, eight, or more) parties.

■ *Risky shift.* You may have heard the phrase "united we stand, divided we fall." **Risky shift** takes place when members who are part of a group agree to a more risky course of action than any individual would have done alone. One explanation for this phenomenon is the sense of shared responsibility and accountability that breeds a feeling of invincibility. Reflect on some of your previous actions. Did you ever do something with a group that you never would have done had you been alone? We can even see this phenomenon on the road. If no other drivers are speeding, you are likely to obey the speed limit. However, if several drivers around you are speeding, you are more likely to follow suit, believing that "no police officer could make all of us pull over and give us tickets." The truth is, while such an event can and does happen, it's relatively rare. By going with the flow and believing you are acting as part of a larger group, somehow your poor judgment is buoyed into the realm of acceptable. In the workplace, risky shift might look like a team agreeing to a schedule that's too ambitious, committing to finding a creative solution to a problem that has never before been solved, or choosing a lease or investment option that is probably "too good to be true."

These four problems or limitations can have devastating effects on teams. In Exercise 10–E, we provide an opportunity for you to think more about these issues, determine steps that team members or team leaders can take to reduce the likelihood that these issues arise, and consider what to do if steps taken to prevent these behaviors are not successful.

Team Developmental Stages

Groups typically pass through a series of stages as they grow and evolve into teams (see Figure 10–1). Theorists postulate that a team goes in and out of at least five stages in its life cycle: forming, storming, norming, performing, adjourning.[39] This process is fluid—teams may revisit a stage, or skip one or more altogether. Each phase has distinguishing characteristics and presents particular challenges to team members and their managers.

Stage One—Forming

In this stage, a team is established to accomplish a particular task. Typically the group members will not know each other, and even if they do, there is a feeling of uncertainty and tentativeness because people haven't had a chance yet to get to know one another and set group objectives.[40] In the **forming** stage, members will engage in behaviors such as defining the initial assignment, discussing how to divvy up the necessary tasks,

Figure 10–1
Team Stage Visual

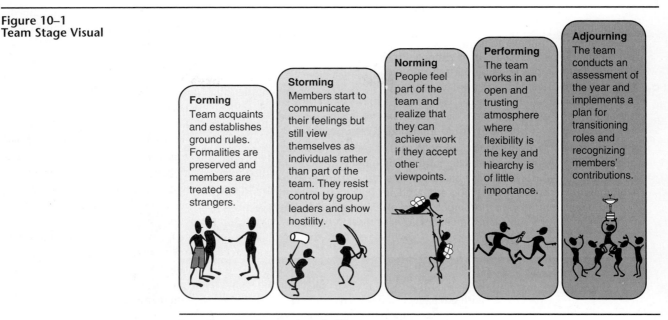

Forming
Team acquaints and establishes ground rules. Formalities are preserved and members are treated as strangers.

Storming
Members start to communicate their feelings but still view themselves as individuals rather than part of the team. They resist control by group leaders and show hostility.

Norming
People feel part of the team and realize that they can achieve work if they accept other viewpoints.

Performing
The team works in an open and trusting atmosphere where flexibility is the key and hiearchy is of little importance.

Adjourning
The team conducts an assessment of the year and implements a plan for transitioning roles and recognizing members' contributions.

Source: http://crushtastic.ca/roundball/?p=813

understanding the broad scope and objectives of the project, and learning about the resources (time, equipment, personnel) available to the team as it works to complete the project.

In this stage, some members test leadership roles, discover personality similarities and differences, and make some initial disclosures, but relatively little progress usually occurs on the task.

As a team member or team leader, your role in stage one is to encourage the group to establish its mission and purpose, set up a work schedule, get to know one another, and establish some initial norms for working together.

Stage Two—Storming

In this stage, a group experiences differences over factors such as direction, leadership, work style, and approach, and perceptions about the expected quality and state of the end product or deliverable. As is true of any relationship, conflict is inevitable. Many couples feel bad when they experience their first fight, and teams are no exception. When the first conflict among group members emerges, some or all of the members begin to feel less enthusiastic about the group and might even doubt the group can come together and achieve its objective. There may be struggles over leadership ("My way is best"), power ("If you don't agree, we'll leave you behind"), and roles ("Who appointed you chief?"). In the **storming** stage, feelings emerge such as resistance to the task or approach being taken by the group, resentment about differences in workload, anger about roles and responsibilities, and changes in attitude about the group or toward individual group members and concerns. Typically in the storming stage, the group is in conflict and chaos, as it has not yet established ways to communicate about these differences. During this stage, few if any processes and procedures are in place, as the need for them wasn't anticipated due to the lack of prior conflict. All of this can result in arguing among members, emergence of subgroups, and disunity. If and when a group in which you are working enters this stage, what can you do?

In the storming stage, your role as a group member or leader is to refrain from taking sides. Encourage the group to develop communication channels. Help your group members focus on the task and not on personal differences. Promote an environment of open communication to ensure that the inevitable conflict is healthy and results in improved communication and commitment to the group's task. Remember that an appropriate level of tension motivates a team, but too much or too little can affect productivity.[41] If your group cannot resolve or work effectively with conflict, request the assistance of a trained process consultant or facilitator. A group that fails to manage its conflicts may fail to achieve its deliverables.

Stage Three—Norming

In this stage, the group faces its issues, conflicts, and power and leadership struggles openly and directly. The members establish and adhere to patterns of acceptable behavior and learn to incorporate new methods and procedures into their working together. In the **norming** stage, members feel a new ability to express constructive criticism; they feel part of a working team and a sense of relief that everything will work out.[42] In this stage, members attempt to achieve harmony by avoiding unnecessary conflict, acting more friendly toward and trusting of each other, and developing a sense of team unity ("Together, we can solve this"). Norms don't have to be established about every single decision or policy, only those that are particularly significant to team members.[43]

As a team member or leader, your role is to encourage team members to take on more responsibility, work together to create means acceptable for solving problems, set challenging goals, and take personal responsibility for team success. As a leader, you set the tone. Don't expect others to "do as you say, but not as you do." If you are seen bickering with colleagues and secretly plotting political moves, team members are less likely to emulate the helpful norming behaviors and may regress to the storming stage.

Stage Four—Performing

In the **performing** stage, teams have worked through their differences. Their membership is stable, the task is clear, and eyes are on the prize. Team members are highly motivated to accomplish their task and focused on team objectives rather than individual interests. Through working closely together, team members have developed insights into one another's strengths and weaknesses (many even finish each other's sentences), feel satisfied with the team's progress, and believe the team will successfully reach or even exceed its goals. In this stage, members engage in constructive self-change for the good of the group; experience greatly enhanced ability to communicate with and give feedback to each other; are able to anticipate, prevent, or work through group problems; and, as a result, develop a close attachment to the team.[44]

As a team member or leader, your role at this stage is to encourage members to provide support to and serve as resources for one another. Make sure the team continues with its progress and maintains its cohesion and morale, and guide it toward success. Do remain vigilant, however. It's easy to kick back and relax, believing that once a team gets to this phase of development, it stays there. That may or may not be true. Changes in membership, scope of the task, or broader organizational changes can cause a team to regress developmentally. In addition, the close attachments members have to a team could possibly blind them to other developing problems.

Stage Five—Adjourning

After successfully completing the task or objective, teams may disband permanently or take a temporary break. Some may get new members or receive a new objective. This stage is usually brought on by an imminent deadline. At the **adjourning** stage, sometimes referred to as deforming, members are likely to feel disappointment if the experience was positive, or gratitude if the experience was negative. The task at this stage is to tie up loose ends and complete final follow-up on projects.

As a team member or leader, your role at this end stage is to encourage the team members to debrief the project, discussing the lessons learned that members can take with them to new projects and convey to new teams tackling similar issues. This stage is many times overlooked but it is a crucial time for teams, as research has shown that team turnover affects social interaction, team learning behavior, and task flexibility. If this stage is not managed correctly, detrimental consequences can impact current and future team effectiveness.[45] It is also helpful at this stage to recognize the team for its efforts. This could take the form of public recognition (a blurb on the team's accomplishments in the monthly newsletter), a reward (some organizations reward teams with a percentage of the savings or revenues realized as a result of the team's work), or other benefit (such as using company funds to take the team out for lunch). By providing encouragement and recognizing accomplishments, hard work, and efforts, you help to continue momentum and build motivation.[46] Of course, ongoing work project teams may not physically adjourn. They may remain intact, continuing with a new set of objectives once a particular project is complete. In this case, rather than adjourning, the team members may choose to debrief at certain checkpoints along the way, evaluating their processes and communication efforts to ensure they're keeping current and are as productive as they can be.

It is healthy for groups to move through some or all of these stages as they evolve into a team. Not all groups go through all the stages, and some go through them at different paces. For example, if a group's members knew each other previously and had similar values and goals—as well as a tight deadline—they might be able to move almost immediately to the norming stage. In another case, where the group members don't know each other well and they have some time before the deliverable is due, they might take longer to reach the norming phase, coalescing as a real team just before the final due date. Some may get stuck in one of the stages and disband before progressing to the next stage or perform at a lower level than what might have been possible. A group stuck in the storming stage but facing an imminent deadline has to continue performing. In this case, it is likely that its performance will suffer due to the inability to function cohesively. In some extreme cases, a group will be dysfunctional and will require outside intervention in order to complete its task. As is true with relationships, teams have developmental cycles. Understanding this ahead of time can help you develop strategies for helping your group evolve into a team and to increase its effectiveness every step of the way.

"The strength of the team is each individual member . . . the strength of each member is the team."

Coach Phil Jackson of the
Chicago Bulls and Los Angeles
Lakers

Add Some E's for T-E-E-E-A-M Success[47]

MIT's Human Dynamics Laboratory believes they have found the science behind creating high-performing teams. By equipping team members with electronic badges, they were able to track communication behavior and were able to show that communication is as critical to team success as skill, personality, discussion content, and individual intelligence. The sociometric data allowed them to predict which teams would be successful based on the amount of three E's: Energy—how much members contributed to the team as a whole; Engagement—how team members communicated with one another; and Exploration—how much teams communicated with other teams. So if you want to improve your team, get them communicating—formally and informally. They found that social time accounted for more than 50 percent of positive changes in communication patterns, and recommended changing the office setting or reorganizing the workspace to allow for interaction, water cooler talks, and coffee breaks.

Characteristics of High-Performance Teams

As former Notre Dame coach Lou Holtz said, "Winning is never accidental. To win consistently you must have a clear plan and intense motivation." As we have said, not all teams are alike. As a team member or leader, your primary goal is to encourage your group to evolve into a motivated, goal-oriented, successful team; we refer to these types of teams as high-performance teams. In **high-performance teams**, there is a commitment to quality and a dedication to producing the best outcome possible. Research shows that most high-performance work teams possess the following characteristics:[48]

- *Common purpose and goals:* High-performing teams have a clearly defined mission, purpose, and goals. Individual team members understand why the team has been formed and what is expected from the team.[49]

- *Intention:* The best teams are not ad hoc or unstructured. Instead, they are planned or structured to achieve a specific goal or address a specific challenge. In structured team building, the importance is placed on intentionally striving to achieve sustainable outcomes by matching team psychology with change and technology.[50]

- *Clear roles:* High-performing teams have clarity about roles and responsibilities. Team members understand their roles and assignments and how they impact the group, have clear and stable boundaries, are aware of how their work affects other members, and know the direction that is needed to get there.[51]

- *Communication processes:* High-performing teams have extensive communication mechanisms. They communicate regularly with each other either in person, via telephone, or through e-mail and keep those unable to attend meetings informed of the group's progress. They constantly update their planning calendar and communicate about adjustments as needed.[52]

- *Accepting and supportive leadership:* Studies have found that team leaders who function more as coaches than managers facilitate the development of participative, motivated teams.[53] These leaders were proactive and committed to the team, and they provided encouraging, positive influence over the team and its members. A manager pulls a group along; a coach gently pushes it from behind. A manager works to maintain control; a coach works to give up control.[54] In fact, members of high-performing teams report being able to speak without fear, in part due to the efforts of leaders who "ensure that sharpshooters put their guns away" by curbing conversations that interrupt others or discount others' ideas.[55]

- *Small size:* The size of the team can be essential to a team's success. The optimal size is between 6 and 10. This is large enough to accomplish the work and provide enough human resources and ideas, and small enough for a team to coalesce and reach consensus on major issues.[56]

- *High levels of technical and interpersonal skills:* High-performing teams are composed of members who have a breadth of both specialty and people skills. Understanding how to work with and through others, problem solving, managing project work flow, giving and receiving feedback, goal setting, time management, and conflict management are some of the most valuable skills in team settings.[57] High levels of emotional intelligence in a team's members can greatly contribute to the team's overall interpersonal process.[58]

- *Open relationships and trust:* In high-performing teams, the members develop cooperative behaviors including understanding what is needed from one another; defining the interrelated activities necessary to complete the project; volunteering to assist one another in doing what's needed; and completing assigned tasks competently, on time, accurately, and with quality. Trust, as fully discussed in Chapter 2, is built through behaviors such as being dependable, doing what is agreed upon, being kept informed and informing others of necessary facts and information, keeping confidential information private, and allowing others to use their specialized knowledge and abilities.[59] Leaders of high-performance teams realize the importance of effective communication in building trust by saying what they mean and meaning what they say; refraining from sending mixed messages, fudging meanings, or using ambiguous words; and encouraging mutual understanding between members and the leader.[60]

- *Accountability:* High-performance team members understand for what (and to what degree) they and others are held accountable. The team receives the message from the organization that performance matters—that it makes a difference whether goals are achieved or not. Expectations are clarified, and members are held responsible as individuals as well as members of the team.[61]

- *Reward structures:* High-performing teams are rewarded for team accomplishments in addition to individual recognition. Organizations that support the team concept organize their recruiting, training, sales, research and development, strategic planning, compensation, performance appraisal, and promotion strategies to support and reward teamwork.[62] For example, Trigon Blue Cross Blue Shield changed its performance appraisal and reward system to recognize equally employees' achievement of individual goals and demonstrated team behaviors.[63] When organizational strategies don't match with or undermine team processes or philosophies, the organization sends a mixed message and members find ways to "game" the system—often at the expense of their team. If an individual team member who "saves the day" for the department is rewarded for individual behavior, it sends the message that collaboration is not as valued as individual contributions or heroics, even if management's rhetoric suggests teams are truly valued.

Tips for Effective Teams

As a member of a team, it is important to be self-directed and work for the betterment of your team. You and your team members will be working with minimal supervision, and it is everyone's responsibility to make the team work. As athletes have learned, if one team member doesn't come through, the quality and performance of the entire team is affected. Teamwork requires full dedication and participation by all members of the team.

The following tips can help make your next team experience more positive and successful.

- *Be focused.* Cooperate with your team members in concentrating on the current issues they face. Cooperation builds trust and mutual respect. Be willing and dedicated to working toward the common purpose.

- *Handle conflict directly* and be willing to compromise. Be willing to explore conflict in a constructive, win–win fashion. Stand up for things that are important to you, but don't insist on getting your way in every discussion. When working together, put personalities aside and confront issues that arise. Resolve conflicts and walk away from sessions with regard, respect, and esteem for yourself and your team members.[64]

- *Focus on both process and content.* Pay attention to the *process* of becoming and working together as a team as well as the *result* or end goal expected from the team. Teamwork is more than producing a deliverable. It also entails the approach or process used when people are working together.[65] The ends don't necessarily justify the means if team members despise and lack respect for team members because of the way decisions and outcomes were rammed through when teams fail to use a consensus approach. At team meetings, review both the processes being used as well as the status of the project.

- *Actively participate,* and encourage others to do the same. At the beginning of a project, talk about roles and responsibilities. Also talk frankly about team members' schedules and their availability to participate fully in the project. Set up checkpoints to ensure that all are contributing equally.

- *Keep sensitive issues private.* At the beginning of a project, discuss the importance of confidentiality. All teams engage in discussions that could be hurtful if made public. Have a pact that private information and views shared will be just that—not relayed to others outside the group. "What's said in the room, stays in the room."

- *Communicate openly and positively.* In order to have full team participation, and for the team to learn and develop, it is essential that team members do not embarrass, reject, mock, or punish someone for speaking up and sharing ideas and perceptions. Foster a climate of psychological safety in order to motivate members to participate, admit errors, and share ideas and beliefs openly and comfortably.[66]

- *Take time to establish operating guidelines* and clarify expectations. Make sure everyone is present for initial discussions of roles, responsibilities, and operating guidelines. For these guidelines to work, it is best that everyone participate in establishing and agreeing to uphold them. Put them in writing and have everyone sign them.

■ *Monitor what's going on with the team.* Watch for reactions, nonverbal cues, level of participation (or lack thereof), and general changes in the group's dynamics. Don't assume that no news is good news. The CEO of a struggling pharmaceutical company thought that was the case when he proposed eliminating business and first-class travel. All of his direct reports seated around the table nodded their heads in agreement, but within weeks, it became clear that only a subset of them actually committed to the decision. The rest didn't challenge the decision; instead, they ignored it. This became a huge problem when employees from different departments traveling together found themselves heading to different sections of the airplane. Moreover, additional time was wasted when once again, the travel policy was on the next meeting's agenda. By honing your observational skills, you can help a team reach its full potential by setting a tone that is conducive to all members enjoying and participating in the team experience.[67]

■ *Practice giving (and receiving) effective feedback.* Express support and acceptance by praising and seeking other members' ideas and conclusions. If you disagree with others' viewpoints, criticize ideas but not the people. Be specific about the ideas that concern you and accept others' concerns about your ideas.

■ *Work with underperformers* to keep them in the flow of the project and prevent them from becoming excluded from the group.[68] If slackers are an issue in your team, talk with them immediately, preferably one on one. Find out if there is a personal problem preventing the member from being more engaged. Offer to be supportive but don't carry the workload. Give that team member specific, manageable tasks and hold him or her accountable. If the underperformance continues, talk with your manager or instructor. The person may need to be removed from the group or reassigned to a different team.

■ *Energize the team* when motivation is low by suggesting new ideas, through humor or use of enthusiasm. Encourage a time-out, if one is needed, or suggest a work or coffee break.

■ *Be reliable and conscientious.* Respect other members by honoring deadlines, commitments, and project milestones.[69] If you are having difficulty making a deadline, don't wait until the last minute—discuss the problem immediately with a team member or with the team. There might be a different way of approaching it. It's easier for a team to be flexible when there is adequate time to review the situation and come up with a different plan.

■ *When needed, give direction to the team's work* by stating and restating the purpose of assignments, setting or calling attention to time limits, and offering procedures on how to complete the assignment most effectively.

■ *Be supportive of your team members.* Always ask how you can help. It's a great way to remind everyone you're a team with collective objectives, not a group of individual contributors competing against one another.

Lessons Learned from the Trenches

As powerfully effective as teams may be, teamwork isn't a panacea for addressing all that ails an organization. In fact, issues resolving outside the team may contribute as much if not more to a team's downfall. First and foremost, while the concept of teamwork is prevalent in both work and nonwork settings, not all situations warrant or are conducive to teams.

In a situation where there is no interdependence or need for collaboration—or worse, direct competition—teamwork is going to be difficult if not impossible. One of the authors worked with a team comprised of heads of corporate public relations (PR) of each of six semiautonomous divisions. Their given task: to centralize the function in order to streamline operations and ensure a consistent message across all divisions. In effect, this team was asked to do away with several of their jobs and choose where and how one corporate public relations office would operate. Not surprisingly, the level of disclosure and cooperation was as low as the competition and gaming were high. The team eventually disbanded and the goal was addressed by an ad hoc group of managers who were not affiliated with the PR function. *Lesson One:* If at first they don't succeed, teams that were doomed from the start should stop trying! Rather than hope that things will turn around, management can recognize that the decision to complete the task as a team was perhaps not optimal, thank the team for its efforts, and allow members to gracefully adjourn the team process.

Second, because teams provide diverse perspectives that must be shared and accounted for in the decision-making process, management must allow ample time and "space" in which to complete an assignment. When faced with tight or impossible deadlines, teams are likely to experience dysfunctional conflict, sidestep effective team processes to complete their task––albeit in a suboptimized way—and fall prey to the self-limiting team behaviors described earlier. Management, therefore, needs to provide adequate resources and their visible support to achieve the stated objectives. For example, at a Kansas plant of the Puritan-Bennett Corporation, a manufacturer of respiratory equipment, a team tasked with improving the software for its respirators failed after seven years of work because management never made the project a priority and was unwilling to free up another key person needed on the team.[70] If it appears that the team is taking too long, it's not wise to provide added pressure, reduce resources, or snatch away their task before it's complete. Such steps will disempower and undermine current and future team efforts. *Lesson Two:* Two heads may be better than one, but they take more time to make better decisions! Estimate the time and resources needed for a team to complete a task, and then double both.

Third, employee and organizational history in teaming should be considered before embarking on the teaming journey. Such history can be facilitative or detrimental to teamwork. For example, in an organization that is implementing teams for the first time, employees lack the proper skill sets and experience from which to draw. The excitement of this new vehicle for completing tasks may fade as frustration filters in. Management may consider providing several team training sessions, mentors, and/or a facilitator until team members become comfortable and confident in their ability to perform. On the other end of the spectrum, organizations that have "been there and done that" using teams may face resistance on the part of employees who have had negative teaming experiences (i.e., group-hate) or specific issues working with particular employees on previous teams. When individuals have experiences with a difficult or unsuccessful team, the basic objectives for using a team process can be greatly diminished by the negative biproducts, as illustrated by this cartoon.

WHAT GROUP PROJECTS ARE SUPPOSED TO TEACH YOU

- COMMUNICATION
- RESPONSIBILITY
- COLLABORATION
- TEAMWORK

WHAT GROUP PROJECTS TAUGHT ME

- COMMUNICATION
- RESPONSIBILITY
- COLLABORATION
- TEAMWORK
- TRUST NO ONE

Used with permission from endlessorigami.com

Since motivation and perceptions of teaming can be reliant on past teaming experiences, it is crucial to recognize the limitations of teaming and take actions to prevent the development or perpetuation of dysfunctional team behaviors, which leads to *Lesson Three:* As they do in any relationship, employees bring their history and "emotional baggage" from past teaming experiences onto new teams. Ignoring these issues or hoping for memory loss isn't the answer. Instead, raise the issue directly, facilitate an open conversation, and involve the potential team members to express their concerns and devise ways for overcoming them . . . before the team begins its task.

Fourth, because effective teaming requires changes in how employees think about and behave in team (versus individual) settings, some tough questions may need to be asked and answered first. Team expert Patrick Lencioni suggests that before deciding that teamwork is the answer, you and your potential teammates should be able to answer yes to the following questions:[71]

- Can we keep our egos in check?
- Are we capable of admitting to mistakes, weaknesses, and insufficient knowledge?
- Can we speak up openly when we disagree?
- Will we confront behavioral problems directly?
- Can we put the success of the team or organization ahead of our own?

As wonderful as teams can be, it should be clear that not all tasks—or the people that perform them—are best served by the team approach. And even when teams start out well, team dynamics—as implied by the name—change. Periods of harmony can be followed by periods of discord, which puts several of the above questions into tighter focus. Members who started out as "team players" may start exhibiting problem behaviors (see the box below for more information and suggestions for addressing some of these behaviors). *Lesson Four:* Teaming is not a natural behavior for individuals raised in an individualistic society. As with any relationship, team members have to trust one another and commit to the team and its higher purpose. To be successful, team members have to work not only toward achieving goals but also toward ensuring a positive working relationship.

Dealing with Problem Team Members

- **Absentee member:** A member can become distracted by a work or personal problem that prevents him or her from following through on commitments made to the team. In this case, the best strategy is to be direct immediately. Discuss the situation with the team member in a way that doesn't make the person feel he or she is being put on the defensive. Explain the problem and find out the team member's perception of the situation. Ask specifically if the team member still has the time necessary for the team. If not, part ways if possible. If this is not possible, determine a way for the team member to make contributions outside of the normal meeting times and make the person accountable for a specific segment of the work that limits reliance on the team.

- **Social loafer:** As mentioned earlier, it is not uncommon for one or more persons on a team to be able to "hide" the fact they're not contributing. This typically happens when the team members' work ethics differ and one or more team members "step up to the plate" and take on additional responsibility to ensure the work gets done, effectively covering for the less productive team members. Work standards will always vary from person to person. A strategy for dealing with this is to raise the issue at the onset of the project. Divide the responsibilities and set up checkpoints to ensure each member is contributing roughly equally. If a discrepancy appears, try to quantify it and reallocate the workload so all members are contributing roughly equally.

■ **Procrastinator:** We're all human, and a seemingly human tendency is to "put off until tomorrow what we should be working on today." This is particularly problematic for work teams. Teams are composed of individuals with different work schedules and work styles. Some people thrive on the pressure of imminent deadlines while others find waiting until the last minute to be overly stressful. In this situation it is best to do two things: (a) set up interim checkpoints, or mini-deadlines, to ensure the work progresses at a reasonable pace, and (b) be realistic when work schedules are drawn up and deadlines determined. Prior to establishing deadlines, ask all team members to check personal and work calendars to catch any problems before they occur. At each meeting reclarify the commitments that might affect a person's inability to adhere to a deadline set earlier. And build in some slack: Set the final deadline for a few days before the *actual* deadline—just in case!

We've included many more examples of challenging team member behavior and how to deal with it in Chapter 13.

Teams may not be a cure for all that ails an organization. But teams can be very effective if the team structure makes sense and members practice the suggestions outlined in the chapter. Other steps team members and their managers can take to improve the likelihood of team success are summarized in the accompanying chart.

The Team Connection[72]

Self-managed and virtual teams, while autonomous, still need a quality link to the organization. Research has found that external team leaders that managed the boundary between the team and the larger organization, referred to as the ambiguous "managerial no-man's land," contributed the most to team success. External leaders that demonstrated capabilities in the following four functions and eleven behaviors created not only successful teams but more autonomous and independent team members.

RELATING

Being socially and politically aware

Building team support

Caring for team members

SCOUTING

Seeking information from managers, peers, and specialists

Diagnosing member behavior

Investigating problems systematically

PERSUADING

Obtaining external support

Influencing the team

EMPOWERING

Delegating authority

Exercising flexibility with team decisions

Coaching

Summary

Workplaces in the United States and abroad have embraced teaming. This is no accident. Organizations that implemented work teams as a way to improve products, services, and processes have witnessed tremendous measurable benefits. Some of these benefits accrue because of synergies—the notion that teams produce more and better solutions than individuals—gained from combining diverse skill sets, perspectives, abilities, and work styles on a single team. Not all teams produce phenomenal outcomes. By understanding the normal phases of group development and ways to gain and maintain group productivity and motivation, you can help your teams reach their full potential.

Key Terms and Concepts

Absentee member	Process improvement team
Adjourning	Procrastinator
Cross-functional teams	Risky shift
Forming	Self-managed team
Group	Social loafing or free riding
Group-hate	Storming
Groupthink	Task force
High-performance team	Team
Norming	Virtual teams
Performing	

Discussion Questions

1. Why has the use of teams in the workplace increased so dramatically? To what can this be attributed?

2. Some organizations decide to implement teams because of the many benefits that are likely to accrue from doing so. However, "doing teams" may not necessarily work as expected. Why is this so?

3. Limitations such as *groupthink* and *social loafing* can sometimes be found on teams. What causes these limitations? What can be done to prevent them (or resolve them)?

4. Imagine you are on a team of six members representing multiple functions in your organization. Your team has been tasked with overhauling the current, cumbersome accounts payable system. So far, your team has pinpointed several areas that can be improved. Just yesterday, one of the VPs suggested adding a finance and accounting person to your team. She said that because they are stakeholders for the new process, they should be included. What do you think? What's likely to happen now?

Endnotes

1. Quote by Tracey Edwards in Jim White, "Teaming with Talent," *Management Today* (September 1999), p. 56.

2. Lillian Chaney and Julie Lyden, "Making U.S. Teams Work," *Supervision* (January 2000), p. 6.

3. Leslie Kwoh, "Starwood Hotels CEO: 'I hate jargon,'" *The Wall Street Journal Online* (June 25, 2013).

4. Karl L. Smart and Carol Barnum, "Communication in Cross-functional Teams: An Introduction to This Special Issue," *Technical Communication* (February 2000), p. 19.

5. Marianne van Woerkom and Karin Sanders, "The Romance of Learning from Disagreement. The Effect of Cohesiveness and Disagreement on Knowledge Sharing Behavior and Individual Performance within Teams," *Journal of Business and Psychology* 25, no. 1 (March 2010), p. 139.

6. White, "Teaming with Talent," p. 56.

7. Harvey Mackay, "Get on the Team and Be a Winner," *Providence Business News* (August 16, 1999), p. 38.

8. Chaney and Lyden, "Making U.S. Teams Work," p. 6.

9. Kevin McManus, "Do You Have Teams?" *IIE Solutions* (April 2000), p. 21.

10. Troy V. Mumford and Marifran Mattson, "Will Teams Work?: How the Nature of Work Drives Synergy in Autonomous Team Design," *Academy of Management Proceedings* (2009), p. 6.

11. John Canemaker, *Walt Disney's Nine Old Men and the Art of Animation* (New York: Disney Editions, 2001).

12. Mohsen Attaran and Tai T. Nguyen, "Succeeding with Self-managed Work Teams." Reprinted by permission of the Institute of Industrial Engineers, 25 Technology Park, Norcross, GA 30092, 770–449–0461. Copyright © 1999.

13. J. Greenberg, *Managing Behavior in Organizations,* 3rd ed. (Upper Saddle River, NJ: Prentice Hall, 2002), p. 224.

14. Mildred Golden Pryor et al., "Teaming as a Strategic and Tactical Tool: An Analysis with Recommendations," *International Journal of Management* 26, no. 2 (August 2009), p. 320.

15. Gale Group, "Java Programming Language: History," *The Free Library* (2005), http://www.thefreelibrary.com/Java+programming+language.-a0163332676.

16. L. L. Martins, L. L. Gilson, and M. T. Maynard, "Virtual Teams: What Do We Know and Where Do We Go from Here?" *Journal of Management* 30, no. 6 (2004), pp. 805–35.

17. S. P. Robbins and T. A. Judge, *Essentials of Organizational Behavior,* 9th ed. (Upper Saddle River, NJ: Pearson Prentice Hall, 2008), p. 145.

18. S. Crock, "Collaboration: Lockheed Martin," *BusinessWeek* (November 24, 2003), p. 85.

19. Jody L. Knowles, Employee Relations Manager, SNL Financial, personal communication (July 26, 2007).

20. See http://www.Medtronic.com/innovation and http://wwwtcmevents.org.

21. McManus, "Do You Have Teams?," p. 21.

22. A. J. Ward, M. Lankau, A. C. Amason, J. A. Sonnenfeld, and B. R. Agle, "Improving the Performance of Top Management Teams," *MIT Sloan Management Review* 48, no. 3 (Spring 2007), pp. 85–90.

23. Smart and Barnum, "Communication in Cross-functional Teams," p. 19.

24. Thomas E. Harris, "Toward Effective Employee Involvement: An Analysis of Parallel and Self-Managing Teams," *Journal of Applied Business Research* 9, no. 1 (1993), pp. 25–33.

25. See Larry Miller, "Teamwork in Healthcare—Keys to Continuous Improvement: The Mayo Clinic—Built on Teamwork," *Management Meditations* (September 4, 2012); and "Approaching Illness as a Team," *New York Times* (December 25, 2012), p. 26.

26. See Chaney and Lyden, "Making U.S. Teams Work"; Michael G. Harvey and David A. Griffith, "The Role of Globalization, Time Acceleration and Virtual Global Teams in Fostering Successful Global Product Launches," *The Journal of Product Innovation Management* 24 (2007), p. 499.

27. Attaran and Nguyen, "Succeeding with Self-managed Work Teams," p. 24.

28. Larry Cole and Michael Scott Cole, "Teamwork Is Spelled Incorrectly: Teamwork Communication," *Communication World* (April 2000), p. 56.

29. K. Kelly, "The New Soul of John Deere," *BusinessWeek* (January 31, 1994), pp. 64–66.

30. Robbins and Judge, *Essentials of Organizational Behavior,* p. 141.

31. Attaran and Nguyen, "Succeeding with Self-managed Work Teams," and Greenberg, *Managing Behavior in Organizations,* p. 237.

32. Irving I. Janis, *Groupthink,* 2nd ed. (Boston, MA: Houghton-Mifflin, 1982).

33. Editorial, "EGF Should Think about 'Groupthink'," *Knight Ridder Tribune Business News* (June 27, 2007), p. 1.

34. Ibid.

35. Paula Caproni, *Management Skills for Everyday Life: The Practical Coach,* 2nd ed. (Upper Saddle River, NJ: Pearson Prentice Hall, 2005), p. 332.

36. S. M. Sorensen, "Group-hate: A Negative Reaction to Group Work." Paper presented at the annual meeting of the International Communication Association, Minneapolis, MN (1981).

37. James A. Buckenmyer, "Using Teams for Class Activities: Making Course/Classroom Teams Work," *Journal of Education for Business* 76, no. 2 (November/December 2000), p. 98.

38. Greenberg, *Managing Behavior in Organizations,* p. 231.

39. Bruce W. Tuckman, "Developmental Sequences in Small Groups," *Psychological Bulletin* 63 (1965), pp. 384–99. The stage theory of team development was first identified by Tuckman. Subsequent research has found the stages occur in a slightly different order. While the original model is reflected in this chapter, some researchers have found that teams more likely progress through conforming before entering the storming stage. See R. E. Quinn and K. S. Cameron, "Organizational Life Cycles and Shifting Criteria of Effectiveness," *Management Science* 29 (1983), pp. 37–61. Also see K. S. Cameron and D. A. Whetten, "Perceptions of Organizational Effectiveness in Organizational Life Cycles," *Administrative Science Quarterly* 27 (1981), pp. 525–44.

40. Peter R. Scholtes, *The Team Handbook* (Madison, WI: Joiner and Associates, 1988).

41. John R. Myers, "What It Takes to Make a Team," *Purchasing* (September 2, 1999), p. 91.

42. Scholtes, *The Team Handbook.*

43. Daniel C. Feldman, "The Development and Enforcement of Group Norms," *Academy of Management Review* 9, no. 1 (1984), pp. 47–53.

44. Scholtes, *The Team Handbook.*

45. Gerben S. van der Vegt, Stuart Bunderson, and Ben Kuipers, "Why Turnover Matters in Self-Managing Work Teams: Learning, Social Integration and Task Flexibility," *Journal of Management* 36, no. 5 (September 2010), pp. 1168–91.

46. Rona Leach, "Supervision: From Me to We," *Supervision* (February 2000), p. 8.

47. Alec "Sandy" Pentland, "The New Science of Building Great Teams: The Chemistry of High-performing Groups Is No Longer a Mystery," *Harvard Business Review* (April 2012), pp. 3–11.

48. Ruth Wageman, "Critical Success Factors for Creating Superb Self-managing Teams," *Organizational Dynamics* (Summer 1997), p. 49.

49. David Rohlander, "Building High-Performance Teams," *Credit Union Executive* (March 2009), p. 36.

50. Barry Ekman and Emmanuela Ginngregorio, "Establishing Truly Peak Performance Teams—Beyond Metaphoric Challenges," *Human Resource Management International Digest* 11, no. 3 (2003), p. 2.

51. American Management Association, "HR Update: Creating Real Teamwork at the Top," *HR Focus* (January 2000), p. 2.

52. Smart and Barnum, "Communication in Cross-functional Teams," p. 19.

53. Paulo Vieira Cunha and Maria Joao Louro, "Building Teams That Learn," *The Academy of Management Executive* (February 2000), p. 152.

54. Renee Evenson, "Team Effort: Beyond Employees to Team, beyond Manager to Coach," *Supervision* (February 2000), p. 11.

55. Phil Harkins, "High-impact Team Leaders," *Leadership Excellence* 23, no. 10 (October 2006), pp. 3–4.

56. Chaney and Lyden, "Making U.S. Teams Work," p. 6.

57. Avan R. Jassawalla and Hemant C. Sashittal, "Building Collaborative Cross-functional New Product Teams," *The Academy of Management Executive* (August 1999), p. 50.

58. Nicholas Clarke, "Emotional Intelligence Abilities and Their Relationships with Team Processes," *Team Performance Management* 16, no. 1/2 (2010), p. 6.

59. Cole and Cole, "Teamwork Is Spelled Incorrectly," p. 56.

60. Harkins, "High-impact Team Leaders," p. 4.

61. Russ Forrester and Allan B. Drexler, "A Model for Team-Based Organizational Performance," *The Academy of Management Executive* (August 1999), p. 36.

62. Becky L. Nichol, "Top Ten Reasons Teams Become Dysfunctional," *National Public Accountant* (February 2000), p. 12.

63. B. Geber, "The Bugaboo of Team Pay," *Training* (August 1995), pp. 27–34.

64. Jassawalla and Sashittal, "Building Collaborative Cross-functional New Product Teams," p. 152.

65. Cole and Cole, "Teamwork Is Spelled Incorrectly," p. 56.

66. Cunha and Louro, "Building Teams," p. 152.

67. Myers, "What It Takes to Make a Team," p. 91.

68. Ted Gautschi, "Strengthen Your Team," *Design News* (October 18, 1999), p. 158.

69. Myers, "What It Takes to Make a Team," p. 91.

70. A. Stern, "Managing by Team Is Not Always as Easy as It Looks," *New York Times* (July 18, 1993), p. B14.

71. P. M. Lencioni, "The Trouble with Teamwork," *Leader to Leader* 29 (Summer 2003), pp. 35–40.

72. Vanessa Urch Druskat and Jane V. Wheeler, "How to Lead a Self-Managing Team," *MIT Sloan Management Review* (Summer 2004).

Exercise 10–A **Bridge Building**	Groups of four to six are tasked with creating a bridge out of the materials provided. You have 30 minutes in which to complete this task. When the project is complete or time is called—whichever comes first—your instructor will roll a ball across your bridge to ensure it meets the project specifications. Following this activity, discuss these questions in your group.

Questions

1. How did your group decide how to build the bridge? Did it make a plan or did it just start building?
2. Did anyone play a leadership role in the task? Explain.
3. What made building the bridge as a group, rather than as an individual, more difficult?
4. In what ways did the group make the project easier? Explain.
5. Was your group a group or team? Explain.

Exercise 10–B **The Story: A Team** **Exercise**	Read the instructions and story below and answer the corresponding questions. Next, complete the same task in your assigned group.

What Does the Story Tell?

Instructions: Read the following story and take for granted that everything it says is true. Read carefully because, in spots, the story is deliberately vague. Don't try to memorize it since you can look back at it at any time.

Then read the numbered statements about the story and decide whether you consider each one true, false, or questionable. Circling the "T" means you feel sure the statement is definitely true. Circling the "F" means you feel sure the statement is definitely false. Circling the "?" means you cannot tell whether it is true or false. If you feel doubtful about any part of a statement, circle the question mark.

Take the statements in turn and do not go back later to change any of your answers. Do not reread any of the statements after you have answered them.

Story

The owner of the Adams Manufacturing Company entered the office of one of his foremen where he found three employees playing cards. One of them was Carl Young, brother-in-law of foreman Henry Dilson. Dilson, incidentally, often worked late. Company rules did not specifically forbid gambling on the premises, but the president had expressed himself forcibly on the subject.

Statements about the Story

1. In brief, the story is about a company owner who found three men playing cards.   T   F   ?
2. The president walked into the office of one of his foremen.   T   F   ?
3. Company rules forbade playing cards on the premises after hours.   T   F   ?
4. While the card playing took place in Henry Dilson's office, the story does not state whether Dilson was present.   T   F   ?
5. Dilson never worked late.   T   F   ?
6. Gambling on the premises of the Adams Manufacturing Company was not punished.   T   F   ?
7. Carl Young was not playing cards when the president walked in.   T   F   ?
8. Three employees were gambling in a foreman's office.   T   F   ?
9. While the card players were surprised when the owner walked in, it is not clear whether they will be punished.   T   F   ?
10. Henry Dilson is Carl Young's brother-in-law.   T   F   ?
11. The president is opposed to gambling on company premises.   T   F   ?
12. Carl Young did not take part in the card game in Henry Dilson's office.   T   F   ?

Questions

1. What process did you use to come up with the group answers?
2. Did anyone act as a leader or facilitator in the exercise? Explain.
3. In what ways was it difficult to achieve a group decision?
4. Which behaviors blocked the group's process? Which ones helped?
5. What are the advantages or disadvantages of working in a group compared to working as an individual?

**Exercise 10–C
Map It Team
Competition**

In groups of three to five, you will be instructed to draw a map from memory. Your instructor will tell you the basis for the map and the details that must be included on the map. Working with your teammates, try to recreate the map as accurately as possible; remember, you are trying to draw a more accurate map than the other teams. You will have 15 minutes to complete your map. Following the activity, discuss these questions with your teammates and class.

Questions

1. Did working with others help in the accuracy of the map? Did working in a team make it easier or harder to draw the map?
2. How did you handle differences in opinion for completing the map?
3. Did competing against other teams increase the desire to work together as a team? Did this help to build team cohesion?
4. How does this activity relate to team projects in school or the workplace?

**Exercise 10–D
Conflict in Team
Projects: Two Case
Studies**

You've been meeting on a team for the past couple of weeks, and while you really get along well with your teammates, it is clear that very little "work" is getting done at these meetings. The other members enjoy spending time with one another, but with the deadline only three weeks away, you're concerned that the team will have to pull an "all-nighter" to get the project done, and even then, it may not be as good as it could be. What would you do?

1. What is your immediate reaction to the scenario? How would you feel if you were writing about this situation?
2. How could this situation have been avoided?

3. What approaches to resolving this conflict are appropriate?

4. What are some things that, if done, would make this approach successful?

5. What are some things to avoid when attempting to resolve this conflict? Why?

You have been working with your project group for the last few weeks. During this time, you've had three meetings, and at each one, Anthony has either come late or left early. Even when he is at the meeting, it seems that his mind is elsewhere. Everyone's input on the project is needed and you're concerned that his lack of participation and preparation is affecting the group outcome. You know that Anthony is a smart guy and performed well when you happened to work with him on another team project last year in a marketing class. But something is different now—different about him, and different about how he interacts with others. He's not violent, but he's also not as easygoing as he used to be. You're not sure how to approach the situation.

1. What is your immediate reaction to the scenario? How would you feel if you were a member of the team writing about this situation?

2. How could this situation have been avoided?

3. What approaches to resolving this conflict are appropriate?

4. What are some things that, if done, would make this approach successful?

5. What are some things to avoid when attempting to resolve this conflict? Why?

Exercise 10–E
Preventing and Resolving Self-Limiting Behaviors on Teams

In the section on self-limiting team behaviors, we discussed several phenomena that can negatively impact a team's process and outcomes. Complete the chart below based on your knowledge and personal experience on teams. When asked, discuss your findings in your small group.

Self-Limiting Behavior	Why It Occurs	Ways to Prevent Behavior	Ways to Manage or Resolve Behavior
Groupthink			
Group-hate			
Social loafing/free riding			
Risky shift			

Exercise 10–F
Case Study on Gaining Appropriate Membership on Teams

This is the team's third meeting. The team's task, deliverables, and membership have been dictated by a steering committee that oversees the division's teaming efforts. Members represent different areas and management levels within the division. A new team member who missed the first two meetings enters the room. Let's eavesdrop:

SCRIBE: "Okay. Here's our agenda. Does this sound okay to everyone?"

NEW TEAM MEMBER: "Well, not exactly. I have a question regarding the team's task. I know I missed the first two meetings, but I'm unclear about our purpose. I mean, without a well-understood purpose, are we ready to talk about membership? I'm not even sure if I should be here!"

SCRIBE: "Well, I suppose we can add 'team purpose' to the agenda. How much time should we allot?"

TEAM LEADER: (Feeling strained by all the necessary structure.) "Could we hold off with the agenda for a few minutes? . . . I know we need the agenda, but I think we should talk about purpose for a few minutes at least; then we can get back to the regular agenda. She (the new team member) brings up a good point."

Some discussion ensues. It becomes clear that the team's purpose *is* unclear. Other additional information is revealed, such as the fact that there had been three other team members who, shortly after being appointed by the steering committee, decided to excuse themselves from the team. Also, the team leader brought in a new person (call her Possible New Member), who is not really a full-fledged member until the steering committee approves it.

SCRIBE: "Back to the agenda. Were there any corrections to the minutes? (No response.) Okay, now for today's meeting roles . . . oh, our timekeeper isn't here today."

NEW TEAM MEMBER: (Looking at Possible New Member) "Would you like to keep time?"

TEAM LEADER: "Well, we're not sure if she is an official team member yet. Remember, the steering committee hasn't okayed her yet. Should she keep time if she's not?"

NEW TEAM MEMBER: "What's the difference? And why do we need the steering committee's blessing? Let's just do it."

TEAM LEADER: "Actually, there are some other names, in addition to Possible Team Member, that we've submitted to the steering committee. After all, we've lost three people since the team began."

NEW TEAM MEMBER: "Do we need additional people? Why? Again, doesn't it depend on what we're trying to accomplish?"

Questions

1. Why is it important to clarify a team's purpose? Once the task is given, why is clarification necessary?
2. What role does this purpose play in defining team membership? Why do you suppose others have "excused themselves" from the team?
3. How effective is the team leader? Explain.
4. Meeting management techniques—using agendas, having a scribe and timekeeper—are intended to make meetings more effective. In what ways could these techniques have the opposite effect?
5. If you were asked to participate in this meeting, what would you do to get the process back on track? Explain.

Exercise 10–G **WebSolutions***	It's 5:30 p.m. on Friday and the "fearless foursome" gather for their weekly debriefing at the local Starbucks. Looking back on their time together in the MBA program, the four friends and WebSolutions' partners/owners laugh at how easy they thought starting their own business would be. Truth be told, the last 18 months on their own have been quite successful, but it was never easy.

It all started a few months after they graduated and accepted jobs in three *Fortune* 500 organizations. The salaries were quite comfortable, and the signing bonuses allowed each to put a down payment on new vehicles (three cars, one motorcycle). However, something was missing. As Ghita tells it, "They said that I had great ideas . . . but rarely did anyone ever *really* listen to or let me run with them. I felt like I had to conform . . . not make any waves . . . not at all what I expected." Ian, her husband and fellow South African, echoes her concerns. "They talked a good talk about empowerment and participative decision making in the interview and orientation session, but when it really mattered, any ideas had to go through the chain of command and pass through multiple managers and VPs . . . most of whom seemed more concerned about shaping these ideas—and their own careers—than allowing any real changes to happen." Fed up, Ghita and Ian talked with Phillip, a fellow alum, about their idea for a new business venture.

*This case was developed by Suzanne de Janasz in 2002.

Things were a bit better for Phillip. He was able to make suggestions and contributions, and even implement some of his ideas in his firm. However, it seemed as if moving up the corporate ladder was practically impossible amid the flattening of organizational levels and implementation of self-managed work teams. It wasn't that he was unhappy, but as Phil recounts, "I wanted more. I wanted to be a driving force for change. I saw some of my friends leaving their corporate jobs and starting their own consulting and technology-based firms, and I realized that's where I could make a difference." In fact, Bettina, a close friend and teammate on several MBA projects, had recently pitched an idea to him. She had been designing Web pages for several small, startup companies as a way to help pay off her student loans more quickly. "It was easy work for me . . . and the clients really loved what I did!" Bettina continued, "They appreciated that I really listened and created what they wanted while also utilizing the latest technology and security features in developing these companies' Web presence." Based on her projections, Bettina saw the possibility of a very successful and prosperous new business.

That was just less than two years ago. Ghita, Ian, Phil, and Bettina began brainstorming this new business idea at the monthly MBA alumni networking function. Collectively, they had the skills and motivation needed to bring the Web design and hosting idea into reality. Since none of them had ever started their own business before, they agreed to proceed slowly and with a plan. They started the Friday afternoon coffee ritual as a way to evaluate their progress and make adjustments to their plan. Eight weeks and a business plan later, they were planning their corporate departures.

Developing a business plan was helpful, but several of the challenges they faced were not anticipated. Luckily, the startup costs of WebSolutions were relatively low, as their "products" were services. The only real cost, aside from that of not having a steady paycheck, was the server space they paid for to host the Web pages they created. And, because three firms with whom they interacted while in their corporate careers jumped ship and became WebSolutions' top clients, a revenue stream (albeit more delayed than expected) was practically guaranteed.

WebSolutions was everything the foursome wanted and more, perhaps too much more. In six months, their revenues tripled! Their list of clients—small and midsized companies expanding their brick and mortar stores with a Web presence—was growing exponentially. Word of their excellent design and hosting services (and relatively reasonable prices) spread quickly, and now it was clear that WebSolutions had to hire several new employees. Unfortunately, the foursome really didn't know much about how to design, recruit, and staff the positions, let alone motivate the employees they would hire.

With an eye toward future growth, the foursome set aside the following Saturday for a marathon planning session. The main issues on the table were these:

- Need for venture funding.
- Formation of departments.
- Potential changes to the open and comfortable culture of the business.
- Infrastructure needs (larger/more powerful PC network and server needed, partners' need to communicate virtually while traveling, benefits/compensation system).

Five full-time employees (three computer programmers/Web designers, two security specialists, and a graphic designer) and a part-time secretary/bookkeeper are hired. For the next three months, WebSolutions runs relatively smoothly. Current customers are quite satisfied with WebSolutions, and additional customers continue to flow in. During one of their weekly coffee get-togethers, it becomes clear to Ghita, Ian, Phil, and Bettina that it may be time to (perish the thought!) create departments. Rather than just organize the current employee base, the foursome takes some time to think about future directions of their firm and their personal or individual goals. In addition to Marketing/PR and New Product/Service Development, they create the following departments: Computer Systems/Security, HR/Administration/Legal, and Finance/Operations. The four discuss their roles in the "new" organization, and a lively conversation ensues over reporting relationships, HR issues, and a need to develop some policies. At the end of a very productive conversation, Ian and Ghita share the exciting news that they are expecting their first child.

As the holiday season approaches, WebSolutions is swamped with even more firms looking to create a Web presence and cash in on their wired customers. Water cooler conversations about the first holiday party are suddenly interrupted by a glitch. One afternoon, despite WebSolutions' cutting-edge technologies, two of their largest clients experienced denial of service attacks, costing them lost sales and a potentially tarnished reputation. Responding to this crisis, Phil identifies six employees and charges them with finding the cause of the attack and determining means to reduce greatly the likelihood of any future attacks.

Members of this team consist of representatives from various departments. Phil, the team leader and head of the Computer Systems/Security department, demonstrates a "take-charge" approach in that he believes he knows more about the task and assignment than anyone on the team. During the team's second meeting, he shares a project milestone chart, which the team accepts. While the group has kept up with its assignments and is working rather effectively, Phil seems impatient with the team's progress. In fact, he would like to exert greater control over the team's activities because he already has done his research, knows the "answer," and wants to complete the project and focus on other activities. However, several of the team members believe that there may be other issues that have not yet surfaced and if Phil's plan is implemented, one of the team members may be seen as the cause of the attack and possibly lose his job.

To be fair, Phil also notices that the team has been unusually quiet and agreeable, and he wonders whether there are some team dynamics issues that are getting in the way. He asks Ghita to sit in on one of the meetings to get her take on the situation. She recommends that the team work offsite for a three- or four-hour block of time. In addition, she would be willing to lead a session on the use of various problem-solving tools/techniques that might be beneficial in this situation.

Questions

1. The good news is that the "fearless foursome" has made what appears to be a successful transition from employees of other firms to partners of their own firm. Six months after opening their doors, revenues tripled. At this point,

   a. What are the strengths of the WebSolutions' top management team? Explain, and discuss how these strengths can be reinforced in the future.

   b. What are potential weaknesses of the team or the organization that need to be addressed as the foursome looks to the future? Why?

   c. Five new employees were hired. Given the relatively few number of employees, what strategies would you recommend using to bring these new "team" members on board? What actions might you avoid and why?

   d. As discussed in the case, structural changes are likely to be implemented. What impact—positive and negative—will the formation of departments have on the organization's environment and employee interactions?

2. We learn that Phil establishes a team to address the recent (and potentially devastating) denial of service attacks experienced by two of WebSolutions' biggest clients. Based on your read of this team's functioning,

   a. What issues are at play and how might these issues impact both the team's outcome (goal or directive) and the process (how they go about the task)?

   b. At the start of the next meeting, Phil receives an urgent call and excuses himself from the meeting. Before he leaves, he asks you, one of his subordinates, to "take over." Now that the meeting is in your hands, what would you do and why? Discuss how you would deal with the unsurfaced issues and potential fears among your teammates.

3. If, instead of Phil assembling and leading the team, he gave you the directive (i.e., create a team to figure out what happened and how we can prevent it in the future),

   a. What would your first two or three steps be and why?

   b. Assuming none of the employees had ever worked on a team before, what issues are you likely to face in the early forming stage? How would you overcome these issues?

Exercise 10–H
Reflection/Action Plan

This chapter focused on teams in the workplace—what they are, why they are important, and how to improve your skill in this area. Complete the following worksheet upon completing all the reading and experiential activities for this chapter.

1. The one or two areas in which I am most strong are:

_____

_____

_____

2. The one or two areas in which I need more improvement are:

_____

_____

_____

3. If I did only one thing to improve in this area, it would be to:

_____

_____

_____

4. Making this change would probably result in:

_____

_____

_____

5. If I did not change or improve in this area, it would probably affect my personal and professional life in the following ways:

_____

_____

_____

Managing Conflict

Learning Points

How do I:

- Deal with unresolved anger in a constructive way?
- Identify the source of conflict as it is occurring?
- Understand what my natural conflict style is and know which strategy to adopt in a conflict situation?
- Change my attitude toward conflict and treat it as a normal and potentially beneficial part of relationships?
- Prevent conflict when appropriate?
- Learn how to manage conflict personally and professionally?

Raj, an account executive for a full-service information technology services organization for the past six years, is about to begin working on his third-quarter contract renewals. During one of his calls, he learns that Stephen—who had been doing business with Raj and his company for quite some time—was recently transferred to his company's offices in Sydney, Australia. "What a shame," thought Raj. "I really enjoyed working with him . . . those early May contract renegotiations over lunch at my favorite restaurant had always gone smoothly . . . both of us feeling that we had worked out an ideal situation for our companies." Stephen's secretary, Myra, informs Raj that Joe is Stephen's replacement and transfers him to Joe's voice-mail. Raj leaves a message about setting up their first meeting, and about an hour later, Joe calls back. Within the first 30 seconds of this call, Raj realizes he's in for some trouble.

"Here are my rules," Joe says, cutting the pleasantries short. "First, we'll meet at my office. Second, I'll let you know what we will talk about and what we won't. Third, I'll tell you the price range we'll be working in. And we won't put anything in writing until we have a deal."

"I'm fine with meeting at your place," Raj says uneasily, putting off his other demands for now. "But we should probably include some of our systems people and someone from your operations division at the meeting. We need to meet their interests as well."

"No," Joe says. "That's not how I do it."

"For years," Raj continues, "your predecessor, Stephen, always brought along your head of operations. I think that's why everything always went so smoothly. We need to talk about more than just price. We want to make sure that our complement of products and services meets your company's unique needs."

"Let me worry about that," Joe says.

Raj is completely taken aback. Joe seems controlling and uncompromising. Is he really irrational or just trying to drive a hard bargain?[1]

1. Clearly, Joe is calling all the shots. Do you think he sees working with Raj as conflictual?

2. What do you think is motivating Joe to respond to Raj in the way he has? Are some people more "into" conflict than others?

3. Raj notes that "he's in for some trouble." What are some steps Raj can take before he meets with Joe to reduce the impending conflict between them? What would you recommend that Raj do at the start of and during his meeting with Joe to not only work through the conflict but also to set the stage for a "smoother" working relationship with Joe?

4. What role does one's personal style and comfort with conflict play in our response to situations like these?

W e're told that conflict is inevitable, that it's part of human nature to have conflicts with others. Yet seldom are we as human beings comfortable with conflict. Many of us would prefer if conflict didn't arise, or that someone else would resolve it. However, and as we saw from the opening case, opposing styles or goals can create conflict—which can persist and affect us emotionally and physiologically whether we avoid the conflictual situation or summon up the courage to confront it. Managing conflict is one of the toughest yet most rewarding skills to acquire. Foremost, it is a skill that does not come naturally; it is learned. In this chapter we discuss conflict, what it is, and why learning to manage it is important. We discuss common sources of conflict and present a model for approaching conflict. We also include strategies and tips for dealing with conflict as well as suggestions for preventing conflict when possible and for being selective about which conflicts you choose to tackle.

"Speaking without thinking is like shooting without aiming."

Ancient Proverb

What Is Conflict?

Conflict is any situation in which there are incompatible goals, cognitions, or emotions within or between individuals or groups that lead to opposition or antagonistic interaction. It is the struggle between incompatible and opposing needs, wishes, ideas, interests, or people. Conflict is a form of interaction among parties who differ in interests, perceptions, goals, values, or approaches to problems. Conflict arises when we begin to feel that the other person is interfering with our ability to attain a certain objective. It begins when we believe the other party is interfering with or standing in the way of an action we want to take, an idea we want to pursue, or a belief we hold. Conflicts may involve individual or group disagreements, struggles, disputes, quarrels, or even physical fighting and wars. Because human beings are unique—possessing a variety of physical, intellectual, emotional, economic, and social differences—conflict is inevitable.

Conflict is a fact of life in organizations. Each organization is composed of people, and each person has a set of goals that is likely to be distinct from the goals of others in the organization. When individuals with different interests compete for the same resource pool, dissension is sure to follow.[2] That tension can be dealt with constructively in a way that stimulates creativity and positive change. In fact, lack of creative tension sometimes reflects an "I don't care" attitude that can lead to stagnation on the job. Effective managers are not afraid of conflict. They have been trained to deal with conflict and have trained their employees to deal with conflict constructively. They accept that conflicts must be faced and strive to find constructive means to manage them. Effective managers are those who are selective as to which conflicts they choose to pursue. Sometimes the best course of action in a difficult situation is to take "the path of least resistance"—to be silent!

Is Conflict Normal?

Society's view of conflict and conflict management has evolved substantially over the last century. These views can be summarized in three perspectives on managing conflict:[3]

1. **Traditional View**—This view was predominant in the early 20th century when it was believed that conflict was always bad and should be avoided at all costs. This perspective posited that conflict was a result of dysfunctional managerial behavior and therefore should and could be stopped at the source. Presumably, if the dysfunctional behavior was stopped (i.e., the manager is fired), the conflict would cease to exist.

2. **Human Relations View**—This was the overriding perspective for the three decades spanning 1940 through 1970. In this view, conflict was viewed as a natural and inevitable part of human existence and was accepted as a normal part of group interaction and relationships. Sometimes the conflict was functional, other times dysfunctional, but it was always present.

3. **Integrationist View**—The contemporary view holds that not only is conflict inevitable, but maintaining a degree of tension can actually be helpful in keeping a group energized and creative. In this view, conflict is seen as a positive force for change within organizations, groups, and relationships. The challenge is finding constructive means for managing conflict while still maintaining some differences that energize a group toward continued discussion and innovation.

It is important to recognize that this evolutionary view of conflict is North American. In other countries like China, Finland, and Japan, conflict is viewed as a disruption of harmony. Even if challenging a person or an idea might bring about positive change, conforming to the norm of harmony and saving face is typically more highly valued than is creativity and innovation.

Although managerial mistakes do sometimes cause unnecessary and even unhealthy conflict, it is important to discard the traditional notion that conflict automatically means one performs ineffectively. Conflict is a certainty for any manager, or any person, for that matter. The best managers recognize this and learn how to manage conflict in such a way that it has positive and fair outcomes for all involved.[4]

Why Is Conflict Management Important?

Conflict is a normal part of life. Every organization, family, relationship, and community has conflicts of ideas, values, thoughts, and actions. Conflict is a given. What isn't given is how we choose to react to conflict. As Marcus Aurelius says in *Meditations*:

If you are distressed by anything external, the pain is not due to the thing itself, but to your own estimate of it; and this you have the power to revoke at any moment.

We can successfully face and resolve conflicts if we take a few steps: recognize that conflicts are normal and inevitable,[5] train ourselves not to overreact when conflicts arise, and have a strategy to use when conflicts—some of which are predictable—arise.

Conflict can be either positive or negative. The outcomes of conflict depend on how the conflict is managed or resolved. **Positive conflict** is functional and supports or benefits the organization or person's main objectives.[6] Conflict is constructive when it leads to better decisions, creativity, and innovative solutions to long-standing problems. Conflict is viewed as positive when it results in the following:

- *Increased involvement*—Organizational members have the opportunity to develop goals, share ideas, and voice opinions, gaining greater insight into others and situations.

- *Increased cohesion*—Members build strong bonds from learning how to resolve differences; "if we can survive this, we must have a true relationship" embodies this benefit of conflict.[7] In some cases, conflict initially reduces cohesion that can in turn reduce the likelihood of "groupthink" occurring. In this case conflict is positive.

- *Increased innovation and creativity*—Members are encouraged to "put their ideas on the table";[8] this can lead to more discoveries, improvements, and creative solutions. "Two heads are truly better than one" when conflict brings about synergy instead of chaos. Similarly, the constraints that are perceived as conflict-producing have been shown to improve creativity.[9]

- *Positive personal growth and change*—Individuals learn their strengths and weaknesses; conflict of ideas challenges individuals to learn and grow by expressing their ideas and thoughts through self-disclosure and sharing of important concepts with others.

- *Clarification of key issues*—Through discussion, members reduce ambiguity and focus energy on the real sources of conflict, then work together to target remaining issues that need to be addressed.

- *Values clarification*—Members clarify who they are and what they stand for, understand who the other party is and what his or her values are, and learn when to sublimate personal interests to the larger needs of the group or organization.

Negative conflict is dysfunctional and hinders the organization's or the person's performance or ability to attain goals or objectives. Conflict is destructive when it leads to stress and anxiety, inability to take action, and loss of esteem or purpose.[10] Conflict is viewed as negative when these problems result:

- *Heightened emotionality, including anger*—When a conflict is unresolved or ineffectively resolved, employees whose concerns have not been addressed appropriately tend to become frustrated, anxious, irritated, and even angry.[11] These emotions make it difficult to act rationally, and as the feelings escalate, the negativity grows—sucking in co-workers (some of whom are never even involved in the conflict!) and impairing the functioning of work groups, divisions, and the organization.[12] Recent research suggests that workplace incivility—rudeness and general disregard for one another—is on the rise, and unresolved conflict is one of its contributors.[13] Furthermore, many employees who experience uncivil behaviors, such as being the target of unkind words or deeds said or done in the heat of the conflict, will experience eroding self-esteem and self-confidence, possibly leading to a reduced ability to perform and to contribute to organizational goals.

- *Personality clashes*—Participants in an unresolved conflict often find themselves locked into their positions and more tied to their own interests than those of others. They come to believe that they are further apart from each other than they are in reality, and decide they are unwilling or unable to work together. Such clashes result in a lack of cooperation within and between work groups, which results in redundancies and poor use of existing organizational resources.

- *Decreased communication*—"Parties communicate less with those who disagree with them and more with those who agree."[14] When talking does occur, it tends to be used for demeaning or further undermining the other's view. With a lack of communication comes unclear or opposing views as to who is or should be responsible for what and unsettling feelings of "unfinished business," where the remaining or unresolved concerns get in the way of being able to move forward.

The benefits of positive conflict far outweigh the time it takes to manage conflict well. As managers, it is our responsibility to learn how to manage conflict effectively and how to help others manage conflict. This is done by creating a climate and culture at work that support constructive conflict—encouraging the clash of ideas (not personalities) and developing processes, training, and tools that help people work through their inevitable differences with each other. This requires a collaborative approach and a commitment to eliminating or at least reducing the occurrence of destructive conflicts.

Sources of Interpersonal Conflict

Not everyone within a group or organization will have the same goals and objectives. By definition, different groups, business units, functions, operating companies, or locations within one organization will have different expectations and operating principles. Each specific entity within an organization may have a unique customer set, employee profile, product orientation, management style, business niche, set of tasks and procedures, and culture or work environment. Business units in the same organization differ significantly in such areas as primary role, task assignments, workloads, vacation scheduling, pay or promotion policies, chain of command, work flow process, and others. For example, General Motors includes very different entities—separate organizations whose primary business is financing (cars and homes), production (building or assembling cars), sales and service (dealership and warranty organizations), and research and development (making continuous improvement on existing car lines as well as developing new ones, such as GM's electric vehicle). Employees in these different units likely work together, sharing expertise as well as information. A variety of situational or organizational factors lead to conflict.[15]

Limited Resources

Despite clear differences between units within an organization, one commonality remains. In general, all are vying for the same resource pool. This pool is usually limited, causing the various units within an organization to compete against each other for finite resources. No matter how prosperous an organization might appear from its facilities, salary levels, or private jets and limousines, few if any organizations have infinite resources. Limits on resources usually result in competition among business units for the restricted resources available through the parent organization. People in organizations compete for what they consider to be their fair share of resources such as money, time, senior management attention, technology, supplies, equipment, and human talent. This inevitably results in conflict.

Differences in Goals and Objectives

A common source of conflict within organizations is differences in personal and/or professional goals and objectives. If we are working on a project with someone whose objective is different from ours, tension or conflict is likely to occur. For example, perhaps one team member wants to "coast" or do as little work as possible toward the team's expected output or deliverable. If this person is on a team of individuals who are committed to a high-quality output, he or she will differ from the others on a host of items, such as approach to the work, ways to get the work done, and standards of work quality and quantity. This tension can be from **intragroup conflict**, differences between members of one group, or from **intergroup conflict**, differences between competing subgroups of an organization.[16] For example, the marketing department might have a different goal than the finance department. Marketing folks might push to increase spending on advertising and promotion in order to improve sales, while finance folks push for increased cost-cutting efforts.

"Now we all need to become a little more open with each other"

Source: Reprinted with permission of Westwood Associates, www.westwood-associates.com.

Miscommunication

Many times, personal and professional conflicts arise due to misunderstandings in communication. Seldom is miscommunication intentional. More often than not, it's the result of not taking time to clarify our understanding of something, gender or cultural differences, or errors in semantics. Often we say one thing and mean another. Or in our haste, we speak quickly and cryptically in hopes that others know what we want. Or perhaps we speak clearly but our nonverbal communication contradicts the verbal message. Or, in the case of e-mail communication, sometimes conflict arises because e-mail doesn't permit you to "read" the other person's verbal or nonverbal cues as you might in telephone or face-to-face communication.[17] In any case, misunderstanding is likely to occur.

Communication issues are further compounded by the jargon that specific groups of people, such as engineers and military personnel, share and understand. The processes and principles of communication may also differ between work groups. For example, one group might have a division newsletter through which employees are kept informed of important organizational changes, while another group might rely on word of mouth to spread key bits of information. This results in each group having a very different understanding of what's going on in the organization. Interaction between these groups could lead to numerous miscommunications, each one a potential source of conflict.

Cultural differences challenge the communication process, as cultures differ in the importance of context (i.e., direct versus indirect communication) and in the attitude toward conflict. People from China, Japan, and India tend to view conflict as disruptive to the harmony within the workplace and would rather keep silent and sweep potentially emotional or divisive issues under the rug than raise them and risk creating an inharmonious atmosphere. Americans, Australians, and the Dutch are more likely to address conflict head-on, while the French manage conflict by first avoiding it (pushing it up the chain of command) and then using force. Schneider and Barsoux recount an example of a French HR director who requested that the term "conflict" not be used in a seminar on managing teams because "once you get to conflict there's no return. It's finished."[18]

Dealing with Angry Customers

Dealing with angry customers in a professional manner is important. Whether right or wrong, when customers have issues, they expect a solution. Staying calm and cool under pressure and showing empathy for their concern can lower the tension and

(continued)

conflict. If a customer has sent an irate e-mail, it is a good idea to suggest meeting him or her (as opposed to firing off an angry reply), as this shows you want to address the problem, listen to their concerns, and fix the situation.

If you've been empathetic and helpful but the customer is verbally abusive beyond your level of tolerance, you may have to be assertive while remaining calm and using a measured tone of voice. "Excuse me sir, I realize that you are frustrated, and I am doing my best to help you. When you raise your voice and threaten me, it makes it difficult for me to find the best solution." You might also increase physical space by taking a few steps away from the customer until you feel that he has calmed down. If you are uncertain how to fix the situation, ask the customer what will make him/her happy and then take swift action. Follow up with the customer to ensure that he is satisfied with the outcome or resolution.

Consider using some of these tips:[19]

1. Always treat the customer with respect, whether you agree with them or not.
2. Hold your customers in high regard—acknowledge their right to be upset.
3. There may be more than one problem—ask questions to find out the extent of the problem.
4. Let the storm blow out—let the customer talk, don't interrupt, never argue but acknowledge that you are listening by using phrases such as "I see" and "of course".
5. Be detached—don't take complaints personally—be objective.
6. Empathize—show you understand what the customer is saying.
7. Don't make excuses—if it is your company's fault, confess and apologize.
8. Offer solutions.
9. Take ownership of the problem—give out your direct line and contact details.
10. Manage expectations—let the customer know what you're going to do and when. It might take time for you to investigate so let the customer know what progress you are making.

Differing Attitudes, Values, and Perceptions

Many conflicts are the result of differences in attitudes, values, and perceptions. Sometimes, without even realizing it, we bring feelings or concerns into an interaction that predisposes us to react in a certain way. For example, if you are afraid of dogs and encounter a neighbor with a dog while out walking one morning, you may react with fear or even hostility. Upon reflection, you realize your reaction was due to a fear of animals you've had since you were a child. But the neighbor, without knowing this background, might misinterpret your strong reaction and conclude you dislike the neighbor rather than fear the dog. Without a chance to communicate—for the neighbor to share his or her perception with you and for you to explain the background behind your reaction—it is likely that you will each emerge from the interaction with a different understanding of what just occurred, and with different, possibly negative, opinions of each other.

Conflicting values are a common and difficult-to-resolve source of conflict between people. Differences in religious beliefs, attitudes toward diverse others, clashes in family values, or work ethic might result in interpersonal differences that surface in the work environment. Whereas conflicts over how to approach a task, otherwise known as substantive conflict, can be functional, relationship conflict that is based on interpersonal differences is almost always dysfunctional.[20] For example, colleagues might view a young consultant who must leave work by Friday afternoon as a slacker when they are left to work late on a client deliverable. The fact is, however, that she is an Orthodox Jew who observes the Sabbath, which her manager knows but her colleagues do not. In this case it would be preferable for her colleagues to be aware of her beliefs. This way the team could make accommodations for her early departure on Fridays, and she could perhaps offer to work late on Thursdays. Fear, confusion, anxiety, and hostility are common attitudes and perceptions and a frequent source of conflict between individuals and groups, and these feelings are often magnified when the individuals are demographically different. These attitudes toward and perceptions about others can be long lasting and self-fulfilling. When such feelings are allowed to develop, conflict is bound to occur.

Style Differences

Another common source of conflict is differences in personal style or personality. An obvious example of this is the predictable tension between two roommates who are on different "body clocks." The early riser who gets up at dawn and the night owl who sleeps until noon are almost certain to get into conflict with each other. Conflicts are also likely to occur between the "slob" and the "neat freak." The manager who is task-oriented and the employee who is a perpetual socializer will probably encounter a great deal of tension and conflict in their boss–subordinate relationship. Then there are those who "love a good fight" and others who abhor conflict, or who avoid, apologize, or save face rather than allow conflict to disrupt the harmony of a work group because of cultural differences. It also appears from the opening case study that Raj and Joe have vastly different styles in how they approach their professional responsibilities. Should Raj find it difficult to work with Joe—who appears to want to control every aspect of their interactions—the two might be unable to find a workable solution for their respective companies. Personality conflicts like these can result in unproductive behaviors at work, including gossip, jealousy, insults, taking sides or playing favorites, slowing work speed, forming cliques, and even looking for another job.

Dealing with an Abusive Boss[21]

Some estimates suggest that a staggering 80 percent of employees leave their jobs because of their bosses. So what creates such a tension between boss and employee? Too often it's the boss's leadership style.

Whereas leadership is all about enabling, engaging, and building confidence, "loudership" is about belittling, controlling, and instilling fear. Bosses who bully, intimidate, and create an environment of fear will undermine the performance, creativity, and commitment of their employees. In the short term, these employees will comply with the demands of their bosses, and looking ahead, they will seek new opportunities. Yet both of these options fail to address the problematic behavior of each party. Accepting abuse becomes a habit that's hard to break, and exiting the firm without confronting the boss's behavior fails to hold a mirror to the boss or sends a message to his superiors that such behavior is acceptable. Consider the following strategies for resolving the conflict:

1. **Try to understand where the boss is coming from.** Sometimes it's hard to get past a venomous delivery to hear the message and decipher its origins. Is the boss reacting to others' impossible or demeaning requests? Sometimes such behavior is a disguised plea to be listened to. Show empathy, "You must be so frustrated to be given conflicting directives," and see if he calms down and answers your question. Listen carefully, and if appropriate, respond by going a step further and offering a plan for taking on additional tasks. Empathy can diffuse tempers and possibly trigger empathy toward you.

2. **Have a plan for dealing with difficult behaviors.** Without a plan, two extremes are likely to occur: One—you crumble in the presence of a louder, or two—you match the venom and escalate the conflict (in which the power differential doesn't favor you). Neither is ideal. When you crumble and show fear, you give the louder ammunition: "I knew you were a baby . . . you're not tough enough to run a sales organization." Think ahead about your goal, what you are willing to accept, and what you will not . . . along with your counteroffer, "I'm not willing to stand here while you yell at me, but if we can have a calm conversation about your concerns over my team's performance, I will gladly accept your criticism and work with the team to find ways to get back on track." Confronting anyone can be difficult, even more so when the person is your boss. Know what you will say, perhaps practicing with a trusted friend or colleague to increase your comfort and confidence for the actual event. Also, consider having this conversation in a public space. The boss might be more willing to listen—as opposed to escalate the conflict—when others are watching.

3. **Document behaviors carefully.** Without documentation, it's your word against his and you'd likely lose . . . and be targeted for more abuse. Make a formal

(continued)

complaint to Human Resources to ensure that behaviors that may have gone unnoticed are finally revealed. What isn't seen cannot be addressed, and may suggest that others have been too scared to file a grievance.

4. **Avoid complaining about the behavior to everyone except the offender.** Some make the mistake of telling the boss's boss. This could backfire. The boss's boss may see your behavior as politically motivated. Moreover, others you complain to may see your complaining as whining and an unwillingness to take charge of a situation, and may actually weaken your position. If you lack the courage to speak directly to the boss, find another way to deal with the stress by talking to and getting support from a partner or close friend who has no ties with the organization.

5. **Have an escape plan.** If loudership behavior has persisted for a long time, and your attempts to deal with it directly and diplomatically have been unsuccessful, it might be time to look for another boss or job. However, when asked the reason for your search in an interview, don't say "Because I have an impossible boss." Rather, be prepared to discuss specific ways in which the interviewer's company and position represent a better fit for your skills, experience, career goals, and so on.

While it may not be easy to address the conflict that arises from an abusive boss, avoiding the conflict will not only ensure it persists, but will also rob the boss of any chance for increased awareness and improvement.

Conflict Management Strategies

Knowing what causes conflicts is half the battle. Knowing what to do when conflicts arise, as they inevitably do, comprises the other half. Those who are effective at conflict management recognize that sources of conflict (for example, limited resources) will probably always be present and seek ways to live with it, minimize its effect, and manage it. When deciding on a strategy for dealing with a specific conflict, keep two factors in mind: your goals, or what you hope to accomplish through the interaction, and the importance of the relationship to you.[22]

The first consideration when selecting a strategy is assessing your goals: What personal or organizational goals are to be accomplished, and how important is it to achieve those exact goals? Remember that conflicts often exist because of opposing goals. The nature and importance of a particular set of goals will determine which strategy is most appropriate for the situation. The second consideration when choosing a conflict resolution strategy is the depth, quality, and duration of the relationship with the other person or persons in the conflict.

Choosing Your Conflict Resolution Strategy

Before selecting a strategy, work through answers to the following questions:

- Is this relationship long term or passing?
- Is the relationship substantive (it goes beyond business issues to more personal matters) or narrow?
- Is the relationship more important to me than the matter under discussion?
- How important is it to maintain a working or friendly relationship with those with whom I am in conflict?
- What possible ramifications will surface after the dust settles?
- What is the power differential in this situation—for example, am I the boss or subordinate?
- If the relationship and the issue are both important, how much time is there to identify possible solutions and reach consensus?

How you answer these questions will impact the conflict strategy you ultimately select.

**Figure 11–1
Conflict-Handling
Strategies**

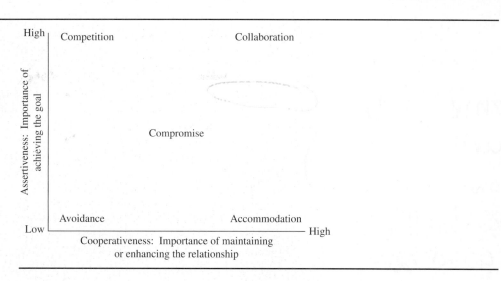

Research on conflict management suggests five possible strategies based on the intersection between relationship and goal importance.[23] Figure 11–1 helps illustrate how each conflict management strategy maps with the assessed importance of the goal and the relationship. Each option has advantages and disadvantages. The appropriate option depends on your preferences and on the context of the specific situation.

- **Avoiding**—In an avoidance or withdrawing strategy, you choose not to deal with the issues or the people involved. You retreat from the situation, hoping it either goes away or resolves itself. This strategy is suitable for situations in which the issues are trivial or of only minor importance to you, when emotions are high, when you feel you have no chance of satisfying your concerns, or when others could resolve the conflict more effectively. Avoiding is dangerous if the matter under discussion requires your attention. It may resurface if not dealt with effectively. What's worse, conflicts that are set aside or ignored can fester due to lack of communication and clarification, making it more difficult—and necessary—to address them at a later time. If the conflict is one that must be addressed, save time and emotional energy by speaking up soon after the conflict is recognized. Avoidance can lead to a "lose–lose" scenario; goals may not be addressed or achieved and the relationship may not be able to progress beyond its current state.

- **Accommodating** (smoothing)—When you use an accommodation strategy to resolve a conflict, you are more concerned with maintaining the relationship than with accomplishing a specific goal through the interaction. This strategy is appropriate when the issue is not that important to you or when harmony is of greater importance to you than "winning" on the issue. For example, if your children challenge your decision to take them to Burger King for lunch (McDonald's has the better toy this week), it's okay to give in to their wishes if both choices are equally suitable. It saves time and emotional energy, and it can be used in a later conflict negotiation ("I did what you wanted; now I want you to do . . . for me"). If you are always accommodating, as in "you win and I lose," it might signal that you are possibly sacrificing some important goals for the sake of the relationship. You might wonder why others never seem to do the same for you. Sometimes we do this because we want to be "nice" and have others like us. However, overreliance on accommodating in conflict situations could be harmful to you and to the relationship in the long term as you are likely to build up resentment over your unmet needs.

One thing to realize is that accommodating sounds different in a one-off, single-issue conflict resolution than it would during one point in a more complex negotiation. For example, a person with whom you are in conflict might not even know that you've accommodated (perhaps because she is used to getting her way and the issue isn't important to you). You can clarify your stance and make a "deposit" for later use if you say, "Well, Jennifer, because you are adamant about visiting your parents for Thanksgiving, I'll go along, but I'll expect that we can visit my parents for the Easter holiday." This strategy also works during a multi-issue negotiation, where you might yield on one issue but expect the other person to yield on an issue important to you.

- **Compromising**—When you compromise or "split the difference" in a conflict, you agree to give up part of your goal and part of the relationship in order to reach an agreement. This strategy is effective for achieving temporary solutions, when both parties are at a comparable level, when there are time pressures, or as a backup when collaboration or competing is neither possible nor successful. This strategy is the political equivalent of "win some, lose some." In other words, you consciously agree to accept that sometimes in the relationship you'll get your way and other times you won't. This is possible in a long-term relationship where there's time for give-and-take exchange. However, many people and groups jump to this strategy too quickly without pursuing synergy or collaboration. One reason is that it's simple to find the mathematical average: "You're asking $300 for the bike and I offered $220. Why don't we split the difference and make it $260?" When the difference is small, this approach may seem simple and risk-free. However, when the difference is large, and more importantly, when there are data available to support a particular value or price (selling a home for $300,000 and being offered $200,000), this strategy can leave both parties frustrated and without a deal. Perhaps we do this because of our feelings about risk: I'm better off getting half of what I want than risking it and getting nothing. Whether this is true or appropriate depends on the situation, the players, and information available.

- **Competing** (forcing)—In a competing strategy, you work to achieve your goals at all costs, even if it means sacrificing the relationship. This is an "I win, you lose" strategy. Joe's approach to Raj in the opening scenario appears to fall into this category, when he said, "Here are my rules. . ." and then dictated the way he and Raj would work together, and responded to Raj's challenge with, "That's not how I do it." His "my way or the highway" approach to dictating the rules of engagement can be perceived as stubbornness, uncooperativeness, and possibly irrational. In a setting where collaboration is needed to maintain an effective long-term partnership between individuals or companies, competing or forcing will be ineffective. However, this approach may be appropriate when you have severe time restrictions, are in a crisis situation, need to issue an unpopular decision, or have to take an action that is vital to an organization's welfare. Some salespeople are guilty of forcing sales. They care about the commission they earn if they sell you a car—today—and use techniques (this is the last one [or day]; if you leave now, the deal expires) that make buyers feel pressured into the sale. More successful salespeople realize that future sales from this person and others in his or her network are likely if agreements are reached collaboratively rather than through force. However, forcing children out on a specific path when the fire alarm rings is not only appropriate, but also safer than discussing or arguing over other options.

- **Collaborating** (integrating)—The ultimate "win–win" strategy, collaboration involves energy, commitment, and excellent skills in communication, problem solving, and negotiation. Collaboration is appropriate when there is plenty of time, when all want a solution that satisfies all parties' objectives and maintains the relationship, and when the issue is very important to all parties involved. It is also critical when the conflicting parties are responsible for implementing the solution. If you feel a solution was only partly effective or was forced on you, you will be less likely to put your heart and soul into its implementation. Coming to a consensus or finding an integrative solution takes considerable problem-solving effort and time. If Martin, the co-worker with whom you wrote a detailed market analysis, promises to deliver the revised analysis to the client by next Monday, not checking with you first or realizing that you were going to be on vacation until Friday, there could be negative consequences if you didn't push back and attempt to find a different solution. You might say, "Martin, I appreciate your being responsive to our client, but I'll be on vacation and unable to work with you on

[Handwritten margin notes:]
Game vs. Iowa where coach allows for some loose ball with a good result

Competing – Glory Road, coach vs. players to gain respect

the revisions before next Monday. Can we discuss some other possibilities regarding dates, who does what and when, and how we might negotiate for more time? The flight and hotel were organized five months ago, and I really need the break." If you are feeling forced into a solution about which you feel strongly, diplomatically challenge the process by saying something like "Margaret, I can tell by your last statement [paraphrase Margaret's statement here] that this issue is important to you. I know you want what's best for your company, and I want the same. Those terms would preclude us from being able to order more in the future. Can we agree to brainstorm additional options that we (and our companies) could both support? I've cleared my calendar for this meeting. . . ." In collaboration, both parties don't necessarily agree, but both feel comfortable enough to express their disagreement and opinions and can work toward an optimal solution.[24]

Although collaborating or the win–win option appears to be the ideal strategy, it is not appropriate in all cases. Each of the strategies has strong and weak points, as shown in Figure 11–2. No one solution is best suited for all situations. The best managers are those who can move fluidly from one style to the next depending on the situation and circumstances. As a manager, you will find yourself using all these strategies. The choice of one over the other depends on the situation and persons involved as well as your own personality. Each of us has a style with which we're naturally most comfortable. (Your instructor can provide the Thomas-Kilmann Conflict Mode Instrument to help you determine which of the styles are dominant for you.) Be aware of your natural tendency and develop proficiency in using other, less comfortable styles, depending on what a situation dictates.

Also recognize that in a particular situation or context, not all of the styles are *available* to the players. As mentioned, when a conflict must be resolved in an instant—as is the case in an emergency situation, such as when Captain Sully Sullenberger told co-pilot

Figure 11–2
Gains and Losses Associated with Conflict Styles[25]

		Competition	Avoidance	Accommodation	Compromise	Collaboration
Gains		Chance to win everything Exciting, gamesmanship Exercise own sense of power	No energy or time expenditure Conserve energy for fights that are "more important"	Little muss or fuss, no feathers ruffled Others may view you as supportive Energy free for other pursuits	No one returns home empty-handed "Keeps the peace" May or may not encourage creativity	Both sides win Better chance for long-term solutions Creativity in problem solving Maintains relationship New level of understanding of situation Improves quality of solution and commitment
Losses		Chance to lose everything Alienates others Discourages others from working with you Potentially larger scale conflicts in the future (or more avoidance of conflict)	Less stimulation Less creative problem solving Little understanding of the needs of others Incomplete comprehension of work environment	Lowered self-assertion and possible self-esteem Loss of power Absence of your unique contribution to the situation Others dependent on you may not feel you "go to bat" for them	Since neither side is totally satisfied, conflicts are likely to recur later Neither side realizes self-determination fully	Time, in the short run Loss of sense of autonomy

Jeff Skiles "My aircraft" after a flock of birds caused both engines to fail while flying over the Hudson River on January 15, 2009—forcing is the only choice. However, when power is unequally distributed between the players, for example, boss and subordinate, the subordinate would take an extreme risk to her relationship with the boss (and employment status!) if she were to resolve a conflict by competing or forcing. (See shaded box on dealing with an abusive boss, on page 271.)

Some Tips for Managing Conflict

■ *Control your temper and emotional response.* This is easier said than done, particularly if harsh words are exchanged. Take a few deep breaths and possibly a short break. When you finish, demonstrate your respect for the other party's feelings. Validate that the conflict is real to them no matter how trivial it may seem to you.[26] For example, "I realize that the Smith account is yours, and that you're angry that I had a conversation with him. . .." Notice that in this statement, the speaker doesn't admit fault but rather demonstrates an understanding of the situation from the other's perspective. Embracing conflict builds honest relationships. By validating both parties' feelings about a situation, you can then move into a problem-solving mode.

■ *Understand the issues.* Don't react impulsively when faced with a conflict situation. Take the time needed to fully assess the scope of the situation: the key players, the source of the conflict, the issues involved, the goals, and the dynamics of the relationship(s) involved.[27] Upon reflection, the issue—or the events leading up to it—may seem less consequential or problematic than at first believed. Perhaps you might have done or said the same thing if the tables were turned! Accept the faults of the parties involved and be willing to admit to them. Better still is to focus on the present and changing behaviors or outcomes than to dwell on or try to change the past or the people involved. Once you have a more objective perspective of the situation, select a conflict strategy from the above choices and apply it as appropriate.

■ *Decide whether to engage.* Said another way, pick your battles. Not all conflicts are manageable or worth the effort needed to resolve them. Take a few minutes to check your reaction and ensure that you have all the facts before making any judgments. Sometimes we make the situation worse by paying too much attention to issues that would be better dealt with via the reinforcement technique of "extinction," providing no reinforcement at all by simply ignoring the event. Sometimes it's best simply to express your opinion, "agree to disagree," and table the matter. If you do decide to engage, choose the time and place carefully. Other times, we don't choose, but rather are drawn into others' conflicts.

In the same way small children bring their conflicts to grown-ups to solve, employees frequently do the same with their manager. A good manager will carefully choose the battles worth handling and select an appropriate strategy for handling them, sometimes ignoring a particular conflict so the individuals responsible for it can address it. In this way, managers can help develop the skills of their employees and the relationships between them.

■ *Search for a common goal or ground.* Another way to resolve conflict is to identify win–win solutions that will be acceptable to both parties.[28] Do this by asking open-ended questions and demonstrating you've heard and understood others' goals or objectives. When this is not possible or time is short, try to accommodate as many of the others' interests as possible and then make the decision that is ultimately the most fair and helpful for the organization. By explaining how you utilized others' input in arriving at the "best" decision—even if it feels like a compromise—you demonstrate your respect for others' views and values. Raj might approach Joe in a way that involves both in identifying the common goal. For example, Raj might say, "Joe, I respect the fact that you and Stephen handle things differently, but our companies have worked together for almost 20 years, and have been able to accomplish *x, y,* and *z* together. What is your goal for our meeting, and what can I do to help you accomplish it?"

- *Threaten to and/or bring in a third party.* If one of the parties seems to be digging in his or her heels, stubbornly refusing to compromise or even listen to the other's viewpoints, further efforts to resolve the conflict by the parties involved are likely to be futile. The mere suggestion that an outsider should be brought in to help mediate may cause the stubborn party to soften up a bit. The mediator could be a manager or someone with higher status, or possibly an employee whose job and skill set qualify him or her to mediate, for example, a labor or employee relations specialist working in the human resources department of the company.

- *Be creative.* Paula Caproni relates a story of an employee who "was very frustrated with her intolerable boss. When a headhunter called to see if she was interested in a promotion in a new company, the employee said that she wasn't—but that her boss might be. The headhunter called the boss, the boss took the job, and the employee was promoted to her boss's job."[29] In many conflict situations, there could be multiple, satisfactory solutions. Rather than pick one and stick with it until the end, think about multiple options, and be creative!

Organizational and Interpersonal Techniques for Preventing Conflict

While conflict can be healthy in an organization or relationship, it also has negative side effects. Unresolved and continuous conflict can lower productivity and morale and lead to high turnover. By utilizing strategies that help prevent or reduce dysfunctional conflict and manage functional conflict, organizations can maximize the benefits of conflict while minimizing the costs.[30] Following are some strategies or techniques that organizations can implement to minimize or deflect conflict.

Organizational Strategies/Techniques

Creating/Maintaining a Culture of Openness

One of the biggest sources of conflict comes from misunderstanding, misinterpreting, and guessing about others' expectations, goals, and decisions when information isn't forthcoming. Some companies, in their attempts to carefully time or control "the message," experience the opposite effect. Guessing begins, rumors emerge, and arguments about the impact of what is believed to have happened or will be happening become water cooler and internal blog conversation—which was the case recently at Microsoft.[31] It would be better to communicate bad news completely and internally before employees read in the local news that their organization will be laying off 10 percent of its workforce! We all know of situations like these. Even something as benign as a manager leaving a note for one of her employees, such as "Joe, we need to meet. How about tomorrow at 10?" can create animosity on Joe's part toward his boss. The manager meant no ill will; in fact, she plans to discuss a promotion opportunity with Joe. But he doesn't know that, and spends that evening and the next morning wondering and worrying unnecessarily. His preoccupation may even translate into less than friendly interactions with family and co-workers.

Some companies like Google, BigStep, and the Marine Resources Council have adopted more informal and personalized ways of connecting with their employees. Examples include regular staff meetings, internal e-mailed newsletters, attitude surveys, community-based events, and brown-bag lunches with top managers. By exchanging information freely and keeping people informed, companies find they are able to reduce some of the conflicts that arise from lack of information. In addition, in a culture where openness is expected and rewarded, employees are encouraged to share their views, even when they run counter to the "wisdom of the ages" or the majority of employees. Caudron notes, "When people are allowed to express their opinions, no matter how disagreeable, magic can occur."[32] This magic, which results in innovation and improvement, is enabled because conflict is allowed and acknowledged as a necessary part of the business process.[33]

Involving Employees in Decisions That Affect Them

As obvious as this may sound, many organizations still hold tight to the way things have always been done, which may include secretive meetings that include only the highest-ranking employees. One exception is Semco, a well-known South American business whose flat hierarchy and involvement of employees in decisions about nearly all company issues (including setting salaries and strategies) helped them successfully transition from a manufacturing company into an e-business.[34] Not every decision should involve every employee; however, including employees in decisions that affect them has multiple benefits. First, because they deal with day-to-day issues and problems, employees are often the best source of ideas and ways to solve organizational problems. Second, because they've been asked (and especially if their inputs are taken into consideration), employees are more committed to the solution and the changes needed to implement it. Finally, the process of involving employees encourages them to stay involved in the search for improvement—even when they aren't asked directly.

One example is resource allocation. As long as resources are finite and need to be shared among various departments within an organization, conflict will be a part of organizational life. To reduce the possible effects of negative conflict, managers should open the process to more employees to seek new and improved ways in which resources can be obtained and allocated. If internal resources can be increased or reallocated (or costs lowered), the number of win–lose conflict situations is likely to drop. Of course, it still might not be possible to increase resources sufficiently to allow all parties to become winners. By involving employees in the process, organizations can reduce the likelihood that organizational members will perceive inequity and take steps to reduce it. Moreover, whenever possible, organizations should establish rewards at the highest level—to encourage collaboration across departments and units—and involve key players in resource allocation decision processes to increase the fairness and effectiveness of these decisions.

Ensuring Alignment of Organizational Systems

In his seminal article, "On the Folly of Rewarding A While Hoping for B," Steve Kerr talked about the problems that stem from an organization that asks for certain behaviors, such as innovation, but rewards employees who maintain the status quo.[35] The message sent is in conflict with the behavior rewarded, and this has the potential for inciting conflict at the interpersonal, group, and organizational levels. While this article is more than 30 years old, its ideas are still relevant today. For example, as organizations have increasingly embraced the notion of teamwork, many forget or are slow to redesign the reward system to publicly and monetarily recognize collaboration and cooperativeness. The traditional system—which rewards individual heroics and independent action—remains untouched while management pays only lip service to the supposed value of teamwork. The employees who see the disconnect learn (or continue) to behave in ways consistent with the reward system, while those who don't expect that their aligned-with-espoused-values behaviors will be recognized. Without aligned organizational structures, processes, and reward systems, employees' divergent values and behaviors result in workplace conflicts.

Offering Team Training and Team Building

As organizations have gotten flatter and less hierarchical, individuals are working in teams dedicated to specific project goals. As discussed elsewhere in the text, the diversity present on teams creates potential for much conflict. By providing team-related training before and coaching during the team's existence, members will have a better idea of what to expect from—and how to excel in—a team experience, thus reducing the likelihood that team-based conflicts will surface. While not all conflict can be avoided, members who collaboratively set team goals, objectives, and norms, as well as practice managing deadlines, others' expectations, and disagreement, are better able to manage conflict if it does appear. Companies' investment in such team training has been shown to pay off.[36]

7-Step Model for Resolving Conflict on a Team[37]

1. Determine the best place to deliver feedback.
   - Deliver individual feedback in private.
   - Discuss project-specific issues in team meetings or in private.

2. Set the context, disclose your humanity, and/or address what the other is thinking.

- "This is not easy for me to say."
- "I've been avoiding telling you.. . ."
- "I know this may sound as if I don't appreciate the work you do, but that is not the case."
- "I'd like to talk with you about.. . ."

3. Stick to the facts and state the impact.

- "I noticed you were 10 minutes late to the last two meetings. When you are late, we cannot fully address the issues, and that impacts everyone's productivity."
- "When I reviewed the change order and double-checked the original plans, I noticed that we did include your request. I'd like to show you.. . ."
- "In our rules of engagement, we agreed that issues be brought up with me first. I noticed the last two you brought up were not addressed to me first."

4. Seek understanding. Ask a question (play dumb).

- "Is anything going on with you that is impacting your ability to be on time?"
- "Is this your understanding?"
- "Is there something that stops you from sharing issues with me as soon as they occur?"

5. Identify an action plan.

- "What can we do to resolve this?"
- "What suggestions do you have?"

6. Summarize decisions, next steps, and accountability.

7. Thank the person.

Providing Diversity Training

As organizations have become more diverse, individuals find themselves working more and more with people who vary in terms of background, physical ability, culture, ethnicity, gender, religious beliefs, education, economic status, sexual orientation, political view, values, goals, ideas, and knowledge base.[38] As challenging as it is for two similar people to agree, the difficulty increases exponentially with increased diversity and numbers of people working together. Recognizing this, many large companies offer diversity training as a way of ensuring that employees understand the importance of differences among individuals and how to manage them effectively.[39]

This training, offered by in-house trainers or outside consultants, helps employees know themselves (e.g., their biases, style, strengths, weaknesses) and how that relates to diverse others. Exercises and discussions included in diversity training are geared toward increasing employees' ability to recognize and value differences, understand and reduce prejudice and discriminatory behavior, and utilize company resources and processes when serious issues (e.g., harassment) arise.

Offering Conflict Management and Negotiation Training

While this may seem an obvious strategy to prevent conflict, recall that few people are comfortable with and have skills to manage conflict. By providing such training, companies recognize that conflict is normal and not necessarily bad. Moreover, the training helps employees deal effectively with differing viewpoints and approaches, which, if managed well, can lead to innovation.[40] These programs teach participants to listen actively and communicate assertively as they attend to—and share their own—differing points of views, feelings, and perceptions; to recognize potential problems and deal with them (while helping others do the same) while they are still minor;[41] and to improve their skills in handling conflict constructively through the application of effective communication, decision-making, problem-solving, and negotiation techniques.

Creating Psychological Safety

Psychological safety refers to the belief that one can share openly and honestly one's true feelings and opinions without risk of retaliation or harm to the relationship. One on one, this safety defines the degree of self-disclosure, trust, and intimacy. If the perception of risk is high, conversations will remain at the surface while conflict and resentment may build below the surface. In the workplace, when employees perceive there is ample psychological safety, they are more likely to speak up, take calculated risks (which increase learning), and act creatively. A high degree of psychological safety lowers employees' perceptions of the fear of reprisal for their actions.

The foundation of psychological safety is trust—among leaders, followers, team members, and peers—and it is cultivated by transparent communication and relationships. Engagement in decision making and the giving and receiving of feedback is important, particularly the sharing of feelings, values, and thoughts with each other. When conflict arises, a high degree of psychological safety means that employees are more likely to address conflict by speaking out as they feel it is not inappropriate to do so but will actually make a positive contribution to the organization.[42] Leaders need to create the conditions for psychological safety by being open, encouraging involvement, and setting an example where there is little or no fear of reprisal.

Source: Henry Martin/New Yorker Collection/www.cartoonbank.com

Individual Strategies/ Techniques

The techniques just described focus primarily on what managers can do in their organizations to reduce sources and consequences of conflict. Following are a few additional techniques that individuals can use to prevent or reduce the likelihood of conflict arising when interacting with others in a personal or professional setting.

Using Effective Communication

Using effective communication skills is always helpful, and three techniques are particularly useful for avoiding conflicts. The first is using "I" language. When we say things like "you just don't understand," or "your idea will never work," we put others on the defensive. They feel attacked and strike back, causing conflict to escalate. Take responsibility for your communication—"I'm not sure I've clearly stated my objection," or "I have a concern about the marketing part of this plan. Can we discuss this?"—and conflicts are less likely to occur. Related to this is the use of absolute language, for example, "you never . . .", "I always . . .", "Everyone knows that . . . ." Such statements are rarely true and often motivate the other person to respond in kind. Try to be less absolute with your observations and more specific when sharing your feedback. For example, "On Friday night and Saturday night, I cooked dinner and you left the room expecting me to clean up. We agreed that we would share cooking and cleaning responsibilities, and lately, I've been feeling that the balance is off. Can we talk about this?"

The second technique is to pay attention to nonverbal cues and check your understanding of their meaning. Perhaps the least understood nonverbal message is silence. "Does everyone understand what I'm saying?" asks a manager after she announces the implementation of a new computer system. Who wants to acknowledge that they're somehow unintelligent by raising their hand? So, the employees' silence is interpreted as agreement, and business returns as usual. But not really. Some employees are angry about the change; after all, the old system worked fine. Others may refuse to use the system, opting instead to get others to do the work for them. Still others start asking questions of and sharing their opinions with employees in other departments. How could this have been avoided? The manager could have expected questions and concerns and asked a different question. She could have noticed the blank looks on some employees' faces and "checked out" body language on others (perhaps some employees are "avoiders") and asked, "I get the sense from your facial expressions that a lot of information was thrown at you and still needs to be digested. Am I correct? What questions and concerns do you have about this new system?"

A third technique is to communicate consequences. Returning to the lazy teammate scenario, realize that saying nothing is akin to approving this behavior. If you've tried reasoning, clarifying the issue, and asserting the team's needs, but nothing has changed, it may be time to communicate consequences before the lazy teammate's inaction creates additional problems and conflict for the team. "We've tried several times to get you to do what we've asked. If your part of the project is not up to the standards we've agreed to by Friday, we're going to ask the team leader to have you reassigned off the team." Of course, this cannot be an empty threat. You must ensure that such a consequence can and will be implemented if the behavior doesn't change.

Managing Others'
Expectations

Some conflicts can be avoided by letting others know what to expect about you and your limits before a problem arises. At the start of a project that involves collaboration, it can be very helpful to disclose pertinent information about your work style, preferences, expectations, and the like. This way, others are aware of differences up front and can adapt accordingly before the differences cause friction. For example, you might tell a colleague you are assigned to work with on a new project, "You should know that I'm a very detail-oriented person, so I really work best when I receive all the details of a problem, not just the general picture."[43] By giving this person an instruction booklet of sorts, you reduce the likelihood of future clashes. Even on a project team for a class, it's helpful to have an initial discussion about each member's work commitments and schedule constraints, goals for the class (e.g., hoped-for grade), likes and dislikes about teamwork, and so on. It's better to find out early on that one member may not be able or want to put forth an equal share of effort, planning to look at the project just the day before it is due—which, unfortunately, happens more than you might think. Knowing what to expect and being able to plan ahead can remove or reduce member guesswork, stress, and conflict.

Related to this is the technique of setting limits. Imagine your boss provides you with yet another project to complete. You can do it, for sure, but not today, or this week, for that matter. At least not with everything else on your plate. Most managers can't read minds. If you won't be able to complete the project when and how it is expected, let your boss know now instead of waiting until a critical deadline has passed. Setting limits—"I'm happy to do this project, but I need to let you know that the other project you wanted me to do will have to be placed on hold"—can help manage your boss's expectations and avoid a future conflict.

Focusing on Others First

Often when we disagree with another person, we rush to explain why our ideas are superior. Like "you" language, this tendency can motivate others to defend themselves. One effective technique for preventing conflict involves anticipating another's disagreement or objection and explaining how your proposal takes this issue into account. "I know you're concerned about *x*, so let me tell you how I think this can be overcome." Even helpful advice could be taken the wrong way, implying that the listener is performing ineffectively. When you are looking to change or improve organizational processes, consider first how others might benefit from the change. Since most people dislike change, you can increase their willingness to listen to your idea if they feel doing so can benefit them and their organization. You can avoid conflicts by appealing to another's self-interest; for example, "I know that the current reimbursement process works. However, if we can reduce the number of approval signatures needed, you'll reduce time spent on your inbox and show us that you trust us to act appropriately."

Planning for and Having Difficult Conversations

Understandably, when faced with the prospect of having a difficult conversation, particularly about someone's behavior in the workplace, most people try to avoid doing so. The longer you wait, the harder the conversation becomes. Rather than wait for a "perfect time" (there is no such thing), send an e-mail or leave a voice message requesting to have a meeting. "I'd like to discuss a sensitive issue with you. When is convenient for you?"[44] Before the meeting, consider the answers to the following questions:

■ What do I hope to accomplish?

■ What would be an ideal outcome?

■ What assumptions am I making about his or her intentions? Remember, you cannot know what is going on in the person's head.

■ What triggered my negative reaction? Does it have anything to do with how I view things? It might be that you are partly responsible for the situation.

■ Can I adjust my framing of the conversation so that I can expect a positive result rather than focus on the difficulty?

■ What will I say first, second? What words should I try to avoid? Try to avoid aggressive or critical language.

When you have the conversation, remember the goal—which is not proving you are right and the other person is wrong. Focus the conversation on how you can help the person, rather than attacking his or her behavior. Don't rehearse the conversation. Know what points you wish to make but realize that this is a conversation rather than a soliloquy. You need to stay open and listen to the person's reactions. Don't interrupt except to acknowledge you have heard what he or she is saying. Resist making assumptions. You cannot know what is going on inside the head of the other person or how they view the problem. Instead, ask for his or her perspective.[45] Clarify your position without negating his or hers. Start to engage the other side in problem solving. Say something like, "Maybe we can talk about how to address these issues?"

Use exercise 11-H to plan an upcoming difficult conversation that you need to have with someone. Doing this will improve your ability to keep the goal in mind and your emotions in check during this conversation.

Summary

Conflict is inevitable. People are unique and have different interests, goals, perspectives, values, and needs. For this reason, conflict can and does occur. Not all conflict is dysfunctional; some conflict can actually increase innovation, creativity, and the bond between conflicting parties. Practicing conflict prevention techniques can help you eliminate or diffuse conflicts before they surface. By knowing likely sources of conflict and appropriate strategies for dealing with different types of conflict, you can manage your response to conflict and improve your interactions with others.

Key Terms and Concepts

Accommodating

Avoiding

Collaborating

Competing

Compromising

Conflict

Human relations view (of conflict)

Integrationist view (of conflict)

Intergroup conflict

Intragroup conflict

Negative or dysfunctional conflict

Positive or functional conflict

Psychological safety

Traditional view (of conflict)

Discussion Questions

1. Is all conflict bad? Discuss.

2. What are typical causes of conflict in the workplace? Ask participants to relate specific examples from their experiences.

3. Imagine you work for an organization that has to make some changes (i.e., budget cuts) due to an economic downturn in its industry. The CEO calls a meeting with all department managers, directors, and vice presidents and tells them they need to cut 30 percent in costs. Moreover, it's their job to decide how to implement this directive. Discuss ways to respond to this directive.

4. Collaborating, one of the five styles of conflict resolution discussed in the text, seems like the approach we should all strive for. What do you think?

Endnotes

1. The opening case is adapted from a scenario included in Lawrence Susskind, "Stubborn or Irrational? How to Cope with a Difficult Negotiation Partner," *Harvard Negotiation Newsletter* 7, no. 12 (December 2004).

2. James H. Keil, "Coaching through Conflict," *Dispute Resolution Journal* (May–June 2000), pp. 65–69.

3. Stephen Robbins, *Organizational Behavior,* 8th ed. (Upper Saddle River, NJ: Prentice Hall, 1998), pp. 435–36.

4. Kathleen M. Eisenhardt, Jean L. Kahwajy, and L. F. Bourgeois III, "How Management Teams Can Have a Good Fight," *Harvard Business Review* (July–August 1997), p. 77.

5. Alfred Fleishman, "Going Back a Little Bit," *St. Louis Business Journal* (January 3, 2000), p. 29.

6. F. Rees, *How to Lead Work Teams* (San Diego: Pfeiffer, 1991).

7. Jeri Darling and Diane Russ, "Relationship Capital," *Executive Excellence* (May 2000), p. 14.

8. Shari Caudron, "Productive Conflict Has Value," *Workforce* (February 1999), p. 25.

9. Marissa Ann Mayer, "Creativity Loves Constraints," *Business Week* (February 13, 2006); online at http://www.businessweek.com/magazine/content/06_07/b3971144.htm (accessed March 11, 2009).

10. Personnel Decisions International, "Five Steps to Mediating Conflict," *Workforce* (October 1999), p. 30.

11. R. J. Lewicki, D. M. Saunders, and B. Barry, *Negotiation,* 5th ed. (Burr Ridge, IL: McGraw-Hill Irwin, 2006), p. 19.

12. Michael Barrier, "Putting a Lid on Conflicts," *Nation's Business* (April 1998), p. 34.

13. See, for example, C. Pearson and C. Porath, "On the Nature, Consequences and Remedies of Workplace Incivility: No Time for "Nice?" Think Again," *Academy of Management Executive* 18, no. 1 (2005), pp. 7–18.

14. Lewicki, et al., *Negotiation,* p. 19.

15. John S. Morgan, revised by Beth Z. Schneider, *Interpersonal Skills for the Manager,* 5th ed. (Institute of Certified Professional Managers, 2000), pp. 139–45.

16. J. K. Barge, *Leadership Communication Skills for Organizations and Groups* (New York: St. Martin's Press, 1994).

17. Raymond A. Friedman and Steven C. Currall, "Conflict Escalation: Dispute Exacerbating Elements of E-mail Communication," *Human Relations* 56, no. 11 (November 2003), p. 1325.

18. S. C. Schneider and J.-L. Barsoux, *Managing Across Cultures* (London: Prentice Hall, 1997), p. 200.

19. M. Dolcezza, "Ten Top Tips: Dealing with an Angry Customer," *Management Today,* January 2012; http://www.managementtoday.co.uk/features/1112107/ (accessed April 23, 2013).

20. J. Yang and K. W. Mossholder, "Decoupling Task and Relationship Conflict: The Role of Intragroup Emotional Processing," *Journal of Organizational Behavior* 25, no. 5 (August 2004), pp. 589–605.

21. S. C. de Janasz, "Is Your Leader a Louder? 5 Ways of Dealing with an Abusive Boss," Huffington Post.com (November 24, 2012). http://www.huffingtonpost.com/suzanne-de-janasz/abusive-boss_b_2090041.html (accessed June 1, 2013).

22. David Johnson, *Reaching Out,* 6th ed. (Boston: Allyn & Bacon, 1997), p. 240.

23. Kenneth Thomas, "Conflict and Conflict Management," in *Handbook of Industrial and Organizational Psychology* (Chicago: Rand McNally, 1976), pp. 889–935.

24. Shari Caudron, "Keeping Team Conflict Alive," *Training and Development* (Sept. 1998), p. 48.

25. Adapted from the work of Ronald Fry, Jared Florian, and Jacquie McLemore, Department of Organizational Behavior, Weatherhead School of Management, Case Western Reserve University, Cleveland, Ohio (1984).

26. Ted Pollock, "When Conflict Rears Its Head: A Personal File of Stimulating Ideas, Little Known Facts and Daily Problem Solvers," *Supervision* (October 1999), p. 24.

27. Ed Rigsbee, "Conflict Management and Resolution," *Business Forms, Labels and Systems* (February 20, 2000), p. 62.

28. Robert F. Pearce, "Developing Your Career Skills," *Compensation and Benefits Management* (Winter 2000), p. 15.

29. Paula Caproni, *Management Skills for Everyday Life: The Practical Coach,* 2nd ed. (Upper Saddle River, NJ: Pearson Prentice Hall, 2005), p. 239.

30. Allen C. Amason, "Distinguishing the Effects of Functional and Dysfunctional Conflict on Strategic Decision Making: Resolving a Paradox for Top Management Teams," *Academy of Management Journal* 39, no. 1, pp. 123–48.

31. J. Greene, "Troubling Exits at Microsoft," *BusinessWeek* (September 26, 2005); online at http://www.businessweek.com/magazine/content/05_39/b3952001.htm (accessed July 23, 2007).

32. Caudron, "Keeping Team Conflict Alive," p. 49.

33. Ibid.

34. R. Semler, "How We Went Digital without a Strategy," *Harvard Business Review* (September–October 2000), pp. 51–58.

35. Steve Kerr, "On the Folly of Rewarding A while Hoping for B," *Academy of Management Journal* 18 (1975), pp. 769–83.

36. See, for example, E. Cooley, "Training an Interdisciplinary Team in Communication and Decision-Making Skills," *Small Group Research* 25, no. 1 (1994), pp. 5–25; and J. Pine and J. C. Tingley, "ROI of Soft Skills Training," *Training* (February 1993), pp. 55–60.

37. According to Jean M. DiGiovanna, founder of ThinkPeople and author of "Five Components Needed for High-Performing Teams," *Design Firm Management & Administration Report* 7, no. 4 (April 2007), pp. 3–6.

38. Scott Sedam, "Why Muddle through Conflict?" *Builder* (June 1999), p. 148.

39. Caudron, "Keeping Team Conflict Alive."

40. Ibid.

41. Pollock, "When Conflict Rears Its Head."

42. J. T. Eggers, "Psychological Safety Influences Relationship Behavior," *Research Notes* (February 2011).

43. Kristine L. Krueger, personal communication (July 22, 2007).

44. J. D. Schramm, *How to Overcome Communication Fears*, HBR Blog Network (September 2010); http://blogs.hbr.org/cs/2010/09/how_to_overcome_communication (accessed April 26, 2013). html.

45. H. Weeks, *Failure to Communicate: How Conversations Go Wrong and What You Can Do to Right Them* (Boston: Harvard Business Press Books, 2010).

Exercise 11–A
Conflict Assessment

1. Briefly describe one conflict situation in which you found yourself recently (in the past couple of years). What were the reasons for and outcomes of this conflict?

_____

_____

_____

_____

2. Using the five conflict styles discussed in this chapter, describe the style you used in resolving the conflict discussed in number 1, pointing to specific behaviors and communication patterns that are evidence of this style. In what ways was this style effective and/or ineffective in this situation?

_____

_____

_____

_____

3. What style did the person with whom you were in conflict use? Evidence? In what ways was she or he effective and/or ineffective in this situation?

_____

_____

_____

_____

4. If you could replay this scenario, what things would you do the same, and why; what things would you have done differently, and why?

_____

_____

_____

_____

5. What conflict style are you most comfortable using? Why?

_____

_____

_____

_____

**Exercise 11–B
Conflict with
Consumers**

You work part-time at the customer service desk of a home improvement store (e.g., Lowes or Home Depot) in your suburban town. It's late September and in walks a man who firmly but politely presents his receipt and insists on returning the barbecue he bought in June for a full refund. He explains that "it doesn't work as well as it should." For your part, it's clear that this man bought the barbecue to enjoy summertime grilling, and now that the summer is over, he no longer needs the barbecue—at least until next summer. Your company's return policy is to take back any product within 90 days of purchase with a receipt and within one year if the product is defective. What do you do?

1. What is your immediate reaction to the scenario? How would you feel if you were a member of the team writing about this situation?

2. How could this situation have been avoided?

3. What approaches to resolving this conflict are appropriate?

4. What are some things that, if done, would make this approach successful?

5. What are some things to avoid when attempting to resolve this conflict? Why?

**Exercise 11–C
Conflict in the
Workplace: Two Case
Studies**

My boss and I are having some interpersonal problems. He does several things that I find really annoying. To start, he is not considerate of my employees or me. I often find myself thinking that I would be reluctant to do the things he does around me that annoy me. Yet he's my boss, so what can I do? He comes in late to the office, after my co-workers and I have been working for a while and have our day planned. Inevitably he'll come in, interrupt, and lay on us a whole new set of priorities for the day. To be fair, he does stay late (we have flextime in our office), and he has a good reason to be late—he has childcare responsibilities to fulfill on school mornings. But his habit of coming in and interrupting the schedule for our day is really off-putting. By the time I've listened to his concerns, reprioritized my and my staff's work, and gotten back on track, it's almost lunchtime and I feel I've wasted almost a half day trying to respond to his concerns. I'm afraid to confront him—he's a good guy and it would only put him on the defensive. And it wouldn't really change anything. But I'm also tired of not feeling productive. I just wish he would be a little more sensitive to our situation and be better organized and more aware of our time constraints. Is that asking too much?

1. What is your immediate reaction to the scenario? How would you feel if you were the person writing about this situation?

2. How could this situation have been avoided?

3. What approaches to resolving this conflict are appropriate?

4. What are some things that, if done, would make this approach successful?

5. What are some things to avoid when attempting to resolve this conflict? Why?

You are a member of a new product development team in a *Fortune* 500 firm. Management has put a lot of pressure on the team to be innovative (after all, it's part of the company vision published for shareholders and others to see), but all that ever seems to happen at the team meetings is a lot of yelling, name-calling, fighting, put-downs, and arguing. The marketing folks believe the engineers don't truly understand what the customer wants. The manufacturing folks are upset that they're never asked whether the product can be manufactured and maintained relatively easily—until after the product is designed and accepted by management. Then, there are the finance folks; all they ever seem to care about is the bottom line. Will we ever be able to complete our task? Is it even possible to be innovative when no one seems to value what anyone else has to say?

1. What is your immediate reaction to the scenario? How would you feel if you were a member of the team writing about this situation?

2. How could this situation have been avoided?

3. What approaches to resolving this conflict are appropriate?

4. What are some things that, if done, would make this approach successful?

5. What are some things to avoid when attempting to resolve this conflict? Why?

**Exercise 11–D
Declining Sales:
A Role-Play**

Visions Medical Equipment is a North American distributor of high-end CAT scan, MRI, ultrasound, x-ray, and mammography equipment. Lately, business has not been good, leading to potential conflict between a salesperson and a buyer.

In groups of three, decide who will be the salesperson, the buyer, and the observer. After reading the information for the two roles (provided by your instructor), engage in a conversation with the goal of resolving the conflict. Following the role-play, the observer should lead the conversation using the questions below.

- What strategies were used?
- What attitudes were depicted?
- What worked and why?
- What didn't and why?

**Exercise 11–E
Humpty Dumpty's
Spaceship Challenge**

In teams of three to six, create a spaceship for Humpty Dumpty (an egg) that can withstand the gravitational forces that occur during a three-foot drop. The spaceship that withstands the highest drop will be the winner. If there is a tie, then the winner will be the spaceship fabricated out of the greatest number of materials. Each spaceship must be fabricated out of at least three materials. Each team only has possession of one material, so you will need to negotiate with other teams to acquire new materials.

Your team will have 10 minutes to plan your spaceship design. Decide what material your spaceship will be made from and determine which teams you will need to negotiate with for materials.

Next, your team will have 20 minutes to negotiate for material and construct the spaceship. Negotiate as effectively as you possibly can; use any strategies or tactics.

Questions

1. Before approaching your opponents, how did you prepare for the negotiation process?
2. Did you use the same conflict-handling styles for all opponents that you negotiated with? Explain.
3. In this situation, which conflict-handling styles were most successful? Why?
4. Did every negotiation work out exactly as you planned and hoped? Why or why not?
5. What factors helped you in the negotiation process? What could you have done differently to make your negotiations more successful?
6. In performing this exercise, what lessons did you learn about negotiation? How does this exercise relate to negotiations in the "real world"?

Source: Used with permission of the author, Kim Eddleston, Associate Professor at Northeastern University. This exercise was presented at the 2000 Eastern Academy of Management/Experiential Learning Association Conference.

**Exercise 11–F
Who Is Responsible? A
Conflict Exercise**

Please read the following story and assign your rankings to the question below, "Who is most responsible?"

Susan came from a small town in South Carolina where her widowed father was an evangelical Christian minister. He raised her very strictly, and it was only with great reluctance that he allowed her to come to USC in Columbia to attend college. He feared that the big city would corrupt her morals. As she boarded the bus, he warned her, "If I ever find out that you've been fooling around with boys or using alcohol or drugs, I'll cut you off from all financial support and never let you enter our home again."

Susan had always obeyed her father and intended to do so while at college. She did stay away from drugs and alcohol, but in October she began dating Larry, a fellow student in her religion class. By December they were sleeping together. When she returned from Christmas vacation, she discovered that she was pregnant. Since neither her father nor the private church-affiliated schools she attended ever mentioned birth control, she had not taken the proper precautions.

Larry did not want to get married, and Susan knew that when her father came to take her home in May the pregnancy would be obvious. Panic-stricken, she decided to have an abortion. She went to one of the agencies that advertised help for unwanted pregnancies in the *Gamecock*. At the agency she learned that an abortion would cost her $500. Knowing that she could not earn this sum in time, she asked Larry for a loan. "I'm sorry, but I don't have that kind of money," he replied. "Besides, you should have been more careful."

Then she asked her best friend Allison for the money. "I don't approve of abortions," Allison said. "I can't lend you money to destroy life."

In desperation, Susan approached one of the dorm-cleaning ladies for help, who was rumored to be an ex-prostitute. "Sure. I've got a concoction that will make you miscarry—no charge," said the woman.

After taking the mixture, Susan did miscarry, but in the process she hemorrhaged severely and died.

Who is most responsible? Rate each of the characters according to their responsibility for Susan's death. Identify the least responsible as #6 and the most responsible as #1; do not use any number more than once.

_____ Susan   _____ Agency Head

_____ Susan's Father   _____ Allison

_____ Larry   _____ The Cleaning Lady

Next, each group of participants should discuss the case and arrive at a group ranking for each of the six characters. Your instructor will provide more information.

After the group finishes, they should discuss:

1. What was the process and/or decision rule/s used to complete the group ranking?

2. Were they able to complete the task? Why or why not?

3. How does the group feel about the results?

4. Did everyone get a say? Did some individuals monopolize the conversation? Did other individuals mediate the conversation?

5. In what ways could this group ranking activity have been handled more effectively? Why?

Source: The story is based on the original exercise "The Drawbridge" (author unknown) and is available from http://www.theasca.org/attachments/wysiwyg/1/6-2B.pdf (accessed July 31, 2010).

Exercise 11–G
Psychological Safety

Please complete the grid below and answer the questions that follow.

	How safe do I feel expressing true opinions? (Safety will vary by issue.)	Why? Have I been "burned" before?	How does this level of safety affect the health of my relationship?
To/among my closest friend/s?			
To/among my classmates?			
Among my team?			
In the classroom?			
In my workplace?			
To my siblings?			
To my parents?			
To my significant other?			

1. What patterns do you see (friends v. family v. co-workers/classmates)?

_____

_____

_____

2. How does your dominant conflict management style influence your beliefs about psychological safety?

_____

_____

_____

3. How much can one issue's "riskiness" affect your belief about the riskiness of expressing your true opinions or beliefs on different issues?

_____

_____

_____

4. What steps might you take to check your assumptions about the psychological safety of certain relationships, settings, or issues?

_____

_____

_____

5. Targeting one specific relationship, setting, or issue, in what ways might revised assumptions about psychological safety benefit you?

_____

_____

_____

Exercise 11–H
Having Difficult
Conversations

As discussed, most people avoid conflict and put off having difficult conversations—even with loved ones and close friends. Think about a recent situation that left you feeling anger, resentment, or frustration toward someone with whom a close relationship is important to have and keep. Use the worksheet below to plan the conversation _you need to have_ with him or her. Consider recruiting someone you trust to role-play the conversation with you; this will give you greater comfort and confidence for the real conversation . . . which you will have within the next few weeks.

1. What do I hope to accomplish?

_____

_____

_____

2. What would be an ideal outcome?

_____

_____

_____

3. What assumptions am I making about his or her intentions?

_____

_____

_____

4. What triggered my negative reaction? In what ways might it have to do with how I view things?

_____

_____

_____

5. How will I reframe the conversation so that I can expect a positive result rather than focus on the difficulty?

_____

_____

_____

6. What will I say first, second? What words should I try to avoid?

_____

_____

_____

Exercise 11–I
Reflection/Action Plan

This chapter focused on conflict management—what it is, why it is important, and how to improve your skills in this area. Complete the worksheet below upon completing all reading and experiential activities for this chapter.

1. The one or two areas in which I am most strong are:

_____

_____

_____

2. The one or two areas in which I need more improvement are:

_____

_____

_____

3. If I did only one thing to improve in this area, it would be to:

_____

_____

_____

_____

4. Making this change would probably result in:

_____

_____

_____

5. If I did not change or improve in this area, it would probably affect my personal and professional life in the following ways:

_____

_____

_____

_____

12 Achieving Business Results through Effective Meetings

Learning Points

How do I:

- Decide whether a meeting is necessary?
- Invite the appropriate people to a meeting?
- Choose an appropriate medium (face-to-face, virtual) for a meeting?
- Determine a clear goal and prepare an agenda that will keep team members on task during a meeting?
- Ensure that everyone is prepared for the meeting?
- Keep meetings running efficiently and effectively?
- Ensure that a team's next and future meetings will be effective?

Paul Atkins sold luxury new and preowned vehicles at a dealership on the East Coast. The money was pretty good, but there were some aspects of the job that always left him wondering what else he should do with his time and talents. One thing he hated was the hours—salespeople were typically scheduled for a minimum of 50 hours per week. This was especially bothersome since many hours, if not days, would go by with not a single customer walking in the showroom. Added to the boredom was another problem—the Monday morning all-hands sales meeting.

Going to a meeting wouldn't be so bad if it was useful. But this was rarely, if ever, the case. Ted, the general sales manager, would seemingly decide what he would do for the half-hour meeting on his way in. Some weeks he couldn't decide on an objective for the meeting (or chose instead to play golf), and the meeting was canceled—without notice to anyone. Other weeks, most participants left feeling their time had been wasted. Paul, who sold only Mercedes and other European imports, would sit through videos on the Toyota Corolla—a car sold by the dealership next door, but owned by the same person. Other times, the meetings were focused on selling techniques, some of which were about as archaic as you can imagine. Yet everyone was required to be there, even salespeople who were off or not scheduled to begin their day until noon (the dealership was open 9 a.m. to 9 p.m. Monday through Friday and until 6 p.m. on Saturday).

When the European import dealership got its own sales manager (who reported to the general sales manager), the salespeople were relieved, believing that they would no longer have to waste their time at the Monday morning meetings. Unfortunately, that was not the case. In fact, the sales manager and the general sales manager frequently butted heads on this issue. After two successive weeks of last-minute meeting cancellations, the European import car staff decided enough was enough. They boycotted the meetings. Eventually, the general sales manager put pressure on the sales manager and made them attend.

1. Many organizations have standing meetings. What benefits could be obtained from these meetings?

2. What are some potential downsides of a standing meeting?

3. Who should be required to come to the "all-hands meeting"? If you answer "it depends," on what should this depend?

4. Assuming the general sales manager is unwilling to change this requirement, what would you recommend he do to improve the meetings?

5. When you rate a meeting you've attended as "useless" or just "bad," what characteristics of the meeting cause this rating?

6. When caught up in a "bad" meeting, what are some things you can do to improve the situation?

Meetings are an important part of the business world. Meetings occur within organizations and between members of different organizations, for example, customers and suppliers. Managers use meetings to share necessary information and to train and coordinate efforts of their employees. Project teams, either school- or work-based, use meetings to set objectives, allocate resources, make decisions, schedule individual components of complex projects, discuss project progress, share needed information and status reports to ensure all are "on the same page," and solve problems. Many firms and campuses now have the capability for virtual meetings, where members are not physically in the same place but are connected via video-conferencing technology or e-mail. In this chapter we discuss the importance of meetings, the how-tos of running effective meetings, and tips and suggestions for making the most of meetings. At the end of the chapter is a series of exercises and activities to help you assess and enhance your skill in running meetings.

The Importance and Benefits of Meetings

Meetings serve an important function. In the increasingly complex and competitive business environment, members of a team or organization need to be kept abreast of critical functional, political, technological, and legal issues facing the firm. This becomes especially important in an empowered and team-based environment. When more work and decision making are being spread to team members and employees at all levels of the organization, meetings are used to ensure that good decisions are made and that others are kept apprised of progress and problems.[1] The need for meetings typically increases as the number of teams and team-based projects increases.

Meetings are important in shaping organizational norms and improving work processes. Such was the case in Paul Atkins's car dealership; whether or not useful information was passed along, the standing meeting was a consistent means for ensuring that all salespeople would be in the same space at least once a week to take in and share information with one another and management. Companies that focus on continuous process improvement find meetings to be an excellent way to train managers and develop shared norms about how to behave and act.[2] Meetings also play a psychological role in organizations in that they help us fulfill a need to be part of a team.[3] Employees interviewed for a recent study reported that they enjoy the social interaction meetings provide, especially when working with others on certain problems.[4]

Let's Be Careful Out There[5]

Meetings, and the way they are held, can help determine the culture of a business. Since 1924, UPS has held daily Pre-Work Communications Meetings at the beginning of every shift. At these highly structured three-minute meetings—held at all 1,700 UPS centers worldwide—managers deliver important information before their drivers head out for the day: weather and road conditions, reminders about safety and customer service, and announcements like employee anniversaries. Implicitly, the meetings also help instill company values—particularly safety and efficiency—by reinforcing them on a daily basis.

Finally, meetings are important when members are involved in complex projects, with multiple deadlines and sets of objectives. The project meeting is an essential tool for keeping projects—and project team members—on track.[6] Most project groups, even those that are exceptionally organized and managed, function best with a regular series of contacts between group members.

Problems with Meetings

"A committee is twelve men doing the work of one man."

John F. Kennedy

This quote underscores a common question of both students and employees alike, namely, "Wouldn't it be easier to fly solo?" One study found that in the average eight-person committee, each individual member wished that three of the other seven weren't there.[7] And according to a *Harvard Business Review* study, the average executive spends three and a half hours weekly in formal committee meetings and at least a day each week in informal meetings and consultations.[8] Some suggest this figure is understated—that meetings take up more than half of executives' working hours.[9] As you climb higher on the corporate ladder, meetings become more frequent and lengthier.[10] A survey of middle managers showed the top three reasons for failed meetings: they get off subject, they lack agendas or goals, and they last too long.[11]

A big cause of ineffective or useless meetings is the lack of preparation and planning. How many times have you walked into a meeting having no idea what the meeting was about or why it was called? Perhaps it's a standing meeting, as in the case of the all-hands meeting at the car dealership. Perhaps you have a general idea of what to expect; after all, it's always been done this way. For example, such a meeting may present the weekly status report, provide a pep talk, or communicate the sales objective. In either case, meetings are doomed to fail when participants (and the person calling the meeting) neither know what to expect nor what to prepare for a meeting.

Have you ever come to a meeting only to find it's been canceled, rescheduled, or moved to another room? What if the goal of the meeting is to discuss complicated technical information, yet no one received any reports or documentation ahead of time? Valuable time is wasted getting individuals up to speed. More time is wasted when the goal of the meeting—plus any previous decisions made—is not clearly communicated. If you walk into a meeting and can't answer the question "Why am I here?" within the first few minutes, this meeting will probably not be optimal. Meeting because you've always met may not be a sufficient reason. What is the point of meeting? What do you want attendees to think, do, or feel as a result of the meeting?[12] If there is simple information to transmit to a group of employees, a meeting may not be the best use of everyone's time. For example, if human resources decides to add another provider to the list of HMOs currently available through employees' health benefits plan, this information is one-way[13] and could be transmitted easily via a written or electronic memo. If, however, human resources is leading a charge to modify the current performance appraisal and merit pay system toward one that accounts for not only individual performance but also individuals' contributions in the many teams in which they work, a memo would likely be insufficient.

Meetings may be unnecessary and even costly, in terms of employees' time and productivity taken away from other tasks and objectives. The car dealership's Monday morning meeting is likely not cutting into the actual selling process, as more car sales occur in the evenings and weekends. However, as we learned, Paul (and his colleagues) finds these meetings a waste of time due to the lack of planning or clear goals, occasional last-minute cancellations, and irrelevant information shared. In this situation, actual productivity (i.e., lost sales) may not be affected; however, the reduced morale that appears to be growing may indirectly affect productivity when employees feel their time is being wasted. Whether everyone's (e.g., the car dealership's standing meeting) or just a few employees' (e.g., a team project with seemingly too many members) presence is unnecessary at a meeting, it can be frustrating.

Has This Ever Happened to You?[14]

You arrive at your workplace on Monday morning. Opening your e-mail, you notice a message from your boss's boss entitled, "Critical meeting this afternoon." The body of the e-mail is as follows: "I know this is late notice, but I need you to attend this meeting. Do whatever you can to free up your schedule." Before the signature block, your boss's boss lists the exact time, as well as the building and room number where the meeting will be held. You can see who else received the invitation, but you only know one other person on the list. What do you do?

Finally, the sheer fact that by definition, meetings involve more than one person, raises the potential for inefficiency and ineffectiveness. Simply put, work becomes more complicated when you have to interact with others. You're probably not alone if you've felt that you could do the work assigned to your group more easily alone than as one of five or six people working together on a project.

There are several explanations for this.

- First, there's the issue of interpersonal dynamics. When we work with others, our uniqueness—work style, personality, preferences, values, and attitudes—often clashes with the unique traits of others. Others may have important information to offer, but if they're combative, overly analytical, or just plain critical, you might prefer they just send the needed information via interoffice mail.

- Second, the more people involved in making a decision, especially a consensus decision, the more time it takes. Despite the benefit of others' input and the existence of **synergy**—the belief that two heads are better than one[15]—some wonder whether the costs (individuals' time and energy) overshadow the benefits.

- Third, there may be redundancies of people and effort. Someone might wonder, "If other members of my group are represented, why must I be here too?"

These three reasons underlie why meetings are the source of frustration and loss of work time[16]—an increasingly valuable resource. In one study, 70 percent of American executives surveyed considered many of the meetings they attend to be a waste of time.[17]

Given the preponderance of poorly planned and executed meetings, it is easy to see why many view meetings as a necessary evil. Not surprisingly, the lack of a clear objective or purpose is a main reason for failed meetings, as evidenced by 89 percent of American executives who blame meeting failure on lack of proper planning and organization.[18]

If managed effectively, however, meetings can be useful for dispensing or gathering information, building morale, making decisions, engaging in creative brainstorming, and encouraging group action.[19] As much as we might want to be left alone to do our work, many of us appreciate being in the fold—knowing what's going on and being involved in decisions and problem-solving efforts. Meetings don't have to be a waste of time or necessarily evil. By learning a few principles and practicing several techniques, meetings can be more efficient, productive, and possibly even enjoyable.

Strategies for Effective Meetings

Before the Meeting

The first principle in running effective meetings is clarifying the purpose. Whether or not a meeting should be held depends on the goal to be achieved. Employee input should be sought, and discussions—at multiple levels and parts of the organizations—need to occur.

Clarify the Purpose of the Meeting

Legitimate purposes for calling a meeting include generating ideas for a project, discussing the pros and cons of potential solutions to a problem, gaining employee input and buy-in for a program or company point of view, or deciding on a strategy or course of action.[20] By clarifying the purpose or goal of a potential meeting, you will be able to determine whether the objective could be accomplished just as easily in a memo, e-mail, or article in the weekly newsletter. Consider whether the potential benefits of getting members together outweigh the costs.[21] One way to approach this analysis is to estimate the value of the results you or your organization wants to obtain. If a result has no value, why spend time working on it? Then design an agenda that produces a positive return on your investment of time and resources. For example, if you are working on an issue worth $1,000, you may want to spend less than $500 resolving it.[22]

Collegial or Competitive?

Sometimes the purpose of a meeting can be to create a sense of collegiality, particularly when people do not often get an opportunity to interact. After a meeting has gone particularly well, probably because there was a clear sense of purpose and the objectives were achieved, there is often a desire to talk informally before leaving the room, or an opportunity for everyone to talk about what is going on in their lives or work. Sometimes, however, this can be taken too far, as revealed by Professor Stanley Fish, discussing department meetings: "Sometimes at the end of a meeting, you're given a chance to indulge in some mild boasting and cheerleading. You go around the table and everyone announces an award that a colleague has won or a book that has been published or a grant that has been financed . . . but inevitably a few people go on too long, display too many 'trophies' and generally hog the stage, with the result that (potential) good feelings give way to jealousy, irritation, envy and all the other base emotions always seething just below the surface. . . . The effect is the opposite of what was hoped for—not collegiality but competitiveness."[23]

Evaluate whether a meeting should be held based on its stated purpose. Even if this evaluation is made, don't assume that invitees know the purpose unless it has been clearly articulated before (and clarified during) a meeting. To say, "to have our all-staff sales meeting," is not clear enough, especially when this is a standing meeting. Without a clear understanding of why there's a meeting and how they can contribute, employees waste time contemplating the purpose and reason for being at a meeting instead of doing their normal work. Moreover, some purposes don't make sense depending on the participants' roles in the organizations. For example, salespeople who compete against each other for commissions and bonuses are unlikely to make effective contributions to a "sharing best practices" meeting. It would be like asking magicians to explain how they do their tricks! Purposes that are clear and appropriate decrease the likelihood of meandering and suspiciously silent conversations. To ensure a successful meeting, decide on a clear, achievable task[24] and communicate it before the meeting begins—both in the meeting invitation and at the start of the meeting. This task should support a project or task team's overall objective, which could come from management, the team members, or a combination thereof.

Four General Types of Meetings

- **Information Sharing**—Several or all members share information that has been gathered or report on group or individual progress. For example, a team designing a new minivan may include members from engineering, manufacturing, marketing, quality assurance, and legal. Subcommittees tasked with specific goals (e.g., to gather data on consumer satisfaction or to administer quality tests) may be asked to update the rest of the team on their findings to assure the group that the subcommittees are on track as well as to furnish the entire group with information needed for group decisions. These meetings tend to be relatively short, in that the purpose is to share information and not to solve problems or make decisions.

- **Information Dissemination**—Critical information is shared with members. Typically, such information is too important for a memo and may require more in-depth explanation or discussion, as in the case of introducing a new reward system. Information dissemination meetings focus primarily on relaying information to the members or employees, with some time allocated to address the audience's questions and ensure that they have a full and clear understanding of the information.

- **Problem Solving/Decision Making**—Employees or members are assembled to solve a problem or make a decision. In contrast with the information dissemination meeting, a problem-solving meeting typically requires full participation of all members present, particularly if the outcome or disposition of the problem affects them. You might also include subject matter experts—those who have specific knowledge in a related area but may not be a member of the group that is meeting. Because of the time needed to make well-informed, consensus decisions, it's important to carve out sufficient time for this type of meeting. Decision-making meetings require more time than information-sharing meetings.

- **Symbolic/Social**—Employees celebrate a special event or managers share recognition for a job well done. When long-time or key employees retire, for example, it would be appropriate to invite those people with whom they have worked to recognize the retiree's contributions publicly. Or perhaps one of the customer service teams just completed one year of complaint-free service. A meeting or social event may be just the thing to recognize this accomplishment. Finally, meetings could be valuable when social interactions are needed and encouraged. One example is the holiday meeting or party. Another example is the case when two firms merge. It would be easy for each firm to continue operating autonomously (while gossiping about "the other guys" behind closed doors). However, if one of the reasons behind the merger is to gain synergy, it behooves the merged firm to encourage the kind of interaction that will increase trust and lead to cooperation among employees of the previously separate firms.

Choose the Type of Communication Mechanism for the Meeting

After clarifying the purpose of the meeting, the next step is to pick the most appropriate type and vehicle or communication mechanism. Traditionally, members of a team, department, or organization would converge on a single location to communicate information, exchange ideas, make decisions, or solve organizational problems. Thanks to the expanded capability and availability of Internet and wireless technologies, people from all parts of the organization and world can be efficiently and effectively connected—anytime and anywhere—in **virtual meetings**. The goal is what should drive the meeting type and approach. For example, an information sharing or dissemination meeting can be accomplished face-to-face or virtually, via an Internet-based, phone, or video conference. Electronic or hard copies of relevant materials can be sent in advance of such a meeting. Even a problem-solving meeting can be held virtually if appropriate electronic meeting and decision-making tools are used. As the accompanying box shows, the one type of meeting that requires face-to-face attendance from most if not all attendees is the symbolic/social meeting. All meetings should have a goal, and when the goal is to build trust and a sense of community, there is no substitute for face-to-face interaction.

Virtual Meetings in Mrs. Fields[25]

Mrs Fields Famous Brands numbers globally more than 950 stores. These stores—Mrs. Fields Cookies and TCBY frozen yogurt—are operated by several hundred franchisees. You can imagine the challenge to communicate with so many employees and franchisees. Previously, the CEO communicated with field teams, but he felt that this did not engage enough people and wanted to expand the number of people he engaged with. What he needed was a tool that created two-way communication. AdobeConnect allows the CEO to hold weekly meetings between himself, the executive team, and 150 corporate employees who are located in the field as well as in corporate offices. This two-way communications tool ensures that while the CEO can present the latest news, executive teams can talk about business unit updates, and the conversation is broadened to discussing store openings, opportunities, and events. Employees can also ask questions of the CEO and team, developing a far stronger engagement and understanding of the company's *big picture*.

Mrs. Fields also uses webinars to communicate directly with franchisees, supplementing the 16 regional face-to-face meetings that take place twice a year with webinars. These feature the CEO and other top executives and can be accessed in real-time on mobile phones, computers, or tablets by franchisees. Employees can also access the recording if they can't participate during the session.

Virtual meetings have created more frequent and direct communication between executives and staff, and executives and dispersed franchisees. They have also saved money by reducing travel time and costs, and seen innovations spread across franchisees more quickly, strengthening Mrs. Fields' competitiveness.

Increasingly, organizations are making use of electronic and wireless technologies to help their members find, create, manage, and distribute information quickly and inexpensively. For some organizations, these technologies complement face-to-face meetings, as in the case of team members who share information effectively and efficiently via e-mails, faxes, and phone calls between meetings. Others, like Microsoft, Verifone, and Cisco Systems, rely heavily on the use of virtual teams and meetings. Three technologies that enable teams to meet and work virtually are discussed next.

Teleconferencing: The ability to include multiple members in a meeting via telephone has been around for a long time. The simplest teleconference, available on most public and private phones, is three-way calling, which allows three people to talk simultaneously on one call. In the business setting, teleconferencing might involve a majority of members sitting and meeting around a table while the members unable to attend in person are "patched in" via a phone strategically placed in the middle of the desk. In other cases, when most or all members of a team are in different locations, a particular technology enables conference phone calls to accommodate from a few up to hundreds of individuals. In still other, more remote locations, teleconferencing is accomplished using a two-way radio system or satellite connections. While Internet access is prevalent in medium and large cities, the "digital divide" still exists. Telephone-based conferencing levels the playing field and allows for the widest audience to participate in teleconferenced, virtual meetings. Not surprisingly, research estimates the market for audio conferencing services exceeded $4 billion worldwide in 2012.[26] Several teleconferencing services are available on the Internet. You can check out www.conferencecall.com, www.freeconference.com, or teleconference.liveoffice.com to learn more.

Electronic Messaging or Chatting: Several free and inexpensive Internet-based platforms facilitate synchronous (at the same time) and asynchronous communication and collaboration. There are many messaging services available on computers, tablets, and mobile phones. ICQ (icq.com) was one of the first instantaneous messaging/chat services. Back in 2004, "more than 400 million messages were sent and received every day."[27] Yahoo (yahoo.com) offers a free service that enables individuals with shared interests to join a group (or form one of their own) to share information, photos, documents, and messages. Apple's iMessage offers free instant messaging for users of Apple's different platforms including iPads, computers, and iPhones to communicate with each other. WhatsApp and Viber are other free mobile-based messaging services. Social network sites such as Facebook also have chat functions. Estimates in 2013 suggest that at least 6 billion SMS messages are sent every day in the United States alone and over 8.6 trillion worldwide each year.[28]

Colleges and universities are making use of these tools for their classes. Programs such as WebCT and Blackboard have functions that enable student groups to meet virtually to share files, transmit e-mails, and have real-time electronic chats to facilitate completing projects.

Video- and Web-Conferencing: Until recently, only very resource-rich organizations could afford the technology to have group videoconferences among employees or between employees and clients in different locations. A special room equipped with a video camera and screen (and a specialist to run the equipment) was required for these meetings, which, while cheaper than flying in employees from different locations, was not inexpensive. Organizations that could not afford this technology (such as that used in the Tandberg system) could use the services of commercial concerns, such as Kinko's, for example, on a fee-per-service basis. This has changed in the last few years, particularly with the availability of Internet-based options. All that's needed for videoconferencing is a set of low-cost webcams that plug into the USB ports of PCs (or are integrated into them) and a Web-based video service such as Skype (www.skype.com) or ooVoo (www.oovoo.com).

More recently, web-based meeting services are becoming even more popular in organizations. Providers include WebEx (www.webex.com), GoToMeeting (www.gotomeeting.com), and AdobeConnect (www.adobe.com). These low-cost programs allow up to a certain number of users in different locations to join a live webconference. These services can also be used for training, e-learning, seminars (webinars), and for recording large meetings for participants who are not able to attend. Web-based conferencing technologies don't just let you talk and view other meeting participants, they also include online presentation capabilities, document sharing, and messaging/chat functions. This means that participants can actively discuss and work on documents during the meeting as though they were in the same room. In addition, one of the more sophisticated online learning platforms—Centra Symposium—allows all this plus the ability for smaller subgroups to work in breakout "rooms" and then be brought back into the main "room" to integrate the subgroups' outputs.

While not without its challenges and drawbacks, the use of these technologies to facilitate the virtual meetings has several advantages:

- *Saving time and costs.* Employees need to spend time or money traveling to and from a face-to-face meeting. As the physical distance between employees grows, so do the savings realized from virtual technologies. One study of the pharmaceutical industry reported that "a full-service e-meeting costs about one-fifth as much as a traditional on-site meeting. A single e-meeting typically yields savings in the range of $125,000 to $200,000. Across a large research program, savings can amount to $5 million to $10 million annually."[29]

- *Recruiting and retaining talent.* Increasingly, organizations are offering alternative work arrangements such as flexible work schedules, telecommuting, and part-time or temporary work to appeal to the most talented and mobile employees—a trend that information and communication technologies have enabled.[30]

- *Extending opportunities.* Technology enables businesses to utilize talented employees whose temporary or permanent physical challenges preclude them from standard working arrangements.

- *Drawing from a larger labor pool.* This is especially true as organizations use formal (e.g., merger) and informal (e.g., networked) arrangements to create organizational relationships that cross regional and national boundaries.[31]

- *Gaining access to subject matter experts and consultants.* Without these technologies, teams would have a more difficult time finding and obtaining needed support from internal or external experts or consultants.[32]

- *Providing quicker responses to changing customer requirements or managerial needs.* These technologies enable a team to meet (virtually) as soon as an issue arises, as opposed to waiting until logistical arrangements can be worked out.

- *Reducing the influence of demographic and status differences.* In the absence of face-to-face communication, members are less self-conscious about their own status (e.g., minority, female, too young) and less likely to self-censor when sharing opinions (particularly unpopular ones), fears, and concerns.[33] This also allows for an open and thorough approach to group decision making and problem solving, as opposed to one that is dominated by those whose hierarchical status or physical characteristics allow them to impose their will on, or unknowingly shut down, others.

Do's and Don'ts for Video and Web Conferencing[34]

Virtual meetings have a different dynamic than face-to-face meetings. Here are some Do's and Don'ts:

Do be courteous to other participants.
Do speak clearly.
Do keep body movements minimal.
Do move and gesture slowly and naturally.
Do maintain eye contact by looking into the camera.
Do dress professionally.
Do make the session animated.

Don't make distracting sounds.
Don't shout.
Don't make distracting movements.
Don't interrupt other speakers.
Don't carry on side conversations.
Don't wear "noisy" jewelry.
Don't cover the microphone.

Virtual meetings should not be considered a substitute for face-to-face meetings. In fact, research shows that teams benefit greatly from face-to-face meetings, particularly in the beginning of a team's existence when building trust and creating group cohesion and commitment is critical to the team's success.[35] *Wall Street Journal* reporter Sue Shellenbarger noted that despite the increasing popularity of telecommuting, some companies are beginning to rethink this. Intel, AT&T, Hewlett Packard, and the federal government report that they still support having employees telecommute; however, concerns over security, needs for consolidating operations, and the need "to keep the team spirit strong . . . [with] face-to-face interaction" has prompted some changes.[36] Practitioners and researchers alike continue to study the benefits and challenges of virtual teams, virtual meetings, and telecommuting employees; the findings of these programs and studies will provide managers with guidance on whether and how to implement such tools in their organizations.

On the Leading Edge of Technology[37]

A Microsoft research project into 3D telepresence technology may soon become an official product. The Viewport research project was unveiled in April 2012 and uses color and infrared cameras and projectors to construct a 3D hologram of a remote user to enable face-to-face meetings. This technology would be extended to Skype, allowing consumers to enjoy "high-definition communication" in its voice and video calling software.

Decide Who Should Participate in the Meeting

After clarifying the purpose for and communication mechanism of a meeting, it is important to spend time considering who needs to be at a meeting. Whom do we invite? The answer: Those who can best contribute to the objective.[38] Returning to our opening case, if all you are planning to do is show a video and hand out updated brochures, perhaps all 40 salespeople should come. But if the purpose of the meeting is to get employees to generate creative ideas, 40 may be too many people. For this type of activity, the optimal size would be between 5 and 7, and no more than 10.[39] Breaking up the group into four or five smaller groups, or having several smaller meetings, may better serve your purpose.

What if your top salesperson can't attend the meeting? Should you have the meeting anyway? If part of the meeting is being used to share and discuss sales tips and techniques, it might be best to postpone the meeting or, if deemed necessary and cost-effective, use video-conferencing to include a key person if he or she is in a different location.

What about support staff and people from a business function such as finance? Again, this depends on the purpose and intended benefit for those who attend. If the receptionist is interested and feels he can contribute based on his experience with call-in customers, perhaps support staff should come. Multiple perspectives can help; they can also lead to communication challenges. Other considerations in answering the "whom to invite" question are organizational politics, need for objectivity, and potential for problems.[40]

Sometimes individuals are invited to meetings for political reasons, for instance, because they hold a particular title or have access to other important individuals in the organization. However, their presence could stifle lower-level employees' creativity. Evaluate the trade-off and consider whether a one-on-one meeting with the politically connected individual would do the trick.

Another consideration is the need for objectivity. Sometimes it is effective, depending on the meeting's purpose, to have outsiders come to the meeting. While they might not be directly affected by the meeting's outcome, they may be able to offer valuable, unbiased, and novel perspectives to the group. Finally, consider potential problems that may result from or during the meeting. For example, consider the company "troublemakers." These are the individuals who have a knack for stirring up the pot needlessly or turning every issue into a power struggle. Perhaps their perspective is valuable, but the way in which they share it is not. If possible, you might want to exclude these persons from the meeting, but schedule a time to meet with them one-on-one.

"I've called this meeting to discuss absenteeism."

Source: Reprinted with permission, www.businesscartoonshop.com.

Inviting the right people—those who have a stake in the outcome or who own the problem, those affected by the outcome, subject matter experts, problem solvers, and idea people[41]—helps ensure that the purpose is served and time-wasting diversions are minimized. For example, if you suspect that the meeting's objective and discussion centers on financial impacts, you might invite representatives from accounting or finance meet with them in advance to gain insight into their attitudes, opinions, or hidden agendas.[42] In addition, it is a good idea to know the participants ahead of time. If you know that Mary in accounting has experience in a particular industry and that her insights would be valuable if shared, you can plan when and how to solicit that input should she not share without prodding.

Develop a Plan for the Meeting

Next, develop plans that will ensure the success of the meeting. First, create and distribute an **agenda** or specific plan for the meeting. The meeting agenda (see Figure 12–1 for a sample) clarifies the goal and lists the points of discussion and their priority for the meeting. A well-defined agenda spells out the tasks, estimated time allocated to each task, the decisions to be made, and expected outcomes or deliverables.[43] It also includes logistical information, such as where and when the meeting will be held and the roles individuals will play.

Circulating a specific agenda to invitees prior to the meeting is important, but it's also important to be flexible about potential changes. By soliciting their input on potential additions or modifications to the agenda, you reinforce that invitees can and should contribute to the goal of the meeting and increase their ownership in the meeting's purpose and their commitment to collaborate with others to achieve it.

In planning the meeting and preparing the agenda, decide on a time and place that is likely to suit the schedules and needs of the invited participants. If manufacturing is typically busy with month-end inventory, it might be best to wait a week, if possible, to ensure that manufacturing can and will participate in a meeting in which their input is necessary. If you are planning a lengthy planning or team-building meeting, for example a half-day or full-day session, you might want to consider having the meeting at another location to minimize distraction and interruptions. Based on the purpose of the meeting, select a site that has adequate space, visual tools, and resources (e.g., copy machine, clerical staff). Select a temperature (a little cooler is better than too warm), seating arrangement (discussions are best when all participants can see one another), and schedule (i.e., include breaks and beverages) that will facilitate lively participation.[44] Include specific directions and a meeting location phone number to ensure that everyone makes the meeting—and on time. After all the arrangements

**Figure 12–1
Sample Agenda**

Start and End Time: _____

Place: _____

Stage one (# of minutes): _____

- (Optional: 5 minutes of unstructured socializing)
- Clarify objective
- Agenda overview, goal/s clarification
- Introduction of members, facilitator, and guest

Stage two (# of minutes): _____

- Review and/or acceptance of last meeting's minutes
- Review of roles for today's meeting
  - Facilitator—
  - Timekeeper—
  - Scribe—
  - Other—
- Continuing business
  - Progress reports from committees, etc.
  - Activity goals and deadlines
- New business
  - Information to be shared
  - Decisions to be made

Stage three (# of minutes): _____

- Briefly summarize meeting
- Review accomplishments

Stage four (# of minutes): _____

- Process check
- Preparation for the next meeting; review:
  - Action items and responsible parties
  - Roles (e.g., facilitator, timekeeper)
  - Next meeting's time, place, and agenda
- Future meeting (issues to be discussed/decisions to be made)

are made, the person making the invitations can ensure that invited participants are available at that particular time without waiting for return e-mails or phone calls. **Calendaring**—the ability to check a colleague's schedule or add meetings to his or her calendar—is now a standard feature in Microsoft Outlook, which is used in many organizations.[45]

During the Meeting

"Be sincere . . . be brief . . . be seated."

Theodore Roosevelt

Pay Attention to Process

When you preside over a meeting, your role is to make the discussion lively, proactive, creative, and focused. To make this happen, think of the meeting as a collection of tasks or services—communicating, facilitating, documenting[46]—and consider who can assist you in performing those services. The more you do to control the meeting, the more other participants will look to you for this control. Instead, encourage the participants to take an active part in contributing to and controlling the meeting. You can do this in many ways during the meeting. To simplify matters, we divide the meeting into four stages, as shown in the meeting process flowchart that follows.[47]

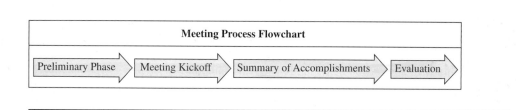

1. The **preliminary or initial phase.** In the first few minutes of the meeting, clearly articulate the meeting purpose and objectives. Then proceed with a general overview of the agenda to set the tone and give members a feel for how the meeting will be conducted. Next, explain why the participants were selected and invited to the meeting. These three steps help establish clear expectations for what will occur.[48] If members do not know one another, briefly allow members to introduce themselves and the department for which they work. In some organizations, meetings begin with up to five minutes of unstructured socializing time. Doing this gets our natural tendency to chat out of the way (we are, after all, social beings), right away. It also helps build camaraderie and loosen up employees who tend to be shy or unlikely to share their views in a meeting.

2. **Meeting kickoff** or the heart of the meeting. If a group of individuals will be meeting on a regular basis, it is important that they establish **operating guidelines,** or the standard or set of norms to which they will be held, collectively. Operating guidelines are the rules of engagement for meetings and establish how meetings should be run, how members will interact, and what kind of behavior is acceptable.[49] A sample set of operating guidelines appears in Figure 12–2. While some of the guidelines may sound like common sense or common courtesy, the fact that the group collectively believes in and articulates the importance of starting and ending meetings on time and not interrupting others makes the implied explicit. It also gives members the ability to "call" each other on behaviors that violate the operating guidelines and therefore undermine the group's ability to effectively operate and achieve its goals. After the guidelines are created, post them where members can see them. By helping the group establish operating guidelines, you help create common expectations among members, encourage desirable behavior, and enhance the group's ability to be self-managing.[50] Good managers not only plan and run effective meetings, they also teach and encourage their employees to do the same.

Figure 12–2
Sample Operating
Guidelines

- We will use an agenda, timekeeper, and meeting leader for each meeting.
- Meetings will start on time (with a review of the agenda) and end on time (with a process check), unless the team agrees to extend the meeting.
- Team members who have been absent or tardy must take measures to "get up to speed."
- Team members will practice active listening.
- It is OK to address the inappropriate use of power by team members.
- A time-out can be called if the meeting is off track or otherwise ineffective.
- Items identified as sensitive will be kept confidential.
- Silence by team members indicates a need for further inquiry.
- The meeting's facilitator should remain neutral but may formally step out of the role to contribute to the discussion.

Encouraging individuals to perform meeting roles also facilitates self-management. Early in the meeting (or in the previous meeting), establish who will play which role—scribe, timekeeper, facilitator, or meeting leader. Typically, groups rotate these roles so that all members develop each of these skills. The recorder or scribe publicly takes notes—using a flip chart or whiteboard—on issues discussed, key decisions made, and action items assigned. The timekeeper keeps track of the time as it relates to the agenda and reminds the group when it is about to exceed the agreed-upon time allotment for a particular topic or discussion. The group should then decide whether the time should be extended (and for how long) or the discussion tabled for a future meeting. The meeting leader is tasked with keeping the discussion task oriented and in line with the agenda. The facilitator helps ensure that participation is balanced, communication is effective, and the process is smooth. Many problems are avoided when members take responsibility for using these meeting roles.[51]

The purpose of the meeting is what the team is attempting to accomplish. The process describes how members go about their task. Both are important. Do members yell and scream when they don't get their way? Do they belittle others who offer opposing views? Does the group go off on tangents, discussing items that are neither important nor on the agenda?

Some Meeting Process Suggestions

- *Encourage the clash of ideas, not personalities.* To do this, remind members that some behaviors are encouraged while others are not. Listening and supporting are preferred to talking too much (dominating) and criticizing. It's better to encourage discussion than to shut people down. Finally, rather than complain, members should pose solutions or engage in a discussion of pros and cons of alternatives. After hearing a proponent's views on a subject, ask for any other or opposing views.[52]

- *Maintain focus and stick to time frames.* When appropriate, stick to the agenda—it's the plan to which all members agreed. While there are times when unforeseeable issues arise between meetings and must be addressed at the meeting, it is important to bring the potentially divergent discussion to the attention of the group and check whether adjustments should be made. If the group decides that an issue is important but does not require immediate discussion, make use of a "parking lot" or a visual bin (such as a piece of newsprint on a blackboard) where issues are collected and stored for future use. Alternatively, you can ask the scribe to record the issue under "next meeting." By taking one of these steps, as opposed to just noting an issue's irrelevance, you demonstrate to the person who suggested that idea that it was heard, noted, is important to the group, and will be discussed in the next meeting or handled outside of the meeting.[53]

- *Consider using a "balanced dialogue" approach for a particular agenda item,* where everyone speaks for an agreed-upon equal length of time (enforced by a timekeeper and a stop watch). When someone's time ends, that's it. They must stop speaking, even if they are in the middle of a sentence. This gives everyone a fair chance to participate and makes meetings go faster.[54]

- *Publicly transcribe key points and decisions made during the meeting.* Doing so helps keep the meeting on track, ensures that decisions are not rehashed, and facilitates the clarification and questioning of important decisions made. This helps keep all members on the same page and assured that their views count as the team moves forward with their goals and tasks. The scribe can make good use of technology during and after the meeting by recording everyone's ideas on a laptop, with the entries appearing before the group either on a large monitor or projected onto the wall.[55] Doing so also makes the distribution of meeting notes or minutes almost instantaneous.

- *For more suggestions on improving the meeting process, see Chapter 13, "Facilitating Team Success."*

3. The **summary of accomplishments** or wrap-up stage. In this stage, the team leader—with the help of the scribe's notes—will review decisions made and summarize the key points discussed. This can be done during the meeting as you move through and complete agenda items, as well as near the end of the meeting. By summarizing each point before moving to the next item, you help ensure that everyone is in agreement, members remain focused, and the scribe takes clear meeting notes.[56] By summarizing at the end, you allow another opportunity for clarification or agreement, help bring closure to the meeting, and clarify the group's accomplishments. Knowing you've completed all or most of the agenda items often gives group members a sense of satisfaction.

4. **Evaluation** and closing remarks. This step is often missed in meetings and could negatively impact future meetings. First, determine whether the meeting objective has been met. One way to do this is by having members do a **process check.** Each person might share a comment or two on how she or he felt about what was accomplished and how it was accomplished. What did the team do well? For example, "We got through all our items, we kept focused, and we came to agreement on a tough issue." What can the team do better next time? One person may note that despite all that was accomplished, he felt his input wasn't valued when he was frequently interrupted. Another may note that the meeting lasted longer than the agreed-upon hour. When team members have an opportunity to air concerns like these, issues are more likely to be nipped in the bud before they escalate into full-blown conflicts. If the person who didn't feel valued didn't say so, and if no one else noticed and addressed the interrupting behavior, this person is likely to dislike the group, find ways to avoid coming to the meeting, or give the appearance that she or he is on track while secretly planning to sabotage the team's efforts. Process checks also tend to minimize the need for the meeting after the meeting. These are the impromptu, out-in-the-hallway, or in-the-bathroom exchanges in which real feelings and issues are discussed. Again, these processes may undermine the team's objective by weakening the trust and confidence members have in each other's ability and desire to achieve the objective.

   After the process check, plan the next meeting. While the discussion and decisions are fresh, decide what should be covered in the next meeting, as well as the logistics of when and where, and meeting roles. If parking lot items neither made it to the current or next meeting, capture their contents in a section of the agenda known as "future meetings" or "future action outside of these meetings." At this point, review the action items. Will there be sufficient time to complete them? Should resources be made available to the person who will take action? Bring closure to these items to ensure that members are sufficiently prepared for the next meeting.

After the Meeting and between Meetings

By following the tips and techniques we've shared, you're likely to plan and run meetings that are effective in accomplishing the objectives you've set. Follow-up after the meeting and before the next meeting is essential in maintaining effective meetings and active progress toward the group's goals.[57]

To maximize the group's effectiveness, consider implementing the following after-meeting or between-meeting strategies:

- Before the next meeting, *have the minutes* (a summary of key points and decisions) *and next meeting agenda typed up and distributed.* If possible, complete and send the meeting summary out the same day while it is fresh in everyone's mind.[58] This aids closure and ensures that members complete action items and are prepared for subsequent meetings. It also helps to call attention to such action items in the minutes in two places: first, as the action and responsibility party arise in the meeting discussion (e.g., "Do a price comparison on the three purchase options discussed. ACTION ITEM—SMITH"), and again with a complete list of all action items, responsible parties, and due dates summarized near the end of the minutes and before notice of the next meeting. Request that members review these immediately to ensure accuracy and again just before the next meeting to be prepared for and ready to contribute to the next meeting.

■ As appropriate, *send out checkpoint memos or e-mails,* especially if external team issues may impact the team's objective or ability to achieve the goals set. Offer support resources for responsible parties, such as whom they might contact or where they might get certain information.

■ Make sure members have *phone, fax, and e-mail lists of all members.* When things come up that may preclude someone's attendance, contacting other members of the team should be easy. Also, by having the list, members are able to contact others for clarification or assistance with action items.

■ If appropriate, *use the time between meetings to meet with individual members* to make sure they are clear about and committed to the goals of the team. Depending on the work or communication styles of some group members, it may be hard to gauge whether or not this is the case from their meeting behavior. Outside of the meeting you may get a different response. Depending on the experience level and track record of members, it may be necessary to ensure that action items are carried out. If not, offer assistance. Tread carefully, however. It is important to show members you trust them and have confidence in their abilities. Saying you do is not the same as showing it. If the individual comes to the next meeting without a completed action item, the lack of progress—for whatever reason—may deter the progress of the group. Talk to the person about this to make sure he or she understands the need to follow through on commitments made to the group so this doesn't happen again.

"OK, now that we all agree, let's all go back to our desks and discuss why this won't work."

Source: Copyright © Mark Anderson, Andertoons.com.

■ Minutes may not always be the best way to send out important information about a meeting. Perhaps the team can design a *meeting summary form* that meets its particular needs. It might include places in which to capture what tasks were decided on, who is going to do the tasks, and the deadlines for these tasks, as well as a running record of key points made throughout the meeting. If the form is simple to use, it may be possible to complete it during the meeting and make copies members can take with them upon departing the meeting. This process helps confirm everyone's responsibilities, clarifies assignments, and establishes accountability. Several commercially available personal organizers, such as FranklinCovey and Day-Timer, include meeting summary forms in their planners.

■ Be sure to *send meeting notes to those members who could not be present* and let them know of any action items they may have been assigned in their absence. Taking this important step helps those who missed the meeting get up to speed, provides them with a record of what was done, and lets everyone have equal access to the process.

■ *Have subcommittee meetings if necessary.* Remember, not all work needs to be done by every member of the team. In fact, this is rarely the case in effective teams given time and expertise constraints. Typically, a subcommittee may go off to develop a draft—a suggested process, a working set of objectives—as a starting point for other members' input and ideas. Using subcommittees can be a highly effective use of time and energy.

- *Track progress* against a milestone chart. The process checks can help you determine how the team is doing relative to its task. It can also uncover potential problems or deficiencies. By examining the trend of evaluations, you can strategize and plan for corrective action, if necessary, before the group gets irrevocably off course.

- *Keep key stakeholders informed* of team progress and setbacks. Perceptions of a team's effectiveness (or lack thereof) are not only impacted by whether and how they accomplish their objectives; they are also a function of how well informed those external to the process are kept.[59] In an environment where teaming and empowerment are the norm, it is easy to take the ball and run with it—and never inform others who may have a need to know. This may include other departments, top management, customers, or suppliers. By ensuring that communication flows freely within the team, as well as beyond the team's boundaries, perceptions and support of the team are likely to remain positive.

Other Helpful Meeting Hints

- *Write down the cost per minute of the meeting* (total all salaries of those present and divide by the number of participants) on a flip chart. This can have a focusing effect; it is an effective way to illustrate that time is money, so let's not waste either!

- *Announce the adjournment time right when the meeting starts.* This clearly informs participants how long they will need to focus and will help them adjust their comments to fit the schedule.[60]

- *Set rules for debate* if one is likely to ensue. For example, "No one can speak for more than five minutes," or "No one can speak twice until everyone who wants to speak has had a turn."[61] It's easy for a meeting to disintegrate into a one-person show or a case where "those who talk the longest and loudest win." By establishing these rules up front and encouraging all members to adhere to them, this problem is less likely to surface.

- *Try to schedule all internal meetings for 30 minutes or less,* unless a key decision must be made. This relatively short meeting period forces members to be prepared if they plan to accomplish anything and puts pressure on members to focus.[62]

- *Have a meeting standing up.* Researchers at the University of Missouri's College of Business and Public Administration found that meetings involving creativity and judgment held with members standing up were 34 percent shorter than those in which members were seated. They also found that the shorter, stand-up meeting resulted in the same quality of decisions and satisfaction with them.[63] Together, these findings suggest that shorter meetings may be more efficient and effective.

- *Follow preestablished timetables* unless the situation warrants change. Start and end the meeting on time, but be open to change if needed. If you run a tight ship but it runs aground, you have not achieved your objective. Be firm but flexible and get member input on proposed time changes.

- *Demonstrate management support and commitment to the team and its tasks.* Ask if you can come to team meetings periodically. Remove or reduce impediments (policies, individuals, insufficient resources) to show your commitment to a team's success. Provide the team with adequate time and logistical arrangements to have effective meetings.

- *Have fun.* When the goal of a meeting is for people to be creative and innovative, they need to loosen up to think in different ways to gain better perspectives.[64] To do this, encourage an off-site meeting and casual dress, have food, and intersperse activities (appropriate physical or experiential exercises) to lighten up the mood and reenergize the members.

Summary

So many people find meetings to be a waste of time. It's not surprising. If you've ever been in workplace meetings, or perhaps had meetings for a class project assignment, you're likely to agree. When done well, meetings can fulfill multiple, important purposes. When poorly planned and executed, meetings become the source of wasted time, humorous water cooler talk, and plain old misery. With so much to do in such little time, wasting time in useless meetings is not an option. Today's manager must be skillful not only at running meetings, but also in deciding whether a meeting is necessary. Planning is essential and can prevent many problems from occurring. If they do occur, you'll be better equipped to resolve these problems and help groups run their own effective meetings.

Key Terms and Concepts

Agenda	Problem-solving/decision-making meeting
Calendaring	Process check/meeting evaluation
Electronic messaging or chatting	Summary of accomplishments
Information-dissemination meeting	Symbolic/social meeting
Information-sharing meeting	Synergy
Meeting kickoff	Teleconferencing
Operating guidelines	Video- and web-conferencing
Preliminary or initial phase	Virtual meeting

Discussion Questions

1. Why is meeting preparation (agenda, purpose, etc.) so important?

2. Some feel that organizations have too many meetings. In your opinion, is this true?

3. We contend that the process is just as important as the outcome of the meeting. Do you agree or disagree, and why?

4. If you were the leader of a project group, what three things would you do before, during, and after each meeting to ensure its effectiveness?

5. If you wanted to increase the effectiveness of a meeting in which you were in attendance but not in charge, how would you contribute?

Endnotes

1. Frank Basil, "Advance Planning Is Key to Successful Meetings," *Indianapolis Business Journal* (March 13, 2000), p. 21.

2. Timothy J. Kloppenborg and Joseph A. Petrick, "Meeting Management and Group Character Development," *Journal of Management Issues* 11, no. 2 (Summer 1999), p. 166.

3. Mark T. Chen, "Project Meeting Cost Analysis," *AACE International Transactions* (2003).

4. Steven G. Rogelberg, Cliff Scott, and John Kello, "The Science and Fiction of Meetings," *MIT Sloan Management Review* 8, no. 2 (Winter 2007), pp. 18–21.

5. Cyrus Farivar, "How to Run an Effective Meeting," BNET/CBS Interactive Network, April 9, 2007; http://www.bnet.com/article/how-to-run-an-effective-meeting/61211 (accessed August 1, 2010).

6. Ibid.

7. Winston Fletcher, "The Meeting Game and How to Win," *Management Today* (December 1999), p. 32.

8. Ibid.

9. Charlie Hawkins, "First Aid for Meetings," *Public Relations Quarterly* (Fall 1997), pp. 33–36.

10. Fletcher, "Meeting Game."

11. Basil, "Advance Planning."

12. Farivar, "Effective Meeting."

13. Ibid.

14. Kristine L. Krueger, Ph.D., personal communication (July 2007).

15. Jan Smith, "If Meeting Is Necessary, at Least Keep It Controlled," *Sacramento Business Journal* (November 5, 1999), p. 42.

16. Becky Jones, Midge Wilier, and Judy Stoner, "A Meeting Primer: Tips on Running a Successful Meeting," *Management Review* (January 1995), p. 30.

17. Basil, "Advance Planning."

18. Ibid.

19. Ibid.

20. Hawkins, "First Aid."

21. Farivar, "Effective Meeting."

22. Steve Kay, "Good News! You Can Turn Your Meetings into Results," *The American Salesman* 44, no. 4 (April 1999), p. 13.

23. Stanley Fish, "Real Meetings," *The Chronicle of Higher Education* (January 9, 2004), http://chronicle.com/article/Real-Meetings/44740 (accessed on 16 June, 2013).

24. David Dunning, "Steer Clear of Pitfalls That Can Doom Meetings," *Puget Sound Business Journal* (January 21, 2000), p. 29.

25. www.adobe.com (accessed April 2013), http://www.images.adobe.com/www.adobe.com/content/dam/Adobe/en/customer-success/pdfs/mrs-fields-case-study.pdf.

26. Andy Nilssen and Alan D. Greenberg, "Ripe for Change: Three Factors Set to Transform Audio Conferencing," February 2013, Accessed November 11, 2013 at https://www.wainhouse.com/files/papers/wr-3-factors-audio-conf.pdf

27. "The ICQ Story," http://www.icq.com/info/icqstory.html (accessed July 17, 2007).

28. H. Kelly, "OMG, the Text Message Turns 20. But Has SMS Peaked?" CNN (December 2012), http://edition.cnn.com/2012/12/03/tech/mobile/sms-text-message-20 (accessed April 2013).

29. Bill Cooney, "Virtual Meetings Offer Solid Benefits for Investigators," *Pharmaceutical Executive* (April 2007), p. 16.

30. Paula Caproni, *Management Skills for Everyday Life: The Practical Coach,* 2nd ed. (Upper Saddle River, NJ: Pearson Prentice Hall, 2005).

31. Ibid.

32. Ibid.

33. L. Sproull and S. Kiesler, "Computers, Networks and Work," *Scientific American* 265, no. 3 (1999), pp. 116–23.

34. St Leo University Office of Information Technology, http://www.inc.com/guides/2010/12/5-tips-for-conducting-a-virtual-meeting_pagen_2.html (accessed April 2013).

35. For example, see Mike Dempster, "Team-building Key for Virtual Workplace," *Business Edge* 5, no. 27 (July 21, 2005); and L. L. Martins, L. L. Gilson, and M. T. Maynard, "Virtual Teams: What Do We Know and Where Do We Go from Here?" *Journal of Management* 30, no. 6 (2004), pp. 805–35.

36. Sue Shellenbarger, "Some Companies Rethink the Telecommuting Trend," *Wall Street Journal,* February 28, 2008, http://online.wsj.com/article/SB120416669485798807.html# (accessed August 1, 2010).

37. Matt Brian, "Microsoft Could Make 3D Skype Calls a Reality with New Meeting Tech," www.theverge.com (April 26, 2013; accessed May 6, 2013).

38. Hawkins, "First Aid."

39. Ibid.

40. Ibid.

41. Ibid.

42. Jones et al., "Meeting Primer."

43. Luis G. Flores and Janyce Fadden, "How to Have a Successful Strategic Planning Meeting," *Training and Development* (January 2000), p. 31.

44. Jones et al., "Meeting Primer."

45. "The Future of Business Meetings," http://www.allbusiness.com/technology/telecommunications-conferencing/12305-1.html (accessed July 31, 2010).

46. Stacey R. Closser, "Creating Memorable Meetings Is Key," *Triangle Business Journal* (February 18, 2000), p. 37.

47. Mark J. Friedman, "How to Run a Problem-solving Meeting," *Training and Development* (October 1996), p. 11.

48. John F. Schlegel, "Making Meetings Effective," *Association Management* (January 1, 2000), http://www.allbusiness.com/management/424176-1.html (accessed November 5, 2010).

49. Peter R. Scholtes, *The Team Handbook* (Madison, WI: Joiner and Associates, 1988).

50. Ibid.

51. Hawkins, "First Aid."

52. Jim Slaughter, "How to Keep Discussions Short," *Association Management* (January 2000), p. 123.

53. Hawkins, "First Aid."

54. Kay, "Good News," p. 17.

55. "The Future of Business Meetings," http://www.allbusiness.com/technology/telecommunications-conferencing/12305-1.html (accessed July 31, 2010).

56. Smith, "If Meeting Is Necessary."

57. Scholtes, *Team Handbook.*

58. Jones et al., "Meeting Primer."

59. D. G. Ancona, "Outward Bound: Strategies for Team Survival in an Organization," *Academy of Management Journal* 33 (1990), pp. 334–65.

60. Slaughter, "Keep Discussions Short."

61. Ibid.

62. John R. Brandt, "Time's Up (Limiting Business Meetings)," *Industry Week* (January 10, 2000), p. 2.

63. Tricia Campbell, "Speed Up Your Meetings," *Sales and Marketing Management* (November 1999), p. 11.

64. Hawkins, "First Aid."

Exercise 12–A
Committee Meeting

You are the chairperson of the social event committee for your school or community-based organization. Much is riding on you and your committee as you begin making preparations for the annual dance. This event is one of the biggest in your town and typically brings in between $10,000 and $20,000 annually that can be spent on resources, travel, and outreach efforts. It's very important that the dance go smoothly. It has for the last 15 years.

You are about to call a meeting of the social event committee to discuss arrangements for the dance. In this meeting, which is about six weeks away, you'll have to decide on location, food, music and entertainment, tables and chairs, decorations, and admission fee. You might even look for corporate sponsors to help fund the event.

1. What needs to be handled in your meeting?

2. Who should be invited?

3. What preparation work should be done?

4. What could you do before the meeting to ensure that everyone will come with ideas and enthusiasm?

5. What should you do during the meeting to ensure that you get closure on the key issues?

6. After the meeting, what can you do to ensure that other committee members follow up on their promises to complete certain tasks?

**Exercise 12–B
Why Am I Here?**

Refer to the shaded box entitled "Has This Ever Happened to You?" and answer the following questions:

1. What is the significance of the e-mail being from your boss's boss?
2. How does this impact your response? Specifically, what will your response be (assuming your schedule is free) and why?
3. What if your schedule included a doctor's appointment that was scheduled three months ago and would mean waiting another three months if you had to reschedule?

Let's say that you decide to keep your doctor's appointment; after all, it is at 2:00 p.m., making it possible for you to attend the first half-hour of the meeting.

4. What, if anything, will you communicate to your boss's boss about your attendance at the meeting? Through what medium will you transmit this information? Why?

You get to the meeting five minutes before the 1:00 p.m., start time. You recognize three other faces, but only one of those faces is someone you actually have spoken with before; he's Matthew from engineering. Your boss's boss hasn't arrived yet, so, not surprisingly, there are several side conversations going on. There are employees sitting on either side of Matthew, so you take one of the remaining empty seats.

5. What do you do now? What do you say to the person next to you?

Your boss's boss arrives at 1:05 p.m., looking harried. He begins to talk about the "critical" issue. Apparently, customer service has received a number of calls about product failures. If the trend continues, he explains, this could spell disaster for the company . . . recall, expensive product replacements, ruined reputation. After responding to some questions, he asks everyone to brainstorm possible solutions.

6. You look at your watch. You have to leave in a couple of minutes. What do you do?

**Exercise 12–C
Planning a Work Team
Meeting**

The following is a list of meetings that occurred recently in a university hospital:

- A meeting to plan a celebration for a staff member who had recently been promoted.
- A meeting to discuss the high number of work-related injuries and what could be done to promote awareness and prevention of worker's compensation claims.
- A meeting to discuss the addition of staff and possible reorganization of a department to support new technologies.
- A meeting to discuss customer satisfaction survey results and how to raise scores in certain clinics related to the item "customers feel listened to."
- A meeting to discuss how to inform staff of computer system upgrades and functionality changes.
- A meeting to decide whether to bid on a new piece of work.
- A meeting to discuss how to prepare for a regulatory audit.
- A meeting to assign resources to departmental projects.

Selecting one or two meetings from the list, and assuming that any of these meetings would last no more than 60 minutes, your group should discuss and document the following:

1. A specific goal to be accomplished in the meeting.
2. The meeting type (e.g., information sharing, symbolic/social).
3. The meeting mode (e.g., whether it could occur virtually).
4. Likely people to invite (e.g., member of human resources, IT staff).
5. Expected process challenges to be faced during the meeting.
6. Important considerations at the end of the meeting.

Source: This list was prepared and contributed by Kristine L. Krueger, Ph.D., Manager, Training & Support Services, Duke University Health System, July 2007.

Exercise 12–D
An Agenda for a Team Meeting

Prepare an agenda for your next project group meeting, using the format given in Figure 12–1. Afterwards, discuss as a group:

1. Does your group use agendas regularly? Why or why not?

2. What impact will this agenda likely have at this next meeting—on the outcome and the process?

Exercise 12–E
Case Study: What About Bob?

You are leading a meeting whose purpose is to decide whether your company should bid for a new piece of business. All the "right" people are there and are prepared to contribute. You have introduced the participants and have discussed why each of them is at the meeting. You have reviewed the agenda, established operating guidelines, and are leading a discussion of the first agenda item, which is how the new piece of business could fit into the company's strategic plan. You notice that Bob, the director of sales, is not making eye contact with anyone, is occasionally drawing stick figures on his note paper, and just softly commented, "Who cares how this fits our strategy? Our strategy is completely off the mark." You look at your watch. Of the time you have allocated for this discussion, there are three minutes remaining for this agenda item.

1. In what ways does preparing an agenda in advance reduce the likelihood of these behaviors? What other "before the meeting" strategies can be used to curb such behavior? Why do you think this strategy or approach would or would not be effective?

2. What options are available for a team member or team leader during the meeting to address this disruptive behavior? Why do you think this approach would or would not be effective?

3. What options are available for a team member or team leader at the end or just following the meeting to address this disruptive behavior? Why do you think this approach would or would not be effective?

Source: This case study was contributed by Kristine L. Krueger, Ph.D., Manager, Training & Support Services, Duke University Health System, July 2007.

Exercise 12–F
Plan and Have a Meeting

Working in groups of four to six, you will be given a topic and a block of time in which to plan and have a meeting. Consider the meeting's topic (see list below) and complete the following:

1. Prepare an agenda. Be sure to include these points:
   - Issues to be discussed.
   - The amount of time allocated to each issue.
   - Role assignments (e.g., scribe, timekeeper, leader, facilitator).
   - Time for a process review.

2. Have the meeting. Record key points and decisions on a flip chart or other "public" device. Plan to have one or more members present the findings of your group.

3. Do a process review. Discuss what worked well and could be improved in this meeting.

4. Report on your group's outcomes (what recommendation or conclusions your group offers) and processes (how your group got to that point).

Topics

- Feedback on this course: What elements are effective in terms of your ability to learn and apply what's being taught? What elements of the course, if improved, would increase your ability to apply what's being taught?
- The role of technology in your team's next presentation: What options are available? What are the strengths and weaknesses of the options? What recommendations would you make for future team-based presentations?
- Add your own.

Exercise 12–G
Reflection/Action Plan

This chapter focused on meetings—why they're important and strategies for planning and running effective meetings. Share your thoughts on the following worksheet upon completing all reading and experiential activities for this chapter.

1. The one or two areas in which I am most strong are:

_____

_____

_____

_____

2. The one or two areas in which I need more improvement are:

_____

_____

_____

_____

3. If I did only one thing to improve in this area, it would be to:

_____

_____

_____

_____

4. Making this change would probably result in:

_____

_____

_____

_____

5. If I did not change or improve in this area, it would probably affect my personal and professional life in the following ways:

_____

_____

_____

_____

Facilitating Team Success

13

Learning Points

How do I:

- Recognize when a team's process is ineffective?
- Help team members work cohesively and effectively with one another?
- Teach and guide teams in utilizing effective process skills?
- Identify and use appropriate process interventions at the right time and in the right manner to deter or resolve dysfunctional behaviors of the team or its individual members?
- Create an environment that allows teams to set and achieve goals effectively?

Your cubicle-mate, Wilson Jamara, is a member of a team that is tasked with putting together an advertising campaign for a major pet food company. Just as you were leaving for the day, Wilson caught you and asked if you'd meet him for breakfast to discuss "a work challenge." (The cubicles don't offer any privacy!) At breakfast, Wilson shares a little history about the team and his frustration. He explains that members of the team were handpicked by management and asked to complete its task in 30 days. One of his teammates, Jennifer Miller, has started to annoy Wilson and others on the team. She has had several years' experience working with pet food company clients—and reminds the team of her past successes frequently during team planning meetings. As Wilson sees it, Jennifer monopolizes many of the conversations and when she doesn't "have the floor," she seems impatient and, at times, condescending in her verbal and nonverbal reactions to others' comments or suggestions. Jennifer often volunteers to do more than her share in putting together both the campaign and the presentation of the campaign . . . which is nice, but has Wilson worried. He feels that it's hard for him and the rest of the team to get their voices heard in these meetings and is concerned that management will think that Wilson and the others aren't carrying their weight. Moreover, if the campaign is seen as unsuccessful, Wilson's bonus will be affected. Wilson asks for your advice.

1. What are some of the main issues that affect how the team works together in this situation? How do you think Jennifer sees the situation?

2. Is it a problem for Jennifer to be so dominant? After all, she has relevant experience and expertise to provide.

3. What would you advise Wilson to do before the next meeting, as well as during the next meeting?

4. What should the other team members do to deal with this situation?

5. What would you do if you were on this team? Why? What would be the likely outcome?

"Our chief want in life is somebody who will make us do what we can."

Ralph Waldo Emerson

What Is Facilitation?

Teams have become an important vehicle for organizations to develop and improve products, services, and processes.[1] The popular press is full of stories of team successes—in organizations large and small, private and public, traditional and virtual. Recognizing the potential that a collection of diverse individuals can bring in the form of innovation and effectiveness, organizational leaders rush to "do teams" in hopes of reaping similar rewards.[2] But as anyone who has ever worked on a team knows, it's not as easy as it looks. In fact, working with others—even those who seemingly share the same goals as you—can be downright frustrating. Getting everyone on the same page and playing by the same rules is critical, yet incredibly difficult—especially when the stakes are high. Each individual has a unique way of looking at the world, making decisions, and expressing him or herself. More members means even more diversity . . . and likely more conflict as team members struggle to be heard and reach agreement among their diverse counterparts. Therein lies the need for facilitation.

Facilitation is the set of "activities carried out before, during, and after meetings to help a group achieve its own outcomes."[3] A **facilitator** or **process consultant** is someone who performs these activities, helping the team by monitoring and improving its internal processes (means)—such as how members communicate, make decisions, or resolve conflict—that are essential for achieving its goals (ends).[4] She or he is typically not a team member, but someone who observes how the team goes about its task, diagnoses potential problems or issues that can hinder the team's effectiveness, and intercedes to help the team overcome these issues. In this chapter, we discuss why facilitation is important, the skills needed to facilitate, and strategies and tactics that can be used to help teams work together, and thus achieve their goals more effectively.

Why Is Facilitation Important?

While teams can bring great benefits to any organization, "simply bringing together a group of professionals does not ensure that this group will function effectively as a team or make appropriate decisions."[5] Team members' varying beliefs, experiences, education, personalities, and work styles can hinder a team's ability to get work done. Even similar individuals often think, behave, and communicate differently; they also have a unique way of interpreting others' thoughts, behaviors, and communication patterns. Ironically, the same diversity that is responsible for team creativity and innovation has been shown to lead to misunderstanding, conflict, and dysfunction.[6] With a multitude of "worldviews," it's not surprising to learn that some teams find it hard to reach agreements and solve problems.[7]

"Running team meetings without a facilitator is about as effective as teams trying to have a game without a referee."[8]

Imagine a discussion among team members who represent different departments and who are assembled to redesign a current product to improve its lagging sales. To the marketing person, this is an issue of poor product placement or advertising that can be fixed by running a customer focus group to learn how to improve product positioning and appeal. To the engineer, the problem is defined as a need to bring the latest technology into the product—at any cost. The manufacturing person suggests that the reason for lagging sales is that the product, as currently designed, is hard to manufacture with consistent reliability; he implores the design engineer to change the design for easier manufacture and assembly. Even with the most talented and motivated individuals, teams with such contrasting viewpoints—and organizational pressure to meet deadlines—can find it impossible to find common ground or even agree upon the rules of engagement. Therein lies the need for team facilitation.

What Facilitators Do

A facilitator is typically a neutral third party tasked with monitoring a team's process and helping improve its effectiveness. The facilitator focuses more on a team's **process** or how it achieves its goals (e.g., methods, procedures, tools, and norms of interaction), than on the **content** or what the team is doing (e.g., goals, tasks, agenda items, subjects discussed, decisions made).[9] Unlike the leader who takes control of the meeting and promotes a particular point of view, the facilitator provides structure and manages participation to ensure that all views are heard.[10] Rather than make decisions or give orders, the facilitator helps the team clarify its own goals and develop its plan for achieving them.[11] For example, if you were facilitating the team in the opening scenario, you might ask the team at the start of the next meeting:

> *"I understand that you are tasked with creating an advertising campaign for one of our clients, and that you've been given 30 days. Now that you've had some time to discuss the task, what do you think about the requirements and constraints? Is 30 days sufficient? How polished is management expecting the campaign to be?"*

These questions can help the team clarify the goal that was supplied to them and think through any issues that might get in the way of achieving this goal. Just because management "said so" may cause problems later on. If a goal is unrealistic or unsupported, it is better to discuss these issues at the start of the task/team and make adjustments than disappoint management and the client later on. This process of helping the team clarify its goal and managing expectations among those with vested interests is a case of an ounce of prevention being worth a pound of cure. The responsibilities of a facilitator vary from team to team, depending on the goals, technical requirements, duration, and employee makeup of that team. Employees or students who have worked on teams before, or who have been working with one team for a long time, may require less facilitation than would members of a newly formed team. In the case of our opening scenario, it seems that some members have more experience than others. A facilitator can help ensure that the more experienced members don't dominate the less experienced members.

The facilitator's role may not be confined to what happens during meetings; many work outside meetings to further group cohesion or help gain sponsorship or support from key groups or individuals external to the team.[12] While facilitators' responsibilities may vary with respect to teams' expected outcomes, technical requirements, and employee makeup, they often do whatever it takes to help the team improve its processes and outcomes. This might start with helping a team clarify and buy into its goals and objectives, and progress through coaching a team to present its recommendations to management and eventually implementing these recommendations.

Finally, facilitators model and educate team members in the use of facilitative skills. It would be very easy for a facilitator to provide continual assistance in improving team processes and outcomes. However, team members would likely become dependent on that help, rendering themselves unable to function effectively without the aid of a facilitator. When a facilitator not only helps the team use meeting management techniques, for example, but also teaches the team why and how to use them, the team will eventually become self-facilitating. In other words, good facilitators often work themselves out of a job.

In sum, as the accompanying box shows, facilitators do whatever it takes to help the team improve its processes (and outcomes). Facilitators may do many things, from helping create a safe and receptive environment in which to effectively communicate and make decisions, to coaching a team to present its findings and recommendations to management or other stakeholders.

Contributions of a Team Facilitator[13]

- Helps team define its goals and objectives and access needed resources to achieve them.
- Helps members assess their needs and skills and create plans to meet and develop them.
- Provides processes that help members use their time efficiently.
- Guides discussions to keep them on track.
- Ensures that assumptions are surfaced and tested.
- Ensures that all members' opinions are shared and considered in decision-making processes.
- Helps to create a positive, productive, and collaborative environment.
- Models and teaches facilitative skills, helping the team diagnose its own processes and eventually become self-facilitating.
- Ensures individual members take responsibility for team processes and outcomes.

Facilitator Skills and Behaviors

Whether you want to become a facilitator for other teams or use facilitative skills to improve the effectiveness of your own team, the good news is that these skills can be learned.[14] The skills required of a formal facilitator or someone who uses facilitative skills will vary depending upon a team's goals, members, history, and context within which it operates. Below we discuss some of the key skills and characteristics of an effective facilitator.

One of the most important characteristics of an effective facilitator is a keen awareness of your strengths, weaknesses, and biases. Without this self-awareness, your ability to set aside personal needs (e.g., power, being liked by group members) or goals for the good of the group and organization may be limited.[15] Though the following material is aimed at formal facilitators, anyone in a team situation can use facilitative behaviors. In any team situation, it's important for individuals to take responsibility for productive processes as well as successful outcomes. To do this requires awareness of the process (and whether it is working), initiative, and a desire to help a team remain positive and proceed toward its goal.

A key facet of facilitator expertise is communication. Skilled in both verbal and nonverbal communication, effective facilitators are able to decode important cues that team members often miss. They listen to what is being said or what is not being said. They tap into the mindset of the group with distinct awareness and vigilance.[16] They recognize subtle indications that fellow team members are likely to ignore or overlook, such as one member not understanding or wanting to understand another's diverse point of view, members feeling threatened by others, or some members' lack of commitment to the team and its goals. Other team participants may deem such signals unimportant or unrelated to the task at hand.

The adept facilitator has keen observation skills and can highlight and focus the group's attention on such cues and their implications. For example, you might be concerned about a team member who rarely participates or isolates herself geographically (e.g., sits on a chair against the wall instead of at the meeting table) at team meetings, but you may choose to overlook her behavior, assuming that as long as the team is making progress, you'll "let sleeping dogs lie." By contrast, an experienced facilitator knows that such behavior might indicate that team member's lack of ownership in the team or its goals. Unchecked, this behavior can resurface later—often in the implementation phase— in the form of uncooperativeness or sabotage, and possibly lead to the downfall of a team.

Another important facilitation skill is the ability to give behavioral feedback to team members in a way that gets them to recognize and modify unproductive behaviors. Providing constructive feedback is probably one of the more difficult yet important skills to master.[17] This is because facilitators need to make team members aware of their potentially dysfunctional behaviors in a manner that addresses the issues but doesn't cause defensiveness or create a negative or disempowering atmosphere. Being specific and using "I" language will allow one or more members to improve their behaviors while remaining fully engaged in and encouraged about the team's task.

Facilitators must also be knowledgeable about decision-making and problem-solving tools. On complex projects, members might lock on to one or more symptoms of an underlying problem and shift the team's resources toward solving the wrong problem. Good facilitators can help a team identify problems, symptoms, causes, and solutions through the use of one or more decision-making or problem-solving tools.[18] Helping teams navigate the problem-solving process will enable them to effectively achieve their goals and increase their confidence in employing similar processes in future endeavors.

Understanding and managing group dynamics—relative to the team's current stage of growth—is another skill facilitators should possess. They should carefully observe how team members interact with one another, particularly when such interaction becomes strained or suppressed. Team members often lament, "These group projects wouldn't be so bad if you could do the work by yourself." Students and employees often complain about their teammates and the team process. These complaints typically involve members' varying commitment levels to the project, unusual or incompatible work styles, and personal or emotional issues.[19] As the term *group dynamics* indicates, the process tends to be unpredictable. An effective meeting can immediately precede an absolutely horrible one. Add or delete a member midstream and see what develops. Now infuse a new constraint on the schedule or budget, and you've got yourself the potential for team conflict, if not its complete breakup. Trained facilitators know what behaviors and emotions to expect from members during each of the four stages of teaming and adjust their techniques accordingly.[20]

For example, a facilitator may notice growing conflict among team members, but may decide not to intercede. After all, such conflict is not only expected but also necessary over the life of a team. Given Wilson's explanation of his team's process and progress, it seems that a trained facilitator would observe the tension among the team and the feelings of frustration toward Jennifer's dominating behavior.

Along with diagnosing the behavior of the group, a skilled facilitator will be able to diagnose the behaviors of individuals and choose appropriate responses when these behaviors are exhibited. According to Schein, three types of behaviors are typically exhibited in team meetings; they are discussed below and shown in Figure 13–1.[21]

- **Task-related behaviors** focus on the *content* of the meeting—the actions necessary to complete a task or goal. These task-related behaviors include contributing to, asking for, summarizing, and clarifying information. The facilitator will monitor these behaviors and intervene if the team's attention to task precludes them from paying attention to process or group dynamic issues. For example, a team might be so focused on their deadline that they will overlook the fact that one member has resigned from the group and is not attending meetings. In this case, a member or the facilitator can ask clarifying questions and help the team acknowledge and deal with this problem, rather than ignore it.

- **Maintenance-related behaviors** relate to the *process* of how the group works together. Some quiet or shy members may need encouragement to participate. Tensions arising from conflicts need to be reduced. Other issues, particularly those that may not be obvious to some, must be diagnosed and resolved. Members of an effective team are likely to exhibit both task- and maintenance-related behaviors during meetings. If conflict surfaces, members may use these behaviors to resolve it. In the case of our opening scenario (and as is often the case in organizations), even obvious team problems can be ignored or brushed aside during the meeting; many are uncomfortable with confrontation—especially toward a dominating person—and will complain about

Figure 13–1
Three Types of Behaviors

	Behavior	Explanation	Examples	Pros (Cons)
Task-Related	Initiating	Proposes a task	"Why don't we start by . . ."	Gets the "ball" rolling
	Giving/seeking information	Offers/asks facts, ideas	"In our department, we were able to cut costs by . . ."	Improves decision making
	Clarifying and elaborating	Clears up confusion	"So you're saying . . ."	Ensures members understand each other
	Summarizing	Restates, offers conclusion	"We've covered all but the last item on the agenda."	Can reduce time spent rehashing discussions
	Consensus testing	Checks on group position	"It sounds like we agree on points 1 and 2, but not 3 . . ."	Saves time, ensures decision buy-in
Maintenance-Related	Harmonizing and compromising	Reduces tension, looks for middle ground	"It doesn't have to be either x or y . . . why don't we use the best elements of both?"	Reduces tension in group Can reduce risk-taking
	Gatekeeping	Facilitates balanced participation	(To silent member) "What's your opinion?"	Ensures members participate
	Diagnosing	Shares observations of group process	"It seems a few of us are unhappy with the decision . . . shall we revisit . . .?"	Ensures hidden problems are surfaced and dealt with
	Standard setting	Helps set norms, test limits	"Let's agree to brainstorm, then evaluate"	Facilitates team self-management
Dysfunctional	Blocking	Prevents consensus	"I'm not going to agree to a solution that . . ."	Could slow down a hasty decision process (and bog down an effective process)
	Dominating	Talks more than his/her share	Overshadows others' potential contributions	Can stifle others' participation
	Withdrawing	Silent, distracted	(Check body language)	Decision making may be quicker (if his/her concerns aren't aired, s/he might sabotage the outcome later)
	Self-seeking	Oppresses with personal needs	"The only way I'll agree to this is if you'll do . . . for me"	Others might emulate this behavior and/or be biased against future inputs from him/her

the "problem people" outside the meeting. This only raises members' frustrations and hinders the team from resolving its issues. If team members ignore the problem or are unsuccessful in addressing it, the facilitator can raise the issue and provide a model for team members to emulate later should another conflict emerge.

■ **Dysfunctional behaviors** are actions taken by members that may hinder or even undermine the team's progress. When members intentionally block the team's progress by refusing to budge on their position on an issue, the facilitator can try to address the issue by using an intervention, such as asking justifying questions.

As we've said, team facilitators should focus primarily on group process (how the team is going about achieving its formal tasks), with much less focus on team content or outcomes (reasons for the team's existence, what the team is talking about). Facilitators use their skills to assist the team with its process (as opposed to the content) by intervening when necessary, such as refocusing a divergent discussion, ensuring balanced participation, or clarifying whether all options have been objectively evaluated. In addition to process expertise, some facilitators may possess specific content or technical knowledge, such as an engineering background, which might potentially benefit a team. However, since a facilitator's primary responsibility is to ensure the open and objective discussion of diverse perspectives, facilitators will typically downplay content knowledge for fear of being perceived as nonobjective or vested in a particular outcome.[22]

Key Facilitative Preventions

A facilitator can do many things behind the scenes or before meetings begin that might help prevent problems from occurring or diminish their impact on the team should such problems surface. The list of prevention strategies, shown in Figure 13–2, ranges from premeeting planning (e.g., working on the agenda with the team leader, ensuring quality of meeting logistics), to start-of-meeting process clarification (e.g., establishing ground rules), to things you could say or do during a meeting (e.g., suggesting or getting agreement on the process, educating the group) to ensure all members of the team are on the same page and working toward a common goal.

Key Facilitative Interventions

Even the most skilled facilitator cannot prevent all problems from surfacing on a team. Sooner or later, one or more group members may decide to take a stand on an issue that is opposed to the position supported by other group members. Management may decide to change the scope of a team's goals and objectives, add or delete team members, or shorten the time in which completion is expected. Or a team member may decide that his or her time is too valuable to be "wasted" at these "frivolous" team meetings. Any of these situations, combined with the diversity challenges mentioned earlier in

Figure 13–2
Facilitative Preventions[23]

Prevention Strategy	Specific Things You Can Say or Do
Establish ground rules and define roles	Upfront (and ongoing) discussion of your role and the ground rules of your involvement with the team leader and later the team members.
	"OK, before we get started, I would like to make sure we all agree on general procedures. While I'm facilitator we're going to operate by consensus. Consensus means . . . if we need to take a formal vote, I will turn the meeting over to your chairperson."
	"Mr. Smith is here as an observer. That is why he is sitting at the back of the room. He has agreed not to participate."
Get agreement on process	"Before we begin to evaluate the alternatives, are we agreed that we'll begin by saying what we like about each alternative, and then go on to our concerns about each one?"
	"Just a moment, before you begin your report. Do you want to entertain questions? During your presentation or afterwards?"
	"To make sure we are clear, Joe is going to present his idea without interruption, then we'll ask clarifying questions, and then we'll go on to Bill's solution."
	"If there are no objections, we'll brainstorm different possible definitions of the problem, stating them as "how to" questions. Any questions about how we are going to proceed?"
Get agreement on content/outcome	"Which issue are you going to discuss first? What's the purpose of this meeting? To design the agenda for the full commission next Wednesday? Does anybody have a different conception of this meeting?"
	"Today, we're just dealing with the issue of vacation policy—not benefits in general. Is that right?"
	"What's success going to look like today?"

Figure 13–2   (Continued)

Prevention Strategy	Specific Things You Can Say or Do
Stay neutral/stay out of content	Refrain from sharing your own ideas or opinions.
	Remind the group of your role: "As your facilitator, I'm supposed to be neutral. This is your meeting. What do you want to do?"
	"I won't be able to help you work through this issue if I start taking sides."
	"I'll share my personal opinions with you after the meeting."
	"Actually, I don't have a personal opinion about the issue yet."
Be positive (win–win attitude)	If you really believe a win–win solution can be found, you will increase the chances of it happening.
	"I know this issue is quite emotionally charged for some of you, but if we take our time and work our way through the problem I'm sure we can find a solution you can all live with."
Suggest a process	"Why don't we try brainstorming?"
	"I would suggest looking at criteria before trying to evaluate the options."
	"How about working backwards from the deadline?"
Educate the group	By offering short comments about why you are doing what you are doing and about the nature of the problem-solving process, you can help the team work through difficult situations and become better at facilitating itself. In addition, you educate when you illustrate how the team can use different problem-solving tools.
	"There's no one right way to solve a problem. Which way do you want to try first?"
	"You can't solve two problems at once."
	"If we don't agree on the problem, we'll never agree on a solution."
	"Sounds like we might need to use the nominal group technique. Are any of you familiar with this?"
Get permission to enforce the process agreements	"If you want to get through all these reports by 11:00, I'm going to have to hold you to your five-minute time limit. Is that OK? Any objections?"
	"Is it all right with you if I push a little harder to get finished on time?"
	"You've agreed not to bring up old history. Do I have your permission to cut you off if you do?"
Get the group to take responsibility for its actions	"This is your meeting, not mine. What do you want to do?"
	"It's up to you to decide if you want to change the agenda."
	"I can't make you reach an agreement. You have to really want to find a win–win solution."
Build an agenda	By working with the team leader to plan an agenda for your meeting, you can anticipate and prevent many potential meeting problems from occurring.
Get ownership of the agenda	Even though an agenda has been prepared in advance, don't assume that everyone in the meeting has seen it or agreed to it. Either you or the team leader needs to check for additions, revisions, and reordering of agenda items.
	"OK, that's the agenda. Any additions or revisions?"
	Once people have had a chance to revise or approve the agenda, then it becomes their agenda, not yours, and they are less likely to feel they have been manipulated.
Assure quality of team logistics	Review with the team leader and members what materials will be necessary for the upcoming meeting. Assure that the location, availability, and setup of meeting rooms are conducive to the team's success.
	"This is the second time we have been bumped from this room. Is there an alternative meeting place we can use for future meetings?"

the chapter, provides ample opportunity for you to use an **intervention**—subtly or not so subtly interrupt the team's process to aid the team when difficulties or potential problems surface.

Some of the interventions, or things a facilitator can say or do to help a team assess and deal with what is going on in the present moment (see Figure 13–3), are fairly simple, straightforward, and innocuous. For example, the use of "say what's going on" is perfect for the team that is experiencing the formation of factions with respect to a particular issue. By sharing your observations with the team, you clarify what is happening while (hopefully) motivating them to reach a resolution. This intervention might sound like this: "It seems we have two perspectives on this decision; John's approach would be to . . . while Mary's approach would involve . . . . Half of you seem to agree with John while the

Figure 13–3
Facilitative Interventions[24]

General Approach	Specific Things You Can Say or Do
Boomerang	Don't get backed into answering questions the group should be answering for themselves. Boomerang the question back to the group. Group member: "Facilitator, which problem should we deal with first?" Facilitator: "That's up to the group. Which do you think we should discuss first?"
Maintain/regain focus	"Wait a second. Let's keep a common focus here." "Just a moment, one person at a time. Joe, you were first and then Don." "I can't facilitate if we have two conversations going at once. Please try to stay focused." "Excuse me, Elizabeth. Are you addressing the issue of . . . ?" "Let's work on one thing at a time."
Play dumb	When the group has gotten off track or the meeting has broken down in some way, playing dumb is a way of getting the group to focus on its own process by having to explain to you. It's a form of boomeranging and is easy to do when you're really confused. "Can someone tell me what's going on now?" "I'm confused. What are we doing now?" "I'm lost. I thought we were . . ."
Say what's going on	Sometimes, simply identifying and describing a destructive behavior to the group is enough to change that behavior. Be sure to "check for agreement" after your process observation. "I think you're trying to force a decision before you're ready." "It seems to me that . . ."
Check for agreement	Almost any time you make a statement or propose a process, give the group an opportunity to respond. Ask, specifically; don't assume they are with you. A powerful way of checking is to look for the negative. Make silence a sign of confirmation. Rather than saying, "Do you all agree?" ask "Are there any objections?" or try "Is there anyone who can't live with that decision?"
Avoid process battles	Don't let the group become locked into arguments about the "right" way to proceed. Point out that you can try a number of things and deal with more than one issue. The issue is which one to try first. "We can try both approaches. Which one do you want to try first?"
Enforce process agreements	Once the group has agreed to a procedure, your credibility and neutrality may be at stake if you don't enforce their agreement. "Wait a second, you agreed to brainstorm. Don't evaluate ideas . . ." "Sorry Beth, I'm afraid your time is up."

Figure 13–3   (Continued)

General Approach	Specific Things You Can Say or Do
Encourage	Early in the team's existence, and especially with shy members, a little encouragement can go a long way. "Could you say more about that?" "Why don't you try." "Keep going. I think this is useful."
Accept, legitimize, deal with, or defer	This is a general method of intervening that works well for dealing with problem people and emotional outbreaks of all kinds. "You're not convinced we're getting anywhere? That's OK, maybe you're right." "Are you willing to hang on for 10 more minutes and see what happens?"
Don't be defensive	If you are challenged, don't argue or become defensive. Accept the criticism, thank the individual for the comment, and boomerang the issue back to the individual or group. "I cut you off? You weren't finished? I'm sorry. Please continue." "You think I'm pushing too hard? (lots of nods) Thank you for telling me. How should we proceed from here?"
Use your body language	Many of these interventions and preventions can be reinforced, and sometimes even made, by the movement of your body or hands. For example, you can regain focus by standing up and moving into the middle of the group; enforce a process agreement by holding up your hand to keep someone from interrupting; encourage someone by gesturing with your hands; and stop a monopolizer's talking by walking over to the person and standing next to or behind him or her.
Use justifying questions	When team members disagree on an issue, a facilitator can use justifying questions to help bring out discussions by uncovering facts and reasons behind team members' opinions. In response to a team member's input that "Well, we tried it before and it didn't work then," the facilitator might respond: "What could you share about that experience, so we don't make the same mistake twice?"
Use leading questions	Use when the team has too narrow a focus and you want to gently guide them into another direction or if the team needs a jump-start. "Have you ever thought about using . . . ?" "Are you sure that is your only option?" "What precludes you from trying . . . ?"
Use the group memory	The group memory (i.e., the easel or notepad on which minutes or key points are being recorded) can also be used to reinforce many of the interventions and preventions. For example, walking up to the group memory can facilitate regaining focus by pointing to the agenda item the group should be dealing with. In addition, getting agreement on content can be greatly supported by writing down or circling the subject to be discussed.
Don't talk too much	The better facilitator you become, the fewer words you will have to use. When you have really done a good job, the group may leave thinking that the meeting went so well it could do without you next time. Use your hands, eye contact, and partial sentences to communicate economically . . . "I'm sorry. You were saying that . . ." "The point you were making was . . ."
Use hypothetical questions	When a team appears to be stagnant or more interested in maintaining the status quo, the facilitator could use hypothetical questions to spur creativity, innovation, and the like. "What if money were no object . . . ?" "If you could change any one thing about your work or environment . . ."

(continued)

Figure 13–3   (Continued)

General Approach	Specific Things You Can Say or Do
Use a reality check	Use when a team needs to reexamine or modify its direction, progress, or process agreements.
	"Time for a reality check: are we doing what we said we would do? *OR* should we be discussing this now? *OR* do we need to change our milestone chart? *OR* is this something we should talk to our sponsor about?"
Use the "round robin" method	If a team member is monopolizing the conversations while others are nearly silent, you might make the suggestion: "Why don't we go once around the table? What do you think might be a way to improve . . .?" Call on members in a clockwise direction, ensuring that no member is skipped and the direction is maintained.
Ask team members to "talk to their neighbor"	Sometimes you'll ask a question and get NO response. Either no one understands it, cares about it, or has had enough coffee. Rephrase the question and ask team members to discuss their responses with the person sitting next to him or her. A lively discussion is sure to ensue.
Use a time-out	When team members are fighting, losing sight of the big picture, or becoming uncooperative for some reason, try calling for a time-out. Ask that members take a five-minute break, after which the meeting will résumé.
Call a team member's bluff	Use when a team member threatens to do something unless or until the team changes direction. (This intervention is risky; you must be willing to accept a team member's decision.)

other half prefer Mary's approach. Am I correct?" A similar intervention, which is simple yet powerful if not overdone, is the "play dumb" intervention. When a team has lost its focus or has become sidetracked on another topic, a facilitator might say something like, "I'm confused. What were we supposed to be discussing now?" This technique can help get the group to focus on its own process and how to improve it. Both of these interventions are fairly easy to do while having the dual benefit of regaining the team's focus and simultaneously improving its members' ability to be self-facilitating.

Another set of interventions involves the use of well-timed questions to help uncover important reasons behind a position (e.g., justifying questions), move the team into a different direction (e.g., leading questions), or get the team to take a leap outside the proverbial box (e.g., hypothetical questions). In the latter case, questions that cause the group to move beyond the "That'll never work here" or "We've tried that before and it didn't work then" types of responses can be really effective. For example, if a team member were to say something like, "That's a great idea but management would never go for it," a facilitator might ask a justifying question, such as, "Why do you think that is the case?" to clarify underlying reasons. If the team member responds, "Well, when the team in the finance department tried to . . . , management apparently shelved their recommendations," the facilitator might respond with the following hypothetical question: "If you had some assurance management is going to listen and take action this time, what specific recommendations should we make about implementing . . .?"

Another set of interventions has the facilitator taking an active and perhaps directive role. Doing so is necessary in certain situations. It is important to remember that the more directive the facilitator is, the more the team members come to expect such behaviors from the facilitator as opposed to developing their own facilitative skills. One example is the use of "time-out." If members are fighting or unusually uncooperative, continuing the meeting might prove unproductive, if not harmful. In such a situation, the facilitator might end the meeting early or call a time-out—a 5- or 10-minute break—after which the meeting résumés. A more risky intervention might be necessary when a team member threatens to leave the meeting or to do something that might sabotage the team's progress should the member not get his or her way. This team member may be waiting for others to cajole him or her back into the meeting or change their way of thinking. In such a situation, it might be appropriate for a facilitator to "call the person's bluff," for example, "No one can make you stay . . . you can leave if you want to, just as long as you realize . . ." This intervention is risky in that the facilitator must be willing to accept the outcome (e.g., a team member's departure) and its impact on the team.

If you are a novice facilitator or an "ordinary" team member starting to use your facilitation skills to reduce the likelihood that your team will be overcome by problem situations, realize that you need not memorize all the interventions in Figure 13–3 to be effective. Start slowly, by understanding why, when, and how to use no more than a handful of the interventions that best suit your own style and comfort level. For example, asking hypothetical questions or playing dumb can be pretty simple to do when a team seems to be at an impasse. As we discussed, these interventions are also fairly nondirective, helping the team find answers to its own questions and making it more likely that they will (1) accept your efforts to intercede or facilitate, (2) increase buy-in to their (as opposed to your) solutions, and (3) increase their independence and realization that they can become self-facilitating.

Another option is to wait until the end of the meeting and share your observations about what is working well and what could be improved, or if that's uncomfortable, consider sharing your thoughts about the team's process after the meeting in a follow-up e-mail to the team members. Because you "can practice as much as you want before you ever hit the send button," e-mailing your process observations helps you increase your confidence in using your facilitative skills.[25] Finally, consider practicing your facilitation skills in conversations with friends or co-workers, where the stakes are low. When your group of friends persistently interrupts or discounts the comments of one group member, she or he may become frustrated, even though words to this effect aren't exchanged. Practicing a simple, "Hang on a second, Marcus wasn't finished . . ." can help both Marcus be heard and you improve as a facilitator. As facilitation expert Roger Schwartz notes, "Any conversation is an opportunity to practice."[26]

Facilitating with Words and Pictures: Graphic Facilitation[27]

Graphic facilitation is a powerful facilitation tool that uses both words and pictures to record and facilitate meetings. Key ideas and concepts are captured in real time on a large display that promotes "big picture thinking" and stimulates participation, creativity, and focus. The visual record encourages teams to clarify differences and define goals. Connections are surfaced and made visible, which helps the work group to remain energized and focused. It adds another dimension to traditional facilitation methods.

The wall charts produced in these meetings tend to be very untidy, reflecting the group's thought processes. These records of the group's meetings and events make it easy for new members to be brought up-to-date and provide memory hooks for people who attended the previous meetings. When recorded over time, they provide a graphic illustration of the group's journey towards its goal.

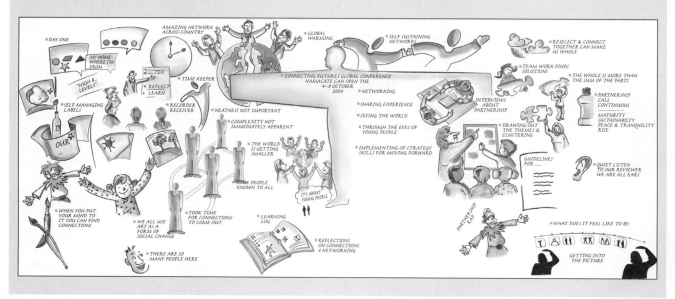

Identifying and Dealing with "Problem People"

Some people, with or without ill intent, can single-handedly hinder even the best teams. We call these **problem people**. Figure 13–4 summarizes some of the more common behavioral descriptors, clarifies the problem and its effect on the team, and suggests possible solutions for handling these people or situations. Have you ever been on a team where one member—who seems to know everything about everything—monopolizes the conversation and gets on everyone's nerves? Some would try to ignore this person, hoping she or he would run out of things to say. More likely, however, is that others would stop trying to be heard—after all, why try to compete with someone who knows everything

Figure 13–4
Dealing with Problem People[28]

Problem Person	Problem	Effect	Solution
The Silent One	Withdrawn. May be bored, indifferent, timid, or insecure.	You lose a portion of the group's power. May have a negative effect on others in the group.	Ask for her opinions. Draw out the person sitting next to her, then ask the quiet one what she thinks of the view just expressed. If you are near her, ask her view so she will feel she is talking to you, not the whole group. Compliment the silent one when she does speak. Give positive verbal and nonverbal reinforcement.
The Advice Seeker	Wants you to solve his problems or those of others. May try to put you on the spot, trying to have you support one viewpoint.	Can put you in position of decision-maker, rather than the group.	Avoid solving other people's problems for them. Never take sides. Point out that your view is relatively unimportant compared to that of the group. Say, "Let me get some other opinions . . . Joe, what do you think of Sam's question?"
The Heckler	Combative individual who wants to play devil's advocate or, though normally good-natured, is upset by personal or job problems.	Can trap you into a one-on-one fight. Can stimulate group in-fighting.	Stay calm. Don't lose your temper. Keep the group from getting excited. Try to find merit in ONE of his points, then move on. Toss his statements out to the group; let them handle it. Talk to him privately and try to find out what's bothering him. Appeal to him for cooperation.
The Fighters	Two or more persons have personality conflicts.	Can divide the group into competitive factions.	Interrupt politely but firmly. Stress points of agreement and minimize points of disagreement. Ask direct questions on the topic. Request that personalities be set aside.
The Drifter	Talks about things not related to subject. Uses far-fetched examples. Gets lost.	Can cause confusion—both for herself and the group.	Interrupt politely. Thank her. Refocus her attention by restating main points being discussed. Smile. Indicate that you are having a problem relating her interesting comments to the subject at hand, or ask her directly to make this connection for the group.
The "Stand Pat"	Won't budge. Refuses to accept the group's decisions. Often prejudiced. Unable or unwilling to see your point or those of others.	Can turn the group into competitive camps. Delays decision making.	Toss his view to the group: "Does anyone else feel as Pat does about this?" Tell him that time is short and ask him to accept the group's position for the moment. Offer to discuss the point with him later.
The Sidetracker	No drifting, just off the subject or agenda.	Can cause confusion and waste group time.	Take the blame for sidetracking her: "Something I said must have led you off the subject. This is what we should be discussing . . . (restate point)."
The Smart-Phone Junkie	More interested in checking e-mail/ messages or taking calls than participating in the meeting.	Sends a message that s/he is "above" the people and issues present—which may be contagious. Distracts the group and hinders progress should the group decide to update him/her.	Set ground rules about phone use, e.g., members should inform group in advance about an expected urgent call or message, and they should leave the room and take responsibility for getting up to speed after the meeting ends. Infractions during the meeting should be addressed early; see "Sidetracker," "Latecomer," and "Early Leaver."
The Verbal Stumbler	Lacks ability to clearly express himself. Has the ideas but finds it difficult to put into words.	Leads to frustration, both for the person and the group.	Help the person out. Rephrase his statements: "Let me see if I understand . . . (paraphrase his point)." Don't say "What you mean is . . ." Keep the idea(s) intact and check for understanding.

Figure 13-4   (Continued)

Problem Person	Problem	Effect	Solution
The Griper	Has some pet gripe. Has a legitimate complaint.	Can turn the meeting into a grievance session.	Point out: "We can't change policies, but we can do the best we can under the system." Indicate you'll bring the complaint (if legitimate) to the proper person's attention. Indicate time constraints. Offer to discuss the problem after the meeting or at a future point.
The Whisperer	Engages nearby people in side conversations while someone else has the floor. May or may not be related to the subject.	Distracts you and other group members.	Don't embarrass him. Interrupt politely and ask if him could share their information with the group. Ask one of those involved in the side conversation his or her opinion of a remark (restate it for the person). Explain that you are having trouble hearing (or talking) when others are speaking at the same time.
The Eager Beaver	Overly talkative. Monopolizes the conversation. May be a show-off or just very well informed and anxious to show it.	Can shut out less aggressive members.	Don't be embarrassing or sarcastic. Interrupt politely with "That's an interesting point. What do the rest of you think about it?" (Look around the group.) Might also use body language: walk over to and stand behind the Eager Beaver and/or use your hands (like a traffic cop) to diminish his talking while encouraging others. Let the group take care of him as much as possible.
The Overachiever	Although she is really trying to help, it makes it difficult to maintain control.	Shuts others out. May monopolize in genuine effort to be helpful.	Recognize the valuable traits of this person. Thank her. Suggest that "we put others to work . . ." Cut across tactfully by questioning others. Use this individual for summarizing.
The Mistaken	Member is obviously incorrect. Definitely in the wrong ballpark.	Can cause inaccurate information to spread. Causes confusion in the group.	Handle with care. Say "I can see how you feel . . ." or "That's another way of looking at it . . ." To correct tactfully, say "I see your point, but how can we reconcile that with . . . (state correct point)?"
The Know-it-All	Can dominate group with comments like "I have worked on this project more than anyone else here . . ." or "I have a Ph.D. in economics and . . ."	May inhibit creativity, causing others to feel inadequate or that their opinions are not valued.	Avoid theory or speculation by focusing the group on a review of the facts. Might suggest another opinion such as, "another noted authority on this subject, (state name), has said . . ."
The Latecomer	Comes late and interrupts meeting.	Slows down group's progress, particularly if latecomer insists on being brought up to speed.	Announce an odd time (8:46 am) for the meeting to emphasize the necessity for promptness. Make it inconvenient for latecomers to find a seat, and stop talking until they do. Establish a "latecomer's kitty" for refreshments.
The Early Leaver	Announces, with regret, that they must leave for another important activity.	Interrupts meeting flow and can halt progress if the Early Leaver is critical to an upcoming discussion that now must be deferred.	Before the meeting begins, announce or confirm the ending time and ask if anyone has a scheduling conflict. If this is a standing conflict, ask group if they would like to change meeting times.

already? One suggestion is to paraphrase what the "expert" has said; this demonstrates that you've been listening and that you value his or her expertise. After restating the "expert" opinion, invite others to offer additional opinions, theirs or other experts'. You could say, for example, "Walt, your point about . . . is really insightful. Your experience in this area is valuable. What do the rest of you know about . . . that can help us complete our task within the constraints we have?" Sometimes, the "know-it-all" offers expertise that may or may not match the question or problem being considered; perhaps the knowledge is more theoretical than practical. In this case, you might try a combination of leading and justifying questions such as, "So, you're telling us that . . . . We should keep that in mind for the future, but right now, can you tell us how your idea will solve the more immediate problem of . . . given that our customers expect our product to work all the time and in all conditions?" By leading the expert to justify his or her opinion, it shows that all inputs are fair game for all team members to debate and discuss. Finally, if the expert continues to dominate the conversation, you might try a more direct approach, beginning with "say what's going on." For example, "Walt, each time someone offers a suggestion, you provide a detailed review based on your expertise and experience of possibilities we should consider. Given that we're still early in the process, I'd appreciate if you hold off sharing some of your critiques."

Here's another example, only this time we challenge you to come up with a potential solution. Let's say you encounter a team member who always complains and turns the conversation to an unrelated topic that is irritating her, leading the team astray. Perhaps the team is working on implementing a new computer system for the human resource department, and every time the company or budget is discussed, this member begins to complain how the company should be spending funds on giving raises and benefits instead of upgrading the computer system. How would you deal with this individual? What preventive techniques might you use? What interventions might you use? Why do you think they would be effective? What if they weren't effective—what else might you try?

Facilitation Tips

As should be obvious from reading this chapter, facilitating is a skill that is both challenging and important in today's team-based environment. Good facilitation—whether coming from a person formally assigned to the role or anyone who is motivated to help the team be more effective in achieving its goals—requires competency in several interpersonal skills as well as the ability to be, and be seen as, a neutral referee as opposed to a team leader. In fact, guiding a group without being seen as the person in charge is more difficult than it may appear. The following suggestions will help you decide whether intervention might be needed at a particular time, and if so, what type of intervention might be effective.

- Keep an open mind about what you think needs facilitating. Your perceptions may or may not match those of the team, leaving open the possibility that the facilitator could do more harm than good.

- Wait and see if team members can resolve their own conflict. Remember that the more a facilitator takes an active role in facilitating a group's process, the more likely the team is to become dependent on the facilitator doing so now and in the future.

- After diagnosing what appears to be a potential problem in the team's process, share your observations in order to check with team members whether your observations are

Facilitating Online Groups

As we know, virtual groups can be just as effective as face-to-face groups. However, team dynamics can negatively impact virtual teams as well, and virtual team facilitation can be helpful. Facilitating groups virtually requires the same facilitation skill set, as well as an understanding of technology tools, a heightened sensitivity to cultural and time differences, and knowledge of strategies to overcome the challenges associated with virtual communication.

First, the facilitator must be clear about the conditions present during the team's initiation. She or he must know and help the team clarify its purpose, member roles, and responsibilities; relevant organizational policies or practices (especially when they differ by business unit or country); resources available; and technology to be used.[29] Ideally, the first meeting—especially in the case of diverse, multicultural teams—should be face-to face.[30] Early on, the facilitator should use a calendar application or doodle poll to find the times with the greatest overlap to maximize member participation. The facilitator can also check on the availability of technology for synchronized collaboration on document creation and editing and online meeting/conferencing facilities, as well as portals and blogs.

During the meeting, the facilitator needs to pay special attention to members who become passive—which, due to distance and the medium, is more likely to occur. Asking questions of specific members or using the round robin technique can be helpful for this; the process check in the end is another opportunity to check for participation issues. In general, it's important that a virtual team facilitator provides timely feedback and ensures that the team has an action plan for following up on actions or decisions.

correct. If you were to skip this step and actively promote a certain path to resolve the situation, you might cause more problems than you fix. If your observations are correct, evaluate which approach would work best in this situation and then suggest these options to the team.

Over time, and as a team moves through its developmental stages and members learn and use effective process skills, a facilitator should move toward being less directive, using questioning and other interventions that put the responsibility about what to do next in the team's hands. However, early in the team's existence, it might be appropriate for you to be somewhat directive or task-oriented; it might help give direction when the team's start seems slow.

Some Barriers or Limitations to Facilitation

Not all organizations or teams use or recognize the value of facilitators. The costs may be prohibitive, preventing work teams from having the luxury of adding (even temporarily) an outside member to facilitate them. If there are no employees with facilitation skills available in the organization, the organization may not want to pay for the services of an outside facilitator. Even if internal employees with the necessary skills can be identified, there are costs associated with pulling them out of their normal duties and reassigning them—even temporarily—to work with one or more teams. In the absence of a trained facilitator, individual team members will be called upon to use facilitative skills as appropriate. In this case, **objectivity**—the ability to view a situation without personal bias and one of the benefits perceptually bestowed upon an "outside" facilitator—is lacking. In this case, some of the problems inherent in culturally and functionally diverse teams (e.g., misunderstanding or devaluing others' opinions, fighting over scarce resources) are not likely to be overcome by an "inside" facilitator.

Even when outside facilitators or process consultants are offered to a team, other problems may exist. First, teams can see the job of process facilitation resting squarely and solely upon the facilitator. Such dependence precludes team development toward self-management. Second, at the other extreme, team members may not trust the outsider or "allow" him or her to intervene. This is especially likely when a team has existed for a period of time and resists the presence or questions the value of this appointed outsider. This problem can be exacerbated if management appoints a facilitator to a team without communicating the reasons or objectives for this step. Team members might become suspicious and choose to be less forthcoming in team meetings and discussions. Facilitators can only facilitate what they see and hear; if the team's work goes "underground," there is not much a facilitator can do to help, should help be needed.

As a facilitator you can reduce these effects by introducing yourself at the first meeting and discussing with the group how they see your role. Check out the team's expectation of the facilitator and discuss the importance of everyone's role in the process.[31] The members' perceptions and expectations will depend on their previous experiences. This role can then be negotiated over time. For example, you can introduce yourself by saying, "Hi, I'm Jan Smith. Your manager asked me to come to help you map your manufacturing process to find ways to decrease defects and cycle time. My background is in . . . and I see myself doing (list role or responsibilities) for you." Listen and honor their opinions and perspectives, further reinforcing that each person has an important role to play in the process.

Another problem facilitators may face is resistance due to a lack of familiarity with or credibility in a part of the organization,[32] despite the fact that such unfamiliarity may underlie valuable objectivity. Since facilitators often work between a team and its management, a facilitator who is seen as ineffective, lacking credibility, or a deterrent to some "master plan" might be "blocked" from helping the team achieve its goals by other organizational stakeholders.

While team facilitation is not a panacea for all organizational challenges, the use of a trained process facilitator can be beneficial.[33] Facilitative skills can be learned and should be used either formally as a trained facilitator or informally whenever you are part of a team. Whether a facilitator is utilized or not, training all team members in facilitation techniques will greatly enhance the teaming experience and output.

Summary

Facilitation helps team members work cohesively and cooperatively to effectively achieve organizational and individual goals. Through the use of facilitation, teams will function more effectively, members will be more satisfied with the team experience and learn new skills, and output will be enhanced. Facilitation is a skill that can increase the effectiveness of all members of teams and organizations. Even if your team does not have the benefit of a process facilitator, having knowledge and skills in facilitation will make you a valuable contributor to your team and organization.[34]

Key Terms and Concepts

Content	Intervention
Dysfunctional behaviors	Maintenance-related behaviors
Facilitation	Objectivity
Facilitative preventions	Problem people
Facilitator or process consultant	Process
Graphic facilitation	Task-related behaviors

Discussion Questions

1. Why are some teams more effective when they have access to a facilitator or process consultant?

2. We suggest that facilitators play other roles, such as educator. Why is the educator role so important?

3. We suggest that facilitators should focus primarily on the process and not the content of the meeting. Do you agree? Explain.

4. While facilitation is helpful, it doesn't fix all problems on teams. Explain.

Endnotes

1. S. G. Cohen, "New Approaches to Teams and Teamwork," in J. R. Galbraith and E. E. Lawler & Associates (eds.), *Organizing for the Future: The New Logic for Managing Complex Organizations* (San Francisco: Jossey Bass, 1993), pp. 194–226.

2. S. de Janasz, "Teaching Facilitation: A Play in Three Acts," *Journal of Management Education* 25, no. 6 (2001), pp. 685–712.

3. R. P. Bostrom, R. Anson, and V. K. Clawson, "Group Facilitation and Group Support Systems," in L. Jessup and J. Valacich (eds.), *Group Support Systems: New Perspectives* (New York: Macmillan, 1993), pp. 146–68.

4. E. Schein, *Process Consultation* (Menlo Park, CA: Addison-Wesley, 1988).

5. E. Cooley, "Training an Interdisciplinary Team in Communication and Decision-making Skills," *Small Group Research* 25 (1994), p. 6.

6. W. E. Watson, K. Kumar, and L. K. Michaelsen, "Cultural Diversity's Impact on Interaction Process and Performance: Comparing Homogeneous and Diverse Task Groups," *Academy of Management Journal* 36 (1993), pp. 590–602.

7. D. Dougherty, "Interpretive Barriers to Successful Product Innovation in Large Firms," *Organization Science* 3 (1992), pp. 179–202.

8. I. Bens, *Facilitating with Ease!: Core Skills for Facilitators, Team Leaders, and Members, Managers, Consultants, and Trainers,* 2nd ed. (San Francisco: John Wiley & Sons, 2005), p. 7.

9. Ibid.

10. Ibid.

11. Ibid.

12. R. Sisco, "What to Train Team Leaders," *Training* (February 1993), pp. 62–63; and D. G. Ancona, "Outward Bound: Strategies for Team Survival in an Organization," *Academy of Management Journal* 33 (1990), pp. 334–65.

13. Adapted and expanded from Bens, "Facilitating with Ease," p. 7.

14. T. G. Cummings and C. G. Worley, *Organization Development and Change,* 8th ed. (Los Angeles: South-Western College Publishing, 2004).

15. D. W. Johnson and F. P. Johnson, *Joining Together: Group Theory and Group Skills,* 6th ed. (Boston, MA: Allyn & Bacon, 1997).

16. American Business Women's Association, "The Art of Facilitation," *Women in Business* (January/February 1999), p. 38.

17. J. M. Jackman, "Fear of Feedback," *Harvard Business Review* (November 2003), pp. 54–63.

18. K. D. Fairfield, "Facilitators: When Do We Need Them?" *Business and Economic Review* 46, no. 4 (2000), pp. 16–20.

19. K. Tyler, "The Gang's All Here . . . ," *HRMagazine* 45, no. 5 (2000), pp. 104–13.

20. Fairfield, "Facilitators."

21. Schein, *Process Consultation.*

22. Sisco, "What to Train."

23. This chart is adapted from and expands on M. Doyle and D. Straus, *How to Make Meetings Work: The New Interaction Method* (Chicago: Playboy Press, 1976).

24. This chart is adapted from and expands on Doyle and Straus, *How to Make Meetings Work.*

25. Roger Schwarz, "Four Ways to Practice—Let's Talk," *Fundamental Change e-Newsletter* 3, no. 6 (Roger Schwarz & Associates, 2007).

26. Ibid.

27. Source: www.donbraisby.co.uk/graphic_facilitation.html (accessed August 1, 2010).

28. This chart is adapted from and expands on David A. Peoples, *Presentations Plus* (New York: John Wiley & Sons, 1988), pp. 147–55.

29. David J. Pauleen, "A Grounded Theory of Virtual Facilitation: Building Relationships with Virtual Team Members" (2001). Unpublished doctoral dissertation. University of Wellington, Victoria, New Zealand.

30. M. Travis Maynard, "Virtual Teams: What Do We Know and Where Do We Go from Here?" *Journal of Management* 30, no. 6 (2004), pp. 805–35.

31. American Business Women's Association, "The Art of Facilitation."

32. Sisco, "What to Train."

33. Tom Terez, "Can We Talk?" *Workforce* (July 2000), pp. 46–55.

34. Tyler, "The Gang's All Here . . ."

**Exercise 13–A
Case Study: Dealing
with Team Conflict**

You've been asked to facilitate a team that has not been doing too well lately. This cross-functional team is composed of eight members from various disciplines, including materials, engineering, program management, operations, and finance, and has been working together for about six weeks. Its task: to reduce the time necessary to procure materials for use on a particular program/line of business. Things were going well in the beginning, as everybody's job could be simplified if there weren't so many delays in the process.

However, in the last meeting, the group identified three key causes that, in essence, suggest that one or more of the represented disciplines are to blame for the delays. These causes included:

1. Undependable suppliers (if it wouldn't take "them" so long to get the needed materials and deliver them on time, things would be fine).

2. Lengthy and cumbersome signature cycle (members of finance and program management are among those who must sign each request).

3. Too many engineering changes (when engineering makes design changes, new materials have to be ordered and "old" materials have to be returned).

Most members of the team, including managers and technical personnel, are hesitant to expose their organization's part (if any) in the delays.

Questions

1. Do you think it's possible to help this team achieve its goal? Explain.

2. As a facilitator, what specific things would you do and say to ensure an effective process? Why?

3. What impact would this likely have on the outcome?

4. What, if anything, can be done "behind the scenes" to improve the team's chances for success?

Exercise 13–B
Video Case: *Twelve*
Angry Men*

Your instructor will be showing a clip from the classic *Twelve Angry Men*. In this movie, members of a jury are about to decide the fate of a young boy charged with murdering his father. Answer the following questions after viewing this clip.

1. In the beginning of this clip, we see the foreman suggesting a process (e.g., why don't we take a straw vote) and clarifying instructions related to this process. Using the role behaviors in Figure 13–1 as a guide, which behaviors did the foreman use and what effect did they have?

2. During this initial or straw vote, we see hesitation on the part of some members when casting their votes. What explains this hesitation, in your opinion, and if you were the foreperson, what might you have done differently?

3. After this vote, some members can be seen pressuring the single dissenting member. If this were to happen in a team you were facilitating, what intervention would you use and why?

4. Midway through the clip, the foreman suggests one process ("Let's all go around the table and convince this man why he's wrong"), and immediately thereafter, another jury member suggests a different process ("It seems to me that he—the dissenter—should be the one who tries to convince us"). Both processes have value. How would you help the group choose between the processes? What, specifically, would you say or do?

5. Periodically, throughout the clip, we see jury members treat one another harshly (e.g., remarks that are ethnically or age discriminatory). If you were to facilitate this group, would you intervene during these moments? Why or why not? If you would intervene, what would you say or do and why?

6. The foreman is actually one of the 12 jury members. At times, he plays a leaderlike role; other times, he is facilitative. Cite examples of each. Should he play both leader and facilitator? Why or why not?

7. Different jury members have different personality styles. Such is also the case on most teams. What are some ways to point out these differences in a way that enables members to benefit from instead of being aggravated by these differences?

8. The jury member played by Jack Klugman, who admits that he "grew up in a slum" and identifies with the defendant, speaks infrequently and only when requested by others to do so. Even then, he seems to lack confidence in sharing his ideas and concerns. If you were to facilitate this "team," what techniques might you use to help this character contribute? Identify at least one "prevention" and one "intervention," and describe how you would use them.

9. Another jury member, played by E. G. Marshall, is intelligent, articulate, and very confident in his opinions. You could see this when he tries to point out the defendant's guilt on the basis of the boy's inability to recall the name of the movie he saw. These qualities can both benefit and hinder a team's process. What impact did his behavior have on you? If you were to facilitate the meeting, what might you have said or done to facilitate this member and why?

10. Which of the four stages of teaming did this "team" go through? Identify the stages and cite evidence to support your answer.

*Distributed by MGM Home Videos, 1957 (Sidney Lumet, director; Henry Fonda, star).

**Exercise 13–C
Alternative Exercise for
*Twelve Angry Men***

View the portion of the film shown in class by the instructor. As you watch the movie, record examples of dysfunctional behaviors demonstrated in the film on the chart below. Cite the actor (describe his role or appearance if you don't know the name) and the specific action or statement that is evidence of a particular dysfunctional behavior. For each behavior, describe strategies that were or could be used to counteract each of the dysfunctional behaviors listed.

Dysfunctional Behaviors and Related Facilitation Strategies: *Twelve Angry Men*

Behavior	Actor/Evidence	Strategy Used or Suggested
Whisperer—periodically engages team member(s) in side conversations		
"Eager beaver" (talker/ monopolizer)—always has something to say		
Heckler/complainer—combative; tells team members why what they're working on will never work		
Silent member—withdrawn; doesn't participate		
Sidetracker—dicusses items not on the agenda		
Fighter—picks a "fight" and/or argues with another team member		
"Stand pat"—won't budge; hostile; unwilling to look at situation from others' perspective; often prejudiced		
Verbal stumbler—unable to express self clearly		
Early leaver—announces they must leave for another activity		

**Exercise 13–D
Intervention
Presentation**

Your instructor will assign one of the interventions listed in Figure 13–3 to each partici-pant. You will need to prepare a two- to three-minute presentation in which you discuss the intervention, why or when it would be used, and how it is used—perhaps role-playing an example that demonstrates what a facilitator would say and do in a situation requiring such an intervention.

The chart below provides an example of how to approach one of the interventions in Figure 13–3: playing dumb.

The Intervention	Description	Why/When Used	How Used
Example: Playing dumb	A nondirective way to help the team realize they're off track	When tangential dis-cussions brought up by a side-tracker or expert overtake the task.	"I'm confused. Can someone tell me what we're trying to accomplish with this discussion?"

You will be asked to present and demonstrate this intervention to a small or large group. After several interventions are presented, discuss how these and other interventions could be used (separately or in combination) with behaviors or situations that impede a team's progress.

1. Which interventions do you feel most comfortable using? Explain.

2. With which interventions do you need more practice? Explain.

3. What are some ways that you can increase your facilitation skills? Create a plan and discuss it with a classmate.

**Exercise 13–E
Facilitation
Self-assessment**

The following questions relate to the facilitation activity you did in your class. Please an-swer them completely yet concisely.

1. What interpersonal skills covered in our class (e.g., listening, problem solving) did you find yourself using when you played the role of facilitator during this activity? Name at least two skills and share an example for each.

_____

_____

_____

_____

2. When you facilitated, what do you believe to be the things you did particularly well? Please describe at least two instances when you felt your facilitation was effective.

_____

_____

_____

_____

3. When you facilitated, what do you believe to be the things you did not do particularly well or that resulted in an outcome different from what you had anticipated? Please describe at least two instances when you felt your facilitation could have been improved.

_____

_____

_____

_____

4. What lessons did you learn about yourself and about the challenges of doing work in teams from this activity? What steps can you take to improve your skills as a facilitator and as a team member?

_____

_____

_____

_____

**Exercise 13–F
Observing Group
Process**

Using one of the following scenarios, form a small group. Conduct a meeting on the topic and generate a list of recommendations within a specified period of time. While your group is conducting the meeting, a second small group will be arrayed in a circle around your group, observing your group process.

Scenario 1

The CEO of a large, _Fortune_ 500 company that has just embraced "teaming" has assembled your team. Customer complaints about your products and services have risen over the last few years, and it is your hope that "teaming" can turn that trend around. Your task is to come up with recommendations for how to implement teaming in the customer service division, one of 10 divisions in this company. Mr. Smith, the executive vice president in charge of this project, would like your recommendations by the end of the semester.

Scenario 2

Your team has been assembled by the athletic director to enhance the quantity and quality of the undergraduate recreational athletics at your university. Dr. Jones expects your team's report and recommendations by the end of the semester.

Using the following chart, the observing group will note at least one behavior each group member exhibits. When time is up, the other small group will share their impressions with your group as to which behaviors they observed and did not observe while your group was meeting.

Observing Group Process

Instructions: Enter the names of team members along the top. Enter comments in the appropriate boxes when you see any or all of the behaviors.

Initiating: Gets a conversation going.						
Information or opinion seeking/giving: Drawing out/sharing relevant information.						
Clarifying and elaborating: Clears up confusion.						
Summarizing: Pulls together what's been said.						
Consensus testing: Moves the group toward decision.						
Harmonizing and compromising: Reduces tension, works out disagreements.						
Gatekeeping: Helps keep communication channels open.						
Diagnosing: Looks at the process, how people are feeling about the group.						
Standard setting: Looks at the group structure.						

Source: "Observing Group Process Chart" from Peter R. Scholtes, *The Team Handbook* (Madison, WI: Joiner Associates, 1988), pp. 7–43.

Questions

1. Which behaviors were observed most frequently? Least?
2. Which behaviors had the greatest positive impact on the team's ability to succeed in its task?
3. Which behaviors, had they been used, would have helped the group to move forward?
4. Did the group appoint a timekeeper? Scribe? Facilitator?
5. What else did the group do to operate effectively?

**Exercise 13–G
Reflection/Action Plan**

This chapter focused on facilitation—what it is, why it is important, and how to improve your skill in this area. Complete the following questions upon completing all readings and experiential activities for this chapter.

1. The one or two areas in which I am most strong are:

_____

_____

_____

2. The one or two areas in which I need more improvement are:

_____

_____

_____

3. If I did only one thing to improve in this area, it would be to:

_____

_____

_____

4. Making this change would probably result in:

_____

_____

_____

5. If I did not change or improve in this area, it would probably affect my personal and professional life in the following ways:

_____

_____

_____

14 Making Decisions and Solving Problems Creatively

Learning Points

How do I:
- Decide between competing options and interests?
- Make a decision before having all the necessary information?
- Make a decision that won't change?
- Evaluate potential options?
- Think creatively about alternatives?

Wow, this was going to be harder than she thought. When Sara was put in charge of this assignment she thought it would be an easy way to get involved at work and enhance her connection with her boss. However, she quickly realized how important it was to make the right decision because of the impact it would have on her company and its employees. The task seemed straightforward: Find a nonprofit organization with which her company could build a relationship. After completing research on several organizations and surveying her colleagues, Sara was left with three clear options. The problem was to narrow the selection to just one. The first option, the American Heart Association, was a good possibility because of the high number of employees who had been affected by a family history of heart disease. The second possibility, the Green County Rescue Mission, was a popular choice because of its high standing in the local community, and the third option, the local chapter of Habitat for Humanity, tied in well with the company's mission. All three options looked good, but her boss distinctly told her to make the decision and present it to the board. She had to make a decision before next Thursday's board meeting, but she didn't know what to do next.

1. What steps has Sara correctly completed toward making a decision?
2. What issues is she facing?
3. What options does she have available to her?
4. What evaluation criteria would help her analyze the three options?
5. What steps should she take toward making the final decision?

"Nothing is more difficult, and therefore more precious, than to be able to decide."

Napoleon Bonaparte

Why Is Decision Making Important?

Making decisions—and being able to live with them rather than second-guessing them—is one of the most difficult tasks we face in life and in business. Whether the decision is a personal choice or it directly affects others—our organizations, colleagues, peers, or family—an effective decision-making process can significantly impact the outcome. In this chapter we discuss what decision making is, why it is important, and strategies to use to make effective decisions. At the end of the chapter, we've included some exercises to help you improve your skills in decision making.

What Is Decision Making?

Decision making is a process by which several possibilities are considered and prioritized, resulting in a clear choice of one option over others. Decision making is a fact of life personally and in business. We make dozens of decisions each day. Some decisions are simple, such as deciding what color paper to use, while others are complex, such as when Steve Jobs of Apple decided when the marketplace and the company were ready for the launch of the next version of the iPhone. Decision making can aid managers in identifying and selecting among potential opportunities, helping them solve immediate problems, and making future problems more manageable.[1] Good decision makers are those who are effective at processing information, assessing risks, and making choices that will have positive outcomes for their organization.[2] But time and time again we see that even some of the most intelligent people or groups of people can make a wrong or even disastrous decision. So while at times intuitive or "gut" decision making is appropriate, in this chapter we focus our attention primarily on structured decision-making processes to provide a framework for making decisions while working in our organizations or as part of a group.

Effective decision making is essential for both organizations and individuals. Changes in organizational structures, processes, technology, and the availability of data have increased the need for members at all levels of an organization to make decisions—and make them effectively.

With the change from hierarchical to flatter, more participative organizational structures, it is crucial for employees at all levels of the organization to have the information and authority they need to react quickly to customer concerns, business issues, and changing market trends. Having a decision-making frame of reference enables employees to react quickly and make decisions that are in the best interest of the organization.

Today more business decisions are being made in team environments. Group decision making is even more complex than decisions made by one or two individuals. Employees in team environments need to understand how to gain buy-in for their positions and how to work with others to arrive at a consensus about a preferred course of action. A decision-making framework can provide the basis for identifying mutual interests. This can serve as the foundation for healthy discussion and eventual selection of one option over others.

Technology is literally speeding up the pace of business. Quick decision making is not only desired, it is expected.[3] Poor or slow decision making can result in failure or a lack of competitiveness. In our fast-paced business environment, the ability to identify potential problems and opportunities, collect the data needed to analyze their limitations and merits, and make expedient determinations based on the information available has become one of the most important managerial skills. Companies that train their employees to be good decision makers and encourage smart decision making can increase efficiency and boost profits. By eliminating unnecessary steps, combining knowledge, and simplifying processes to help speed up decisions, managers with well-honed decision-making skills can have a tremendous impact on a company's bottom line.[4] Yet as with BP's recent oil rig explosion and massive oil spill in the Gulf of Mexico, the decision to skip some basic procedures and quality tests removed critical safeguards and proved to be disastrous. Sometimes the fast pace of business and the push to make money can lead to hasty decisions by failing to consult or listen to others.

Figure 14–1
A Decision-Making Process

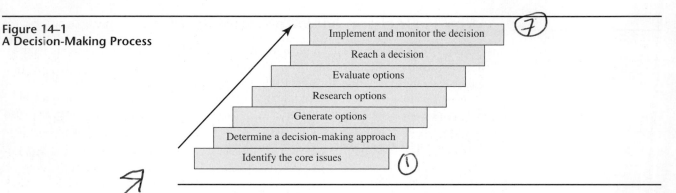

The vast amount of information available today through the media, Internet, and other outlets makes decision making an essential skill rather than just one that's nice to have. The most effective managers are those who are able to scan quickly a wide variety of data from numerous sources and determine which information is relevant for their needs. Through decision-making processes, managers learn to translate, assimilate, and activate the information they receive.[5]

Decision-making skills play a vital role in managerial success. A recent study showed that of 2,207 executives surveyed, only 28 percent believed that the decisions made in their companies were generally good, while 60 percent felt that "bad decisions were as frequent as good decisions." These executives also stated that bad decisions were consistently made by "some of the smartest people in the best companies." It was also clear that while they understood the need for good decision-making processes, they were still unclear on how to develop these skills.[6] Therefore, it is helpful to have a model to lead the process.

A Decision-Making Process

Figure 14–1 represents a straightforward **decision-making process** for almost any type of decision. This framework can be used for decisions you face in your personal life, at school, and in the workplace. As you read the seven steps, analyze how Sara from the opening scenario could apply the process to be more effective in her decision making.

Step One—Identify the Core Issues

What is the concern you are addressing? What is it you're trying to change or react to? In the first step of decision making, you need to determine your objective, stating clearly and specifically what you want the end result to be.[7] In the opening scenario, Sara needs to select a nonprofit organization that will be acceptable to her boss and co-workers. She also wants to ensure that her choice is the right option for establishing a long-term commitment for donating and volunteering by her company and co-workers. By specifying the end goal or desired state, you have a logical foundation for making a good decision—for sorting through options and determining which one or ones best meet your overall objective.[8]

Step Two—Determine a Decision-Making Approach

How will you (and your group) make the decision? What options are available to you? What are the possible ways you can respond to a situation? What different steps can be taken? Establish a course of action before attempting to make the decision. This sounds simple, but often people rush to make a decision before agreeing on how the decision will be made. The very act of discussing a potential process paves the way for consideration of options that might not otherwise have surfaced. Was Sara's boss correct in assigning this task to only one person? Should this have been done by a task force? What type of process did Sara use, and could she have handled the process differently?

Step Three—Generate Options

By definition, making decisions implies that more than one option is available to you. It is very rare and unusual for any problem or situation to have only one solution or possibility. People who only consider one alternative or solution are setting themselves up for failure or marginal success. Often the initial solution presented is not the best one.

The best decisions are those made after consideration of varied or multiple options. Be creative and brainstorm as many potential alternatives or solutions as possible (more about this later in this chapter). We see in the opening case that Sara has three options. Is this enough? How could she have found other options? Using a decision-making matrix such as the one in Exercise 14–A can help in generating options.

Step Four—Research Options

Conducting research is a crucial step for virtually all team or organizational decisions. Often one of the reasons we're unable to move forward and make a decision is that we simply don't have the information needed to make a good decision. By taking the time to gather data, you are able to increase your confidence that once the decision is made it will be the right one, as it is based on the information available at the time. At this step Sara would need in-depth research on all of her options in order to move forward with her decision. Do you have any suggestions on sources that help in the evaluation of nonprofit organizations? Where can you find this information? At this point you will want to evaluate your data for any deficiencies to ensure that you have enough information to truly make a decision or pause and continue to search for other options.

Step Five—Evaluate Options

At this point, a little healthy pessimism is needed. Once you've been creative and nonjudgmental in generating options and gathering information about them, you can assess the pros and cons of each option.[9] Assess the gains that would be derived from each and any limitations that are inherent in each option. Also consider other factors that are important to you when making the decision and evaluate the degree to which each option relates to the factors of importance. At this point, Sara would need to determine which option would satisfy the needs of her organization. Would personal connection to the nonprofit's mission be more important than local community involvement? Would reputation or the nonprofit's efficiency or effectiveness rating in achieving its mission be more critical? While evaluating the options, we often work with incomplete or imperfect information in the decision-making process. We can reduce the risk factors by hypothesizing potential scenarios. For example, if Sara has incomplete information, she could ask questions such as, "What would happen if I decided to select option 1? How would other organizational members feel if we were to select option 2? How would option 3 affect our business or influence our stakeholders?" At this stage, it's also appropriate to narrow the alternatives. Only consider the options that are truly realistic and fulfill the goal or desired end state you defined in step one. Scenario planning, which is examining the options by thinking of all the "what ifs" that could affect each option, is an important tool, especially if you are dealing with a unique or nonroutine situation. Although this step is based on hypothetical factors, it can help you see potential pitfalls in your decision-making process. It is important to keep in mind that unique situations will have an increased factor of risk and require extra attention to avoid misinterpretations or unidentified circumstances[10]

Another key consideration in decision making is that with the availability of so much information in today's technological age, it is possible to get caught up in having too many alternatives, too many ideas, and too much work. This can lead to a lack of focus and momentum, which can lead to indecisiveness and a loss of power.[11] We may become overwhelmed by the options and never proceed to selecting one, a condition known as **analysis paralysis**.[12] Prioritizing the factors that are important to you and evaluating your options against these priorities can help you narrow the options to those that are the most viable given the circumstances and your goals in a specific situation. Using a weighted average decision-making technique such as the one in Exercise 14–B is an effective process for prioritizing outcomes and probabilities. There are many decision-making tools and techniques you can use to help you sift through your options. You can create a list of pros and cons that would result from the decision, you could use a decision tree to think through the outcomes of each possible option, or you could plot out the strengths, weaknesses, opportunities, and threats that are associated with the decision and the potential options (see Figure 14–2).

Figure 14–2
Decision-Making Tools

DECISION-MAKING TOOLS

List of Pros/Cons: List the pros and cons of making a decision

PROS	CONS

Decision Trees: List the options for a decision and think through the probable outcomes.

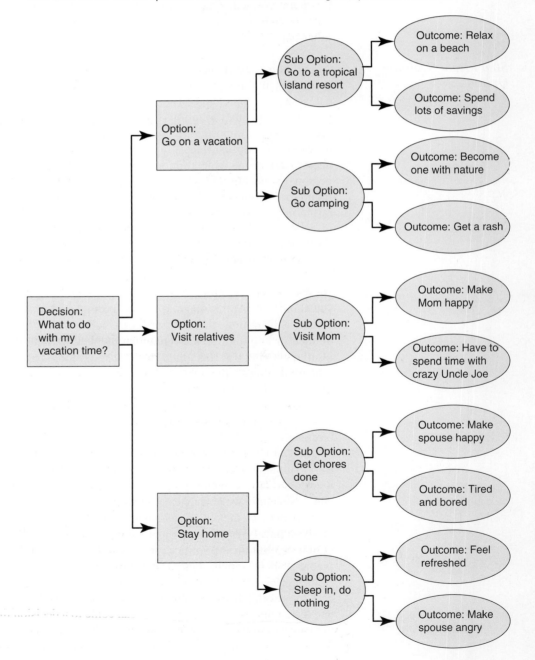

Figure 14–2   (Continued)   **SWOT Analysis:** List the Strengths, Weaknesses, Opportunities, and Threats for different decisions

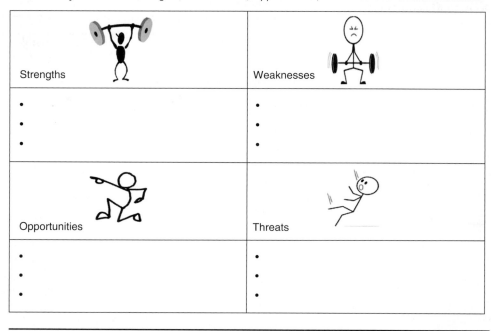

Step Six—Reach a Decision

Once all the information is in and you've had a chance to consult with others as necessary and weigh the alternatives, it's time to make a decision. Determine which option best meets your overall needs and resolve to act on that option. But before taking the plunge, envision taking the plunge first. Do a self-visualization to make sure the decision you're making is one you can live with. One way to do this is to make a decision, but take 24 hours to think about it. Let your subconscious act as though you've made the decision, but don't let anyone know and don't act on the decision yet. The next morning, before you even rise, ask yourself how you feel about the decision you made yesterday. Listen to what your heart tells you. Do you feel positive? Calm? That it was the right choice? Or do you feel negative? Panicked? That it would be the wrong choice? If you feel fine about the choice you've made, it's an intuitive sign you've made the best decision given the information available and you can probably act on it. If you still have serious reservations about your decision, then you're not ready to act, and you should defer action until you've had a chance to resolve the conflict you're experiencing.

In reaching your decision, you will want to make sure your process was not distorted by any biases from self-interest or emotional attachments from pattern recognition.[13] Pattern recognition occurs when our brain process analyzes new situations based on past experiences that seem somehow similar to this new situation. While this works most of the time, you may be misled when tackling new decisions because you believe you understand the new situation, when in reality you may not. You may be simplifying the situation because it seems familiar. Another problem with using past situations as a basis for decision making is that they may be tagged with emotions and biases. You may therefore unconsciously allow a bias to interfere in your accurate evaluation of possible alternative options or you may limit yourself by anchoring to your initial or preferred choice. If you feel you may be making an error in judgment, it is always good to use a system of checks and balances.

If the decision seems sound, it is time to move forward. Once Sara has gone through the previous stages, we hope that she can come to a decision that meets the necessary criteria and that she has the research and evidence to present her option to the board. How would you suggest presenting the decision? What evidence would best support her decision? What should she do if she feels her decision may not receive approval? How could she pretest her decision to get feedback from potential stakeholders?

*Step Seven—Implement
and Monitor the Decision*

Once you've reached a decision, it's time to act on it and monitor it to make sure it results in the outcome you expected. Develop a plan that specifies the steps you'll take, a time frame, and the key players. Then, monitor the plan to see if it is following the direction you wanted. Also observe whether external factors have changed or if you're receiving information that might affect your decision, and adapt your plan accordingly. Taking the time to plan and to monitor the decision after making a decision ensures that you'll do the follow-through necessary for the decision to be successful. Once the board approves Sara's decision, another decision will need to be made on how and what type of relationship to establish with the nonprofit, as well as how to encourage employee volunteerism throughout the company.

What Kind of Decision Maker Are You?

What kind of decision maker are you? You may be more methodical, pondering your situation and analyzing options before deciding on one. You may be more impulsive, reacting quickly and intuitively. Or perhaps you are somewhere in the middle, taking action based on your intuition, after taking some time to explore the situation. Whatever your natural style, when considering a life or career decision or change, it is important to incorporate elements of all of these approaches. If you are usually organized, analytical, and deliberate in making decisions (often referred to as "left-brained,") be somewhat creative and see what your intuition can contribute to your decision. If you are intuitive and tend to approach issues in a roundabout way (often referred to as "right-brained,") or make decisions hastily based on your past experience, take the time to develop and implement a plan in consultation with others who can help keep you on track. Whether we act intuitively, analytically, or through a combination of the two, it is important to take time to make a decision with which we can live. The accompanying box (refer to next page) offers pointers about steps to take before making a decision.[14]

*"The dip in sales seems to coincide with the
decision to eliminate the sales staff."*

Source: Leo Cullum/New Yorker Collection/www.cartoonbank.com

The "Readiness for Change" Test: Don't Make a Decision Until . . .

- You've assessed your risk-taking ability, clarified your options, and generated creative options.
- You've communicated with and obtained full support from those who are affected by the decision.
- You've gathered the information you need.
- You've predicted the "best and worst" outcomes and developed contingency plans.
- You're ready to follow through, and stick with, your choice.
- You've "slept on it" and your intuition is telling you it's the right thing to do.
- You have an exit strategy for "just in case."

Collaborative Decision Making

In many situations, it is helpful or necessary to involve others in the decision-making process. **Collaborative decision making** involves identifying your and the other parties' priorities and determining the option(s) available that meet both sets of needs. This can be possible by paying careful attention to your and the others' ability to handle risks; thorough assessment of each of your primary needs and motivators; continuous, positive communication; and a willingness to be creative in generating options rather than taking a stand for one fixed option. The collaborative process can also be aided by decision support systems that allow users to store, transmit, and manipulate information while working toward group decisions.

One of the reasons it's often difficult to make decisions is that you're not the only one involved or impacted by the decision. By including stakeholders in the process, you will be able to get more buy-in to the solutions. Collaborative decision making can also help to overcome self-interest or emotional attachments that may be hindering individual decision making as well as infuse the process with the knowledge, insights, and experiences of others. Working with others should increase the group's learning through the exchange of new ideas and perceptions on the issues.[15] When you're making decisions with someone else—whether a spouse or partner, team member, employer, customer, or client—it's useful to know how to

Tips for Collaborative Decision Making[16]

- *Consider you and the person(s) involved as one unit.* Do what's ultimately best for the unit (for example, the team, the organization, the couple, the family, and so on).
- *Be open to new ways of looking at the situation.* Establish what's important to you and the other(s).
- *Sharpen your communication skills.* Making decisions that incorporate others' concerns requires shifting your focus from your own interests to a set of joint interests—those of yourself and others. In particular, skills in self-disclosure, values clarification, assertiveness, sending verbal and nonverbal messages, active listening, persuasion, conflict management, and interest-based negotiation are particularly helpful in collaborative decision making.
- *Rely on your intuition.* The analytical process described in this chapter is useful and important. But don't rely solely on a logical approach in decision making. Your feelings (and those of the others involved in the decision) are just as important as the pragmatic facts of the situation.[17] Sir Richard Branson, founder and chairman of Virgin Group, was considering expanding the company into the airline business. He consulted with many colleagues and business partners and even though he was advised to be cautious in an industry comprised of strong competitors, he relied on his research, his intuition, and his business expertise to create an airline that responded to customer needs and to develop a highly competitive airline division.[18]
- *Have a "veto" rule.* Some teams and couples rely on a "veto" guideline to prevent them from moving forward before all involved are "on the same page." A veto guideline gives each party the freedom to "call time" and request that a decision not be enacted until all issues are resolved.

take into consideration the best interests of all parties who will be affected by the outcome. See the accompanying box (refer to previous page) for tips for collaborative decision making.

David Straus, prominent author and researcher, has devised five principles of collaboration to help with the challenges associated with collaborative decision making.[19]

- *Involve relevant stakeholders.* It is important to identify and find means to involve key stakeholders in the decision process. This not only includes those that are directly affected by the decision or who have relevant information or expertise on the issue, but also those who have the power to make or break the decision. Including the right stakeholders will not only improve the quality of information infused in the process, but will gain a broader buy-in and acceptance of the decision.

- *Build consensus phase by phase.* Consensus does not magically happen; it must be created throughout the decision-making process. By working through the phases of the process, group members will come to a consensus—not 100 percent agreement—but rather a decision that all members can stand behind.

- *Design a process map.* Since there is no right way to solve problems, a process map serves as a guide for stakeholders in working through the process. The map should take into consideration the unique issue or content associated with the task along with the needs or objectives of the organization and the members involved in the decision-making process. The map will clarify the tools needed to steer the process.

- *Designate a process facilitator.* In order to ensure a smooth process, a third-party facilitator, dedicated to focusing on the process, will help the group continue moving forward and allow the group members to focus their energy on the task at hand.

- *Harness the power of group memory.* Posting a written record of all ideas and decisions made by the group can ensure that the group avoids dysfunctional behaviors such as repetition, loss of focus, disproportionate participation levels, and disruptions by providing a visual reminder of the task and decisions involved in the process.

By controlling the process and implementing the appropriate principles, we can guide the group through the complexities of collaborative decision making. Edward de Bono's Six Thinking Hats[20] tool can be used to help groups and individuals plan a process to get everyone's ideas organized into a collaborative process while taking into account all the ways individuals approach decision making. This technique helps group members be more mindfully involved in parallel thinking through a process that separates thinking into six functions or roles, hence six different colored hats as shown in Figure 14–3. Imagine, for

Figure 14–3
Six Thinking Hats Diagram

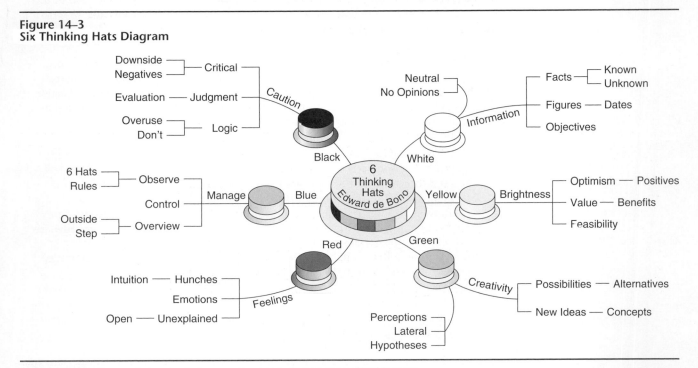

Source: From http://www.mindmapinspiration.com. Reprinted with permission of Paul Foreman.

example, your team has been struggling with unproductive meetings and wants to decide on some means for making meetings shorter and more productive. Using the six hats method, you ask all team members to "put on" the white information hat. They are only allowed at this stage to give facts and data with no opinions. Once the team is satisfied they have provided all the information, they are to put on the green hat to come up with creative possibilities for changes. This process can continue by putting on the red hat allowing members to express feelings and emotions, then the yellow hat to discuss the value and benefits that will come from potential changes, or the black hat to judge and question if tactics will work. The blue hat is the hat worn for managing the process, to direct the team to the appropriate hat as needed to move the process forward. This method can allow for flexibility in bringing emotion and skepticism into a rational process to develop a supported and vetted decision.

In the next section we discuss problem solving, why it's important, strategies that can be used, and tips to make your problem-solving efforts more productive. We also include information on creativity to aid in innovative thinking. At the end of the chapter are some exercises to help you enhance your skills in rational and creative problem solving as well as suggestions for further resources.

"If I were given one hour to save the planet, I would spend 59 minutes defining the problem and one minute resolving it."

Albert Einstein

What Is Problem Solving?

Dr. Walter A. Shewhart suggests that **problem solving** is a cyclical process composed of four steps: Plan, Do, Check, and Act (**PDCA**).[21] This process was introduced to Japan by W. Edwards Deming, one of the most highly recognized gurus of quality management techniques. As you can see from Figure 14–4, the most important step in the process is the *plan*. It is in this stage that we define and identify potential solutions for problems. This is easier said than done. What looks like the problem might actually be a symptom. Correctly defining the problem can be a challenge; with the remaining elements in this step we validate whether we identified the real problem and create a plan for fixing it. Asking why the problem exists or subdividing the problem into smaller problems may help to get at the root causes. Using the 5-Why Analysis process devised by Toyota in the 1970s, groups are forced to ask "why" at least five times to get past the symptoms and find out the root causes for why the process did not work. Accurately addressing the root cause is fundamental, as illustrated by Benjamin Franklin's poem from *Poor Richard's Almanac*:

For want of a nail a shoe was lost,

for want of a shoe a horse was lost,

for want of a horse a rider was lost,

Figure 14–4
PDCA Cycle

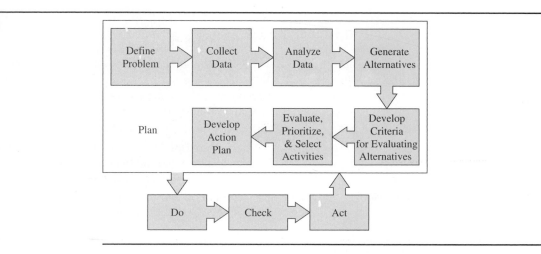

for want of a rider an army was lost,

for want of an army a battle was lost,

for want of a battle the war was lost,

for want of the war the kingdom was lost,

and all for the want of a little horseshoe nail.

Once the plan is complete, the next stage is to *do*—or implement—the plan. Next, we *check* to see if the changes made resulted in lasting, measurable improvements. If not, we may need to take a step back. Did we solve the right problem? Did we unknowingly create a new one? Did we implement a short-term fix that will need modifications in the future? Based on our check, we then *act* by taking appropriate steps to adjust or ensure the problem is solved.

Why Is Problem Solving Important?

Organizational problems come in many forms—whether in processes (how managers lead, how employees communicate, how work flows, how conflicts are solved, how employees deal with customers or suppliers) or outcomes (inadequate or unsatisfactory products or services, excessive employee absenteeism or turnover, or insufficient profit margins). Problems such as these can significantly hamper an organization's ability to operate and succeed in the long term. The ability to solve problems—and apply problem-solving techniques to improve processes that work—can significantly and positively impact an organization's bottom line, as well as its long-term viability.

All too often, managers and employees rush to fix what they do not completely understand, in effect relieving symptoms temporarily. Often the problem resurfaces, possibly with greater intensity and impact than during its initial appearance.[22]

"The best way to have good ideas is to have lots of ideas."

Linus Pauling, Nobel Laureate
and Nobel Peace Prize winner

Problem-Solving Techniques

Brainstorming

These techniques can be used individually or in combination, depending on the nature of the problem and the resources available.

Brainstorming is a tool used to stimulate and capture creative thoughts and ideas. It involves the creative generation of many ideas to solve a problem. There are several variations of brainstorming, yet they all have in common the ground rules highlighted in the accompanying box.

Brainstorming Guidelines

- Articulate the theme or the question (e.g., Why are sales down? How can we cut costs in the manufacturing area?).
- Set a time limit (usually 5 or 10 minutes, depending on the size of the group and the complexity of the theme or question).
- Record the ideas for everyone to see (using a flip chart or whiteboard).
- Remember that quantity is important (generate as many ideas as possible).
- Encourage everyone to actively participate (no benchwarmers!).
- Accept all ideas (positive or negative critiquing is *not* permitted).
- Piggyback or build on the ideas of others.

If the pace of suggesting new ideas begins to slow or participants seem stifled by constraints, the leader or facilitator of the brainstorming session may ask a hypothetical question such as, "What if money were no object?" or "What if you could not fail . . . what would you suggest doing?" During the process, it is important to enforce the ground rules should they be broken. Many people can't seem to resist evaluating others' ideas—it's human nature. However, such evaluation can stifle creativity or cause participants to censor their ideas before sharing them with the group.

After the flow of ideas slows and all useful hypothetical questions have been raised, it is time to ask questions and clarify and consolidate ideas. Evaluation should still be kept to a minimum, as the craziest of ideas may spawn other creative ideas or solutions that can be useful. Be careful not to remove or downplay ideas prematurely.

A normal or open[23] brainstorming session tends to result in the most ideas, the most creative ideas, and the most synergy among group participants and their ideas.[24] However, those who are introverted or feel inhibited by senior members of the organization may be overshadowed by those who are more verbal or dominant. To ensure that all members present fully participate in the idea-generating process, consider using variations on brainstorming, such as round robin, nominal group technique, and Post-it Note brainstorming.

- In **round robin** brainstorming, group members participate in a structured order, for instance, starting with the person at the head of the table and moving clockwise. Using this technique helps equalize the verbal and less verbal participants, but may inhibit some of the creative disagreement that comes when participants can shout out ideas as they come.

- The **nominal group technique**, or NGT, is another variation on open brainstorming that ameliorates the negative impact that status differences may have on a problem-solving group. The technique "nominalizes" or equalizes hierarchical or status differences among members of a group, enabling individuals to speak out without concern for such differences or fears of being ridiculed.[25] To brainstorm NGT style, all team members are given index cards or pads on which to write their ideas. After the theme or question is posed, each person in the group must write down as many answers to the question as they can. After the silent writing of ideas slows, you ask each member in sequence to share one written idea, recording all ideas on the flip chart for everyone to see. Keep going around the group, asking for and recording one unique idea from each person until all written ideas are recorded. If individuals note that their idea was already listed, underline or put a check next to the idea.

- When using the **Post-it Note brainstorming** variation,[26] participants' brainstormed ideas are written on Post-it Notes—one idea per note—instead of on a flip chart. For the open method, this variation requires one scribe to record each idea on a Post-it Note and then stick it to a wall or whiteboard. Post-it Notes can also be used in the nominal group technique; all participants are given a pad of Post-it Notes (instead of cards or slips of paper) on which to write their ideas. Scribing ideas on Post-it Notes may take a bit longer than using the traditional method, but one benefit is the ability to easily manipulate the idea in subsequent problem-solving steps or techniques such as affinitizing, which is described next.

Using Affinitizing to Synthesize Brainstormed Ideas

The **affinitizing** method provides a useful means to organize and produce agreement on categories of ideas; doing so facilitates a group's ability to address organizational problems.

**Figure 14–5
Finished Affinity Diagram**

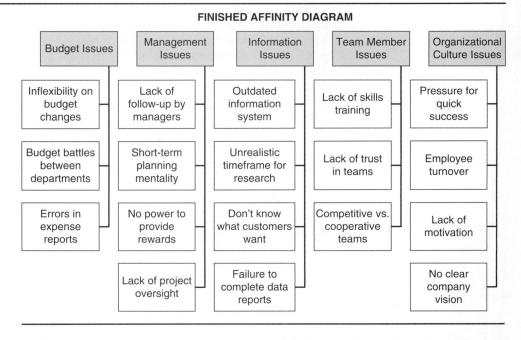

The process is fairly simple. After brainstorming ideas on Post-it Notes (or cards), group members follow the steps listed in the accompanying box.

Affinitizing Steps

1. Stick the notes on a wall or whiteboard so that each note can be seen (or spread out cards on a large desk).

2. Silently (no talking allowed!), group related ideas by moving notes into categories.

3. Discuss, clarify, and modify groups as necessary once the movement slows.

4. Brainstorm a title that encapsulates or expresses the theme for each group of notes. When all agree on the titles for each grouping, they are written on Post-it Notes (one per grouping) and placed at the top of each grouping as shown in Figure 14–5.

At this point, instead of working with 20 or 30 unmanageable ideas, the group has pared down the ideas into 3–8 manageable groups of ideas. As an added bonus, the highly participative nature of brainstorming and affinitizing helps build consensus among team members on identifying problems.

Building Consensus through Multivoting

Multivoting can be used with a brainstormed list of topics or a pared-down list of affinitized categories. The process is highlighted in the accompanying box.

Multivoting Steps

1. Begin with the brainstormed list. As appropriate, combine overlapping items. Another option is to use the categories that emerged from the affinitizing process.

2. Number each idea or category.

3. Divide the total number of ideas or categories by 3; this is the number of votes each member gets. If there are 13 ideas, each member picks his or her top 4; if there are 8 categories, each member picks 3. (Individuals have only one vote per idea or category.) It might be useful to discuss selection criteria before members vote. For example, instruct members to consider those ideas or categories with the greatest potential impact or least time to implement when making their choices.

4. After members have had time to select and jot down their top choices, have a recorder tabulate the results. An easy method is to jot down the numbers and ask

which members had each one among their top choices. Another method is to go around the room and ask members their choices, placing hatch marks adjacent to the appropriate number.

5. The idea or category with the highest number of votes wins. In the event of a tie, utilize the multivoting process once more to arrive at a winner.

Because participants each pick their top choices, the winning idea or category tends to be on almost everyone's list. While multivoting does not by itself produce consensus, it gets the group closer, quickly.

At this point, you should be familiar with an assortment of tools and techniques to use when attempting to solve a problem. While you may think that all organizations use a logical, rational approach similar to the problem-solving processes we've outlined, this is not necessarily the case. Other approaches are available, and depending on the problem at hand and the people involved, other approaches to solving problems may be warranted. In the next section, we describe several intuitive or creative approaches that can be used to complement or substitute stages in the problem-solving process.

"Some men see things the way they are and ask why. I see things as they could be and ask why not?"

Robert F. Kennedy

What Is Creativity and Why Is It Important?

Carol Goman, well-known creativity author and consultant, defines **creativity** as "bringing into existence an idea that is new to you."[27] She cites research done in the late 1940s by a group of psychologists attempting to prove that by age 45, few individuals could think creatively. By testing subjects at various ages, they found that 90 percent of 5-year-olds were highly creative; by age 17, that number dropped to 10 percent; and by age 20, the figure dropped to about 5 percent, where it stayed.[28] If this research holds true, in order to gain competitive advantage, organizations will need to work on means to assure members are able to rejuvenate their childlike creativity.

What makes individuals and businesses ultimately successful is creativity and innovation.[29] Consider this: A stay-at-home mom uses craft materials and decals she has lying around the house to decorate the holes in her daughters' popular Crocs™ shoes. Eventually all of her daughters' friends are asking for the decorations and the Jibbitz™ business is formed. At an average retail price of $3 each with over 8 million sold worldwide, a little creativity has gone a long way.[30]

When we see things differently, we break with tradition and find solutions and often new problems. Creative problem solving helps us to view a situation from a new perspective and increases the likelihood that we will generate innovative, cost-effective ways to do business. Imagine that you were the engineer at Procter & Gamble who came up with the idea of putting messages on Pringles potato chips; however, you were not sure how to do it. How would your assumptions about "how things have always operated" constrain you from changing and finding more innovative ways to operate? In order to find the solution, Procter & Gamble relied on its innovation network outside the company to find an Italian baker using a similar technique to color pasta.[31] Sometimes you need a new perspective. In our rapidly changing global environment, innovation is one of our most valuable resources and design thinking, or "seeing the world not as it is but as it could be," is key in tackling the future.[32] When Roger Jellicoe led a tight-knit team of Motorola engineers in a skunkworks project in creating the super-thin RAZR cell phone, they had to dismiss many of the company rules to develop this new project. They had to throw out the previously accepted models for creating a phone, and use materials and techniques Motorola had never tried before in their top-secret project to create the phone that revolutionized the industry and rejuvenated the company.[33]

Strategies for Increasing Creativity in Problem Solving

Creative problem solving requires the use of both convergent and divergent thinking. **Convergent thinking** is starting with a problem and working to move toward a solution. Most of us take this approach. If you walk into your apartment and notice a foul odor, you're likely to first check to see if the trash needs to be taken out. Then you'll look in the refrigerator, and so on. Eventually, you may find (and eradicate) the problem. Another approach to solving problems is **divergent thinking**. This involves generating new ways to view a problem and seeking novel alternatives to the problem. Creative problem solving will use both types of thinking—convergent and divergent—moving us from basic assumptions based on past experiences to a more novel perspective on the situation.

Let's say your manager informs you that the incidence of shoplifting has been increasing at the apparel store in which you work as a salesperson. The convergent approach will involve the usual—install video cameras, post warning signs, install antitheft tags on the clothing. A divergent approach might include analogies for the problem statement, "How do we keep people from stealing?" Trying to keep people from shoplifting is *like* similar situations:[34]

- Trying to keep kids from sneaking cookies out of the cookie jar.
- Trying to prevent people from jaywalking.
- Trying to keep flies away from cow manure.

Next, you solve the analogy. How do you keep kids from sneaking cookies out of the cookie jar? Hide the jar, put a lock on the jar, or give the kids cookies. How do you prevent people from jaywalking? Post warning signs, increase police presence, increase the number of tickets issued, or create physical barriers along the street. How do you keep flies away from cow manure? Cover the manure, move the animals to another site, or create a fly-friendly haven.

Finally, transfer the analogy solutions to the problem. To keep people from stealing, we could hide the expensive clothing or put it in a special room, give out free samples of apparel (something very cheap), give out free clothes for those who turn in shoplifters, or move the store to another area (or venue, such as catalog or Internet sales). The solutions will be found by moving between convergent and divergent thinking.

Four Stages of Creative Problem Solving[35]

These four stages can guide individuals and groups through the creative process.

- *Preparation*—Gather information, define the problem, generate alternatives, and examine all available information.
- *Incubation*—Engage in subconscious mental activity in which the mind combines unrelated thoughts in pursuit of a solution.
- *Illumination*—Recognize insight and articulate a creative solution. This is sometimes called the Aha! stage.
- *Verification*—Evaluate the creative solution relative to some standard of acceptability.

In this phase, you test to see if the idea can work. You might do a reality check (pulling the creativity down to fit within constraints and boundaries), ask for feedback from others (is this feasible or how can we make it feasible?), or try a pilot project.

"Ideas are like rabbits. You get a couple, learn how to look after them, and pretty soon you have a dozen."

John Steinbeck

Some Methods for Generating Novel Ideas

Not everyone gets to the illumination phase in the same way or time. Some people are naturally creative—they are tinkerers. Others either haven't developed this skill, have had it "beaten out of them," or could benefit from some techniques. Several methods and examples for generating novel ideas follow.[36]

- *Part changing*—List parts or attributes that can be changed. Think about the first laptop computer. It did everything a desktop PC could do, only it was lighter and portable. How about the popular fruit smoothies? Before that, if you wanted something cold and thick, you'd get a milkshake. If you want to improve a product or service, list the parts or attributes. Brainstorm possible changes—even ones you think could never work. How about online banking and loans, online brokerage services, virtual real estate or vacation tours, or online doctors? These services originated by thinking of attributes that could be improved. James Dyson, the creator of the Dyson bagless vacuum cleaner, set out to make a powerful vacuum that no longer needed the bothersome bags. He used technology similar to a cyclonic separator he saw at an industrial sawmill that removed dust from the air. After five years of making prototypes he was able to sell his product not only by why it was different but by why it would work better.[37]

- *Checkerboard*—Make a grid with parts or attributes listed on the vertical and horizontal axes to find new interactions or combinations. By considering "forced" combinations, new ideas could emerge—if you let them. How about the all-in-one office machine (printer, scanner, fax, copier)?

- *Checklist*—Make lists to make sure nothing is left out or forgotten. Using questions such as those below can serve as a checklist for ensuring that all possibilities are considered:

  - What else can this be used for?
  - What could be used instead? What else is like this?
  - How could it be adapted or modified for a new use?
  - What if it were larger, thicker, heavier, or stronger?
  - What if it were smaller, thinner, lighter, or shorter?
  - How might it be rearranged or reversed?

- ***Analogy method***—Fix a problem or create something new by thinking of other products, people, animals, or social units that perform similar acts to make analogies. The shoplifting example we discussed is one application of the similarity method; another example is waiting for you to try at the end of the chapter. What follows is an actual situation in which this method was successfully used to solve a business problem.

A cosmetics manufacturer watched as sales of its lipsticks declined. Its marketing staff wasn't sure why this was occurring, so they decided to investigate. Using customer information cards filled out at various cosmetics counters, they contacted customers and asked if they would be willing to participate in a focus group. It turns out that the customers liked the lipsticks—the colors, the texture, the staying power, the options (sheer, frosted, and matte), and the price were all judged satisfactory. What customers didn't like was the metal tube in which the lipstick was packaged. Within weeks of purchase, the tubes looked old and tarnished. This made customers think that the lipsticks were old. After buying the product the first time, few customers made repeat purchases.

The manufacturer undertook several experiments to respond to this problem, but was unable to find a material that wouldn't tarnish. Employees were challenged to solve this problem. One employee, a hunting enthusiast, noticed that ammunition was always bright and shiny—even cases that had been in his closet for years. He contacted the ammunition manufacturer, explaining his dilemma, and requested a visit. While there, the employee learned what materials were used for the ammunition casings. These materials were then used for the lipstick cases. It worked! Within a short period of time, the declining sales trend was reversed. The moral of this story is to be willing to challenge assumptions about where to look for clues to solving problems.

- *Assumption smashing*—Generate new ideas by dropping all assumptions you have about a topic or issue. Start by creating a list of the assumptions you have about the situation. Then, think about the situation by dropping one assumption at a time or by starting with the opposite of the assumptions. For example:[38] Develop new concepts for restaurants. Start by listing the assumptions about restaurants: They serve food, people pay the bill when they leave, and so on. Now reverse the assumptions. What if restaurants did not serve food? They could rent space for people to cook their own dinner, bring their own food, or have a picnic. "People pay first" turns into customers paying for ingredients only and cooking their own food, or people paying only for the space. Or if customers did not pay, how could restaurants make money? Now you can use the new ideas to evaluate the situation, find the problems, and come up with possible creative changes for improvement. Assumption smashing helps in your lateral thinking by starting with what is familiar to you and moving to a new perspective.

Management's Role in Supporting and Stimulating Creativity

Many of the ideas we've discussed seem simple enough. With practice, we can all use analogies, checkerboards, or other approaches to find creative solutions to enduring problems. What happens when employees are creative but the rest of the organization is not? Unfortunately, this is often the case. How many of the statements in the accompanying box have you heard before in your organization? What are possible effects of using such statements?

Idea Killers

- We tried it before.
- It would cost too much.
- That's not my job.
- That's not how we do things here.
- You may be right, but . . .
- That'll never work.
- You can't do that here.
- Our customers would never go for that.
- It's good enough.
- If it ain't broke, don't fix it.

Goman calls these and similar statements **idea killers**.[39] When creative suggestions or ideas are met with these responses, creativity is killed—not just now, but in the future as well. Statements such as these send the message that any idea that "breaks the rules" will not be accepted, let alone listened to. If you are on the receiving end of one of these statements, chances are you'll learn to keep your mouth shut. Who wants to be ridiculed? Even when employees are told to be creative and innovative, any encouragement coupled with idea killers is likely to be canceled out.

Instead, as a colleague and manager of other employees, you can play a role in creating an environment that truly encourages and stimulates creativity. Creative managers will be able to focus on the big picture; be open, energetic, sometimes unorthodox; and challenge others to experiment with new ideas.[40] The concept of creating an open or relaxed environment is so profound that innovative firms such as Google, Oracle, and AT&T take great care in creating a unique workplace. Businesses from airlines to grocery stores are challenging the conventional approaches to invigorate and bring out the best in their workforce. Studies show that leaders who facilitate knowledge sharing and creative problem-solving capacity will help to improve employees' creative performance.[41] Therefore, how you respond to others' creative ideas sends a strong message for future attempts. Statements such as those in the accompanying box show that you are listening to others' ideas and you are open to continued discussion.

Idea Growers

- How could we improve . . . ?
- How can (that suggestion) build on (a previous idea)?
- What have we missed?
- Who else would be affected?
- What would happen if . . . ?
- Who else has a suggestion?
- I don't know much about that. How about you?
- How many ways could we . . . ?
- May I ask a question?

Idea growers, as Goman calls statements like these,[42] really help continue conversations focused on creative problem solving and stimulate further creative ideas. Saying you value creativity isn't the same as demonstrating it! Think about it. If an employee were to come to you with an idea you believe is ill-conceived, how would you respond? We're not suggesting you should lie and praise the employee as if she were a two-year-old who managed to eat her food without plastering the walls with it. At the same time, you can give feedback in a way that encourages the employee to keep working on the idea while addressing concerns you may have.

One technique that you could use is called **P-P-C**, which stands for *Positives, Possibilities, and Concerns.*[43] It works like this. Imagine you manage the women's wear section of a major department store. You have solicited the input of your employees on ways to improve customer service. One employee, Nancy, suggests clearing enough space to place comfortable chairs, a table, and reading material to increase the spouses' and boyfriends' willingness to wait while their partners try on clothes. She further suggests serving coffee or wine. You have some reservations, but there are some strengths in the idea. Using the P-P-C approach, you respond:

- *Positives:* "I like your concern regarding the spouses."
- *Possibilities:* "We could even include merchandise catalogues (e.g., automotive, tools, stereo) for them to read while they wait."
- *Concerns:* "I'm not sure we could take down the display area to make enough room to implement the idea. How do you think it could be handled?"

It is important not only to find out "how creative your employees are," but also to ask "how are they creative" to consider their creativity style for devising ways to help them express and apply creativity.[44] You might take this idea a step further. Since most thinking in organizations is logical and rational, set aside a room (or part of another room or basement) and call it the **innovation chamber**.[45] Even if creativity is not totally valued in other parts of the organization, this is one place where it is not only valued but also desired. This chamber will become a safe haven for generating innovative, creative ideas. You might even decorate it in a way that stimulates creative thinking (that is, with neither white walls nor a linoleum floor). For example, paint the walls with abstract designs, use colored lights (pink, purple), play soft music, use floor pillows instead of a table and chairs, and have plenty of space for writing (or use flip chart paper taped to the walls). Put a sign on the door and send an official memo to employees about the purpose and use of this room. Post rules in the room, such as these:

- The innovation chamber is a criticism-free space.
- All ideas—even crazy ones—are welcomed, discussed, and credited to the individual and the group.
- All who enter must participate.
- If no really deviant ideas emerge, then the session is less than successful.

Creative Laughter[46]

Is your organization lacking in creativity? Well, stop crying about it and start laughing. If you don't think working should be synonymous with fun, just ask the management at Google, which *Fortune* magazine ranked number one on the "Best Companies to Work For" list in 2013, up from fourth in 2010. Studies have consistently shown that humor in the workplace improves communication, increases job satisfaction, and builds loyalty and retention. When employees are able to cope with stress, both physically and mentally, decision making and problem solving are enhanced, which leads to creativity. Since creativity is a driving force for innovation and staying one step ahead of

(continued)

competition, Google works hard at keeping employees happy and thinking in unconventional ways. Its California campus includes an outdoor wave pool, indoor gym, and child care facilities. Employees get free meals three times a day and free shuttle service to and from San Francisco. They are allotted 20 percent of work time to work on their own ideas and even encouraged to brainstorm on boards in the halls. Since Google believes maintaining the "Googley" culture is its most valuable asset, Chief Culture Officer Stacy Sullivan works to ensure the experience translates into new offices as the company expands.

Strategies for Increasing Individual Creativity

We mentioned earlier that as we age, we lose our capacity to be creative. There are many reasons why this occurs, but more importantly, how can you get this lost creativity back? Here are a few suggestions:

- *Do creative exercises.* Challenge your mind. Resist the temptation to opt for quick, tried and true solutions. Experiment, play, and search for new solutions. Like any other muscle in the body, the mind becomes weak and rigid in the absence of exercise.[47]

- *Break some rules.* Write in your books, order something that's not on the menu, question the validity (and objectivity) of news reports, challenge your religious beliefs, vote differently from your parents or how you might have voted 10 years ago.

- *Learn your language* (or a new one). Commit to learning one new word a day. Ensure you pronounce it correctly.

- *Keep an open mind.* When you meet someone new, take in all aspects of that person's personality and don't label her or him as a ditz, lazy, and so on.

- *Keep a journal.* Writing down your thoughts helps you remember key discoveries, such as feelings, emotions, and beliefs. One of your most creative moments is right when you wake up. This is one of the best times to jot down your thoughts, especially if you can remember key aspects of a dream you had that night.

- *Develop confidence in your senses.*[48] Don't wear a watch; guess the time given available clues. Guess the temperature before looking at the sign above the bank. Guess your friends' heights and weights using your own as a comparison, and if you're brave enough, ask for confirmation. Cook something without a recipe or measuring devices. Use your sense of smell and taste to make needed modifications.

- *Expose yourself to new perspectives.* Take an elevator to the top of a tall building; what do you see that you couldn't see before? Read a novel or see a movie that you would ordinarily never read or see. Eat a type of food that you've never eaten before. Travel outside your comfort zone, which may be different for different people. For some, it's outside the town; for others, it's outside the continent. An excellent illustration of this is the scene in the film *Dead Poets Society* in which Robin Williams's character has his students stand up on their desks to get a different perspective of the world. A bit unusual for a conservative school, but that was the point![49]

Being creative is not just a workplace skill; it's a life skill as well. Once you have rejuvenated your creativity, you can apply it to all aspects of your life. Bill Gates, the founder of Microsoft, has been able to translate his creative business techniques into addressing world health issues and looking for solutions for improving the U.S. educational system.[50] How we approach situations is a function of how many possibilities we can see; if you always stay in the middle, you will never see what is over the edge. Have you ever tried to buy a car and found out that your credit was less than perfect? Did you give up or begin looking for a creative way to finance this purchase? How about when your team needs a new slogan for the latest promotional campaign? Do you stop after a few suggestions? What about having a contest? What about asking customers to submit their ideas? When you exercise your creative potential, you can benefit both professionally and personally.

Summary

We face decisions every day. Some of these are tough—mired in ambiguity, complexity, and ethical considerations—while others are easy. The process by which you make decisions can significantly impact whether the decision is right—effective and successful in the long term—for you and those affected by the decision. While simple decisions, such as whether to wear a blue or red shirt, may not require a multistep decision process, more complex and consequential decisions do.

Organizations face problems (or opportunities) on a daily basis. Those firms that take a disciplined approach to problem solving—clearly defining the problem, identifying potential and creative solutions, selecting solutions based on appropriate criteria, and creating a detailed plan to implement the solution—are likely to succeed and prosper. Finding solutions—especially creative ones—to problems or inventing new products and processes requires creative employees and the right environment. Your effectiveness as a manager can be greatly enhanced by your ability to make effective decisions and solve problems creatively.

Key Terms and Concepts

Affinitizing	Idea growers
Analogy method	Idea killers
Analysis paralysis	Innovation chamber
Brainstorming	Multivoting
Collaborative decision making	Nominal group technique
Convergent thinking	PDCA cycle
Creativity	Post-it Note brainstorming
Decision making	P-P-C technique
Decision-making process (steps)	Problem solving
Divergent thinking	Round robin

Discussion Questions

1. Why is problem solving important in organizational settings?

2. One of the "rules" of brainstorming is no critiquing—positive or negative. Criticism is not allowed because of the potential for squelching open dialogue about the issue at hand. Why is positive critiquing, for example, "Wow, that's a great idea," problematic?

3. We suggest that group problem solving may not appeal to everyone. Why is this the case?

4. We suggest that managers' behaviors could both stimulate and hinder creative problem solving. Explain.

Endnotes

1. Raymond Suutari, "Tale of Two Strategies: How Does Your Company Make Its Strategic Business Decisions," *CMA Management* (July–August 1999), p. 12.

2. Victoria Crittenden and Arch G. Woodside, "Building Skills in Thinking: Toward a Pedagogy in Metathinking," *Journal of Education Business* 83, no. 1 (September 2007), p. 37.

3. Sal Marino, "Rely on Science, Not Your Gut," *Industry Week* (January 24, 2000), p. 18.

4. D. Keith Denton and Peter Richardson, "Making Speedy Decisions," *Industrial Management* (September 1999), p. 6.

5. Kenneth Brousseau et al., "The Seasoned Executive's Decision-Making Style," *Harvard Business Review* 84, no. 2 (February 2006), p. 119.

6. Dan Lovallo and Olivier Sibony, "The Case for Behavioral Strategy," *McKinsey Quarterly* no. 2 (2010), p. 30.

7. Scott Beagrie, "How to . . . improve your decision making," *Personnel Today* (May 23, 2006), p. 33.

8. Ralph L. Keeney, "Foundations for Making Smart Decisions," *IIE Solutions* (May 1999), p. 24.

9. Carl Evans and Warren Wright, "How to Make Effective Decisions," *British Journal of Administrative Management* 68 (October/November 2009), p. 32.

10. Stan Shapiro, "Decision Making under Pressure," *The Futurist* 44, no. 1 (January/February 2010), p. 42.

11. Jennifer White, "Maintaining Focus: The Best Way to Overcome the 'Too Much Syndrome,' " *Business Journal* (March 10, 2000), p. 39.

12. Joel Barker, *Paradigms: The Business of Discovering the Future* (New York: Harper Business, 1993).

13. Andrew Campbell, Jo Whitehead, and Sydney Finkelstein, "Why Good Leaders Make Bad Decisions," *Harvard Business Review* 87, no. 2 (February 2009), pp. 62–63.

14. This material and the chart that follows were adapted from Karen O. Dowd and Sherrie Gong Taguchi, *The Ultimate Guide to Getting the Career You Want (and What to Do Once You Have It)* (New York: McGraw-Hill, 2003).

15. Christina Evangelou and Nikos Karacapilidis, "A Multidisciplinary Approach for Supporting Knowledge-based Decision Making in Collaborative Settings," *International Journal of Artificial Intelligence Tools* 16, no. 6 (2007), p. 1071.

16. Dowd and Taguchi, *The Ultimate Guide.*

17. E. Dane, K. W. Rockmann, and M. G. Pratt, "When Should I Trust My Gut? Linking Domain Expertise to Intuitive Decision-making Effectiveness," *Organizational Behavior and Human Decision Process* 119 (2012), pp. 187–94.

18. Richard Branson, "Richard Branson on Decision-making for Entrepreneurs," *Entrepreneur. com* (February 7, 2012), http://www.entrepreneur.com/article/222739.

19. See Michael Doyle and David Straus, *How to Make Meetings Work: The New Interaction Method* (New York: Wyden Books, 1976); and David Straus, *How to Make Collaboration Work: Powerful Ways to Build Consensus, Solve Problems, and Make Decisions* (San Francisco, CA: Berrett-Koehler Publishers, 2002).

20. Edward de Bono, *Six Thinking Hats: An Essential Approach to Business Management* (Boston: Little, Brown, 1985).

21. Paul Kiesow, "PDCA Cycle: An Approach to Problem Solving," *Ceramic Industry* (October 1994), p. 20.

22. Quinn Spitzer and Ron Evans, "New Problems in Problem Solving," *Across the Board* (April 1997), p. 36.

23. Glenn Ray, *The Facilitative Leader: Behaviors That Enable Success* (Upper Saddle River, NJ: Prentice Hall, 1999).

24. Ibid., p. 103.

25. Larry Hirschhorn, *Managing in the New Team Environment: Skills, Tools, and Methods* (Reading, MA: Addison Wesley, 1991).

26. Ethan M. Rasiel, "Some Brainstorming Exercises," *Across the Board* (June 2000), p. 10.

27. Carol Kinsey Goman, *Creativity in Business: A Practical Guide for Creative Thinking* (Menlo Park, CA: Crisp Publications, 2000), p. 46.

28. Ibid., p. 11.

29. Oren Harari, "Turn Your Organization into a Hotbed of Ideas," *Management Review* (December 1995), pp. 37–40.

30. "About Us," Jibbitz, www.jibbitz.com (accessed October 11, 2007).

31. William C. Taylor and Polly LaBarre, *Mavericks at Work: Why the Most Original Minds in Business Win* (New York: Harper Collins, 2006).

32. David Cooperrider, "Managing-as-Designing in an Era of Massive Innovation," *Journal of Corporate Citizenship* 37 (Spring 2010), p. 24.

33. Adam Lashinsky, "RAZR's Edge: How a Team of Engineers and Designers Defied Motorola's Own Rules to Create the Cellphone That Revived Their Company," *Fortune* (June 1, 2006), http://money.cnn.com/2006/05/31/magazines/fortune/razr (accessed May 29, 2013).

34. This example is adapted from Goman, *Creativity in Business,* pp. 62–63.

35. J. W. Haefele, *Creativity and Innovation* (New York: Reinhold, 1962); Max H. Bazerman, *Judgment in Managerial Decision Making* (New York: Wiley, 1986), pp. 89–91.

36. G. David and S. Houtman, "Thinking Creatively: A Guide to Training Imagination" (Madison, WI: Wisconsin Research and Development Center for Cognitive Learning, 1968); and Goman, *Creativity in Business,* p. 28.

37. Burt Helm, "How I Did It: James Dyson," *Inc.com* (February 28, 2012), http://www.inc.com/magazine/201203/burt-helm/how-i-did-it-james-dyson.html (accessed June 3, 2013).

38. Edward DeBono, *Serious Creativity: Using the Power of Lateral Thinking to Create New Ideas* (New York: HarperBusiness, 1993).

39. Goman, *Creativity in Business,* p. 76.

40. Malcolm Higgs and Jill Hender, "The Characteristics of the Creative Manager," *Journal of General Management* 29, no. 4 (Summer 2004), p.11.

41. A. Carmeli, R. Gelbard, and R. Reiter-Palmon, "Leadership, Creative Problem-solving Capacity, and Creative Performance: The Importance of Knowledge Sharing," *Human Resource Management* 52, no. 1 (January–February 2013), pp. 95–122.

42. Goman, *Creativity in Business,* p. 77.

43. Example adapted from Goman, *Creativity in Business,* p. 82.

44. D. J. Treffinger, E. C. Selby, and P. F. Schoonover, "Creativity in the Person: Contemporary Perspectives," *LEARNing Landscapes* 6, no. 1 (Autumn 2012), pp. 409–19.

45. Floyd Hurt, "Creativity: A Hole in Your Head," *Agency Sales Magazine* (June 1998), pp. 58–60.

46. Material from Sue Kehaulani Goo, "Building a 'Googley' Workforce," *Washington Post* (October 21, 2006), p. D1; also Dan Danbom, "Getting Serious about Humor," *Vital Speeches of the Day* 17, no. 21 (August 15, 2005), p. 668; and Robert Levering and Milton Moskowitz, "Best Places to Work for 2010," writers and researchers for Great Place to Work Institute, study completed for *Fortune* (http://www.greatplacetowork.com/what_we_do/lists.php? listname=bestusa, online edition); "Fortune 100 Best Companies to Work For," *CNNMoney* (http://money.cnn.com/magazines/fortune/best-companies/?iid=bc_sp_header, accessed May 15, 2010).

47. Tom Wujec, *Pumping Ions: Games and Exercises to Flex Your Mind* (New York: Doubleday, 1988).

48. Marilyn vos Savant and Leonore Fleischer, *Brain Building in Just 12 Weeks* (New York: Bantam Books, 1991).

49. The authors thank Robert A. Herring of Winston-Salem State University for making this suggestion.

50. Donna Gordon Blankinship, "Gates: US Education System Needs Work," Associated Press (November 13, 2006).

Exercise 14–A Decision-Making Matrix

- **Step 1:** Use the following table to choose four mutually exclusive options to pursue in the first year after your graduation from college. In other words, what will you do with your life after you graduate? At the bottom of this page, succinctly describe each option.
- **Step 2:** In the column entitled "Decision Factor," briefly describe the aspect or criterion that differentiates your choice of one option over the other. For example, one decision factor might be "income in first year." Another might be "intellectual challenge," and so on. Bear in mind that each decision factor must be applicable (but not necessarily the best) for each outcome. For example, if one outcome option is to join the army, you cannot use a decision factor like "overcome fear of guns." If you did, the only possible column that could get the check mark would be the one for "Join the army."

- **Step 3:** Using the criteria in step 2, place an *X* in the column for each row that will most thoroughly fulfill that criterion/factor. That is, which option is the best for that decision factor?
- **Step 4:** Add the number of *X*'s in each column and record that number at the bottom of the table in each column.
- **Step 5:** For the time being, ignore the left-hand column.
- **Step 6:** Your instructor will debrief this exercise with the class.

	Decision Factor	Options			
		A	B	C	D
	TOTALS:				

Option A: _____

Option B: _____

Option C: _____

Option D: _____

Source: This exercise was developed and contributed to this book by Dr. Brian K. Miller, Assistant Professor, Management Program, College of Business, James Madison University, Harrisonburg, Virginia (2004).

Exercise 14–B
Weighted Average
Decision Making

Sometimes it's difficult to make a decision in which many variables are involved that are all important to you. But since it's unlikely you'll be able to make a decision that satisfies all your needs, weighted averaging gives you a way to differentiate those factors that are more important to you than others and to weigh these differences when analyzing the factors. Working on your own, think of a decision that you need to make now or that you will face in the near future.

1. On a separate sheet of paper, list all the variables or factors (up to 10) that are important to you in making a specific decision. These factors determine what you want to achieve from the decision's outcome.

2. In the left column of the following chart, list these factors in priority order, #1 being the most important.

3. Across the top of the page, list each alternative you are considering (up to four alternatives).

4. Start with the first factor. Working across this row, determine which option best meets this factor and assign the number 1 to that option. Then determine the option that next best meets the factor, assigning it the number 2. Continue with this determination using the numbers 3 and 4.

5. Move to the second (and subsequent factors) and repeat step 4.

6. Multiply each cell (#1–#4) by the priority number in the corresponding row (#1–#10). Note these numbers in each cell.

7. Sum each column. The column with the *lowest* sum is the option that *best* meets your higher-priority needs (your top priority is #1).

Factor/Priority	Option A	Option B	Option C	Option D
1.				
2.				
3.				
4.				
5.				
6.				
7.				
8.				
9.				
10.				
Sum				

Exercise 14–C
Brainstorming—A Warm-up

How creative are you? Using the space below, brainstorm as many ideas as you can in five minutes on the *alternative uses of the object presented by your instructor.* Write down all ideas, even outlandish ones. If you get stuck, switch your point of view—how could it help you survive if you were lost at sea, in a desert, in a snowstorm, or on the moon? How could it be used for personal/home purposes or for commercial or work situations? How could you change it with some type of technological advancement? Challenge your assumptions about the object—how can it be changed to produce different purposes?

Questions

1. How did you do?
2. Did you use the entire time? Could you have continued writing after time was up?
3. How could this technique be applied in the workplace?

Exercise 14–D
Collaborative Problem Solving

The following questions pertain to the problem-solving exercise you were led through in class.

1. Did your problem-solving group arrive at a workable plan for implementing a solution? If yes, to what do you attribute the group's success? If not, what precluded you from generating a workable solution to the problem presented?

2. In what ways did solving the problem as a group instead of individually improve the process and outcome?

_____

_____

_____

3. In what ways did solving the problem as a group instead of individually hinder or undermine the process and outcome?

_____

_____

_____

4. How did you overcome these hindrances?

_____

_____

_____

**Exercise 14–E
Corporate Crime:
A Problem-Solving
Exercise**

1. Each group will receive 40 statements of data concerning a situation. The goal is to solve the problem from the data given. Each member of a group gets _seven-eighths_ of that group's statements. The rules for the activity are the following:

  a. The members are not permitted to exchange cards or to show their cards to other members of their group.

  b. All data must be communicated orally to the other members of the group; these statements may be repeated as often as the group feels is necessary.

  c. If all members of the group feel that a statement (data) is not relevant to arriving at the solution of the problem, the statement is to be placed face down and not repeated.

  d. Group members may _not_ take notes during the process.

  e. Only one problem solution may be presented from each group.

2. At the end of the allotted time, your group must write a solution of the problem on a sheet of blank paper and submit it to the instructor. After doing so, discuss:

  a. Your reactions to the experience.

  b. Any difficulties you had in separating irrelevant from relevant data.

  c. How your group decided which data were relevant.

  d. How the use of only verbal communication affected the difficulty of the task.

**Exercise 14–F
What's Old is New**

You are part of a team charged with creating a new team sport that will increase the use of some of the sporting equipment that your company produces. Your new sport must use at least two items from your company's product list (you may use other equipment or props if necessary):

Baseball bat	Soccer ball
Football	Tennis ball
Frisbee	Tennis racquet
Horseshoes	Swimming goggles
Volleyball net	Boxing gloves
Pogo stick	Hula-hoop
Jump rope	Bike helmets

Your team must provide the following criteria in developing the sport:

- The equipment that will be necessary.
- The playing surface or field dimensions and type.
- The number and type of team players, and any specialized positions.
- The time frame for the sporting activity (innings, periods, etc.).
- The point systems and means for measurement; how to determine a winner; how to obtain a score; differentials in scoring, penalties, and so on.
- All rules that are required in playing the sport.
- The process for playing the game—sequence, format, instructions, or training.
- The name of the game.

Questions

1. Did your team go through the four stages of creative problem solving? Explain.
2. What method or techniques did you use to generate novel and creative ideas?
3. What was difficult about this exercise? Easy? Explain.
4. Based on your experience, how would you express a team's ability to be creative as compared with an individual's?

**Exercise 14–G
Sensing Creativity**

By using all five of our senses we are able to allow sensations to trigger our creative thinking.

1. Write down some information to explain a recent experience you had such as meeting a friend for lunch or coffee, biking, going to a theater, attending a meeting, and so on.

_____

_____

_____

2. Now close your eyes and think about the experience by examining it through your five senses. Go through each sense one at a time: What did you hear? Think about the various sounds around you. What did you see? Think about colors, objects, all activities going on around you. What did you smell? Did those smells remind you of anything? Describe what you felt or touched. Explain the textures around you. What did you taste? Use the diagram below to record your experience and all the sensations and any connotations these sensations brought to mind.

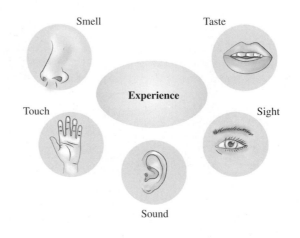

Try this activity in a future experience. Take quick note of the situation and then close your eyes and go though each one of your senses to fully experience the situation. Open your eyes and try to add to that description.

Questions

1. In comparing your first description of the experience to the description using your senses, how has the description changed?

2. Even though we have multiple experiences in a day, why don't we fully sense all of them? How could including the full range of sensations improve our creative ability? How can you apply this to being more creative at work or school?

Exercise 14–H
Reflection/Action Plan

1. The one or two problem-solving or creativity areas in which I am most strong are:

_____

_____

_____

_____

2. The one or two problem-solving or creativity areas in which I need more improvement are:

_____

_____

_____

_____

3. If I did only one thing to improve in this area, it would be to:

_____

_____

_____

_____

4. Making this change would probably result in:

_____

_____

_____

_____

5. If I did not change or improve in this area, it would probably affect my personal and professional life in the following ways:

_____

_____

_____

_____

UNIT 1

INTRAPERSONAL EFFECTIVENESS: UNDERSTANDING YOURSELF

1. Journey into Self-awareness
2. Self-disclosure and Trust
3. Establishing Goals Consistent with Your Values and Ethics
4. Self-management

UNIT 2

INTERPERSONAL EFFECTIVENESS: UNDERSTANDING AND WORKING WITH OTHERS

5. Understanding and Working with Diverse Others
6. Listening and Nonverbal Communication
7. Communicating Effectively
8. Persuading Individuals and Audiences

UNIT 3

UNDERSTANDING AND WORKING IN TEAMS

9. Negotiation
10. Building Teams and Work Groups
11. Managing Conflict
12. Achieving Business Results through Effective Meetings
13. Facilitating Team Success
14. Making Decisions and Solving Problems Creatively

UNIT 4

LEADING INDIVIDUALS AND GROUPS

15. Effective and Ethical Use of Power and Influence
16. Networking and Mentoring
17. Coaching and Providing Feedback for Improved Performance
18. Leading and Empowering Self and Others
19. Project Management

Unit 4

I t's been a long and enlightening journey. Along the way, you've had opportunities to fuel your tank (assess and manage intrapersonal effectiveness), have enlightening conversations with a wide range of diverse individuals (interpersonal and communication effectiveness), and work collaboratively and effectively with individuals who share the same goals as you (working in teams). These skills will help you interact effectively and build relationships with colleagues, supervisors, co-workers, subordinates, faculty, parents, significant others, and even your children! What about when others look to you for leadership? In this fourth and final stop in our personal development journey, we take a look at the characteristics and skills of effectively leading individuals and groups. Today's leaders mentor, coach, and provide feedback to others. They manage projects. They empower employees and they influence others through networking and the appropriate use of power and politics. By mastering these skills, you can focus on developing others, and in turn, focus your energies on charting your course toward new and different destinations.

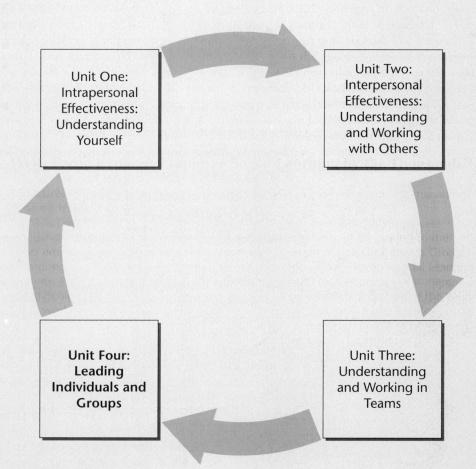

15

Effective and Ethical Use of Power and Influence

_____ **Learning Points**

How do I:

- Acquire and use power to get others to do what I want them to do even when my position lacks such authority?
- Use my connections to successfully champion a cause?
- Identify people to go to if I want to get something done in an organization?
- "Read" others as well as the organization's culture?
- Learn how to create and manage a positive impression of myself?
- Consider the negative or unethical implications of my actions?

Jill felt confident that her team would be awarded the Markinson account. Winning the contract had required research and work from all divisions of the company, and this account would take the company to its next level. Jill's team had developed the majority of the ideas proposed for the account standards and laid out the best plan for managing the account. With the success her team had experienced in the past year, along with being recognized for developing the key portions of the proposal accredited for winning the account, Jill had every reason to believe her team would be the lead for the project.

Marcus also knew how critical the lead would be for this account. His team had struggled with the last project, missing the final deadline while going slightly over budget. Being the lead on the Markinson account was just the thing needed to reenergize his team and prove its capabilities to upper management. Marcus realized his team was at a disadvantage when compared to Jill's, but he was not going to let that stop him. And he knew just how to make his move, at his weekend golf game with Samuel, his long-time friend from college, and assistant regional director for the company.

Jill was completely stunned when the regional director made the announcement at the Tuesday meeting that Marcus's team was awarded the lead on the Markinson account. How could this be? As Jill slowly packed up her belongings and made her way to the conference room door, she heard Marcus and Samuel in the hall. "I don't know how to thank you, Samuel. My team really needed this chance," said Marcus. "Well, you owe me," Samuel replied. "I really stuck my neck out this time. This account is critical to the company, so don't let me down. You better handle the account better than you played golf on Saturday."

1. How would you respond to this situation if you were Jill? Explain.
2. What type of power or lack of power played a part in the decision?
3. How did organizational politics play a role in the situation?
4. What actions could Jill have taken to win the account for her team?
5. What ethical issues are presented in this situation?

Have you ever experienced or witnessed a situation such as this? Maybe you've seen an opposite situation—one where a manager uses his or her influence to get an employee demoted or fired. Perhaps you've wondered why certain individuals become the lucky (or unlucky) targets of power exerted by high-ranking members of an organization. In this chapter, we discuss power and organizational politics, why they're important in organizations, and how to assess situations and effectively use power and influence to achieve your goals and those of your organization.

What Is Power and Why Is It Important?

Power is the ability to get someone to do something you want done or the ability to make things happen in the way you want.[1] In order to get anything done, be it as simple as getting someone to pass the salt at the dinner table or as elaborate as getting your company to expand its product line, power is a basis on which to start the action. Some individuals may use the power of their position or title to influence or control others' actions, while others will rely on their personal or informal power to act. In the current business environment, where managers must compete for scarce resources and achieve goals that require the actions and abilities of others, understanding and utilizing various types of power becomes a critical skill. Knowing which power bases you have available to you for a particular action and understanding the positive or potential negative consequences that can result from the use of a power base can lead to a manager's short- and long-term effectiveness.

Position or Formal Power

Have you ever had a boss (or superior) command you to complete a task that didn't appeal to you? As much as you may have wanted to ignore his or her wishes, you probably realized that as a boss, he or she had the right to make such demands as well as to impose consequences should you not comply. This set of power mechanisms or processes are conferred on the basis of one's position or managerial level in the organization and are referred to as **position power** or **formal power**. Formal power can include **legitimate**, **reward**, and **coercive power** bases. Descriptions and examples of these bases of power are provided in Figure 15–1.[2] While formal power is frequently used or is responsible for the accomplishment of many tasks in the business environment, power is best used when it does not appear as power. Rarely do people respond well to being forced or told what to do. Nevertheless, many individuals in positions of power use their formal power base alone to support their decisions. Failure to move beyond the use of formal power can lead to irrational decision making as well as a dysfunctional environment controlled by one individual's behaviors or choices. People in higher positions should examine the implications of exerting their formal power and use it appropriately.

Another source of power that often but doesn't always come with one's position is **information power**—the access to vital information and control over its distribution to others.[3] Typically, by virtue of their position, managers get access to information that is unavailable to peers and subordinates (e.g., financial and operational measures). With the opportunity to distort or frame the information, managers can use information power as a means of influencing others' goal-directed behaviors.[4] Some subject matter experts or those with networks that expand beyond the immediate organization have the opportunity to obtain and wield information power.

Figure 15–1
Formal and Informal Power Bases

Formal Power Base	
Legitimate	Based on a person holding a formal position or title. Employees comply because they accept the legitimacy of the person in charge.
Reward	Based on a person's ability to provide (or withhold) rewards. Others comply because they desire the rewards available from the person in power.
Coercive	Based on a person's ability to punish or harm. Others comply because they want to avoid punishment.
Informal Power Base	
Expert	Based on a person possessing knowledge or superior skills in an area of expertise. Employees comply because they respect and trust the person's knowledge or skill.
Referent	Based on a person's ability to influence because of others' desire to identify or associate with him or her. Others comply because they like, believe in, or want to emulate the person and what he or she represents.

Person or Informal Power

What happens when you aren't a manager or supervisor? Due to restructuring and downsizing in many organizations, there are proportionately fewer employees in positions of formal authority. Influencing peers or teammates to comply with your wishes can be a more challenging, and likely more important, proposition. **Person power**, or **informal power**, comes from the qualities of a person or how others view her. Two well-established bases of "person" power—**expert power** and **referent power**—are described in Figure 15–2.

These two power bases can be as powerful as formal ones,[5] but unlike formal or position power, informal or person power engenders commitment as opposed to compliance. Put another way, individuals who are influenced more by a person's qualities than his or her position willingly accept the assignment requested and put their "all" into achieving a positive result, as opposed to doing the bare minimum to "get by." For example, the Dalai Lama, although a deposed leader of an occupied country, wields great political influence due to his moral, compassionate, and humble reputation. Research has shown that some of the best-performing leaders of teams relied most heavily on expert and referent power bases to influence the teams and their members.[6] The table in Figure 15–2 offers tips for increasing your referent and expert power.

Remember that the use of power is situational, meaning that any power base can be effective if used appropriately and positively. Consider the situation, as well as your personal and position power, and choose wisely. The right power base can provide the necessary fuel to support your position or goals. In the next section, we discuss politicking, or how to turn power into influence.

POWER FAILURE

Figure 15–2
Some Tips for Increasing Power[7]

Referent	Expert
Develop your people skills. The better you get along with others, the more referent power you'll have.	Take advantage of any training or educational opportunities provided by your organization.
Improve your relationship with and gain confidence from your manager and peers. Their success is influenced by you and your performance.	Attend trade and professional association meetings. Use networking skills to increase your connections and visibility.
Use personal appeals and sincere flattery to make a connection with and befriend others.	Let others know about your expertise by volunteering for projects that will allow you to showcase your skills or talents. Also, consider displaying diplomas or awards in your office.

"Politics is the art of the possible."

Prince Otto von Bismarck, 1867

What Is Organizational Politics and Why Is It Important?

Organizational politics, also referred to as **politicking**, is the use of power and information to move resources toward preferred objectives.[8] It is speaking up on behalf of our and our employees' or company's interests and is part of the process of rule making and decision making in organizational life. It must be realized that management is not a purely technical or core activity, that contextual performance is needed in the social, political, and moral practices of an organization.[9] People use political behavior to affect decisions, obtain scarce resources, and earn the cooperation of people outside their direct authority.[10] Simply put, politicking is advocating for your interests in a way that meets your and your company's objectives. One who is effective at politicking in business is fully engaged in the life of the organization, understands the key issues and drivers within the organization and the industry, and exercises sound judgment when making decisions that affect the people in and resources of the organization. One who is political is cautious, not rash, and makes decisions carefully, not impulsively. To some, the word *politicking* may conjure up negative connotations, as the term can be used to define behavior that is motivated primarily or even exclusively by self-interest. In this view politicking is an irrational or deviant action since it is taken by individuals and not directed by the organization itself; political actions are not in keeping with organizational goals. Others feel it is the way for individuals to overcome the unfair distribution of resources that occurs in organizations. No matter what the view, it is important to note that politicking is a subtle and many times masked process with little or no formalized regulation and should be monitored.[11]

Organizations, like people, can have a "dark side." It is not uncommon to find people willing to put their needs above those of others, to do whatever it takes to get what they want. Research has shown that perceptions of high levels of organizational politics can lead to employee dissatisfaction with negative repercussions of job stress, turnover, and lack of employee commitment.[12] If the environment is perceived as highly political, employees will either increase their political efforts to make the situation "equitable" or "bearable" or they may withdraw with more incidents of absenteeism or shirking of duties.[13] Managers should therefore monitor the levels of politicking to manage and mitigate the potential negative impacts of organizational politics. In this chapter we prefer to focus on the positive view of organizational politics.

Politicking is important because of the complexities involved in being in business today. The global marketplace, the changing attitudes and growing diversity of employees, the intense competition for profits, the explosion of technology, the constant changes in business strategy, and the changing cast of characters who run companies are just a few of these intricacies. Politicking is a way to strengthen and expand your existing network of contacts within your organization. It can be used to learn about available resources and how to get them allocated to objectives that support your and your employees' interests.[14] In one study, 53 percent of those interviewed noted that organizational politics enhanced the achievement of organizational goals and survival.[15] Politicking can be a way to validate your "fit" within the organization and understand the playing field, which can be key when developing your personal and organizational goals.[16]

Entrepreneurs will need to politick in order to gain credibility as competent players in their industry while proving they are innovative enough to stand out as potential new leaders.[17] In team situations, leaders or members who are able to politick effectively are able to more easily access resources and information to increase team effectiveness.[18] Developing skills in politicking enables managers to understand the changing nature of their business, obtain needed information and resources, adapt as needed, and even reduce workplace stressors.[19]

Influence and Politics in the Digital Age

Websites, e-mail, Facebook, Twitter, and blogs have changed the way the world gets and transfers its information. From business to politics, the digital age is a force to be recognized. Companies spent over $100 billion in 2012 on global digital advertising to educate and influence consumers around the world with the largest investments in the Middle East, Africa, and Eastern Europe.[20] These tools are used to not only market to potential consumers but also to track buyer perceptions and behavior. But companies aren't the only ones taking advantage of the broad reach of digital media. Barack Obama's 2012 reelection campaign relied on e-mail marketing, Twitter, Facebook, and YouTube as an integral factor in spreading their message and gaining support.[21] Obama and his opponent Mitt Romney both used Twitter to solicit campaign donations and to criticize opponents' statements, platforms, and tactics. Twitter-fueled frenzies were used by all candidates to punctuate their points and the missteps of their opponents. Research has also been compiled to examine how Twitter impacted the uprisings and political changes in the Middle East. The tweets not only gave political headlines in real time but also captured the sentiments of the people. In Syria, the key word was "massacre" on Twitter and hundreds of thousands liked "Syrian Revolution" on Facebook. In Egypt, Twitter was used to organize rallies and influence people to participate in demonstrations.[22]

Engaging in Organizational Politics: Considerations

Effective politicking requires forethought before being put into action. Whether you will engage in politicking may be a direct result of your locus of control. **Locus of control** is related to a person's belief regarding how much control he or she has over external events or the external environment.[23] Therefore, an individual's belief will have a direct impact on the amount and level of politicking he or she will engage in within the organization. If you are a person with a strong internal locus of control, you will see yourself as having a direct impact on or extensive control over external matters. Most likely, you will engage in organizational politics and believe your actions and behavior will directly result in your future success. Entrepreneurs tend to have a strong internal locus of control and believe they have the power to succeed in their own ventures. Studies have also shown that students with internal locus of control tend to pursue better study practices and do better than their classmates with an external locus of control.[24] People with a strong external locus of control believe they have little or no control over external events and would therefore reduce their level of political actions, believing it to be a waste of time and effort. Externals believe their efforts will have little or no effect on changing future outcomes.

Once you know your belief on the impact of politicking, there are three dimensions to consider when determining if and how to engage in politicking: analyzing yourself, reading others, and assessing the organization (see Figure 15–3).[25]

Figure 15–3
Action for Effective
Organizational Politicking

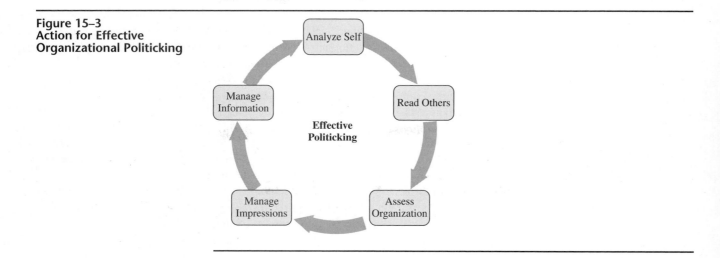

Analyzing Yourself

Politicking begins with a clear understanding of yourself and the influencing qualities you possess naturally. What are your strengths and limitations, and how do these help or hinder your ability to be political within an organization? What strengths can you bring to your interactions with others, and what limitations might make it difficult for you to influence others, particularly within an organizational context? Several personal characteristics, such as being confident, articulate, and sensitive, make it easier for a person to be an effective politicker (see the following box, "How Political Are You?"). Having an honest assessment of your goals and your capability for achieving them will help in utilizing your positive aspects while diminishing or controlling your negative factors. For example, if you have a tendency to dominate conversations, try to focus on listening intently to others while they are speaking. (Refer back to the Unit 1 chapters and exercises to help you reassess your intrapersonal strengths and weaknesses.)

Another aspect of self-understanding with regard to influencing is the role of power. Understanding the power base from which you are working and determining the power base that would best match a specific situation or person with whom you are interacting will increase the effectiveness of your politicking.

How Political Are You?[26]

Take a look at the list below. Circle the number that most describes the degree to which each word describes you.

	Agree		Neither		Disagree
Articulate	1	2	3	4	5
Sensitive	1	2	3	4	5
Competent	1	2	3	4	5
Extroverted	1	2	3	4	5
Self-confident	1	2	3	4	5
Assertive	1	2	3	4	5
Collaborative	1	2	3	4	5
Intelligent	1	2	3	4	5
Logical	1	2	3	4	5
Socially adept	1	2	3	4	5

Total the numbers circled. If your score is less than 30, you have a natural ability to be political in organizations.

Reading Others

Effective managers who are good at influencing within their organizations know the importance of being able to "read" people,[27] or understand others' perceptions, reactions, and motivations. To be effective in politicking, it is important to understand others quickly: their power base; their perceptions regarding their position, the situation, and organization; and their stance on the issues at hand. This requires attention to what is known (others' position, experience, previous decisions), as well as what lies beneath the surface (such as goals, values, fears).

In some instances there is insufficient time to form impressions and check our understanding of these perceptions with the person or with a trusted colleague. In these cases, we have to rely on our instincts about the person—understanding where they're coming from and what they want to obtain from the situation. Let's say your star employee just left for an overseas assignment and you need to find a temporary replacement. There's no time for a formal search, especially given the temporary nature of the assignment, so you'll have to rely on your impression of potential candidates in your network, which you hope will be accurate. You'll do this by identifying a potential applicant or pool of applicants, asking a few respected others for their opinions, talking with those you are considering, and offering the position to the person who you think best fits your profile.

Some Tips on Reading Others

- *Listen intently.* Listen for what is said and how it is said, not for what you think the person *should* be saying. Use pauses frequently; silence often encourages a person who wants to say more.

- *Observe aggressively.* Interpret others' body language and check for consistency (or lack thereof) between what's being said verbally and what's being displayed nonverbally.

- *Turn up your sensitivity.* Be aware of more than simply the conversation that is taking place. Use all your senses to pick up the nuances that are occurring within and between groups of people in the room.

- *Analyze first impressions.* Think about what the person is trying to present or hopes to gain before accepting what you see. If something seems inconsistent, ask.

Assessing the Organization

People who use politicking strategies effectively are likely to be those who have a good handle on the way an organization is structured—how it operates, how things get done, and how its people and culture function. They use their connections to people and information to obtain resources, get decisions made and implemented, navigate through complex bureaucracies, and generally facilitate processes in a way that meets organizational objectives.[28] Often, managers use political behaviors to influence people and processes when they lack formal direct authority. The following tactics can help you determine whether and how to politick appropriately.

- *Observe and listen.* Pay close attention to the organizational norms. Know what type of behavior is acceptable and what individuals and the organization frown upon. Pay attention to successful and unsuccessful practices and actions: Do employees speak up in meetings when their managers are present? What time do employees usually arrive at and leave the organization? Do they work on Saturdays? One employee at Microsoft, a company known for its intense work culture, decided to come in early to get work done so he could leave early to pick up his children from school. Others paid little attention to the time he arrived, but were quick to point out his "early" departure. He was perceived unfavorably, despite the fact that he worked as many hours as his co-workers, and eventually he was asked to leave.[29] Although this employee eventually won a lawsuit against his employer, it's a good example of the role that organizational politics can play in organizations. Unfair? Perhaps, but we have to know and follow both the written and unwritten rules to succeed in an organization.

■ *Evaluate the organization.* You may know who reports to whom on the organization's chart, but this may not represent how authority actually flows or the way in which certain practices are carried out. Know the formal roles individuals play in the organizations, as well as the informal roles. For example, don't overlook departmental clerical and administrative staff members. To the politically astute, these individuals can be a wealth of information. When treated with respect, they can help get you what you need, whether access, information, or "insider" tips.

Once you've assessed the organization, you can increase the odds that your efforts at politicking are successful. The following section describes three broad strategies you can use to develop your political skill: choosing wisely, managing impressions, and managing information.

Choosing Wisely

Do you remember the children's story about the boy who cried wolf? After several trial calls—just to see if others would come—the townspeople ignored his subsequent calls, figuring they were yet another trial or joke. When his call was real, no one came. Similarly, if you were to wield your power (or political influence) for each and every "cause," others might eventually reduce the attention they pay to subsequent causes. You'd be better off conserving your "political capital"—your reputation, influence, energy, and resources—for more important actions or causes. In addition, consider the most appropriate time to wield power. Sometimes waiting is helpful, as you might get what you want without asking. Or, you might get a portion of what you want. Be gracious, and then determine whether and how to get the rest.

Just as it is important to determine which situations warrant politicking, it is also crucial to decide how you will approach the situation. Various politicking strategies (see the following box) can be utilized to achieve your goal. You should carefully select a strategy based on the organization, the situation, and the individuals involved, and you should weigh the potential consequences of your political action. Each strategy can have elements of effectiveness if used appropriately and negative repercussions when used in haste.

Politicking Strategies[30]

Assertiveness—being able to speak up for your and your employees' rights without interfering with the needs of others in your organization.

Upward appeals—demonstrating that more senior and powerful people in your organization support the decision for which you are advocating.

Bargaining or **exchange**—using the "give and take" or compromise approach; for example, "I will do this for you if you do this for me."

Reciprocation—offering something to someone else and then expecting him or her to support your stance on a topic.[31]

Coalition building—gaining support for a position from others.

Ingratiation—putting the other in a friendly mood before approaching, or building a friendly rapport first before transacting business.

Rationality—using logic and reasoning to support your appeal.

Inspirational appeals—using emotional appeals based on values and ideas to gain support.

Consultation—seeking participation and input in the process before making a decision about a position to support.

Managing Impressions   Another important politicking strategy relates to influencing others' impressions of you. You've heard the saying, "You only have one chance to make a first impression." This saying stems from our human tendency to form opinions about others before we've actually gotten to know them. Whether this is fair or not, we form impressions about others—consciously or subconsciously—based on subtle factors such as their dress, speech, handshake, phone manner, writing style, prior reputation, and behavior and mannerisms. **Impression management** is a process by which we attempt to influence the reactions and images people have of us and our ideas.[32] We do this when we wear our best suit on a job interview or when we send a copy of a congratulatory e-mail or note to our boss. Impression management is being used when we try to choose the right words when in a public setting or even how we may act when managing or working on a team with others. Impression management can also be used to solidify our self-concept and further validate personal values or goals. While self-presentation not only creates a perspective for others to evaluate us on, it can be just as important for self-fulfillment and goal setting.[33] Through impression management, we become aware of all the ways in which we convey an initial impression of who we are to others and make a conscious choice about what parts of us we want to display to others.

In the same way that networking can help others take notice of your résumé and invite you to an interview, impression management can get you noticed—and possibly get you the job. Impression management is a big part of interviewing, from dressing up to create a certain impression to answering questions or asking the right questions to appear knowledgeable and competent. This can also be true in the reverse; interviewers can use impression management to portray the company in a particular light to attract a desirable candidate.[34] Both parties should be aware of the implications resulting from impression management and attempt to use a structured process to reduce the possibilities of exaggerations.[35] If both parties are honest in the process and it really is a true fit, it could be a win–win result. In the end, both parties will need to live up to their promises.

Finally, try to adopt a "win–win" attitude. When making a request for organizational resources (for example, staff, budget, time, project approval), it's best to frame your request in terms of the "greater good" and show that you've thought through the impact of your request on other areas and departments within your organization.

Managing Others' Impressions of You

- *Be punctual*—Demonstrate self-control and respect for others' time.
- *Dress appropriately*—Inquire ahead whether business or business casual is the norm. Dress to impress—err on the conservative side—but don't overdress. It could make others feel uncomfortable.
- *Flatter legitimately*—Say positive things about the person based on fact or personal observation. Be genuine. Others can sense when you're not.
- *Have a good sense of humor*—It helps put people at ease. Do try to use humor appropriately—as a lead-in to, not as a replacement for, substance. Beware of humor that can be construed as prejudiced against a certain group.
- *Be friendly and approachable*—Talk about things you have in common with the other, such as experience, hobbies, or views on current events. One way to do this in a business setting is to stay current with business periodicals such as *The Wall Street Journal, Fortune, BusinessWeek, International Herald Tribune,* and others.
- *Make friends*—and value all contacts.

Managing Information   Managers who are effective at politicking stay well informed about the organization and the industry and use information they gather to help them make better business decisions.[36] **Information management** involves obtaining useful information and managing the information received so that it is accessible and available as needed. As technology advances and we are bombarded 24/7 by all kinds of information, the ability to manage information is becoming even more critical. The most effective managers are those who understand the importance of information and know how to access, sift through, store, and use information to their advantage. In high-tech fields, innovations become old news by the time they are available to end users. Knowing what's coming, what's in the works, and who's involved in these efforts can make the difference between success and failure. Relying solely on the information easily accessible, or worse, ignoring such information, is a recipe for disaster.

Being able to effectively organize current and emerging information that relates to your work is important in many professions. In sales, for example, when your customer has indicated particular likes or needs, has asked you to contact her in six months, or has referred you to another potential customer, this information is vital to your success. Does your information management technique rely on numerous nondescript piles of paper on your desk? If so, you may want to come up with a different system. It doesn't have to be formal. For example, a series of Post-it Notes stuck to your bulletin board might work.

Tips for Managing Information

- *Set up a simple, user-friendly file system* (both print and electronic).
  - The system should include both specific project folders as well as general "resource" folders that are topical rather than pertain to a specific assignment. Resource folders might include technology, reports, or current events that may affect your organization or career.
  - Purge these folders on a regular basis to ensure they are current.
  - File the folders from past projects in a place separate from your active files. Limit the clutter in your active pile.
- *Glance briefly at all information* that comes to you either electronically or in print.
  - Quickly make "importance" decisions: must handle, handle if time, or discard.
  - Decide who else should see this information and arrange for them to be copied or informed.
  - Discard items that are not relevant or can be obtained later. Process or file the remaining items immediately. One rule of time management is to handle each piece of paper only once.
  - Make printouts of sensitive e-mails and file them in your personal files. Then remove them from your electronic in-box.
- *Refer to your project and related resource files prior to attending a meeting about the topic.* These few minutes can help get you up to speed and reduce wasted time in meetings.
- *Keep written notes on all meetings attended.* Date the pages and jot down key issues discussed and decisions made. Bring these notes with you to subsequent meetings to prevent having to revisit topics that have already been addressed.
- *Keep a telephone log* to track phone messages received and follow-up calls needed or made.
- *Manage your e-mail.* Respond to professional e-mail messages during the day, preferably during one or two blocks of time set aside for this task. Only respond to personal e-mail after hours, or better still, maintain a separate personal account. Many Internet service providers (ISPs) offer this service for free.
- *Keep running "to-do" and "tickler" lists.* Maintain all "to-do" items on one master list, and keep a separate "tickler" list to remind you of upcoming deadlines and activities. Related folders can be kept in the current file until you work on a specific "to-do" item.

"In political decisions, do not look for logic—look for politics."

Jerry Madden,
NASA project manager, retired

Ethical Issues in Organizational Politics

When engaging in political behaviors, it is important to keep in mind any ethical implications of your actions. As physicists tell us, "For every action, there is an equal and opposite reaction." Before taking action, ask yourself whether the action you're considering might cause an imbalance in your or someone else's area of the organization. For example, if you are advocating salary raises for your staff, what are the implications for the staffs of other managers? It's also important to consider whether you are achieving your objective at the expense of someone else's objectives. Always think through the implications of your objectives on the work of others. You don't want to "win the battle but lose the war," an old saying that reminds us to consider the long-term implications of a change effort as well as the short-term benefits or implications. While your staff might appreciate the raises you were able to obtain for them, the other staff with whom they work might perceive inequity and reduce their cooperation and effort to equalize the situation.

Ethical issues in politicking are brought to the forefront when dealing with Machiavellian personalities. A **Machiavellian** individual uses any means possible for personal gain. Individuals who rate high on this trait believe that the end justifies the means, so any behavior is acceptable if it furthers his or her position, including questionable or unethical behaviors. If you are a high Machiavellian, you see the workplace as more political and will tend to manipulate encounters in order to gain advantage in work situations. Be careful; although Machiavellianism can be seen as a positive trait when trying to gain better communication or benefits for all organizational members, it also can be viewed as a negative factor and can severely damage relationships within the organization.[37]

Are Your Political Actions Ethical?

- Why am I considering doing this?
- Who will benefit by this action? Am I doing this for my own exclusive benefit?
- Who (if anyone) might be harmed?
    - How can I adjust my strategy to ensure others' needs will be taken into account?
    - What alliances can I form that will make this action more likely to meet my own as well as others' needs?
- Is this request in the best interest of my colleagues and organization?
- Are the tactics I'll use and the outcomes that will result fair and equitable?
- Would the tactics I use and words I convey be acceptable if known publicly?

When done correctly, politicking can be a powerful tool for achieving your objectives and being successful within an organization. Asking yourself the questions listed in the box "Is Your Politicking Ethical?" should help you reduce or prevent potential negative side effects from developing from your efforts. As a manager, it is your role to create an environment that supports a healthy level of politicking, one that helps others understand the power and appropriate use of politicking within the organization.

Keeping Organizational Politics in Check

Sometimes organizations experience unfair or negative politicking—devious, self-interested efforts to sway opinion or a decision toward one point of view at the exclusion of all others. While politics will always exist at some level in organizations, you can ensure your staff's use of fair, positive political actions and work to reduce the level of unfair, negative influence. Some tips for doing this follow.

- *Reduce task ambiguity*—Employees need to be clear on what they can and cannot do and how tasks are prescribed. There should be no misunderstanding about what's expected of employees, their role, the amount of authority they have, and the level of work in which they're expected to get involved. For example, make it clear if they will be doing routine things in addition to more creative work. This will reduce the inevitable in-fighting that develops when people feel they're being taken advantage of in the workplace.

- *Increase communication channels*—Open up two-way communication. Ensure that all involved have input into key decisions and resource allocation requests before they're made. Be clear on where everyone stands, and ensure that all have the equivalent amount and quality of information needed to make informed decisions. This will prevent employees from feeling left out of important decisions and increase the degree to which they support or buy into your company's change efforts.

- *Ensure a clear and consistent reward and promotion structure*—Have a reward system that is well organized, fair, and clearly communicated. One of the best ways to reduce unfair politicking is to put careful thought into designing a compensation structure that all current and new employees understand, that is accessible and beneficial to employees at all levels within the organization, and that motivates current as well as potential employees. Such a compensation plan increases employee motivation, reduces concerns about potential inequities, and helps to focus attention on business objectives rather than on an individual employee's or department's perceived salary inequities.

- *Provide sufficient resources*—A scarcity of resources leads to a high degree of politicking within organizations. It's not always possible, but managers should try their best to offer a work climate in which the staff has the resources necessary to do a job well. For example, as a hospital administrator, you would want to make sure that as the occupancy rate at your hospital increases, sufficient additional staff will be called in to accommodate the increased patient volume.

- *Formalize the structure*—The more formal the structure, the more reasoning and performance-based data will be used for politicking.[38] In informal work settings that are less established, such as in some high-tech and dot-com startups, reasoning and performance-based data are supplemented with personal contact, emotional appeals, and future-oriented thinking.

Summary

Your ability to understand and use power and politics can give you an important edge in the current business environment. With fewer layers of management and greater competitive demands, supervisors and nonsupervisors alike are challenged to marshal the necessary resources to get things done in a positive and effective manner. By following the power and politicking strategies and tips offered, you can facilitate your success and that of those who work with and for you.

Key Terms and Concepts

Assertiveness	Legitimate power
Bargaining	Locus of control
Coercive power	Machiavellianism
Coalition building	Organizational politics
Consultation	Person power
Expert power	Politicking
Formal power	Position power
Impression management	Rationality
Informal power	Reciprocation
Information management	Referent power
Information power	Reward power
Ingratiation	Upward appeals
Inspirational appeals	

Discussion Questions

1. In the text, we posit that formal or position bases of power engender compliance while informal or person power engenders commitment. Do you agree? Can you share an example?

2. Let's say you have a great idea for a new product. You'd like to meet with the director of sales and marketing, but for the last couple of weeks, she's been too busy to talk to you. Using power and politicking strategies, what would you do to pitch the product idea to her?

3. Different organizations have different levels of politics. How do you feel low or high levels of politics impact the employees and the organization itself? What are some examples of high or low political actions?

4. We discuss ethical considerations in organizational politics. What do you believe are ethical dilemmas that exist in politicking? What ethical issues have you seen at your organization as a result of power, influence, and politics?

Endnotes

1. J. R. Schermerhorn Jr., J. G. Hunt, and R. N. Osborn, *Core Concepts of Organizational Behavior* (Hoboken, NJ: John Wiley & Sons, 2004), p. 256.

2. J. R. P. French and B. Raven, *The Bases of Social Power* (Ann Arbor, MI: University of Michigan Institute for Social Research, 1959), pp. 150–67.

3. A. Pettigrew, "Information Control as a Power Resource," *Sociology* 6 (1972), pp. 187–204.

4. L. N. Lussier and C. F. Achua, *Leadership: Theory, Application, Skill Development* (Cincinnati, OH: South-Western College Publishing, 2001).

5. Rune Lines, "Using Power to Install Strategy: The Relationships between Expert Power, Position Power, Influence Tactics and Implementation Strategy," *Journal of Change Management* 7, no. 2 (June, 2007), p. 164.

6. Vanessa Druskat and Jane Wheeler, "Managing from the Boundary: The Effective Leadership of Self-Managing Teams," *Academy of Management Journal* 46, no. 4 (August 2003), p. 452.

7. Lussier and Achua, *Leadership.*

8. D. Farrell and J. C. Petersen, "Patterns of Political Behavior in Organizations," *Academy of Management Review* (July 1982), p. 405; and D. J. Vredenburgh and J. G. Maurer, "A Process Framework of Organizational Politics," *Human Relations* (January 1984), pp. 47–66.

9. Fernanda Duarte, "Teaching Organizational Power and Politics through a Critical Pedagogical Approach," *Journal of Management & Organizations* 16 (2010), pp. 715–26.

10. Joseph E. Champoux, *Organizational Behavior: Using Film to Visualize Principles and Practices* (Cincinnati, OH: South-Western, 2000).

11. Brian Miller, Matthew Rutherford, and Robert Kolodinsky, "Perceptions of Organizational Politics: A Meta-Analysis of Outcomes," *Journal of Business and Psychology* 22, no. 3 (2008), p. 212.

12. B. K. Miller, M. A. Rutherford, and R. W. Kolodinsky, "Perceptions of Organizational Politics: A Meta-analysis of Outcomes," *Journal of Business Psychology* 22 (2008), pp. 209–22.

13. G. Harrell-Cook, G. R. Ferris, and J. H. Dulebohn, "Political Behavior as Moderators of the Perceptions of Organizational Politics—Work Outcomes Relationships," *Journal of Organizational Behavior* 20 (1999), pp. 1093–1105.

14. Donald Fedor et al., "Perceptions of Positive Organizational Politics and Their Impact on Organizational Outcomes," *Journal of Applied Social Psychology* 38 (2008), pp. 76–96.

15. B. E. Ashforth and T. R. Lee, "Defensive Behavior in Organizations: A Preliminary Model," *Human Relations* 43, no. 7 (1990), pp. 621–48.

16. Kate Davey, "Women's Accounts of Organizational Politics as a Gendering Process," *Gender, Work & Organizations* 15, no. 6 (November 2008), p. 651.

17. Dirk De Clercq and Maxim Voronov, "The Role of Cultural and Symbolic Capital in Entrepreneurs' Ability to Meet Expectations about Conformity and Innovation," *Journal of Small Business Management* 47, no. 3 (July 2009), pp. 398–420.

18. Vanessa Druskat and Jane Wheeler, "Managing from the Boundary," p. 452.

19. P. L. Perrewé, G. R. Ferris, D. D. Fink, and W. P. Anthony, "Political Skill: An Antidote for Workplace Stressors," *Academy of Management Executive* 14, no. 3 (2000), pp. 115–23.

20. Todd Wasserman, "Report: Digital Advertising Broke $100 Billion in 2012," *Mashable* (January 9, 2013), http://mashable.com/category/digital-advertising/.

21. Stephanie Miller, "Re-election Story: Email Marketing Essential to Political Campaigns," *Ideal Email Marketing* (December 15, 2012), http://www.idealemailmarketing.com/a-wow-re-election-story-email-marketing-essential-to-politcal-campaigns-2/405/.

22. Jon Friedman, "Twitter's Window on Middle East Uprisings: Scholar Tracks the Tweets That Changed the World," *MarketWatch* (May 18, 2011), http://www.marketwatch.com/story/twitters-window-on-middle-east-uprisings-2011-05-18.

23. J. B. Rotter, "Generalized Expectancies for Internal versus External Control of Reinforcement," *Psychological Monographs* 80, no. 1 (1966), pp. 1–28.

24. P. W. Grimes, M. Millea, and T. Woodruff, "Grades—Who's to Blame? Student Evaluation of Teaching and Locus of Control," *Journal of Economic Education* (Spring 2004), pp. 129–47.

25. Stephen P. Robbins and Phillip L. Hunsaker, *Training in Interpersonal Skills: Tips for Managing People at Work* (Upper Saddle River, NJ: Prentice Hall, 1996), p. 128.

26. R. W. Allen, D. L. Madison, L. W. Porter, P. A. Renwick, and B. T. Mayes, "Organizational Politics: Tactics and Characteristics of Its Actors," *California Management Review* (Fall 1979), pp. 77–83.

27. Iris Randall, "The Key to Networking: Knowing How to 'Read' a Person Makes Networking Easier," *Black Enterprise* (March 1996), p. 56.

28. David Krackhardt, "Assessing the Political Landscape: Structure, Cognition, and Power in an Organization," *Administrative Science Quarterly* 35, no. 2 (1990), pp. 342–69.

29. Video case, "Joys and Risks of the Daddy Track," *Nightline* (August 14, 1991).

30. Reprinted from D. Kipnis, S. M. Schmidt, C. Swaffin-Smith, and I. Wilkinson, "Patterns of Managerial Influence: Shotgun Managers, Tacticians, and Bystanders," *Organizational Dynamics* (Winter 1984), pp. 58–67. With permission from Elsevier Science.

31. Russell Cropanzano and Marie Mitchell, "Social Exchange Theory: An Interdisciplinary Review," *Journal of Management* 31, no. 6 (2005), pp. 874–900.

32. Asha Rao, Stuart Schmidt, and Lynda Murray, "Upward Impression Management: Goals, Influence Strategies, and Consequences," *Human Relations* 48, no. 2 (1995), p. 147.

33. Ashok Laiwani and Sharon Shavitt, "The 'Me' I Claim to Be: Cultural Self-Construal Elicits Self-Presentational Goal Pursuit," *Journal of Personality & Social Psychology* 97, no. 1 (July, 2009), pp. 88–102.

34. Stephen Knouse, "Targeted Recruiting for Diversity: Impression Management, Realistic Expectations, and Diversity Climate," *International Journal of Management* 26, no. 3 (December 2009), p. 348.

35. Murray Barrick, Jonathan Shaffer, and Sandra DeGrassi, "What You See May Not Be What You Get: Relationships Among Self-Presentation Tactics and Ratings of Interview and Job Performance," *Journal of Applied Psychology* 94, no. 6 (November 2009), p. 1409.

36. Thomas H. Davenport, Robert G. Eccles, and Laurence Prusak, "Information Politics," *Sloan Management Review* (Fall 1992), pp. 53–65.

37. Heather L. Walter, Carolyn M. Anderson, and Matthew M. Martin, 'How Subordinates' Machiavellianism and Motives Relate to Satisfaction with Superiors," *Communication Quarterly* 53, no. 1 (2005), p. 57.

38. Rao, Schmidt, and Murray, "Upward Impression Management," p. 147.

**Exercise 15–A
Assessing Your
Views of Power**

Indicate your opinion on each question by using the following scale:

5 strongly agree

4 somewhat agree

3 neither agree nor disagree

2 somewhat disagree

1 slightly disagree

Statements	Your score
1. It is important for a leader to use all power and status symbols that the organization provides in order to be able to get his or her job done.	
2. Unfortunately, for many employees, the only thing that really works is threats and punitive actions.	
3. In order to be effective, a leader needs to have access to many resources to reward subordinates when they do their job well.	
4. Having excellent interpersonal relations with subordinates is essential to effective leadership.	
5. One of the keys to a leader's influence is access to information.	
6. Being friends with subordinates often reduces a leader's ability to influence them and control their actions.	
7. Leaders who are reluctant to punish their employees often lose their credibility.	
8. It is very difficult for a leader to be effective without a formal title and position within an organization.	
9. Rewarding subordinates with raises, bonuses, and resources is the best way to obtain their cooperation.	
10. In order to be effective, a leader needs to become an expert in the area that he or she is leading.	
11. Organizations need to ensure that a leader's formal evaluation of subordinates is actively used in making decisions about them.	
12. Even in the most enlightened organizations, a leader's ability to punish subordinates needs to be well preserved.	
13. The dismantling of formal hierarchies and the removal of many of the symbols of leadership and status have caused many leaders to lose their ability to influence their subordinates.	
14. A leader needs to take particular care to be perceived as an expert in his or her area.	
15. It is key for a leader to develop subordinates' loyalty.	

Scoring: Reverse score for item 6, then add your scores on each item as follows:

Legitimate power	Add items 1, 8, and 13:	Total:
Reward power	Add items 3, 9, and 11:	Total:
Coercive power	Add items 2, 7, and 12:	Total
Expert power	Add items 4, 6, and 15:	Total:
Referent power	Add items 5, 10, and 14:	Total:

The higher your score in each category (maximum of 15), the more you believe in utilizing that source of power.

Questions

1. For each base of power, discuss an appropriate situation for its effective use.
2. Did the outcome of this assessment surprise you? Why or why not?
3. What are the pros and cons of using your dominant source(s) of power?
4. How does the outcome of this assessment match up to the dominant source of power used by your supervisor (parent, team leader, etc.)?

Source: From Afsaneh Nahavandi, *The Art and Science of Leadership,* 3rd Edition, © 2003. Reproduced by permission of Pearson Education, Inc., Upper Saddle River, New Jersey.

Exercise 15–B
Power and Its Consequences

Working with a partner, you will be asked by your instructor to get your partner to do something that he or she may not want to do. Your mission is to utilize each of the five bases of power (legitimate, reward, coercive, expert, referent)—one at a time—to accomplish this task. Then, reverse roles and do the same thing.

Questions

1. Which of the bases of power were easiest for you to use to accomplish your task? Explain.
2. Which of the bases of power resulted in the most immediate compliance from your "subordinate"? Why do you think this was the case?
3. Once the tables were turned, how did you feel about being the one toward whom power was being used?
4. Which of the bases of power did you feel most comfortable complying with?
5. Which of the bases of power did you feel least comfortable (or most bothered by) complying with?
6. Discuss the applications and implications of this exercise in team or organizational settings.

Source: This exercise is adapted from S. Meisel, "Quick Tips and Energizers for OB Classes," presented at the 2001 OBTC annual conference in Carrollton, GA.

Exercise 15–C
Recognizing Effective and Ineffective Political Behavior

Analyze the following situations and determine whether the behavior utilized in each demonstrates effective or ineffective politicking. Explain the reasons for your assessment.

1. Rita is taking golf lessons so she can join the Saturday golf group, which includes some higher-level managers.

   Effective or Ineffective (circle)? Explain. _____

   _____

   _____

2. Paul tells his manager's manager about mistakes his manager makes.

   Effective or Ineffective (circle)? Explain. _____

   _____

   _____

3. Jasmine realizes that her team will not be able to complete its task by the deadline. She asks her boss for a meeting to give her a heads-up on the situation.

   Effective or Ineffective (circle)? Explain. _____

   _____

   _____

4. Sally avoids spending time socializing so that she can be more productive on the job.

   Effective or Ineffective (circle)? Explain. _____

   _____

   _____

5. John sent a very positive performance report to three higher-level managers to whom he does not report. They did not request copies.

   Effective or Ineffective (circle)? Explain. _____

   _____

   _____

6. Tamika has to drop off a daily report by noon. She delivers the report at around 10 a.m. on Tuesday and Thursday so that she can run into some higher-level managers who meet at that time near the office where the report must go. On the other days, Tamika submits the report around noon on her way to lunch.

   Effective or Ineffective (circle)? Explain. _____

   _____

   _____

7. Samuel joins a particular church where many of the top managers are members.

   Effective or Ineffective (circle)? Explain. _____

   _____

   _____

Source: From Lussier/Achua, *Leadership: Theory, Application, and Skill Development* 1E, p. 355. © 2001 South-Western, a part of Cengage Learning, Inc. Reproduced by permission. www.cengage.com/permissions.

Exercise 15–D Politicking—What's My Angle?

1. Divide into pairs or small groups.

2. Decide on a situation in which politicking is needed (examples: getting a co-worker to cover a shift for you, getting a team member to take on a certain part of a project, getting the boss to put your name in for a promotion or sales trip, getting someone to give you a reference).

3. Develop a short script for the situation using the politicking strategies from the chapter. Create at least four different scripts from the possible list in the chapter.

4. Role-play the scenario with members from another group. Decide who will be group A and group B.

   ■ Group A Presenters—Present each strategy one at a time, allowing a break between each strategy so the other team members can make notes.

   ■ Group B Observers—Allow the other team's member to present their appeal to you. Make notes in the attached chart after each strategy to report the following observations:

      ■ What strategy do you believe they were using?

      ■ How effective was the tactic?

      ■ How did the tactic affect you? Did it make you uncomfortable? What was your impression or feeling about the presenter?

5. When group A has presented all of their strategies, allow group B to present while group A observes.

Observer Tracking Chart

Politicking Strategy	Level of Effectiveness	Perceptions/Feelings
1.		
2.		
3.		
4.		
5.		
6.		

1. How many of you felt your strategies were successful?
2. Which strategies were most effective and why?
3. How do these different strategies come into play in varying situations?
4. What did you learn about yourself, others, and politicking from this exercise?

**Exercise 15–E
"Powers" of
Observation**

Observe a business meeting or a situation where politicking is present. Many of the reality TV shows or sports analysis shows will be political in nature. Record the effective and ineffective politicking behaviors you observe being performed by members of the group.

Following your instructor's guidelines, write a paper that addresses the following questions:

1. What makes the behaviors effective or ineffective?
2. What role does someone's authority (or power in his or her position) or lack of authority play in his or her use and effectiveness of political behaviors? What strategies would have most impact in this situation? Why?
3. What steps could be taken to regulate or reduce the need for politicking in the future by this group? Are there any negative or unethical factors to consider in this situation?

**Exercise 15–F
Reflection/Action Plan**

This chapter focused on power and politicking—what they are, why they are important, and how to improve your skills in these areas. Complete the following worksheet upon completing all readings and experiential activities for this chapter.

1. The one or two areas in which I am most strong are:

_____

_____

_____

2. The one or two areas in which I need more improvement are:

_____

_____

_____

3. If I did only one thing to improve in each of these areas, it would be to:

_____

_____

_____

4. Making these changes would probably result in:

_____

_____

_____

5. If I did not change or improve in these areas, it would probably affect my personal and professional life in the following ways:

_____

_____

_____

16 Networking and Mentoring

Learning Points

How do I:

- Identify a job opening or arrange an interview through a friend or a friend of a friend?
- Reach out to and connect with others when I am a newcomer in an organization?
- "Work a room"—meet many different people in a short amount of time?
- Overcome my reluctance or discomfort with networking?
- Build a diverse network of mentors who can provide insight and assistance on career-related issues?
- Learn how to be an effective protégé
- Develop effective relationships with, and provide value to, others in my network?

Mr. Zaven Yaralian is a prime example of how networking can help individuals progress through their careers (see chart diagramming his career below). Yaralian was a professional football coach for the New Orleans Saints. As in most other professions, success in obtaining coaching jobs relies on both technical expertise and networking skills. Yaralian's career has benefited time after time from contacts he made at the beginning of and throughout his career. He acquired his former position directly as the result of networking.

Coach Yaralian played football for the University of Nebraska, a highly recognized program that produces outstanding players as well as coaches. He honed his game through one of the best college coaches, Tom Osborne. After graduation, he kept in close touch with Coach Osborne. Following his unsuccessful attempt at pursuing a career in the NFL, Yaralian contacted Osborne. Osborne, who knew Yaralian's heart belonged to football, suggested coaching. Coach Osborne gave Yaralian his first job in coaching as a graduate assistant in his own program.

Yaralian then began moving up in his profession. He began his first full-time job in football at Washington State University. He got the job through a referral and recommendation from Coach Osborne. From there he progressed to other schools, including the University of Colorado. While in Colorado, Yaralian's team made a bid for the national championship. His boss and well-respected head coach, Bill McCartney, helped Yaralian reach the next level of performance in his career. Through recommendations from him and Osborne, Yaralian was offered and accepted a position with Mike Ditka of the Chicago Bears. Ditka then helped Yaralian obtain an offer from Dan Reeves of the New York Giants. Yaralian then reunited with the Hall of Famer, Mike Ditka, five years later in New Orleans, where Yaralian became the defensive coordinator for the New Orleans Saints. The once unknown defensive back coach was given the opportunity to coach with some of the best coaches and teams in the NFL because of a network of key relationships he had made and cultivated throughout his career.[1]

Zaven Yaralian's Career through Networking[2]

Top: Career opportunity
Bottom: Connection used

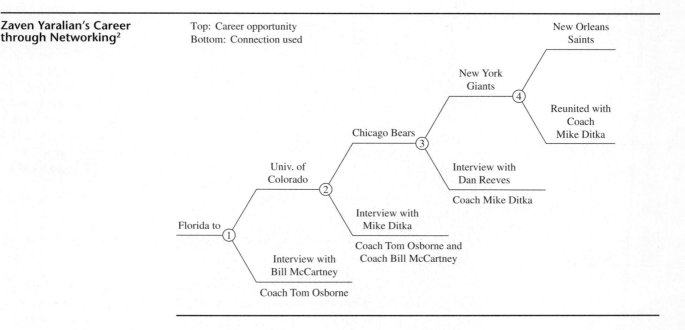

1. In business, neither technical skills nor networking abilities are sufficient by themselves. Do you agree with this statement? Why or why not?

2. When Yaralian proves he is an effective coach, why would others help him move up—and out—of their organization? Wouldn't you prefer keeping outstanding performers as opposed to helping them leave?

3. What are some benefits of networking?

4. What are some potential downsides of networking?

5. In what ways have you used networking to get a leg up on a job or other opportunity?

"It's not what you know, it's who you know."

The old adage about the valuable role others can play in opening doors for us is still repeated because it's often true. As illustrated in the above case, moving up successfully can happen as the result of both acquiring knowledge and fostering important relationships with others who can be helpful to you as your career progresses. While we wouldn't say that credentials aren't important, the fact is that having the credentials to do a job is just the first step. Equally important is getting access—to information, people, and jobs—and other people are often the conduit through which this access is obtained. In this chapter, we discuss the definition and importance of networking and mentoring, how they are used, and tips for effectively building mentor networks to increase your social capital and that of others.[3]

What Is Networking?

Networking is the building and nurturing of personal and professional relationships to create a system or chain of information, contacts, and support. In the business world, the goal of networking is to develop and maintain relationships with people who can be helpful to you, your employer, or your organization.[4] Successful networking requires a certain mindset or philosophy: an attitude of giving advice, information, and help rather than expecting this from others.[5] Effective networking is most likely to occur between two or more people who build rapport by finding common interests through meaningful, balanced, two-way communication. A networker who appears too needy or self-centered might face resistance from others who might otherwise be able to help him or her.

Whether through face-to-face, phone, written, or electronic means, the networker attempts to connect with others who can provide needed information and opportunities. A person's network is evolving constantly. Studies estimate that over a lifetime, a person will have several thousand acquaintances. Moreover, as age and income increase, so too will the number of acquaintances. Some contacts are cultivated deliberately and others evolve naturally.[6] The largest portion of a person's network actually consists of secondary contacts—friends of friends who are close to the situation about which you need information. By cultivating this network through networking, you are able to enhance your **social capital**: the resources that can provide new ideas, timely information, job opportunities, business leads, influence, and social support as a result of these relationships.[7] In this knowledge economy, the unique set of relationships and knowledge that is social capital can provide individuals with substantial career advantages[8] and organizations with competitive advantages.[9]

The Importance and Uses of Networking

Creating a personal network and developing networking skills can provide numerous professional benefits for individuals and organizations. Networking is invaluable for those who are seeking advancement within an existing organization as well as those who are seeking a new career opportunity. Building a network of contacts can keep you current with industry trends and expedite your career advancement from one position to another, either within an existing organization or in a move from one organization to the next.[10]

Networking within an Organization

Networking while on the job increases your access to available resources and information.[11] Networking with others helps you augment your thoughts and ideas with those of others, creating a concept that incorporates "best practice" thinking from the outset of its development. Networking helps you increase your effectiveness when researching a new concept, starting a new project, or developing a new product idea.[12] By consulting with others who are experts in the topic in which you are involved, you incorporate their thoughts into your knowledge base in the given area. For example, when charged with developing or testing a new product, an important first step is to identify internal and external experts who can serve as sources of information on the relevant topic, preventing you from "reinventing the wheel" and helping you build allies who can later advocate for the change you are proposing.

Networking is essential when taking on a new assignment or project. It is a good habit to get to know others, both inside and outside your department, and at all levels—peers, subordinates, and superiors. By networking with co-workers as well as with individuals at more junior and senior levels of the organization, you can learn about the broader business in which your organization is involved and about the challenges and opportunities that lie ahead.[13] Staying in touch with people and trends in your company enables you to prepare for and adapt to organizational changes. Access to information and "connectedness" enables you to acquire a more strategic view of the business, one that is holistic rather than limited to your specific functional area. This helps you position your department and organization to respond strategically to marketplace changes as they inevitably occur.[14]

Networking and Technology

E-networking or social networking is exploding in popularity with increased reliance on technology. "While older adults go online to find information, the younger crowd go online to live."[15] This revelation has not been lost on colleges and universities across the country, which are relying on online networking sites to stay connected with alumni to encourage volunteerism and donations.[16] One university successfully used Facebook to make contact with and boost acceptance rates of candidates invited to join its honor society. They realized that to reach the target audience, they needed to talk the audience's language and meet them where they live.

Individuals and organizations are now using news groups, online forums, e-mail, and blogs to make contacts, build relationships, and even check backgrounds of potential employees. Electronic communication can also help you maintain contact with multiple members of your network with the click of the mouse. Although many still feel there is nothing like face-to-face communication for building solid relationships and networking, a growing population is more comfortable approaching social situations through electronic means.

This heightened understanding can increase your effectiveness as a businessperson and your value to the organization as you learn to make decisions from multiple rather than one-dimensional business perspectives. For example, an aerospace firm during the early 1990s found defense budgets shrinking substantially. The CEO's directive—cut 30 percent across the board—could have spelled disaster if not for the willingness of division and department managers to network. Some programs were nearly dead, while others—early in the life cycle though potentially a financial success—were struggling to make ends meet. Managers met and discussed the directive, deciding that cutting costs by one-third did not necessarily mean firing one-third of the employees, and that cutting all programs or departments at the same rate did not make sense. They networked, shared information and resources, and found ways to meet the directive in a way that met the needs of the organization.

Organizations may be represented on charts as groups of self-contained work units, such as marketing, finance, research and development, purchasing, information systems, planning, logistics, communications, public relations, human resources, and legal counsel, but in fact, most departments rely heavily on outputs of other departments. Most decisions made by one segment of an organization affect other segments of an organization. What happens between the boxes on the organization chart—the "white spaces"[17]—could mean the difference between failure and success of the organization. Managing the white spaces through organizational networking not only facilitates organizational synergy but also helps you when you're promoted to positions elsewhere in the company or when you move to other companies and industries.

Networking to Find a Job or Change Careers

Networking can also help you learn about new job opportunities. In today's fast-paced, global, high-tech environment, your attitude about and comfort with networking can significantly impact your ability to establish contacts, get interviews for jobs, and identify and cultivate mentors within organizations.[18] By developing your network and improving your ability to sell yourself, you can benefit by finding a new job as well as by increasing your skills in selling and promoting—useful skills in any business today. Networking skills are crucial for career and personal success. Career specialists estimate that 70–80 percent of the best jobs come from effective and consistent personal networking with others rather than through executive search firms (commonly referred to as "headhunters"), sending in blind résumés, posting a résumé on the Web, or responding to job ads.[19]

Effective networking produces a ripple effect. Like a stone thrown in the water, creating numerous waves and movements, one personal contact can lead to others that eventually result in knowledge about multiple career opportunities.[20] You might recall the commercial for Fabergé Organics shampoo ("I told two friends, and they told two friends, and so on"). Another way of explaining the value of networking is the premise of "six degrees of separation,"[21] the notion that most of us can find a connection to anyone else in the world through six levels of contacts. This is referred to as the **secondary network**, and its existence indicates the importance of not relying solely on those you know when doing research, getting to know an organization, or searching for a job. For example, if your **primary network**—those individuals you know personally—consists of approximately 250 people, expand this into your secondary network. If each of your 250 direct contacts has a personal network of 250, the first tier alone will have over 62,500 contacts. Just imagine the opportunities!

Using LinkedIn to Expand Your Professional Networking

LinkedIn is the world's largest professional network. Launched in 2003, by 2013 it had over 200 million members in 200 countries and territories. It is free to sign up and create your profile but there are some features, such as direct e-mailing to members, that are only available if you purchase a premium membership. Once your profile is set up, you can join professional interest groups to meet other people and share discussions with them, search posted jobs, and look for people in industries, companies, and specific roles. Not having a presence on LinkedIn means that you don't have visibility as more and more recruiters (agencies, headhunters, and companies) use LinkedIn to find candidates.

Executive recruiters and headhunters use LinkedIn either to research candidates who have applied for a position, or source job candidates. Jobs can be posted on the jobs boards but recruiters also use LinkedIn in more advanced ways. These companies use LinkedIn to build a referral chain. Using the advanced search function they can identify potential candidates by specifying an industry, company, and even a role. Then they trawl through the returned list to pick the most interesting candidates. They can then contact them using inmail, or, if the individuals have posted contact details, contact them directly. LinkedIn is a particularly useful tool for higher-level roles at senior manager, director, VP, and CEO levels.

An effective technique for finding the right job or career for you is informational interviewing. This means interviewing people about their own careers and jobs. In **information interviews**, the goal is to learn from the person with whom you're speaking, not to obtain a job. You can do this by asking what they like and dislike about their job, getting advice from them about how you might embark on a similar career path or join a similar organization. A sample set of questions to ask during information interviews appears in the accompanying box. When used early in the job search process, networking for information, rather than for specific jobs, can help you clarify your job goals and improve your interviewing skills. Wouldn't it be better to realize that you are not cut out to spend eight hours a day in front of a computer than to take a job and then quit? This focused task will help you achieve your short-term goal as well as clarify your interest or compatibility with a particular job or career field.

Questions to Ask in Information Interviews

1. How did your interest in this career develop?
2. How did you prepare for this career?
3. What do you like and dislike about this career?
4. What are the current and future trends in this career?
5. What are the key issues with which you're working right now?
6. Describe a typical day in this job.
7. If you could change one thing about this career, what would it be?
8. What advice do you have for someone like me?
9. Would you have a few minutes to critique my résumé?
10. Who else can I talk to about a career in _____?

This principle can be applied both as a student and as a manager. As a student, it is important to identify key resource people who can help you attain your goals. Through networking with your resident advisor, upper-class students, coaches, and teachers, you can learn the names of people you can consult or organizations that can be of benefit to you on school projects or when dealing with personal problems. Those students who are willing to reach out to others rather than trying to solve all their own problems are better able to make changes and solve problems than are those who refuse assistance from others and try to fix or change things on their own. Students who utilize their contacts are more likely to get internships and jobs than those who do not.

Other Uses of Networking

Networking is a great way to locate providers of goods and services. It can serve individuals and organizations by helping them identify good deals or valuable savings to help reduce costs. Have you ever wanted to buy a car, needed to find office supplies at a discount, or relocated to a new area and needed a doctor, a dentist, or a hairdresser? A network of friends, peers, and acquaintances can help you streamline your search. Networking can be instrumental in helping managers find key people to hire.[22] Firms in high-growth areas, such as information security and wireless or digital technologies, experience great difficulty in recruiting and retaining talented professionals. Even with promises of signing bonuses and stock options, some firms come up empty-handed. Often, the personal recommendation from a friend—alone or combined with a signing bonus—can help entice a prospective employee to accept a job offer. Also called **reverse networking**, this practice offers numerous benefits to firms over traditional recruiting strategies.

Small business owners and entrepreneurs benefit greatly from networking. For example, how do real estate agents, independent financial planners, and consultants find leads and turn them into paying customers? How do entrepreneurs locate venture capitalists to invest in their businesses? By nurturing relationships with individuals in the profession (e.g., peers in other organizations, former employees, or people you meet at conferences or in trade associations) and in your community (e.g., volunteer organizations, religious groups, city or school councils, athletic teams), you can increase your contacts exponentially.[23] More importantly, the likelihood of gaining new business from a referral is 60 to 70 percent as opposed to 10 percent from a nonreferral.[24] Networking can also provide a clearer understanding of your clients' concerns or needs, and in turn increase the effectiveness of your operations.

Simply put, networking is an important and valuable skill for those who want to succeed within an organization, find a new employer, or expand a customer base. Networking enables us to break out of old patterns and find new, more efficient solutions to fulfill our organizational and career-related needs.

Developing an Appropriate Mindset for Networking

There is more to networking than just understanding the tactics and techniques for developing and practicing the skill. Networking involves building and maintaining relationships.[25] Successful networking requires a positive, cooperative mindset. So far, we have discussed networking as a way to use your connections to meet your needs. This sounds rather one-sided. The most successful networkers have an attitude derived from viewing relationships as opportunities to give to, rather than take from, others.[26]

There are two kinds of networkers: those who are self-oriented, and those who are focused on others. The "self-oriented" networker approaches a room and surveys it for potential customers or clients, thinking, Who can I sell? Who might be able to give me a job lead? What can I get them to buy? How do I convince them they need me or what I offer? The "other-oriented" networker approaches a room and identifies people who need to be connected with others in the room, thinking, Who in this room could use my help? Who can I introduce to whom? How can I help you? I know someone who might be able to help you; can I have them contact you?

Networking in Action [27]

Met Mrs. Gonzales at Trade Fair June 7. She suggested I contact Mr. Kerne at Trim Tech.

June 11
Took Mr. Kerne to lunch. Discovered we had much in common. He made an appointment for me to see a John Grant at Jaco Co.

June 18
Mr. Grant, a vice president, took me to their human resource director. Two interviews followed.

June 30
Accepted position with Jaco.

Contact Record [28]

Here is a good format to use to keep up with your contacts. You can keep track of your contacts in an organizer, Rolodex, notebook, or computer database. This will allow you to access all the pertinent data when you need to and to keep the data current.

Name: _____

Contact: _____

Company/Organization: _____

Address: _____

_____

Phone: _____

E-mail address: _____

How do I know this person? _____

_____

_____

_____

Why is he/she a good first contact? _____

_____

_____

Contact record. List date(s) of all contacts and brief subject/nature of contact. Keep track of items sent and "to do" items here. _____

_____

_____

_____

Those who are approached by the self-interested networker might feel taken advantage of. A relationship was not formed; instead, pleasantries were exchanged as a way of getting some need met. Should this networker contact the person at a later date, there's a possibility that the person will be less willing to help. Effective networking should be a reciprocal process; by helping others you in turn help yourself. An appropriate blending of the two orientations can create mutually beneficial interactions and develop a long-term win–win situation.

Barriers to Networking

Networking may sound simple enough, but for some the prospect of networking can be intimidating. For many people, the skill of networking does not come naturally. Meeting others, making small talk, and especially marketing or promoting oneself are processes that require practice in order to be performed successfully. People fear or avoid networking for a number of reasons:

- *Being shy/introverted, lacking in self-esteem or confidence in personal skills and abilities.*[29] Networking can be achieved through means other than face-to-face meetings, such as an e-mail or letter. Once your confidence and competence increase, try combining these approaches with more direct, face-to-face methods, such as through meetings and conferences.

- *Difficulty in asking others for help and being or feeling unable to reciprocate the favor immediately.* Realize that networking goes beyond a single interaction; you may have the opportunity to return the favor at a later time. Moreover, you'll be helping your contact by connecting him or her to your network.

- *Wanting to reach goals without any special help from others.* While this is a noble cause, refusing to network can negatively impact your career as well as the value of the social capital you can offer. Furthermore, it is unlikely that networking alone will get you a job. It opens doors, but if you don't possess the necessary knowledge, skills, and abilities, any "special help" from others would reflect poorly on them. From the organization's perspective, when two candidates are equally qualified, a "known quantity" is preferred to hiring an "unknown."

- *Concern about sharing sensitive or competitive information.* The nature and amount of information you share is up to you and your contact. Specific expectations can and should be discussed early in the relationship. Over time, trust—a key ingredient of effective relationships—will build, and this concern will likely lessen.

Whatever your personal barriers or discomfort with networking might be, it is important to resolve the issues that can prevent you from becoming an effective networker. Those who do not learn how to network will fall behind in today's competitive and global environment.[30] Luckily, these skills can be learned and applied in a variety of contexts. Networking takes conscious effort. It is very much like working out: If you do not continue to work at it, you will lose what you have already gained. Also, once the habit has been established, it becomes a natural (and beneficial) part of your routine.

Strategies for Building an Effective Network

The following steps will help get you started in developing and maintaining a beneficial network:

- *Organize your current network.* Identify people you already know and enter their names and contact information into a database. See the box "What If I Don't Have Any Contacts?" for ideas.

- *Expand your network.* After assessing your network, think about how you want to expand it. Realize that diversity and reciprocity are two key principles in building a successful network.[31] It's best to seek out people in different groups, companies, and industries, because the occupational world is diverse. Begin by asking your co-workers for names of people they know or have heard about in your fields of interest. At the same time, check the Internet and other publications to identify other people and organizations to add to the list. Professional associations that are related to your field of expertise or interests are an excellent source of names of people with whom to network. You or someone you know might already be a member of one or more of these organizations. Using associations as sounding boards can help you both to get information you need and to assess the strengths and weaknesses of the information you receive.[32]

  Review the list with anyone involved in the project to obtain additional names. Then contact each name on the list (via phone, e-mail, or memo), one at a time, introducing yourself, explaining the reason you're making the contact, and describing where you found the person's name. Explain why you need the information and offer a little background that helps them understand why you're contacting them. It helps to say something positive about why you're contacting each person specifically—such as you know they're an expert, you heard good things about them, or you know they have the experience that could benefit your project.

- *Nurture the relationships.* Commit to spending time, one-on-one, to get to know your contacts. The more they know you and your goals, the better they can help you. Similarly, find out their wants and needs. End every conversation with people in your network by asking how you can help them. Finally, keep in touch periodically with your friends, contacts, and associates to maintain these relationships.

- *Take charge of the situation.* Make networking a conscious effort and take control over potential opportunities. Having a game plan in mind and being proactive in conversation will help you influence the outcomes. Learning the art of small talk can be just as important as honing your technical skills. Since most people like to talk about themselves, open the conversation by inquiring about their family, occupation, hobbies, recreation, or dreams. This will allow you to develop a rapport or relationship with the person for future reference and to provide appropriate details about yourself. Listening in this situation can be the most effective means for building the relationship at this point, so refer to Chapter 6 for tips on effective listening techniques.

Look for everyday opportunities to expand your network. Effective networkers learn to analyze every situation for possibilities and never underestimate a person's connections. Frequently, people locate jobs or opportunities from mere acquaintances or from people to whom they have only weak ties as often as from close friends and relatives.[33] Even the most mundane situations can add to your network. Talking to the person behind you while standing in a slow-moving line at the airport, or discussing the headlines in the paper while waiting at the car dealership to get your car serviced, or even chatting to other parents at your child's ball game can lead to opportunities and connections beyond your initial network.

What If I Don't Have Any Contacts?

Everyone has contacts! A contact is simply a person who is willing and able to help you. Following are a few examples of possible contacts. If you're having trouble identifying names of potential contacts, you might be overlooking the obvious—friends, relatives, and neighbors. Remember, these people may not have the information you need, but they may know others who do. Another strategy for meeting potential contacts is to get involved in organizations—community service, career, professional, recreational, civic, fraternal, academic, religious—where you are likely to meet people who share an interest in or commitment to a cause with you.

Who Are Contacts?[34]

Friends, relatives, neighbors, sorority or fraternity members.

Co-workers of parents, spouse or significant other, and other family members.

Current and former classmates.

Priests, ministers, rabbis, and fellow church or synagogue members.

Fellow club members.

Personal lawyer, insurance agent, realtor, accountant, doctor, dentist, beautician.

Teachers and former teachers.

Employers and former employers.

Co-workers and former co-workers.

Members of your employer's human resources department.

Grade school, high school, college, and graduate school alumni and alumni associations.

Business associates and members of professional organizations.

(continued)

To prepare mentally for a networking meeting, follow these three steps:

1. Analyze the *process*. Ask yourself with whom you'll need to network—the types of individuals you will be seeking and for what purpose.[35] Be sure to identify what you hope to gain as well as ways in which you can contribute. Remember that networking is a two-way street. Others will be more apt to help you when you show your willingness to help them.

2. Identify the *place* where the networking might or will occur. Identify community organizations; professional associations; clubs; social, professional, or fraternal organizations; alumni associations; and chambers of commerce—any source that might be a good place to meet others interested in topics similar to your interests.

3. *Practice* networking. Focus on the specific steps and techniques of networking. Practice these steps and learn to be comfortable with networking. Success breeds success. The more you practice, the better you'll be at networking. You might begin practicing and build up your confidence by using a "safer" method to network, such as a letter or e-mail.[36]

Before, During, and After a Networking Meeting

We've discussed the importance of networking and ways for you to increase your network and networking skills. The following table is organized chronologically, highlighting key things to do or consider before, during, and after a networking meeting.

Before	During	After
■ Make networking a high priority; allot time in your weekly or monthly planner for networking activities. ■ Set specific networking goals (why, with whom, about what, when, where, how). ■ Start with a small circle of well-known associates and friends; small goals will lead to big goals. ■ Practice small talk—develop conversation starters before entering a room or attending a conference or meeting. ■ Know the organizational culture—the norms, customs, dress.	■ Focus completely on the other person's needs initially when establishing professional relationships. ■ Get all vital information (name, title, address, company, phone number, e-mail address, etc.). ■ Verify how to pronounce the person's name correctly. ■ Be visible, not pushy. Check nonverbal language for cues. ■ Respect the other's time—if you ask to chat for 10 minutes, don't exceed that. ■ Refrain from praising, fawning, self-deprecation, flirting, or cuteness. ■ Be sincere; give only genuine, specific compliments. Instead of "You were great," try "The lead you gave me on the consulting job was very helpful. I was able to . . . Thanks!"	■ As you walk away, jot down a few notes on the back of the person's business card to jog your memory when writing a follow-up note.[37] ■ Follow up with new contacts within 48 hours, and again when you achieve a goal they helped you attain. ■ Send thank-you notes (by mail, not e-mail). Be sure to maintain professionalism in all follow-up correspondence (phone messages, e-mail), including proper grammar, pronunciation, etiquette. ■ If you follow up by phone, consider writing a script or key ideas to mention. Be organized—sketch out in advance how you plan to approach the conversation. ■ Assess yourself: How did you do? What kind of impression do you think you made? ■ Follow through on your promises and be conscious of how you can help others in your network.

What Is Mentoring?

"Mentoring is an enduring phenomenon that has survived several major, historical paradigm shifts. The fact that it has endured, documented, for millennia . . . suggests that mentoring fulfills some deep, important yearnings for connection between the generations."

James Clawson[38]

We may have dozens or even hundreds of individuals in our network. All of them have the potential to contribute in some way to the development of our career, and some of them could be considered mentors. In this next section, we discuss what mentoring is, why it is important, and strategies that can build effective mentor networks.

Mentoring has been traditionally defined as a unique interpersonal relationship between two individuals, a *mentor* and a *protégé*. In Greek mythology, Odysseus entrusted a wise and faithful advisor named Mentor to educate and care for his son Telemachus while he was away. Thereafter, the term *mentor* was synonymous with a person who lends support to another in pursuing his or her goals. In today's context, a **mentor** is generally a higher-ranking employee who has advanced organizational (or industry) experience and knowledge and who is committed to providing guidance and support to the **protégé's** career development.[39] Recently, mentoring has been described in more reciprocal terms, indicating the belief that benefits of such relationships accrue to mentors as well as to protégés.[40] Even organizations benefit from mentoring, as mentoring facilitates the socialization process and helps acculturate junior members of the organization.[41] In fact, over 60 percent of the *Fortune* top 100 companies have formal mentoring programs.[42] Similar examples are shown in Figure 16–1. In addition, there is a growing number of mentoring programs that go beyond company and geographic borders and are geared toward specific audiences, such as women in STEM—Science, Technology, Engineering and Math (e.g., MentorNet[43] and another program sponsored by the National Math + Science Initiative, ExxonMobil, and *Fortune*[44]) and low-income students preparing for college (e.g., College MAP[45]).

**Figure 16–1
Formal Mentoring
in Action[46]**

- IBM—The Executive Resource Program has been particularly helpful in retaining women—it helped increase the number of women in executive positions by 27 percent.
- Coca Cola Co.—Mentoring programs help with diversity training for all employees.
- Hewlett-Packard—The Accelerated Development program combines mentoring, planning, and leadership workshops, helping the company save on the cost of hiring new employees. HP recently augmented this program with an e-mentoring program and developed a program with public school systems.
- Lucent Technologies—Actively recruiting employees to participate in mentoring programs helps attract and retain talented employees.
- Hewlett-Packard, Intel, and National Semiconductor—Mentoring programs for high schools, colleges, and grade school students and teachers encourage interest in IT careers.
- Intel—A unique system matches mentors with protégés by skill demands rather than by seniority or job title, making them more responsive to the fast-paced environment and enabling them to pass along best practices quickly.
- Environmental Protection Agency—The Environmental Leadership Program facilitates transfer of knowledge about best practices between large environmentally responsible companies and small organizations. Some of the companies involved include Motorola, Simpson Tacoma Kraft, John Roberts Company, and the Salt River Project.
- General Mills—Its mentoring program (developed through its training council) was ranked number 5 in *Training* magazine's top 125 Best Training Programs in 2007. A 50 percent decrease in customer complaints is also attributed to the mentoring and training programs.

We all know that teaching through experience can be one of the most effective methods of transferring knowledge. Which would you prefer, being handed a company's five-inch-thick manual, or having someone "show you the ropes"? In addition to teachers, mentors play many roles, including role model, confidant, coach, advisor, counselor, encourager, and friend. These roles fall into two broad categories of mentor functions, career and psychosocial.[47] **Career functions** are aspects of the relationship that enhance career advancement such as sponsorship, exposure, visibility, coaching, protection, challenging assignments, and career strategizing. **Psychosocial functions** are the aspects of the relationship that enhance a sense of competency, identity, and effectiveness in a professional role, including role modeling, acceptance and confirmation, counseling, friendship, support, and personal feedback.

When done well, mentoring can help protégés gain needed job information and experience, as well as support and encouragement (i.e., psychosocial support[48]) to advance in their job and career.

Mentoring: First Person[49]

I am the first person in my family to get a Ph.D., so it was hard to find people who understood my daily challenges. I was looking for someone who had walked this path before. My mentor, Stan Rendon, is a senior process development engineer who works in 3M's Corporate Research Process Laboratory. He is an incredibly good mentor, and we have a lot in common. Like me, he was the first in his family to get an advanced degree.

We chat about once a week, mostly by e-mail. Our conversations vary. Sometimes I ask him questions or advice. Sometimes I just tell him what's going on in my life. He encourages me to keep trying during hard times, and it's inspiring to hear about some of the impressive work he does at 3M. Stan is a great source of advice for career planning and goal setting. When I struggled with the choice between an academic or industrial career, he encouraged me to prepare for both so that I would have more opportunities upon graduation. Thanks to Stan's insight, I'm now considering the possibility of pursuing a dual career path in academia and industry.

One trick I've learned is that Friday is usually the most relaxed work day for Stan, so I e-mail him on Fridays. I put it on my schedule so I don't forget.

All in all, my mentor and I have developed an intellectually nourishing relationship that has already given me added confidence and direction.

At the time of her writing, Talesha Hall was a Ph.D. candidate in chemical engineering at Purdue University. She and her mentor, Stan Rendon, both work for 3M.

The Importance of Mentoring

Why are we interested? First, trends in the business environment make mentoring not only desirable but also essential for the success of both organizations and employees. Second, those involved in a mentoring relationship gain indisputable benefits. We'll begin with the business trends.

One trend responsible for the increasing reliance on mentoring is the fact that more organizations are viewing their people—as opposed to their products, services, or assets—as the chief source of sustainable competitive advantage.[50] Peter Drucker asserts that knowledge is the only meaningful resource in today's economy; knowledge and the people within whom knowledge resides have become primary assets and sources of competitive advantage.[51] As the competition for highly skilled and dedicated professionals heats up, firms are focusing more attention on developing their current employees. If sharing knowledge provides added value in the knowledge economy, then involvement in productive mentoring relationships should benefit both individual participants and the organization.[52]

Another trend is the dramatic change in the nature of individual career development. The days when employees climbed the same corporate ladder over the course of 30 years are gone; we now see new career patterns described as "Protean" or "boundaryless," meaning that individual careers can change shape or form at any time.[53] Part of what is driving these changes is organizational downsizing and rapid technological change that can cause previously valuable skills to suddenly become obsolete, necessitating changes in an individual's career path. Each time employees relocate, they are required to learn new organizational rules, procedures, and politics[54] while simultaneously mastering the technical aspects of the job. In order to effectively assimilate new skills and environments, establish connections with influential decision makers, and navigate the boundaryless career landscape, today's employees need not just one, but multiple mentors.[55] This view is reflected in a quote by Bill Radiger, president of Karma Media, LLC:

> *"One mentor is not enough. You have to rely on a number of mentors to allow you to see values in action, to develop business acumen and product knowledge. If you do choose to rely on one mentor, that mentor had better know everything, otherwise you will end up with their bad habits along with the good."*[56]

In addition, these changes and impacts on careers explain the evolution and necessity of alternative forms of mentoring that often extend beyond traditional organizational, geographical, and functional boundaries.[57] These include the following forms of mentoring:[58]

- Mentoring by peers as well as superiors.
- Formal and informal mentors.
- Intra- and interorganizational mentors.
- Mentoring by groups.
- Reciprocal and co-mentoring.
- Multiple, simultaneous mentors.
- Face-to-face and **virtual** (electronic) mentors.

Wells Fargo Expands Employee Social Learning by the Thousands[59]

Triple Creek River is a company that provides social learning technology for managing dynamic learning networks, including mentoring.

Wells Fargo, a global financial services company with over 275,000 employees worldwide, wanted to expand their social learning in the form of mentoring to the wider employee population of 6,600 team members of the Wholesale Services Group. Mentoring was considered the deepest form of learning in Wells Fargo's Social Learning Strategy. Previously it had taken them approximately 480 man hours per year manually matching less than 100 learners and advisors (approximately 2 percent of the Wells Fargo workforce). The Triple Creek team recommended that Wells Fargo employees make their own learning connections through River's automated matching system and join learning engagements based on individual learning needs. Launched in 2011, of the 6,600 invitees in the group, 938 signed up by October 2011 on the mentoring platform. The platform allowed the participants to find their own mentoring matches rather than being placed by an outsider.

Benefits of Mentoring

One reason for the popularity of mentoring is that it can provide benefits to both protégé and mentor. Anecdotal evidence suggests that mentoring can assist protégés in many ways, both professionally and personally. Figure 16–2 explains many of the benefits that can be derived from obtaining a mentor.

Recent research on mentoring's effects confirms much of what has been expected. Studies that empirically examined the impact of mentoring confirmed that protégés receive more promotions, have higher incomes, have higher career satisfaction, have higher job satisfaction, and are less likely to express an interest to leave an organization than their nonmentored counterparts.[60]

Effective mentoring programs can bring about benefits for the mentor as well, some of which are listed in Figure 16–3. Mentoring has been found to be a reciprocal process: "in learning you teach and in teaching you learn." Through their relationship with a protégé, mentors have been able to hone their interpersonal skills, gain insight into their ideas and perceptions, and increase their awareness through diverse experiences.[61]

**Figure 16–2
Mentoring Benefits
for Protégés**

- Career and leadership development—career preparation and leadership training.
- Increased self-confidence, self-awareness, and growth.
- Mutual sharing and enhancement of relationship.
- Exposure to diverse perspectives and experiences.
- Identification of skill gaps.
- Direct access to powerful resources within their future profession.
- Development of friendships that can provide valuable contacts and expand associations in related networks.
- Development of interpersonal skills—by working with a more experienced individual, protégés learn by observation and practice.
- Protection for the individual and the organization against potentially damaging experiences.
- Gaining valuable inside information into the workings of the organization for movement in the organization; insight into informal workings.
- Saving time. By allowing protégés to learn from others' experience, they don't have to reinvent the wheel; they can speed up the advancement process and get a jump on the learning curve.

**Figure 16–3
Mentoring Benefits
for Mentors**

- Experience shared learning and positive results.
- Gain personal satisfaction from helping another.
- Develop patience, insight, and understanding.
- Gain exposure to cultural, social, or economic characteristics different from their own.
- Improve their leadership and communication skills.
- Gain personal experience for future career options, including training, teaching, or counseling.
- Train employees in ways that will meet future needs for their organization, thereby ensuring its future competitiveness.
- Receive help to revitalize and redefine their own careers through reflection.

Another reason mentoring is being offered by more and more corporations is its applicability to company diversity programs. Many corporations offer mentoring programs, which have been proven to bolster a person's chances for advancement, to all employees, with an emphasis on minorities and women, who have long been underrepresented in many industries and organizations. Companies are finding that offering mentoring programs is an excellent way to boost the performance and advancement rates of minorities and women, as well as to build confidence and boost morale.

Blue Xchange: BlueCross Blue Shield of North Carolina

BlueCross Blue Shield of North Carolina (BCBSNC), serving 3.7 million members, wanted to support the effectiveness of the informal mentoring relationships that were in existence. They launched the Blue Xchange in 1999. In 2004 the program was recognized by *Training* magazine as a best practice in mentoring. The program goals were to:

- Identify, retain and develop high-performing employees.
- Focus on diversity.
- Develop networking opportunities.
- Provide cross-divisional exposure.
- Enhance recruitment and retention.

The program has six components, including the orientation, creation of a development plan, a formal agreement between mentors and mentees, mentoring meetings, mini workshops, and an evaluation of progress. The program is open to all employees after one year of service. Forty percent of the current mentors were once mentees. Cohorts showed an increase in promotions, transfers, and title changes within the second year following participation in the program (18 percent and 25 percent of protégés in 2001 and 2002 received outstanding performance ratings, compared to 10 percent of the population for the same time). Retention is also higher among participants, and they were found to be highly engaged in their work and committed to the organization (protégé turnover is 46 percent lower than in the BCBSNC general population).

In 2009, the program—which costs less than $4,500 to run and results in a yearly savings of over $1.4 million—won an Ovation Award for HR Excellence.[62]

Qualities of an Effective Mentor

What makes effective mentors? What characteristics or qualities facilitate their ability to help others—inside and outside their firm or industry—reach their full potential? Mentoring expert Kathy Kram compiled a list (see Figure 16–4) of characteristics or skills—ranging from willingness and desire to be a mentor to possessing highly developed interpersonal skills—that aid in a mentor's effectiveness. Whether you are a mentor or looking for a mentor, it is important to develop these skills.

Figure 16–4
Characteristics of Effective Mentors[63]

- Expertise and experience in their profession; successful in their professional endeavors.
- Enthusiasm and genuine interest for the profession.
- Desire and energy to help others.
- Available time to help others.
- Ability to relate to others in all types of settings.
- Good interpersonal skills; good listening skills; a high level of emotional intelligence or ability to read others and situations and act appropriately.
- Skilled in giving honest and detailed constructive feedback.
- Supportive in their work for others.
- Ability to work well with a diverse group of people.
- High yet achievable standard of performance for themselves and others.
- Worthy of emulation.
- Willingness to expose their protégé to a broad-based network of professionals and to share information about organizational norms.
- Ability to separate personal needs and concerns from professional demeanor when interacting with a protégé.
- Can share stories and experiences that provide a point of reference, not necessarily a model that must be followed.
- Will keep confidential information secret and protect protégé as appropriate.

Types of Mentoring Relationships

Many of us have functioned as mentors at one time or another, perhaps without the formal designation. We might have a kid brother or sister whom we taught to ride a bicycle, or perhaps we helped a new classmate or employee learn the rules of the game. Mentoring and mentoring relationships can be formal or informal. The institution officially designates **formal mentors** (also called *organizational* or *managerial mentors*) through a prescribed mentoring program. Mentors' relationships with protégés are arranged through a formal matching process and with the assistance of an external organizing force (for example, human resources). Formal mentoring relationships usually have a specific time frame, a method for termination, and one or more checkpoints for goal setting and meetings.

Most of us have been involved in the other type of relationship, known as an **informal or peer relationship**.[64] These relationships often develop spontaneously and without a specific plan. They occur when a mentor and protégé find each other (either when a potential protégé seeks another's advice or a potential mentor notices another's potential and offers to take the protégé under his or her wing) and negotiate the terms of their relationship. Many informal or peer relationships develop over time and are very effective and rewarding if there is consistency in needs, goals, and resources. Based on the level of commitment, intensity, types of issues, and needs addressed by those involved in a peer relationship, three types of relationships can be identified and represented on a continuum:[65]

- **Informational peers** benefit most by exchanging information about their work or organization. The relationship is characterized by low levels of self-disclosure and trust and demands little in terms of time and support.

- **Collegial peers** tend to trust more and share more, delving somewhat into issues beyond work, including family and personal life. Peers request and receive direct and honest feedback.

- **Special peers** exhibit high levels of trust, self-disclosure, and self-expression; they share ideas and advice on a multitude of issues and allow for the exchange of dilemmas, fears, and concerns.

As a peer mentoring relationship deepens toward the "special" category, we find a greater number and depth of mentoring functions being served. In addition to the formal and informal types of relationships, we see the development of a new form: **co-mentoring**.[66] Co-mentors are a pair of close, collegial friends who are committed to facilitating each other's development and who take turns mentoring each other at particular stages of their careers/lives.[67] In essence, each person is both mentor and protégé. Sometimes, this relationship might involve the newer or less experienced member sharing his or her technology skills or what's considered the latest thinking in a field, while the more experienced member shares his or her expertise and experience in the organization and industry.

Virtual Mentors, Real Benefits[68]

In today's fast-paced, networked world, connecting with mentors virtually is not only possible, it's necessary. If you e-mail, Facebook, Tweet or participate in online forums, you already realize the power and facility of connecting with others. So, if you shudder at the thought of approaching a stranger to be your potential mentor, consider e-mentoring (using e-mail, phone, videoconference to initiate and build critical developmental relationships). While traditionalists may believe that "real" mentoring is only carried out face-to-face, research confirms that the benefits of mentoring—enhanced learning, job performance, career progression, satisfaction, and even pay—are real and tangible, even when the relationship between mentor and protégé is virtual.[69] Moreover, virtual mentoring has a few advantages over traditional mentoring.

1. **Avoiding gossip**. While many organizational mentoring programs arose out of a need to support diversity initiatives, the pairing of a young female with a high-ranking male can be the subject of coffee break conversations. Employees—especially those who feel they've been passed over for promotions and other opportunities—can't help but gossip about their perceptions of what's "really going on" between the mentor and protégé. Such gossip ("I know why she got the promotion . . .!") is not only damaging to the reputation and credibility of the mentor and protégé, but also to the mentoring program. *When protégé and mentor meet electronically, other employees have nothing to see and nothing to say.*

2. **Just the facts**. When people meet face-to-face, visual cues such as ethnicity, height, weight, and dress often cause us to make assumptions about others' values and goals that impair message sending and receipt. Successful mentoring relationships are characterized by value similarity; demographic similarity does not enter

into the equation. *When we converse over chat or e-mail, we are not distracted by the other's appearance, but instead are tuned in directly to what is being communicated.*

3. **The whole truth.** Research on computer-mediated communication shows unequivocally that because relationships are free to develop without the distractions of gender and other demographic differences, trust forms more quickly than it does in face-to-face relationships. Protégés are more likely to share the whole truth, and not just "what they think their mentor wants to hear." What kind of advice—if any—could a mentor provide if all you share is that everything is perfect? Moreover, the presence of "electronic courage" can embolden those who are normally shy in person to compose an honest dilemma or complaint. *Protégés are more willing to share openly and candidly their failures as well as their successes, and therefore stand to receive more and more useful advice from their e-mentors.*

4. **Managing impressions.** Imagine meeting with your newly assigned mentor, the VP of Marketing, for the first time. You've heard she's smart, no-nonsense, and highly regarded. You want to impress her but you're worried that you'll get tongue tied and share things that put you in a less-than-positive light. Because several choices for engaging in conversations with an e-mentor are virtual (not face-to-face) and asynchronous, the *e-protégé has a chance to think through and edit their communications, ensuring that all interactions—especially the early ones, crucial for building rapport and trust—are presented positively.*

5. **Balancing work and life.** While not without its challenges, virtual mentoring provides employees more flexibility in where and how they fulfill their multiple roles, reducing the time wasted in scheduling and rescheduling meetings, activities, and meals in order to have a mentoring conversation. *Virtual mentoring naturally gives freedom to the parties in deciding when, for how long, and how frequently they will connect . . . with little wasted time.*

6. **Getting access.** There was a time when only the elite, high potential, or members of underrepresented groups were eligible for organizational mentoring programs. With more than a third of the world's population now online, we are no longer so digitally divided. Moreover, the boundaries of time and geography are rendered irrelevant. *Mentoring via virtual methods means that anyone, at any age, and in any part of the world, can connect with and share ideas with anyone else with access to a computer.*

Start developing your e-mentoring relationship now. Complete Exercise 16-G!

Four Stages of Mentoring Relationships

Most mentoring relationships evolve through four stages. They are described below:[70]

1. **Orientation and initiation.** In this phase, the mentor and protégé are assigned or select each other, disclose information, and begin to build trust. This phase usually lasts between 6 and 12 months, during which time initial wishes become realized (e.g., coaching is provided) and the relationship takes on significance for both parties. Traditional relationships begin face to face and within a single organization; however, technology has enabled such relationships to occur virtually, using e-mail and other methods (e.g., phone and videoconference) to connect geographically distant partners.[71] (See Online Mentoring, Exercise 16–G.)

2. **Cultivation.** During this phase, which may last between one and five years, the relationship becomes more rewarding for both parties. There is continued growth and development in career and psychosocial support functions, mutual trust, sharing and challenging of ideas, and learning—for both protégés (who gain knowledge and insight) and their mentors (who gain loyalty and a sense of helping another).

3. **Separation.** Most mentoring relationships typically fade after a few years. At this point, the protégé is ready to assert more independence and work more autonomously, or perhaps the mentor experiences a significant change in his or her career (for example, retirement). Or, one or both may change jobs, creating geographical and psychological distance in the relationship. When opportunities to interact are constrained, mentor and

protégé may step back from the formal relationship, or they may continue, depending on their commitment to the relationship.

4. **Redefinition.** Depending on the nature of the separation, the mentor and protégé will often redefine their mentoring relationship. Typically, the mentor's job is "done" and peer status is achieved. Protégés express appreciation for their mentors, who now see their protégés as equals, similar to peer colleagues or friends.

How to Find a Mentor

If your company does not have a formal mentoring program, you can find a potential mentor or mentors through informal channels.

- *Clarify your career goals and coaching needs.* Ask yourself why you're seeking a mentor, what your objectives are, and how someone more senior in the organization (who's not your boss) can be helpful to you.
- *Identify potential candidates.* Have you served on a committee or task force with someone who's a few levels above you and whose ideas you respect? Did you have a chance to develop a rapport with that person? If so, approach the person directly, indicating your interest in succeeding at the organization, and ask whether he or she would be willing to meet with you from time to time to offer career advice and insights into the company and industry.
- *Involve your boss.* Often your boss will be supportive of your interest in being mentored, especially if your boss is people-oriented and understands the importance of developing staff.
- *Network with others.* If you're relatively new and haven't had the chance to develop your own network, your associates and co-workers might have some contacts that could be helpful to you. In addition, you might find potential mentors at industry or trade shows, professional conferences, and management development programs.

Limitations of Mentoring

It's hard to deny the value of mentoring, especially in this environment of continuous, complex, and transformational change. However, mentoring may not always have the positive impact it is designed to have. Mentoring partners and organizations should be aware of the limitations or possible roadblocks associated with building and maintaining mentoring relationships. As much as we would like to believe otherwise, mentoring relationships don't always work. Just as relationships with friends and loved ones can become dysfunctional, so too can those with a mentor. When dysfunctions arise (e.g., co-dependence, abuse of power, inappropriate intimacy), it is important for organizations and individuals to take steps to redefine or dissolve the relationship when it is not working for one or both of the parties involved.[72]

Another issue in mentoring is that mentors, despite their desire to help, may not have adequate time to devote to a protégé. Formal programs typically take the time commitment into account when designing and implementing mentoring. However, mentors may be promoted or become involved in projects that require additional time. This forces the mentor to choose between job-related needs and those of the protégé. When mentors choose the former but don't communicate this choice to protégés, the protégés wonder why their support system is suddenly unavailable. By contrast, a protégé might become promoted or be given greater responsibility or visibility. Some mentors, feeling threatened by the protégé's success and seeing the protégé as a competitor or rival who could threaten their professional or personal image, might subtly (or not so subtly) attempt to sabotage their protégé's career. This is more likely to occur when a mentor is in the same function and organization as the protégé and is compounded when the mentor lacks personal or organizational assurance of his or her role in the organization.

Mentoring may result in a mismatch of resources or a mismatch between the mentor and protégé in goals, perceptions, and personality. For example, a mentor may be selected on the basis of his or her position in the organization, yet may lack the specific skills or resources the protégé desires. Similarly, a protégé may feel that the mentor has delivered less time or attention than what was expected or promised. In fact, mentoring scholars Lillian Eby and Tammy Allen found that 55 percent of the 242 protégés studied reported that their mentors had occasionally neglected them.[73] Finally, despite their strengths, mentors may inadvertently display weaknesses, such as a negative work style and bad habits, which the protégé then emulates.

Mentoring relationships can also suffer when protégés become overly submissive to the mentor. This is especially likely when both parties are in the same chain of command. When a protégé fears power inherent in the mentor's position, she may become submissive to the mentor, unwilling to disagree with the mentor's viewpoints or share pertinent information that might be damaging (e.g., concerns about performance). In such a situation, the benefits of mentoring are not realized because of the protégé's concerns about how her true views or beliefs could impact performance appraisals or desire for retribution.[74] What starts out well may not remain so. The dynamics of a mentoring relationship can become destructive if interests of the parties change. This may be especially problematic in a formal mentoring program where inertia supports the status quo and where the parties may fear loss of prestige or reputation should either request the dissolution of the relationship.

Keys for Protégés to Make Mentoring Work

- *Ask for what you need while respecting the mentor's time.*[75] Focus on just a few quality meetings rather than numerous surface discussions. If you need additional time or attention, discuss this up front to manage expectations and jointly determine if he or she can address these needs, now or in the future.

- *Be mindful of the mentor's credibility and reputation.* Act professionally at all times and be willing to confess mistakes and acknowledge the mentor's assistance. This is especially important when your mentor works in the same organization as you.

- *Be realistic and commit to regularly reassessing and altering your network.* Having a mentor doesn't guarantee you'll receive promotions and advancement opportunities. Mentoring does offer you insights into how an organization operates and helps you understand decisions that are made—both about the company overall and about you and your career. Also, realize that as your career evolves, bringing different situations and challenges, so too will your need for different mentors; caring and feeding your network will require occasional pruning.[76]

- *Be selective.* Choose mentors who are respected in their organizations and who have a reputation for being effective collaborators or developers. Selecting mentors on the basis of title alone may lead to disappointment or frustration with their inability to provide the time and assistance you need.

- *Make mentoring a two-way street.* Seek out opportunities to provide mentors with technical information, new knowledge, or emotional support, as "the goal of building networks is to contribute to others."[77] Helping others increases the likelihood of receiving assistance in the future as well as increasing the trust and credibility of the relationship.[78]

- *Demonstrate your trustworthiness.* Always treat as confidential any sensitive company information the mentor shares with you. Demonstrate your trust as well. If you don't honestly share your fears or concerns, your mentor won't be able to help you.[79]

- *Be willing to accept gracefully all feedback mentors are willing to provide you.* Encourage feedback by requesting it. Show your appreciation by acknowledging how their feedback proved helpful.

- *Seek out multiple mentors.* A collection of mentors is invaluable, providing different perspectives, knowledge, and skills while serving multiple mentoring functions.[80] They can provide emotional support or protection from political enemies in a way no one individual can.[81]

These limitations can exist in any type of mentoring relationship or in any context. Other limitations might be specific to the organization as a whole. Even in organizations that formally support and implement mentoring, such support may be more lip service or marketing hype than reality. This could happen for several reasons. First, should an organization suddenly face a severe market threat, it is likely to respond in a reactionary mode. That is, short-term thinking and shortcuts take precedence over planning and long-term fixes. While mentoring may be seen as valuable, the current "fire" may need immediate attention, whereas the long-term goal of building human capability is relegated to the back burner. Another possibility is the potential disconnect between the leaders' espoused philosophy about mentoring and a reward system that runs counter to it. Related to this are fears or mismanaged expectations that reduce managers' willingness to carry out the mentoring policy or philosophy. Mentoring will fail if the environment does not support it.

Gender Differences in Mentoring

Recent research from Catalyst[82] suggests that while men and women are equally likely to benefit from mentors who facilitate their learning and career development, men benefit more. Why? Women are more likely to choose mentors who are at their level while men choose mentors who are a level or two above them in the hierarchy. Both genders benefit from mentor support; however, men's choices are linked with more opportunities and faster advancement up the hierarchy. Men's mentors—aside from exposing them to a more senior network—actively promote their protégés and lobby for getting them into more visible positions.

This phenomenon might also contribute to the dearth of women's participation on boards. Some European countries have implemented quotas to increase female representation on boards . . . with mixed results. Lacking experience in more senior positions, women may not be "boardroom ready."[83]

A limitation for mentoring facing many organizations is a lack of sufficient female and minority role models.[84] The glass ceiling effect, argued by Kanter and others, explains why so few women have positions at the most senior organizational level. For female and minority employees hoping to partner with someone who understands them and their challenges, finding a high-ranking female or minority mentor—especially one who is willing to devote the time and attention necessary—might be difficult. Discouraged, they may ignore their desire for a mentor or look outside the organization or industry for a mentor. It has been suggested that the gender of the parties involved may impact the functionality of a mentoring relationship. Sexual harassment or improper behaviors have been reported in cross-gender partnerships; they have also been unjustly perceived by those outside the mentoring relationship.[85] There is also the potential for improper behaviors, such as abuse of power and discrimination, in cross-racial relationships.[86] Therein lies the usefulness of nontraditional forms of mentoring, especially online mentoring.[87] Protégés receive similar types and levels of support and development from online mentors as they do from traditional, face-to-face mentors, as demonstrated in a recent study.[88]

Despite these challenges, mentoring—whether formal or informal, one-on-one or group, internal or external, face-to-face or online—offers benefits to the individuals involved. The list in the shaded box on the previous page provides some keys for making the most out of mentoring.

Summary

Networking and mentoring do not guarantee that our careers will advance. But they are extremely effective tools for individuals interested in building their social capital. In this chapter we have seen how networking and mentoring can benefit individuals and organizations, and we discussed strategies for effective networking and mentoring. Those who actively network and seek out mentoring relationships will reap benefits, as will their contacts and their organizations. The exercises that follow will help you improve your skills in both areas.

Key Terms and Concepts

Career functions	Orientation and initiation stage
Collegial peers	Primary network
Co-mentoring	Protégé
Cultivation stage	Psychosocial functions
Formal mentors	Redefinition stage
Informal or peer relationships	Reverse networking
Informational peers	Secondary network
Information interviews	Separation stage
Mentor	Social capital
Mentoring	Special peers
Networking	Virtual mentoring

Discussion Questions

1. The opening quote in this chapter is, "It's not what you know, it's who you know." Discuss what this means from both an organizational and individual perspective.

2. What are some other benefits that can be obtained from networking?

3. If networking is so beneficial, why do some not engage in it?

4. We contend that mentoring has benefits not only for the protégé but for the mentor as well. Discuss these benefits.

5. If you are involved in a "virtual" meeting where the participants don't meet face-to-face, how can you ensure the meeting is effective?

Endnotes

1. Blake Yaralian, "Networking," unpublished student paper, James Madison University, COB 202 (Fall 1999).

2. Ibid.

3. W. Baker, *Achieving Success through Social Capital: Tapping the Hidden Resources in Your Personal and Business Networks* (San Francisco: Jossey Bass, 2000).

4. M. Forret and T. Dougherty, "Correlates of Networking Behavior for Managerial and Professional Employees," *Group and Organization Management* 26, no. 3 (2001), pp. 283–311.

5. Deb Haggerty, "Successful Networking," *The National Public Accountant* (September 1999), p. 30.

6. Moshe Even-Shoshan and Tamar Gilad, "Network Your Way to Better Recruitment," *Workforce* (June 1999), p. 106.

7. Baker, *Achieving Success*; and S. C. de Janasz and M. L. Forret, "Learning the Art of Networking: A Critical Skill for Enhancing Social Capital and Career Success," *Journal of Management Education* 32, no. 5 (2008), pp. 629–50.

8. Namely salary, promotions, and career satisfaction; see, for example, P. Adler and S. W. Kwon, "Social Capital: Prospects for a New Concept," *Academy of Management Review 27* (2002), pp. 17–40; and S. E. Seibert, M. L. Kraimer, and R. C. Liden, "A Social Capital Theory of Career Success," *Academy of Management Journal 44* (2001), pp. 219–37.

9. P. F. Drucker, *Managing for the Future: The 1990s and Beyond* (New York: Dutton, 1992).

10. de Janasz and Forret, "Learning the Art of Networking."

11. Catherine M. Petrini, "Building a Chain of Contacts," *Training & Development Journal* (January 1991), p. 27.

12. Dorothy Riddle, "Networking Successfully," *International Trade Forum* (July–September 1998), p. 13.

13. Marcia A. Reed, "Through the Grapevine," *Black Enterprise* (July 1999), p. 62.

14. Baker, *Achieving Success.*

15. Amanda Gefter, "This Is Your Space: What Is Online Social Networking All About and How Is It Changing Our World?" *New Scientist* 191, no. 2569 (September 2006), p. 46. However, it is important to note that the most recent statistics suggest that the Baby Boomer population is the fastest growing age segment of social networking sites, such as Facebook users, many of whom log on at least once a day. http://seniorhousingnews.com/2010/01/07/baby-boomers-represent-fastest-growing-segment-on-social-networking-sites/ (accessed November 4, 2010).

16. Jennifer Saranow, "New Technology Aids Alumni Networking," *The Wall Street Journal Online,* Career Journal.com, http://www.careerjournal.com/jobhunting/networking/20040920-saranow.html (accessed May 24, 2007).

17. Geary A. Rummler and Alan P. Brache, "Managing the White Space," *Training* (January 1991), pp. 55–67.

18. A. Andrew Olson, "Long-Term Networking: A Strategy for Career Success," *Management Review* (April 1994), p. 33.

19. Laura Koss-Feder, "It's Still Who You Know . . . in the Boom Economy, Job Hunting Is a Way of Life. Here's How to Do It," *Time* (March 22, 1999), p. 114F.

20. Brian Kreuger, "Job Hunter," www.collegegrad.com, May 2000 (accessed June 2001).

21. David Berman and Sean Silcoff, "Have Rolodex, Will Go Far," *Canadian Business* (November 13, 1998), p. 50.

22. Baker, *Achieving Success.*

23. M. Forret and S. Sullivan, "A Balanced Scorecard Approach to Networking: A Guide to Successfully Navigating Career Changes," *Organizational Dynamics* 31 no. 3 (2002), pp. 245–58.

24. Marc Parise, regional president of First Midwest Bank, as cited in Forret and Sullivan, "Balanced Scorecard Approach," p. 255.

25. Jeffrey Gitomer, "Building Good Relationships Puts the Work in Networking," *The Kansas City Business Journal* (February 25, 2000), p. 24.

26. Haggerty, "Successful Networking."

27. Mike Godwin, Megan Fandrei, Josh Bare, Scott Longendyke, Cheryl Morgan, and Brian Sweet, "Politicking and Networking," unpublished student paper, James Madison University, COB 202 (Fall 1999).

28. M. Godwin et al., "Politicking and Networking" (1999), adapted from Tom Irish and Peter Grassl, "How to Build Your Network," www.smartbiz.com/sbs/arts/irish5.htm.

29. Forret and Dougherty, "Correlates of Networking Behavior."

30. Riddle, "Networking Successfully."

31. M. Tosczak, "Career Strategies to Weather Unpredictable Times," *Kenan-Flagler Business Magazine* (Fall 2002), pp. 12–16.

32. Forret and Sullivan, "Balanced Scorecard Approach."

33. Mark S. Granovetter, "The Strength of Weak Ties," *American Journal of Sociology* (1973).

34. Andrea Nierenberg, "Masterful Networking," *Training and Development* (February 1999), p. 51.

35. Jeffrey Gitomer, "Networking Not Working? Try Smart-Networking," *Birmingham Business Journal* (January 7, 2000), p. 10.

36. V. Whiting and S. de Janasz, "Mentoring in the 21st Century: Using the Internet to Build Skills and Networks," *Journal of Management Education* 3 (2004), pp. 275–93.

37. Gitomer, "Networking Not Working?"

38. Quote by James Clawson, professor at University of Virginia Darden School (1996).

39. Ellen A. Fagenson, "The Mentor Advantage: Perceived Career/Job Experiences of Protégés versus Nonprotégés," *Journal of Organizational Behavior* (1989), pp. 309–20; Kathy E. Kram, *Mentoring at Work: Developmental Relationships in Organizational Life* (Glenview, IL: Scott Foresman, 1985); Raymond A. Noe, "An Investigation of the Determinants of Successful Assigned Mentoring Relationships," *Personnel Psychology* (1988), pp. 457–79; and Terri A. Scandura, "Mentorship and Career Mobility: An Empirical Investigation," *Journal of Organizational Behavior* (1988), pp. 169–79.

40. Kathy E. Kram, "A Relational Approach to Career Development." In D. T. Hall (ed.), *The Career Is Dead—Long Live the Career,* pp. 132–57 (San Francisco: Jossey Bass, 1996); B. R. Ragins, "Diversified Mentoring Relationships in Organizations: A Power Perspective," *Academy of Management Review* (1997), pp. 482–521.

41. D. M. Hunt and C. Michael, "Mentorship: A Career Training and Development Tool," *Academy of Management Review,* no. 3 (1983), pp. 475–485.

42. S. Branch, "Mentoring at Work. The 100 Best Companies to Work for in America," *Fortune* 139, no. 1 (1999), pp. 118–30.

43. For more information, see http://www.mentornet.net/documents/about/ (accessed July 28, 2010).

44. Jessica Shambora, "Beyond Gossip Girls: College Women Talk Math andScience," http:// postcards.blogs.fortune.cnn.com/2010/06/23/beyond-gossip-girls-college-women-talk-math-and-science/ (accessed July 28, 2010).

45. For more information, see http://www.ey.com/Publication/vwLUAssets/Corporate_responsibility_college_MAP/$FILE/Corporate_responsibility_college_MAP.pdf (accessed July 28, 2010).

46. Jade Boyd, "Firms Work to Keep Women—Flextime, Mentoring Programs Interest Retention Efforts in IT," *Internetweek* (November 27, 2000), p. 90; and Talila Baron, "IT Talent Shortage Renews Interest in Mentoring," *Information Week* (April 24, 2000); "Mentoring—Setting an Example," Environmental Protection Agency, www.p2pays.org (December 4, 1997); Fara Warner, "Inside Intel's Mentoring Movement," *Fast Company.com* 57 (March 2002), p. 116; Holly Dolezalek, "General Mills; Serving It Up," *Training* (March 5, 2007).

47. Terri A. Scandura, "Dysfunctional Mentoring Relationships and Outcomes," *Journal of Management* (May 1, 1998), p. 449.

48. Kram, *Mentoring at Work.*

49. *MentorNet News,* http://www.mentornet.net/news/newsart.aspx?nid=22&sid=1 (accessed March 7, 2008).

50. Peter F. Drucker, *Managing for the Future: The 1990s and Beyond* (New York: Dutton, 1992); J. Pfeffer, T. Hatano, and T. Santalainen, "Producing Sustainable Competitive Advantage through the Effective Management of People," *Academy of Management Executive* (1995), pp. 55–72.

51. Drucker, 1992.

52. Troy R. Nielsen, "The Developmental Journey of Mentoring Research and Practice," paper presented at the annual Academy of Management Meeting, Chicago (1999).

53. M. B. Arthur and D. M. Rousseau, "The Boundaryless Career as a New Employment Principle." In M. B. Arthur and D. M. Rousseau (eds.), *The Boundaryless Career* (New York: Oxford University Press, 1996), pp. 3–20; D. T. Hall, "Protean Careers of the 21st Century," *Academy of Management Executive* 10 (1996), pp. 8–16.

54. Suzanne de Janasz and Sherry Sullivan, "Multiple Mentoring in Academe: Developing the Professorial Network," *Journal of Vocational Behavior* 64, no. 2 (2004), pp. 263–83.

55. See Kenneth Brousseau, Michael Driver, K. Eneroth, and Rickard Larsson, "Career Pandemonium: Realigning Organizations and Individuals," *The Academy of Management Executive* 10 (1996), pp. 52–66; and Kram and Hall, op. cit.

56. Suzanne de Janasz, Sherry Sullivan, and Vicki Whiting, "Mentor Networks and Career Success: Lessons for Turbulent Times," *Academy of Management Executive* 17, no. 4 (2003), pp. 78–91.

57. de Janasz, Sullivan, and Whiting, "Mentor Networks and Career Success."

58. S. C. de Janasz, "Alternative Approaches to Mentoring in the New Millennium." In M. Karsten (ed.), *Gender, Ethnicity, and Race in the Workplace,* (Praeger/Greenwood, 2006), pp. 131–47.

59. www.triplecreekriver.com (accessed February 17, 2013).

60. Mentoring benefits were confirmed in numerous studies, including, e.g., G. F. Dreher, "A Comparative Study of Mentoring Among Men and Women in Managerial, Professional, and

Technological Positions," *Journal of Applied Psychology* 75, no. 5 (1990), 539–46; T. Scandura, "Mentorship and Career Mobility: An Empirical Investigation," *Journal of Organizational Behavior* 13 (1992), 169–74; T. A. Scandura and R. E. Viator, "Mentoring in Public Accounting Firms: An Analysis of Mentoring-Protégé Relationships, Mentorship Functions, and Protégé," *Accounting, Organizations and Society* 19, no. 8 (1994), 717–34; D. B. Turban, T. W. Dougherty, and F. K. Lee, "Gender, Race and Perceived Similarity Effects in Developmental Relationships: The Moderating Role of Relationship Duration," *Journal of Vocational Behavior* 61 (2002), 240–62; Fagenson, "The Mentor Advantage."

61. Patricia M. Buhler, "A New Role for Managers: The Move from Directing to Coaching," *Supervision* (October 1, 1998), p. 16.

62. https://www.capital.org/eweb/upload/CAI/cai-main/public/2009/04/Press_Release_-_2009_Ovation_Awards_winners.pdf (accessed May 31, 2013).

63. Adapted from and built upon Kram, *Mentoring at Work.*

64. Adapted from and built upon Kram, *Mentoring at Work,* pp. 134–39.

65. Adapted from and built upon Kram, *Mentoring at Work.*

66. Andy Hargraves and Michael Fullan, "Mentoring in the New Millennium," *Theory into Practice* 39 (2000), p. 50; and J. Rymer, "Only Connect: Transforming Ourselves and Our Discipline Through Co-Mentoring," *Journal of Business Communication* 39, no. 3 (2002), pp. 342–63.

67. de Janasz, Alternative approaches.

68. de Janasz, S. C., (February 21, 2013), "Virtual Mentors, Real Benefits" http://www.huffingtonpost.com/suzanne-de-janasz/virtual-mentoring-_b_2670122.html (accessed 15 May 2013).

69. S. C. de Janasz, E. A. Ensher, and C. Heun, "Using e-Mentoring to Connect Business Students with Practicing Managers: Virtual Relationships and Real Benefits," *Mentoring & Tutoring: Partnership in Learning* 16, no. 4 (2008), pp. 394–411.

70. Kathy E. Kram, "Phases of the Mentoring Relationship," *Academy of Management Journal* 26 (1983), pp. 608–25.

71. Whiting and de Janasz, "Mentoring in the 21st Century."

72. Scandura, "Dysfunctional Mentoring Relationships."

73. L. T. Eby and T. D. Allen, "Further Investigation of Protégés' Negative Mentoring Experiences: Patterns and Outcomes," *Group and Organizational Management* 27, no. 4 (2002), p. 456.

74. Ibid.

75. de Janasz, Sullivan, and Whiting, "Mentor Networks."

76. Ibid.

77. Baker, *Achieving Success.*

78. Forret and Sullivan, "Balanced Scorecard Approach."

79. de Janasz, Sullivan, and Whiting, "Mentor Networks."

80. Ibid.

81. J. A. Wilson and N. S. Elman, "Organizational Benefits of Mentoring." *The Academy of Management Executive* 4, no. 4 (1990), pp. 88–94.

82. Cited in http://www.cbsnews.com/8301-505125_162-44441155/why-mentoring-helps-men-more-than-women/siwhy (accessed May 31, 2013).

83. http://www.businessweek.com/debateroom/archives/2011/02/boards_of_directors_need_quotas_for_women_1.html (accessed May 31, 2013).

84. Gary N. Powell, *Women and Men in Management,* 2nd ed. (Newbury Park, CA: Sage Publications, 1993), p. 207.

85. de Janasz, "Alternative Approaches."

86. Scandura, "Dysfunctional Mentoring Relationships."

87. de Janasz, Ensher, and Heun, "Using e-Mentoring."

88. Ibid.

89. Quiz adapted from Forret and Sullivan, "Balanced Scorecard Approach," p. 258.

Exercise 16–A
Your Personal Network

1. Working on your own, write down all your primary contacts—individuals you know personally who can support you in attaining your professional goals. Then begin to explore their secondary connections. Make assumptions about possible secondary connections that can be made for you by contacting your primary connections. For example, through one of your teachers (primary), you might be able to obtain some names of potential employers (secondary).

2. Then meet with your partner or small group to exchange information about your primary and secondary networks and to exchange advice and information on how to best use these connections, as well as how you could be helpful to them.

3. Add names or types of names to your list based on ideas you get by talking with others in your group.

Primary and Secondary Connections

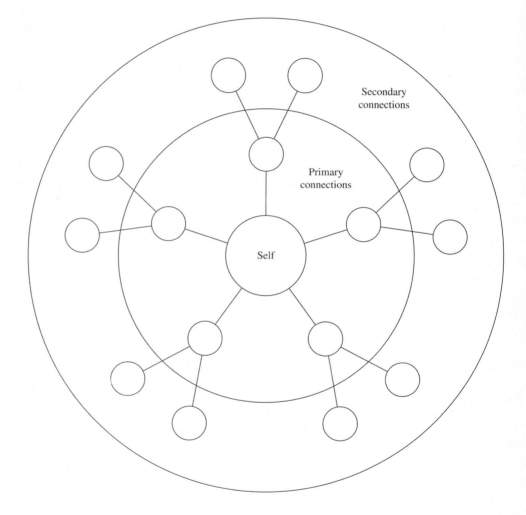

Questions

1. What were some of the best primary sources identified by your group?

2. What were some of the best sources for secondary contacts identified by your group?

3. What are some suggestions for approaching primary contacts?

4. What are some suggestions for approaching secondary contacts, and how is contacting secondary sources different from contacting primary contacts?

5. What did you learn about yourself and others from this exercise?

**Exercise 16–B
Networking
Scorecard**[89]

Do you engage in the following behaviors? Please place a √ in the box if you routinely engage in the listed activity.

How often do you . . .

Networking in Your Organization

☐ Ask to serve on new work projects or committee assignments?

☐ Volunteer for cross-functional task forces?

☐ Attend your organization's social functions?

☐ Participate in company-sponsored athletic activities?

☐ Ask your direct reports how you can facilitate their development?

☐ Meet your peers in the organization for lunch or coffee?

☐ Send thank-you notes or gifts to those who have helped you?

Networking in Your Profession

☐ Attend meetings or conferences of professional organizations?

☐ Serve on committees for your professional organization?

☐ Collaborate on projects with peers in your profession?

☐ Socialize with peers in your profession?

☐ Accept speaking engagements on your area of expertise?

☐ Write articles on your area of expertise for newspapers, trade publications, or newsletters?

☐ Send cards, newspaper clippings, or e-mail to keep in touch with members of your profession?

Networking in Your Community

☐ Participate in local service groups (e.g., Rotary, Kiwanis)?

☐ Become involved in promoting a personal cause (e.g., increasing literacy, preventing breast cancer, helping the elderly)?

☐ Become involved in the arts, theater, symphony, or other quality of life events in the community?

☐ Participate in city governance through serving on boards, councils, or committees?

☐ Meet members of your religious organization?

☐ Welcome newcomers into your community?

☐ Meet others in your community who share your interest in a hobby or athletic activity?

1. How much are you networking? Total number of √'s = _____

2. Where are you focusing your networking efforts?

   Number of √'s for:

   Organization = _____   Profession = _____   Community = _____

3. Where should you be focusing your networking efforts based on your professional and personal goals? _____

4. What three networking activities will you commit to add to your repertoire in the next three months?

   a. _____

   b. _____

   c. _____

5. What outcomes do you expect to achieve by expanding your networking activities? Be specific. _____

**Exercise 16–C
Networking Scenarios**

Working on your own, develop a networking strategy for the following three scenarios.

Next, collaborate with a partner or small group to identify the best strategy for dealing with each of the three scenarios. Each group should develop one best strategy for each scenario and be prepared to report its findings.

Scenarios

I. You are running for student government president. What steps would you take to make your candidacy a success?

1. _____
2. _____
3. _____
4. _____
5. _____
6. _____

II. You are working as an intern and are interested in becoming a permanent full-time employee at the organization. What people would you approach and what steps could you take to obtain an offer?

1. _____
2. _____
3. _____
4. _____
5. _____
6. _____

III. You just moved to a new community and your company's business growth relies heavily on referrals. How do you make contacts in a place where you don't know anyone? How can you build a client base?

1. _____
2. _____
3. _____
4. _____
5. _____
6. _____

Questions

1. What was difficult about this exercise?
2. What creative means were devised to build networks of contacts in these scenarios?
3. Which of these ideas would be easy to implement? Which would be difficult? What makes some strategies easier to do than others?
4. What personal qualities are needed to actually use these strategies?
5. How can someone who is shy about approaching new people use (some or all of) these strategies successfully?

Exercise 16–D
It's a Small World

1. Find someone in the room whom you barely know. Discuss people and connections you have to see if you can find common ground (e.g., shared personal interests or viewpoints, acquaintances you have in common).

2. Determine whether you have any acquaintances in common and determine how many levels or layers of connections it will take you to arrive at a commonality. Discuss organizations you belong to, classes you have been in, where you grew up, sports you play, and so on.

3. Mention a goal you would like to achieve, such as an internship connection you would like to make, a contact in a particular industry in which you are interested, or a person you would like to meet. Work with the other person to see if he or she might know someone who has a valuable connection for you.

Questions

1. Was it difficult or easy to approach someone relatively new with whom to discuss this topic? Why?

2. Did the exchange get easier as it proceeded? Why and how?

3. Did you establish a connection to a person of interest to you such as a potential summer employer? If so, with whom, and how did you make this connection?

4. What is your plan for following up on the contacts you made through your discussion(s) with your teammate(s)?

Exercise 16–E
The 30-Second Commercial

Imagine you are going to a career conference. Representatives from a few hundred firms known to recruit at your school will be there. Your job is to network—meet as many people as practical while attempting to find what would be the perfect job and organization for you. To do this, it is crucial to be able to communicate quickly and neatly what contribution you can offer to a prospective employer. Each new person you meet will want a thumbnail sketch of who you are, what skills and experience you offer, and any other special information. They don't have time for your life story, nor will they want to ask 20 questions to get the information they need to decide whether to continue talking to you about possible opportunities.

1. To network effectively in this situation, you will need to create a 30-second commercial, possibly in response to, "So, tell me about yourself." Think about how you'd like to present yourself to this particular audience. Create a script—one that will take between 20 and 30 seconds to verbalize—that you can use in this setting. Focus on a short, *genuine* appraisal of your capabilities.

2. Now, practice your script. How long does it take? How does it sound—confident but not arrogant? What changes might you make?

3. Now pair up with someone in the class. Practice meeting each other (take turns playing student and potential employer) and using your introduction. Exchange feedback and advice to refine both "commercials."

Questions

1. How did it feel pitching yourself? Why?

2. How did it feel being pitched to? Explain.

3. Why is it important to have this commercial rehearsed and ready?

4. What are the benefits and downsides to using this commercial?

Exercise 16–F
It's Not What You Know . . . It's Who You Know: A Hands-on Networking Exercise

Participants will be given role assignments (available from your instructor). Consistent with the practice of networking, these role assignments (and potential combinations thereof) contain three possible outcomes as described below.

■ "I help/need you, you help/need me." In this scenario, two people each have something the other wants.

■ "I help you now, you help me later." In this scenario, two people can each help each other in the near future.

■ "I can't help you directly, but I know someone who knows someone who can possibly help you." In this scenario, three or more people are involved.

1. Read the following role descriptions. Take a few minutes to think about how you would market yourself and your "needs." Think about creative, yet not necessarily obvious or "in-your-face" ways to make your needs and wants known.

2. You now have approximately 15–20 minutes to network. Take your time and make a positive impression—even if the person with whom you first connect is of no immediate use to you. You can politely ask the "unuseful" participants to direct you to others whom you may have met who may be able to provide what is being requested.

3. Continue until you find the person or persons who can help meet your needs. Along the way, make note of others' needs and make a conscious effort to direct those people to each other.

Questions

1. How did you find the person(s) you were looking for? What interpersonal skills were helpful in enabling you to achieve your objective? Explain.

2. What were some of the lessons you learned about networking—what works well and not so well (e.g., role of eye contact, being persistent, being positive)?

3. How did it feel when you approached someone new with your need?

4. What was most difficult for you to do in this exercise?

5. In real life, what would be most difficult for you in approaching someone new about something you needed?

6. What did you learn about yourself and others from this exercise?

Source: Suzanne C. de Janasz and Stephen C. Davis, "It's Not What You Know . . . It's Who You Know: A Hands-on Networking Exercise," presented at Organizational Behavioral Teaching Conference, Carrollton, GA, 2000. Also appears in S. C. de Janasz and M. L. Forret, "Learning the Art of Networking: A Critical Skill for Enhancing Social Capital and Career Success," *Journal of Management Education* 32, no. 5 (2008), pp. 629–50.

Exercise 16–G
Online Mentoring

You will identify and develop an online business mentor relationship with a current business manager, with whom you will correspond periodically on course-related topics.

Start thinking about who might be an appropriate mentor for you. Consider professional and personal acquaintances of your family and friends—lawyers, accountants, doctors, owners of small businesses, executives. It is not necessary that the mentor you select is in the field in which you are majoring; however, such "matching" may be helpful in establishing rapport with your mentor and providing you with insight into your chosen field. For example, those students with an interest in international business may want to select an online mentor who currently works overseas or who is employed by a domestic branch of an international corporation.

Getting Started

1. Select a mentor. Your instructor will provide you with criteria for mentor selection.

   In addition to professional and personal acquaintances of your family and friends, consider former bosses, fraternity/sorority colleagues (preferably those who have graduated several years ago), and neighbors.

2. Contact the potential mentor, discuss the assignment, explain their potential role, and clarify the time commitment (about 15 minutes for each of three e-mail exchanges

during the semester). Explain why you have selected the mentor or believe he or she would make a good mentor; for example, you have similar career interests, you are aware of his or her success/expertise, and so on. Ascertain the mentor's ability to commit to providing you valuable feedback in a timely fashion.

3. Develop your first set of questions. Please give your questions careful thought. A few things to consider about your questions:

   a. You are making an impression, so ask intelligent questions, and ask them in an appropriate format. The question: "Do you use empowerment in your workplace?" is a closed question, which is likely answered with a simple yes or no. Rewording the question, "In what ways do you empower your employees?" is likely to result in a more thoughtful and complete response. You might want to go a step further and establish a context for your question, such as, "In class, we discussed some of the benefits and pitfalls of empowerment, which is a way to give employees greater discretion over their work environment. To what extent do you empower your employees and what impact has that had on their productivity and satisfaction?" Typically, if the answers your mentor gives you are less than satisfactory, the question was too vague, ambiguous, or closed-ended.

   b. Try to ask questions that help clarify topics currently under discussion. You are welcome to ask questions that relate to topics not yet covered, but you may find it more difficult to compose such questions.

   c. Ask questions that are personally meaningful to you. If you chose a mentor who has experience in a field you would like to enter, fashion questions that are industry specific, such as, "Given the rapid rate of change in the computer industry, how do you keep abreast of both technology and management issues?" or "In what ways does managing technical professionals differ from managing nontechnical or administrative employees?"

   d. Don't assume that your mentor understands all the terms you discuss in class. If you are interested in interpersonal style differences and would like to know your mentor's style, do not ask "Are you a Theory X or Theory Y manager?" (explained in Chapter 18) without some context or explanation of these styles. Even more commonly used terms like *empowerment* may not mean the same thing to people at different levels in the organization or in different types of organizations. Instead try a question like: "In class, we learned that individuals have different preferences in the way they handle conflict. The five styles we discussed are (briefly describe each). Which style is most (least) comfortable for you and why? Share an example where your style did (or did not) accomplish your intended goal."

   e. Feel free to build on previous questions, especially if you feel your mentor's answer was incomplete or you would just like to delve deeper. The goal is that you find value in the exchanges with your mentor.

Source: From Journal of Management Education: a publication of the Organizational Behavior Teaching Society by Vicki R. Whiting and Suzanne C. de Janasz, "Mentoring in the 21st Century: Using the Internet to Build Skills and Networks," Vol. 28, No. 3, 2004, pp. 275–293. Copyright © 2004 by Sage Publications, Inc. Reprinted with permission of Sage Publications, Inc., via Copyright Clearance Center.

Exercise 16–H
Is Mr. Miyagi a Good Mentor?

Karate Kid (1984) is a story about Daniel . . . a boy who is being bullied and who seeks help from Mr. Miyagi, a handyman/martial arts master.

Watch the following clip and answer the questions:

http://www.youtube.com/watch?v=3PycZtfns_U&feature=related

1. In what ways is Mr. Miyagi a good mentor? Explain.

_____

_____

_____

2. In what ways might Mr. Miyagi's mentoring skills or approach be improved? Explain.

_____

_____

_____

After watching the next clip (http://www.youtube.com/watch?v=8aYl7N0JPWs),

3. In what ways have your impressions about Mr. Miyagi's mentoring changed or stayed the same? Explain.

_____

_____

_____

4. Would you want to be mentored by someone like Mr. Miyagi? Why or why not?

_____

_____

_____

**Exercise 16–I
How Would You
Mentor João?**

João Oliveira was torn. A senior manager at Consumer Products Firm (CPF), a global manufacturer, Oliveira had been running its largest factory in Portugal for the last five years. Now he had been offered a post as manufacturing director at CPF in Argentina, an upward promotion and in a far bigger market. It was a rare opportunity, one that would allow Oliveira to develop both his global skills and his general management potential.

For the bulk of his career, the 46-year-old Oliveira had worked for CPF in Portugal. A native of Lisbon, he had trained as an engineer at the top national university. After spending three years as a junior engineer with a local industrial firm, he had been recruited to join CPF at 25.

Oliveira worked very hard running the factory. For the bulk of the last five years, he had been putting in 65-hour weeks. His wife, who had given up a career in law to bear and care for their two children, now 9 and 5, had complained more and more bitterly about Oliveira being "married" to his job. Finally, two years before, the couple had divorced. Now single, Oliveira lived alone in a small apartment not far from his ex-wife and children. The divorce had been a painful wake-up call; Oliveira described his son and daughter as the two most important things in his life, and made a point of seeing them frequently.

Oliveira knew that for the time being he had gone as far as he could in the CPF hierarchy in Portugal. To become director of manufacturing or country general manager it was clear he would have to work outside the country first. To date, other than spending a semester of university in England and serving on a couple of global manufacturing project teams, he had never done so. It was obvious that the offer to go to Argentina was, in part, an invitation to remedy this deficiency. And Oliveira knew that, at 46, he was unlikely to receive another such offer from CPF, most of whose international executives had taken their first expatriate assignments 10 to 15 years younger.

Oliveira had heard of the offer just before coming on a two-week executive development course at a global business school. He would have to decide immediately upon his return whether or not to take the job. On the fourth day of the course, the topic was "Developing Talent Globally." The professor had emphasized something he called the "Mobility Principle": _You cannot learn as much staying in one place as you can by moving around._

Oliveira was committed to developing himself, and had ambitions to rise further within CPF. He also felt keenly the pain of the divorce and a strong attachment to his children. As he pondered his options, he wished that somehow the decision could be made for him.

Questions:

Imagine João has come to see you for advice for what to do with CPF's offer.

1. What questions would you ask to help him evaluate this opportunity and deal with the potential changes it represents? (Consider questions that are open-ended, exploratory, nonjudgmental, not leading, and that don't have "right" answers.)

_____

_____

_____

_____

2. Why are questions potentially more powerful than giving advice?

_____

_____

_____

3. How would you end the mentoring session? Why?

_____

_____

_____

Source: This case (©2006) was prepared by Professor Maury Peiperl and is used with permission from IMD International.

Exercise 16–J
On Becoming a Master Mentor . . .

Become involved as a mentor. There are multiple opportunities to do this, including the following:

- Junior Achievement.
- Big Brothers, Big Sisters.
- Literacy program.
- School-based mentoring program.
- Community organizations—contact information available through local campus service learning office.
- Working as a counselor for a day camp.

Prior to beginning your work as a paid or volunteer mentor, decide which skills you want to concentrate on most.

At the conclusion of the first month or 15 hours of service, evaluate your mentoring abilities—what's working well and what could be improved. If you developed a trusting relationship with a peer or supervisor, ask him or her for feedback on your strengths and opportunities for improvement. You might even ask the people whom you mentor two simple questions: In my role as your mentor (Big Brother, teacher, counselor), what are some things I'm doing that are helpful for you? What are some things that I don't do or should stop doing? In other words, how best can I help you achieve what you want to achieve?

Following your instructor's guidelines, write a reflection paper summarizing your experiences and providing an in-depth assessment of your strengths and opportunities for improvement as a mentor. Utilize the feedback you've received from others as well as your personal experiences prior to and including this experience.

**Exercise 16–K
Reflection/Action Plan**

This chapter focused on networking and mentoring—what they are, why they are important, and how to improve your skills in these areas. Complete the worksheet below upon completing all reading and experiential activities for this chapter.

1. The one or two areas in which I am most strong are:

_____
_____
_____
_____

2. The one or two areas in which I need more improvement are:

_____
_____
_____
_____

3. If I did only one thing to improve in each of these areas (coaching and mentoring), it would be to:

_____
_____
_____
_____

4. Making these changes would probably result in:

_____
_____
_____
_____

5. If I did not change or improve in these areas, it would probably affect my personal and professional life in the following ways:

_____
_____
_____
_____

Coaching and Providing Feedback for Improved Performance

Learning Points

How do I:

- Identify effective characteristics of coaching and feedback?
- Help others set and achieve goals?
- Utilize techniques and strategies to coach others with whom I work?
- Praise someone for giving extra effort?
- Give constructive feedback without making the recipient feel defensive?
- Let others know I am open to receiving constructive feedback?
- Give myself feedback and check these perceptions with others?

Shawn Martin was enjoying his position as branch manager for a national finance company. At first he was not sure about the move to the new location or the relative isolation that came with working away from headquarters, but he was getting used to the independence and level of control he had over operations. Over the nine months since he took the position, business had been unstable, to say the least, but he felt his branch's performance reflected the unstable economy in the community. During his short time as manager, Shawn had received very little input or guidance on how to develop plans for the branch office or how to work through the issues associated with managing his office. He basically made decisions on his own and hoped for the best. All in all, Shawn thought things were going well.

Alecia Michaels, the regional manager, scheduled a lunch meeting with Shawn on her way through town. As Shawn waited at the restaurant for Alecia to arrive, he thought about some of the positive and negative issues regarding his branch to discuss in their meeting. As they sat down and ordered, Alecia asked Shawn his opinion on how the branch was doing. Shawn explained his view on the fluctuating business and mentioned a few of his concerns with his particular branch's system. What he heard next, however, was unexpected. "One of the reasons I wanted to see you today was to let you know that corporate is very concerned with the low volume from your branch, and to let you know I have overheard other regional managers expressing doubt about your ability to handle this assignment." After she let this statement sink in, Shawn replied, "I had no idea the branch was so far off target. Can you tell me which managers have concerns and what abilities you feel I lack in handling this position? This is the first I have heard of this, so can you be more specific?" As Alecia began to reply, her cell phone rang. "Excuse me a minute, Shawn, I have to take this call."

As Shawn waited for Alecia to finish her phone conversation, he tried to sort out the source of these comments. He had been promoted based mainly on his sales record; it had nothing to do with his managerial skills. Sure, he was new to management and could use some guidance and training, but while he was at headquarters, he had had an excellent performance record and was respected by all who worked with him. He was really shaken. This was the first time in his professional career that he had received some potentially damaging feedback. Alecia finished her conversation and turned to Shawn. "I know this is a lot to throw at you at once, but I have to cut our lunch short and leave now to handle the latest crisis at one of my other branches. I will call you tomorrow and set up a time when we can discuss the future of your office."

Shawn couldn't help but feel hopeless. His branch was not doing well, others saw his managerial performance as less than stellar, and his status at the company was in question. He had just relocated his family and could not move them again so soon, not to mention that he did not want to be demoted back to sales. How could he ever turn this around? Whom could he turn to for help and guidance?

1. We learn that Shawn's manager had some concerns. Do you feel his manager provided adequate support for Shawn to improve? Why or why not?

2. What are the key issues or problems concerning giving and receiving feedback?

3. What kind of feedback and help should Shawn elicit from Alecia at his next meeting? From the corporate office? From his co-workers? From other branch managers?

4. How could coaching help Shawn be a more effective manager?

"Good management consists of showing average people how to do the work of superior people."

Ron Zemke[1]

Good managers are in business to help their business succeed—and they know that the way to do this is to help those around them succeed. Good managers and team leaders take regular employees and team members and give them the advice, guidance, and information necessary to become exemplars in their work—people who are superior workers. Long reserved for athletes or top performers in business, coaching is a technique that organizations have recently adopted and formalized as a way to motivate employees to superior performance. Coaching involves guiding, instructing, and training,[2] with a focus on teaching individuals, groups, or teams specific skills needed to improve their performance. Coaches also provide feedback to let employees know how they're doing and whether they need to make adjustments to succeed in an organization. In this chapter we look at both coaching and feedback—what they are, why they are important to individuals and organizations, and ways you can develop your skills in coaching and providing feedback to others.

What Is Coaching?

"Coaching is unlocking a person's potential to maximize their own performance. It is helping them to learn rather than teaching them."

Harvard educator
Timothy Gallwey

Coaching is a means for managers to provide their employees with guidance, insight, and encouragement through frequent interactions in order to improve their work performance. It is designed to strengthen and enhance learning through a continual day-to-day process that goes beyond the once-a-year appraisal system.[3] Coaching conveys a set of beliefs, values, and vision and enables goal setting and action steps for the realization of extraordinary results.[4] Because of the interdevelopmental nature of the coaching process, both coaches and the individuals they coach benefit by building skills and developing as people.

Traditionally, coaching is a recognized process used in sports. In athletics, coaches demonstrate or encourage the effective use of skills, reinforce positive behaviors, and identify and correct negative behaviors. The term *coaching* is now seen as a useful concept in other walks of life, such as business. Over the years even top CEOs such as Eric Schmidt (former Google CEO), Jonathan Schwartz (former Sun Microsystems CEO), and Steve Bennett (former Intuit CEO) employed personal coaches to help them improve their management ability by helping them see how others see them.[5]

In response to merger mania, the proliferation of dot-coms, ever-changing technology, and calls for downsizing and cost cutting, organizations are expecting their employees to do more with less. With fewer employees and frequent changes in job roles, managers cannot watch over every aspect of the job (and employees don't want them to!). Instead, managers need to use their sideline vantage point to empower their employees to perform at high levels when the "coach" is off the field.[6] The trend of managers and team leaders acting as coaches—instead of traditional top-down supervisors—is especially important given the demands that the globally competitive, technologically complex environment places on organizations' educated and adaptable employees.[7] When managers and team leaders act as coaches (like facilitators or enablers), rather than supervisors (like directors or superiors), employees' abilities and creativity can be unleashed instead of controlled, resulting in increased morale, productivity, and enhanced interpersonal working relationships.

The Importance and Benefits of Coaching

Traditionally, employees looked to their supervisors for direction, decision making, and control. Today's more fluid, less hierarchical working environment calls for a different philosophy or mindset. To remain competitive, organizations need to harness the creative and synergistic capacity of all their employees, not just the ones in leadership positions. The very capabilities that led an organization to success a few years ago could cause its undoing if it refuses to engage in continual learning and renewal. By adapting and creating a new environment that includes leader–employee partnerships—where leaders are more like coaches and less like bosses—individuals thrive and organizations remain competitive and survive.[8] Coaches are leaders who focus their energy on helping others improve their performance and achieve goals.[9] A coaching philosophy and process benefits both individuals and the organization in important ways:[10]

- Coaching reduces employees' fears related to their (and others') status in the organization. By emphasizing collaboration, partnership, and mutual growth, the perception of "manager versus worker" is replaced with a more team-oriented view of "Together we can. . . ."

- Coaching enables workers to feel they are part of the organization rather than used by it. They take ownership in and contribute to organizational performance and success. Employees enjoy working in a healthy environment, one where relationships are rooted in mutual respect and rapport, and constructive and respectful language is encouraged. While some employees are used to and respond to fear and threats, the outcome of the management by fear approach is compliance, not commitment.

- Effective coaching endorses rather than diminishes people's skills and abilities. Imagine the Little League coach who publicly scolds or belittles a child upon making an error. Now imagine another coach who encourages children to play to their potential, scolds parents for their unhealthy and belittling remarks, and utilizes not only the best players but also those who have yet to develop their full potential. For which coach would you rather play? When managers coach effectively, they "accentuate the positive and eliminate the negative," to quote a popular 1940s song. They see more possibilities than limitations in the individual and the organization and take personal responsibility for overcoming those limitations.

- Coaching helps people overcome personal obstacles to their success. Good coaches use goal setting and constructive feedback.[11] When good coaches help employees set and achieve goals, they feel a sense of accomplishment. A recent survey by the

International Coach Federation noted that self-esteem and self-confidence was the number one result reported from using a personal coach.[12]

- When used in team settings, coaching improves team communications and provides a structure for managing conflict. Coaching helps reinforce team goals and commitments by providing external support and insight into effective team processes. Coaching teaches team members and the team as a whole how to build trust and competency so they are able to self-manage.[13]

- Coaching behaviors encourage others to coach. In essence, coaching behaviors beget coaching behaviors. With greater trust and support, employees are more likely to take risks and suggest creative solutions to organizational problems.[14] As employees feel supported and trusted, they become more supportive of other employees and more trusting of management.

Beyond individual and team benefits, coaching provides many benefits for the organization as well.[15] Coaching helps to improve workforce recruitment and retention. People want to join and stay in an organization where they will be respected, trusted, listened to, and valued. It also reduces misunderstanding and mistakes by resulting in a more positive and supportive climate at work through the use of a common language to which everyone can relate. Coaching emphasizes the unique potential of individuals to evoke hidden talents, thereby increasing their ability to contribute to the organization's success.

Do You Have What It Takes?

Coaching requires several competencies as shown by this extensive list.[16] Work through Exercise 17–A, "Coaching Clinic," to see if you have or how you can have what it takes to be a coach.

Communication skills	Caring
Feedback skills	Approachability
Analytical skills	Flexibility
Planning skills	Trustworthiness
Goal-setting skills	Ability to challenge
Organizational skills	Ability to empower
Motivational skills	Accountability
Integrity	Ability to confront
Commitment	Technical skills
Patience	Industry knowledge
Empathy	

Skills and Characteristics of Effective Coaches

Effective coaching can help enhance organizational communication with internal and external customers. As employees become more involved in decisions and communications, they play a more active role in relationships with customers both inside and outside of the organization. The coaching process should evolve wherein a coach starts with a more directive approach of pushing an employee towards solutions the coach suggests to a more non-directive approach that helps employees become independent in making decisions (See Fig. 17–1). This will lead to improved performance management, positively affecting external customer service while internally promoting focused performance discussions, the development of new skills, and planning for personal career advancement.

Another important result of coaching is seen in the expansion of entrepreneurial thinking within organizations. Coaching fosters creativity and helps build a shared vision. Building on the benefit of trust and support of individuals, coaching creates an

Figure 17–1
Coaching Continuum:
The Evolving Role of a Coach

DIRECTIVE			NON-DIRECTIVE
Push (Solving problems for them)			*Pull (Helping them solve their own problems)*
Tell	Sell	Ask	Participate

Dependent	*Employee Change*	Independent

Telling	Giving guidance	Questioning	Encouraging
Instructions	Suggesting	Clarifying	Reflecting
Advice	Feedback	Listening	Empathizing

atmosphere in which individual creativity is not only supported but also deeply encouraged. Coaching provides organizational members with the opportunity to start new projects or initiate partnerships with suppliers or customers.

Effective coaches acquire a mindset, skills, and values that will help build employee commitment to the organization. Coaching skills or techniques are not seen as genuine when accompanied by an attitude or behaviors that run counter to the goals of coaching. Merely possessing a coaching philosophy is not enough; it is also necessary to have good skills in communication, feedback, and goal setting. Effective coaches have all the following characteristics or abilities:

- *A desire to bring out the best in others' performance.* Effective coaches support employees' needs, create choices, seek commitment, and provide means for self-expression.[17]

- *Ability to give constructive and positive feedback.* Coaching enables employees to understand their mistakes and learn how to improve or develop their skills. Effective coaches are able to talk face-to-face with others about performance problems, and they also affirm and acknowledge others' contributions to the organization.

- *Honesty and trustworthiness.* Effective coaches are keenly aware of themselves and how they impact others. Through their actions, they demonstrate their trustworthiness, high personal standards, ability to develop mutual relationships, and willingness to share their wisdom.[18]

- *Willingness to NOT assign blame.* "Blame the process, not the person." Good coaches are process- and problem-oriented; they focus on how to solve problems rather than on the personality of the people involved. To do this, they get involved and collaborate to find solutions.

- *Good communication skills.* Good coaches create an environment in which communication is open and two-way, encouraging employees to bring forth problems as well as opportunities without fear of blame or retribution. Such dialogue builds mutual trust and commitment.

- *A parallel style of thinking and acting.*[19] Good coaches attend to both human and business needs. They realize that in order to accomplish the organizational goals, they must balance the need for learning with the need for results.

- *Responsibility and accountability.* Good coaches accept full responsibility for their actions and for what occurs in their environment and encourage others to do the same.[20]

- *Constructive conflict management.* Effective coaches encourage competing ideas to promote creativity and innovation and discourage personal conflicts. They stress the team approach and facilitate mutual understanding among all parties involved.

- *A personal level of caring.* For employees to respect the coach and his or her knowledge, the coach must show genuine care and concern toward them.[21]

Effective Coaching Behaviors

Now that you know the benefits of coaching and what makes coaches effective, you might be wondering exactly what to do when planning to call an employee (or teammate) in for coaching. Since the ultimate goal of coaching is to be supportive in helping employees obtain the ability to solve their own problems, coaches will need to develop a process that will supportively pull employees toward their own problems. Situations vary and call for

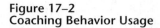

**Figure 17–2
Coaching Behavior Usage**

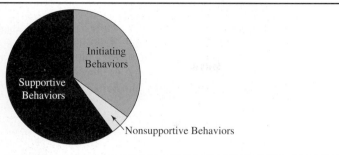

Source: Reprinted with permission from Steve J. Stowell, "Coaching: A Commitment to Leadership," *Training and Development Journal,* Vol. 6, June 1988, pp. 34–38.

different strategies. A study of a major service organization that examined the behavior of effective and ineffective coaches and their coaching sessions found the following:[22]

- Coaching sessions require managers to use face-to-face discussions of performance problems. For many managers, this is considered an unpleasant task and is therefore avoided. The best sessions last between 35 and 45 minutes.

- Effective coaches don't legislate quality; they model it. "Do as I say, not as I do" does not work in this environment. For the leader–employee partnership to work, there has to be mutual respect and trust.

- Effective coaches and their sessions contain high levels of **supportive behaviors** (words or actions that denote concern or acceptance) and moderate levels of **initiating** or *problem-solving* **behaviors** (words or actions that encourage problem solving or resolutions). Coaches should avoid using nonsupportive behaviors (words or actions that express aggression or power). (See Figures 17–2 and 17–3.) The leader establishes a framework for the coaching discussion, which might look something like this: "We have a situation that deserves some attention. What can we do to solve it? I'm confident in your ability. I'll support you. What do you think would help in this situation?"

- Successful coaches use supportive behaviors far more frequently than unsuccessful coaches. These behaviors fall into three categories: verbal (statements that indicate the coach's commitment to and backing of the employee), tangible (statements that offer help, resources, links to other people and information), and active (behaviors and actions that indicate complete and empathic listening including asking questions, acknowledging, using appropriate body language, showing genuine interest). This last category might be most important; it demonstrates the coach's willingness to understand before trying to be understood.

**Figure 17–3
Key Leadership Behaviors
for Successful Coaching and
Coaching Sessions**[23]

Supportive Behaviors—A leader's words and actions showing concern and acceptance of employees:
- Collaboration regarding solutions to problems.
- Help and assistance through training and resources.
- Concern over the employee's needs and objectives.
- Empathy for the employee and attention to obstacles and problems.
- Expressions of the value of the employee and his or her contribution to the work.
- Acceptance of responsibility in situations.
- Interaction that provides time for the employee to air his or her feelings.

Initiating Behaviors—Initiating and structuring actions and discussions:
- Providing feedback and analysis of issues and concerns.
- Clarifying leader expectations and requirements.
- Exploring impact and effects of employee's actions.
- Planning actions around solutions and desired changes.
- Seeking commitment to the action plan.
- Clarifying positive and negative consequences connected to future action and plans.

**Figure 17–4
Coaching Template**

A coaching plan can help utilize everyone's time more effectively and guide the process toward more directed goal achievement. This template can be used for coaching individuals or teams.

- Stage 1: Expectations and Importance (1–3 minutes): Discuss the reason for the coaching, the expectations of the actions to be accomplished, and the importance to the organization.

- Stage 2: Questioning and Listening (4–10 minutes): Get the other person(s)' perception, ideas, and clarifications on their expectations for future actions.

- Stage 3: Solution and Agreement (5 minutes): Agree on action steps for accomplishing goals and changes.

Source: Alan Vengel's "20-Minute Coaching Conversation,"[24] p. 13.

- The best coaches ask questions that enable the employee to discover how to improve. They collaborate with the employee to analyze situations and performance and jointly find solutions.

- Successful coaches challenge employees and stimulate resolutions. They accomplish those goals by initiating action-oriented problem analysis discussions. These problem-solving discussions are best when they focus on one or two issues. Any more would be overwhelming.

- The best coaches allow for flexibility in the coaching process to focus on the needs of the individual employee. Each employee has unique characteristics and needs based on his or her level of expertise, challenges faced in each situation, as well as attitude, readiness, and commitment to the process. The best sessions are those in which the coach plans, prepares, and rehearses prior to the coaching session so he or she can be responsive to the specific employee and coaching situation.[25] Because many find such sessions difficult to do, this preparation can be key to reducing the coach's discomfort with the process, enabling him or her to do the same for the employee. Refer to the Coaching Template in Figure 17–4 for drafting a coaching session.

Counseling

Coaching should not be mistaken for counseling. Some situations call for counseling rather than coaching, and it is important that managers understand the difference between the two. (See Figure 17–5.) **Counseling** is used to address personal or attitudinal problems rather than those related to an individual's ability (or lack thereof). Counseling is a complex task and is best reserved for professionals. It involves listening skills, feedback skills, trustworthiness, and a good deal of patience.

Two methods facilitate the counseling process; the manager's comfort and ability with counseling and the severity of the problem being addressed in the session will determine the choice between them. **Directive methods** include probing, questioning, and discussing specific problems and possible solutions. In addition, a manager may have the person

**Figure 17–5
A Comparison between
Coaching and Counseling**

	Coaching	Counseling
Objective:	To reinforce positive behaviors and correct negative behaviors, to gain positive work outcomes and enhance relationships.	To facilitate understanding of behaviors and to obtain a willingness to change.
Means:	Pass information, set standards, and provide insight, encouragement, direction, and guidance.	Two methods: Directive—assuring, probing, and questioning; nondirective—listening and supporting.
Employee problems stem from:	Lack of ability, information, or understanding and incompetence.	Attitudes, defensiveness, personality clashes, and other emotional problems.

discuss her behavior, beliefs, and perceptions in order to help the manager put the individual's emotions and attitudes into perspective.

Another method, the **nondirective approach**, involves being a good listener and sounding board. Listening may be the most valuable and helpful means for identifying the source and solution for employee problems. Sometimes people just need to disclose the way they are feeling to relieve stress and gain a new perspective on a situation. In so doing, they often find solutions to their own problems. Many of the effective listening techniques provided in Chapter 6 would be key behaviors in providing nondirective counseling.

Although managers should be familiar with directive and nondirective approaches, they should seldom get involved in counseling an employee themselves. Good managers recognize their limitations in helping others and refer employees with personal or emotional problems to other professionals or resources, such as the organization's employee assistance program.[26] Many organizations have employee assistance and wellness programs to assist with personal and health problems ranging from mental illness, substance abuse, day care, and family issues to physical health issues and financial planning.

Helping Others Set Goals

A major component of coaching is helping others set goals. Receiving performance feedback through coaching can be difficult for employees. By incorporating goal setting into the coaching activity, a manager can motivate an employee to set a new course or direction.

Managers and organizations can have a dramatic impact on subordinates' goal attainment.[27] To increase employees' chances of attaining goals, the organization's environment must be conducive to individual growth and development in the context of organizational goals. Underscoring this philosophy with managerial support via coaching—both in setting the example and supporting others to do the same—also facilitates the goal-setting process. Managers need to be aware of behaviors that can positively impact others in setting and achieving personal and organizational goals. The Nestlé® corporation teaches managers the "GROW" model (Goal, Reality, Options, What's next) to use goal setting to motivate and coach employees for continued growth and improvement.

Goals you set for yourself are more likely to be achieved when they are SMART (specific, measurable, achievable and attainable, realistic, and time bound). This is also true of goals set by your teammates or employees. Coach others to ensure their goals conform to and contain SMART elements. Work with them to ensure that the desired outcome is clear and that they have the necessary skills and resources to accomplish their goals. Good managers help others set "stretch" goals—those that require total effort but are not so unrealistic that subordinates avoid committing to what they perceive to be impossible. Studies demonstrate that performance increases with the level of goal difficulty, providing that the individual is committed to achieving it and has the ability to do so.[28] Goals should be challenging yet realistic.

Once SMART goals are set, your work isn't done. As a coach, you might need to provide periodic feedback and encouragement, especially if the goal is particularly complex and will take a long time to reach. Encourage others to break up large, complex goals into smaller objectives, and set checkpoints and processes to follow up. Some employees may prefer feedback initiated by the manager, while others prefer to provide periodic updates. There may even be employees who are accustomed to the "no news is good news" approach. Use your judgment and assessment of their capabilities and past performance to determine how often and by what mechanism interim performance is checked and modified, if necessary. In addition, goal setting is an ongoing process.[29] Your work helping others set goals is likely never done, though your level of involvement may change over time. Encourage employees to establish and update goals periodically, annually at the minimum.

Goals that are SMART are more likely to be achieved. The same can be said for goals that are personally meaningful or externally rewarding. When employees set goals that advance personal needs and desires for growth and development, their intrinsic motivation to achieve those goals will be high. Employee commitment can be increased further when they stand to gain recognition, perquisites, or other financial rewards when goals are achieved. Managers or coaches can clarify the existence of such organizational rewards or create new ones. A perfect example of this is in sales organizations. Top sellers within a specified period of time are likely to be awarded bonuses, priority parking spaces, minivacations, or other special treatment, like access to desirable training opportunities. These rewards can encourage individual commitment to (and healthy competition between co-workers in obtaining) rewards in such organizations. When such rewards are not available, managers can increase goal commitment and achievement by using an informal chat or note to express their satisfaction and appreciation for the employee's positive efforts and improvements.

Finally, commitment to goals will vary directly with the amount of participation and input from the employee in setting the goals. You cannot set someone else's goals and expect to have high commitment and motivation.[30] In addition, some researchers have hypothesized that allowing participation in the goal-setting process increases a person's perception of control and fairness.[31] Have you ever been asked by someone else to get high grades, quit smoking, or lose weight? Were you successful? Chances are, unless and until the goal is yours, you're likely not to give it your all. Depending on the employees' understanding of organizational goals and their role in achieving those goals, managers can trust employees to set their own goals or managers can solicit employee input and set goals participatively. Extend the notion of participative goal setting to include goal checking. In other words, jointly develop a system that will enable individuals to gauge their performance in relation to jointly established goals and know whether (and why) they have successfully completed them.[32] Recognizing goal progress will provide fulfillment and a sense of well-being, which can be an affective reinforcer in subsequent goal attainment.[33]

Effectively helping others to set goals is a key element in managerial coaching. Figure 17–6 summarizes and highlights the steps necessary for helping others set and achieve goals.

What Is Feedback?

"Many receive advice; only the wise profit from it."

Syrus

Today's companies are being pressured by the marketplace to come up with the best ideas and the most innovative products. How do these companies and their employees know whether their efforts are successful? Ultimately, consumers indicate their

---

Figure 17–6
Five Steps for Helping Others Set Goals

PREPARE—Be informed about the organization's goals and direction to ensure a match with the goals of the individual. Also be sure to review the individual's past performance and accomplishments to ensure that goals are attainable and challenging.

CLARIFY—Provide an overall picture on how individuals' goals and objectives fit with the organizational objectives. Ensure that they know their part in the whole.

DECIDE—Work together to decide what would be attainable, desirable, and challenging goals. Put the goals in writing and make them public.

COMMIT—Determine how you can commit to support, assist, and facilitate others in achieving their goals. Such support might include making phone calls, arranging for training, coordinating with the efforts of other individuals or departments, and obtaining needed equipment.

PARTICIPATE—Schedule regularly planned meetings to discuss progress, revise goals if necessary, and set higher or additional goals. Make goal setting a part of the process, and continue the cycle on a regular basis.

Source: Cynthia A. Mulhearn, "Seeking New Heights: How and Why Goal-Setting Works," *Managers Magazine* (June 1994), p. 13. Reprinted with permission of LIMRA.

approval of a company's products and services through their purchasing behavior and other company-initiated mechanisms, such as customer satisfaction surveys. By asking for and responding to this "advice," organizations remain viable competitors in our continuously changing environment. The old adage "no news is good news" no longer suffices. Organizations—and their employees—need to know how they're doing so they can continually develop and improve. Whereas customers provide this information to organizations, managers are responsible for letting employees know how they're doing and whether adjustments need to be made. This section discusses **feedback**: why it's necessary for organizations and individuals, how to give and receive it effectively, and the benefits of doing so.

Feedback is information that enables individuals or groups to compare actual performance with a given standard or expectation. Feedback involves offering your perceptions and describing your feelings in a nonjudgmental manner and supplying data that others can use to examine and change behaviors. It also assists in goal setting and performance improvement.[34]

Most people are eager to know how they are doing. As a student, you receive much feedback on your schoolwork. Grades on exams and assignments, written suggestions for improvement, and face-to-face meetings with faculty provide you with feedback on your performance or how well you are doing relative to others in your class or your teacher's expectations. Through feedback, you receive direct information about how you are performing and how to direct your future efforts in terms of corrective action (do more of this, stop doing that). If the feedback is constructive—it is truthful, fair, and not given as a personal attack—the information gained can be invaluable in enhancing our performance and helping us grow personally and professionally.[35]

Why Giving Job Feedback Is So Important in Organizations

The importance of giving, receiving, and incorporating feedback into organizational life is increasing today due to heightened competition and shifting requirements. Workplace change is now a constant. Positions and roles are continually being reengineered, often with little or no additional training offered to employees as they start new jobs or new roles within their organization. As a result, seasoned employees are expected to give feedback to new employees or team members on company expectations and requirements. This is beneficial because it ensures that employees experience many aspects of the business and become successful at teaching, coaching, and mentoring others. On the other hand, continual adaptation to new roles can be a mentally and emotionally taxing experience for new and existing employees. Knowledge of effective feedback mechanisms can reduce the strain caused by having to train new people continually.

In this new environment, feedback also travels upward from employees to managers. Feedback mechanisms are put in place for employees to share progress toward goals, relay current problems, and inform management about how they feel about their jobs, co-workers, and the organization in general. With growing public and governmental pressure to carefully scrutinize corporate governance, even corporate officers and boards of directors need feedback to regulate their actions and decisions. Providing feedback to these top executives can ensure that decisions both address the interests of the organization and conform to ethical standards.[36]

Why Feedback Is Important for Individuals

The ability to give, receive, and ask for feedback is important to us personally. (See Figure 17–7.) Giving feedback greatly benefits those with whom you work. When information about performance is given in such a way that the person can learn and grow from the feedback, it can be an enormous boost for professional confidence and competence. Helping others to better understand the company and how to excel at their jobs can result in enhanced employee morale, improved employee relations, greater teamwork, and enhanced productivity.

Figure 17–7
Benefits of Giving, Getting, and Asking for Effective Feedback

	Benefits of:	
Giving Feedback	**Getting Feedback**	**Asking for Feedback**
■ Ensures that individuals focus on meeting organizational goals and objectives.	■ Builds our confidence by reinforcing our strengths.	■ Demonstrates our commitment to improve.
■ Reinforces positive and effective actions and behaviors.	■ Directs us toward areas needing improvement.	■ Demonstrates our dedication to doing things right.
■ Provides corrective action of ineffective or problematic behaviors.	■ Helps us understand our blind spots—weaknesses of which we're unaware.	■ Shows our commitment to continued service in an organization.

When we receive feedback, we learn how others perceive us. Because it isn't unusual to find that others interpret our behaviors differently than we intended,[37] feedback provides us with information needed to change our behaviors and attitudes (if we desire to do so). Feedback highlights what we need to do to be more efficient or effective. It adds to our understanding of our strengths and weaknesses and aids us in developing self-improvement plans through which we can learn new skills and evaluate our use of these skills. Through enhancement and improvement, we can reinforce positive actions and correct insufficient or disruptive behaviors. As illustrated in the opening case, providing feedback to Shawn over the nine months might have eliminated many of the problems being addressed at the meeting. It would have provided Shawn with insight into his new managerial role and improved the branch along with improving Shawn's skill base.

Asking for feedback has many benefits. By asking for feedback, we demonstrate our commitment to improve and our dedication to do things right. This strengthens our affiliation or sense of belonging with an organization. If we see ourselves as temporary or short-term employees, we won't care what others think of us. When we ask for feedback, we signal a desire to remain involved with an organization in a longer and more meaningful capacity. Asking for feedback also builds and enhances our self-esteem. Feedback can reinforce the things we do well. This is a confidence-builder and critical for developing a positive self-identity. Just as companies ask for feedback from customers, seeking feedback from others (superiors, peers, friends, partners) will help us maintain and build strong relationships.

Even feedback that is constructive can be beneficial. Constructive feedback enables us to find out—in a nonthreatening way—how we can change and ways to improve. When offered appropriately, constructive feedback can also result in significant behavior changes. Feedback can have a strong impact on our actions and on our attitude. We all have blind spots. The better we understand our behaviors and their impact on others, the better equipped we will be to choose alternative behaviors.[38] Since Shawn, in the opening case, knew he was not the most experienced manager, he should have taken the initiative to seek feedback when the company failed to provide it. Feedback is a reciprocal process and does not always need to be started by the superior.

Sources of Feedback

Feedback typically comes from one of three primary sources:[39] (1) others—superiors, peers, customers, friends, contacts, and parents; (2) the task itself—feedback can be directly built into the task; and (3) self—an honest, realistic appraisal of how we're doing relative to others' and our own expectations.

Others

Interacting with others provides input about how we are doing. This can be an excellent source of feedback. While it is helpful to ask for and obtain feedback from others, overly positive and overly negative feedback should be treated with care. Your self-identity and self-awareness should be strong enough that you can assess your own behavior and evaluate judgments about you against your own perceptions about yourself. When you receive feedback that is overly positive (e.g., "You did a great job today") from someone who is not aware of mistakes you made in your performance, accept the feedback gracefully but don't "believe your own press." Vow to make changes so that the next time you receive this feedback, you will feel it is richly deserved. Sometimes we receive negative feedback (e.g., "Why can't you ever do anything right?"). When this happens, use your self-awareness to evaluate this feedback. If there's a kernel of truth, accept it and make changes. If not, forget about it and focus on the positives you know you have to offer instead. It is also best to seek feedback from someone who will give you honest, unbiased feedback. If you are asking someone for feedback on your résumé, it is better to have someone point out your mistakes rather than have a potential employer see the mistakes.

The Task Itself

When developing project plans, it is a good idea to build in mechanisms for evaluating the progress of the project and the people responsible for getting the work done. As a member of a project team, you might suggest building in regular checkpoints—periodic points during which the team evaluates the progress made to date and makes needed changes—and continually monitoring the project until its end. The team can also discuss and debrief the project throughout and at the end as a means for getting feedback about which elements went well and which ones could be improved the next time around. Evaluating a completed project provides an excellent source of feedback, as the actual project output is tangible evidence of the quality (or lack thereof) of the process. For example, a quality improvement team will know whether a project is successful if the number of defective parts declines. Similarly, a customer service team can evaluate its progress by tracking the ratings given by customers in customer satisfaction surveys.

Self

Our own thoughts and perceptions can be good sources of feedback, although it is difficult for us to be completely objective when self-evaluating. While we can sometimes be our own worst critics, studies show that workers often overestimate their own performance. Few employees or even students think they are just average. Giving feedback to yourself is easy, but doing it objectively can be difficult. Generally, if self-esteem is an issue, you'll be harder on yourself than others would be. However, this may not apply to people from cultures whose values differ from yours. It is helpful to supplement your own evaluation with comments from others. Take, for example, the student who asked his close friends for some feedback about himself. His actions showed intelligence as well as courage. It must have been a good strategy—that student is now president of a major consumer products company! When giving yourself feedback, it helps to assess yourself relative to others in similar roles, rather than making your assessment in a vacuum. Evaluate honestly those things you're doing well and those areas in which you can improve, and make plans to make the necessary changes. You can also check your self-evaluations with those of others.

> *"To know what to do is wisdom. To know how to do it is skill. But doing it, as it should be done, tops the other two virtues."*
>
> Anonymous

Characteristics of Effective Feedback

Effective feedback provides both instruction and motivation.[40] A supervisor who demonstrates the proper sequence of steps in responding to a customer's technical questions has provided instruction to an employee. When the employee performs these steps correctly in a subsequent call, the boss responds, "Nice job! I really liked how thorough you were in asking questions to discover the best solution." This kind of feedback reinforces desired behavior and motivates the employee to continue to improve performance. To ensure that your feedback fulfills these two objectives, it should possess the following characteristics (also see Figure 17–8).

**Figure 17–8
Characteristics of
Effective Feedback**

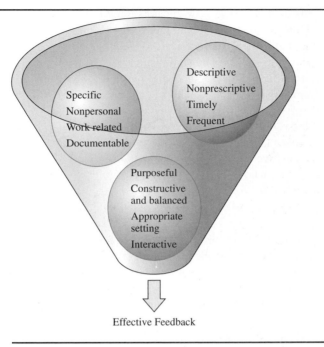

Effective Feedback

12 Characteristics of Effective Feedback

1. Specific
2. Nonpersonal
3. Work related
4. Documentable
5. Descriptive
6. Nonprescriptive

7. Timely
8. Frequent
9. Purposeful
10. Constructive and balanced
11. In the appropriate setting
12. Interactive

Specific

General comments like, "You did a good job" or "That is all wrong" tend not to be helpful. Instead, focus your comments on a specific activity or behavior so others know exactly how they can improve their performance in the designated area. "That was a tough decision. I'm impressed with how you weighed the pros and cons and selected the best course of action." "I'd like to talk with you about your proofing of these reports."

Nonpersonal

How you deliver feedback is as important as what you say. Avoid blaming ("You're the reason we have mistakes around here") and referring to assumed personality traits ("How come you're so lazy?"). Direct your feedback at the behavior itself and not the worker.

An example of this is, "I am concerned about the fact you've been late every night this week."[41] Focus on what people do, not who they are.[42]

Work Related

When giving feedback to someone on the job, only refer to behaviors that are directly related to the job: "We need to talk about your absences," rather than "I understand you've been going nightclubbing every night this week."

Documentable

When giving specific work-related feedback, make sure it is based on fact rather than hearsay. "Our records show you've been using company phones for making personal calls" will be accepted more readily than, "Betty tells me you're on the phone a lot." Also keep a written record of any conversations you have when using feedback to help employees correct undesirable behaviors. **Documentable** feedback could be important if in the future you need to fire a poor-performing employee.

Descriptive	To give **descriptive** feedback, focus your feedback on a specific behavior that the recipient can change or control, describing behavior rather than evaluating it—for example, "I've noticed the filing system is getting a bit disorganized." Discuss what the person did and the feelings aroused by those actions rather than labeling or name-calling. "You interrupted me and I get frustrated when I lose my place," rather than "You're inconsiderate."[43]
Nonprescriptive	Give **nonprescriptive** feedback. Avoid moralizing or giving feedback that is judgmental or prescriptive. When you lecture employees about what you think they should do, they are likely to become defensive and tune out your feedback.
Timely	Give feedback promptly, immediately after the event or incident, if possible. While promptness is important, it is okay to wait briefly if it means delivering feedback in a private setting and once emotions have cooled. "Let's debrief how the meeting went to-morrow, after we've both had a chance to think about it." Don't delay giving feedback, as it will reduce the likelihood that others will understand and learn from their mistakes. In addition, don't withhold the feedback. Saying nothing when performance is inadequate or when someone treats you inappropriately is equivalent to indicating your acceptance of his or her behavior.
Frequent	The best performance feedback is given frequently and on an ongoing basis. Ideally, there should be no surprises at your formal performance appraisal (typically once each year); feedback about specific incidents should have already been delivered. This allows the for-mal review to focus more proactively on the future, on clarifying and reinforcing personal strengths and development goals.
Purposeful	Focus feedback on only one or two specific topics. "Let's talk about what happened dur-ing the last week of the project." As they say in marriage counseling, "Don't throw in the kitchen sink." If you're discussing a team member's lack of follow-through on a project, don't take the opportunity to offer a laundry list of other unrelated concerns.
Constructive and Balanced	Feedback is more likely to be accepted when it contains a balance of positive and negative comments. When giving feedback, it's helpful to start the conversation with positive feedback. This reinforces to the employee that she has strengths and that you and the organization value her. Initial positive feedback reduces employees' defen-siveness and increases their openness to any constructive criticism that follows. "I am really pleased with the quality of your work on the Miller project. I'm wondering if there's a way you could bring others from the team into more phases of the Genovese project."
In the Appropriate Setting	While there are some cultural exceptions, it is appropriate to give positive feedback to employees either in private or public. Constructive feedback should always be shared in a private setting to avoid embarrassment, resentment, and defensiveness. "I'd like to talk with you. Let's go somewhere where we're out of earshot."[44]
Interactive	Good feedback takes into account the needs of both the giver and the receiver. Feedback is best when it is a two-way interchange and it allows time for dialogue. One way to do this is to solicit an employee's perspective on a subject or incident before deciding how to handle it. "I've shared your teammates' view of the situation. What is your perspective on what occurred? How do you think we should approach this situation?" By asking for and integrating the employee's perspective with your own, you can reduce misunderstandings, develop better solutions, and most importantly, gain their commitment to a solution—*their* solution.

"I praise loudly. I blame softly."

Catherine the Great,
1729–1796

Challenges in Providing Feedback

Giving performance feedback, especially constructive feedback, is one of the most difficult things for a manager to do well. Studies show that many managers dread feedback sessions with their employees and often resist or avoid them. Giving feedback is one of the toughest managerial responsibilities, yet it is one of the most important. Anxiety over giving feedback exists for several reasons:

1. Managers are uncomfortable giving negative feedback and discussing performance weaknesses. While many of us can and do give out compliments and praise, few look forward to doling out criticisms and therefore avoid or delay giving feedback. Many individuals will use more passive or general language in giving negative feedback, and this indirect approach may cause the recipients of the feedback to misinterpret the seriousness or true cause of the problem. They will therefore lack clear direction on how to improve. Research suggests that women are particularly uncomfortable giving critical feedback due to their preference for "saving face" for others.[45]

2. Employees tend to have an inflated view of their own performance; most people rate themselves above average when, statistically, about half will be below average. The perceptual differences between a manager and employee underscore the difficulty in giving feedback.

3. Feedback is sometimes closer to criticism than to legitimate information that can help employees gauge their performance. Many employees will see the feedback as a judgment or direct criticism and may become emotional, defensive, or even hostile. Managers may fear the reaction they might get when delivering negative feedback to some employees.[46] Recent research on workplace incivility demonstrates that such behaviors have become more commonplace and of concern in the workforce.[47]

4. As organizations have downsized and increased spans of control, managers have less time available to provide effective feedback to greater numbers of employees. With other, more pressing matters tugging at them, managers may feel unable to make "time for all those intimate, eyeball-to-eyeball encounters"[48] amidst all the other things for which they are accountable.

Despite how difficult giving feedback might appear to be, it is important for managers to give constructive feedback. Feedback—and the lessons derived from it—are the lifeblood of an organization. Without feedback, employees are left in the dark, frustrated over not knowing where they stand. This can lead to interpersonal conflicts, absenteeism, and turnover.[49]

Tips for Preparing and Leading a Feedback Session

By following the tips and techniques below, you'll find it easier to **give feedback** and ensure that employees accept and act upon it positively for improved performance:

- *Prepare a script.* If possible, identify in advance the situation that will be discussed and develop a "script" for how you intend to approach the situation, using an outline such as the one in Figure 17–9. Most people fear the unknown and unexpected. By preparing a script and thinking through possible responses, you are likely to reduce the discomfort associated with providing constructive feedback. See Figure 17–10 for a sample script.

Figure 17–9
Outline for Feedback Session

Brief Description of Situation:

Opening: Overview/Purpose of Meeting (state why you are meeting and what you hope to accomplish).

Feedback (explain the situation objectively, using facts to back up your assertions about a specific behavior and its impact on fellow employees or team members).

Interaction/Clarification (invite a response—what the employee's perception of the situation is).

Suggestions (offer a suggestion for change or brainstorm a solution with the employee).

Clarify Expectations/Close/Next Steps (agree to meet again at a specific time to review progress).

**Figure 17–10
Sample Script**

The situation: As director of marketing, you have been receiving some signals that your star sales-person, Margaret, has been ruffling the feathers of some of her customers and peers. John, a buyer for Belk's (a department store), sent you a letter detailing the harsh treatment he received from Margaret when he requested changes in his current order. You also heard from another of your employees that Liz, a co-worker of Margaret's, was seen crying in the employee lounge immediately following a heated discussion with Margaret. Stories like these are out of the ordinary when it comes to Margaret; however, you have also heard through the grapevine that Margaret may be experiencing some personal problems. Margaret has been an outstanding performer for the last four years; however, you are concerned about an emerging pattern of interpersonal issues involving her. You plan to approach Margaret in the following way:

Opening: "Margaret, I'd like to talk with you about your performance over the last two months. My goal is to get some clarity about two specific situations and offer assistance in improving your current performance."

Feedback: "Margaret, for the last four years, you've had steadily increasing sales and have been a star performer. Lately, however, I've received some distressing information about how harshly you treated a Belk's buyer, and of a strained discussion with Liz."

Interaction/Clarification: "I'm not sure what to make of these instances; could you help shed some light on what's going on?" (Listen to her response.)

Suggestions: "Margaret, I am committed to helping assist you in removing whatever's in the way of you performing at your peak. . . . Is there anything I can do to help?" (Wait for her suggestions. If none are forthcoming, offer some, such as additional training, time off.)

Clarify Expectations/Close/Next Steps: "Sounds like we have a good plan. So we're both on the same page, what changes should I expect to see over the next few weeks?" (Listen to her response.) "Let's plan on meeting again in three weeks . . . how about Friday the 19th at 2:00 p.m.?"

- *Examine your motives.* Evaluate why you need to give feedback and the outcome you hope to achieve by doing so. Getting something "off your chest" is not a sufficient reason. Assess potential barriers or obstacles, the strength of your relationship with the intended recipient, competitive pressures that might impact the situation, the perceived imbalance of power, and the credibility you both possess in the organization. This assessment can bring to the surface problems that could arise when giving (or receiving) feedback. Understanding your reasons and the factors affecting the potential feedback session aids in developing a successful strategy for giving feedback.[50]

- *Ask for input.* Get the employee's or team member's opinion about and perspective on the situation. This enables others to examine their own perspectives and allows you to determine whether a situation is completely understood. It also paves the way for getting the other person's ideas on how to proceed, making him or her feel part of the process and the organization instead of isolated or victimized by it. By ensuring two-way communication, both parties confirm data and perceptions, assuring that the dialogue meets expectations on both sides.[51]

- *Offer help, support, and suggestions.* If appropriate, offer to be of assistance by meeting with the employee periodically to check progress or by recommending internal or external resources that might be available (e.g., an employee assistance program). Be supportive of the employee as a person. Make it clear it is only his or her behavior that is of concern to you. Explain the impact of desired results—how the requested change will benefit the employee as well as others. Emphasize joint problem solving. This reduces the other party's defensiveness and resistance to your suggestions.

- *Clarify expectations and specify next steps.* Ask the employee for feedback on your feedback. Have you made your expectations clear? Have you provided adequate resources or information? Once the situation and options for improvement are understood, it's time to discuss suitable next steps and a plan to follow up. As a manager, you demonstrate the seriousness of the situation and signal your commitment to the requested change by asking the employee to meet with you, call, or send you a progress memo on a regular basis. Use goal setting (as discussed in Chapter 3) to set up specific actions to ensure that positive change occurs after the feedback session. Incorporate the steps described in the goal statements and objectives as a guideline for future plans of action.

Constructive feedback can have positive results if handled and presented properly. Start the session positively, discuss what needs to change, and involve the employee in developing action steps he or she can focus on and work toward for development. This ensures ending the feedback session on a positive note.[52]

© 2010 Ted Goff www.tedgoff.com

"It's very nice of you to want to see me. I hope you're going to tell me how great I am and that you're giving me a raise."

Source: © 2010 Ted Goff, www.tedgoff.com. Reprinted with permission.

Tips for Receiving Feedback

When **receiving constructive feedback**, it is important to demonstrate an openness to hearing the information and benefiting from it. Try to understand the speaker's point of view—even if you don't agree with his or her observations—rather than argue your views. While it may feel a bit uncomfortable having the attention focused on you and your behavior, try to be objective and not take things personally. Check your body language. Even if you don't think you feel defensive, crossing your arms over your chest and interrupting may communicate otherwise. Listen carefully, and if something is unclear, ask for specific examples that support the speaker's feedback. Finally, summarize key points to demonstrate that you've understood the feedback.[53] If the person giving you feedback is well trained, she'll deliver the information fairly and effectively. If the person lacks this training, there are a few steps you can take to ensure things go well.

- *Keep an ongoing performance folder.* Keep letters or e-mails that commend your performance in the folder. If a problem surfaces, keep careful documentation of whom you talk to and what is said. Keep a running list of projects in which you've been involved, noting your contributions to each. This is a good idea even if you don't receive constructive feedback. But if you do, this record might provide you with information that can be useful when asked to share your perspective on the situation.

- *Evaluate your own progress on a regular basis.* Whenever assigned to a new project, task force, or work group, make it a habit to request feedback early on and throughout the project. This makes it easier for co-workers and teammates to approach you with concerns if any surface and often prevents a formal feedback session from being necessary.

- *Let someone know if a change in your personal circumstances is affecting your work.* We are often reluctant to bring personal problems to work or school. Yet if something serious is happening and is affecting the quality of our work, it's better to talk with someone before the problem gets out of hand. This way, co-workers can manage their expectations about and make allowances for what is hopefully a temporary downturn in your performance.

Asking for Feedback

As we have discussed, it is important for employees and team members to receive feedback. This inspires us to improve, grow, and develop both as people and as professionals.[54] However, many teammates, managers, and organizations are reluctant or fail to provide feedback. Feedback is a two-way process. If feedback is not forthcoming, it is up to you to request it. Questions such as, "How am I doing?" "How can I improve?" and "Can we debrief—what worked and what didn't?" demonstrate your willingness to receive feedback and might also provide you the opportunity to give feedback. As a manager, you must show that you value feedback and input from all who are affected by your performance. As renowned management author and consultant Peter Drucker said, "The leader of the past was a person who knew how to tell. The leader of the future will be the person who knows how to ask." Studies show that managers who requested feedback, analyzed it, and made action plans based on the information were perceived to be more effective than those who didn't.[55]

Often a manager will be relieved when you bring up the need for feedback. He or she might have been too busy, or perhaps was avoiding the situation because of the fears mentioned earlier. Whatever the reason, there are times when you might need to empower yourself by requesting a feedback session. Below are a few suggestions to ensure things go smoothly:

- Demonstrate you're open to continual change and learning.
- Learn why you're not getting the feedback. Do most employees in the organization not get feedback, or are you the only one? By understanding why feedback has been absent, you will be better able to devise a plan for requesting and receiving feedback more regularly.
- Assess why you want feedback before you request it. Make sure you're not overly dependent on someone else's view of you. According to Deborah Tannen, some women tend to seek more feedback than men, on a continual basis, and see it as more important.[56]
- Regular feedback is useful. Requesting it too frequently is not, as it may send a message that you lack confidence in your abilities.
- Ask for suggestions on how you can improve. End any feedback session with a question about ways in which you can improve. This assures the giver of the feedback that you are listening and taking the feedback seriously. Restate or clarify their suggestions to show the giver that you understand and are committed to making the needed changes.

Summary

Coaching is an effective way to facilitate personal and organizational performance improvement and success. By providing feedback and support, coaches let individuals and groups know how they're doing so they can determine whether to modify current strategies, actions, and behaviors. Simply put, if it's not working, then why do it? Despite the benefits of coaching and giving feedback, many lack the skill and confidence to do so effectively. By following the tips and techniques for effectively providing, accepting, and asking for feedback, you will improve your performance and that of your co-workers, teammates, and subordinates.

Key Terms and Concepts

Asking for feedback	Giving feedback
Coaching	Initiating behaviors
Counseling	Nondirective approach
Descriptive	Nonprescriptive
Directive methods	Receiving constructive feedback
Documentable	Supportive behaviors
Feedback	

Discussion Questions

1. Why is coaching and providing feedback so important in the current environment?

2. You have just been promoted to supervisor of bank teller operations. Recently, your bank has been trying to become more product focused; in other words, instead of just performing transactions, the tellers have been asked to inform customers about various loan "products" in the hope of increasing the more profitable products and services of the bank's business. Transaction fees don't pay the bills like they used to. How would you go about your new role, taking into account elements of coaching and providing feedback?

3. Discuss the meaning of the quote, "Many receive advice; only the wise profit from it."

4. We generally think of feedback as coming from another person. However, there are at least two other sources. What are they and how do they work?

5. Discuss the effectiveness of this performance feedback: "Mary, your work is outstanding! Keep it up and you may get that promotion sooner than you think!"

Endnotes

1. Ron Zemke, *Coaching Knock Your Socks Off Service* (Amacom: New York, 1997).

2. Victoria DeVaux, "Coaching Benefits: From Winning the Race to Winning in the Office," *Training and Development* 64, no. 1 (January 2010), p. 20.

3. Gary S. Bielous, "Effective Coaching: Improving Marginal Performers," *Supervision* (July 1998), p. 15.

4. Corporate Coach University International, www.ccui.com (accessed May 2000).

5. Ray B. Williams, "Why Every CEO Needs a Coach," *Psychology Today* (August 13, 2012), http://www.psychologytoday.com/blog/wired-success/201208/why-every-ceo-needs-coach.

6. Peter Heslin, Don VanderWalle, and Gary Latham, "Keen to Help? Managers' Implicit Person Theories and Their Subsequent Employee Coaching," *Personnel Psychology* 59 (2006), pp. 871–902.

7. Bruce Hodes, "A New Foundation in Business Culture: Managerial Coaching," *Industrial Management* (September–October 1992), p. 27.

8. Ibid.

9. Clinton Longenecker and Gary Pinkel, "Coaching to Win at Work," *Manage* (February 1997), p. 20.

10. Corporate Coach University International.

11. Robert W. Lucas, "Effective Feedback Skills for Trainers and Coaches," *HR Focus* (July 1994), p. 7.

12. DeVaux, "Coaching Benefits," p. 20, quoting results of International Coach Federation Global Coaching Survey from 2007.

13. Vanessa Druskat and Jane Wheeler, "Managing from the Boundary: The Effective Leadership of Self-Managing Teams," *Academy of Management Journal* 46, no. 4 (August 2003), p. 452.

14. K. T. Dirks and D. L. Ferrin, "Trust in Leadership: Meta-analytic Findings and Implications for Organizational Research," *Journal of Applied Psychology* 87 (2002), pp. 611–28.

15. Corporate Coach University International.

16. Katherine Ely et al., "Evaluating Leadership Coaching: A Review and Integrated Framework," *The Leadership Quarterly* 21 (2010), pp. 585–99.

17. Steven J. Stowell, "Coaching: A Commitment to Leadership," *Training & Development Journal* (June 1988), pp. 34–38.

18. Ibid.

19. Ibid.

20. Corporate Coach University International.

21. Longenecker and Pinkel, "Coaching to Win," p. 21.

22. Stowell, "Coaching," p. 36.

23. Ibid.

24. Alan Vengel, "20-Minute Leadership," *Leadership Excellence* 27, no. 6 (June 2010), p. 13.

25. Ely et al., "Evaluating Leadership Coaching."

26. Anthony Grant, "Coach or Couch?" *Harvard Business Review Research Report* (January 2009), p. 97, retrieved from hbr.org.

27. Gary P. Latham and Edwin A. Locke, "Goal Setting—A Motivational Technique That Works," *Organizational Dynamics* (Autumn 1979), pp. 68–80.

28. Shawn K. Yearta, Sally Maitlis, and Rob B. Briner, "An Exploratory Study of Goal Setting Theory and Practice: A Motivational Technique That Works?" *Journal of Occupational and Organizational Psychology* (September 1995), p. 237.

29. Jeffrey Russell and Linda Russell, "Talk Me Through It: The Next Level of Performance Management," *Training and Development* 64, no. 4 (April 2010), p. 45.

30. R. H. Axelrod, *Terms of Engagement: Changing the Way We Change Organizations* (San Francisco: Berrett-Koehler, 2000).

31. M. Erez and F. H. Kanfer, "The Role of Goal Acceptance in Goal Setting and Task Performance," *Academy of Management Review* (1983), pp. 45–46.

32. Yearta et al., "An Exploratory Study," p. 237.

33. P. Alex Linely et al., "Using Signature Strengths in Pursuit of Goals: Effects on Goal Progress, Need Satisfaction, and Well-Being, Implications for Coaching Psychologists," *International Coaching Psychology Review* 5, no. 1 (March 2010), pp. 6–15.

34. A. R. Cohen, S. L. Fink, H. Gadon, and R. D. Willits, *Effective Behavior in Organizations,* 5th ed. (Boston, MA: Irwin, 1992), p. 295.

35. C. R. Zemke Bell, "On-Target Feedback," *Training* (June 1992), p. 36.

36. Rob Goffee and Gareth Jones, "Individual and Collective Leadership in the Boardroom: Why Feedback Is Vital Even at the Top," *Ivey Business Journal Online* (September–October 2005), p. 1.

37. S. D. Carr, E. D. Herman, S. Z. Keldsen, J. G. Miller, and P. A. Wakefield, *The Team Learning Assistant Handbook* (New York: McGraw-Hill, 2005).

38. J. Luft, *Group Processes* (Palo Alto, CA: National Press Books, 1970).

39. Cohen et al., *Effective Behavior,* p. 295.

40. Angelo Kinicki and Robert Kreitner, *Organizational Behavior: Key Concepts, Skills and Best Practices* (Boston, MA: Irwin/McGraw-Hill, 2003), p. 159.

41. Harriet V. Lawrence and Albert K. Wiswell, "Feedback Is a Two-Way Street," *Training and Development* (July 1995), p. 49.

42. Carr et al., *Team Learning Assistant,* p. 45.

43. Cohen et al., *Effective Behavior,* p. 295.

44. Robert W. Lucas, "Effective Feedback Skills for Trainers and Coaches," *HR Focus* (July 1994), p. 7.

45. Deborah Tannen, "The Power of Talk: Who Gets Heard and Why," *Harvard Business Review* (September/October 1995), pp. 138–48.

46. J. Jackman and M. Strober, "Fear of Feedback," *Harvard Business Review* (April 2003), pp. 101–106.

47. L. Andersson and C. Pearson, "Tit for Tat? The Spiraling Effect of Incivility in the Workplace," *Academy of Management Review* 24, no. 3 (1999), pp. 452–71.

48. Richard Nemec, "Getting Feedback," *Communication World* (March 1997), p. 32.

49. Bill Yeargin, "If You Criticize, Make It Constructive," *Boating Industry* (October 1997), p. 24.

50. Lawrence and Wiswell, "Feedback."

51. Ibid.

52. Crain Communications, "Tips for Providing Feedback to Employees," *Investment News* (November 23, 1999), p. 34.

53. Carr et al., *Team Learning Assistant,* p. 46.

54. Richard Koonce, "Are You Getting the Feedback You Deserve?" *Training and Development* (July 1998), p. 18.

55. Dick Sethi and Beverly Pinzon, "The Impact of Direct Report Feedback and Follow-Up on Leadership Effectiveness," *Human Resource Planning* (December 1998), pp. 14–16.

56. Koonce, "Are You Getting the Feedback," p. 18.

**Exercise 17–A
Coaching Clinic**

Think of a coach you have had in the past—from sports, school, clubs, or work. Draw upon your experiences with this coach to answer the following questions.

What about their coaching style made them effective (characteristics, behaviors, attitudes)?

_____

_____

_____

_____

_____

What about their coaching style made them less than effective? _____

_____

_____

_____

From your observations, and using the grid that follows, make a list of characteristics that you believe are necessary for effective coaching. Compare and supplement your list with characteristics provided in the chapter. Next, evaluate yourself as to your level of competency with the skill, trait, or characteristic. Then determine an action plan on how you can improve this characteristic, trait, or behavior.

Necessary Characteristic	Your Level of Competency (Low, Medium, High)	Action Plan for Improvement
1.		
2.		
3.		
4.		
5.		
6.		
7.		
8.		
9.		
10.		

Exercise 17–B
I Need a Coach

In groups of three you will conduct a coaching session. One person will serve as the observer, one as the coach, and the third will be coached with regard to an ability issue.

1. One participant is to explain a trait, skill, or ability (for example, patience in dealing with a co-worker, effectively presenting a new idea in a team meeting, creating a good first impression, conducting research) in which they would like to become more proficient.

2. The coach is to devise a coaching session using the template in Figure 17–4 and use various coaching techniques to help the other person.

3. The observer should note characteristics of the coach and techniques used to help the other person. Discuss with the pair tactics used, what might have been effective, and what areas need to be improved upon. This is an opportunity for all members to give feedback.

Observation

1. What coaching techniques were utilized? _____

_____

_____

_____

2. In what ways were they effective? _____

_____

_____

_____

3. In what ways could the coaching have been improved? _____

_____

_____

_____

As a trio, discuss the aspects of coaching or of being coached that were most difficult and why.

Exercise 17–C
Coach Me Through It

In pairs, you will either coach or be coached by your partner to complete a task. Instructions will be provided by your instructor. You will be limited by a time period and will have two attempts to complete the task. When you have completed the attempts, discuss the following questions:

1. What was the most helpful part of being coached? What was the most frustrating aspect?

_____

_____

_____

_____

2. What actions did the coach take to help the other accomplish the task?

_____

_____

_____

_____

3. What were the results from the first attempt? The second attempt?

_____

_____

_____

_____

4. What about the coach's tactics helped or hindered the success of the task?

_____

_____

_____

_____

5. From the activity, what have you learned about being an effective coach?

_____

_____

_____

_____

**Exercise 17–D
Helping Others Set
Goals—Modeling
Exercise**

In groups of three or four, you will be role-playing the following scenarios. For each role-play, there will be two participants and at least one observer. After each role-play, the observer should provide feedback and lead the group in a discussion based on the following questions.

Observer Questions

1. What techniques were used in helping others set goals? Which ones were effective and why? Which ones were ineffective and why?

2. What could have been done differently? What impact would that have had on the outcome?

3. Evaluate the goals that were set. Are they SMART goals? How can they be improved upon?

4. How will completion be ensured? What type of control or check-up system has been put in place?

5. In what ways have the goals been tied to rewards? How clear is the goal measurement system?

Scenario One

The roles include:

Mother and/or father (Mom and Dad)

College-level son or daughter (Terry)

A silent observer

Using the following scenario, help Terry set SMART goals:
   Terry is about to leave for his/her sophomore year at college, where he/she is hoping to major in marketing in the College of Business. By the end of this semester, Terry has to apply to the college, but is concerned that his/her GPA may not be high enough. Mom and Dad have talked with each other and have concluded that Terry was unfocused in virtually every area of life during his/her freshman year. They would like to help Terry to become more serious about his/her performance and bring up his/her grades. So, before Terry leaves for college, they want to talk with Terry and get him/her to set some goals for sophomore year.

Scenario Two

The roles include:

Jamie Harper—the supervisor

Pat Phillips—the subordinate

A silent observer

Using the following scenario, help Pat set SMART goals:

Pat is a researcher for a marketing firm and is assigned to do background research on various projects. At any given time, Pat may be assigned as many as three projects.

Jamie is having a feedback session (in Jamie's office) with Pat regarding his/her inability to meet project deadlines. In the past six months, Pat has met only one of eight deadlines. Pat is consistently two to three days behind schedule, and works extra hours (in a panic) just before every deadline. Pat always seems to be busy and very disorganized; he/she is frequently taking on side projects from various people in the organization who need a little extra help or favor. Jamie would like to help Pat set some goals to help him/her start creating and achieving realistic deadlines and work schedules.

Exercise 17–E
Giving Positive Feedback

Positive feedback is as important as constructive feedback. This activity provides an opportunity for you and your teammates to give and receive positive feedback.

1. Working first on your own, on small pieces of paper or index cards write one team member's name on each card. On the other side, write a positive statement about the team member.

2. Working in teams or small groups, each team member takes a turn sharing his or her positive feedback with the other team members, handing the person the card on which they've written the positive statement. Repeat the process until all feedback is shared and all cards have been received.

3. As a group, discuss the feedback. What surprised you? What did you learn about yourself? What are some things you heard about others that you'd like to improve? What are some qualities you would like the team to improve?

4. As a group, summarize the feedback without revealing names. Elect a scribe to record a list of the positive qualities most mentioned, and a list of things team members have said they'd like to work on as a group.

5. Each group reports their findings to the large group.

6. Discuss the qualities that make for effective team leadership and how one can improve these qualities.

Exercise 17--F
Peer Feedback

In this activity, you will use feedback forms (pages that follow) to provide feedback to each of your teammates.

1. Complete a "peer feedback sheet" on each team member. On the back of the sheet, offer examples that back up the two most outstanding behaviors and the two most in need of improvement that have been identified in the checklist. Complete a feedback sheet for each member of the team, including yourself.

2. Divide into working teams.

3. The facilitator will explain the feedback session.

4. One person from the group needs to volunteer to receive feedback.

5. Each person, in turn, reads his/her feedback as written.

6. The person receiving the feedback must listen. She or he cannot defend, interrupt, or in any way devalue the feedback giver. If necessary, she or he can ask clarifying questions. Finally, the receiver must thank the feedback givers.

7. This process repeats until each person has taken a turn as feedback receiver.

8. Each person reflects on the feedback received, looks for commonality, and considers the next steps for improving team/leadership behavior.

9. Discuss the findings and determine ways you can work together to support each other in developing exemplary characteristics as a team.

Peer Feedback

To:
From:

Behavior	Outstanding	Satisfactory	Needs Improvement
1. Enthusiasm/attitude	_____	_____	_____
2. Motivation/willingness to work	_____	_____	_____
3. Responsibility/accountability	_____	_____	_____
4. Effort	_____	_____	_____
5. Completion/quality of assigned tasks	_____	_____	_____
6. Punctuality	_____	_____	_____
7. Ability to meet deadlines	_____	_____	_____
8. Dedication to team	_____	_____	_____
9. Attendance/participation	_____	_____	_____
10. Sharing of ideas and feedback	_____	_____	_____
11. Communication with team	_____	_____	_____
12. Creativity	_____	_____	_____
13. Accuracy	_____	_____	_____
14. Respect for others	_____	_____	_____
15. Flexibility	_____	_____	_____
16. Ability to get along with teammates	_____	_____	_____
17. Organization	_____	_____	_____
18. Ability to create group "synergy"	_____	_____	_____
19. Leadership	_____	_____	_____
20. Other (specify): _____	_____	_____	_____

Peer Feedback

To:
From:

Behavior	Outstanding	Satisfactory	Needs Improvement
1. Enthusiasm/attitude	_____	_____	_____
2. Motivation/willingness to work	_____	_____	_____
3. Responsibility/accountability	_____	_____	_____
4. Effort	_____	_____	_____
5. Completion/quality of assigned tasks	_____	_____	_____
6. Punctuality	_____	_____	_____
7. Ability to meet deadlines	_____	_____	_____
8. Dedication to team	_____	_____	_____
9. Attendance/participation	_____	_____	_____
10. Sharing of ideas and feedback	_____	_____	_____
11. Communication with team	_____	_____	_____
12. Creativity	_____	_____	_____
13. Accuracy	_____	_____	_____
14. Respect for others	_____	_____	_____
15. Flexibility	_____	_____	_____
16. Ability to get along with teammates	_____	_____	_____
17. Organization	_____	_____	_____
18. Ability to create group "synergy"	_____	_____	_____
19. Leadership	_____	_____	_____
20. Other (specify): _____	_____	_____	_____

Peer Feedback

To:
From:

Behavior	Outstanding	Satisfactory	Needs Improvement
1. Enthusiasm/attitude	_____	_____	_____
2. Motivation/willingness to work	_____	_____	_____
3. Responsibility/accountability	_____	_____	_____
4. Effort	_____	_____	_____
5. Completion/quality of assigned tasks	_____	_____	_____
6. Punctuality	_____	_____	_____
7. Ability to meet deadlines	_____	_____	_____
8. Dedication to team	_____	_____	_____
9. Attendance/participation	_____	_____	_____
10. Sharing of ideas and feedback	_____	_____	_____
11. Communication with team	_____	_____	_____
12. Creativity	_____	_____	_____
13. Accuracy	_____	_____	_____
14. Respect for others	_____	_____	_____
15. Flexibility	_____	_____	_____
16. Ability to get along with teammates	_____	_____	_____
17. Organization	_____	_____	_____
18. Ability to create group "synergy"	_____	_____	_____
19. Leadership	_____	_____	_____
20. Other (specify): _____	_____	_____	_____

Peer Feedback

To:
From:

Behavior	Outstanding	Satisfactory	Needs Improvement
1. Enthusiasm/attitude	_____	_____	_____
2. Motivation/willingness to work	_____	_____	_____
3. Responsibility/accountability	_____	_____	_____
4. Effort	_____	_____	_____
5. Completion/quality of assigned tasks	_____	_____	_____
6. Punctuality	_____	_____	_____
7. Ability to meet deadlines	_____	_____	_____
8. Dedication to team	_____	_____	_____
9. Attendance/participation	_____	_____	_____
10. Sharing of ideas and feedback	_____	_____	_____
11. Communication with team	_____	_____	_____
12. Creativity	_____	_____	_____
13. Accuracy	_____	_____	_____
14. Respect for others	_____	_____	_____
15. Flexibility	_____	_____	_____
16. Ability to get along with teammates	_____	_____	_____
17. Organization	_____	_____	_____
18. Ability to create group "synergy"	_____	_____	_____
19. Leadership	_____	_____	_____
20. Other (specify): _____	_____	_____	_____

Peer Feedback

To:
From:

Behavior	Outstanding	Satisfactory	Needs Improvement
1. Enthusiasm/attitude	_____	_____	_____
2. Motivation/willingness to work	_____	_____	_____
3. Responsibility/accountability	_____	_____	_____
4. Effort	_____	_____	_____
5. Completion/quality of assigned tasks	_____	_____	_____
6. Punctuality	_____	_____	_____
7. Ability to meet deadlines	_____	_____	_____
8. Dedication to team	_____	_____	_____
9. Attendance/participation	_____	_____	_____
10. Sharing of ideas and feedback	_____	_____	_____
11. Communication with team	_____	_____	_____
12. Creativity	_____	_____	_____
13. Accuracy	_____	_____	_____
14. Respect for others	_____	_____	_____
15. Flexibility	_____	_____	_____
16. Ability to get along with teammates	_____	_____	_____
17. Organization	_____	_____	_____
18. Ability to create group "synergy"	_____	_____	_____
19. Leadership	_____	_____	_____
20. Other (specify): _____	_____	_____	_____

Peer Feedback

To:
From:

Behavior	Outstanding	Satisfactory	Needs Improvement
1. Enthusiasm/attitude	_____	_____	_____
2. Motivation/willingness to work	_____	_____	_____
3. Responsibility/accountability	_____	_____	_____
4. Effort	_____	_____	_____
5. Completion/quality of assigned tasks	_____	_____	_____
6. Punctuality	_____	_____	_____
7. Ability to meet deadlines	_____	_____	_____
8. Dedication to team	_____	_____	_____
9. Attendance/participation	_____	_____	_____
10. Sharing of ideas and feedback	_____	_____	_____
11. Communication with team	_____	_____	_____
12. Creativity	_____	_____	_____
13. Accuracy	_____	_____	_____
14. Respect for others	_____	_____	_____
15. Flexibility	_____	_____	_____
16. Ability to get along with teammates	_____	_____	_____
17. Organization	_____	_____	_____
18. Ability to create group "synergy"	_____	_____	_____
19. Leadership	_____	_____	_____
20. Other (specify): _____	_____	_____	_____

**Exercise 17–G
Practicing Giving
Performance Feedback**

In your triad or small group, you'll participate in a performance feedback session. Person A is the listener—the one who's receiving the feedback. Person B is the talker—the one who's giving the feedback. Person C is the observer/recorder—the one who observes and comments on the interaction between Persons A and B.

1. Choose a scenario from the list below. Person B prepares a script using the outline in Figure 17–9 as a guide.
2. Person B gives feedback to Person A. Person A practices the tips for accepting feedback given in the book. Person B practices the tips for giving feedback given in the book. Person C observes the interaction and evaluates Persons A and B using the feedback observation sheets below.

Observation Sheet: Listener

1. _____ The Listener asked the Talker to cite specific examples of the behavior being discussed.
2. _____ The Listener asked clarifying questions and paraphrased the Talker.
3. _____ The Listener actively listened—asked probing questions of the Talker.
4. _____ The Listener appeared nondefensive and open to improvement suggestions.
5. Other examples of effective feedback behaviors of the Listener (specify):

Observation Sheet: Talker

1. _____ The Talker offered balanced feedback (positive feedback followed by constructive feedback and suggestions for improvement).
2. _____ The Talker was not judgmental or evaluative.
3. _____ The Talker focused on specific behavior.
4. _____ The Talker asked the Listener for input and suggestions.
5. Other examples of effective feedback behaviors of the Talker (specify):

Feedback Role-Play Scenarios

1. A roommate conflict (e.g., due to messiness, playing loud music, not paying their bills).
2. A performance review for a peer (e.g., feedback on lack of presentation skills, feedback on poor interviewing skills, feedback on inability to remain calm in a conflict or negotiation).
3. A subperforming employee (e.g., due to lateness, frequent absences, distracted by nonwork issues). Another option is to use the example in Figure 17–10.
4. A serious employee offense (e.g., concerns about possible theft, potential sexual harassment, potential discrimination).

Questions

1. What was the hardest thing you faced in developing this script?
2. Can you see this script working in real life? Why or why not?
3. What about the script makes it easier to give appropriate feedback?
4. How does the Talker's preparation affect the ultimate goal of improving performance?
5. What would you do if the Listener gets defensive or argumentative?
6. Was there satisfactory closure at the end of the session? Explain.

Exercise 17–H
Giving Self-feedback

1. Working on your own, complete the self-feedback worksheet below. The sheet concerns your involvement in project teams. (Alternatively, you can conduct a self-evaluation of your own performance as an employee, student, or roommate, focusing on two questions: What do you do well? In what areas can you improve?)

2. At the bottom of the worksheet, describe your positive team qualities and areas you'd like to improve. Give specific details on how you intend to make changes.

3. Share the results with a partner.

4. Discuss the activity with the large group using the questions below:

   ■ In what areas are you stronger? Weaker?

   ■ What can you do to improve in those areas?

   ■ What suggestions do you have for others who wish to improve?

   ■ In what ways have these behaviors helped keep previous teams on track?

   ■ Discuss a situation where the lack of these qualities hindered a team from being effective.

   ■ What did you learn about yourself as a team member from this exercise?

Self-feedback Worksheet

In team projects:

1. _____ I participate willingly.
2. _____ I stay with the task assigned.
3. _____ I start by clarifying the assignment with the group.
4. _____ I try to encourage the group to get back on track when needed.
5. _____ I use the experience as a potential learning activity.
6. _____ I try consciously to be aware of my own behavior style and the styles of others.
7. _____ I try to engage in active listening.
8. _____ I try to provide positive feedback to group members.
9. _____ I help the group keep track of time.
10. _____ I help the group summarize results and action items.
11. _____ I volunteer to record for the group.
12. _____ I raise concerns openly rather than ignore or avoid them.
13. _____ I volunteer to be a group spokesperson.
14. _____ Other (specify):

Things I do well:

_____

_____

_____

_____

Ways I can improve:

_____

_____

_____

_____

**Exercise 17–I
Reflection/Action Plan**

This chapter focused on coaching and feedback—what they are, why they're important, and how to improve your skills in these areas. Complete the worksheet below upon completing all reading and experiential activities for this chapter.

1. The one or two areas in which I am most strong are:

_____

_____

_____

_____

2. The one or two areas in which I need more improvement are:

_____

_____

_____

_____

3. If I did only one thing to improve in this area, it would be to:

_____

_____

_____

_____

4. Making this change would probably result in:

_____

_____

_____

_____

5. If I did not change or improve in this area, it would probably affect my personal and professional life in the following ways:

_____

_____

_____

_____

18 Leading and Empowering Self and Others

Learning Points

How do I:

- Identify the skills and characteristics of effective leaders and develop these skills to increase my ability to lead?
- Provide leadership to others, even when I'm not an official leader?
- Allow employees to take responsibility for their work, as opposed to controlling their every move?
- Reduce any fears I have about mistakes made by my empowered subordinates?
- Empower myself when an organization or manager does not empower me?
- Motivate others to take risks and do what they think is best?
- Give the responsibility of doing a task to another while ensuring the quality of the work?

Brian finally got his coveted day off to spend on the golf course with his wife, Sharon. He couldn't have asked for a more perfect day—great weather, early tee time, and his putting was perfect. Then came the dreaded call from Brian's work. "Now what?" asked Sharon. "Production was just informed that our base material is back-ordered and will not be available for at least two weeks, so the office wanted to know if they should order from our backup supplier," Brian stated. "Why do they always have to call me? They have seen me handle this same situation multiple times. They know we need the material by Friday, and they know the number is on my speed dial. I can't have one day where my staff handles problems on their own. It drives me crazy." To that Sharon replied, "Perhaps the problem is not with your staff; perhaps it is with you. Have you ever asked yourself why they don't make decisions on their own?"

Now what did she mean by that? But before he could ask for clarification, Sharon was already walking down the fairway. Brian was a hard-working and efficient manager. He made sure all details were taken care of and tried to solve issues or problems to eliminate excess stress on his staff. He treated them with respect and provided positive feedback to constantly encourage his team. Then why could they not make decisions on their own?

Did they not have the resources or knowledge to make the decisions, or did they lack the confidence or the authority to make decisions? If either of those options were true, what did it say about his ability to lead?

1. What factors contribute to Brian's staff's inability to make decisions?

2. What aspects of Brian's leadership are ineffective?

3. What does empowerment have to do with this situation?

4. How can Brian change his approach to leadership to empower his staff?

5. What actions can the office staff take to empower themselves and be more effective in their operations?

"Leadership is as delicate as Mozart's melodies. The music exists and it doesn't. It is written on the page, but it means nothing until performed and heard. Much of its effect depends on the performer and the listener. The best leaders, like the best music, inspire us to see new possibilities."[1]

M. Kur

If you were asked to think of someone who has made a positive impact on society, who would that be? Martin Luther King Jr.? Thomas Jefferson? Gandhi? Nelson Mandela? Barack Obama? Bill Gates? Most likely, the person you thought of would be considered a leader. But what exactly is leadership, and why is it important?

Throughout history, civilizations have focused on their leaders.[2] Whether elected or appointed, the kings, queens, chiefs, and presidents of their nations are entrusted with decisions that affect everyone they serve. Leading armies, creating new nations (and destroying existing ones), and defining what is and isn't acceptable are among the many responsibilities of leaders.

Leaders of organizations face similar challenges. While they need not bring their troops to the battleground, organizational leaders must understand the environment in which they operate, establish goals and objectives, and motivate their employees to achieve excellence to "battle" in the global marketplace. Moreover, these leaders must lead the "troops" in a way that enables them not only to do necessary tasks, but also to participate in day-to-day decisions that affect them. Employees expect to play a more meaningful role in the business of the organization than in the past, rendering the command and control approach to leadership useless. We begin this chapter by discussing leadership, what it is, why it's important, and how to develop self-leadership even if you don't hold an official title. Next, we examine empowerment and delegation—two tools that leaders can use to keep themselves and their colleagues motivated and involved in their work. We also look at the benefits, challenges, and strategies of implementing these tools in organizations.

What Is Leadership?

"Great leaders often inspire their followers to high levels of achievement by showing them how their work contributes to worthwhile ends."

Warren Bennis and Burt Nanus,
Leaders

As a field of study, leadership has been around for centuries. We have been intrigued by the magical, elusive power of certain individuals to move nations of people, inspire others to follow their lead, or bring about complex social change. We are intrigued by those that have been able to move others to action whether as an energizing leader such as Jack Welch of GE, as an innovative and inspirational leader such as Konosuke Matsuhita, founder of Panasonic, or as an entrepreneurial leader such as Steve Jobs of Apple. Scholars have offered numerous theories about what leadership is and what makes individuals successful in leadership roles. As it would be almost impossible to offer a single definition of leadership, we present a compilation. **Leadership** is:

■ A process of social influence to move individuals and groups toward goal achievement.[3]

■ Sharing a vision and engaging followers in that vision.[4]

■ The ability to move an organization to a higher level of performance by transforming vision into significant actions.

■ A relationship, as opposed to the property of an individual.[5] Leadership exists only where followers exist, and its effectiveness varies in direct relation to the level of trust present in the relationship.[6] Similarly, while some individuals may be more or less trusting than others, trust exists (and evolves) in relationships.[7]

■ An observable, learnable set of practices and skills—many of which fall into the interpersonal arena.[8] Anyone who wants to lead can significantly improve his or her ability to do so through training, practice, and feedback.[9]

■ An integration of theory, process, and practice, and the realization that what is effective in one situation may be ineffective in another.[10]

■ Effective leadership requires the ability to size up the situation (and people involved), compare it against prior experiences and practices, and develop an approach that would fit but remain flexible enough to adjust as the situation requires.[11] Effective leaders also take the time to reflect on their actions and behaviors to objectively assess what worked and what didn't. In short, effective leaders are continuous learners.

Characteristics of Effective Leaders

Each of us has the ability to become a great leader. Even some who came from humble beginnings, like Abraham Lincoln and Barack Obama, have risen to positions of leadership and influenced many people and nations. You might be thinking, "But I'm only a student," or "What can a single mom do?" or "I'm not that smart." Great leaders do not fit a singular mold. They are women and men, young and old, able-bodied and physically challenged, and come from all nations and socioeconomic backgrounds. What does it take to be a great leader? Effective leaders are characterized (see Figure 18–1) by their ability to:[12]

■ *Challenge the process.* Some of the most successful leaders bucked the system. They took risks, challenged convention, and ignored rules. For example, in 1955,

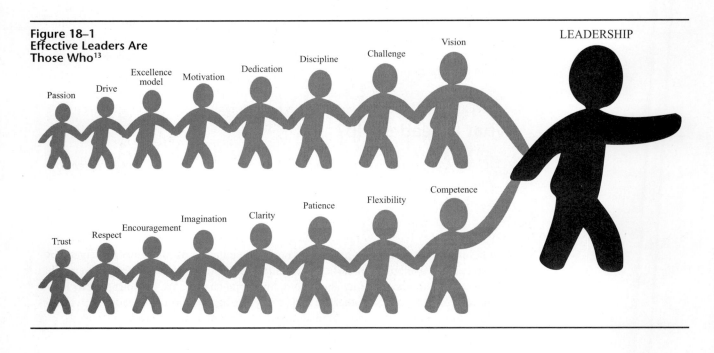

**Figure 18–1
Effective Leaders Are
Those Who**[13]

Passion Drive Excellence model Motivation Dedication Discipline Challenge Vision LEADERSHIP

Trust Respect Encouragement Imagination Clarity Patience Flexibility Competence

Rosa Parks broke the law by refusing to give up her seat to a white passenger while riding a bus in Montgomery, Alabama. She was jailed, but her spirit wasn't broken. Her strong belief in the rights of all humans, regardless of their skin color, coupled with her role as secretary of the local National Association for the Advancement of Colored People (NAACP), helped prompt a bus boycott that lasted nearly a year. Shortly thereafter, the Supreme Court struck down segregation laws.

- *Inspire a shared vision.* Rather than dictate direction, effective leaders appeal to group members' values, beliefs, and emotions, motivating them to align themselves with a mission that reflects the greater good. Leaders who passionately believe in their teams, products, or services exude enough fervor to "infect" others with this passion. In 1980, enraged over the death of her 13-year-old daughter at the hands of a repeat drunk-driving offender, Candy Lightner enlisted some friends and founded Mothers Against Drunk Driving—MADD. Through Lightner's inspiring vision and tireless efforts, MADD has grown to approximately 600 affiliates and 2 million members and supporters nationwide, has helped pass more than 2,300 laws against drunk driving and underage drinking, and is credited with saving more than 268,000 lives through research-based programs, policy initiatives, exemplary victim services, and public education.[14]

- *Enable others to act.* Effective leaders share information and power with their collaborators, empowering them to set and achieve cooperative goals. Employees need to know where they fit in the bigger picture and need to have the ability to make decisions in order to contribute in meaningful ways. By listening to and supporting all employees—regardless of their rank—leaders create an atmosphere of mutual trust and respect and enable others to perform to their potential.[15] These servant or coaching leaders are able to motivate and inspire their workforce even in the most troubling of times.

  Tom Green and Mary Miller were to manage the two-year closing process of one of Delphi's brake manufacturing plants, and the main concern was to limit the number of accidents during that time period. However, by following three basic principles—(1) Listen, don't talk, (2) ask, "What do employees need?" and (3) ask, "Do those served, grow?"—their leadership was not only able to have safety factors maximized with no time lost to accidents but also to have quality increased to an all-time high of 99.999 percent and costs reduced by over $160 million over the two-year period. By enabling others and supporting the employees, they were able to make the doomed facility a profitable center.[16]

- *Model the way.* A leader is "a part of, not apart from" the gfoup.[17] In other words, leaders' power exists not so much because of their role, but because it is granted them by those who follow. To be effective, leaders must "walk the talk" by exhibiting the behaviors they expect in others and ensuring consistency between their words and deeds. For example, leaders who expect their managers to empower subordinates must do the same by sharing power, accepting mistakes, and involving managers in decisions large and small. Similarly, leaders who expect persistence and dedication must not give up, even amid adversity. Linda Henman, president of Henman Performance Group, has created routines for her employees to give her direct feedback by rewarding and modeling open communication. "If executives want openness and transparency, they should start by being open and transparent in their own communication."[18]

  As Albert Schweitzer, noted theologian and Nobel Peace Prize winner, said, "Example is not the main thing in influencing others. It is the only thing." Everyone can think of a parent, teacher, peer, or coach who was able to influence others by leading through example. The late John Wooden, famed college basketball coach, has been deemed by many the greatest coach ever. His success as a coach and leader was based on his belief that he was a teacher—not just of basketball, but of life. He developed a Seven Point Creed,[19] which he believed was the key to success on and off the court. By following these principles based on Christianity and demonstrating his caring for others, his leadership modeled the way for many players and coaches. Moving to the business arena, when Procter & Gamble first premiered Bounce™ fabric softener sheets, many questioned whether the product would appeal to customers. The request for a patent was turned down until someone in the company championed it. Bounce™ became one of P&G's most successful brands.[20]

■ *Encourage the heart.*[21] Last but not least, leaders must find ways to reward individuals and groups that achieve success and progress toward common goals. Along the way, effective leaders provide coaching, feedback, and recognition to show others appreciation for their efforts. Leaders who focus on consideration through building relationships and trust in an open environment—who create a pleasant workplace and show concern for others' personal welfare, while still achieving organizational objectives—inspire high levels of respect.[22] Management at Metso Corporation of Finland, a global supplier of technology and services for mining and construction, believes leadership should drive results by building inspiration and trust. The company believes in developing and coaching employees by using a 360° feedback process that allows all employees to evaluate everyone they are associated with, including their peers and superiors.[23]

As you can see from these characteristics and examples, even those without a formal leadership position can lead others successfully. Perhaps you can recall a time when others hung on your every word, asked for your advice, or looked to you for direction. Or perhaps you were in a situation where someone should have taken the lead but didn't. In situations like these, you can bemoan the lack of direction or vision . . . or you can practice self-leadership.

"Leadership is not a rank. It is a responsibility."

Peter Drucker, leading
management consultant

Leaders versus Managers

The great 19th-century British prime minister Benjamin Disraeli said, "I must follow the people. Am I not their leader?" Although he was to some extent joking, his statement holds the true essence of leadership. Leadership is not limited to the person with the title or superior position in the situation, and the power of leadership is not merely designated by a formal power base. Leadership in organizations is about influencing the behavior of others, and superiors and subordinates alike can have a direct influence on motivating others to achieve organizational goals. Therefore, it is true that not all managers are leaders and not all leaders are managers. The terms *manager* and *leader* should not be used interchangeably. A clearer determination for the terms would denote that we manage things and lead people. Leaders move beyond the basic tasks of the day by creating a vision that sets higher standards to lift members' performance.

Leadership Through Actions[24]

It is true; sometimes actions speak louder than words. This was exemplified when Lenovo's CEO, Yang Yuanqing, distributed $3 million of his bonus to employees, including assistants, production line workers, and receptionists. As CEO, he would normally get about $5.2 million but since the personal computing and information technology company posted a 73 percent increase in net profit, he was provided the extra $3 million. He in turn wanted to show his appreciation to the rank-and-file employees for their hard work and dedication. And even though the $314 individual bonus does not seem like much by U.S. standards, to Chinese workers in the Shenzhen province who average $253 a month, this gesture is greatly appreciated. In times when firms and leaders are criticized for outlandish bonuses and compensation packages in comparison to no or only minimal wage increases for workers, this action will serve as a strong motivator for this leader's employees.

Self-leadership

Self-leadership is what happens when individuals act on their own to achieve the organization's mission, vision, purpose, values, and goals.[25] It occurs when you challenge yourself to muster the self-direction and self-motivation you need to perform a task or achieve a goal.[26] Imagine that you come up with an idea for a new product—one that would revolutionize the way individuals brush their teeth. You pitch the idea to your boss, but she gently dismisses the idea, noting that the dental hygiene market is already saturated with products manufactured by your and competing organizations. You work evenings and weekends perfecting the design, even doing a patent search to determine the patentability of your innovative design. You pitch the idea to your boss's boss, and while intrigued, he intimates that management would never commit the necessary resources to develop the product and bring it to market. Frustrated, you decide to discuss the idea with family and friends, searching for support—both emotional and financial. Your enthusiasm is contagious, and they agree that your new product idea has the potential to revolutionize dental hygiene and produce substantial revenues. You develop your business plan while simultaneously planning your eventual departure from your organization.

Sound like a fairy tale? Actually, this scenario approximates the path many successful entrepreneurs took in leaving relatively secure jobs with established organizations to pursue their passion. It's easy to see how important it is for organizations to support and reward this kind of self-leadership. By expanding their view of work control to reconfigure the important role of self-influence,[27] organizations and the individuals who practice self-leadership can reap significant benefits.

Self-leadership is important for several reasons. First and foremost, it helps create an ideal organization. Employees who practice self-leadership perform because they believe in and enjoy what they're doing, not because of threats.[28] Through this creation of meaning, the organization's goals become the employees' goals[29] and are sought with the same energy and conviction. While it may be easy to envision such a situation in a nonprofit organization such as MADD, Doctors Without Borders, Greenpeace, or UNICEF, for-profit organizations whose mission goes beyond raising shareholder value to include socially responsible actions[30]—including The Body Shop, Patagonia, and Ben & Jerry's—have been able to attract, motivate, and retain employees on the basis of such alignment.

In addition, employees who practice self-leadership are more productive because they have more control and decision-making power.[31] Returning to our opening story, had Brian's staff felt confident in making decisions on their own, they would have been able to take the necessary steps themselves, rather than waiting for approval from Brian. At the same time, they would prove they have the ability to handle even more responsibility in the future. Because of their ability to exert control over their environment, employees with self-leadership tend to be more satisfied with their jobs[32] and more committed (loyal) to their organizations.

"No man is fit to command another that cannot command himself."

William Penn

What Is Empowerment?

In simple terms, **empowerment** is the process by which a leader or manager shares his or her power with subordinates.[33] This definition provides a starting point for understanding empowerment, yet you might be asking yourself: Power to do what? In the traditional workplace, which was centered on manufacturing, all you needed was obedience to get work done.[34] Workers' tasks were preplanned and simplified; managers observed employees closely to ensure adherence to prescribed ways of completing tasks.

The current environment—characterized by increasing turbulence, complexity, speed, competition, and change—renders the old command-and-control system useless. Shortened product life cycles and constant focus on change create a need for the **knowledge worker.**[35] Knowledge workers are employees who need and use information to perform their work. This category can include everyone from product developers or producers, to programmers, to consultants, to clerks who deal with customers. Knowledge-focused companies recognize that people are their greatest assets and keep their workforces involved and informed.[36] The environment demands workers who are adaptable and self-managing, flexible and autonomous, and enabled and motivated to accomplish what they choose.

As companies focus more on team structures, require more flexibility, and become more decentralized, empowerment is essential in creating participative environments.

Why Is Empowerment Important?

One reason empowerment has been embraced lies in its ability to provide motivation. Managers realize that employee motivation facilitates the achievement of organizational goals. Many motivational theories incorporate the factor that individuals tend to be motivated toward the fulfillment of their needs. (See Figure 18–2.) Maslow's **hierarchy of needs theory**[37] proposes that people are intrinsically motivated in direct relationship to their needs, from the most basic lower-level needs (physiological, safety) progressing up the hierarchy to the social or higher-level needs (social, self-esteem, self-actualization). Modifying Maslow's theory, Clayton Alderfer tried to simplify the needs into three categories: existence, relatedness, and growth.[38] Even with the modifications of the earlier theory, it still shows that in addition to basic human needs, motivation will need to address higher-level or social needs as well. David McClelland proposed that we acquire needs over time and are motivated by actions that help us satisfy these need categories: Need for Power, Need for Achievement, or Need for Affiliation.[39] And while none of these needs theories are perfect or complete,[40] they help clarify why many workers are no longer simply motivated to just work; they want to be challenged, become satisfied with their accomplishments, and contribute to personal and organizational goals.[41] Therefore, leaders should address individuals' needs and, through the use of empowerment, intrinsically motivate employees toward increased ownership of job responsibilities.

Through empowerment, organizations are able to support the motivating potential inherent in satisfying higher-level needs. Managers facilitate employee motivation through empowerment and thus increase autonomy, respect, power to make decisions, status, and freedom to grow and develop within the organization. Thus, an empowered worker is a satisfied worker.[42]

Thanks to the ubiquity of technology and information, many of us have become quite proficient at identifying the best value when purchasing products and services. We can "name our own price" for anything from groceries to airline tickets. One might conclude that as a result, the need for good customer service has declined. In fact, it has increased. Once price and ease of obtaining a good or service no longer matters, how do successful firms differentiate themselves in the eyes of their customers? How do organizations build customer loyalty to current and future products and services? They do this through their human assets—their employees.

When employees feel aligned with an organization's mission and goals, supported to target appropriate outcomes, and rewarded when they and the organization achieve desired performance and outcomes, they do whatever it takes to produce a deliverable or satisfy a customer.[43] Contrast this philosophy with one in which employees are closely monitored, given information on a need-to-know basis, and rewarded randomly, if at all.

Figure 18–2
Needs Fulfillment

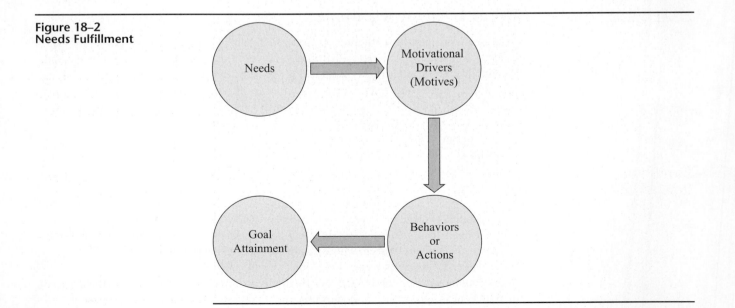

Figure 18–3
Empowerment Outputs

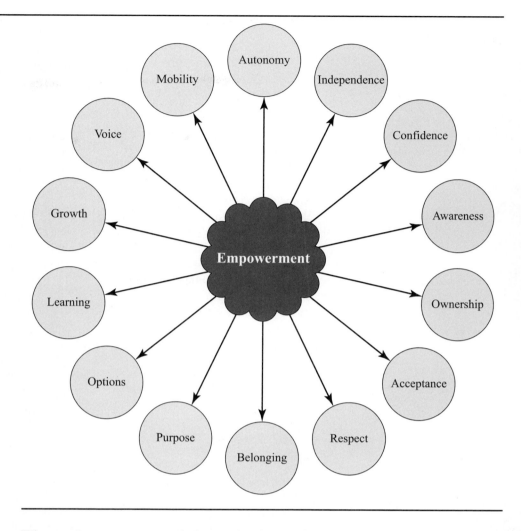

When workers are empowered, they are involved in decision making, asked to suggest new services and processes, and encouraged to solve problems creatively and effectively. In the opening scenario, Brian's staff is not empowered. They are not able to problem-solve or make decisions on even daily or recurring issues. Such decisions are better left to someone in charge, right? Wrong!

If the office staff had had the power to make decisions, a quicker solution would have emerged that would have been beneficial to the staff, to Brian (an uninterrupted day off), and, ultimately, to the organization. However, giving employees power may not be as easy as it seems. Many managers view sharing power and authority as risky and question the notion that empowerment is beneficial. We'll discuss why shortly. We'll also help you understand why today's leaders need to recognize that empowering their workforce is an opportunity, rather than a threat.[44] In addition, an organization that empowers its employees may be better suited to attract and retain its highly skilled and trained professionals, thus maintaining its competitive edge.

Benefits of Empowerment

Empowerment has numerous benefits (Figure 18–3). After reading the following list of benefits, you might wonder whether you or the organization for which you work can afford *not* to empower employees!

■ Empowerment reinforces member participation and growth, commitment to quality, and a more open, honest environment. This results in greater job satisfaction, motivation, and commitment—a sense of achievement.[45]

■ With empowerment, people have a greater sense of achievement, improved confidence and self-esteem, and a sense of belonging.[46] Mary Kay cosmetics exemplifies empowering its representatives. They are provided with support and training through conventions and educational materials, they are able to control their schedule and the amount of effort they wish to exert, and they receive recognition and rewards for their efforts. Because they are treated as owners of their businesses, Mary Kay employees feel confident and have a sense of belonging and control over their work. This empowerment helps release their energies toward even greater achievements.

■ Empowerment speeds up reaction time and decision making and provides speed and flexibility, allowing quicker response to customers. Empowered employees who deal directly with customers will be able to better meet their needs and demands, leading to more satisfied customers.[47] Imagine you are boarding a plane when you realize you have been ticketed for a seat that is already "rightfully" occupied. Some airlines would have you deplane and wait until all passengers are seated and then consult a supervisor about fixing the problem. In an empowered airline organization, the agent, who is likely part owner of the airline, immediately takes the problem into his or her hands and finds a solution. Perhaps you are bumped to first class, or perhaps you are given another option or compensation. Either way, the problem is solved quickly without management intervention, and the customer is satisfied. Empowerment is often cited as a key reason for the phenomenal success of Herb Kelleher's Southwest Airlines.

■ Empowered employees are more likely to offer ideas, exercise creativity, and develop more innovative processes and products than those who are not.[48] In an empowered organization, employees are encouraged to take risks and are not afraid of failure. They look for opportunities to improve products, processes, and services that seem to work well, in addition to reacting to problems that need immediate attention. Because they have the authority to act in the best interests of their work unit and organization, empowered individuals positively affect their environment through proactive behaviors.[49]

An example of an empowering organization is 3M. When a scientist there created the failed glue that eventually became the key ingredient in Post-it Notes, he was not "punished" by his management. Instead, he was encouraged to see if he could come up with a use for his "failure." Wouldn't you want to get a percentage of Post-it Notes' revenues?

■ With empowerment, employees are more responsible, which leads to greater loyalty, trust, and quality.[50] By transferring power and authority to employees, they become accountable and responsible for their decisions and actions. Since they solve their own problems and find their own solutions, empowered employees will be more committed to a quality outcome and to stay long enough to see the fruits of their labor. This kind of loyalty is invaluable to an organization's ability to attract and retain talented personnel.

■ Empowerment reduces operational costs by eliminating unnecessary layers of management, staff, quality control, and checking operations.[51] This was the premise behind Toyota setting up their now highly implemented kanban system in the 1950s, which allowed employees to set production levels to meet real-time demand based on visual signals from the production floor. The traditional hierarchical design assumes that employees cannot be trusted to make sound organizational decisions. Each successive layer of management has a role in ensuring that employees representing the previous layer follow the stated rules and procedures and, if not, that they are corrected by their management. For example, at one large aerospace company, the process of ordering a $2 package of pencils could cost as much as $75 when accounting for the seven layers of management and approval all orders had to go through before being placed. However, by defining parameters, the ordering process was streamlined to allow a single individual to order products within certain reasonable limits, without the need for management consent. In terms of quality control, empowered workers take responsibility and receive rewards for the quality of their product and are therefore committed to producing products and services of the highest quality possible. In many empowered organizations, employees not only take responsibility for their operations, but they also engage in activities designed to streamline and improve processes—building in quality from the start. This eliminates the need for surveillance or inspection by a "Big Brother" or quality assurance engineer.

■ Empowerment reduces turnover and aids in retention. In 2000, when the economy was booming, employee turnover was near a 20-year high. Schellenbarger reports that due to the costs of replacing an employee—about 1.5 times a year's pay—companies are pouring millions of dollars into efforts designed to increase employee loyalty.[52] By management tending to such issues as fair pay, involvement in decision making, and trust in leadership—all elements associated with an empowered workforce—employees remain more committed and loyal to organizations.

Whole Foods—Innovation Through Empowerment[53]

Whole Foods' co-CEO Walter Robb believes the company maintains its competitive edge through management's relationship with the employees. The secret to their success is the strong culture of empowerment by supporting and encouraging the creativity and intelligence of every team member (employee). Believing in the employees gets you innovation; as Robb states, "it is the living breath and heart of the company; that's where the humanity happens." He believes you need to address the basic human need to belong, so they give the employees something larger than themselves to be a part of. One example is the gain-sharing program that every employee participates in to save money by improving efficiency or by creating sales. This is a shared opportunity and every 30 days the results are directly seen in their paychecks. On average this adds up to over $1 an hour for the employees. They also have a policy that restricts executive pay to no more than 19 times that of the average employee salary. By showing they are on more equal ground through reasonable pay, management builds credibility and keeps the faith. And it is not just words; management flies coach and drives their own cars to back up their words with sincere actions.

Disadvantages or Costs of Empowerment

At this point, you might be thinking to yourself, if empowerment is all this and more, then why don't we see more organizations doing it? Many managers and organizations want to empower their workforce, but are not sure how to do it without jeopardizing achievement of the jobs and organizational goals. Truth is, many managers and organizations resist empowerment for a number of reasons.[54] For one, empowerment results in greater costs in selection and hiring. Little difficulty is likely to be encountered finding individuals capable of performing simple, controlled tasks. When employees are to be empowered—trusted with organizational information and the means to improve it—selectivity in hiring is necessarily increased.

Empowerment can also result in lower and inconsistent delivery. In the control model, employees follow a specific script and set of instructions, eliminating any inconsistency (and creativity, for that matter). Employees in an empowered environment have a different experience. In their efforts to satisfy the customer, empowered employees may take more time and personalize the service for the customer's needs. Depending on the business and strategy, this could be good or bad. A recent article suggests that fast-food franchises do significantly more business in their drive-through windows than through their walk-up counters. Reducing the service delivery time by a small increment can have a substantial positive impact on profits.[55] There is also the possibility for giveaways and bad decisions, however.[56] What if Brian's employees took the initiative and ordered materials from the company's backup supplier? Would this be a bad or a good decision? One such decision is not likely to impact an organization's profits; however, empowered employees may go too far, to the point that profits are affected.

Empowered employees may also make changes in their environment that improve their work unit while negatively impacting another work unit. This is not likely to happen when employees have information about how all the pieces fit together, but such freedom could result in a costly error.

Empowerment typically comes with boundaries. While an organization gives empowered employees the authority to make decisions, these decisions must generally be made within certain broad operating principles. However, what if employees were to stray beyond those boundaries? What if employees abuse their power? For example, an empowered and overzealous employee, acting without regard for company guidelines, might satisfy one customer in the short term but damage relationships with the home office in the long term. Organizations that empower employees must give their employees authority, responsibility, and guidelines or parameters within which they perform.

An important dimension that hinders empowerment is the fact that some individuals cannot handle or do not want the responsibility. Despite the intrinsic and extrinsic benefits of empowerment, some employees prefer to show up, be told what to do, get their paycheck, and go home. Empowerment may be perceived as freedom by some but as ambiguity by others. Some prefer keeping things simple and known. They fear the responsibility inherent in thinking about and making decisions that could change, and possibly improve, the way things have always been done. It's important to remember that just because you value empowerment, others may not. Leaders should take extra consideration when using empowerment techniques with nonmanagement or foreign employees, especially if this is a new process.[57]

Finally, one reason some managers avoid empowerment—even when their organization embraces it—is fear of change and the unknown. "It's working now, so why should I change? What if my empowered employees mess up; will I be fired? What if they do so well—become self-managing—that I'm no longer needed? How can they know better than me? I've been here longer and have more experience than they do." It takes a certain mindset or philosophy to empower successfully. What makes some leaders more willing and able to empower their subordinates than others? Some individuals possess a leadership style or proclivity toward empowering (or disempowering) behaviors, while others understand that empowerment can actually expand their power base, so they might gain more than they would lose.

"To control your cow, give it a bigger pasture."

Suzuki Roshi, Zen master

To Empower or Not to Empower?

It seems clear that empowerment is an important and necessary element, at least in some form, in today's global environment. Only the fittest and most innovative companies will survive; empowerment increases the energy level of the workforce and channels it into good use.[58] Is empowerment a one-size-fits-all proposition? Luckily, no.[59] There are multiple approaches to empowerment, and several criteria are worth considering when determining the degree to which you should implement empowerment in your workplace. It is important to keep in mind that different degrees of empowerment can have varying effects on quality and service depending on the type of business or industry you are in.[60]

Different levels of empowerment can be used with your workforce; deciding which level will be appropriate for your situation or workforce can facilitate successful implementation.[61] These approaches differ in terms of the degree to which ingredients of empowerment are present.

In **suggestion involvement**, the organization makes a small shift from the production line or control model. Employees are encouraged to contribute ideas, possibly via an anonymous suggestion box. In general, day-to-day activities remain unchanged unless a manager decides to implement a suggestion. This step is helpful in that employees are encouraged to be creative and think about ways to improve products and processes; however, employees may not know whether their ideas are acknowledged or may not be asked to get involved in implementation.

In the **job involvement** approach to empowerment, employees are given greater freedom in their job and tasks. Their responsibilities become more open or fluid, such as a team in which all employees are cross-trained to perform a variety of tasks. Their jobs become enlarged and enriched,[62] and they receive feedback on their performance. These results can increase employee satisfaction and productivity. Managers' roles in this approach are more like advisors; they give some choices to employees but must be kept apprised, especially if problems surface.

Employees in a **high involvement** organization have much greater voice and discretion over their work environment. Managers provide the necessary resources, information, and rewards to employees while acting as coaches or facilitators of employees and teams. Because they understand their role in the organization and its success, empowered employees are in the best position to redesign their work, solve problems (or find new ones!), and share in the profits realized by their innovative and productive efforts. Employees take ownership in their work unit and the organization, and often manage themselves.

Is empowerment an appropriate strategy for your organization? Certain considerations (see Figure 18–4) should be evaluated in deciding whether a low level of empowerment (production line approach) or a high level of empowerment is more appropriate. The production line approach works effectively when the primary business value is speed and efficiency, for example, in a fast-food restaurant, but empowerment takes time. The production line approach breaks tasks down into noncomplex, predetermined components, whereas empowerment works where employees require time to process varying situations and generate appropriate solutions.

The production line approach works well when employees' ties to the customer are secondary to the product or service being delivered, for example, at a gas station. Organizations that value longer term customer relationships, for example, a four-star resort or a wealth management firm, will find empowerment more beneficial for both employees and customers.

The production line approach also works in environments where technology enables workers to perform many of the most important tasks routinely. In organizations with a lot of variety and complexity, where employees perform tasks that are primarily nonroutine, empowerment will be required.

Another situation in which the production line approach works well is in business environments that are predictable, where most of the problems that may arise can be anticipated, prepared for, and responded to in a prescribed manner. Empowerment is preferred in unpredictable environments; airlines, for example, face weather and mechanical issues that can require a variety of responses that would be difficult to specify in a manual.

Lastly, the production line approach is best when an organization's managers are primarily hierarchical, "top-down" **Theory X**[63] **managers**. A Theory X manager believes subordinates dislike work and shirk responsibility, leading them to be more directive with the tendency to dictate work efforts. An organization predominated by participative, open **Theory Y managers**—holding the belief that people enjoy work, crave responsibility, and strive for excellence—is the perfect environment for an empowerment approach to problem solving. These managers, and their employees, are more comfortable with higher levels of employee involvement.

**Figure 18–4
Empowerment
Considerations**[64]

Contingency	Production Line vs. Empowerment Approach
Basic business strategy	Efficient high volume vs. customized differentiated
Tie to the customer	Transaction vs. relationship
Technology	Routine vs. nonroutine
Business environment	Predictable vs. dynamic
Type of people	McGregor's Theory X managers vs. Theory Y managers

Guidelines for Implementing and Improving Empowerment[65]

1. *Walk the talk*—Managers need to "practice what they preach."
2. *Set high performance standards*—Set standards that force others to excel, and show that you have confidence in their ability to reach them.
3. *Recognize empowerment* (in the structure of the organization)—Reflect empowerment in attitudes and processes within the organization.
4. *Change old habits*—Managers must be ready to relinquish power, and subordinates must be ready and able to accept new responsibilities.
5. *Start small*—Changes need to be made little by little; empowerment does not happen overnight.
6. *Build trust*—Managers must project confidence and be open and honest with their co-workers.

Implementing Empowerment

So, exactly how does an organization empower its workforce? According to Bowen and Lawler, four ingredients of empowerment must be present in an environment for effective employee involvement:[66]

- *Information about the organization and its performance.* Unlike the old model, in which only top management is interested in and can understand an organization's financials, operating costs, and competitive position, empowerment gives employees this information and the training to understand what it means to their work unit and how their actions impact the bottom line. If you don't know where you are, how will you know if you're improving?

- *Rewards based on the organization's performance.* Many organizations still reward employees for nonperformance-related criteria such as tenure. While employee loyalty has some benefits, what message does an organization send when it rewards employees who are less productive but more senior than those who actively and productively contribute to the organization's bottom line? In an empowered organization, employees engage in collaborative efforts—for the collective good—and share in the organization's success through profit sharing and stock ownership. Recall the slogan for Avis: "We're the employee owners of Avis . . . we work harder!"

- *Knowledge that enables employees to understand and contribute to organizational performance.* Along with the training to understand organizational performance, empowered employees receive training and access to resources to fix problems and improve processes. This knowledge may come in the form of education (problem-solving and quality classes) or resources (bulletins for charting progress, meeting times, outside experts).

- *Power to make decisions that influence organizational direction and performance.* This ingredient brings us back to our original definition of empowerment. Training, knowledge, and rewards are great, but if all employees can do is recommend—rather than implement—solutions, commitment to the outcome will be constrained. Empowered employees are given the authority, usually within defined parameters, to make decisions and implement changes that improve the performance of individuals, teams, work units, and the organization.

Through these ingredients, we can see that empowerment is more than just sharing power. Empowered employees are enabled. They have the freedom to successfully do what they want to do, rather than having to do what you want. Whetton and Cameron refer to this as a pull strategy, rather than a push strategy; employees accomplish tasks because they are internally meaningful or motivating, not because someone or something external to them deems it important.[67] To make empowerment work, managers have to believe in and want empowerment, and employees must feel empowered—they must perceive that there is a liberating rather than constraining environment. It is their perception of the environment that shapes the empowerment.[68] Spreitzer discusses four psychological attributes of empowerment: meaning, self-determination, competence, and impact.[69]

This view holds that it is essential for organizations to be empowering; they need to provide the right climate, tools, training, and support. However, for empowerment to actually exist, employees must feel it or experience it. In other words, empowerment can only come alive and be more than just words on a page in a company brochure when employees carry it out. It is the manager's role to engender the four psychological attributes mentioned above in those they intend to empower.[70] However, individuals can still refuse to accept empowerment.

Six Social Structural Characteristics That Create an Empowering Environment[71]

Low role ambiguity—a clear set of responsibilities and duties, defined guidelines, and standards for accountability.

Wide span of control—decentralization to allow for greater contribution to overall operation to avoid micromanagement.

Sociopolitical support—the existence of relevant support networks of bosses, peers, subordinates, and members of the work group.

Access to information—Availability of information on operations and procedures to determine strategy and frameworks for the accomplishment of organizational goals; freely sharing information across levels and functions.

Access to resources—ability to marshal resources essential to tasks to eliminate dependency and powerlessness.

Participative unit climate—a climate and culture that emphasize and encourage individual contribution and initiative rather than top-down command and control.

There are five stages to implementing empowerment:[72]

1. **Investigation**—analyzing whether empowerment should be implemented and in what form. In this phase, the organization evaluates its current business processes and strategies for success and weighs the current situation against preferred goals. Using the chart in Figure 18–4, the company first identifies its core business strategy, its customer links, the prevalence of technology throughout the organization, the business and environment in which the business is operating, and the type of people currently working for the organization. Then it considers data such as employee morale, customer satisfaction, and industry best practices. After this analysis the organization can determine whether empowerment will bring the desired changes and outcomes needed to achieve greater success.

2. **Preparation**—setting the stage for generating and demonstrating organizational support. This is a crucial step. Changing from a production line approach to a decision-making and problem-solving approach that is more empowering requires a significant culture shift. The way people act and are rewarded will change dramatically. In this phase managers and employees all receive information about the desired shift, why it's occurring, the changes that will result, the training and tools that will be available to help them through the change, the benefits of the change, and information on how and when the changes will take place.[73]

3. **Implementation**—assessing all current systems and adjusting to support an environment based on empowerment. In this phase job descriptions are redesigned, reporting relationships are examined, and reward systems are aligned with the changes. For example, an employee who was formerly paid on an hourly basis might be placed in a bonus pool and receive periodic recognition for "best practice" examples of excellent customer service. Operating procedures and policy manuals are updated, ongoing training is developed and offered, and information and communication systems

are realigned to support the ongoing changes that will result from the empowerment initiative.

4. **Transition**—moving from the former system to the new one. This phase marks the end of the introduction or "rollout" of the new system and starts the permanent implementation of the new system. This phase involves receiving feedback on how the new system is working and making modifications as required. Numerous adjustments are made as employees and managers gain experience with the new guidelines and techniques. In this phase employees are also mobilized—allowed to have an impact, given the freedom to take action, supported in their decisions, and encouraged to take risks.

5. **Maturation**—the new system is firmly rooted. This phase involves maintaining the new system and continuously improving it. Constant reexamination of current processes will determine how changes or new adaptations need to be implemented to remain vital.

"Be a first-rate version of yourself instead of a second-rate version of somebody else."

Judy Garland

Self-empowerment

So far, we've discussed what empowerment is, why it's used, and its benefits and disadvantages. We've also discussed that in order for empowerment to result in increases in productivity, innovation, satisfaction, and commitment, organizations and their managers have to be empowering and individuals have to accept empowerment. Employees must demonstrate and prove that they have the ability and desire to handle the responsibility that empowerment brings. What if empowerment does not exist in your organization or your work group? Do you give up and wait for others to tell you what to do? Here's where self-empowerment comes in. It involves following these steps:

- Create a vision of preferred achievements for yourself and your group. Set high standards for performance and establish goals and deliverables needed to achieve that standard.

- Understand your need for dependency—and let go of it. We all start out dependent. As children, we look to our parents for rules and norms of accepted behavior. When we succeed—or fail—we look to others for recognition or acceptance. When you empower yourself, you set the goals and the rules and you evaluate your performance. No one will tell you what to do or whether you were successful. Believe in yourself and your capabilities to succeed. When you do, you can have pride in your accomplishments and the knowledge that you made it happen.

- Identify and manage your allies and adversaries, and network and politick where appropriate. Even the best-laid plans are subject to roadblocks. After setting a vision and goals, determine what and who can help—and hinder—your ability to achieve those goals. Find ways to reduce obstacles or enlist the support of others, including your peers and managers, to remove or reduce those obstacles. Who might champion your efforts? Maybe your boss is uncomfortable with empowerment, but her boss is not. This is not to say that you should skip the chain of command; rather, you do what you need to get the job done. Inform your boss of your plans and where they fit in. If your boss chooses not to get involved, don't let that stop you. Get others involved and keep your boss informed of your progress. Persuade others to support you. Most people will offer help or resources to individuals and projects that have the potential to make a positive difference in the organization.

- Develop risk-taking strategies; find the courage and confidence to live out your vision. The old saying, "nothing ventured, nothing gained" holds true. Why be an average performer when you are capable of so much more? Why do only what others expect of you when your expectations and aspirations are higher? By accepting self-empowerment and daring to go where others may not have gone, you have to accept that failure is a possibility. Then again, so too is success. Evaluate the costs and benefits of taking on a self-empowered "adventure"; if the net result is positive, what have you got to lose? Former Chicago Bulls superstar Michael Jordan was cut from his high school varsity basketball team as an underclassman. What would have happened if he lacked the courage to persist when others told him he didn't make the cut? Luckily for his fans, he pursued his vision.

One final note about empowerment. Research suggests that empowered managers are more likely to empower their subordinates than managers who are not empowered.[74] Referred to as the falling dominos effect, this phenomenon suggests that beyond the benefits already mentioned, empowerment can be downwardly contagious. When you feel empowered, you are likely to take steps to do the same for those reporting to you, and so on. Because of this cascading effect, when empowerment starts at the top of the organization, the benefits are likely to be exponential. For self-empowerment to be effective, managers must create situations and circumstances that encourage self-leadership.

"I start my day by making a list of everything I need to do . . . and who I can get to do it for me."

Source: www.CartoonStock.com. Reprinted with permission.

Empowerment through Effective Delegation

As you progress in your career, you're likely to find that no matter how skilled and experienced you are, you can neither do everything nor make all necessary decisions. Even if you could—which would probably make you superhuman—you would be preventing your subordinates from developing and reaching their full potential. One means of empowering others is through the technique of **delegation**. Delegation involves assigning work—and the authority and responsibility for the work—to others. Healthy environments are characterized by delegation; if done properly, it can be one of the most effective management tools for getting things done, and it is considered a critical part of being a good leader.[75]

Delegation is not as simple as it sounds. In fact, many managers avoid delegation or do it poorly. Delegation involves transferring authority, responsibility, and accountability to others, typically subordinates. It is not abdication or "dumping"; rather, it can help create a positive, team-oriented environment. In this section, we discuss why delegation is important and how to do it effectively.

Benefits of Delegation

Benefits of delegation accrue to both the delegatee and the delegator. Following are some of these benefits:

- Delegation allows staff to handle specific routine tasks, which enables managers to observe and evaluate employee performance as well as to deal with tasks that are more complex.

- Transferring responsibility to staff aids in their development and increases staff readiness for promotions.[76]

- Delegation increases the delegatees' level of job satisfaction; they gain both greater autonomy and the feeling that they are making a contribution to organizational success.

- Delegation can lead to better decision making because people closer to the issue have input on decisions. This pushes organizational decision making downward, leading to better ways to do things and a more democratic and inclusive process.[77]

- Delegation allows for growth and development of the manager who's delegating. By giving responsibility for tasks to others, the manager's time is available for other tasks, for conceiving new ideas, or for innovation.

- Delegation demonstrates a manager's trust in his or her employees. It shows the manager's ability to manage and develop other individuals, to effectively communicate, and to work through others.

Challenges in Delegating

Despite these benefits, many of us choose not to delegate or we do it poorly. Delegating responsibility is easy to understand, yet hard to do; however, not delegating can be disastrous.[78] People fail to delegate for a number of reasons:

- *Lack of time:* Perhaps you feel you can do it yourself more quickly. While training will be needed to ensure a task is done correctly, not training means the next time the task needs to be done, you will be the one doing it. The adage, "Give a man a fish; feed him for a day. Teach a man to fish; feed him for a lifetime," reminds us that delegation is important.

- *Perfectionism:* Perhaps you feel you can do it better, which may be true; however, letting others perform a task enables them to learn, grow, and develop. Let go of the idea that asking a less-qualified person to do a task seems illogical.[79]

- *Fear of surrendering authority:* Perhaps you fear a loss of power. If you believe that you are the only one who can do something, that belief reinforces your perception that you maintain control or power in a situation. Truth is, few employees are indispensable.

- *Lack of confidence in staff:* Perhaps you don't trust in the abilities of your staff or you fear they might purposely fail, to make you look bad. Build trust by delegating a simple, low-risk task and progress from there.

- *Dual accountability:* Perhaps you feel that this task is your responsibility and that it's not right to share that responsibility with someone else. Certain tasks, such as personnel issues, should not be delegated; many other tasks can and should be delegated. By delegating, you *help* others build their skills and feel more satisfied about their contributions.

Activities Included in Delegation

To be effective, delegation requires three activities: assigning responsibility, transferring authority, and establishing accountability, as shown in Figure 18–5.[80] All three elements are necessary, and they should occur simultaneously.

1. **The assignment of responsibility**. When assigning the responsibility to accomplish a task, the delegatee must understand exactly what is to be accomplished and accept the responsibility for doing so. This requires two-way communication to ensure that both parties clearly understand the task and the expectations that go along with it. Manager and subordinate might discuss and clarify all potential contingencies and ascertain whether the subordinate has the necessary skills and knowledge to perform the assigned task.[81]

**Figure 18–5
Delegation Elements**

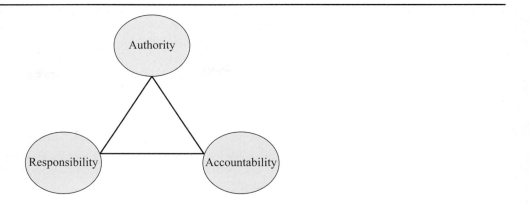

2. **The transfer of authority**. The delegatee must have the proper authority to obtain the necessary resources to complete the task. This includes formal control over necessary resources, clarification of parameters or guidelines, and an understanding of any limits on the employee's authority to act.[82] As appropriate, others should also be apprised of the transfer of the authority. For example, suppose a manager is traveling for two weeks and he delegates the collection and processing of timecards to a subordinate. Before he leaves, he needs to make his staff aware of this temporary change and make arrangements with the payroll office to accept the subordinate's signature on the timecards.

3. **The establishment of accountability**. Delegation is not complete without holding delegatees accountable for the completion of the assignments. They need to be aware of the rewards and consequences of their actions and must realize that they will have to justify decisions for the tasks for which they are responsible. If the delegatee forgets to turn in the timecards and her co-workers don't get paid, they are likely to become unhappy. When delegating tasks, it is important that consequences—both good and bad—are clearly understood. A word of caution: Be sure to delegate both pleasant and less pleasant tasks. "Dumping" provides little variety and could lead to employee complaints.[83]

A Process for Effective Delegation

Effective delegation begins with an open, supportive environment. Create a work environment that has mutual support, mutual trust, and clear lines of communication.[84] Communication and delegation go hand in hand—most problems associated with delegation such as lack of motivation, dissatisfaction, and inferior work can be traced back to a lack of understanding.[85] Two-way communication—aided by effective speaking, listening, and feedback skills—is necessary throughout the entire delegation process.

Next, decide what to delegate. Examine tasks that can and should be delegated; determine why (the goal of the delegation) and how (the process) you will delegate tasks. Decide what the delegation will require, such as training, information, resources, and experience.

Assess and select capable individuals. Just because an employee lacks experience is no reason to avoid delegating or to only delegate mundane tasks to him or her.[86] To delegate successfully, you will need to match the person to the task, design a training program if necessary, make sure the person will be able to complete the task and goal, and work with him or her to anticipate any potential problems and ways to overcome them. Employees need to feel confident and competent to succeed.

Delegate over stages, allowing employees to work more and more on their own without constant supervision. In other words, start small. Show your support of and trust in them by allowing them to prove themselves and their ability to work with little or no supervision on simple tasks or on an initial task related to a larger project. For example, you can start with low levels of delegation in which you ask someone to get baseline information. Then you can move the person to a medium level by asking him or her to get information, analyze it, and suggest options. This way you are able to assess the person's skills and decision-making abilities and determine their capacity to handle the next level or an entire assignment on their own.[87] This process allows you to maintain an appropriate level of control and responsibility over the task. Next, you'll want to establish controls. You are ultimately responsible for the task; delegation does not mean that you are no longer accountable or responsible for the end results. Make it clear at the time of delegation how and when checks will occur, and develop feedback mechanisms to ensure the task is on target and being performed properly.[88]

As needed and requested, provide help and coaching. Encourage a delegatee to complete the task by demonstrating your confidence in his or her abilities. Accept only finished work—do not allow for reverse delegation—and make others understand that their success depends on their contribution. Don't quickly let delegatees back out of their responsibilities just because you fear the delegation process may fail. You can be a support factor—ask questions, give guidance, and teach employees to be problem solvers and decision makers.[89]

Finally, provide feedback. Give rewards and credit for jobs completed successfully, and provide constructive feedback for insufficient work. If you accept substandard work and fix or finish it, you deprive the delegatee of the opportunity to learn from mistakes, as well as send a message that mediocre (or worse) performance is acceptable.

Summary

In today's dynamic business environment, effective leaders are needed to help individuals and organizations succeed and achieve their full potential. Leaders establish a vision and, through their actions and behaviors, inspire others to embrace and achieve that vision. Effective leaders use empowerment to increase employee participation, creativity, and motivation in order to remain viable and competitive. By understanding the benefits and tactics for empowerment, along with being aware of the potential consequences of improper empowerment and delegation, you will be able to increase job satisfaction while effectively achieving organizational goals.

Key Terms and Concepts

Accountability	Knowledge worker
Assignment of responsibility	Leadership
Authority	Maturation stage
Delegation	Preparation stage
Empowerment	Self-leadership
Hierarchy of needs theory	Suggestion involvement
High involvement	Theory X manager
Implementation stage	Theory Y manager
Investigation stage	Transition stage
Job involvement	

Discussion Questions

1. If empowerment is so effective, why don't we see more of it in the workplace?

2. Some faculties offer their students the opportunity to suggest changes to the syllabus—in terms of assignments, point values, due dates, and so on. Rarely do students take up this offer. How could you explain this?

3. Some people use the terms *empowerment* and *delegation* interchangeably. Are these terms synonymous?

4. Thanks to a recent pay raise, you now have enough funds to pay for a housecleaner every other week. You are therefore in a position to delegate this dreadful cleaning task to someone else. What steps would you take to ensure you get what you want (and pay for)?

Endnotes

1. M. Kur, "Leaders Everywhere! Can a Broad Spectrum of Leadership Behaviours Permeate an Entire Organization?" *Leadership and Organization Development Journal* 18 (1997), p. 271.

2. A. Nahavandi, *The Art and Science of Leadership,* 3rd ed. (Upper Saddle River, NJ: Prentice Hall), 2003.

3. P. G. Northouse, *Leadership: Theory and Practice* (Thousand Oaks, CA: Sage, 1977).

4. Kur, "Leaders Everywhere!", p. 271.

5. A. Shriberg, D. L. Shriberg, and C. Lloyd, *Practicing Leadership: Principles and Applications,* 2nd ed. (New York: John Wiley & Sons, 2002).

6. J. M. Kouzes and B. Z. Posner, *Credibility: How Leaders Gain and Lose It, Why People Demand It* (San Francisco: Jossey-Bass, 1993).

7. D. W. Johnson, *Reaching Out: Interpersonal Effectiveness and Self-Actualization* (Upper Saddle River, NJ: Pearson Education, 2002).

8. Nahavandi, *Art and Science.*

9. Kouzes and Posner, *Credibility.*

10. Shriberg, Shriberg, and Lloyd, *Practicing Leadership.*

11. D. Goleman, "Leadership That Gets Results," *Harvard Business Review* (March/April 2000), pp. 78–90.

12. Kouzes and Posner, *Credibility.*

13. J. Lord, "Really MADD: Looking Back at 20 Years," *DRIVEN* magazine (Spring 2000), http://www.madd.org/aboutus/0,1056,1686,00.html (accessed August 24, 2004).

14. Ibid.

15. R. Bommelje and L. Steil, *Listening Leaders: The 10 Golden Rules to Listen, Lead, and Succeed* (Minneapolis, MN: Beaver's Pond Press, 2004).

16. Benjamin Lichte, "5 Examples of Leadership Success in Troubled Times," *CIO* online (June 29, 2009), http://advice.cio.com/benjamin_lichtenwalner/5_examples_of_leadership_success_in_ troubled_times?page=0%2C1.

17. Kouzes and Posner, *Credibility.*

18. Harrison Monarth, "Taking the Brutality out of Brutal Honesty," *CNNMoney* (June 18, 2013), http://management.fortune.cnn.com/2013/06/18/taking-the-brutality-out-of-brutal-honesty/.

19. Eric Neel, "Forever Coach," *E-Ticket, ESPN.com* (Oct 14, 2005), retrieved from http://sports .espn.go.com/espn/eticket/story?page=wooden.

20. Shriberg, Shriberg, and Lloyd, *Practicing Leadership.*

21. Kouzes and Posner, *Credibility* .

22. Joseph A. Saro, Philip Worchel, Earl Pence, and Joseph Orban, "Perceived Leader Behavior as a Function of the Leader's Interpersonal Trust Orientation," *Academy of Management Journal* 23, no. 1 (March 1980), p. 161.

23. "Metso's Code of Conduct," *Metso* (March 14, 2013), http://www.metso.com/corporation/about_eng.nsf/WebWID/WTB-041101-2256F-B8107?OpenDocument.

24. Andrew Jauregui, "Yang Yuanqing, Lenovo CEO Donates $3 Million Bonus to 10,000 Employees in China," *The Huffington Post* (July 20, 2012), http://www.huffingtonpost.com/2012/07/20/yang-yuanqing-lenovo-ceo-donates-3-million-dollar-bonus-to-employees_n_1690811.html.

25. Kur, "Leaders Everywhere!", p. 271.

26. C. Manz and C. Neck, *Mastering Self-Leadership* (Upper Saddle River, NJ: Prentice Hall, 2003).

27. J. P. Kotter, *The New Rules: How to Succeed in Today's Post Corporate World* (New York: The Free Press, 1995).

28. S. G. Cohen, L. Chang, and G. E. Ledford Jr., "A Hierarchical Construct of Self-management Leadership and Its Relationship to Quality of Work Life and Perceived Work Group Effectiveness," *Personnel Psychology* 50, no. 2 (1997), pp. 275–308.

29. G. M. Spreitzer, M. A. Kizilos, and S. W. Nason, "A Multidimensional Analysis of the Relationship between Psychological Empowerment, and Effectiveness, Satisfaction, and Strain," *Journal of Management* 23, no. 5 (1997), pp. 679–705.

30. For a broader discussion of social responsibility and organizations that practice it, see A. B. Carroll, *Business and Society: Managing Corporate Social Performance* (Boston: Little, Brown, 1981).

31. Kotter, *The New Rules.*

32. H. K. S. Laschinger, J. E. Finegan, J. Shamian, and P. Wilk, "A Longitudinal Analysis of the Impact of Workplace Empowerment on Work Satisfaction," *Journal of Organizational Behavior* 25, no. 4 (2004), pp. 527–43.

33. Jay A. Conger and Rabindra N. Kanungo, "The Empowerment Process: Integrating Theory and Practice," *Academy of Management Review* 13 (1988), p. 473. For a closer look at the relationship between empowering practices and the employees' psychological experience of empowerment, see Scott Seibert, Seth Silver, and Alan Randolph, "Taking Empowerment to the Next Level: A Multiple-level Model of Empowerment, Performance and Satisfaction," *Academy of Management Journal* 47 (2004), pp. 332–51.

34. Joanne Cole, "Building Heart and Soul," *HR Focus* (October 1998), pp. 9–10, quoting Hornstein, author of *Brutal Bosses.*

35. Craig Pearce, "The Future of Leadership Development: The Importance of Identity, Multi-Level Approaches, Self-Leadership, Physical Fitness, Shared Leadership, Networking, Creativity, Emotions, Spirituality and On-Boarding Processes," *Human Resource Management Review* 17, (2007), p. 355.

36. Larry English, "Information Quality Management: The Next Frontier," *DM Review* (April 2000), p. 38.

37. Abraham H. Maslow, *Motivation and Personality,* 2nd ed. (New York: Harper and Row, 1970).

38. Clayton Alderfer, *Existence, Relatedness, and Growth* (New York: Free Press, 1972).

39. David McClelland, *Human Motivation* (Glenwood, IL: Scott, Foresman, 1985).

40. E. Lawler and J. Shuttle, "A Causal Correlation Test of the Need Hierarchy Concept," *Organizational Behavior and Human Performance* 7 (1973), pp. 265–87.

41. Realize that this theory is culture-bound. For example, in other cultures—e.g., Asian and Hispanic—the order of the hierarchy differs and social needs dominate other needs.

42. Laschinger et al., "Longitudinal Analysis," pp. 527–43.

43. See, e.g., David E. Bowen and Edward Lawler III, "The Empowerment of Service Workers: What, Why, How and When," *Sloan Management Review* (Spring 1992), pp. 31–39.

44. Gretchen M. Spreitzer, "Social Structural Characteristics of Psychological Empowerment," *Academy of Management Journal* (April 1996), pp. 483–504.

45. Rob MacLachian, "Regeneration X," *People Management* (April 2, 1998), p. 34.

46. Wong Pang Long, "Managing Problems: To Empower or Not, Is the Question," *The New Press Times* (December 22, 1996), p. 32.

47. Ibid.

48. Nigar Demircan Cakar and Alper Erturk, "Comparing Innovation Capability of Small and Medium-Sized Enterprises: Examining the Effects of Organizational Culture and Empowerment," *Journal of Small Business Management* 48, no. 3 (July 2010), p. 325.

49. Spreitzer, "Social Structural Characteristics," pp. 679–705.

50. R. Forrester, "Empowerment: Rejuvenating a Potent Idea," *Academy of Management Executives* 14 (2000), pp. 67–80.

51. Bowen and Lawler, "Empowerment of Service Workers," pp. 31–39.

52. Sue Schellenbarger, "To Win the Loyalty of Your Employees, Try a Softer Touch," *The Wall Street Journal* (January 26, 2000), p. B1.

53. See "How Workers Spur Whole Foods Innovation," *Fortune.com/leadership,* "Leadership by Geoff Colvin" (June 17, 2013), http://money.cnn.com/video/news/2013/06/17/f-leadership-whole-foods-walter-robb-employee-culture.fortune; "Why Whole Foods Restricts Executive Pay," *Fortune. com/leadership,* "Leadership by Geoff Colvin" (June 17, 2013), http://money.cnn.com/video/news/2013/06/17/f-leadership-whole-foods-walter-robb-executive-salary.fortune.

54. Bowen and Lawler, "Empowerment of Service Workers," pp. 31–39.

55. Jennifer Ordonez, "Next! An Efficiency Drive: Fast-Food Lanes Are Getting Even Faster," *The Wall Street Journal* (May 18, 2000), p. A1.

56. Bowen and Lawler, "Empowerment of Service Workers," pp. 31–39.

57. Andrea Drake et al., "Empowerment, Motivation, and Performance: Examining the Impact of Feedback and Incentives on Nonmanagement Employees," *Behavioral Research in Accounting* 19 (2007), p. 85.

58. Long, "Managing Problems," p. 32.

59. Forrester, "Empowerment," pp. 67–80.

60. Akiko Ueno, "Is Empowerment Really a Contributory Factor to Service Quality?" *The Service Industry Journal* 28, no. 9 (November 2008), p. 1322.

61. Bowen and Lawler, "Empowerment of Service Workers," pp. 31–39.

62. See, for example, Greg R. Oldham and J. Richard Hackman, "Relationships between Organizational Structure and Employee Reactions: Comparing Alternative Frameworks," *Administrative Science Quarterly* (March 1981), p. 66.

63. Douglas McGregor, *The Human Side of Enterprise* (New York: McGraw-Hill, 1964), pp. 68–78.

64. Bowen and Lawler, "Empowerment of Service Workers," pp. 31–39.

65. Leaders Direct, www.leadersdirect.com/empower.html (accessed June 2000).

66. Bowen and Lawler, "Empowerment of Service Workers," pp. 31–39.

67. David A. Whetton and Kim S. Cameron, *Developing Management Skills,* 4th ed. (Reading, MA: Addison-Wesley, 1998), p. 377.

68. Spreitzer, "Social Structural Characteristics," pp. 483–504.

69. Ibid.

70. K. S. Cameron, D. A. Whetton, and M. U. Kim, "Organizational Dysfunctions of Decline," *Academy of Management Journal* (1987), 30, pp. 126–138.

71. Spreitzer, "Social Structural Characteristics," pp. 483–504.

72. Carol Yeh-Yen Lin, "The Essence of Empowerment: A Conceptual Model and a Case Illustration," *Journal of Applied Management Studies* (December 1998), p. 223.

73. Carole Schweitzer, "Empowerment by Example," *Associate Management* (May 1998), p. 50.

74. Bernard M. Bass, David A. Waldman, Bruce J. Avolio, and Michael Bebb, "Transformational Leadership and the Falling Dominoes Effect," *Group & Organization Management* (1987).

75. Carl Holmes, "Fighting the Urge to Fight Fires," *Harvard Business Review* (November– December 1999), p. 30.

76. Maria DePaola and Vincenzo Scoppa, "Delegation, Skill Acquistion and Turnover Costs," *International Journal of the Economics of Business* 14, no. 1 (February 2007), p. 127.

77. Ibid.

78. Holmes, "Fighting the Urge," p. 30.

79. Terry Foster, "Using Delegation as a Developmental Tool," *Training Journal* (May 2004), p. 28.

80. S. C. Bushardt, D. L. Duhon, and A. R. Fowler Jr., "Management Delegation Myths and the Paradox of Task Assignment," *Business Horizons* (March–April 1991), pp. 34–43.

81. William W. Hull, "Passing the Buck vs. Making an Assignment," *Supervision* (March 1999), p. 6.

82. Ibid.

83. Nahavandi, *Art and Science.*

84. Holmes, "Fighting the Urge," p. 30.

85. Robert Rohrer, "Does the Buck Ever Really Stop?" *Supervision* (April 1999), p. 11.

86. Monique R. Brown, "Management by Delegation: Don't Be a Micro Manager: Share the Responsibility," *Black Enterprise* (February 1998), p. 76.

87. M. E. Haynes, "Delegation: There's More to It Than Letting Someone Else Do It," *Supervisory Management* (January 1980), p. 9.

88. Hull, "Passing the Buck," p. 6.

89. Pat Weisner, "Delegating Up," *Colorado Business Magazine* (December 1997), p. 9.

Exercise 18–A
Do You Know an
Effective Leader?

Think of someone whose leadership skills you admire. It can be in any setting—work, school, family, and so on. Use the following worksheet to evaluate the person's effectiveness.

1. In what way(s) did this person "buck the system," challenge the process, or ignore the rules in leading? Explain.

   _____

   _____

   _____

2. What was this person's vision for the organization or group she or he led? In what ways did she or he inspire others to embrace that vision?

   _____

   _____

   _____

3. What are some examples of ways that this person provided information, power, or support to those she or he led? How did this create an environment that enabled others to act? If you were a follower, what impact did this environment have on you?

   _____

   _____

   _____

4. Did this person "walk the talk"? Provide an example that demonstrates this important quality of effective leadership. How important was this consistency between his or her words and deeds to others' (your) trust in him or her?

   _____

   _____

   _____

5. In what ways did this person recognize and reward his or her followers or teammates? If you were one of these individuals, what impact did this person's efforts at encouraging the heart have on your motivation to succeed?

   _____

   _____

   _____

Questions

1. Which of these five abilities is most and least critical to leaders' effectiveness? Explain.

2. Which of these five abilities do you value most? Explain.

3. When a person leads in the absence of a formal position of authority, which of these five abilities is most difficult to exhibit? Explain.

**Exercise 18–B
What Is Your Self-leadership Quotient (SLQ)?**

Instructions: Read the following items and, using a scale from 0 (never) to 5 (always), rate how characteristic each item is of how you approach activities at work and at play. When you're done, add up your score.

Not characteristic 0—1—2—3—4—5 Very Characteristic

Setting My Course—
   Determining Where I
   Aim to Go

Getting Centered

___1. I check my feelings.

___2. I clarify what is important to me.

___3. I get in touch with my personal power.

Identifying Purpose

___4. I seek problems to solve.

___5. I clarify my purpose.

___6. I assume responsibility to act.

Deciding on Direction

___7. I survey the situation.

___8. I brainstorm what is possible.

___9. I envision my purpose accomplished.

Setting Goals

___10. I match challenges to my ability.

___11. I align my personal goals with my purpose.

___12. I set specific targets.

Traversing My Course—
   Getting from Here to My
   Destination

Establishing Milestones

___13. I survey my resources.

___14. I map out action steps.

___15. I establish standards of achievement.

Getting Cooperation

___16. I create a network of allies.

___17. I build team spirit.

___18. I share my vision.

Motivating Myself

___19. I create meaning in what I do.

___20. I measure my progress.

___21. I reward my progress.

Enjoying the Moment

___22. I accentuate the positive.

___23. I look for satisfaction in small things.

___24. I get absorbed in my activities.

Staying On Course—
   Correcting My Course
   and Bypassing Obstacles

Thinking Flexibly

___25. I maintain a "can-do" attitude.

___26. I adapt my thinking to the situation.

___27. I avoid perfectionism.

Correcting My Course

___28. I identify detours.

___29. I make contingency plans.

___30. I learn from my mistakes.

Bypassing Obstacles

___31. I accept the challenge.

___32. I view problems as opportunities.

___33. I do something differently.

Piloting my Adventure

___34. I focus my attention.

___35. I develop strategies.

___36. I follow my bliss.

Scoring

144–180: Excellent—Your ability to lead yourself is outstanding. By studying the qualities you can probably become an even better self-leader as well as an outstanding leader of others.
109–143: Good—You employ most self-leading skills. With practice you can become an excellent self-leader.
73–108: Potential—You have many self-leading skills, but employ them inconsistently. With some skill training and practice you have the potential to be an excellent self-leader.
36–72: Needs Improvement—You have many self-leading skills, but use them infrequently. If you make the effort to learn and practice the skills, you can greatly improve your self-leading ability.
0–35: Deficient—You do not demonstrate self-leading ability and will find yourself going in circles and looking to others for direction. You probably have the capability to become a self-leader but you will have to make acquiring the skills a priority.

Exercise 18–C
It's Plane to Me

Each group will consist of five production employees and one supervisor. You will be instructed to create a paper airplane. The instructor will supply the supervisors with their instructions for their production process. Production workers are to follow the instructions provided by their supervisor. Any questions or suggestions should be discussed with your supervisor.

Questions

1. How did you feel while doing your job?
2. How do you feel about your supervisor?
3. How did you respond or react to your supervisor's instructions?
4. Would you enjoy working for this company? Why or why not?
5. What was your productivity level? What was the quality?

Exercise 18–D
Case Study: "Am I the Manager?"

Gail was hired at the apparel manufacturing company to be the office and production manager. She was very excited about her new position; the job responsibilities seemed to be a perfect fit with her skills and strengths. Her responsibilities included running the office and the ordering department and coordinating the production facilities. Larry, the owner of the company, handled all the financial aspects of the business. L.J., the plant manager, was Gail's direct supervisor.

On the first day of work, Larry instructed Gail to make the order and production department more efficient. Gail soon began to realize that there were a few employees in the ordering department who were very inefficient and lacking in motivation. One employee in particular, Kathy, would come in 10–20 minutes late, have several personal calls that lasted anywhere from 5 to 25 minutes, and refuse to answer the phones when anyone else seemed to be free. She would simply say to the other order people, "I need you to get that call; I'm busy doing my account summaries." Larry had already warned Gail of Kathy's unacceptable behavior and informed her that Kathy had several documented violations and notations in her personnel file. Larry felt that Gail should try to work with her, but if she was not able to change her behavior, he wanted Gail to document one final complaint and terminate her.

Gail decided to have a feedback session with Kathy, during which Kathy was very defensive yet said she would try to change her behavior. Kathy insinuated that even though she did these things, Larry liked her and he was not really bothered by them. Over the next two weeks Kathy did not change her behavior, so, with the documented results of the feedback session and the other citations in her file, Gail decided she would terminate Kathy. Kathy caused a scene in the office and ran into Larry's office. After a considerable time period, Gail was called into Larry's office. He told Gail that Kathy was not fired and that "Gail just needed to help Kathy improve upon her behaviors." Gail left the meeting feeling as if she had just been undermined in front of the entire staff.

Another situation that had been developing dealt with Gail's reorganization of the production department. To gain efficiency between the ordering staff and the production department, there needed to be an order and prioritization schedule. After developing a new system, Gail proceeded to explain the new system to both the ordering department and to Maggie, the production supervisor, and her staff. Not much was said, and Gail felt confident her new system would work. Soon she discovered that nothing had changed. Maggie was making her own determinations regarding production regardless of the orders put in and prioritized by the order department. Gail went to discuss it with Maggie, and the reply she got from Maggie was, "This is my department, I have been here much longer than you, and I'll have them produce what I want them to. Go cry to Larry if you don't like it. Until I hear it from Larry, I will do as I please." This dream job was starting to seem more like a nightmare.

The final straw came regarding ordering materials. Gail quickly realized that they did not have the necessary materials to make the high-demand products. She worked on an inventory count with L.J. and between the two of them they were able to come up with an accurate count and an order plan to get production back on schedule. Gail then proceeded to place an order for the necessary supplies. At least she had control over something around here. Two days later, Larry called her into the office, furious about the orders. "How dare you order supplies!" Larry stormed. "You do not have the right to requisition materials; I handle the finances, and this just put me in a bad spot with a supplier I owe money to. I make the decision on when we purchase materials. Understand?" Gail was beginning to understand all too well. She was mad, frustrated, hurt, and disillusioned all at the same time. "What have I gotten myself into with this organization?" she thought.

Questions

1. What guidelines of empowerment did Larry or Gail violate?
2. What guidelines of delegation did Larry or Gail violate?
3. What should Gail plan to discuss with Larry? What issues need to be raised?
4. What does Gail need to do to obtain the necessary elements of empowerment and delegation? What does Larry need to do to facilitate Gail's success?
5. What advice would you give to Larry and Gail regarding their working situation?

Exercise 18–E
Empowerment
In-Basket Simulation
and Self-assessment

Your instructor will provide the materials needed to complete this in-basket activity. Playing the role of J. Carter, a newly promoted manager in General Software Systems, you will have approximately 20 minutes to respond to a stack of memos in your in-basket. You must provide a written response to each memo, keeping in mind the person and position to whom the response is targeted. After this activity is completed, answer the following questions completely but concisely based on your experience.

1. How did you feel about your job (playing the role of J. Carter) and the organization for which you worked? What did you like and dislike about carrying out the functions of your role?

_____

_____

_____

_____

2. What characteristics of your job and organization made you feel empowered and/or disempowered? Explain, citing specific examples.

_____

_____

_____

_____

3. If, as researchers suggest, the characteristics and behaviors of empowered people are so functional, and those of disempowered people are so dysfunctional, why don't we see more empowerment in the workplace?

_____

_____

_____

_____

4. What specific things can you do to empower your co-workers or teammates? What steps can you take to overcome disempowerment that currently exists in your workplace or team?

_____

_____

_____

_____

Exercise 18–F
Delegating Tasks

From a past or present job, group project, or organizational task (from a fraternity, fundraiser, committee activity), think of a task you would like to or could delegate to another person.

The task to be delegated, including all contingencies and related activities: _____

_____

_____

The goal and benefits (to me, to the delegatee) of delegating the task: _____

_____

_____

The person or persons who will be chosen (What skills, abilities, and competencies do they possess?): _____

_____

_____

Assigning the responsibilities (How will I clearly communicate all the requirements for this task? How can I motivate them to do this task?): _____

_____

_____

Transferring authority (What power must they have? Who else will need to be informed? What parameters will be set for limitations?): _____

_____

_____

Establishing accountability (What are the rewards and consequences? How will completion be measured? What are the standards for completion?): _____

_____

_____

Establishing responsibility (What degree of responsibility will I give? What level of delegation will I use and why?): _____

_____

_____

Establishing controls (What control mechanisms will I need to develop? When and how will I evaluate progress?): _____

_____

_____

Questions

1. What will be the most difficult aspect of this delegation for you?
2. What potential problems, barriers, or consequences can you foresee for this delegation?
3. What other steps or aspects must be taken into consideration to make this an effective delegation?
4. What unanticipated developments could occur to impact task accomplishment?

**Exercise 18–G
In Their Own Words**

Interview a manager about the way she or he empowers employees. (You might need to define the term.) Ask the manager questions such as:

- How many direct reports do you have?
- Do you consider them to be effective performers? Why or why not?
- Do you consider them to be trustworthy? Why or why not?
- In what ways do you empower your employees?
- Is this process successful? Why or why not?
- If you were called out on a two-week assignment, is there an employee you would feel comfortable putting in charge of your unit? Why or why not?
- What concerns would you have in doing so?
- In what ways does an empowering management philosophy help or hinder your success as a manager?

Based on his or her answers, would you say this manager used empowerment successfully? Defend your answer with examples shared in your interview.

**Exercise 18–H
Reflection/Action Plan**

This chapter focused on leadership and empowerment—what they are, why they're important, and how to improve your skills in these areas. Complete the following worksheet upon completing all reading and experiential activities for this chapter.

1. The one or two areas in which I am most strong are:

_____

_____

_____

_____

2. The one or two areas in which I need more improvement are:

_____

_____

_____

_____

3. If I did only one thing to improve in this area, it would be to:

_____

_____

_____

_____

4. Making this change would probably result in:

_____

_____

_____

_____

5. If I did not change or improve in this area, it would probably affect my personal and professional life in the following ways:

_____

_____

_____

_____

19

Project Management

Learning Points

How do I:

- Keep projects on track?
- Help my team meet deadlines?
- Ensure that project members agree on and maintain the necessary standards or quality?
- Handle multiple projects simultaneously?
- Incorporate my personal project time lines into my professional project time lines?
- Keep long-term objectives in mind while working on day-to-day objectives?
- Handle unexpected events that interfere with my preplanned schedule?

Curtis Benson was fully aware of the importance of fulfilling this government contract on time and within budget. With the economy being so tight, the scrutiny on project success rates had dramatically increased. However, Curtis felt confident he could keep this project under control. He was a seasoned project manager and had a pretty high success rate. But with strict government regulations and the number of subcontractors working on this task, there was an increased chance for complications.

So far, the project was going along relatively smoothly. Sure, there were some minor issues to deal with and a few delays due to scheduling errors with some of the subcontractors. The first real sign of trouble came when the technical team (subcontractor A) tried to install the required radar system that was not compatible with the electronic systems installed by subcontractor B. It seemed that subcontractor A had received a change order directly from the government on the type of radar system to be used. However, this change order had never been reviewed by Curtis nor was it shared with the electricians who were still going by the original design plans.

Wow! What a mess. Curtis had to think fast. How to fix this without incurring extra cost and putting the project way off schedule? It could be fixed, but Curtis knew that time and budget were going to take a hit; there was no easy way around it. As he walked down to his supervisor's office he kept thinking, "How did I let this happen? Why didn't I see this coming? What could I have done differently? So much for my good record."

1. What factors contributed to this situation?

2. What could Curtis have done differently to avoid the complications?

3. What can Curtis do to save this project and what should he do on future projects?

4. Has something like this ever happened to you before? How did you react? What did you learn from this experience?

"Plan the work. Work the plan."

This old saying is the cornerstone of management today. If you don't plan, you will be so busy reacting to situations that you will not have time to take advantage of new opportunities.[1] It's easy for most people to develop plans. What separates successful plans from unsuccessful ones is the implementation. For a plan to become reality, it needs to be operationalized—brought to life. This chapter introduces the concept of project management and discusses how this concept can be used to organize projects and assignments that are managed by teams. The definition and importance of project management, steps involved in managing projects, and strategies and tips for honing your project management skills are discussed. We also include information on tools available to help you manage projects.

What Is Project Management?

Have you ever been involved in a team project where team members had different definitions of quality? Or different interpretations of the phrase "on time"? Or where everyone procrastinated until the last minute? When used effectively, project management can help prevent or reduce the likelihood of these problems. **Project management** is the coordination of your work and that of others such that organizational objectives can be achieved while meeting time, budget, and quality standards or expectations.[2]

Project management is a systematic process through which almost all the steps involved in starting and completing a project are anticipated and outlined in advance.[3] We use the word *almost* because no one can predict everything that will happen between the present and the project deadline. In project management, the known steps are anticipated and accounted for; in addition, the schedule includes some "slack" to account for unforeseen difficulties or events that invariably arise. Project management involves tracking a project from its inception to completion, whether it's managing the $43 billion California high-speed rail project, planning the 2016 Summer Olympic Games in Rio de Janeiro, monitoring the Panama Canal expansion project (also called the Third Set of Locks project), or organizing your 10-year high school reunion. These all include scheduling steps, allocating tasks to various team members, creating and overseeing time and financial budgets for projects, monitoring progress maade toward goals, and providing overall project resource management. Project management is the process that takes strategy and vision and makes it a reality.

Why Project Management?

According to World Bank data (2009), more than 20 percent of global activity (up to 30 percent in emerging economies) is project centered with approximately 22 percent of the world's gross domestic product (GDP) being project-based.[4] A large percentage of our global economy is therefore hinging on value created through effective project management. In today's rapidly changing and highly competitive workplace, managers are being asked to reduce costs while increasing productivity. This imperative forces managers to develop new models of operating for every aspect of the organization.[5] One way to "do more with less" is to encourage employees to be efficient in plotting their work flow, whether on independent or team-based projects. As employees work increasingly in teams, it is essential to have a system to help team members work collectively on a project that has multiple milestones or deadlines. This is especially true when individual members are involved in multiple projects. They, and their managers, must juggle many balls simultaneously. Being involved in multiple individual and team-based projects, project managers and project team members have a lot—perhaps too much—on their plates today. Project planning and management become essential as project managers attempt to adapt to changing technology, coordinate with multiple people and departments, meet financial goals, and manage business strategy while simultaneously monitoring multiple projects with day-, week-, or year-long or more time spans. And all of this must get done while getting the day-to-day work done![6]

Projects that encompass many tasks and run over several weeks or months require planning and coordination with other projects and activities, both personal and professional. As a manager or employee, your ongoing job priorities and commitments have to be factored in when planning new projects. The same is true for students. Coursework and extra assignments need to be incorporated into your plans, as do personal commitments. Vacations, medical appointments, sports competitions, community involvement, carpooling, child care, and elder care are examples of personal commitments that should be taken into account when planning project schedules either independently or with others.

Benefits of Project Management

Applying a project management approach to your work has numerous benefits for organizations and individuals. We've mentioned the need to "do more with less" or perhaps "work smart, not hard." Project management helps organizations in several ways:

- *Resources such as time, money, and personnel are appropriately allocated to the organization's numerous priorities and objectives.*[7] Through advance planning, individual project calendars can be adjusted to coordinate with other organization commitments. For example, in planning a major new product rollout, a company can ensure that it occurs at a time when other projects aren't absorbing needed time and energy of the managers and employees involved in the rollout effort.[8]

- *Long-term objectives can be kept in mind while short-term objectives are being implemented.* Through thinking strategically about an organization's long-term objectives, short-term activities that help move the organization toward the longer-term goal can be planned and implemented. Using project management, a company can ensure that weekly or monthly tasks and objectives—in addition to those responsible for them—are included in plans that support a new marketing strategy. If a company strives to expand sales by 20 percent by adding an online business to complement its brick and mortar business within two years, it could set up multiple milestones that track this progress. Within 3 months, research for website content will be completed; within 6 months, the website will be up and running; within one year, sales should increase by 5 percent; within 18 months, sales should increase by 15 percent, and so on. In the case of the Three Gorges Dam in China, the Chinese government consistently focused on the long-term benefit of supplying up to 10 percent of the country's energy needs and ability to recover the expense with 10 years of generated power even though the project was highly controversial in costing $28 billion and displacing 1.3 million people.

- *Contingencies can be anticipated.* By articulating in advance the known steps to complete a project and building in some slack in the schedule, each unanticipated event that occurs during the project time line does not have to be treated as a crisis that affects the ultimate deadline or deliverable. Let's say a company is implementing a new integrated computer system that tracks inventory, sales, costs, and operations. The consultants who are installing the package estimate that complete installation and implementation will take eight months. This includes installing software, training all employees, testing and debugging the system, and making modifications. For project planning purposes, it's best to add 10 to 20 percent additional time to each phase. This will ensure that slack is built into the schedule to accommodate the unexpected, such as incompatibility with previous hardware, heavier than usual sales, or vacations and holidays. By allocating extra time to projects at the outset, you have a better chance of getting ahead of your workload and staying there.[9] Sarah Gavit, an experienced project manager at NASA's Jet Propulsion Laboratory, notes, "Manage the risk. There always will be certain parts more susceptible to going wrong. Before we ever lay out a schedule, we look at four or five areas with high risk. We develop contingency plans and watch extra closely. Other project managers sometimes don't look until they're up against the wall."[10]

- *Project output is made more consistent.* By developing quality standards in advance, team members, managers, and employees have the opportunity to discuss and clarify their perceptions of the project objectives and their expectations for the end product, or project deliverable(s). For example, when developing a new interviewer training program, a company can outline the legal requirements, research industry benchmarks or best practices, and develop a set of specifications for the project that all members of the planning team agree to in advance. By getting all involved on board before any project output is generated, the quality of the components comprising the end product will be higher and more harmonious than if everyone established his or her own quality standards independently.

  Project management has numerous benefits for the individuals involved as well as the organization. In addition to enabling individuals to be more efficient and organized, project planning and management has other benefits for individuals:

- *Collegiality is enhanced.* Through meeting with other team members and organizational employees who have a stake in the success of a project, you have the opportunity to build relationships that contribute to a sense of belonging in the organization.[11] Let's say you are part of a group tasked with implementing a new budget tracking system for the company. By meeting regularly as a team and with department heads and other stakeholders, you are able to form relationships that contribute to the success of the project at hand and last beyond the duration of the project. These relationships facilitate your knowledge and understanding of where you and your work fit with that of others in the organization. This enhances your perspective and enables you to think more globally as you do your work. In addition, being connected or networked with others in the organization increases trust and helping behaviors—part of collegiality.[12]

- *Morale is enhanced.* No one likes feeling that they're all alone in overcoming a mountain of work at the office. Planning work in advance and achieving the desired outcome successfully boosts your morale and the morale of others involved in the effort. For example, tackling a thorny problem such as designing a new budget monitoring system can be a tedious task. When you articulate, plan for, and carry out the various components of the task systematically and incrementally, what might be an overwhelming task appears more manageable. And when you are able to make progress on this task—even one small component at a time—your self-efficacy increases along with your morale. "Projects that succeed are just about the most satisfying work experience you can have. It's as much fun as you can have and still get paid," notes Steve McMenamin, vice president of customer service at Southern California Edison Co.[13]

- *Job satisfaction is increased.* Once we have mastered the basics of any job, many of us want more. Once we prove our capabilities, many people want to be involved in greater levels of responsibility, more variety of work, and more complex work.[14] Being involved in multiple projects or tasks affords you this opportunity to stretch and grow further and, as a result, experience enhanced job satisfaction. Let's say that in recognition for your outstanding capabilities as a waitress, the owner of a busy restaurant asks you to participate in a task force that is evaluating ways to improve customer service. Project management gives you the tools needed to juggle both roles simultaneously, facilitating your ability to take on both roles and, in so doing, increasing your ability to multitask and contribute to the organization beyond your daily job.

- *Learning is enhanced.* Project management results in learning about others' jobs and work styles, not just your own. Working with others on projects increases your understanding of how your and others' roles and responsibilities fit into the whole. This increases your knowledge of the complexities and interdependencies in the organization, enabling you to make more substantive and appropriate contributions to the organization's success. For example, you might be involved in a group project at school where the ultimate deliverable is a presentation on a cutting-edge business topic. By planning the project in advance with other team members, you exchange ideas about preferred ways to approach the project, manage time, communicate with each other, make decisions, and solve problems. This collaboration increases everyone's skills and knowledge base.

■ *Creativity and synergy are enhanced.* Through planning a project in advance with your manager and team members, you are more likely to envision a new way to approach the situation than if you simply did the work in the same way it's always been done. Imagine you are part of a team charged with implementing a membership expansion campaign for a fraternity. By planning the project in advance, you can ask big-picture questions such as, "What do we want to accomplish?" "How can we do things better than before?" "What worked and what didn't work previously?" "Ideally, what would we like the new program to look like?" By brainstorming with other team members to answer these questions, you're likely to tap into the synergistic potential that resides in most diverse groups. This process energizes a group toward identifying more creative, innovative, and better solutions than any one team member working on his or her own could have produced.

Let's face it. Despite, or perhaps because of, all the technology that is now available, working today is harder and more pressure filled than ever. The average workday for today's white-collar worker is longer today than it was in the 1960s.[15] With the availability of e-mail, fax machines, and voice-mail, our expectations for quick turnaround have changed from a week or so to an hour or two! Customers want service now. Managers want deliverables yesterday. With all this pressure, it's a wonder that any projects with a time line of more than a few days get done. Managing projects can be tedious and time-consuming work. The time that an organization or individual invests in planning will yield paybacks and returns through reduced implementation time and costs.[16] A project management mindset can serve as a way to spread the work around, making working on projects more effective and enjoyable.

"Plans are only good intentions unless they immediately degenerate into hard work."

Peter Drucker,
management consultant

Managing the Project

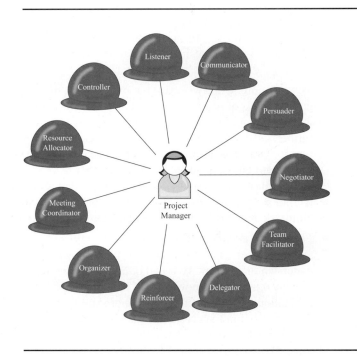

In order to effectively manage a project, the project leader or manager must be a skilled individual who not only possesses the motivation to handle the challenge, but also has honed his or her interpersonal skills. Studies have shown that project managers with higher emotional intelligence (EQ), as discussed in Chapter 4, have stronger leadership tendencies and are more successful in influencing the project outcomes. Those with higher EQ have better-honed interpersonal competencies in conflict and team management while having the necessary levels of empathy and attentiveness to get the job done.[17] The project manager must be able to direct and oversee the operation to create synergy through collaboration. The position therefore requires some important skills that have been addressed in this textbook:

- *Communication.* The project manager must clearly communicate the scope and nature of the project, tying the project objectives to the overall organizational strategy while simultaneously making it relevant and practical for individual project members. Project leaders will therefore need to listen as well as they speak (review the material for listening skills in Chapter 6). And as discussed in Chapter 7, open, two-way communication will be the key to enhancing the process.

- *Persuasion.* Projects are not always met with enthusiasm. Project managers will need to use influence and persuasion to build and maintain commitment and momentum for project completion. Utilizing various persuasive techniques—rewards, incentives, feedback, or reasoning—will be necessary for aiding the manager in working through long or complicated processes. Influencing others through effective persuasion and negotiation will require the skills addressed in Chapters 8 and 9.

- *Feedback.* In order to stay on schedule and within budget, the project team will require not only positive reinforcement, but also guidance and correction. The project manager will need to determine the appropriate timing, level, and source of feedback to guide the team through the entire process. Research has shown that project feedback and knowledge transfer must be explicit for project members to gain accurate perceptions of performance as well as learn to become more autonomous in the process.[18] Feedback, as covered in Chapter 17, is not only essential during the project to measure incremental progress, but is also essential after the project to ensure learning for individuals and the organization for future activities.

- *Team Building.* Project management is essentially a team process; therefore, project managers need to be effective team leaders (Chapter 10). Whether facilitating meetings (Chapters 12 and 13), encouraging active participation (Chapter 14), coaching (Chapter 17), or managing conflicts (Chapter 11), project managers will need high levels of persistence and patience for leading the team.

- *Empowerment and Delegation.* Projects need control and consistency for accomplishing the objectives while still involving all of the project members. Although project managers will want to keep a close eye on the process, they will need to involve and empower members in order to gain support for initiatives and encourage participation and responsibility. Project managers will need the ability to utilize empowerment and delegation for effective leadership, as covered in Chapter 18.

As you can see, leading a project can be a complex and challenging experience. It will not only require competency in the technical skills, but also will require well-rounded ability in all of the interpersonal fields. However, by using the appropriate steps to guide you through the process, project management can provide you with the opportunity to improve your leadership skills while enhancing your visibility within the organization.

Eight Steps to Managing Projects

The eight steps for managing projects (see Figure 19–1) can help you clarify, organize, and implement projects or complex tasks. First, we must define *what* we are managing before we plan *how* we manage it. Make sure you take the necessary time to clearly define the project as the first step lays the foundation for the rest of the process. Do not fall for "the sooner the project is started, the sooner it will be finished" mentality.[19]

**Figure 19–1
Steps to Managing Projects**

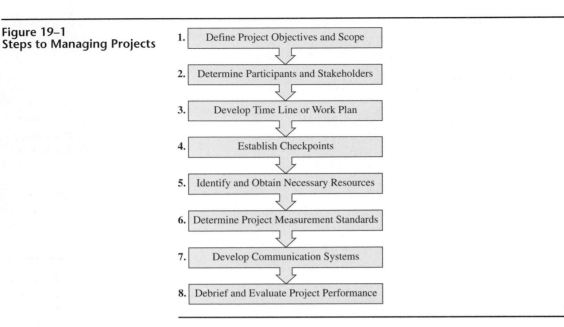

1. Define Project Objectives and Scope
2. Determine Participants and Stakeholders
3. Develop Time Line or Work Plan
4. Establish Checkpoints
5. Identify and Obtain Necessary Resources
6. Determine Project Measurement Standards
7. Develop Communication Systems
8. Debrief and Evaluate Project Performance

Step One—Define Project Objectives and Scope

As a group, discuss the goals of the project. What deliverables and outcomes are expected? What would you ideally like to accomplish? The answers to these questions may be different. If so, focus first on the essentials or must-haves, and then, if there is room in the schedule, incorporate the optionals or nice-to-haves. For example, an essential element would be to meet the deadline imposed by the instructor or manager. An optional element would be to have deliverables prepared a week ahead of time. After going through all the steps of project management, you'll then be able to assess whether getting done a week early is possible. Using a "cause and effect" diagram such as Ishikawa's **Fishbone Diagram** is helpful in early stages of project management to gather and organize project factors and in finding hidden issues that may impact activities, resource allocation, or steps in the overall process (see Figure 19–2). The diagram will have a "spine" or central line to show factors that are connected to the final result or problem. The "main bones" leading to the spine are the main factors to consider, and each of these can have secondary or additional subfactors. The factors can vary in relation to the particular project or problem. Try to develop your own cause and effect diagram by working through Exercise 19–A.

Project Management in Action[20]

Pam Statz, an analyst for HotWired—a company that creates and manages websites for other entities—used to struggle with meeting deadlines until her department began using project management. Pam and her staff continually failed to meet expected deadlines because they were unable to work together toward stated objectives. They had to spend their weekends and late nights in the office to try to accomplish their goals. Using Microsoft Project, they defined specific objectives and the person responsible for achieving them. They focused on using a time line and a plan. The project management tools and approach provided a means for group members to communicate and share files without having to be physically together. Project management enabled Pam's department to become a cohesive unit that met deadlines in a relatively stress-free manner. That, in turn, enabled HotWired to efficiently and effectively design websites—and satisfy their customers—often before project deadlines.

Several steps can help you define the project:

■ Relate the project goals to overall organizational goals and strategy.[21] For example, if your team's goal is to produce a set of recommendations for consideration by senior management, determine your boss's objectives—as well as those of his or her boss—to make certain your project goals support the organization's broader goals. Projects should not be

Figure 19–2
Fishbone Diagram

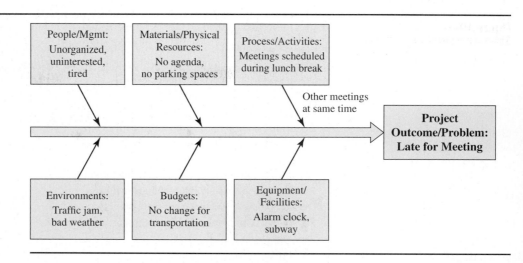

carried out in a vacuum, and project leaders must clearly communicate the value the project adds to the overall organization, explaining not only what needs to be done, but also why. Without taking this step, you risk "doing things right" instead of "doing the right things."

- Clarify the scope of the project. Making recommendations is not the same as implementing them. Aside from the time required, these differing outcome expectations can be a source of frustration and chaos for a team. Using the overall strategy of the organization can provide boundaries when making decisions. Tactics and decisions should be within the scope of what the organization wants to accomplish and where it is going in the future.[22]

- Clarify project objectives with the project manager or instructor to guarantee that everyone's on the same page about the expected outcome. This might surprise you, but the phrase "zero defects" means different things to different people. Quality of 99.9 percent is impressive, unless you consider that a 0.1 percent error rate equates, for example, to Americans consuming over 14,000 cans of "bad" soda in a single year. Clarifying project objectives and scope can be one of the most critical steps in the process of project management.

Step Two—Determine Project Participants and Stakeholders

Now that you are clear about what to do, it makes sense to consider who should be included in the project. Even though some people may not seem necessary at first, the fact that their work or organization is affected by the outcomes of the project, thereby making them **stakeholders,** may suggest that their inclusion is more important than you might think. Key considerations for this stage include the following:

- Make sure to keep vital employees and teammates part of the project and to involve key stakeholders—those who have a stake in the outcome such as your manager or instructor—or keep them apprised of the group's efforts throughout the project.[23] For example, a functional organization charged with procuring materials for projects became frustrated with a system that took anywhere from four weeks to 18 months to obtain even simple, low-cost items. The group worked together and devised a new system designed to save countless hours and, hence, costs. But they weren't done. The proposed system required extensive changes in the way accounts payable did its work. The group presented its plan to management and the accounts payable department, then asked representatives from the latter group to join them to flesh out the details and implement the new system. Had they not included this step, the group might have faced an uphill battle—even though their proposed new system could save valuable resources.

- Once the project group has been assembled, note members' availability (and lack thereof) on a master calendar. Indicate specific dates when one or more of the team members will not be available to work on the project. Holidays, vacation days, anticipated personal days, travel days, meeting days, or commitments to other projects should be noted and accounted for when designating project steps and entering to-do items on the project calendar. Some dates may have to be skipped completely if key

**Figure 19–3
Sample Work Plan**

Project: Team presentation on business topic of current interest

Due Date: December 3

Team Members' Names and Initials: James Smith (JS), Mary Conover (MC), Jesse Baron (JB), Nomi Hussein (NH), Maria Santanella (MS)

Step	Date	Initials
1. Meet with team; decide topic	10/8	All
2. Discuss key components of topic	10/12	All
3. Assign individual research topics	10/15	MS
4. Regroup to share results	10/29	All
5. Compile further research and develop outline	11/5	JS, MC
6. E-mail group to solicit and incorporate feedback	11/12	JS, MC
7. Develop presentation and share draft with others, edit	11/19	JB, NH
8. Plan presentation, prepare slides, and share with group	11/26	MS
9. Rehearse	11/29	All
10. Prepare copies for distribution	12/1	JB
11. Present	12/3	All
12. Arrange, have debrief and lunch session	12/5	NH

group members are unavailable, while others may be included if tasks performed by others are unaffected by individual absences.

- Discuss what the group members' interests are—their strengths and desired contributions to the project. One might volunteer to contribute by doing research, another by doing data entry, a third by doing analysis, and so on. The team must consider two things: (1) If possible, allow members not only to do what they do best, but also afford them the opportunity to develop other skills. (2) If individuals don't volunteer, or if all members lack needed skills, roles will have to be assigned regardless of personal interest or strengths. For example, give someone with a computer background the chance to take on a marketing role if possible and if the person desires. While he or she may be better equipped to prepare the final report or presentation, allowing members to stretch and possibly cross functional lines builds their skills for future projects.

- Consider the team members' planning and organizing skills. Discuss expectations regarding meeting project deadlines as well as what each person can contribute to the task. When allocating project steps to specific team members, assign tasks that stretch but don't overextend any one team member.

Step Three—Develop a Time Line or Work Plan

The next step is to create a specific plan that takes into account all the various steps—large and small—as well as the relationships among the steps. For example, in building a car, you would never install the headrests before installing the seats. Figure 19–3 shows a work plan for a five-member team presentation project. It includes all the steps necessary to complete the project, a time frame to allow for completion of the project, and assignment of responsibilities for individual team members. Some tactics for developing a **project time line** or **work plan** include these:

- Working with a large blackboard, whiteboard, easel and newsprint, or computer program (something that everyone involved can see), begin brainstorming all the steps that will be needed to complete the project. If possible, start with the end goal and work backward from there. This process, called **backscheduling,** involves looking backward from a target date, beginning with your goal or objective, and then plotting the means to achieve it. Backscheduling involves three steps:

1. Identifying the individual tasks necessary to achieve the objective.
2. Estimating how long it will take you to complete each task and determining the best time to do it.
3. Listing each task on a calendar, appropriately backdating each task from the project due date.[24]

Let's take you away from business to share an example of backscheduling. If you were preparing a meal such as the Spanish *paella*, you wouldn't put all the ingredients in at the same time. This complex dish includes meats (sausage, chicken), seafood (fish, shrimp, mussels), and vegetables (carrots, peppers), each of which has an optimal cooking time. If you were planning to serve the dish in 40 minutes, you would put the meats in first, as they would take the longest to cook. Then you'd add the vegetables, and finally the seafood. If you didn't consider each ingredient's optimal cooking time, the results would not be what you intended. Shrimp that has cooked for 40 minutes tastes mushy, and the fish would fall apart and taste dried out. If you put the meats in last, say with only 10 minutes to go, you may subject your guests to undercooked meats (and the problems they bring). When you backschedule, you determine what happens last, next to last, next to next to last, and so on. For the example in Figure 19–3, the team would need to start with the presentation date and work backward to determine when they would need to begin the project to ensure quality and timely completion. By doing so, they would determine that they will need eight weeks to allow for successfully creating this particular presentation.

If the project is complex and it's easier to start at the beginning, do so. List each step and allocate all steps to specific dates on the calendar. Realize that some tasks are serial (one must precede another) while others are parallel (two non-interrelated tasks that can occur simultaneously). Breaking the project into smaller sections or steps can lead to better performance and increase the satisfaction and ownership of project members.

- Determine and specify the dependencies that exist between all the tasks, participants, and activities in a project plan. Each step relates to others in the plan. Understanding these interrelationships can help the group know where potential problems could arise or where a delay or lag could change the process.[25] If employees at the manufacturer supplying the upholstery material for the car seats are on strike, it will impact not only the availability of the car seats, but also the installation of the headrests.

- As a group, clarify the objectives when specific tasks are assigned. Clearly communicate the expected deliverables and the desired results. Monitor tasks delegated and record who is responsible for specific tasks. Set precise and realistic deadlines for short-term deliverables, adjusting the time line as necessary throughout the project. Exercise 19–B can help your team devise a work plan.

- Build in time for the unexpected. Planning and communication with teammates are essential here. Watch for the tendency to try to make up lost time late in the project cycle. It's not atypical for a project to stay on schedule for the first 80 percent of the time and then fall apart due to overconfidence ("We're practically done"), reduced attention to the schedule ("We know what we have to do . . . who needs to see the schedule?"), or just procrastination. Once group members recognize this slippage, they become stressed and rush to completion, resulting in lower-quality output than would have been the case if they had adhered to the original time line. Many people and teams grossly underestimate the time needed toward the end to complete details that bring a final deliverable up to quality standards. Let's say your team is assembling a report based on a survey conducted over a six-month time period. Who's going to check the accuracy of the data? Who will proofread? Edit? Check for content? Run the report by the research and legal departments? Share a preview copy with a few stakeholders to ensure buy-in? Copy and prepare presentation materials, or ensure they're available online? All these minute details take much more time than most people imagine. It's wise to build them into the schedule from the outset of the project.

  Talking through these kinds of details with a project group has several benefits. It helps the group become realistic about what can and cannot be accomplished. It helps individuals think of additional steps that might otherwise have been omitted from the planning phase. And it helps team members begin defining the quality standards for the project in real terms.

- Avoid the tendency to wait until late in the project to buy time for these important details. Budget for them up front. Stay vigilant and look at the whole project to determine where time can be bought earlier in the process. Taking time for this discussion will pay off in a higher-quality outcome, and with less stress than "winging it"![26]

■ A veteran project manager, Uwe Weissflog, manager of strategic planning for Structural Dynamics Research Corporation, offers some final advice: "Be very flexible. In this day where we're on these faster, better, cheaper programs, with very high turnaround and very high-risk technologies, you can come up with a great master plan, but things never go according to plan. You have to be flexible when changes come in to rapidly replan and not be discouraged by it."[27] The goal of your project is set, but the action plan or means of getting to your end result must constantly be adapted to address deviations from the original path. Effective project managers recognize when and how to change directions as well as when to ask for help when extra resources are needed.[28]

Step Four—Establish Checkpoints and Control Mechanisms

Step four involves setting up a series of checkpoints, or points at which progress on the project will be checked, and entering these onto the project calendar (see Exercise 19–E). Even after your group lists all the tasks, identifies interdependencies, and assigns specific due dates, it is wise to establish periodic checkpoints. These may be progress meetings where members can check status, clarify expectations, or raise issues. If unanticipated problems arise, these checkpoint meetings can be used to solve problems and make necessary adjustments to the schedule.

■ Evaluate your project for important steps or tasks to be completed and insert interim deadlines or checkpoints in the project plan. In step three, we broke the project into smaller tasks or objectives. In this step, break tasks down further into milestones or incremental steps to determine when checks and tests should be completed. For example, break a 30-day project into three 10-day subsections, instituting a checkpoint after each one. This will help shorten the time between when an error or misunderstanding occurs and when it can be discovered and corrected.[29] It will also help to prevent or reduce the possibility of time line slippage.

■ Review and update the project plan regularly. Monitor other projects and events that might interfere with your project schedule and adjust accordingly. One suggestion is to post the project plan in an area visible to all group members. Don't confine the schedule to the conference room in which you meet only monthly. Instead, put it in a hallway that all members pass through, such as the hallway to the bathroom or break room. By keeping the plan highly visible, potential interferences and problems can be raised and dealt with before they impact the expected outcomes.

Step Five—Identify and Obtain Necessary Resources

Project managers and their teams must identify and obtain the resources they need to complete the project within the specified time frame, cost parameters, or budget in order to meet quality standards. It is therefore necessary to:

■ Look through the tasks and objectives and discuss what will be required to carry out the assignment. Be realistic about what can be accomplished given the resources available and time constraints inherent in the project; this will facilitate effective **resource management** over the course of the project. Use outside views, past project data, and other reference information to improve the accuracy of your forecasts. Watch out for optimism bias, which can lead to thinking it will be done sooner or cost less than it actually will, and be careful of political pressure from internal or external stakeholders to estimate what others expect and not what is actually needed for a successful project.[30] If your group anticipates a shortfall of personnel, budget, time, computer support, administrative support, or supplies, now is the time—before you roll up your sleeves and begin the project—to discuss these needs with your manager. If the resources can be provided, great. If not, it's important to "push back" on management and negotiate which elements of the deliverable can be achieved, given the resources available. Don't assume you can get these resources later. Get what you need before you start or, if the resources are not forthcoming, manage stakeholders' expectations about the group's ability to achieve a desired outcome.

■ Know when to let a project go or when to start over. Sometimes a project team discovers early on that the project expectation is unrealistic or the scope of the project is more complex than originally envisioned. Perhaps the team thought its job was to make recommendations when their manager saw the task as ending with implementation of the recommendations. These perceptions differ substantially. Or perhaps a pilot project is expanded to include the entire organization. The project team might need to reconsider its objectives and change course. If this happens to you, consult with your manager or instructor. Perhaps the task can be reconceived. Don't let politics, pride, or the thought of failure keep you from asking for help or from scrapping a project that is not going to contribute to the organization. Use active decision making throughout to help you make these determinations.[31] Communicate frequently and clearly about these determinations with appropriate stakeholders.

Step Six—Determine How Project Results Will Be Measured

Before the project starts, understand how the project will be evaluated and who will assess it. This will ensure that steps are built into the process to obtain the data needed to evaluate the success of the project. If your group's task is to improve customer satisfaction, how will you know whether you've done it? Are they happier? Do they file fewer complaints? Is the wait time for help shorter? Especially in a case like this, your group might first have to measure and establish a baseline. How do you know if the wait time is shorter after your recommendations are implemented if you don't assess the wait time before you begin? In some organizations, teams are rewarded with a percentage of total savings—another good reason to establish and assess results.

Step Seven—Set Up an Ongoing Communication System

There is no substitute for effective communication in project management. Typically, projects get in trouble when people are unsure of their role or responsibilities relative to other roles and responsibilities. To avoid confusion, members must see over the horizon and convey to others their ideas, perceptions, and the objective with clarity and confidence. Group projects also require listening skills. Several communication skills are especially important:

- Communicate with team members and stakeholders. The ability to deal with people—using your interpersonal skills—can be the primary factor in the success of a project.[32] Important skills to use throughout the process are listening, giving and receiving feedback, persuading, delegating, seeing things from another's perspective, and getting people to respond to you.[33]

- Start the project with face-to-face or telephone contact if possible. This is important for both traditional and virtual teams. Research shows that e-mail contact can occur once the group is formed and people are clear on their roles and responsibilities. Misunderstanding is less likely to occur when members are able to meet and fully discuss project expectations and concerns in real time, with the benefit of nonverbal language.

- Meet regularly (in person or virtually) to check on project status and progress. Meetings can keep a project on task by enabling members to check and recheck their understanding of dates and deliverables. To be effective, meetings should be primarily decision oriented. In addition to sharing status, meetings can be used to maintain agreed-upon deadlines, discuss changes that might be necessary in the plan or work schedule, address questions and issues, and clarify roles and expectations.

- Revisit initial decisions made by the group if they are not working. An important aspect of project management is continuously reviewing the initial prioritization of steps. Continuously cross-check all interrelated project components to make sure that the critical aspects and requirements are being implemented. Constantly review and modify where necessary, ensuring your ability to deliver by your deadlines.[34]

- Keep people informed by issuing progress reports. This can be done face to face, but written methods (e.g., an e-mail sent to the team) may provide an easier and more efficient means for tracking individual and collective progress. Err on the side of going overboard on updating people on how your objectives or tasks are measuring up to the goals of the project.[35]

- Ensure a positive, open atmosphere. Provide encouragement throughout the project. If the project occurs over an extended period of time, plan some fun get-togethers to build camaraderie, trust, and rapport among team members.

- Monitor performance and catch problems early. If you do not take this step, you risk marginalization, in which the poor performers bring down the group's standards rather than the other way around. Since a change to a single step can have a ripple effect on the whole project and system, communicating instantly is critical in keeping projects on time and on budget.[36] Provide constructive feedback as soon as possible. A good project manager will be able to question others and give feedback without alienating the members.[37]

- Give less experienced team members more initial attention and direction. As they acquire experience and confidence, you can be less involved in overseeing their work.

- Be clear on accountability and clarify where overall responsibility for the ultimate quality of each deliverable lies. Make sure everyone understands and is held accountable for the responsibilities they assume.

- Develop records that document the group's progress on the project. This will help the group stay on track without having to replicate earlier discussions. It also aids future groups working on similar projects. The records can be print or electronic and should include the original project plan and changes that are made, meeting schedules and minutes, team to-do lists, memos and e-mail correspondence, and samples of interim and final deliverables.

Step Eight—Debrief and Evaluate the Process and Results at Project End

Remember that all processes and efforts can be improved. Keep notes of lessons learned throughout the process and share them with group members at the end of the project. Use the top four ranked factors associated with project success as a questionning process: Were our goals and objectives clear? Was our schedule realistic? Did we have the necessary support from senior management? Did we allocate the necessary funds and resources?[38] Discuss what worked well and what didn't. Discuss what everyone learned from the group's mistakes and how similar mistakes can be prevented in future team projects.

Figure 19–4 Project Management Tips from a Rocket Scientist

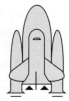

Here are a few of Jerry Madden's (former NASA project manager) "128 Lessons Learned for Project Managers"[39]

#4. Most managers succeed on the strength and skill of their staff.

#5. A manager who is his own systems engineer or financial manager is one who will probably try to do open heart surgery on himself.

#15. Wrong decisions made early can be salvaged, but "right" decisions made late cannot.

#20. Managers who rely on the paperwork to do the reporting of activities are known failures.

#36. A puzzle is hard to discern from just one piece, so don't be surprised if team members deprived of information reach the wrong conclusion.

#54. All problems are solvable in time, so make sure you have enough schedule contingency—if you don't, the next project manager that takes your place will.

#60. Sometimes the best thing to do is nothing. It is also occasionally the best help you can give. Just listening is all that is needed on many occasions. You may be the boss, but if you constantly have to solve someone's problems, you are working for him.

#97. Talk is not cheap. The best way to understand a personnel or technical problem is to talk to the right people. Lack of talk at the right levels is deadly.

#98. Projects require teamwork to succeed. Remember most teams have a coach and not a boss, but the coach still has to call some of the plays.

#108. Gentlemen and ladies can get things done just as well as bastards. What is needed is a strong will and respect—not "strong-arm" tactics. It must be admitted that the latter does work but leaves a residue that has to be cleaned up.

#116. Let your staff argue you into doing something even if you intended to do it anyway. It gives them the feeling that they won one! There are a lot of advantages to gamesmanship, as long as no one detects the game.

#128. The project manager who is the smartest man on his project has done a lousy job of recruitment.

A punch-list that details the problem areas that need to be addressed or fixed during or after completion of the project can be a helpful tool. This will help to determine if the same problems seem to happen frequently. Knowing the rate of frequency can give you and your project team greater awareness of problem areas for making adjustments.[40] This allows all involved to offer feedback and to share ideas for improving group behaviors and processes in the future. Some of Jerry Madden's practical tips for improving project management from a 37-year career as a revered project manager at NASA are discussed in Figure 19–4.

Project Management Tools

Several tools are available to help you track progress on projects. Software programs have been developed to aid project managers working in many fields and on various projects. Most of these programs are designed to help managers organize schedules, rates, and contact information while tracking progress, and they tend to be based on standard project management tools. One of the more common and simple tools is the **Gantt chart.** Named after its developer, Henry Gantt, this chart describes the temporal relationships of events or tasks that unfold over time.[41] It can also show projected and actual schedules. Figure 19–5 shows how another project team managed the same task as the team whose work plan is depicted in Figure 19–3. From this chart, the team can track the planned activities, control individual activities, and identify delays or deviations from the original plan. Team members can see where they have lost time and can plan and make adjustments to complete the project on time. The Gantt chart is also helpful in debriefing the project and in improving the team process for the next assignment.

To make a Gantt chart,

1. Brainstorm all the tasks necessary to complete the final project.

2. Reorganize this list in order from beginning to ending tasks.

3. Create a grid (or use graph paper) wherein the columns represent weeks (or days if the project is very short) and the rows represent specific tasks. Plan to post this where all group project members can see it.

4. List each task in order and estimate the time needed to complete each task. Traditionally, this would be represented by a rectangle whose endpoints show the start and finish time of the task; the longer the rectangle, the longer it would take to complete this task.

5. You could also include two rows for each task—one that shows the projected or planned time (using an opaque rectangle) and one that shows the actual time (using a shaded rectangle).

While it may not be critical to have the planned and actual schedules on a Gantt chart, adding the actual schedule helps in at least two ways. First, you will be able to make real-time adjustments to the schedule, especially when the start or finish of a preceding, interdependent task is delayed. Second, the comparisons will help in the overall project debriefing and provide feedback and lessons learned for future projects and planning.

Another common tool used in project management is the **PERT (Program Evaluation and Review Technique)** chart. A PERT chart diagrams all the steps involved in completing a project and estimates the length of time needed in each phase of the project. By mapping tasks in a flowchart pattern, the PERT chart helps identify sequences of dependent activities (see Figure 19–6).[42] It indicates the most optimistic estimates of the time to complete the project under the best conditions, pessimistic estimates of performance under the worst conditions, and the most likely scenario under normal conditions.[43] The PERT process can also determine the longest anticipated single line of activity from start to finish,[44] which is known as the **critical path method (CPM).**

Figure 19–5
A Gantt Chart on the
Development of a
Team Presentation

	Week	1	2	3	4	5	6	7	8	9
1 Decide Topic	Plan	▓								
	Actual	░								
2 Research Topic	Plan	▓								
	Actual	░	░							
3 Meet to Share Results	Plan		▓							
	Actual			░						
4 Compile Further Research and Develop Outline	Plan		▓							
	Actual			░	░					
5 Get Team Feedback and Incorporate Ideas	Plan				▓					
	Actual				░					
6 Develop Presentation and Discuss Draft	Plan					▓				
	Actual									
7 Plan Presentation, Develop Slides	Plan						▓			
	Actual									
8 Rehearse Presentation	Plan						▓			
	Actual									
9 Prepare Audience Handouts	Plan							▓		
	Actual									
10 Present	Plan							▓		
	Actual									
11 Prepare and Pass Out Evaluation	Plan							▓		
	Actual									
12 Debrief	Plan							▓		
	Actual									

To make a PERT chart and determine the critical path,[45]

1. Define the project and all of its significant activities and tasks.

2. Develop the relationships among the activities. Decide which activities must precede and follow others.

3. Draw the network connecting all the activities.

4. Assign time and/or cost estimates to each activity.

5. Compute the longest time path through the network; this is called the critical path.

6. Use the network to help plan, schedule, monitor, and control the project.

The critical path represents tasks and activities that, if delayed, will cause the entire project to be delayed. Teams can use this information to identify noncritical tasks for replanning, rescheduling, and reallocating resources to gain flexibility and allow for alterations. Therefore, PERT and CPM can play a major part in controlling a project. Figure 19–5 illustrates a team presentation project showing the relationship between the activities and the estimated time needed to complete the presentation. The critical path shows that they will need a minimum of 33 days to complete all the steps and identifies which steps are critical and which ones have some slack time.

Figure 19–6
PERT Chart for Development of Team Presentation

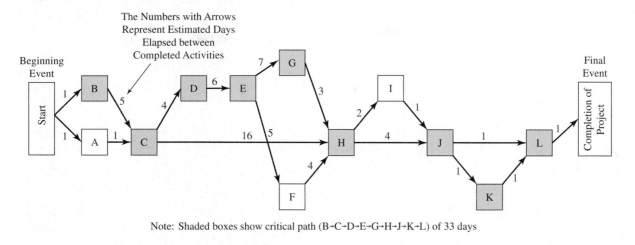

Note: Shaded boxes show critical path (B→C→D→E→G→H→J→K→L) of 33 days

Both of these methods are immensely helpful in planning a project. By creating either chart, most groups discover missing steps, clarify whether the anticipated time line is realistic (or not), and identify critical dependencies and resources. One recommendation for creating a first-draft Gantt or PERT chart is to use Post-its or other easily movable notes. Since so many hidden tasks or issues arise in the building of these charts, the use of Post-its can reduce group members' frustration in the process. Software programs can also be used to create PERT charts; the team identifies the tasks and time estimates, and the programs prepare the charts. Numerous Web-oriented software programs are available. These programs enable group members to enter tasks, estimate time lines and other dependencies, and create the project management chart.[46] One benefit of these programs is that changes—added tasks, modified time lines—create instant adjustments to the overall schedule, enabling members to see the immediate impact of a midterm slippage. Another benefit is that many of these programs can be "connected" to company systems, enabling stakeholders such as department heads and customers to access information on how a project that concerns them is progressing, while the project team maintains control over the project.[47] Of course, as is true of any computer program, the availability of electronic project management does not replace the need for human interaction. Keeping people informed through personal contact is an important complement to electronic communication about project status.[48] Modeling, quantitative methods, and software and technology algorithms are helpful tools, but interpersonal and project management skills are crucial as someone still needs to listen to the data.[49]

Summary

In today's environment, company and individual success comes more readily to those who can do more with less while working smarter, not harder. One way to do this is to make effective use of project management skills and tools. This becomes especially important when you are involved in one or more complex projects. Taking time to clarify project expectations, determine contributors and stakeholders, establish specific objectives or milestones, create contingency plans, and communicate regularly with stakeholders are among the steps needed to make all your projects a success. In the final analysis, others expect project outcomes or deliverables—on time and on budget—not excuses or explanations!

Key Terms and Concepts

Backscheduling	Project management
Critical path method (CPM)	Project time line
Fishbone diagram	Resource management
Gantt chart	Stakeholders
Program Evaluation and Review Technique (PERT)	Work plan

Discussion Questions

1. How does project management help organizations and individuals do more with less?

2. Why is it important to determine project stakeholders as well as project participants?

3. What are some reasons projects veer off schedule? Discuss ways to deal with these reasons.

4. Let's say you and your project team are three months into an eight-month project and you realize that you're already 2.5 weeks behind schedule and 15 percent over budget. What would you do?

Endnotes

1. David L. Coles, "Step Back to Get Ahead; The Key to Completing Projects on Time Is Working Backward from Your Deadlines," *Coles and Associates* (March–April 1988), p. 14.

2. Joe E. Beck, Worley Johnson, and R. Steve Konkel, "Project Management Insights," *Occupational Health and Safety* (June 2000), p. 22.

3. Alexander Laufer, "Project Planning: Timing Issues and Path of Progress," *Project Management Journal* (June 1991), p. 39.

4. World Bank, "World Development Indicators," Washington, DC: World Bank Publications (2009).

5. Roland Gareis and Martina Huemann, "Project Auditing: A Tool for Compliance, Governance, Empowerment, and Improvement," *Journal of Academy of Business and Economics* (February 2007).

6. Kathleen Melymuka, "Born to Lead Projects: Some People Have Innate Talents for Managing Projects," *Computerworld* (March 27, 2000), p. 62.

7. Howard Millman, "On Track and in Touch," *Computerworld* (June 26, 2000), p. 88.

8. Sonia Tellez, "Think Globally When Designing a PM Solution," *Computing Canada* (December 10, 1999), p. 28.

9. Coles, "Step Back," p. 14.

10. Quoted in an article by Kathleen Melymuka, "Project Management Top Guns," *Computer-world* (October 20, 1997), pp. 108–9.

11. Lawrence Todryk, "The Project Manager as Team Builder: Creating an Effective Team," *Project Management Journal* (December 1990), p. 17.

12. M. C. Higgins, "The More the Merrier? Multiple Developmental Relationships and Work Satisfaction," *Journal of Management Development* 19, no. 4 (2000), pp. 277–96.

13. Melymuka, "Project Management Top Guns," p. 62.

14. See J. Richard Hackman, "Motivation through the Design of Work—Test a Theory," *Organizational Behavior and Human Performance* (August 1976), p. 250; J. R. Hackman, "Is Job Enrichment Just a Fad," *Harvard Business Review* (September–October 1975), p. 129.

15. See Frank Swoboda, "Workers Generally Worse Off Than a Decade Ago, Study Finds," *Washington Post* (September 7, 1992), p. 25; and Susan Cartwright, "Taking the Pulse of Executive Health in the U.K.," *The Academy of Management Executive* (May 2000), p. 16.

16. Lloyd A. Rogers, "Project Team Training: A Proven Key to Organizational Teamwork and Breakthrough in Planning Performance," *Project Management Journal* (June 1990), p. 9.

17. Nicholas Clarke, "Emotional Intelligence and Its Relationship to Transformational Leadership and Key Project Management Competences," *Project Management Journal* 41, no. 2 (April 2010), p. 19.

18. P. Letmathe, M. Schweitzer, and M. Zielinski, "How to Learn New Tasks: Shop Floor Performance Effects of Knowledge Transfer and Performance Feedback," *Journal of Operations Management* 30 (2012), pp. 221–36.

19. Stefan Thomke and Donald Reinertsen, "Six Myths of Product Development," *HBR The Magazine* (May 2012), http://hbr.org/2012/05/six-myths-of-product-development/ar/1.

20. Pam Statz, "Wanna Be a Project Manager?" *WebMonkey* (2001), http://hotwired.lycos.com/webmonkey/01/18/index3a.html?tw=jobs.

21. Terry Williams and Knut Samset, "Issues in Front-end Decision Making on Projects," *Project Management Journal* 41, no. 2 (April 2010), p. 38.

22. Andrew Longman and James Mullins, "Project Management: Key Tools for Implementing Strategy," *Journal of Business Strategy* 25, no. 5 (September 2004), p. 54.

23. Robert Thompson, "More Heads Better Than One in Project Management," *Computing Canada* (December 10, 1999), p. 27.

24. Coles, "Step Back," p. 14.

25. Paul S. Adler, "Never-Ending Mission to Find Magic Solution," *Computing Canada* (October 1, 1999), p. 17.

26. Don Reinertsen, "The Best-Laid Plans Become the Enemy of Vigilance," *Electronic Design* (March 20, 2000), p. 57.

27. Quote attributed to Uwe Weissflog, manager of strategic planning at Structural Dynamics Research Corp., as captured by Kathleen Melymuka, "Project Management Top Guns."

28. Rogers, "Project Team Training," p. 9.

29. P. E. D. Love and Z. Irani, "A PM Quality Cost Information System for the Construction Industry," *Information Management* 40, no. 7 (2003), p. 649.

30. Brent Flyvbjerg, "From Nobel Prize to Project Management: Getting Risks Right," *Project Management Journal* 37, no. 3 (August 2006), pp. 5–15.

31. Daphne Main and Carolyn L. Lousteau, "Don't Get Trapped," *Strategic Finance* (November 1999), p. 74.

32. Melymuka, "Project Management Top Guns," p. 62.

33. Melymuka, "Born to Lead Projects," p. 62.

34. Ed Yourdon, "The Value of Triage," *Computerworld* (March 20, 2000), p. 40.

35. "Ask Bill Gates (Project Management Tips)," *Management Today,* February 2000, p. 38.

36. Tellez, "Think Globally," p. 28.

37. Melymuka, "Born to Lead Projects," p. 62.

38. Joyce Fortune et al., "Looking Again at Current Practice in Project Management," *International Journal of Managing Projects in Business* 4 , no. 4 (2011), pp. 553–72.

39. Jerry Madden, "128 Lessons Learned for Project Managers," *Academy Sharing Knowledge Magazine NASA* (March 3, 2005), http://askmagazine.nasa.gov/issues/14/practices/ask14_lessons _madden.html.

40. Cassandra Dillenberger, "Keys to Improving the Performance of Project Managers," *Contractors Business Management Report* no. 5 (May 2009), p. 10.

41. Peter R. Scholtes, *The Leader's Handbook* (Washington, DC: McGraw-Hill, 1998), p. 205.

42. Scholtes, *The Leader's Handbook,* pp. 99, 205.

43. Haidee E. Allerton, "How To," *Training and Development* (November 1999), p. 15.

44. Scholtes, *The Leader's Handbook,* p. 205.

45. Barry Render and Ralph M. Stair, Jr., *Introduction to Management Science* (Boston, MA: Allyn & Bacon, 1992), p. 368.

46. "Get a Grip," *Fortune* (Summer 2000), Supplement, pp. 74–90.

47. Matthew J. Liberatore, "A Decision Support System Linking Research and Development Project Selection with Business Strategy," *Project Management Journal* (November 1988), p. 14.

48. Thompson, "More Heads Better Than One," p. 27.

49. Steve Lohr, "Sure, Big Data Is Great. But So Is Intuition," *NY Times Online* (December 29, 2012), http://www.nytimes.com/2012/12/30/technology/big-data-is-great-but-dont-forget-intuition.html.

**Exercise 19–A
Fishing for a Cause**

1. In groups of 3–4, use the fishbone diagram to plot the cause and effect factors for a project or problem.

2. Define the project or problem (this can be a team, school or work project, or a related organizational problem).

3. Brainstorm all potential categories of factors that could have an impact on the outcome. These can be any categories such as legal/political, technological, environmental, international, sociocultural, economic, or related to the problem or organization such as sytems, financials, management, training, customers, and so on. You can use some of the brainstorming techniques found in Chapter 14.

4. Create secondary bones to denote any secondary or sublevel factors that are pertinent to the outcome of the project or problem.

5. Be prepared to present your diagram to the class and see if they can think of other issues or factors you may not have included.

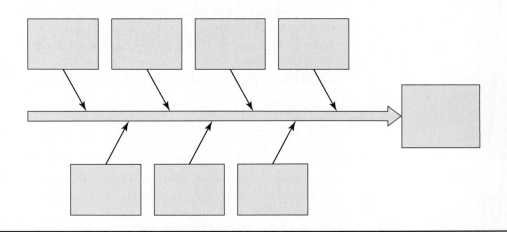

**Exercise 19–B
Team Project
Worksheet**

1. As a team, use the following sheet to develop a work plan for your team project. Use the guidelines outlined in this chapter, and be sure to break down large objectives into smaller components.

2. For each project step, collectively decide on a due date as well as the persons ultimately accountable. Even if a task requires input from all team members, one person must accept the responsibility for coordinating this task.

3. Before approving the plan, each member should compare his or her project tasks with other requirements or deadlines listed in his or her day planner. Potential conflicts should be discussed and adjusted accordingly. Slack time should be incorporated as well.

4. Present your team's work plan to the class or group. Obtain feedback from them about steps that might have been overlooked or time lines that may be unrealistic. Adjust accordingly. Remember to make adjustments both on the team work plan and in your own day planner.

Team Project Work Plan

Project:

Due Date:

Names and Initials of Team Members:

Project Steps:	Date:	Initials:
1.		
2.		
3.		
4.		
5.		
6.		
7.		
8.		
9.		
10.		
11.		
12.		
13.		
14.		

(continue with additional steps on reverse or on blank sheet of paper)

Exercise 19–C
Personal Project
Time Line

You will need your up-to-date individual day planner and project sheet or computer project management program.

1. Working on your own, consider a project in which you're currently involved or in which you anticipate being involved soon.* The project can be personal, such as planning a trip; academic, such as preparing to give a class presentation; or professional, such as conducting an analysis of available products that compete against those of your company.

2. Develop a work plan for the project, following the steps outlined in this chapter. Starting from the project deadline and going backward, list every step needed to complete the project. Use a pencil if working on paper. Be as thorough as possible. Assign initials and projected dates for each step.

3. Now transfer each of these dates (in pencil if using paper) to your personal day planner. If there are conflicts between this project and other classes, projects, or activities that are already in your planner, adjust the dates accordingly on both the project work plan and in your personal day planner.

4. Share your project work plan with a partner and obtain feedback on how realistic and how detailed your plan is, as well as on any suggested steps for adding or deleting. Modify your plan accordingly.

*If you can't think of a project, imagine it is the start of the fall semester and you are asked to prepare a 20-page term paper and presentation on a cutting-edge business topic by the end of the semester. You have 12 weeks in which to plan and complete this project. Other ideas: building a new house, opening a retail store, producing a TV documentary, manufacturing and marketing a new product.

Exercise 19–D
Ace the Project

Form a group of 4–7 members. You will be given three tennis balls, and your instructor will provide the instructions for completing the task. You will then repeat the activity within new time constraints. Follow the directions to complete the task.
When you have finished the tasks, discuss the following questions:

1. In a complex task, to what degree can a team improve its performance? Ten percent? Fifty percent? How?

2. What is the most effective process for improving your team performance?

3. How critical are assignment phrasing, instructions, goals, communication, or even rewards to improving performance?

Source: Adapted from John Kevin Doyle, "Critical Chain Exercises," *American Journal of Business Education* 3, no. 4 (April 2010), p. 43. Affiliation Benedictine University.

**Exercise 19–E
R&D Project Planning**

Your organization has just assigned you to a newly formed task team, which is taking over a secret project presently being handled by Research and Development. Your entire team has been assigned responsibility and authority to first design a plan for managing the project and then, after top management has reviewed and accepted your plans, carry out the project.

Your instructor will provide you with a copy of the Project Planning Situation Participant Booklet from Human Synergistics International. This exercise, printed on NCR (carbonless) paper, presents a list of 20 management activities arranged in random order. Your task is to rank order these activities according to the sequence you would follow in planning, organizing, implementing, and controlling the project.

Source: Adapted with permission from the Project Planning Situation™ (#SM17101). Copyright © 2003 by Human Synergistics International, c/o 39819 Plymouth Road, Plymouth MI, USA 48170.

**Exercise 19–F
Product Recall**

The Scenario

You are part of Yum Yum Bubblegum's management team. Yum Yum Bubblegum manufactures and sells bubble gum in the United States and Canada. You have three manufacturing plants:

- Chewing, Mississippi
- Bubbleton, Alabama
- Poppingsburg, South Dakota

The same products are manufactured at all plants and then sent to Yum Yum's distribution center in Shipit, Arkansas, where they are then shipped to customers via distribution trucks. Assume that the company has no contingency or preventive product recall plans.

The Problem

- The company has just been notified that six people have been hospitalized for toxic poisoning related to substances found in Yum Yum Bubblegum.
- Three of the hospitalized individuals purchased gum in Dallas, Texas; one in San Antonio, Texas; one in San Diego, California; and one is believed to have purchased the gum in an airport in Utah.

Questions and Task

Using the tips and techniques provided in the chapter, work as a team to manage the cleanup project.

1. As managers, how should you attack this problem? What's your plan? Create a list of key steps and a time frame for each step.

_____

_____

_____

_____

2. Next, choose your project team. Who should be on this team? What is each team member's role? Who should be the leader?

_____

_____

_____

_____

3. Determine a contingent plan of attack that specifies how to approach the problem and how to control the process.

_____

_____

_____

_____

4. Finally, determine a preventive plan for the future, assuming that this fiasco does not blow the company's ability to continue to do business.

_____

_____

_____

_____

5. Discuss the importance of project management in preventing or dealing with crises.

_____

_____

_____

_____

Source: Permission provided by creator Sherry Ghodes, JMU BMA Student, presented Fall 2000.

**Exercise 19–G
Tools of Project
Management**

1. Research existing project management tools and resources on the Internet, such as Microsoft Project. Bring an example of a new product that you think looks particularly effective to your class or group.

2. Contact your computer department and ask them for recommendations of new software programs that can be used easily for tracking projects. Try one out and report to your group on its effectiveness and potential applicability to your group's project.

3. Visit a local office supply or stationery store and investigate the current day planner systems that are available. Make a note of the particular strengths and limitations of each. Report to the class or group on the top one or two that you believe are the best available for your group's purposes.

**Exercise 19–H
Reflection/Action Plan**

This chapter focused on project management—what it is, why it's important, and how to improve your skills in this area. Complete the following worksheet upon finishing all the reading and experiential activities for this chapter.

1. The one or two areas in which I am most strong are:

_____

_____

_____

_____

2. The one or two areas in which I need more improvement are:

_____

_____

_____

_____

3. If I did only one thing to improve in this area, it would be to:

_____

_____

_____

_____

4. Making this change would probably result in:

_____

_____

_____

_____

5. If I did not change or improve in this area, it would probably affect my personal and professional life in the following ways:

_____

_____

_____

_____

Index

Page numbers followed by *n*, refers to Endnotes.